University Casebook Series

April, 1992

ACCOUNTING AND THE LAW, Fourth Edition (1978), with Problems Pamphlet (Successor to Dohr, Phillips, Thompson & Warren)

George C. Thompson, Professor, Columbia University Graduate School of Business.
Robert Whitman, Professor of Law, University of Connecticut.
Ellis L. Phillips, Jr., Member of the New York Bar.
William C. Warren, Professor of Law Emeritus, Columbia University.

ACCOUNTING FOR LAWYERS, MATERIALS ON (1980)

David R. Herwitz, Professor of Law, Harvard University.

ADMINISTRATIVE LAW, Eighth Edition (1987), with 1989 Case Supplement and 1983 Problems Supplement (Supplement edited in association with Paul R. Verkuil, Dean and Professor of Law, Tulane University)

Walter Gellhorn, University Professor Emeritus, Columbia University.
Clark Byse, Professor of Law, Harvard University.
Peter L. Strauss, Professor of Law, Columbia University.
Todd D. Rakoff, Professor of Law, Harvard University.
Roy A. Schotland, Professor of Law, Georgetown University.

ADMIRALTY, Third Edition (1987), with 1991 Statute and Rule Supplement

Jo Desha Lucas, Professor of Law, University of Chicago.

ADVOCACY, see also Lawyering Process

AGENCY, see also Enterprise Organization

AGENCY—PARTNERSHIPS, Fourth Edition (1987)

Abridgement from Conard, Knauss & Siegel's Enterprise Organization, Fourth Edition.

AGENCY AND PARTNERSHIPS (1987)

Melvin A. Eisenberg, Professor of Law, University of California, Berkeley.

ANTITRUST: FREE ENTERPRISE AND ECONOMIC ORGANIZATION, Sixth Edition (1983), with 1983 Problems in Antitrust Supplement and 1991 Case Supplement

Louis B. Schwartz, Professor of Law, University of Pennsylvania.
John J. Flynn, Professor of Law, University of Utah.
Harry First, Professor of Law, New York University.

BANKRUPTCY, Second Edition (1989), with 1991 Case Supplement

Robert L. Jordan, Professor of Law, University of California, Los Angeles.
William D. Warren, Professor of Law, University of California, Los Angeles.

BANKRUPTCY AND DEBTOR–CREDITOR LAW, Second Edition (1988)

Theodore Eisenberg, Professor of Law, Cornell University.

UNIVERSITY CASEBOOK SERIES—Continued

BUSINESS ASSOCIATIONS, AGENCY, PARTNERSHIPS, AND CORPORATIONS (1991)

William A. Klein, Professor of Law, University of California, Los Angeles.
Mark Ramseyer, Professor of Law, University of California, Los Angeles.

BUSINESS CRIME (1990), with 1991 Case Supplement

Harry First, Professor of Law, New York University.

BUSINESS ORGANIZATION, see also Enterprise Organization

BUSINESS PLANNING (1991)

Franklin Gevurtz, Professor of Law, McGeorge School of Law.

BUSINESS PLANNING, Temporary Second Edition (1984)

David R. Herwitz, Professor of Law, Harvard University.

BUSINESS TORTS (1972)

Milton Handler, Professor of Law Emeritus, Columbia University.

CHILDREN IN THE LEGAL SYSTEM (1983), with 1990 Supplement (Supplement edited in association with Elizabeth S. Scott, Professor of Law, University of Virginia)

Walter Wadlington, Professor of Law, University of Virginia.
Charles H. Whitebread, Professor of Law, University of Southern California.
Samuel Davis, Professor of Law, University of Georgia.

CIVIL PROCEDURE, see Procedure

CIVIL RIGHTS ACTIONS (1988), with 1991 Supplement

Peter W. Low, Professor of Law, University of Virginia.
John C. Jeffries, Jr., Professor of Law, University of Virginia.

CLINIC, see also Lawyering Process

COMMERCIAL AND DEBTOR–CREDITOR LAW: SELECTED STATUTES, 1991 EDITION

COMMERCIAL LAW, Third Edition (1992)

Robert L. Jordan, Professor of Law, University of California, Los Angeles.
William D. Warren, Professor of Law, University of California, Los Angeles.

COMMERCIAL LAW, Fourth Edition (1985), with 1991 Case Supplement

E. Allan Farnsworth, Professor of Law, Columbia University.
John Honnold, Professor of Law, University of Pennsylvania.

COMMERCIAL PAPER, see also Negotiable Instruments

COMMERCIAL PAPER, Third Edition (1984), with 1991 Case Supplement

E. Allan Farnsworth, Professor of Law, Columbia University.

COMMERCIAL PAPER AND BANK DEPOSITS AND COLLECTIONS (1967), with Statutory Supplement

William D. Hawkland, Professor of Law, University of Illinois.

COMMERCIAL TRANSACTIONS—Principles and Policies, Second Edition (1991)

Alan Schwartz, Professor of Law, Yale University.
Robert E. Scott, Professor of Law, University of Virginia.

CRIMINAL LAW AND APPROACHES TO THE STUDY OF LAW, Second Edition (1991)

John M. Brumbaugh, Professor of Law, University of Maryland.

CRIMINAL LAW, Second Edition (1986)

Peter W. Low, Professor of Law, University of Virginia.
John C. Jeffries, Jr., Professor of Law, University of Virginia.
Richard C. Bonnie, Professor of Law, University of Virginia.

CRIMINAL LAW, Fourth Edition (1986)

Lloyd L. Weinreb, Professor of Law, Harvard University.

CRIMINAL LAW AND PROCEDURE, Seventh Edition (1989)

Ronald N. Boyce, Professor of Law, University of Utah.
Rollin M. Perkins, Professor of Law Emeritus, University of California, Hastings College of the Law.

CRIMINAL PROCEDURE, Fourth Edition (1992)

James B. Haddad, late Professor of Law, Northwestern University.
James B. Zagel, Chief, Criminal Justice Division, Office of Attorney General of Illinois.
Gary L. Starkman, Assistant U. S. Attorney, Northern District of Illinois.
William J. Bauer, Chief Judge of the U.S. Court of Appeals, Seventh Circuit.

CRIMINAL PROCESS, Fourth Edition (1987), with 1991 Supplement

Lloyd L. Weinreb, Professor of Law, Harvard University.

DAMAGES, Second Edition (1952)

Charles T. McCormick, late Professor of Law, University of Texas.
William F. Fritz, late Professor of Law, University of Texas.

DECEDENTS' ESTATES AND TRUSTS, See also Family Property Law

DECEDENTS' ESTATES AND TRUSTS, Seventh Edition (1988)

John Ritchie, late Professor of Law, University of Virginia.
Neill H. Alford, Jr., Professor of Law, University of Virginia.
Richard W. Effland, late Professor of Law, Arizona State University.

DISPUTE RESOLUTION, Processes of (1989)

John S. Murray, President and Executive Director of The Conflict Clinic, Inc., George Mason University.
Alan Scott Rau, Professor of Law, University of Texas.
Edward F. Sherman, Professor of Law, University of Texas.

DOMESTIC RELATIONS, see also Family Law

DOMESTIC RELATIONS, Second Edition (1990), with 1992 Supplement

Walter Wadlington, Professor of Law, University of Virginia.

EMPLOYMENT DISCRIMINATION, Second Edition (1987), with 1990 Supplement

Joel W. Friedman, Professor of Law, Tulane University.
George M. Strickler, Professor of Law, Tulane University.

EMPLOYMENT LAW, Second Edition (1991), with Statutory Supplement and 1991 Case Supplement

Mark A. Rothstein, Professor of Law, University of Houston.
Andria S. Knapp, Visiting Professor of Law, Golden Gate University.
Lance Liebman, Professor of Law, Harvard University.

UNIVERSITY CASEBOOK SERIES—Continued

ENERGY LAW (1983), with 1991 Case Supplement

Donald N. Zillman, Professor of Law, University of Utah.
Laurence Lattman, Dean of Mines and Engineering, University of Utah.

ENTERPRISE ORGANIZATION, Fourth Edition (1987), with 1987 Corporation and Partnership Statutes, Rules and Forms Supplement

Alfred F. Conard, Professor of Law, University of Michigan.
Robert L. Knauss, Dean of the Law School, University of Houston.
Stanley Siegel, Professor of Law, University of California, Los Angeles.

ENVIRONMENTAL POLICY LAW, Second Edition (1991)

Thomas J. Schoenbaum, Professor of Law, University of Georgia.
Ronald H. Rosenberg, Professor of Law, College of William and Mary.

EQUITY, see also Remedies

EQUITY, RESTITUTION AND DAMAGES, Second Edition (1974)

Robert Childres, late Professor of Law, Northwestern University.
William F. Johnson, Jr., Professor of Law, New York University.

ESTATE PLANNING, Second Edition (1982), with 1985 Case, Text and Documentary Supplement

David Westfall, Professor of Law, Harvard University.

ETHICS, see Legal Ethics, Legal Profession, Professional Responsibility, and Social Responsibilities

ETHICS OF LAWYERING, THE LAW AND (1990)

Geoffrey C. Hazard, Jr., Professor of Law, Yale University.
Susan P. Koniak, Professor of Law, University of Pittsburgh.

ETHICS AND PROFESSIONAL RESPONSIBILITY (1981) (Reprinted from THE LAWYERING PROCESS)

Gary Bellow, Professor of Law, Harvard University.
Bea Moulton, Legal Services Corporation.

EVIDENCE, Seventh Edition (1992)

John Kaplan, Late Professor of Law, Stanford University.
Jon R. Waltz, Professor of Law, Northwestern University.
Roger C. Park, Professor of Law, University of Minnesota.

EVIDENCE, Eighth Edition (1988), with Rules, Statute and Case Supplement (1990)

Jack B. Weinstein, Chief Judge, United States District Court.
John H. Mansfield, Professor of Law, Harvard University.
Norman Abrams, Professor of Law, University of California, Los Angeles.
Margaret Berger, Professor of Law, Brooklyn Law School.

FAMILY LAW, see also Domestic Relations

FAMILY LAW, Third Edition (1992)

Judith C. Areen, Professor of Law, Georgetown University.

FAMILY LAW AND CHILDREN IN THE LEGAL SYSTEM, STATUTORY MATERIALS (1981)

Walter Wadlington, Professor of Law, University of Virginia.

UNIVERSITY CASEBOOK SERIES—Continued

FAMILY PROPERTY LAW, Cases and Materials on Wills, Trusts and Future Interests (1991)

Lawrence W. Waggoner, Professor of Law, University of Michigan.
Richard V. Wellman, Professor of Law, University of Georgia.
Gregory Alexander, Professor of Law, Cornell Law School.
Mary L. Fellows, Professor of Law, University of Minnesota.

FEDERAL COURTS, Eighth Edition (1988), with 1991 Supplement

Charles T. McCormick, late Professor of Law, University of Texas.
James H. Chadbourn, late Professor of Law, Harvard University.
Charles Alan Wright, Professor of Law, University of Texas, Austin.

FEDERAL COURTS AND THE FEDERAL SYSTEM, Hart and Wechsler's Third Edition (1988), with 1992 Case Supplement, and the Judicial Code and Rules of Procedure in the Federal Courts (1991)

Paul M. Bator, Professor of Law, University of Chicago.
Daniel J. Meltzer, Professor of Law, Harvard University.
Paul J. Mishkin, Professor of Law, University of California, Berkeley.
David L. Shapiro, Professor of Law, Harvard University.

FEDERAL COURTS AND THE LAW OF FEDERAL–STATE RELATIONS, Second Edition (1989), with 1991 Supplement

Peter W. Low, Professor of Law, University of Virginia.
John C. Jeffries, Jr., Professor of Law, University of Virginia.

FEDERAL PUBLIC LAND AND RESOURCES LAW, Second Edition (1987), with 1990 Case Supplement and 1990 Statutory Supplement

George C. Coggins, Professor of Law, University of Kansas.
Charles F. Wilkinson, Professor of Law, University of Oregon.

FEDERAL RULES OF CIVIL PROCEDURE and Selected Other Procedural Provisions, 1991 Edition

FEDERAL TAXATION, see Taxation

FIRST AMENDMENT (1991)

William W. Van Alstyne, Professor of Law, Duke University.

FOOD AND DRUG LAW, Second Edition (1991), with Statutory Supplement

Peter Barton Hutt, Esq.
Richard A. Merrill, Professor of Law, University of Virginia.

FUTURE INTERESTS (1970)

Howard R. Williams, Professor of Law, Stanford University.

FUTURE INTERESTS AND ESTATE PLANNING (1961), with 1962 Supplement

W. Barton Leach, late Professor of Law, Harvard University.
James K. Logan, formerly Dean of the Law School, University of Kansas.

GENDER DISCRIMINATION, see Women and the Law

GOVERNMENT CONTRACTS, FEDERAL, Successor Edition (1985), with 1989 Supplement

John W. Whelan, Professor of Law, Hastings College of the Law.

GOVERNMENT REGULATION: FREE ENTERPRISE AND ECONOMIC ORGANIZATION, Sixth Edition (1985)

Louis B. Schwartz, Professor of Law, Hastings College of the Law.
John J. Flynn, Professor of Law, University of Utah.
Harry First, Professor of Law, New York University.

UNIVERSITY CASEBOOK SERIES—Continued

HEALTH CARE LAW AND POLICY (1988)

Clark C. Havighurst, Professor of Law, Duke University.

HINCKLEY, JOHN W., JR., TRIAL OF: A Case Study of the Insanity Defense (1986)

Peter W. Low, Professor of Law, University of Virginia.
John C. Jeffries, Jr., Professor of Law, University of Virginia.
Richard C. Bonnie, Professor of Law, University of Virginia.

IMMIGRATION LAW AND POLICY (1992)

Stephen H. Legomsky, Professor of Law, Washington University.

INJUNCTIONS, Second Edition (1984)

Owen M. Fiss, Professor of Law, Yale University.
Doug Rendleman, Professor of Law, College of William and Mary.

INSTITUTIONAL INVESTORS (1978)

David L. Ratner, Professor of Law, Cornell University.

INSURANCE, Second Edition (1985)

William F. Young, Professor of Law, Columbia University.
Eric M. Holmes, Professor of Law, University of Georgia.

INSURANCE LAW AND REGULATION (1990)

Kenneth S. Abraham, University of Virginia.

INTERNATIONAL LAW, see also Transnational Legal Problems, Transnational Business Problems, and United Nations Law

INTERNATIONAL LAW IN CONTEMPORARY PERSPECTIVE (1981), with Essay Supplement

Myres S. McDougal, Professor of Law, Yale University.
W. Michael Reisman, Professor of Law, Yale University.

INTERNATIONAL LEGAL SYSTEM, Third Edition (1988), with Documentary Supplement

Joseph Modeste Sweeney, Professor of Law, University of California, Hastings.
Covey T. Oliver, Professor of Law, University of Pennsylvania.
Noyes E. Leech, Professor of Law Emeritus, University of Pennsylvania.

INTRODUCTION TO LAW, see also Legal Method, On Law in Courts, and Dynamics of American Law

INTRODUCTION TO THE STUDY OF LAW (1970)

E. Wayne Thode, late Professor of Law, University of Utah.
Leon Lebowitz, Professor of Law, University of Texas.
Lester J. Mazor, Professor of Law, University of Utah.

JUDICIAL CODE and Rules of Procedure in the Federal Courts, Students' Edition, 1991 Revision

Daniel J. Meltzer, Professor of Law, Harvard University.
David L. Shapiro, Professor of Law, Harvard University.

JURISPRUDENCE (Temporary Edition Hardbound) (1949)

Lon L. Fuller, late Professor of Law, Harvard University.

JUVENILE, see also Children

JUVENILE JUSTICE PROCESS, Third Edition (1985)

Frank W. Miller, Professor of Law, Washington University.
Robert O. Dawson, Professor of Law, University of Texas.
George E. Dix, Professor of Law, University of Texas.
Raymond I. Parnas, Professor of Law, University of California, Davis.

LABOR LAW, Eleventh Edition (1991), with 1991 Statutory Supplement

Archibald Cox, Professor of Law, Harvard University.
Derek C. Bok, President, Harvard University.
Robert A. Gorman, Professor of Law, University of Pennsylvania.
Matthew W. Finkin, Professor of Law, University of Illinois.

LABOR LAW, Second Edition (1982), with Statutory Supplement

Clyde W. Summers, Professor of Law, University of Pennsylvania.
Harry H. Wellington, Dean of the Law School, Yale University.
Alan Hyde, Professor of Law, Rutgers University.

LAND FINANCING, Third Edition (1985)

The late Norman Penney, Professor of Law, Cornell University.
Richard F. Broude, Member of the California Bar.
Roger Cunningham, Professor of Law, University of Michigan.

LAW AND MEDICINE (1980)

Walter Wadlington, Professor of Law and Professor of Legal Medicine, University of Virginia.
Jon R. Waltz, Professor of Law, Northwestern University.
Roger B. Dworkin, Professor of Law, Indiana University, and Professor of Biomedical History, University of Washington.

LAW, LANGUAGE AND ETHICS (1972)

William R. Bishin, Professor of Law, University of Southern California.
Christopher D. Stone, Professor of Law, University of Southern California.

LAW, SCIENCE AND MEDICINE (1984), with 1989 Supplement

Judith C. Areen, Professor of Law, Georgetown University.
Patricia A. King, Professor of Law, Georgetown University.
Steven P. Goldberg, Professor of Law, Georgetown University.
Alexander M. Capron, Professor of Law, University of Southern California.

LAWYERING PROCESS (1978), with Civil Problem Supplement and Criminal Problem Supplement

Gary Bellow, Professor of Law, Harvard University.
Bea Moulton, Professor of Law, Arizona State University.

LEGAL ETHICS (1992)

Deborah Rhode, Professor of Law, Stanford University.
David Luban, Professor of Law, University of Maryland.

LEGAL METHOD (1980)

Harry W. Jones, Professor of Law Emeritus, Columbia University.
John M. Kernochan, Professor of Law, Columbia University.
Arthur W. Murphy, Professor of Law, Columbia University.

LEGAL METHODS (1969)

Robert N. Covington, Professor of Law, Vanderbilt University.
E. Blythe Stason, late Professor of Law, Vanderbilt University.
John W. Wade, Professor of Law, Vanderbilt University.
Elliott E. Cheatham, late Professor of Law, Vanderbilt University.
Theodore A. Smedley, Professor of Law, Vanderbilt University.

UNIVERSITY CASEBOOK SERIES—Continued

LEGAL PROFESSION, THE, Responsibility and Regulation, Second Edition (1988)

Geoffrey C. Hazard, Jr., Professor of Law, Yale University.
Deborah L. Rhode, Professor of Law, Stanford University.

LEGISLATION, Fourth Edition (1982) (by Fordham)

Horace E. Read, late Vice President, Dalhousie University.
John W. MacDonald, Professor of Law Emeritus, Cornell Law School.
Jefferson B. Fordham, Professor of Law, University of Utah.
William J. Pierce, Professor of Law, University of Michigan.

LEGISLATIVE AND ADMINISTRATIVE PROCESSES, Second Edition (1981)

Hans A. Linde, Judge, Supreme Court of Oregon.
George Bunn, Professor of Law, University of Wisconsin.
Fredericka Paff, Professor of Law, University of Wisconsin.
W. Lawrence Church, Professor of Law, University of Wisconsin.

LOCAL GOVERNMENT LAW, Second Revised Edition (1986)

Jefferson B. Fordham, Professor of Law, University of Utah.

MASS MEDIA LAW, Fourth Edition (1990)

Marc A. Franklin, Professor of Law, Stanford University.
David A. Anderson, Professor of Law, University of Texas.

MUNICIPAL CORPORATIONS, see Local Government Law

NEGOTIABLE INSTRUMENTS, see Commercial Paper

NEGOTIABLE INSTRUMENTS AND LETTERS OF CREDIT (1992) (Reprinted from Commercial Law) Third Edition (1992)

Robert L. Jordan, Professor of Law, University of California, Los Angeles.
William D. Warren, Professor of Law, University of California, Los Angeles.

NEGOTIATION (1981) (Reprinted from THE LAWYERING PROCESS)

Gary Bellow, Professor of Law, Harvard Law School.
Bea Moulton, Legal Services Corporation.

NEW YORK PRACTICE, Fourth Edition (1978)

Herbert Peterfreund, Professor of Law, New York University.
Joseph M. McLaughlin, Dean of the Law School, Fordham University.

OIL AND GAS, Sixth Edition (1992)

Richard C. Maxwell, Professor of Law, Duke University.
Stephen F. Williams, Judge of the United States Court of Appeals.
Patrick Henry Martin, Professor of Law, Louisiana State University.
Bruce M. Kramer, Professor of Law, Texas Tech University.

ON LAW IN COURTS (1965)

Paul J. Mishkin, Professor of Law, University of California, Berkeley.
Clarence Morris, Professor of Law Emeritus, University of Pennsylvania.

PENSION AND EMPLOYEE BENEFIT LAW (1990), with 1991 Supplement

John H. Langbein, Professor of Law, University of Chicago.
Bruce A. Wolk, Professor of Law, University of California, Davis.

PLEADING AND PROCEDURE, see Procedure, Civil

POLICE FUNCTION, Fifth Edition (1991), with 1991 Supplement

Reprint of Chapters 1–10 of Miller, Dawson, Dix and Parnas's CRIMINAL JUSTICE ADMINISTRATION, Fourth Edition.

PREPARING AND PRESENTING THE CASE (1981) (Reprinted from THE LAW-YERING PROCESS)

Gary Bellow, Professor of Law, Harvard Law School.
Bea Moulton, Legal Services Corporation.

PROCEDURE (1988), with Procedure Supplement (1991)

Robert M. Cover, late Professor of Law, Yale Law School.
Owen M. Fiss, Professor of Law, Yale Law School.
Judith Resnik, Professor of Law, University of Southern California Law Center.

PROCEDURE—CIVIL PROCEDURE, Sixth Edition (1990), with 1991 Supplement

Richard H. Field, late Professor of Law, Harvard University.
Benjamin Kaplan, Professor of Law Emeritus, Harvard University.
Kevin M. Clermont, Professor of Law, Cornell University.

PROCEDURE—CIVIL PROCEDURE, Successor Edition (1992)

A. Leo Levin, Professor of Law Emeritus, University of Pennsylvania.
Philip Shuchman, Professor of Law, Rutgers University.
Charles M. Yablon, Professor of Law, Yeshiva University.

PROCEDURE—CIVIL PROCEDURE, Fifth Edition (1990), with 1991 Supplement

Maurice Rosenberg, Professor of Law, Columbia University.
Hans Smit, Professor of Law, Columbia University.
Rochelle C. Dreyfuss, Professor of Law, New York University.

PROCEDURE—PLEADING AND PROCEDURE: State and Federal, Sixth Edition (1989), with 1991 Case Supplement

David W. Louisell, late Professor of Law, University of California, Berkeley.
Geoffrey C. Hazard, Jr., Professor of Law, Yale University.
Colin C. Tait, Professor of Law, University of Connecticut.

PROCEDURE—FEDERAL RULES OF CIVIL PROCEDURE, 1991 Edition

PRODUCTS LIABILITY AND SAFETY, Second Edition (1989), with 1989 Statutory Supplement

W. Page Keeton, Professor of Law, University of Texas.
David G. Owen, Professor of Law, University of South Carolina.
John E. Montgomery, Professor of Law, University of South Carolina.
Michael D. Green, Professor of Law, University of Iowa

PROFESSIONAL RESPONSIBILITY, Fifth Edition (1991), with 1992 Selected Standards on Professional Responsibility Supplement

Thomas D. Morgan, Professor of Law, George Washington University.
Ronald D. Rotunda, Professor of Law, University of Illinois.

PROPERTY, Sixth Edition (1990)

John E. Cribbet, Professor of Law, University of Illinois.
Corwin W. Johnson, Professor of Law, University of Texas.
Roger W. Findley, Professor of Law, University of Illinois.
Ernest E. Smith, Professor of Law, University of Texas.

PROPERTY—PERSONAL (1953)

S. Kenneth Skolfield, late Professor of Law Emeritus, Boston University.

PROPERTY—PERSONAL, Third Edition (1954)

Everett Fraser, late Dean of the Law School Emeritus, University of Minnesota.
Third Edition by Charles W. Taintor, late Professor of Law, University of Pittsburgh.

SECURED TRANSACTIONS IN PERSONAL PROPERTY, Third Edition (1992) (Reprinted from COMMERCIAL LAW, Third Edition (1992))

Robert L. Jordan, Professor of Law, University of California, Los Angeles.
William D. Warren, Professor of Law, University of California, Los Angeles.

SECURITIES REGULATION, Seventh Edition (1992), with 1992 Selected Statutes, Rules and Forms Supplement

Richard W. Jennings, Professor of Law, University of California, Berkeley.
Harold Marsh, Jr., Member of California Bar.
John C. Coffee, Jr., Professor of Law, Columbia University.

SECURITIES REGULATION, Second Edition (1988), with Statute, Rule and Form Supplement (1991)

Larry D. Soderquist, Professor of Law, Vanderbilt University.

SECURITY INTERESTS IN PERSONAL PROPERTY, Second Edition (1987)

Douglas G. Baird, Professor of Law, University of Chicago.
Thomas H. Jackson, Dean of the Law School, University of Virginia.

SECURITY INTERESTS IN PERSONAL PROPERTY (1985) (Reprinted from Sales and Sales Financing, Fifth Edition)

John Honnold, Professor of Law, University of Pennsylvania.

SELECTED STANDARDS ON PROFESSIONAL RESPONSIBILITY, 1992 Edition

SELECTED STATUTES AND INTERNATIONAL AGREEMENTS ON UNFAIR COMPETITION, TRADEMARK, COPYRIGHT AND PATENT, 1991 Edition

SELECTED STATUTES ON TRUSTS AND ESTATES, 1992 Edition

SOCIAL RESPONSIBILITIES OF LAWYERS, Case Studies (1988)

Philip B. Heymann, Professor of Law, Harvard University.
Lance Liebman, Professor of Law, Harvard University.

SOCIAL SCIENCE IN LAW, Second Edition (1990)

John Monahan, Professor of Law, University of Virginia.
Laurens Walker, Professor of Law, University of Virginia.

TAXATION, FEDERAL INCOME (1989)

Stephen B. Cohen, Professor of Law, Georgetown University

TAXATION, FEDERAL INCOME, Second Edition (1988), with 1991 Supplement (Supplement edited in association with Deborah H. Schenk, Professor of Law, New York University)

Michael J. Graetz, Professor of Law, Yale University.

TAXATION, FEDERAL INCOME, Seventh Edition (1991)

James J. Freeland, Professor of Law, University of Florida.
Stephen A. Lind, Professor of Law, University of Florida and University of California, Hastings.
Richard B. Stephens, late Professor of Law Emeritus, University of Florida.

TAXATION, FEDERAL INCOME, Successor Edition (1986), with 1991 Legislative Supplement

Stanley S. Surrey, late Professor of Law, Harvard University.
Paul R. McDaniel, Professor of Law, Boston College.
Hugh J. Ault, Professor of Law, Boston College.
Stanley A. Koppelman, Professor of Law, Boston University.

TAXATION, FEDERAL INCOME, OF BUSINESS ORGANIZATIONS (1991), with 1991 Supplement

Paul R. McDaniel, Professor of Law, Boston College.
Hugh J. Ault, Professor of Law, Boston College.
Martin J. McMahon, Jr., Professor of Law, University of Kentucky.
Daniel L. Simmons, Professor of Law, University of California, Davis.

TAXATION, FEDERAL INCOME, OF PARTNERSHIPS AND S CORPORATIONS (1991), with 1991 Supplement

Paul R. McDaniel, Professor of Law, Boston College.
Hugh J. Ault, Professor of Law, Boston College.
Martin J. McMahon, Jr., Professor of Law, University of Kentucky.
Daniel L. Simmons, Professor of Law, University of California, Davis.

TAXATION, FEDERAL INCOME, OIL AND GAS, NATURAL RESOURCES TRANSACTIONS (1990)

Peter C. Maxfield, Professor of Law, University of Wyoming.
James L. Houghton, CPA, Partner, Ernst and Young.
James R. Gaar, CPA, Partner, Ernst and Young.

TAXATION, FEDERAL WEALTH TRANSFER, Successor Edition (1987)

Stanley S. Surrey, late Professor of Law, Harvard University.
Paul R. McDaniel, Professor of Law, Boston College.
Harry L. Gutman, Professor of Law, University of Pennsylvania.

TAXATION, FUNDAMENTALS OF CORPORATE, Third Edition (1991)

Stephen A. Lind, Professor of Law, University of Florida and University of California, Hastings.
Stephen Schwarz, Professor of Law, University of California, Hastings.
Daniel J. Lathrope, Professor of Law, University of California, Hastings.
Joshua Rosenberg, Professor of Law, University of San Francisco.

TAXATION, FUNDAMENTALS OF PARTNERSHIP, Third Edition (1992)

Stephen A. Lind, Professor of Law, University of Florida and University of California, Hastings.
Stephen Schwarz, Professor of Law, University of California, Hastings.
Daniel J. Lathrope, Professor of Law, University of California, Hastings.
Joshua Rosenberg, Professor of Law, University of San Francisco.

TAXATION OF CORPORATIONS AND THEIR SHAREHOLDERS (1991)

David J. Shakow, Professor of Law, University of Pennsylvania.

TAXATION, PROBLEMS IN THE FEDERAL INCOME TAXATION OF PARTNER-SHIPS AND CORPORATIONS, Second Edition (1986)

Norton L. Steuben, Professor of Law, University of Colorado.
William J. Turnier, Professor of Law, University of North Carolina.

TAXATION, PROBLEMS IN THE FUNDAMENTALS OF FEDERAL INCOME, Second Edition (1985)

Norton L. Steuben, Professor of Law, University of Colorado.
William J. Turnier, Professor of Law, University of North Carolina.

TORT LAW AND ALTERNATIVES, Fifth Edition (1992)

Marc A. Franklin, Professor of Law, Stanford University.
Robert L. Rabin, Professor of Law, Stanford University.

TORTS, Eighth Edition (1988)

William L. Prosser, late Professor of Law, University of California, Hastings.
John W. Wade, Professor of Law, Vanderbilt University.
Victor E. Schwartz, Adjunct Professor of Law, Georgetown University.

TORTS, Third Edition (1976)

Harry Shulman, late Dean of the Law School, Yale University.
Fleming James, Jr., Professor of Law Emeritus, Yale University.
Oscar S. Gray, Professor of Law, University of Maryland.

TRADE REGULATION, Third Edition (1990)

Milton Handler, Professor of Law Emeritus, Columbia University.
Harlan M. Blake, Professor of Law, Columbia University.
Robert Pitofsky, Professor of Law, Georgetown University.
Harvey J. Goldschmid, Professor of Law, Columbia University.

TRADE REGULATION, see Antitrust

TRANSNATIONAL BUSINESS PROBLEMS (1986)

Detlev F. Vagts, Professor of Law, Harvard University.

TRANSNATIONAL LEGAL PROBLEMS, Third Edition (1986), with 1991 Revised Edition of Documentary Supplement

Henry J. Steiner, Professor of Law, Harvard University.
Detlev F. Vagts, Professor of Law, Harvard University.

TRIAL, see also Evidence, Making the Record, Lawyering Process and Preparing and Presenting the Case

TRUSTS, Sixth Edition (1991)

George G. Bogert, late Professor of Law Emeritus, University of Chicago.
Dallin H. Oaks, President, Brigham Young University.
H. Reese Hansen, Dean and Professor of Law, Brigham Young University.
Claralyn Martin Hill, J.D. Brigham Young University.

TRUSTS AND ESTATES, SELECTED STATUTES ON, 1992 Edition

TRUSTS AND WILLS, See also Decedents' Estates and Trusts, and Family Property Law

UNFAIR COMPETITION, see Competitive Process and Business Torts

WATER RESOURCE MANAGEMENT, Third Edition (1988), with 1992 Supplement

The late Charles J. Meyers, formerly Dean, Stanford University Law School.
A. Dan Tarlock, Professor of Law, IIT Chicago-Kent College of Law.
James N. Corbridge, Jr., Chancellor, University of Colorado at Boulder, and Professor of Law, University of Colorado.
David H. Getches, Professor of Law, University of Colorado.

WOMEN AND THE LAW (1992)

Mary Joe Frug, late Professor of Law, New England School of Law.

WILLS AND ADMINISTRATION, Fifth Edition (1961)

Philip Mechem, late Professor of Law, University of Pennsylvania.
Thomas E. Atkinson, late Professor of Law, New York University.

WRITING AND ANALYSIS IN THE LAW, Second Edition (1991)

Helene S. Shapo, Professor of Law, Northwestern University.
Marilyn R. Walter, Professor of Law, Brooklyn Law School.
Elizabeth Fajans, Writing Specialist, Brooklyn Law School.

AGENCY, ASSOCIATIONS, EMPLOYMENT AND PARTNERSHIPS

CASES, STATUTES AND ANALYSIS

FOURTH EDITION

By

ALFRED F. CONARD
Henry M. Butzel Professor Emeritus,
University of Michigan Law School

ROBERT L. KNAUSS
Dean and Distinguished University Professor,
University of Houston Law Center

STANLEY SIEGEL
Professor, New York University Law School

Mineola, New York
THE FOUNDATION PRESS, INC.
1987

C., K. & S. Agency-Partnerships 4th Ed. UCB
2nd Reprint—1992

FOREWORD

We have sought in this coursebook to provide to our students an overview of the entire range of business and nonprofit organizations. We believe that lawyers should be familiar not only with the corporate form of organization, which continues to dominate most elements of big business, but also with the partnership form, in which both large and small businesses have shown renewed interest, and with individual proprietorships, which far outnumber partnerships and corporations combined.

As in earlier editions of this book, we probe beyond the rules applicable to particular organization forms, discussing in detail the legal principles applicable to the structure and operations of all enterprises. We have included legal and economic materials on the principles of agency in tort and contract, which are inescapably involved in nearly every contact between enterprises of every form and the public with which they deal, whether for good or evil.

We aspire not only to enlighten our readers about the rules of decision, but also to provoke serious examination of the social and economic policies that may be served or disserved by legal rules. In this edition we continue to present comparative materials from other legal systems, and we offer considerably expanded materials on economic theory, with the hope that these may enhance understanding and evaluation of existing and proposed legal structures in this country.

Throughout the text, we have deleted or summarized older cases and added contemporary cases, notes and articles. The materials on general and limited partnerships have been expanded to reflect the increased use of these forms in both small and large enterprises, as well as the dramatic changes in substantive law represented by widespread adoption of the Revised Uniform Limited Partnership Act and major changes in the tax laws relating to partnerships.

The materials in this book are drawn entirely from the companion volume on Enterprise Organization (fourth edition), and are offered in this form for those instructors whom may wish to present a separate course on noncorporate organization or to use a separate text on corporation law.

We have included in the coursebook for ready reference the texts of the Uniform Partnership Act and both the original and revised versions of the Uniform Limited Partnership Act.

This edition carries forward the organization and approaches that have been welcomed by teachers in three preceding editions under this title, and in three before them under the title of "Business Organization." We hope that this successor edition will help future attorneys to understand the structure of the organizations that conduct most of our economic life, and to promote the interests not only of their clients but of the society in which they all play a role.

ALFRED F. CONARD
ROBERT L. KNAUSS
STANLEY SIEGEL

June, 1987

SUMMARY OF CONTENTS

APPENDIX

*

TABLE OF CONTENTS

CHAPTER 2. VICARIOUS LIABILITY FOR INJURIES

CHAPTER 3. THE EMPLOYMENT RELATIONSHIP UNDER SOCIAL LEGISLATION

CHAPTER 4. AGENCY IN CONSENSUAL TRANSACTIONS

TABLE OF CONTENTS

CHAPTER 5. FIDUCIARY RELATIONSHIPS

CHAPTER 6. PARTNERSHIP

TABLE OF CASES

[Names of cases reprinted are in italic type; names of cases referred to in text notes and footnotes are in roman type.] References are to Pages.

TABLE OF CASES

TABLE OF AUTHORS QUOTED

*

AGENCY, ASSOCIATIONS, EMPLOYMENT AND PARTNERSHIPS

*

Chapter 1

FORMS OF ORGANIZATION

INTRODUCTION

In the industrialized states, most people spend their working hours in the shops and offices of companies, governmental organizations, or employed by health or educational institutions. Members of the "independent professions", however much they cherish the image of individuality, usually earn their fees by working as agents for other people. In addition, they disclose a worldwide tendency to cluster in firms, and almost inevitably join professional associations.

To appreciate the economic significance of the acts of employees and agents, we need to consider some of the statistics of our economic organization. In 1983, about 100 million people were earning their livings in civilian pursuits. About 90 percent of these were working for somebody else, for wages and salaries. Some 9 percent considered themselves self-employed, but a considerable fraction of these were working for someone else for fees—as brokers, repairmen, lawyers, and accountants—usually in an agency relationship. The remainder were unpaid family workers.[1] This means that a very great preponderance of the nation's economic activity is carried on by employees and agents.

A contemporary economist has remarked that "one aspect of the many-sided revolution through which we are passing is the organizational revolution."[2] Only a century ago our economy was dominated by individual farmers and artisans. Today it is enmeshed in a web of corporations, labor unions, trade associations, and other organized movements. "In our political and economic thinking," he says, "in our ethical thinking as well, we are still often a hundred years behind the times—still thinking in terms of the society in which organizations are small and rather weak, in which the family is the dominant institution."

Organization is not new; it certainly existed when the Babylonians dug irrigation ditches, and when the Egyptians built pyramids. Life was never more pervasively organized than in the Middle Ages, when the church, the feudality, and the guilds regulated men's economic activities, their customs, and their expressions of belief.[3]

The "renaissance" of the Fifteenth Century and the later "enlightenment" of the Eighteenth Century may be characterized as move-

1. Statistical Abstract of the United States, 1985, pp. 394–395.

2. K. Boulding, The Organizational Revolution (1953), pp. 3–15.

3. O. von Gierke, Das Deutsche Genossenschaft, I (1868), 153–637.

1

ments to throw off these inherited structures. Enthusiasts apparently believed that by wiping out the bonds of organization, they would realize the vision of a man as an independent individual. What happened, as we know, was that royalty and nobility were not yet cold in their graves when organized political parties arose to take their places. The organized guilds were succeeded by the organized company and the organized labor union.

It is clearly false therefore to think of the "organizational revolution" as involving the rise of organizations to take the place of individualism. On the other hand, the last centuries' changes in the nature and the number of organizational forms in which people live, move, and have their being are so radical that they well merit the name of "revolution". The most obvious phase of the revolution is the one chiefly noted by the coiner of the phrase—the increase in the number of organizations to which a single individual is likely to belong. An upper middle-class American earns his living working for a corporation, and may plausibly belong to a professional society organized at the city, state and national level, to a church, college alumni association, political party, fraternal club, service club, country club, as well as being a shareholder in several business corporations; these are in addition to his family, and to the various governmental organizations (nation, state, county, city and school district) in which he participates.

A second aspect of the revolution is the immense size and power which have been acquired by modern economic organizations. A familiar paradox of statisticians, before the court-ordered divestiture of 1984, was to note that the American Telephone and Telegraph Company, a corporation of the state of New York, had a larger gross income than the government of that state.

A third aspect of the revolution, and the most important for the present study, is the fluidity of the rising modern organizations in contrast with the family, the church, and other traditional organizations. One aspect of this fluidity is the ability of every member to change his affiliation. A Capulet does not become a Montague and a Jew seldom becomes a Catholic, but a shareholder can switch with the greatest of ease from Royal Dutch Shell to Standard Oil of California, or from Imperial Chemical to Phillips Electric. In somewhat lesser numbers, members switch without trauma their political parties, and their country clubs. Fluidity appears also in the changeability of leadership. Most of the newer organizations are constructed on a democratic model, whereby the "members" (however identified) are entitled to freely elect their leaders. Although contemporary analysts are fond of demonstrating that the succession is more bureaucratic than democratic,[4] no one denies that authority revolves infinitely more freely in the modern corporation and other organizations than in the family, the aristocracy, the monarchy, or the patriarchal church.

---

4. A A Berle and G. Means, The Modern Corporation and Private Property (1932) pp. 87, 124, 220–221; G. Ripert, As-pects du capitalisme moderne (1951) pp. 90–109.

This volume is an introduction to the legal relationships inherent in an organizational society, i.e., a society dominated by organizations. We are not speaking only of an individual's relationship to his principal, his employer, or his organization. In a society where my answering service speaks to your answering service, organizations deal constantly with other organizations. A corporation may be employed by and become an agent of another corporation. Organizations are frequently *members* of other organizations; universities, unions, and many business corporations are large stockholders in other corporations. In most jurisdictions a corporation can itself become a partner or join in a joint venture with one or more other corporations. An organization as a member or as an agent of another organization may owe fiduciary duties to its principal or to fellow members. If all of this sounds somewhat mind-boggling, it is because it is mind-boggling. The materials which follow are designed to provide a method of analysis. The emphasis is on the business organization, but we do include some materials on non-profit organizations. Relationships within the family and in political organizations are left for other courses.

People organize themselves in all sorts of different ways which may shade into one another, or be deliberately mingled, like colors on a palette. Although there is always a tint which one has trouble in identifying as more red than blue, it is nevertheless useful to have names for the principal colors.

By far the most pervasive organizational form is the one known to lawyers as "agency", embracing all the people who work for somebody else (or have somebody else working for them). Agency embraces all kinds of agents—from the disappearing domestic servants, who may be directed in every move, to employees of businesses of all types, to the professional lawyer or broker, who may be advising his "principal" what ought to be done for him. An organizational entity itself may be an agent. Agency involves all kinds of employers, from the newsboy who pays a helper to a corporation which pays thousands of employees in skilled and unskilled capacities. It also includes individuals working for the government. It involves all kinds of jobs, from the degrading to the ennobling—from Oliver Twist picking pockets for Fagin to Lee Iacocca donating Chrysler funds to restore the Statue of Liberty. No categorical distinctions are drawn between employment for profit-making purposes, for eleemosynary objectives, and for personal gratification. There may be agencies for illegal purposes as well as for legal. The common element of agencies is that the main benefit or detriment of the act is intended to fall upon one of the parties, while the other is a mere instrument. In the terms of a metaphor as old as civilization, one party is "over" the second, and the second is "under" the first.

The great majority of agency relationships are found within business organizations, the largest classes of which are known as proprietorships, partnerships, limited partnerships and corporations. Although most moderns "earn" their livings in these business enterprises, the activities that make their lives worth living may be their family, their religion, their game of golf or bridge, their political cause, or their favorite charity. These activities are often carried out through organizations which are referred to by the cumbersome but technically accurate term "non-profit unincorporated association". As these organizations become richer and more complex, they frequently incorporate.

All of these forms of organization are involved to some degree in this casebook.

REFERENCES

K.E. Boulding, The Organizational Revolution (1953).

M. Weber, Law in Economy and Society (trans. by Shils and Rheinstein, 1954).

W.H. Whyte, The Organization Man (1956).

THE CHOICE OF BUSINESS FORM

Among the endless variety of structures in which business enterprises may be organized, four basic types merit initial attention. These are the individual proprietorship, the simple partnership, the limited partnership and the business corporation. A few of the attractions and detractions that characterize them in their typical forms are indicated by the following table. The attractions are indicated in italic type, the detractions in roman.

PROPRIETORSHIP	PARTNERSHIP	LIMITED PARTNERSHIP	CORPORATION
No documentation or filing essential to existence		Documentation and filing essential to existence	
No initial and annual franchise or license tax			Initial and annual franchise or license taxes
Owners individually liable for business debts		*Limited partners and shareholders not individually liable*	
Judicial proceedings in name of individual owner	Judicial proceedings in names of all partners	Judicial proceedings in name of general partner(s)	*Judicial proceedings in name of corporation*
Transfer of ownership requires conveyancing formalities	Transfer of ownership requires consent of copartners	*Transfer of limited shares may be allowed freely and informally*	*Shares freely negotiable*
Ownership and authority terminated by death of proprietor	Ownership and authority impaired by death of a partner	Ownership and authority impaired by death of a general partner	*Ownership and authority unaffected by death of member*

PROPRIETORSHIP	PARTNERSHIP	LIMITED PARTNERSHIP	CORPORATION
Distributed profits taxed only as income of members			Distributed profits taxed as corporate income & again as members' income
Enterprise profits taxed as income of members even though undistributed			*Undistributed profits taxed only as corporate income*
Enterprise losses offset against members' individual taxable incomes			Enterprise losses not offset against members' taxable incomes

In contemplating the indicated characteristics of different forms of organization, readers should remember that many of these characteristics can be varied by structural adaptations. For example, a closely held corporation can obtain most of the tax attributes of a partnership by conforming to a regime provided by Subchapter S of the Internal Revenue Code. On the other hand, a limited partnership, and even a simple partnership, may be so organized that it falls under the corporation tax regime. With regard to transferability of shares, partnership agreements can be devised so as to confer some of the negotiability of corporate shares upon ownership interests, while corporation charters and bylaws can be designed to restrict transfers of ownership in a manner characteristic of partnerships. But the typical attributes of the various forms remain significant because they are the attributes most frequently encountered in organizations of these forms, and because it is always easier (and often safer) to plan an organization that has the attributes typical of the form than to plan one with atypical attributes.

"AGENCY PROBLEMS"

In every enterprise that embraces more than one operative, some individuals are presumably working wholly or partly for the benefit of others in the organization. All these operatives are "agents," although their duties range from those of janitor to those of partner or chief executive. The persons for whose benefit the agents work—who may be individual proprietors, partnerships or corporations—are known in legal literature as the "principals," and in colloquial speech as the "owners" or the "bosses." Many of the agents are also members of the partnerships or shareholders in the corporations for whom they work, so that they share simultaneously some of the characteristics of agents and of principals.

The relationship of the operatives to their principals raises a host of problems, most of which fall into two main classes. One of these is the extent to which the principals are responsible for the promises and torts of their agents. This class may be regarded as the "external" aspect of agency, because it involves relations with third persons who are outside the principal-agent relationship.

Another problem is the extent to which the agents actually serve the purposes of the principals, or serve purposes of their own that conflict with those of the principals. This may be regarded as the "internal" aspect of agency.

In the following excerpt, this internal aspect is explored from the viewpoint and in the vocabulary of financial economics. The persons whom lawyers would call "principals" or "owners" are called "residual claimants." This term reflects the theory that the partners or shareholders in an enterprise are entitled to the residue of assets after creditors have been paid.

AGENCY PROBLEMS AND RESIDUAL CLAIMS

Eugene F. Fama and Michael C. Jensen Excerpts from 26 Journal of Law & Economics 327–328, 332–333 (1983).*

I. INTRODUCTION

A. *Organizational Survival*

Social and economic activities, such as religion, entertainment, education, research, and the production of other goods and services, are carried on by different types of organizations, for example, corporations, proprietorships, partnerships, mutuals, and nonprofits. Most goods and services can be produced by any form of organization, and there is competition among organizational forms for survival in any activity. Absent fiat, the form of organization that survives in an activity is the one that delivers the product demanded by customers at the lowest price while covering costs. This is the telling dimension on which the economic environment chooses among organizational forms.

An important factor in the survival of orgnizational forms is control of agency problems. Agency problems arise because contracts are not costlessly written and enforced. Agency costs include the costs of structuring, monitoring, and bonding a set of contracts among agents with conflicting interests, plus the residual loss incurred because the cost of full enforcement of contracts exceeds the benefits.[1] In this paper we explain the special features of the residual claims of different organizational forms as efficient approaches to controlling special agency problems. We analyze only private organizations. In related papers we examine other features of the contract structures of different organizational forms that contribute to their survival; in particular, (1) the control of agency problems in the class of organizations character-

1. This definition of agency costs first appears in Michael C. Jensen & William H. Meckling, Theory of the Firm: Managerial Behavior, Agency Costs and Ownership Structure, 3 J. Financial Econ. 305 (1976).

ized by separation of "ownership" and "control," and (2) the effects of special characteristics of residual claims on decision rules for resource allocation.[2]

B. *Residual Claims: General Discussion*

The contract structures of organizations limit the risks undertaken by most agents by specifying either fixed payoffs or incentive payoffs tied to specific measures of performance. The residual risk—the risk of the difference between stochastic inflows of resources and promised payments to agents—is borne by those who contract for the rights to net cash flows. We call these agents the residual claimants or residual risk bearers.

The characteristics of residual claims distinguish organizations from one another and help explain the survival of organizational forms in specific activities. We first analyze and contrast the relatively unrestricted residual claims of open corporations with the restricted residual claims of proprietorships, partnerships, and closed corporations. We then turn to the more specialized residual claims of professional partnerships, financial mutuals, and nonprofits.

II. OPEN CORPORATIONS

Most large nonfinancial organizations are open corporations. The common stock residual claims of such organizations are unrestricted in the sense that (1) stockholders are not required to have any other role in the organization, (2) their residual claims are freely alienable, and (3) the residual claims are rights in net cash flows for the life of the organization. Because of the unrestricted nature of the residual claims of open corporations, there is generally almost complete separation and specialization of decision functions and residual risk bearing.

. . .

III. RESTRICTED VERSUS UNRESTRICTED RESIDUAL CLAIMS

The proprietorships, partnerships, and closed corporations observed in small-scale production activities differ in many ways both from one another and from open corporations. For example, proprietorships have a single residual claimant, whereas partnerships and closed corporations have multiple residual claimants. As a consequence, the residual claim contracts in partnerships and closed corporations must specify rights in net cash flows and procedures for transferring residual claims to new agents more explicitly than the residual claims in proprietorships.

However, for control of the agency problems in the decision process, the common characteristic of the residual claims of proprietor-

2. Eugene F. Fama & Michael C. Jensen, Separation of Ownership and Control, in this issue. See also Eugene F. Fama & Michael C. Jensen, Organizational Forms and Investment Decisions (Working Paper No. MERC 83–03, Univ. Rochester, Managerial Economics Research Center 1983).

ships, partnerships, and closed corporations that distinguishes them from open corporations is that the residual claims are largely restricted to important decision agents. This restriction avoids the agency problems between residual claimants and decision agents that arise because of separation of risk-bearing and decision functions in open corporations. Thus, costly mechanisms for separating the management and control of decisions are avoided.[12]

Restricting residual claims to decision makers controls agency problems between residual claimants and decision agents, but at the expense of the benefits of unrestricted common stock. The decision process suffers efficiency losses because decision agents must be chosen on the basis of wealth and willingness to bear risk as well as for decision skills. Residual claimants forgo optimal diversification so that residual claims and decision making can be combined in a small number of agents. Forgone diversification and limited alienability lower the value of the residual claims, raise the cost of risk-bearing services, and lead to less investment in projects with uncertain payoffs than when residual claims are unrestricted. Finally, because decision agents have limited wealth, restricting residual claims to them also limits resources available for bonding contractual payoffs and for acquiring risky organization-specific assets.

An organizational form survives in an activity when the costs and benefits of its residual claims and the approaches it provides to controlling agency problems combine with available production technology to allow the organization to deliver products at lower prices than other organizational forms. The restricted residual claims of proprietorships, partnerships, and closed corporations are more likely to dominate when technology does not involve important economies of scale that lead to large demands for specialized decision skills, specialized risk bearing, and wealth from residual claimants. In these circumstances, the agency costs saved by restricting residual claims to decision agents outweigh the benefits that would be obtained from separation and specialization of decision and risk-bearing functions. On the other hand, unrestricted common stock residual claims are more likely to dominate when there are important economies of scale in production that (i) can be realized only with a complex decision hierarchy that makes use of specialized decision skills throughout the organization, (ii) generate large aggregate risks to be borne by residual claimants, and (iii) demand large amounts of wealth from residual claimants to purchase risky assets and to bond the payoffs promised to a wide range of agents in the organization. In such complex organizations the benefits of unrestricted common stock residual claims are likely to outweigh the costs of controlling the agency problems inherent in the separation and specialization of decision and risk-bearing functions. In these circumstances, the open corporation is more likely to win the competition for survival.[13]

---

12. However, in partnerships and closed corporations, some mechanisms for resolving conflicts among residual claimant decision makers (for example, buy-out rules) are required.

13. In Fama & Jensen, Separation of Ownership [26 J.L. & Econ. 301 (1983)], we discuss how the diffusion of information among decision agents influences the sur-

NUMBER AND DIMENSIONS OF ENTERPRISES
OF VARIOUS TYPES

(Numbers in thousands; receipts and income in billions of dollars)

	1970	1975	1980	1982
Proprietorships [1]				
Number	9,400	10,882	12,702	10,106
Business receipts	238	339	506	434
Net income	33	45	55	51
Partnerships [2]				
Number	936	1,073	1,380	1,514
Business receipts	93	147	292	297
Net income	10	8	8	-7
Corporations [3]				
Number	1,665	2,024	2,711	2,926
Business receipts	1,751	3,199	6,361	7,024
Net income	66	143	239	154

1. "Proprietorships" for 1980 and prior years include farms; for 1982, farms are excluded. According to a separate table, the number of "individual or family" farms in 1982 was 1,946,000, which, if added to the number of proprietorships, would yield a figure of 12,052,000 proprietorships for 1982. Comparable figures for farm receipts and net income in 1982 are unavailable.

In 1980, the largest number of proprietorships were in the "services" industry, closely followed by the numbers in "agriculture, forestry and fishing," and in "wholesale and retail trade." "Services" produced by far the most net income, although "wholesale and retail trade" produced the most receipts.

2. "Partnerships" in this table, which is based on income tax returns, means organizations that file partnership tax returns. They are likely to include most organizations that are regarded as simple or limited partnerships under the law of enterprise organization, but to exclude a few such organizations that are assimilated to corporations under the Internal Revenue Code. The low figures for net income, including the negative figure for 1982, may reflect the inclusion of limited partnerships designed as "tax shelters" to produce paper losses to be charged against taxable income.

In 1980, "finance, insurance and real estate" was the leading industrial division among partnerships, both in number of organizations and in business receipts, but "services" produced the most net income. Negative aggregate net income was reported by partnerships in "finance, insurance and real estate" and in "mining."

3. "Corporations" in this table embrace organizations that are taxed as corporations, even though they may call themselves by other names, such as "associations" or "trusts." On the other hand it omits two kinds of corporations that attorneys frequently encounter—those that file no income tax returns, either because they are inactive, or because they are the subsidiaries of corporations that file consolidated returns embracing the subsidiaries' activities.

vival of organizational forms. For simplicity, we have ignored these issues here.

In 1980, "wholesale and retail trade" embraced the largest number of corporations, but "manufacturing" produced the most receipts and, by a wide margin, the most net income.

SOURCES: Statistical Abstract of the United States, 1986, pp. 517, 518, 638; Id., 1984, p. 533.

Data on the concentration of assets in a small fraction of the corporate population is presented below, at page 586.

SECTION 1. PROPRIETORSHIPS

Although proprietorships are the most numerous form of business organization, there is no distinctive body of law about them. One does not find any treatises or digest titles devoted to them. This is probably because proprietorships are the implicit subject of most of the bodies of law known as contracts, torts and property. But sole proprietors do have their problems, both as to their duties and as to their rights. The following cases illustrate some of the elementary problems that may be faced by other forms of organization, but are particularly apposite to the individual proprietor.

MANCHESTER SUPPLY CO. v. DEARBORN
New Hampshire Supreme Court, 1940.
90 N.H. 447, 10 A.2d 658.

[The plaintiff's petition, as amended, sought judgment against Leah Dearborn for goods purchased by her husband, Fred Dearborn. A judgment against Fred had been obtained in a previous action. A master heard the evidence in the present suit and recommended dismissal of the petition; the lower court followed his recommendation.]

The master, after reciting in summary the testimony of the defendants, both of whom were called to the stand by the plaintiff, made the following findings:

"Fred Dearborn had conducted a plumbing business as an independent contractor for many years, and had done business with the plaintiff company as such independent contractor. The goods in question were purchased on an open account between the plaintiff and Fred Dearborn, and so far as anything appears to the contrary, the plaintiff intended to give exclusive credit to Fred Dearborn. The items sued for were sold by the plaintiff on Dearborn's credit, and the plaintiff expected him to pay for them.

"The only basis for a finding of agency with an undisclosed principal is the plaintiff's assumption that Leah was the undisclosed principal of her husband because of the fact that he was her husband and the goods were purchased for use in her property. Against that assumption, we have the facts as found, and the testimony of Leah Dearborn with particular reference to Dearborn's dealings with the plaintiff over a period of years as an independent plumbing contractor.

"The Master finds no basis to treat this transaction of Fred Dearborn with the plaintiff any differently from others over a period of years wherein Dearborn did business with the plaintiff; and therefore finds that Dearborn was not acting as the agent of Leah Dearborn, but as an independent contractor."

It appears that the articles purchased from the plaintiff were various items of heating equipment which the defendant Fred installed in a house owned by his wife and in which they both lived. . . .

WOODBURY, J.　After contrasting English law with the continental systems, Professor Mechem in his work on agency writes that "it is unquestionably the general rule of our law that an undisclosed principal, when subsequently discovered, may, at the election of the other party, if exercised within a reasonable time, be held upon all simple non-negotiable contracts made in his behalf by his duly authorized agent, although the contract was originally made with the agent in entire ignorance of the principal." 2 Mechem, Agency (2d ed.), § 1731. To the same effect see 1 Williston, Contracts (Rev. ed.), § 286; § 3 C.J.S. Agency, § 244; 2 Am.Jur., Agency, § 393; 1 Am.Law Inst., Restatement of Agency, § 186. Later in the above section of Professor Mechem's work it is said, "The rule itself is doubtless an anomaly, but even so it is undoubtedly as well settled as any other rule of the law of agency." It has for many years been in effect in this state. Chandler v. Coe, 54 N.H. 561; Bryant v. Wells, 56 N.H. 152, 155.

From the authorities cited above, as well as from the very nature of the situation, this right of action does not depend upon the third person's knowledge when dealing with the agent, that the latter was acting for another instead of for himself. Obviously everyone, when dealing with an agent for a wholly undisclosed principal, believes that he is dealing with the agent only, relies solely upon the agent individually, and, if credit be extended, extends that credit to no one but the agent. However, and herein lies the anomaly, the creditor has a right of action against the undisclosed principal, when discovered, even though he never learned of the existence of the latter until after the bargain was completed, if he can prove, as in every other case of agency, that the agent's acts were within the scope of authority. 1 Am. Law Inst., Restatement of Agency, §§ 194, 195; 1 Williston, Contracts, supra; 2 Am.Jur., Agency, § 401; 3 C.J.S. Agency, § 245; Platts v. Auclair, 79 N.H. 250, 252, 108 A. 167. The fundamental question in the case at bar, then, is not whether the plaintiff, when it sold the items of heating equipment to Fred, believed that it was dealing with Fred alone and individually, but it is whether or not Leah ever authorized Fred to make those purchases for her and in her behalf.

This is the question which the plaintiff brought to the attention of the master by its request for a finding referred to earlier in this opinion, and that question does not appear to have been properly passed upon. While it is true that there are findings to the effect that Fred was not acting as the agent of his wife when he purchased the items of heating equipment, it is evident from those findings themselves as well as from their context, that the master's conclusion of lack of agency was based at least in part upon his findings with respect to the plaintiff's belief at the time of purchase that it was dealing with Fred alone and in his individual capacity. These latter findings concerning the transactions between Fred and the plaintiff shed no light upon the real question in this case which is whether or not Fred, when dealing with the plaintiff, was, unknown to it, acting as the agent of his wife. From this failure to comprehend the nature of the issue presented, it follows that there must be a new trial as to the defendant Leah. . . .

THE LIABILITY OF THE UNDISCLOSED PRINCIPAL IN CONTRACT

William Draper Lewis, 1909.
9 Col.L.Rev. 116, 133–134.[1]

[In an action of assumpsit] it is not the defendant's promise to the plaintiff on which the plaintiff recovers, but the fact that the defendant caused the plaintiff to do an act (though that act is merely a promise with the intent of being legally bound), which he would not have done had not the defendant acted. . . .

Where the agent acts openly in his principal's name the usual explanation of the principal's liability on the promise is the fiction that the principal has made the promise. But if the thought just expressed is correct, the fiction is an unnecessary invention,—the principal is liable on the contract because he has so acted as to induce the plaintiff to change his position for a stipulated reward. . . .

Where the principal is disclosed and the contract is made in his name, he has so acted as to induce the plaintiff to change his position. But the same is equally true in the case of the undisclosed principal; he has also moved his agent in the same way. To no greater and to no less extent than the disclosed principal has he caused the plaintiff to alter his position. To permit the person who has dealt with the undisclosed principal's agent in such a way as to raise a contract on which the action of assumpsit could be brought, on discovery of the principal, to elect whether he shall regard the contract as with the agent or with the principal, instead of being an anomaly and contrary to the fundamental common law idea of the reason for the obligation of the contract, would appear to fit in as perfectly with the fundamental idea lying at the foundation of the liability, as the denial of such a right to one who has made a formal contract under seal with agent of the undisclosed principal, fits in with the fundamental idea lying at the foundation of liability on formal contracts. . . .

1. The quotation is excerpted from an article of the same name. William Draper Lewis (1867–1949) was dean of the Department of Law of the University of Pennsylvania from 1896 to 1914, when he resigned to run for Governor of Pennsylvania on the Progressive ticket. He was drafts- man (after Ames' resignation) of the Uniform Partnership Act (completed 1914). But he is likely to be best remembered as the organizer of the American Law Institute, of which he was director from 1923 to 1947, and through which he fathered the Restatements of the Law.

REFERENCES ON UNDISCLOSED PRINCIPALS

Articles:

Sir Frederick Pollock, editorial note (1887) 3 L.Q.Rev. 358–359 (denouncing rights of undisclosed principal).

Holmes, History of Agency (1882) 4 Harv.L.Rev. 345, 5 id. 1, reprinted in 3 Select Essays in Anglo-American Legal History (1909) 368; see especially 3 Select Essays 390–395, 410.

Mueller-Freienfels, The Undisclosed Principal, 16 Mod.L.Rev. 299 (1953) (liability of undisclosed principals is gaining favor in Europe, where it was formerly unrecognized).

SPIVAK v. SACHS

Court of Appeals of New York, 1965.
16 N.Y.2d 163, 263 N.Y.S.2d 953, 211 N.E.2d 329.

CHIEF JUDGE DESMOND. Plaintiff, a California attorney not admitted to the Bar of New York State (or of Connecticut), has an affirmed judgment against defendant for the reasonable value of legal services (plus traveling and other expenses) rendered to defendant in New York City where defendant resided. Defendant appeals here, arguing that plaintiff cannot recover since what he did amounted to the illegal practice of law in this State in violation of section 270 of the Penal Law.

Both courts below held—and it is not really disputed or disputable—that these were legal services. The Trial Term and the Appellate Division majority decided, however, that what plaintiff did in New York was not the "practice" of law within the meaning of section 270 of the Penal Law which, as all agree, states the basic law, but was a mere "isolated situation". The Appellate Division dissent, however, pointed (21 A.D.2d 348, pp. 350–351, 250 N.Y.S.2d 666, pp. 668, 669) to the undisputed fact that the services consisted of "advice and assistance rendered to defendant and her attorneys . . ., including litigation pending in Connecticut and the proposed drafts of a settlement agreement", also legal advice as to "the matter of the proper jurisdiction for the matrimonial litigation, the advisability of the dismissal of the Connecticut proceedings with the institution of a new action in New York, the matter of property settlements . . . the custody of the infant son of the parties" as well as the giving of plaintiff's opinion "as to the nature of the representation defendant was receiving at the hands of her present counsel in New York with a recommendation that she retain a certain other attorney here".

The dissent below emphasized that the advice given by plaintiff was in part based on his knowledge or claimed knowledge of New York law. The dissenting Justices concluded that all this showed that plaintiff had practiced law illegally in New York. With that conclusion we agree.

We summarize the facts as found below. Plaintiff had never represented defendant before but had met her and her husband socially in California, Connecticut and New York. In 1959 defendant's husband sued her for a divorce in Connecticut and she retained attorneys in New York and Connecticut to represent her in the litigation and to negotiate a separation agreement. In November of that year defendant telephoned from New York to plaintiff in California. She told him that she was being pressed into a property settlement, that one child had been taken from her and she feared she might lose the custody of the other child and that she was confused and wanted plaintiff to come to New York to talk to her about her affairs. There were two other such telephone conversations during which defendant explained the details of the proposed agreements and again urged plaintiff to come to New York. He agreed to do so, informing her that he would advance his own expenses, then charge them to her plus a reasonable fee for his services. He told her that he was not licensed in New York and could do no more than consult with her, advise her and recommend New York counsel. Flying to New York, he spent about fourteen days there on defendant's affairs. During several meetings with defendant he examined various drafts of separation agreements as proposed by defendant's Connecticut counsel and discussed her problems as to financial arrangements and custody of the children. Based on his knowledge of both New York and California law, so he testified, he expressed his opinion that the suggested financial provisions for her were inadequate and that "she wasn't being adequately represented". Later defendant arranged meetings of plaintiff with defendant's New York attorney and plaintiff told that New York attorney that Connecticut was not the "proper jurisdiction" for the divorce suit. After several more meetings with the New York lawyer at some of which defendant was present, plaintiff tried without success to persuade defendant to discharge her New York counsel and retain a different New York lawyer named by plaintiff. For these services plaintiff demanded a fee of $10,575 but was awarded judgment for $3,500 as his fee at the rate of $250 per day, plus about $1,600 in travel, hotel, telephone and incidental expense.

It is settled that the practice of law forbidden in this State by section 270 of the Penal Law to all but duly licensed New York attorneys includes legal advice and counsel as well as appearing in the courts and holding oneself out as a lawyer (People v. Alfani, 227 N.Y. 334, 125 N.E. 671; Bennett v. Goldsmith, 280 N.Y. 529, 19 N.E.2d 927; Matter of New York County Lawyers' Assn. [Cool], 294 N.Y. 853, 62 N.E.2d 398; Matter of New York County Lawyers Assn. [Roel], 3 N.Y.2d 224, 165 N.Y.S.2d 31, 144 N.E.2d 24). All this plaintiff concedes but he argues here, as he did successfully below, that although not admitted to the New York Bar he may still collect a fee for legal services performed here, since what he did was a "single, isolated incident" and not the "practice" of law. We think this is a misreading of the statute and a misapplication of the holdings in People v. Alfani (supra) and People v. Goldsmith (249 N.Y. 586, 164 N.E. 593), particularly the latter.

Alfani and Goldsmith were both laymen and both were prosecuted and convicted for alleged violations of section 270. Alfani's conviction was upheld since he had made it his regular business to draw legal papers for hire. Goldsmith's conviction was reversed upon the ground that there was no evidence that he "held himself out to the public as being entitled to practice law within the meaning of section 270 of the Penal Law. (See People v. Alfani, 227 N.Y. 334, 125 N.E. 671.)" This court followed the Appellate Division's dissent in Goldsmith's case and agreed with it that the drawing by a layman of one single document for a small fee without any "holding out" was not the "practice" of law. The contrast was with Alfani who made such work his regular business. The exculpation of Goldsmith was consistent with People v. Title Guar. & Trust Co. (227 N.Y. 366, 125 N.E. 666) where a corporation which abstracted titles and guaranteed mortgages was held not to have violated section 280 of the Penal Law by drawing a single document without giving any legal advice.

The *Alfani, Goldsmith* and *Title Guarantee* cases (supra), laying down the rule that drawing a single document for a small fee or no fee is not law practice, have no relevance to the case at hand. Here we have a California lawyer brought to New York not for a conference or to look over a document but to advise directly with a New York resident as to most important marital rights and problems. Not only did he give her legal counsel as to those matters but essayed to give his opinion as to New York's being the proper jurisdiction for litigation concerning the marital res and as to related alimony and custody issues, and even went so far as to urge a change in New York counsel. To say that this falls short of the "practice of law" in New York is to defeat section 270 and the policy it represents. The statute aims to protect our citizens against the dangers of legal representation and advice given by persons not trained, examined and licensed for such work, whether they be laymen or lawyers from other jurisdictions.

This is not answered by pointing to rules permitting out-of-State lawyers to appear in our courts on occasion or even to be admitted to practice here. The first is by express permission of the court and always on recommendation of a member of our Bar. As to admission here of a lawyer from another jurisdiction, that comes about only after the fulfillment of certain express requirements.

There is, of course, a danger that section 270 could under other circumstances be stretched to outlaw customary and innocuous practices. We agree with the Supreme Court of New Jersey (Appell v. Reiner, 43 N.J. 313, 204 A.2d 146) that, recognizing the numerous multi-State transactions and relationships of modern times, we cannot penalize every instance in which an attorney from another State comes into our State for conferences or negotiations relating to a New York client and a transaction somehow tied to New York. We can decide those cases when we get them but they are entirely unlike the present one.

This was an illegal transaction and under our settled rules we refuse to aid in it but leave the parties where they are (McConnell v.

Commonwealth Pictures Corp., 7 N.Y.2d 465, 199 N.Y.S.2d 483, 166 N.E.2d 494, and cases cited).

The order should be reversed and the complaint dismissed, with costs in all courts.

JUDGES BURKE, SCILEPPI and BERGAN concur with CHIEF JUDGE DESMOND; JUDGES DYE, FULD and VAN VOORHIS dissent and vote to affirm upon the opinion at the Appellate Division.

REFERENCES

Murphy v. Campbell Investment Co., 79 Wn.2d 417, 486 P.2d 1080 (1971) (partnership that lacked license when contract was executed could not recover although it had perfected license by the time work was performed).

Costello v. Schmidlin, 404 F.2d 87, 32 A.L.R.3d 1139 (3d Cir.1968) (engineer licensed in New York could recover for consultation in New Jersey with engineer licensed in New Jersey).

Rights under federal law and constitution:

Spanos v. Skouras Theatres Corp., 364 F.2d 161 (2d Cir.1966), cert. denied 385 U.S. 987, 87 S.Ct. 597, 17 L.Ed.2d 448 (1966) (out-of-state lawyer retained to work with in-state lawyers on federal rights of client was entitled to fee); comments, 67 Colum.L.Rev. 731, 55 Geo.L. 374, 4 Houston L.Rev. 722, 65 Mich.L.Rev. 769, 41 N.Y.U.L.Rev. 1235, 19 Stan. L.Rev. 856, 40 So.Cal.L.Rev. 569, 53 Va.L.Rev. 424.

Cowen v. Calabrese, 230 Cal.App.2d 870, 41 Cal.Rptr. 441, 11 A.L.R.3d 903 (1964) (Illinois lawyer could recover for services rendered in California in relation to federal bankruptcy case).

Out-of-state attorneys in civil rights cases:

Leis v. Flynt, 439 U.S. 438, 99 S.Ct. 698, 58 L.Ed.2d 717 (1979) (out-of-state attorneys who were barred from representing Larry Flynt in Ohio pornography prosecution had no federal Constitutional right to be admitted to state court for this purpose); per curiam opinion reversing 574 F.2d 874 (6th Cir.1978), which affirmed 434 F.Supp. 481 (S.D.Ohio 1977). Comment, 29 Buffalo L.Rev. 133 (1980).

Sanders v. Russell, 401 F.2d 241 (5th Cir.1968) (mandamus granted to require district court judge to admit out-of-state attorney in civil rights case where there was dearth of local representation).

Sobol v. Perez, 289 F.Supp. 392 (D.C.La.1968) (civil rights defense lawyer from District of Columbia represented black defendants in Mississippi courts in cases arising out of school desegregation; was prosecuted for unlicensed practice in Mississippi courts; federal court enjoins state district attorney and judge because of interference with federal rights); comment, 4 Harv.Civ.Lib.-Civ.Rights L.Rev. 65 (1968).

Note, Commerce Clause Challenge to State Restrictions on Practice by Out-of-State Attorneys, 72 Nw.U.L.Rev. 737 (1977).

Sherman, The Right of Representation by Out-of-State Attorneys in Civil Rights Cases (1968) 4 Harv.Civ.Lib.-Civ.Rights L.Rev. 65.

Economics and sociology of licensing:

Gellhorn, Occupational Licensing—A Nationwide Dilemma, 109 J. Accountancy 39 (1960) (noting effects of licensing in restricting economic opportunity of members of disfavored groups).

Baron, Licensure for Health Care Professionals: The Consumer's Case for Abolition, 9 Am.J.L. & Med. 335 (1983).

Johnson and Corgel, Antitrust Immunity and the Economics of Occupational Licensing, 20 Am.Bus.L.J. 471 (1983) (contending that licensing is a device for restricting competition).

Friedman, Freedom of Contract and Occupational Licensing 1890–1910: A Legal and Social Study (1965) 53 Cal.L.Rev. 487 (contrasts courts' tolerance of licensing laws with condemnation of laws regulating wages and hours).

NOTE ON BUSINESS NAMES

Recent decades have seen a rapid spread of statutes requiring people who do business under "assumed" or "fictitious" names to file the assumed name, and the personal names of the actors, in a public office. These statutes are generally assumed to apply to such names as "Bluebird Tearoom," "Reliable Plumbers," and "General Trading Company," when used as designations of business enterprises, even though there is nothing deceptive about them.

Many of the assumed name statutes prescribe a criminal penalty, but fail to say whether violation has any effect on civil remedies. In several states, early decisions under the acts held that a merchant could not recover on a contract which he made under his assumed, but unfiled, name. In all or most of these states, further reflection persuaded the courts or legislatures that the penalty did not fit the crime. For example, the Supreme Court of Kentucky denied recovery on a note for $284 taken under the name of "Big Four Auto Company," [1] but boggled at denying recovery to a merchant who had deposited in the defendant bank $80,000 under the name of "Dreamland Theatre." [2]

Recent statutes commonly preclude suit by the user of an unfiled assumed business name only until the name has been filed, after which suits based on prior business may be maintained. See, for instance, Cal.Bus. & Prof.Code § 17918; Mich.Comp.L. § 445.5.

REFERENCES

Recommendation and Study—Fictitious Business Names, 9 Cal.L.Rev.Comm.Rep. 601 (1969).

McClintock, Fictitious Business Name Legislation, 19 Hastings L.J. 1349.

SECTION 2. PARTNERSHIPS

One of the outstanding features of the organizational revolution is the impulse of people to join in common endeavors. This impulse is commonly attributed to the desire to pool money, resources, skills, and intelligence for greater achievements; it may also respond to some less rational need for affiliation or psychic reinforcement. Modern laws generously provide convenient receptacles for these efforts, by way of corporations for business, religious, eleemosynary, educational or social purposes.

However, millions of people continue to pool their resources through less formal, or substantially unstructured, groups. Of these, the one best known to the law is the ordinary partnership. As recently as the early 1960's there were professional rules imposed by medical boards, bar associations and stock exchanges which prohibited corpo-

---

1. Hunter v. Big Four Auto Co., 162 Ky. 778, 173 S.W. 120, L.R.A. 1915D, 987 (1915).

2. Hayes v. Providence Citizens Bank & Trust Co., 218 Ky. 128, 290 S.W. 1028, 59 A.L.R. 450 (1927), overruling Hunter v. Big Four Auto Co., supra.

rate membership and restricted members of these professions to sole proprietorship or to the partnership form. These professional partnerships often possessed sophisticated articles which yielded nothing in perfection to the most elaborate corporation papers. As we write in 1986, most of these rules have been repealed, and a substantial proportion of professional associations are in corporate form.

The great mass of ordinary partnerships are probably in that form because the parties never gave their organizational structure much attention. Their agreements are informal, and often unwritten. Consequently the partnership law is designed to cover in a very loose way the most diverse and inarticulated organizational structures, some of which would not be recognized as partnerships by their participants. In the penumbra of the partnership concept, where association fades into mere co-ownership or co-operation, we encounter something called the "joint venture."

A majority of the juridical disputes surrounding partnership arise from the desire of investors to share profits without incurring the full responsibilities of membership. For those who recognize this problem, the law now provides a special structure called the limited partnership, which is briefly noticed in the following section.

NOTE: HISTORICAL DEVELOPMENT OF PARTICIPATION WITHOUT INDIVIDUAL LIABILITY

Among the various forms of organization in which men tend to cluster themselves, one type which assumed an early prominence in common law was the partnership. It seems to have been always too clear for argument that all partners are liable for the undertakings of other partners within the scope of the partnership business. This led to the question, who is a partner?

In the late 1700's, a doctrine became deeply entrenched, even if not universally applied, that "every man who has a share of the profits ought also to bear his share of the loss," with a gratuitous corollary that every such person ought to be suable by a creditor. Two leading English cases became widely cited for this doctrine: Grace v. Smith[1] (1775) and Waugh v. Carver[2] (1793).

To this rule there were a few exceptions, like the case of the partner's widow, who might receive an annuity of a profit share without becoming a partner. But any business man who contributed capital to a business, in return for a promised share of profits, had a better than even chance of being held liable as a partner on the complaint of a credit. If he escaped, it was by proving he was really a landlord, a creditor or some other clearly distinguished category. Most certainly, the common law of the eighteenth and nineteenth centuries did not recognize the category, so well recognized throughout the mainland of Europe, of an associate in commenda—a man who advanced money and shared profits, but did not incur personal liability because he did not intend to be a principal.

As time wore on, courts were forced to recognize more and more exceptions to the rule that the participant in profits is liable for obligations. The rule was

1. Grace v. Smith, 2 Wm. Blackstone 998, 96 Eng.Repr. 587 (King's Bench 1775).

2. Waugh v. Carver, 2 Henry Blackstone 235, 126 Eng.Repr. 525 (Common Pleas, England 1793).

flatly repudiated in the leading House of Lords decision of Cox v. Hickman [3] (1860), which served as a signal in the United States as well as England for courts to deal more charitably with the profit-sharing investor.

A uniform law for partnerships in the United States was first taken up by the Conference of Commissioners of Uniform State Laws in 1902, and was finally approved in 1914. At the beginning of 1985, the Uniform Partnership Act had been adopted in all states except Louisiana.

UNIFORM PARTNERSHIP ACT
National Conference of Commissioners of Uniform State Laws, 1914.

Read carefully sections 6, 7, 9 and 15.

KAUFMAN–BROWN POTATO CO. v. LONG
United States Court of Appeals, Ninth Circuit, 1950.
182 F.2d 594.

STEPHENS, CIRCUIT JUDGE. The individuals, Charles H. Kaufman and Albert H. Brown, doing business as Kaufman-Brown Potato Company, a partnership, joined with two others in a petition filed in federal district court alleging that they were creditors of Gerry Horton and J.D. Althouse, individually, and creditors of them doing business as Gerry Horton Company, a partnership, and Gerry Horton and J.D. Althouse doing business as Gerry Horton Farms, a partnership. The petition contained appropriate allegations upon which bankruptcy adjudication was pronounced against both Horton and Althouse and against the two partnerships of which they were members. . . .

. . . The referee and the district court in response to a petition of the trustee in bankruptcy subsequently made an order declaring among other things, that there was a second partnership by the name of Gerry Horton Farms which was composed of the first mentioned partnership of the same name and the partnership of Kaufman-Brown Potato Company. This second "Gerry Horton Farms" is distinguished by the bankruptcy court by adding after the name "engaged in raising potatoes". We shall designate it "Gerry Horton Farms (partnership combination)." By the amended order "Gerry Horton Farms (partnership combination)" as a distinct and separate enterprise is added to those adjudged bankrupt in the original adjudication.

Applicable local or California state law was applied to the facts in the consideration of this issue,[1] and when this is done we must hold to the referee's and the court's conclusions unless they are without substantial support or, though they are substantially supported, we find

---

3. Cox v. Hickman, 8 H.L.Cas. 268, 11 Eng.Repr. 430 (House of Lords 1860).

1. [Footnote by the court:] Although the strict place of contracting appears to have been Illinois, performance was to appear in California. It was in California that the creditor rights arose. A rigid adherence to the place of contracting test as to what law governs is, we think, obnoxious where as here the more important contacts are with California. In any event, applicable Illinois law is no different. The Uniform Partnership Act has also been adopted there. See Smith-Hurd Ann.St. of Ill. (1917), c. 106½, §§ 1–43.

upon a review of the whole case that clearly a mistake has been made. . . .

It appears from the evidence that Horton and Althouse, prior to any association with Kaufman-Brown Potato Company, were doing business in partnership both as Gerry Horton Company and Gerry Horton Farms, under the former name as farm produce distributors and under the latter name as producers. In 1944 they held two parcels of California farm land under lease. As to each parcel separately Horton and Althouse as Gerry Horton Farms contracted in writing with Kaufman and Brown doing business as Kaufman-Brown Potato Company, who were distributors, relative to planting, raising, and harvesting potatoes on such land.

It was agreed on each contract that Kaufman and Brown would purchase from Horton and Althouse for a certain amount an undivided interest [50% as to one parcel; 40% as to the other parcel] in all potato crops to be planted, raised and harvested upon such leased land during the year 1944. Horton and Althouse agreed to pay all costs and expenses of planting and raising in excess of the amount above mentioned to be paid in by Kaufman and Brown for the above undivided interests. The costs incurred for harvesting were to be shared in the ratio of such interests. The net proceeds after repayment to Kaufman and Brown of the amount they paid in and of any amounts paid by Horton and Althouse in addition thereto for the expenses of planting and raising were to be divided "between the partners" [quoting from such contracts] in like manner. The over-all losses sustained in the venture were to be borne by the parties in their interest ratio. It was also provided that Horton and Althouse would keep full and accurate accounts of the enterprise at their place of business. The written contracts provided for an option to Kaufman and Brown Potato Company to purchase the crop raised and harvested on each parcel of land for a price equal to the prevailing market price but if there were no prevailing market price upon harvest Kaufman and Brown agreed to handle all the potatoes as agents for Horton and Althouse for a stated commission "for said services rendered on behalf of the partners hereto" and pay to Horton and Althouse all money received from the sale thereof "subject to accounting and distribution as hereinbefore set forth." [Quotations are from each contract.] In the event that Kaufman and Brown exercised their option to purchase, Horton and Althouse could add to the purchase price any markups allowed by O.P.A. regulations but that the total amount of such markups would be divided between the parties in the ratio of their interests. Horton and Althouse were to furnish all the necessary farming equipment. The contracts also provided for the execution of a crop mortgage as security for faithful performance by Horton and Althouse and for a promissory note also to be executed in an amount which as above mentioned Kaufman and Brown were to pay in. After each contract had been fully complied with, the mortgage and note were to be surrendered and cancelled. It was declared that the mortgage and note were executed solely as security for performance and that Horton and Althouse were not to be held liable for any losses resulting from causes beyond their control. The contracts did not provide for a firm bank account nor for a firm name of the business to be conducted under the provisions of the contracts. Both agreements were prepared by Horton and Althouse's attorney pursuant to Horton's instructions.

A partnership may be formed for a single venture. Westcott v. Gilman, 1915, 170 Cal. 562, 150 P. 777, Ann.Cas.1916E, 437. . . . Whether or not a partnership relationship exists is determinable by the intent of the parties to do things which constitute a partnership. Chapman v. Hughes, 1894, 104 Cal. 302, 37 P. 1048, 38 P. 109. . . . It is immaterial that the parties deign not to call their relationship, or believe it not to be, a partnership, especially where as here the rights of third persons are involved. It is true that a mere agreement to share profits and losses does not make a partnership but both the sharing of profits and losses are usual in partnership agreements and practices.

It is plain that the contracts in question were drawn with some of the usual covenants and conditions both of a straight financing contract with options and of a partnership agreement. Appellants point especially to the provisions for crop mortgages as supporting the former relation but their argument is offset by the proviso that such were to be security only for performance on the part of Horton and Althouse and that Horton and Althouse would not be liable for any losses occasioned by causes beyond their control. The non-mention of capital contribution of each of the parties is stressed, but all partners need not contribute capital in the strict sense of the word; some may invest their labor and skill. See Gray v. Palmer, 1858, 9 Cal. 616, 638. These contracts provide that Kaufman and Brown were to put up so much money for initial expense but note that all of it was to be returned out of the product as expense before division of sales returns. Horton and Althouse were to devote themselves to the farming aspect using their own equipment, and Kaufman and Brown were to use their sales organization and experience if necessary to effect distribution of the crop. However, the provision that the amounts paid in by Kaufman and Brown were to be repaid before division of sales returns is consistent with a partnership relationship. [Citing U.P.A. § 18(a).] There is a provision in each of the contracts that in certain circumstances Kaufman and Brown would act as agents for Horton and Althouse to dispose of the potatoes upon harvest through Chicago markets for a stated commission and would pay to Horton and Althouse money obtained from sales. This provision appears to be more unusual in a partnership contract than inconsistent with one, for Horton and Althouse were to keep the accounts and all such provisions were stated to be "subject to accounting and distribution as hereinbefore set forth." The use of the word "partner" in *each* agreement could have been but a handy word to include personnel without naming them but the factfinder, on analyzing the complicated contracts, would not be justified in rejecting its possible bearing on the issue entirely. The contracts also provide that Horton and Althouse keep the "books of account and all other records" of the enterprise at their place of business and that each of the partners hereto "shall at all times have access to and may inspect and copy any of them." The latter quoted language is taken verbatim from California Civil Code section 2413 [California Corporations Code section 15019], which relates to "partnership books".

It is evident that Kaufman and Brown advanced more than was required by the contracts. This fact could be accounted for by their desire to protect their interests in either relation. Further, there is testimony to the effect that both Messrs. Kaufman and Brown came to California and made recommendations relative to operations under the contracts. Of course, their interest in the contracts could have justified their personal presence on the ground, either as partners or joint venturers, but it is consistent with partnership interest.

We are of the opinion that the record contains the essentials of a partnership and also substantial proof that such was the intention at least of Horton and Althouse, the authors of the contracts. Upon a review of the record as a whole we do not find that a mistake has been made. Compare Westcott v. Gilman, supra.

[After finding that there was a "partnership combination," the court found that the order adjudicating it a bankrupt was invalid for procedural reasons. But it gave effect to its finding by refusing to permit payment on Kaufman-Brown's claim until all other creditors should be paid in full.]

REFERENCES

Gutierrez v. Yancey, 650 S.W.2d 169 (Tex.Civ.App.1983) (agreement to finance farming operation in exchange for a share of profits did not create a partnership, in the absence of language indicating an intent to form partnership or to share losses).

Martin v. Peyton, 246 N.Y. 213, 158 N.E. 77 (1927) (agreement to finance a brokerage firm did not create partnership, where rights of financiers were carefully framed as powers of veto, powers to accept undated resignations, and an option to buy).

Lewis & Queen v. N.M. Ball Sons, 48 Cal.2d 141, 308 P.2d 713 (1957) (partnership that lacked occupational license could not recover for services, although supervising partner was licensed).

THE UNIFORM PARTNERSHIP ACT
William Draper Lewis, 1915.
24 Yale L.J. 617, 621.

. . . The second test of the Act is the extent to which existing uncertainties in the law of partnership are rendered certain. Before answering this question it is perhaps well to emphasize the fact that there is one matter connected with partnership which legislation cannot make certain. By no human ingenuity would a Partnership Act which does not abolish common law partnerships enable the person who reads it to tell in every supposable case whether there is or is not a partnership. . . .

. . . The uncertainty lies in the fundamental characteristic which distinguishes partnerships from every other business association. All other business associations are statutory in origin. They are formed by the happening of an event designated in a statute as necessary to their formation. In corporations this act may be the issuing of a charter by the proper officer of the state; in limited partnerships, the filing by the associates of a specified document in a public office. On the other hand, an infinite number of circumstances may result in co-ownership of a business. Partnership is the residuum, including all forms of co-ownership of a business except those business associations organized under specific statutes.

SECTION 3. LIMITED PARTNERSHIPS

The desire for a way of investing in a business without incurring the liability of a partner led, over a hundred years ago, to statutes of "limited partnership." The first one in an Anglo-American jurisdiction was New York's adopted in 1822 in conscious limitation of the commenda (*société en commandite*) which had grown up under the European law merchant, and was codified in the Napoleonic Commercial Code of 1807. At this date, the doctrines of Grace v. Smith and Waugh v. Carver were in full vigor, and incorporation still (for the most part) a matter of legislative grace.

Although legal theorists have made much of the changes wrought by Cox v. Hickman, it is notable that limited partnership laws continued to be enacted after that decision, and after legislation which made incorporation easy. England adopted her Limited Partnership Act in 1907, 47 years after Cox v. Hickman, and 17 years after the English Partnership Act.

In the United States, the National Conference of Commissioners on Uniform State Laws promulgated a Uniform Limited Partnership Act in 1916, and that Act ultimately was adopted by all states except Louisiana. In 1976, only four years after the last adoption of the ULPA, a revised Uniform Limited Partnership Act was adopted. In late 1986, a majority of states had adopted the 1976 revision, or some variation of it.

Following the onset of World War II, there was a rapid increase in interest in the limited partnership. Prior to that time, investors who feared personal liability were generally satisfied with the corporate form, which had become very freely available. But the corporate form has the disadvantage of subjecting the enterprise to a number of special burdens of regulation, procedure, and taxes—especially income taxes. The earnings of a corporation are subject to tax as corporate income; the dividends paid from the earnings are subject to tax as income of the shareholders. In a partnership, if typical arrangements are followed, the earnings are taxed only once, as income of the partners. Moreover, both world wars and the Korean War brought with them an additional tax on "excess profits," which applied to corporations but not to typical partnerships and limited partnerships. We say "typical" because a partnership may be so conducted as to incur corporation taxes even though it may not be, for other purposes, a corporation.

During the 1970s and 1980s, limited partnerships became favorite instruments for sophisticated investors because of income tax rules that permitted high earners to set off "losses" of limited partnerships against income from other sources. These rules were restricted, but not completely abolished, by the Tax Reform Act of 1986, the impact of which remains uncertain at this writing.

REFERENCES ON LIMITED PARTNERSHIPS

History:

Crane, Are Limited Partnerships Necessary?—The Return of the Commenda (1933) 17 Minn.L.Rev. 351.

Note, The Limited Partnership (1936) 45 Yale L.J. 895.

Statutes:

8 Uniform Laws Annotated 48–188 (citations of old-style limited partnership acts superseded by uniform act, and reproductions of old-style acts still in effect as of 1922).

Foreign law:

Eder, Limited Liability Firms Abroad (1952) 13 U.Pitts.L.Rev. 193 (comparing the "limited liability company" with the "limited partnership" in Latin-American law).

Revised ULPA (1976):

Kessler, The New Uniform Limited Partnership Act: A Critique (1979) 48 Ford.L. Rev. 159.

Pierce, Limited Partner Control and Liability Under the Revised Uniform Limited Partnership Act (1979) 32 Southwestern L.Rev. 1301.

UNIFORM LIMITED PARTNERSHIP ACTS
National Conference of Commissioners on Uniform State Laws

Read sections 1, 2, 7 and 11 of the 1916 Act; and sections 101, 201, 303 and 304 of the 1976 Revision.

RATHKE v. GRIFFITH
Washington Supreme Court, 1950.
36 Wn.2d 394, 218 P.2d 757, 18 A.L.R.2d 1349.
Comment, 26 Wash.L.Rev. 222.

ROBINSON, JUSTICE. This case involves two actions, consolidated for purposes of trial, in which respondent sought and obtained judgment against appellants Griffith, on account of advances made by respondent to the partnership known as Midfield Packers, a frozen foods concern, in which Mr. Griffith was allegedly a general partner. The amounts of the judgments are not at issue, and the sole question raised on appeal concerns the status of Mr. Griffith in the partnership. If he was, as is asserted, a general partner, he is liable to respondent; on the other hand, he urges that he was a limited partner only, and it is conceded that, if he is correct in this contention, he may not be held responsible for the debts in question. The facts in the case are as follows:

On or about August 14, 1942, Mr. Griffith, in company with several others, executed a writing, denominated "Articles of Limited Co-partnership," which provided that the parties thereto were associating under the firm name of Midfield Packers, an organization formed for the purpose of canning and otherwise processing fruits and vegetables. Therein appellant Griffith is described as a limited copartner, and his liability is fixed at $1,000. On December 8, 1942, the articles were filed in the office of the Thurston county auditor. Mr. Griffith's only contribution to the partnership consisted of his assuming the indebtedness of the Midfield Packers on a certain truck. He paid this indebtedness in full, the entire payment amounting to over $1,000. . . .

The Midfield Packers entered into business, and, in the course of time, contracted the indebtedness which has become the subject of this action. Mr. Griffith testified that, upon learning that creditors of the partnership were claiming that he was a general partner, he immediately executed a bill of sale by the terms of which he conveyed all of his interest in the partnership to the two individuals named as general partners in the original articles and in the later modification. This bill of sale purports to have been executed in November, 1946, and was filed in the office of the Thurston county auditor.

It would appear that, in a number of respects, the parties involved in the organization of the Midfield Packers failed to comply with the strict terms of the limited partnership statutes in force at the time. Their most significant lapse was their failure to publish the certificate of partnership, in accordance with the terms of Rem.Rev.Stat. § 9969. . . .

In the present case, the trial court took the view that the failure of the parties to comply with this, and with certain other statutory requirements not necessary to be discussed here, had the effect of imposing liability as a general partner upon Mr. Griffith, the alleged limited or special partner. It would appear that the trial court's decision was in accord with the majority of the cases decided in other states under the old type of limited partnership laws. The question before us is whether the passage of the Uniform Limited Partnership Act in 1945 changed the situation with respect to attempted limited partnerships formed prior to its adoption. In this connection, it is pertinent to consider briefly the history of the concept of the limited partnership in the United States.

This form of association, though common on the continent of Europe since the middle ages, was unknown to the common law of England and the United States, and was originally borrowed from the civil law of France. Clapp v. Lacey, 35 Conn. 463; 3 Kent's Commentaries (14th Ed.) 38. Ames v. Downing, 1 Brad., N.Y., 321, includes an interesting account of the historical background of the limited partnership; see, also, Jacquin v. Buisson, 11 How.Prac., N.Y., 385. From their earliest inception, in New York and Connecticut in 1822, limited partnership statutes, being in derogation of the common law, were strictly construed by most courts. Pierce v. Bryant, 5 Allen 91, 87 Mass. 91; Holliday v. Union Bag & Paper Co., 3 Colo. 342; Richardson v. Hogg, 38 Pa. 153. The view was commonly taken that the special or limited partner was essentially a general partner, with immunity from personal liability only on condition of full and exact compliance with the statutory requirements as to the details of formation of the association. Crane on Partnership, p. 81, § 26, note 15. . . .

But it was coming to be recognized that the strict interpretation being given to the limited partnership statutes by the courts, though it unquestionably carried out the intent of those responsible for the adoption of these statutes, was rendering this form of association commercially impracticable. See, Commissioners' note to section 1 of the Uniform Limited Partnership Act, Vol. 8, Uniform Laws Annotated, p. 2. The limited partnership statutes were quite commonly coming to be regarded as a trap, In re Marcuse & Co., 7 Cir., 281 F. 928; for the fact that any minor deviations from the statutory provisions might have the effect of subjecting the "limited" partners to unlimited liability, naturally rendered the limited partnership a hazardous means of obtaining limited liability, and, therefore, discourage its employment. Accordingly, in 1916, a Uniform Limited Partnership Act was drafted in order to remedy these deficiencies. . . .

[The court then discussed In re Marcuse & Co. (C.C.A.7th, 1922) 281 F. 928, and Giles v. Vette (1924) 263 U.S. 553, 44 S.Ct. 157, 68 L.Ed. 441 (affirming Marcuse), and continued:]

It would seem from the language of the Marcuse and Giles cases, which we have quoted, that it was the intention of the circuit court of appeals, and of the supreme court, to lay down a rule that section 11 was to apply to *all* cases where an individual had entered upon a supposed limited partnership with the intent that he should be liable only as a special partner, provided, of course, that no creditors had been misled, to their loss, by any misrepresentations to which he was a party. The broad language employed seems quite adequately to cover those situations where the individual attempted to become a limited partner in a partnership defectively organized under the old acts, as well as under the Uniform Act; and the persuasive effect of this language would seem to be sufficient in itself to suggest a resolution of any ambiguity in the statute in favor of the contention of such an individual that he should not be held as a special partner in this type of situation. In addition, this solution is plainly in accord with the policy of the Uniform Act, which, as we have shown earlier in this opinion, was expressly designed to relieve the hardship consequent in holding liable as general partners those who intended in good faith to become limited partners, but were held not to occupy that status by reason of errors in the formation of the partnership for which they were not responsible. . . .

Respondent points out, however, that section 11 requires that, in order for a person erroneously believing himself to be a limited partner to escape liability as a general partner, he must, upon discovering his mistake, promptly renounce his interest in the profits of the business. It is the claim of respondent that no proper renunciation was made in this case. But the statute does not specify any particular form which this renunciation should take. It will be recalled that Mr. Griffith never took any profits from this business, and so was not under any obligation to pay them into court, as was done by Hecht and Finn in the case of Giles v. Vette. He did, however, execute a bill of sale by the terms of which he conveyed all of his interest in the limited partnership to the general partners in the concern. This appears to have been done as soon as he learned that the creditors of the Midfield Packers were attempting to hold him as a general partner. We think this relinquishing of all of his claims against the assets of the Midfield Packers was sufficient compliance with the requirements of section 11. Apparently, this was the view taken by the district court and the circuit court of appeals when they considered the matter in the Baumere Foods case, supra.

The judgments appealed from are accordingly reversed, and the causes dismissed as to the appellants.

SIMPSON, C.J., and MALLERY and HAMLEY, JJ., concur.

HILL, JUSTICE (dissenting). I dissent. I could agree with the majority's interpretation of the applicability of § 11 of the Limited Partnership Act, Rem.Supp.1945, § 9975–11, were it not for § 30 of the act, subd. (2). . . .

The majority writes this subsection out of the statute. I cannot agree that we have the right so to do. And, to be what the majority refers to as laconic, I believe the portion of the section quoted means what it says.

NOTE ON ACTIONS TO BE TAKEN BY A PERSON ERRONEOUSLY BELIEVING HIMSELF TO BE A LIMITED PARTNER

The exculpatory provision of § 11 of the ULPA, as originally promulgated, left considerable doubt as to the precise nature of the actions required to be taken on the part of the partner to avoid general liability. What is the meaning of renunciation of "his interest in the profits of the business, or other compensation by way of income"? In Rathke v. Griffith, the renunciation appears to have taken the form of the limited partner deeding over his entire interest to the general partners. An Arizona decision [1] immunizing the limited partner also involved a renunciation of the entire interest. In a Maryland case,[2] renunciation of future profits, without the return of past profits, was held sufficient to satisfy § 11. What of renunciation of past profits?

An inherent problem of § 11 is that its remedial action is quite unrelated to the original defect: failure to file, or inadequate or improper organization. Moreover, the remedial action may itself be an excessive price for the limited partner to pay. Consider the decided cases. Is it appropriate to insist that the

1. Graybar Electric Co. v. Lowe, 11 Ariz.App. 116, 462 P.2d 413 (1969).

2. Gilman Paint & Varnish Co. v. Legum, 197 Md. 665, 80 A.2d 906 (1951).

limited partner deed away his entire interest, or forever forego profits in the enterprise?

The 1976 Revision of the ULPA responds to some, but not all, of these concerns. Read carefully § 304, and note that it replaces the vague renunciation of old § 11 with an equally vague (and punitive) withdrawal "from future equity participation in the enterprise." However, as an alternative the partner may cause an appropriate certificate of limited partnership or of amendment to be executed and filed. How can the partner do this? Does the ULPA give him authority to sign for, bind, and file for the other partners?

The 1976 Revision also limits the rights of creditors to seek personal recovery against the erroneously-believing limited partner to those who actually believed in good faith that he was a general partner and who transacted business during the period prior to corrective action.

REFERENCES

Defective formation:

Giles v. Vette, 263 U.S. 553, 44 S.Ct. 157, 68 L.Ed. 441 (1923) (limited partnership agreement had been filed in attempt to comply with a prior act which had since been repealed by the U.L.P.A.; the court applied Sec. 11 of the U.L.P.A. to limit liability even though a partnership of the type formed was improper under the new act).

Renunciation of profits:

Gilman Paint & Varnish Co. v. Legum, 197 Md. 665, 80 A.2d 906 (1951) (partner renounced future profits, but did not return past profits; held, renunciation sufficient); comments, 31 Boston U.L.Rev. 561, 26 N.Y.U.L.Rev. 717.

Graybar Electric Co. v. Lowe, 11 Ariz.App. 116, 462 P.2d 413 (1969) (renunciation of interest in partnership held effective to escape liability for partnership debts).

Vidricksen v. Grover, 363 F.2d 372 (9th Cir.1966) (articles of limited partnership were not recorded; limited partner learned of omission in March; in August, sued general partner for accounting; in September, bankruptcy proceedings began, and limited partner filed renunciation; held, not "prompt"); comment, 32 Mo.L.Rev. 386.

Filing by limited partnership in other states:

The 1976 Revision of the ULPA contains detailed provisions on foreign limited partnerships—similar to comparable provisions in the corporation codes on registration of foreign corporations—which were not present in the original 1916 version. See ULPA (1976 Revision) §§ 901–908. Note in particular § 907(c). The cases and note below concern the original ULPA.

Cheyenne Oil Corp. v. Oil & Gas Ventures, 204 A.2d 743 (Del.1964) (Unregistered foreign limited partnership may sue as limited partnership; dictum that penalty for nonfiling is general partnership liability).

Burnham & Co. v. Kleinhans, 114 N.H. 472, 322 A.2d 618 (1974) (Under statute forbidding foreign partnership from doing business in state without registration, defendant sued by foreign partnership had burden of proving that plaintiff was doing business in state).

Note, Regulation of Foreign Limited Partnerships, 52 Boston Univ.L.Rev. 65 (1972).

PLASTEEL PRODUCTS CORP. v. HELMAN

United States Court of Appeals, First Circuit, 1959.
271 F.2d 354.

HARTIGAN, CIRCUIT JUDGE.

This is an appeal from a judgment of the United States District Court for the District of Massachusetts entered following the allowance of appellees' motions for summary judgment.

Plaintiff, a Pennsylvania corporation, sued appellees, among others, all Massachusetts citizens, as "co-partners doing business as Copley Steel Products Company" for $6,555.29 as unpaid balance for merchandise sold and delivered to Copley. Several of the defendants filed motions for summary judgment on the ground that they were limited partners only, and submitted uncontradicted supporting affidavits.

Appellees Clifton E. Helman, William M. Glovsky and Richard G. Mintz were trustees of the Shirley H. Eisenberg Trust; appellees Clifton E. Helman and William M. Glovsky were trustees of the C.A.S. Trust. Other defendants in the action were Benjamin M. Sriberg and Saul Glassman, who were trustees of the Jeannette W. Sriberg Trust, and Herbert W. Eisenberg. On or about December 29, 1955 an agreement was executed by all the defendants, and a certificate was duly filed with the Secretary of the Commonwealth of Massachusetts purporting to establish a limited partnership to do business as Copley Steel Products Co. By this agreement Herbert W. Eisenberg was to be general partner, contributing services but no cash, and receiving an initial 10% of the net profits; the limited partners were Clifton E. Helman and William M. Glovsky, described as trustees of the C.A.S. Trust; Clifton E. Helman, William M. Glovsky and Richard G. Mintz, described as trustees of the Shirley H. Eisenberg Trust, and Benjamin M. Sriberg and Saul Glassman, described as trustees of the Jeannette W. Sriberg Trust. Provisions in the agreement called for contributions of $100 by the trustees of the Sriberg Trust with a 25% participation in the balance of the profits; and $5,000 by the trustees of the C.A.S. Trust and $5,000 by the trustees of the Eisenberg Trust with 37½% of the balance of the profits to each of the latter two groups. Other provisions named Paul L. Sriberg as general sales manager of the partnership; provided for purchase of the interest of the trustees of the Sriberg Trust if Paul L. Sriberg's employment were terminated; and authorized the exercise of various financial powers by the general partner only when the general partner acted jointly with Paul L. Sriberg. Affidavits of the appellees stated that they have not participated in any business affairs of the limited partnership.

. . .

The district court denied the motion for summary judgment by Benjamin M. Sriberg and Saul Glassman, Trustees of the Jeannette W. Sriberg Trust, but allowed the motions for summary judgment of the appellees, on the ground that appellees were limited partners only. Accordingly, a separate judgment under Rule 54(b), F.R.Civ.P., 28 U.S. C.A., was entered for the appellees.

The question of law involved here is whether Mass.Gen.Laws Ann. c. 109, § 7 (Uniform Limited Partnership Act), makes appellees liable as general partners as a result of their execution of the December 1955 agreement. . . .

Plaintiff-appellant contends that appellees took part in the control of the business by the selection of Paul L. Sriberg as general sales manager and by providing for joint control by him and the general partner of financial aspects of the business.

Appellees contend that the absence of tenure provisions for Paul L. Sriberg negates any purpose of appellees to control the partnership; that the disputed provisions of the agreement evince only a desire for Paul L. Sriberg's services and a willingness both to concede some profits to obtain his services and to allow some protection for the Sriberg Trust interest. Appellees also contend that none of the decided cases interpreting and applying § 7 would support a holding of general liability here.

There are very few cases which afford much assistance in the interpretation and application of § 7. The cases applying statutes in force prior to the Uniform Limited Partnership Act cannot be relied on since the uniform act was drawn to overcome the strict interpretations which were frustrating the purpose of statutory limited partnerships. Gilman Paint & Varnish Co. v. Legum, 1951, 197 Md. 665, 80 A.2d 906.

The cases that do interpret and apply § 7 contain some elements which aid in reaching a decision here. In Rathke v. Griffith, 1950, 36 Wash.2d 394, 218 P.2d 757, 18 A.L.R.2d 1349, the copartners had drawn by-laws that provided that the affairs of the partnership should be handled by a board of directors and named the defendant, a purported limited partner, as one of the directors. But in view of testimony that the defendant had never functioned as a director, the court refused to hold that this arrangement itself constituted participation in control of the business sufficient to make the defendant generally liable. In the instant case the only conduct relied on to charge appellees as general partners is the signing of the limited partnership agreement. By analogy to the Rathke case, this does not constitute participation such as to impose general liability.

Paul L. Sriberg could have been discharged at any time by the general partner. This would lead to the surrender of the interest of the trust for his children and the end of any necessity for joint signing by Sriberg and the general partner. This factor makes the case somewhat analogous to Grainger v. Antoyan, 1957, 48 Cal.2d 805, 313 P.2d 848, in which the defendant was authorized to co-sign the checks, but they also could be signed without him. There the court held that, with no other evidence of taking part in control of the business, the defendant was not subject to general liability. The power here to discharge Sriberg and terminate any apparent control clearly distinguishes this case from Holzman v. De Escamilla, 1948, 86 Cal.App.2d 858, 195 P.2d 833, in which the purported limited partners were necessary to the issuance of any checks and, indeed, could issue checks without the general partner's approval. There general liability was imposed.

In our view of these cases the ground solely relied on by the appellant to charge appellees with general liability is insufficient to constitute taking part in the control of the business.

. . .

Judgment will be entered affirming the judgment of the district court.

NOTE: CONTROL BY LIMITED PARTNERS

As the *Plasteel* case indicates, case law under the ULPA of 1916 struggled with the question whether participation in selection or removal of general partners constituted taking part "in the control of the business." Some states attempted to solve this problem by enumerating various acts that would not constitute control. In one of the widest departures, California provided that voting on various matters, including "election or control of general partners" would not amount to taking part in control. Cal.Corp.Code § 15507 (1977).

Section 303 of the RULPA has narrowed the concept of participation in control of the business by permitting a vote on a wide variety of matters (including removal of a general partner) and permitting other forms of participation in the business by general partners. Moreover, section 303 has narrowed the class of creditors who may recover even when a limited partner has participated in control. Several states have further narrowed the conception. California, for instance authorizes limited partners to vote on the *admission* of a general partner, so long as the person voted on does not thereby become the sole general partner. Cal.Corp.Code §§ 15683(b)(5)(H), (I) and (J) (1985 Supp.)

The principal concern of lawyers in expanding the powers of limited partners is probably less often the exposure of limited partners to debts than the exposure of the limited partnership to taxation as a corporation, with the concomitant loss of capacity to pass partnership losses on to limited partners for income tax purposes.

REFERENCES

Participation in management:

Holzman v. De Escamilla, 86 Cal.App.2d 858, 195 P.2d 833 (1948) (limited partners in farming partnership who overruled the general partner on what crops to plant were liable to creditors).

Weil v. Diversified Properties, 319 F.Supp. 778 (D.C.D.C.1970) (when limited partnership was in financial straits, limited partners intervened with orders and prohibitions; held, this is not sufficient ground to require that they contribute to losses equally with general partner).

Trans-Am Builders, Inc. v. Woods Mill, Limited, 133 Ga.App. 411, 210 S.E.2d 866 (1974) (limited partners met with general partners to discuss financial problems, visited construction site and objected to certain work being performed; held, no violation of the control test of ULPA section 7.)

Feld, The "Control" Test for Limited Partnerships (1969) 82 Harv.L.Rev. 1471.

Pierce, Limited Partner Control and Liability Under the Revised Uniform Limited Partnership Act (1979) 32 Southwestern L.J. 1301.

Basile, Limited Liability for Limited Partners: An Argument for the Abolition of the Control Rule, 38 Vand.L.Rev. 1199 (1985).

Authority of Limited Partner:

Berman v. Herrick, 231 F.Supp. 918 (D.C.Pa.1964) (limited partner has no authority to bind the partnership or general partners).

Civil rights of partnerships:

United States v. Silverstein 314 F.2d 789 (2d Cir.1963), certiorari denied 374 U.S. 807, 83 S.Ct. 1696, 10 L.Ed.2d 1031 (general partner of large limited partnership not allowed to claim self-incrimination as a defense to a summons for the partnership books and records by the federal government in an investigation of tax liability; analogy made to corporation). Notes, 62 Mich.L.Rev. 526 (1964); 63 Col.L.Rev. 1319 (1963).

General partners as investment advisers:

Abrahamson v. Fleschner, 568 F.2d 862 (1977), cert. denied 436 U.S. 913, 98 S.Ct. 2253, 56 L.Ed.2d 414 (1978) (general partners in investment partnership held to be "investment advisors" under Investment Advisers Act of 1940).

SECTION 4. NONPROFIT ASSOCIATIONS

Section 6 of the Uniform Partnership Act defines a partnership as ". . . an association of two or more persons to carry on as co-owners a business for profit."

Associations of two or more persons for purposes that are non-profit-oriented fall outside the definition. Most social, civic, political and religious organizations are in this category. As these organizations become larger many of them choose to incorporate under state non-profit corporation statutes. One effect of incorporation is that the liability of members is then limited under state statute. The extent of liability of members of unincorporated non-profit associations is discussed in the following cases.

SECURITY–FIRST NAT. BK. v. COOPER

California District Court of Appeal, 1944.
62 Cal.App.2d 653, 145 P.2d 722.

SHAW, J. pro tem.—The plaintiff brought this action against Santa Monica Lodge No. 906, Benevolent and Protective Order of Elks, an unincorporated association, and 1188 persons alleged to be members of it, of whom 188 were designated by their true names and 1000 by names alleged to be fictitious. . . .

[A judgment of nonsuit was entered in favor of the members sued.]

Another ground of the motion [for nonsuit] was that the individual members of the unincorporated lodge are not bound by the action of its officers in entering into the lease and no liability was cast on them personally thereby. The liability of the members of an unincorporated association on contracts made by it varies according to the answer to the question whether the association is one organized for profit. Here there is no doubt that the association was not organized for profit.

Such an association is not a partnership and its members are not liable as partners. The rule of liability of members of such an association, not organized or conducted for profit, is stated in 7 C.J.S. 78, as follows: "Membership, as such, imposes no personal liability for the debts of the association; but to charge a member therewith it must be shown that he has actually or constructively assented to or ratified the contract on which the liability is predicated. If, however, a member, as such, directly incurs a debt, or expressly or impliedly authorizes or ratifies the transaction in which it is incurred, he is liable as a principal. So a member is liable for any debt that is necessarily contracted to carry out the objects of the association." Substantially the same rule was stated in *Leake v. City of Venice* (1920), 50 Cal.App. 462, 465 [195 P. 440], by quoting from another case, as follows: "Where the parties unite in a voluntary unincorporated association, and for convenience contract under an associate name, the acts of the association, it not being a legally responsible body, are the acts of its members who instigate and sanction the same." The meaning of the words "constructively assented" in the above quotation from Corpus Juris Secundum is illustrated by the statement of the court in *Richmond v. Judy* (1879), 6 Mo. App. 465, that "Persons who organize as a campaign committee on the eve of an election may perhaps be supposed to know that their associates, in the name of the committee, will incur certain obvious expenses in giving notice of political meetings, and to sanction such outlay by the very fact of their organization."

In this case the lease was executed in behalf of the unincorporated lodge by its presiding officer and secretary, after a vote of the lodge at a regular meeting authorizing them to do so. Plaintiff was unable to prove that any of the defendants appearing at the trial was present at that meeting, as far as we can discover by our unaided search of the record. However, 58 of the defendants, including defendants Robinson, Foreman, Vivalda and Boswell, were members of the lodge at the time the lease was executed. All of them had, on joining, signed the by-laws of the lodge. These by-laws contained provision for "The operation, management and control of the Home or Club occupied by this Lodge." The Constitution and Statutes of the National Order of Elks, which appear to be binding on all individual lodges and the members thereof, provided that "A Lodge may establish and maintain a home or club, for the social enjoyment of its members . . ." and set forth in some detail the mode of controlling and managing such a home or club. These provisions of the governing regulations of the order and of the lodge are sufficient to bring the case within the rule above quoted from Corpus Juris Secundum, that members of an association who "impliedly authorize" or "constructively assent to" a transaction by which a debt is incurred are liable as principals. Or, to use the other form of expression appearing in the same quotation, the establishment and maintenance of a "home or club" was one of the objects of the association (lodge). The lease was executed to accomplish this object and was an appropriate means to that end. Consequently, all who were members of the lodge at the time the lease was executed by the lodge were liable thereon as principals, even though they did not expressly authorize it by appearing at the meeting and voting for the resolution directing its execution.

[The judgment of nonsuit was reversed as to defendants who were members of the lodge at the time the lease was executed. They were held liable even for rents that accrued after the lodge was incorporated, since these rents accrued under the lease made before incorporation.]

NOTE: THE CONTENT OF "CONSENT"

Judicial opinions disclose considerable variation in views of what activities show "consent" of a member to a transaction or activity of the association. In Meriwether v. Atkin, 137 Mo.App. 32, 119 S.W. 36 (1909), the court affirmed a judgment of nonsuit in favor of the president of a lodge who appointed a committee to consider leasing a building, and presided at a later meeting that approved the minutes of an intervening meeting that authorized the committee to contract for the construction of a building. The president was absent from the meeting that authorized the committee to contract.

REFERENCES

Cousin v. Taylor, 115 Or. 472, 239 P. 96, 41 A.L.R. 750 (1925) (members of association who were present at a meeting that voted without dissent to employ expert to contest telephone rates were liable for expert's fees).

Orser v. George, 252 Cal.App.2d 660, 60 Cal.Rptr. 708 (1967) (members of duck-hunting club not liable for another member's negligence in shooting at frogs and mudhens).

Libby v. Perry, 311 A.2d 527 (Me.1973) (liability for negligence in arrangements for National Guard dance was limited to committee members present when unanimous vote was taken, treasurer, others who attended planning meetings, and one who made application for use of the armory; a member who was absent from all the meetings was not liable).

Henn and Peifer, Nonprofit Groups: Factors Influencing Choice of Form, 11 Wake Forest L.Rev. 181 (1975).

Jackson, Why You Should Incorporate a Homeowners' Association, 3 Real Estate L.J. 311 (1975).

Note, Liability of Members and Officers of Unincorporated Associations for Contracts and Torts, 42 Cal.L.Rev. 812 (1954).

Note, Enforcing a Contractual Claim Against an Unincorporated Association in Wisconsin, 1960 Wis.L.Rev. 444.

AZZOLINA v. SONS OF ITALY

Connecticut Supreme Court, 1935.
119 Conn. 681, 179 A. 201.

HINMAN, J. This action was brought by seven persons as plaintiffs against the named defendant, hereinafter called the Lodge, which was a voluntary unincorporated association formed for fraternal and social purposes, located in Meriden, and one hundred and eight individual members of that association. . . . The nature and scope of the action, as construed and tried by the parties, are indicated in the report and finding of the referee, and appear to be that the plaintiffs, members of the Lodge, claimed to have been compelled to pay a debt of the Lodge, for which the individual defendant members, as well as the Lodge, were liable, and the plaintiffs were seeking to recover from each of them his proportionate share of the common indebtedness so paid by the plaintiffs. . . .

The referee found and reported that of the defendant members of the Lodge seventy-five, named in a schedule (A) included in the report, voluntarily participated in the building project while it was being carried on by the Lodge, also that twenty other members not named as defendants so participated, but four of the latter had paid the plaintiffs $40 each and thereby discharged their obligation to them. Therefore the total number of participating members, including the seven plaintiffs, was found to be one hundred and two; the whole number of members of the Lodge at the time of the building operations was one hundred and seventy. The referee, further, stated alternative conclusions as to the per capita share of the amount—$3660.91—which he found to have been the amount of the net expenditure by the plaintiffs, due from each defendant liable to contribute to the plaintiffs, according to whether all of the members of the Lodge or only those voluntarily participating were held liable by the court as a matter of law. In rendering judgment, however, the trial court adopted neither alternative but adjudged "that the plaintiffs recover of the defendants . . . $5025.19," a sum apparently arrived at by addition of interest to the base amount of $3660.91. In this we find error.

In the case of a voluntary association formed for the purpose of engaging in business and making profits, its members are liable, as partners, to third persons upon contracts which are within its scope and are entered into with actual or apparent authority, and a joint judgment against them is justified. Bennett v. Lathrop, 71 Conn. 613, 42 A. 634; Davison v. Holden, 55 Conn. 103, 10 A. 515; Lawler v. Murphy, 58 Conn. 294, 313, 20 A. 457; 3 Page, Contracts, p. 3168; 25 R.C.L. p. 64. When a member of such an association cannot obtain reimbursement from it for liabilities which he has properly discharged, he is entitled to contribution from all the other members. 47 C.J. p. 809. But when, as here, the purpose of the association is not business or profit, the liability, if any, of its members is not in its nature that of partners but that arising out of the relation of principal and agent, and only those members who authorize or subsequently ratify an obligation are liable on account of it. A person may authorize the obligation arising from a contract either by becoming or remaining a member knowing that such a contract would be reasonable and proper in order to carry out the purposes for which the association was formed or, if the contract is outside the scope of those purposes, by assenting to it or participating in the undertaking. 3 Page, Contracts, pp. 3169, 3170; Page, Contracts, Supplement, Vol. 1, p. 1237; Stege v. Louisville Courier Journal Co., 196 Ky. 795, 245 S.W. 504; Vader v. Ballou, 151 Wis. 577, 579, 139 N.W. 413, 7 A.L.R. 216. Ash v. Guie, 97 Pa.St. 493, 39 Am.Rep. 818, is a case in some respects analogous to the present one and illustrative of the principle and its application. The proof failed to show that the building of a temple was within the purposes of the Masonic Lodge, of which the defendants were members, or that any committee or members had a right to contract debts of the Lodge for building the temple, but it was held (p. 500) that those members who engaged in the undertaking of erecting the building or borrowing of money therefor, or assented to or subsequently ratified it were liable for the debts thereby incurred. Among other decisions to like effect are Ehrmanntraut v. Robinson, 52 Minn. 333, 54 N.W. 188; Sizer v. Daniels, 66 Barb. (N.Y.) 426, 432; Stege v. Louisville Courier Journal Co., supra; Lynn v. Commercial Club, 31 S.D. 401, 407, 141 N.W. 471; Devoss v. Gray, 22 Ohio St. 159, 169; First National Bank v. Rector, 59 Neb. 77, 80 N.W. 269.

Actions for contribution are based upon the principle, equitable in origin but now recognized in courts of law, that where one person has been compelled to pay money which others were equally bound to pay, each of the latter in good conscience should contribute the proportion which he ought to pay of the amount expended to discharge the common burden or obligation. Waters v. Waters, 110 Conn. 342, 345, 148 A. 326; Bulkeley v. House, 62 Conn. 459, 467, 26 A. 352. As between members of an unincorporated association, each is bound to contribute only his aliquot share. Hodgson v. Baldwin, 65 Ill. 532; Lorimer v. Julius Knack Coal Co., 246 Mich. 214, 224 N.W. 362, 64 A.L.R. 210; Hall v. Harris, 6 Ga.App. 822, 65 S.E. 1086; 5 C.J. pp. 1340, 1364; 13 C.J. p. 836. The judgment should have awarded to the plaintiffs, as against each of the defendants named in Schedule A of the referee's report as participating members, his aliquot share of the entire net amount expended by the plaintiffs to pay the note described in the third count ($3660.91, being $3994.66, the sum contributed by the plaintiffs to pay the note, less $128.75 paid them by the Lodge toward interest on renewal notes and $160 received from nondefendant members) with interest from February 15th, 1928, the date on which that note was paid, the share of each ascertained by dividing the total amount by one hundred and two, the number of defendants found to have participated in the building project plus the twenty participating members not made defendants and the seven plaintiffs. . . .

There is error; the case is remanded to the Superior Court with direction to enter judgment in accordance with this opinion.

In this opinion the other judges concurred.

REFERENCES

Elliott v. Greer Presbyterian Church, 181 S.C. 84, 186 S.E. 651 (1936) (each member liable to third party for entire debt).

Cortiza v. Rosenblat, 291 So.2d 425 (La.App.1974) (under Louisiana civil code, member of noncommercial partnership not liable to third party for whole of partnership debt, but only for proportionate share).

NOTE: EXTENT OF MEMBER'S LIABILITY
IN CIVIL LAW SYSTEMS

American cases seem to assume that if a member is liable to an outsider for an association obligation, he should be liable for the whole extent of it; it is only his obligation to contribute to other members that is limited to his aliquot portion.

The system is quite different in civil law systems, where a distinction is drawn between *civil* and *commercial* associations. The former are derived from the *societas* of Justinian's civil code, which became the *société civile* of the Napoleonic Civil Code (arts. 1832–1872). The member of a civil association is liable to association creditors only for his proportionate share of the debt (art. 1863). The commercial partnership (*société en nom collectif*) is a product of the law merchant, codified in the Napoleonic Code de Commerce (arts. 20–22)[1] which provided that each member is liable for the entire amount of the association's obligations.

These contrasting principles of liability survive in most of the legal systems built on the *jus civilis,* including Louisiana[2] and Puerto Rico.[3]

Under these systems of law, the demarcation between civil and commercial associations becomes crucial. The line varies considerably from system to system, and is always controversial. Without going into details, we should emphasize at least that it is not at all a distinction between what Americans would call "profit" and "non-profit" associations. A civil association is defined in the French civil code as an association formed for *bénéfices* —which is the usual word used to designate the profits of a business, although broad enough to include the benefits of sharing a golf course or club house. In general, commercial associations are the ones formed for selling merchandise and lending money; civil associations are those formed to receive revenues from the use of property or services. Thus a law partnership would be a civil partnership rather than a commercial one. Social and athletic clubs, if not incorporated, would generally fall into the category of civil associations.

LYONS v. AMERICAN LEGION POST NO. 650 REALTY CO.
Ohio Supreme Court, 1961.
172 Ohio St. 331, 175 N.E.2d 733, 92 A.L.R.2d 492.

In January of 1960, Martha A. Lyons, administratrix of the estate of William A. Lyons, deceased, began an action in the Court of Common Pleas of Knox County against American Legion Post No. 650 Realty Company, Inc., and 81 individuals, members of American Legion Post No. 650 at Danville. The post itself, an unincorporated association, was not made a party defendant.

1. Now superseded by Loi no. 66–537 sur les sociétés commerciales (Business Associations Law) of July 24, 1966, arts. 10–22.

2. La.Civ.Code § 2872. For a recent invocation of the distinction, see House of Lights, Inc. v. Diecidue, 222 So.2d 603 (La. App.1969).

3. L.P.R. § 10:1393 (commercial partners liable for entire debt); § 31:4351 (civil partners liable for proportionate contribution); § 31:4372 (civil partners not liable for entire debt).

. . . . The action is grounded on the claimed joint and several negligence of the defendants in permitting carbon monoxide fumes to escape from a defective gas heater in a building owned or leased by the realty company, whereby decedent, a nonmember of American Legion Post No. 650 and a paying patron at a fish fry conducted by such post in such building, was injured and subsequently died by reason of such injury.

. . . .

ZIMMERMAN, J. In the cases of Koogler et al., Trustees v. Koogler (1933), 127 Ohio St. 57, 186 N.E. 725; State v. Fremont Lodge of Loyal Order of Moose (1949), 151 Ohio St. 19, 84 N.E.2d 498; and Damm v. Elyria Lodge No. 465, B.P.O.E. (1952), 158 Ohio St. 107, 107 N.E.2d 337, it was either indicated or held that, since a voluntary unincorporated association had no status as a legal entity, an action against it as such would not lie, and that ordinarily any action had to be brought against the individual members of such an association collectively and conjointly.

Or stating it in another way, "In the absence of an enabling statute, a voluntary association cannot be sued by its association name. It has no legal existence, and the persons composing it must be joined individually." Kimball v. Lower Columbia Fire Ass'n, 67 Or. 249, 252, 135 P. 877, 878. See also, United Mine Workers of America v. Coronado Coal Co., 259 U.S. 344, 385, 42 S.Ct. 570, 574, 66 L.Ed. 975, 984, 27 A.L.R. 762, 771.

Then, effective on September 30, 1955, the General Assembly enacted legislation which is now Sections 1745.01 through 1745.04, Revised Code. Section 1745.01 provides:

"Any unincorporated association may contract or sue in behalf of those who are members and, in its own behalf, be sued as an entity under the name by which it is commonly known and called."

Section 1745.02 reads:

"All assets, property, funds, and any right or interest, at law or in equity, of such unincorporated association shall be subject to judgment, execution and other process. A money judgment against such unincorporated association shall be enforced only against the association as an entity and shall not be enforceable against the property of an individual member of such association." . . .

It is the purpose and intent of the statutes quoted and referred to above to limit actions solely against unincorporated associations as entities in the names they commonly use, as determined by the two lower courts herein, or may the individual members of such associations still be sued as under the former practice? We think the new statutes are no more than cumulative and do not abrogate the right to sue the members of the associations if the suitor chooses to proceed in that way. It is to be noted that Section 1745.01, Revised Code, uses the permissive word, "may," and that, under Section 1745.02, Revised Code, when a suitor does take advantage of the enabling statutes by suing an unincorporated association by the name it uses, the collection of any judgment obtained against such association must be satisfied out of its property alone and the property of its members is immune from seizure. Surely, had the General Assembly intended to eliminate actions against the individuals composing an unincorporated association, it would have so expressed itself.

That statutes like Section 1745.01 et seq., Revised Code, represent an alternative mode of procedure appears to be the established rule. . . .

However, a recognized difference exists between an unincorporated association organized for the transaction of business and one organized for fraternal or social purposes. This is illustrated in Azzolina v. Order of the Sons of Italy, Conte Luigi Cadorna, No. 440, 119 Conn. 681, 691, 179 A. 201, 204, where it is stated in the opinion:

> "In the case of a voluntary association formed for the purpose of engaging in business and making profits, its members are liable, as partners, to third persons upon contracts which are within its scope and are entered into with actual or apparent authority, and a joint judgment against them is justified. . . . But when, as here, the purpose of the association is not business or profit, the liability, if any, of its members is not in its nature that of partners but that arising out of the relation of principal and agent, and only those members who authorize or subsequently ratify an obligation are liable on account of it."

The same principle is recognized in relation to torts. . . .

In the instant case the petition alleges that the defendants, American Legion Post No. 650 Realty Co., Inc., and the individual members of American Legion Post No. 650 "jointly and severally, conducted or caused to be conducted within said building a social affair known as a fish fry for which they charged each person attending the sum of one dollar ($1.00)," and that "defendants, and each of them, were negligent in failing to provide a safe heating system in the building; in equipping and maintaining the building with a defective heating system; in failing to adequately inspect said heating system; in failing to provide proper ventilation in the building; and in failing to warn invitees in the building, including decedent, of the presence of carbon monoxide fumes therein."

Such petition probably states causes of action good as against demurrer so that defendants should plead to conserve their interests, but on the trial of the action to establish liability on the part of individual defendants evidence would have to be produced linking them as active participants in the affair resulting in plaintiff's decedent's alleged injuries, and, furthermore, that they knew or in the exercise of ordinary care should have known of the defective condition of the instrumentality claimed to have caused the injury. And, of course, the other elements necessary to support recovery would have to be proved.

The judgment of the Court of Appeals is reversed, and the cause is remanded to the trial court for further proceedings.

REFERENCES

Fairfield Lease Corp. v. Empire Employees, 74 Misc. 328, 345 N.Y.S.2d 305 (Dist.Ct. 1973) (action on lease was not maintainable against unincorporated group sued by name of association and "John Doe, President", although lease was signed in name of the association).

Magness v. Chicora Chapter No. 33, 193 S.C. 205, 8 S.E.2d 344 (1940) (members liable without proof of individual assent).

Mitterhausen v. South Wisconsin Conference Association of Seventh Day Adventists, 245 Wis. 353, 14 N.W.2d 19 (1944) (trustees held liable, on the ground that they are members).

Crane, Liability of Unincorporated Association for Tortious Injury (1963) 16 Vand.L. Rev. 319.

Oleck, Non-Profit Association as Legal Entities (1964) 13 Clev.-Marshall L.Rev. 350.

Note, Hazards of Enforcing Claims against Unincorporated Associations in Florida (1964) 17 U.Fla.L.Rev. 211.

SECTION 5. CORPORATIONS

A. ATTRIBUTES

The Meaning of Corporateness

The drift of all kinds of human organization—governmental, cultural, and economic—into the corporate form during the 19th and 20th centuries has been remarkable, and promotes speculation about its causes. What is it that makes corporate organization so desirable?

Probably the primal consideration has been to establish a fund of property which is distinct from the property of any of the members, and therefore free from the hazards of the members' debts, and from the uncertainties of descent and distribution on the members' deaths. The reverse of this coin is the maintenance of the members' individual property separate from that of the corporation, and presumptively free from claims of the corporation's creditors. Going along with these attributes is the capacity of the organization to sue or be sued collectively without regard to the citizenship or residence or presence within the jurisdiction of the members. These characteristics, which might be described as "separateness" from the individual members, have been conceptualized as "entity" or "personality," and whole books have been written about them—rather more in Europe than in the United States.

The critical student will observe that the attributes of corporateness are not entirely confined to corporations. The Uniform Partnership Act makes the property of the group a separate fund from that of the members, and the Uniform Limited Partnership Act permits limited partners to insulate their individual property from the debts of the firm. Moreover, contemporary procedural laws permit suit by and against partnerships and associations even though they are not incorporated. The distinction of corporations is that they possess these characteristics more universally and unconditionally than do other forms of organization.

Another aspect of corporateness is the provision by law of a prefabricated form of organization, with shareholders or members, directors, officers, articles, bylaws and prescribed modes of amendment and dissolution. True, a diligent draftsman can build all these characteristics into articles of partnership, or the deed of settlement of a business trust; but in those cases, the whole thing must be custom-made. The corporate form is like a GI uniform the state provides to everyone, and which is wearable without alteration although the most choosy customers may take it to a tailor for refinement.

The Variety of Corporations

The attributes of corporateness are attractive to people in almost every field of activity. The first corporations recognized by English law were municipal corporations, which remain today among the most important instruments of human society. We will not, however, give further attention in this book to governmental corporations, which are political subdivisions, as the dynamics are so fundamentally different from corporations of the private sector.

Close on the heels of municipal corporations, there appeared in English law ecclesiastical and charitable corporations, the precursors of a vast fauna of educational, recreational, political and social corporations which are conventionally designated as "nonprofit corporations". These two classes of corporations—municipal and nonprofit—were apparently the only kinds of corporations known to Lord Coke, whose observations on the nature of "corporations" have had a pervasive effect on judicial thinking about business corporations.

The junior branch of the corporate family—which was destined to become more numerous and perhaps more powerful than the other two—is composed of business corporations. These are the organizations that spring first to the American mind when the word "corporation" is heard. And the examples which spring most prominently to mind are those immense aggregations owning billions of dollars worth of assets, spread over several continents, with hundreds of thousands of shareholders and tens of thousands of employees often marked with the epithet of "multinational."

But the multinationals and the billionaires are a very small fraction of the corporate population. At the other end of the spectrum are the small family corporation exemplified by the "Ma and Pa Grocery," with few members and few assets; what they lack in size, they make up in the number of units. Actually, family corporations are not quite at the end of the spectrum because there are a surprising number of corporations which have no assets at all; they are mere receptacles, waiting to be filled, or recently emptied. Between these extremes of immensity and tininess are many other sizes and shapes of corporations that tend to be overlooked. There are thousands of corporations whose shares are actively traded in the financial markets, but which are neither billionaires nor multinational. There are tens of thousands whose shares are freely marketable, but for which no organized market exists. There are hundreds of thousands of "close corporations" involving perhaps 3 to 30 members whose shares are not ordinarily for sale, but which are more than one-family affairs.

Corporations with many shareholders usually have substantial assets, but the converse does not hold. Some immense corporations have only one or two shareholders; an outstanding example is AT&T Technologies, one of the largest industrial firms in the nation, which is wholly owned by American Telephone and Telegraph Company. Such companies have been aptly called "megasubsidiaries".

If business corporations vary widely in size, they vary just as widely in their purposes. Although profit-making is usually one objective, there are others that enter into the formation and continuance of many business corporations. Many of the mill, turnpike and bridge companies of the early United States were organized by community subscription not so much in the hope of making a profit from the enterprise organized, as to furnish a means of grinding grain and conveying it to market. Recent examples of business enterprises organized partly or wholly for services purposes are low-income housing projects, sometimes created with a limitation on the dividends payable to shareholders; another illustration is the development of "minority enterprise" in which disadvantaged population groups are given an opportunity for exercising management skills. Special corporate arrangements—the government-owned railroad companies (which are organized in business corporation form)—are another illustration.

Corporate Structure

Corporations statutes commonly provide for a corporate structure involving shareholders, directors, and officers.

Shareholders. A corporation creates its own membership by the terms of its articles of incorporation. In a business corporation, membership is achieved by the purchase of shares of stock. Corporate shares are a contract between the shareholder and the corporation. The rights given to a shareholder may include a preference in dividends, the right to share assets if the corporation is dissolved, and voting rights. Unless restrictions are present, the shareholder of "common stock" is entitled to vote for the election of directors and for major corporate changes including amendments to the articles of incorporation. Shareholders in their capacity as shareholders are not employees or agents of the corporation.

Directors. State corporation statutes usually provide that "the business and affairs of a corporation shall be managed by a board of directors" or "managers under the direction of the board of directors." In fulfilling this function, directors act as a group and not individually.

A responsibility of the board is to elect the president of the company and other officers. It is typical that a board of directors of a large company meets only quarterly, and it is unusual for a board to meet more often than monthly. The actual operation of the company is delegated to the officers and other employees. Directors as individuals in their capacity as directors are not employees of the corporation. Directors are not agents, but they do owe certain fiduciary duties to the corporation.

Officers. Major officers of the corporation are usually specified in state corporation statutes, and their election by the board of directors is required. Officers are employees of the corporation, and the corporation only acts—makes contracts, commits torts—through the officers and other employees who have been delegated authority by the board of directors.

B. INCORPORATION AND ADMITTANCE

A corporation is established by filing Articles of Incorporation (occasionally called a Certificate of Incorporation) with the state agency responsible for administration of corporations, usually the Secretary of State or the Department of Commerce. Although the process itself is the essence of simplicity, a number of organizations—most notably the Corporation Trust Company and the United States Corporation Company—will, for a fee, perform the service for any attorney who wishes to delegate the job.

At one time, and even today under some old codes, it was necessary in drafting the articles of incorporation to detail the powers and the purposes of the corporation. Some care was necessary in this drafting process, since the actions of a corporation beyond its powers or purposes were subject to avoidance or annulment as *ultra vires,* beyond the corporation's authority. Most corporate statutes today limit the effect of the *ultra vires* doctrine, allowing only the shareholders or the state to proceed against the corporation for exceeding its powers. And many states today have statutory provisions allowing the corporation to be established with all legal purposes and powers, without any need to detail those powers and purposes.

May we therefore assume that the job of incorporating is purely ministerial, that anyone with a form-book and a secretary will do the job well? Consider the simplicity of the Official Form for Articles of Incorporation under the Model Business Corporation Act.

The simplicity of the process is deceptive. Since a great deal of the planning of a business enterprise must take place as it is organized, quickly drafted articles of incorporation may end up costing the enterprise a great deal later in its life. Should the corporation have perpetual or limited life? Should it have a limited number of authorized shares? Does preservation of proposed control structures demand preemptive rights? Will special agreements on control and voting be inserted in the articles of incorporation? Should provision be made for the possibility of deadlock among shareholders or directors? Does the corporation wish to indemnify its officers and directors against liabilities they may incur in office? What shall be the name of the corporation?

We shall encounter many of these questions again as we discuss control, capital structure and corporate operations. The important point is that the lawyer's skill makes the difference between articles that simply satisfy the state corporation laws and articles that carry out the intentions of the entrepreneurs and set a course for successful future operations of the corporation.

An additional problem of draftsmanship is presented by the bylaws, which usually contain many of the details of management and internal regulation not contained in the articles of incorporation. Since the articles are amended by the shareholders, and the bylaws usually amended by the directors, bylaws are more easily changed. Careful thought must be directed to the degree of permanence desired for a particular provision before a decision is made in which of the two documents it will appear.

Note, too, that however inartfully drafted they might be, articles of incorporation must be filed.

THOMPSON & GREEN MACHINERY v. MUSIC CITY LUMBER

Court of Appeals of Tennessee, 1984.
683 S.W.2d 340.

Lewis, Judge.

We granted this Tenn.R.App.P. 9 appeal to consider whether the doctrines of de facto corporation and corporation by estoppel are alive and well in Tennessee or whether their demise was caused by the passage of the Tennessee General Corporations Act, specifically Tenn. Code Ann. §§ 48–1–204 and 48–1–1405.

The pertinent facts are as follows: Joseph E. Walker is President of Music City Sawmill Co., Inc. and Music City Lumber Company, Inc., both Tennessee corporations. On January 27, 1982, Mr. Walker, supposedly on behalf of Sawmill, purchased a wheel loader from plaintiff, Thompson & Green Machinery Co., Inc. However, on January 27, 1982, Sawmill was not a corporation, a fact unknown to either plaintiff or defendant Walker on January 27th. It was not until late July or early August, 1983, that it was discovered that the date of the incorporation of Sawmill was actually January 28, 1982, one day after the sale of the wheel loader.

Pursuant to the sale, Walker signed a promissory note in the amount of $37,886.30 on behalf of Sawmill to plaintiff. A purchase money security interest was also taken in the equipment. The promissory note was signed in the following manner:

January 27, 1982

MUSIC CITY SAWMILL, INC.
(Corporate, Partnership or Trade (Seal)
Name or Individual Signature)

BY: /s/ Joe Walker
    (Signature: Title of officer, "Partner" or "Proprietor")

Individually

Sawmill was unable to make the payments and returned the wheel loader on August 27, 1982. On October 14, 1982, plaintiff sold the wheel loader for $15,303.83 and applied the proceeds to the note, leaving a balance of $17,925.81. So far as the record discloses, between January of 1982 and August, 1982, plaintiff and Sawmill dealt with each other as corporations.

Plaintiff brought suit against both Sawmill and Lumber on May 5, 1983, in the Chancery Court to recover the balance due on the note and parts sold to Sawmill. On August 5, 1983, plaintiff amended its complaint to include Mr. Walker as a defendant after plaintiff learned that Sawmill was not a corporation on January 27, 1982. This suit against Mr. Walker individually was his first notice that Sawmill was not incorporated on that date.

Mr. Walker does not seriously assert that the doctrine of de facto corporation is still viable in Tennessee. He does forcefully insist that plaintiff is estopped to deny Sawmill's corporate existence because plaintiff (1) "dealt with Sawmill as a corporation" and (2) "did not intend to bind [Mr. Walker] personally on the promissory note."

It is the insistence of plaintiff that neither the doctrine of de facto corporation nor corporation by estoppel are viable in Tennessee since the passage of the Tennessee General Corporations Act. Plaintiff contends that defendant Walker is personally liable because of the interaction of Tenn.Code Ann. § 48–1–1405 which provides that "[a]ll persons who assume to act as a corporation without authority so to do shall be jointly and severally liable for all debts and liabilities incurred or arising as a result thereof," and Tenn.Code Ann. § 48–1–204 which provides that "[a] corporation shall not . . . incur any indebtedness . . . until (a) The charter has been filed by the secretary of state, and (b) . . . there has been received the amount stated in the charter as being the minimum amount of consideration to be received for its shares before commencing business."

Plaintiff insists that since the charter was not filed by the Secretary of State when the promissory note was executed, the corporation neither had the authority to incur indebtedness nor the power to authorize any actions on its behalf and, therefore, pursuant to Tenn. Code Ann. § 48–1–1405, Mr. Walker is liable "for all debts and liabilities incurred" since he assumed to act as a corporation without authority.

It is conceded that Sawmill did not have a corporate existence on January 27th. It therefore follows that Mr. Walker could not and did not have authority to act for Sawmill on January 27th when he executed the promissory note to plaintiff.

> It is a general rule that one who deals with an apparent corporation as such and in such manner as to recognize its corporate existence de jure or de facto is thereby estopped to deny the fact thus admitted. . . . The estoppel extends as well to the privies as to the parties to such transactions. The general rule is applied in actions brought by either of the contracting parties against the other, and in actions by the persons dealing with the corporation, wherein the existence of the corporation is assailed for the purpose of establishing individual partnership liability on the part of its members.

18 Am.Jur.2d Corporations § 76.

Tennessee has long recognized the foregoing rule. . . .

The General Assembly, in enacting Tenn.Code Ann. § 48–1–1405 saw fit to place statutory liability upon those who assume to act as a corporation without authority. Section 48–1–1405 does not contain an exception that one who assumes to act as a corporation without authority shall be jointly and severally liable for debts and liabilities *except* when the plaintiff thereafter dealt with the corporation as a corporation or when the plaintiff did not intend to bind one who assumed to act personally. No exceptions are contained in § 48–1–1405. For this Court to hold that under the circumstances here Mr. Walker is not liable, it would be necessary that this Court rewrite the Tennessee General Corporations Act and hold that the Act does not mean what it says. We are not at liberty to do so. We find nothing ambiguous in Tenn.Code Ann. § 48–1–1405. It is clear that "[a]ll persons who assume to act as a corporation without authority so to do shall be jointly and severally liable for all debts and liabilities incurred or arising as a result thereof." We find no good faith exception in the act. To allow an estoppel would be to nullify Tenn.Code Ann. § 48–1–1405.

We are of the opinion that the doctrine of corporation by estoppel met its demise by the enactment of the Tennessee General Corporations Act of 1968.

It results that the judgment of the Chancellor is reversed and the cause remanded to the Chancery Court for the entry of judgment for plaintiff in the amount of $17,925.81 together with accrued interest and attorney's fees as provided by the note and for any other necessary proceedings. Costs are taxed to defendant Walker.

TODD, P.J., and KOCH, J., concur.

REFERENCES

Timberline Equipment Co., Inc. v. Davenport, 267 Or. 64, 514 P.2d 1109 (1973) (holding that Model Business Corporation Act provisions adopted by Oregon exclude concept of de facto corporation).

Robertson v. Levy, 197 A.2d 443 (D.C.App.1964) (holding that MBCA provisions exclude doctrines of de facto corporation and corporation by estoppel).

Cranson v. International Business Machines Corp., 234 Md. 477, 200 A.2d 33 (1964) (holding that creditor that had dealt with defendant as a corporation was estopped from asserting his individual liability).

Bankers Trust Co. of Western New York v. Zecher, 103 Misc.2d 777, 426 N.Y.S.2d 960 (1980) (security agreement executed in name of corporation before it was incorporated was enforceable because corporation existed de facto).

REVISED MODEL BUSINESS CORPORATION ACT

Committee on Corporate Laws of the Section on Corporation, Banking and Business Law of the American Bar Association, 1985.

§ 15.01 Authority to Transact Business Required

(a) A foreign corporation may not transact business in this state until it obtains a certificate of authority from the secretary of state.

(b) The following activities, among others, do not constitute transacting business within the meaning of subsection (a):

(1) maintaining, defending, or settling any proceeding;

(2) holding meetings of the board of directors or shareholders or carrying on other activities concerning internal corporate affairs;

(3) maintaining bank accounts;

(4) maintaining offices or agencies for the transfer, exchange, and registration of the corporation's own securities or maintaining trustees or depositaries with respect to those securities;

(5) selling through independent contractors;

(6) soliciting or obtaining orders, whether by mail or through employees or agents or otherwise, if the orders require acceptance outside this state before they become contracts;

(7) creating or acquiring indebtedness, mortgages, and security interests in real or personal property;

(8) securing or collecting debts or enforcing mortgages and security interests in property securing the debts;

(9) owning, without more, real or personal property;

(10) conducting an isolated transaction that is completed within 30 days and that is not one in the course of repeated transactions of a like nature;

(11) transacting business in interstate commerce.

(c) The list of activities in subsection (b) is not exhaustive.

§ 15.02   Consequences of Transacting Business Without Authority

(a) A foreign corporation transacting business in this state without a certificate of authority may not maintain a proceeding in any court in this state until it obtains a certificate of authority.

(b) The successor to a foreign corporation that transacted business in this state without a certificate of authority and the assignee of a cause of action arising out of that business may not maintain a proceeding based on that cause of action in any court in this state until the foreign corporation or its successor obtains a certificate of authority.

(c) A court may stay a proceeding commenced by a foreign corporation, its successor, or assignee until it determines whether the foreign corporation or its successor requires a certificate of authority. If it so determines, the court may further stay the proceeding until the foreign corporation or its successor obtains the certificate.

(d) A foreign corporation is liable for a civil penalty of \$_____ for each day, but not to exceed a total of \$_____ for each year, it transacts business in this state without a certificate of authority. The attorney general may collect all penalties due under this subsection.

(e) Notwithstanding subsections (a) and (b), the failure of a foreign corporation to obtain a certificate of authority does not impair the validity of its corporate acts or prevent it from defending any proceeding in this state.

ALLENBERG COTTON COMPANY, INC. v. PITTMAN

Supreme Court of the United States, 1974.
419 U.S. 20, 95 S.Ct. 260, 42 L.Ed.2d 195.

MR. JUSTICE DOUGLAS delivered the opinion of the Court.

This is an appeal from a judgment of the Supreme Court of Mississippi, 276 So.2d 678 (1973), which held that under the applicable Mississippi statute [1] appellant might not recover damages for breach of a contract to deliver cotton because of its failure to qualify to do business in the State. Appellant claims that that Mississippi statute as applied to the facts of this case is repugnant to the Commerce Clause of the Constitution.   . . .

. . .

---

1. Mississippi Code Ann. § 79-3-247 (1972), formerly Miss.Code Ann. § 5309-239 (1942), provides in part:

"No foreign corporation transacting business in this state without a certificate of authority shall be permitted to maintain any action, suit or proceeding in any court of this state. Nor shall any action, suit or proceeding be maintained in any court of this state by any successor or assignee of such corporation on any right, claim or demand arising out of the transaction of business by such corporation in this state."

II

Appellant is a cotton merchant with its principal office in Memphis, Tenn. It had arranged with one Covington, a local cotton buyer in Marks, Miss. to "contract cotton" to be produced the following season by farmers in Quitman County, Miss. The farmer, Pittman, in the present case, made the initial approach to Covington, seeking a contract for his cotton; in other instances Covington might contact the local farmers.[3] In either event, Covington would obtain all the information necessary for a purchase contract and telephone the information to appellant in Memphis, where a contract would be prepared, signed by an officer of appellant, and forwarded to Covington. The latter would then have the farmer sign the contract. For these services Covington received a commission on each bale of cotton delivered to appellant's account at the local warehouse.[4] When the farmers delivered the cotton, Covington would draw on appellant and pay them the agreed price.

The Supreme Court of Mississippi held that appellant's transactions with Mississippi farmers were wholly intrastate in nature, being completed upon delivery of the cotton at the warehouse, and that the fact that appellant might subsequently sell the cotton in interstate commerce was irrelevant to the federal question "as the Mississippi transaction had been completed and the cotton then belonged exclusively to Allenberg, to be disposed of as it saw fit, at its sole election and discretion," 276. So.2d, at 681. Under the contract which Covington negotiated with appellee, Pittman, the latter was to plant, cultivate, and harvest a crop of cotton on his land, deliver it to a named company in Marks, Miss., for ginning, and then turn over the ginned cotton to appellant at a local warehouse. The suit brought by appellant alleged a refusal of Pittman to deliver the cotton and asked for injunctive relief and damages. One defense tendered by Pittman was that appellant could not use the courts of Mississippi to enforce its contracts, as it was doing business in the State without the requisite certificate. The Supreme Court of Mississippi sustained that plea, reversing a judgment in favor of appellant, and dismissed the complaint.

Appellant's arrangements with Pittman and the broker, Covington, are representative of a course of dealing with many farmers whose cotton, once sold to appellant, enters a long interstate pipeline. That pipeline ultimately terminates at mills across the country or indeed around the world, after a complex sorting and matching process designed to provide each mill with the particular grade of cotton which the mill is equipped to process.

. . .

3. The latter practice seems to have been the more usual one. (App. 54, 102–105.)

4. The commission was paid in some instances by appellant, in other instances by the individual farmer. (Id., at 53, 68.)

Much reliance is placed on Eli Lilly & Co. v. Sav-On-Drugs, Inc., 366 U.S. 276, 81 S.Ct. 1316, 6 L.Ed.2d 288 (1961), for sustaining Mississippi's action. The case is not in point. There the Court found that the foreign corporation had an office and salesmen in New Jersey selling drugs intrastate. Since it was engaged in an intrastate business it could be required to obtain a license even though it also did an interstate business.

The Mississippi Supreme Court, as noted, ruled that appellant was doing business in Mississippi. Appellant, however, has no office in Mississippi, nor does it own or operate a warehouse there. It has no employees soliciting business in Mississippi or otherwise operating there on a regular basis; [12] its contracts are arranged through an independent broker, whose commission is paid either by appellant or by the farmer himself and who has no authority to enter into contracts on behalf of appellant.[13] These facts are in sharp contrast to the situation in *Eli Lilly,* where Lilly operated a New Jersey office with 18 salaried employees whose job was to promote use of Lilly's products. 366 U.S., at 279–281, 81 S.Ct. at 1318–1320. There is no indication that the cotton which makes up appellant's "perpetual inventory" in Mississippi is anything other than what appellant has claimed it to be, namely, cotton which is awaiting necessary sorting and classification as a prerequisite to its shipment in interstate commerce.

In short, appellant's contacts with Mississippi do not exhibit the sort of localization or intrastate character which we have required in situations where a State seeks to require a foreign corporation to qualify to do business. Whether there were local tax incidents of those contacts which could be reached is a different question on which we express no opinion. Whether the course of dealing would subject appellant to suits in Mississippi is likewise a different question on which we express no view. We hold only that Mississippi's refusal to honor and enforce contracts made for interstate or foreign commerce is repugnant to the Commerce Clause.

The judgment is reversed and the cause remanded for proceedings not inconsistent with this opinion.

So ordered.

Reversed and remanded.

MR. JUSTICE REHNQUIST, dissenting.

.   .   .

For reasons which are not entirely clear to me, the Court holds that Mississippi may not require Allenberg to qualify as a foreign

---

12. One of appellant's Memphis employees, Jerry Hill, came to Mississippi on two or three occasions to deliver contracts to the broker, Covington. The more usual practice however, appears to have been for the contracts to be mailed. (App. 56–57, 66–67, 72–76.)

13. *Id.,* 60–61, 65–66, 106–107. See also n. 4, *supra.*

corporation as a condition of using Mississippi courts to enforce its contract with appellee Pittman.[2]

   . . .

It has been settled since Mr. Chief Justice Taney's opinion for the Court in Bank of Augusta v. Earle, 13 Pet. 519, 10 L.Ed. 274 (1839), that a corporation organized in one State which seeks to do business in another State may be required by the latter to qualify under its laws before doing such business. . . .

NOTE ON THE ORIGIN OF INHIBITIONS ON SUITS
BY OUT–OF–STATE CORPORATIONS

The idea that a corporation formed in one state cannot sue in another without some formal recognition by the latter is commonly traced to an opinion rendered by Chief Justice Taney in 1839, in which he declared:

> ". . . a corporation can have no legal existence out of the boundaries of the sovereignty by which it is created. It exists only by operation of law; and where that law ceases to operate, and is no longer obligatory, the corporation can have no existence." [1]

Taney quickly qualified the implications of this proposition by declaring that a second state may choose to recognize the foreign corporation, and will be presumed to do so in the absence of countervailing evidence. But he had laid the foundations for states to exclude corporations of other states unless those corporations complied with the terms laid down by the admitting state. Soon after his decision, states began adopting statutes that forbade out-of-state corporations to do business without having been admitted and paying appropriate fees.

It might have been argued that states are forbidden by the constitution to exclude corporations of other states, but this argument was foreclosed by another of Taney's pronouncements—that a corporation cannot claim the rights of citizens, even though it may be composed of citizens.[2]

It remains true today that a state may impose licensure and admission requirements on out-of-state corporations doing intrastate business.[3] However, the state's powers are not without limitation, and if the character of the out-of-state corporation's activities is entirely interstate, the state may not insist upon registration as a condition of maintaining suit.[4] Where the line between intrastate and interstate activities is to be drawn remains uncertain, and state sanctions with respect to activities by unlicensed corporations vary.[5]

2. In its concluding paragraph the Court states: "We hold only that Mississippi's refusal to honor and enforce contracts made for interstate or foreign commerce is repugnant to the Commerce Clause." The Court offers no definition or analysis as to why this particular contract was "made for interstate or foreign commerce," and the language is traceable to none of our previous cases dealing with the Commerce Clause.

1. Bank of Augusta v. Earle, 38 U.S. (13 Pet.) 519, 583, 10 L.Ed. 274 (1839).

2. Bank of Augusta v. Earle, 38 U.S. (13 Pet.) 519, 586, 10 L.Ed. 274 (1839); acc., Paul v. Virginia, 75 U.S. (8 Wall.) 168, 19 L.Ed. 357 (1868).

3. Eli Lilly & Co. v. Sav-On-Drugs, Inc., 366 U.S. 276, 81 S.Ct. 1316, 6 L.Ed.2d 288 (1961).

4. Allenberg Cotton Co., Inc. v. Pittman, 419 U.S. 20, 95 S.Ct. 260, 42 L.Ed.2d 195 (1974).

5. See generally Note, Sanctions for Failure to Comply With Corporate Qualifi-

In the 19th Century, many corporations which operated extensively in more than one state went through the formality of reincorporation in additional states.[6] This procedure was chosen partly to acquire corporate powers in the additional state, and escape the theory that the original incorporating state could not give them corporate powers outside its own boundaries.[7] Under these procedures, the corporation submitted itself fully to the domestic corporation law of all the incorporating states, which was quite different from admission, which leaves the foreign corporation subject to the corporation laws of only the state which created it.[8]

The nickname of "domestication" was appropriately adopted for the process of reincorporation, by which the foreign corporation became fully subject to the domestic corporation law.[9] However, since reincorporation fell into desuetude as a consequence of more liberal policies on admission and the extension of corporate power, the term "domestication" has been applied, occasionally, to the much simpler procedure of admission.[10] This application leads to confusing the results of reincorporation cases with those of admission cases. We suggest that careful lawyers should apply "domestication," if at all, only to a full reincorporation.

REFERENCES

Retroactive admittance:

Salitan v. Carter, Ealey and Dinwiddie 332 S.W.2d 11, 80 A.L.R.2d 455 (Mo.App.1960) (after admittance, corporation can sue on business conducted before admittance).

Doing business:

Farmers Bank v. Sinwellan Corp., 367 A.2d 180 (Del.1976) (Maryland corporation that operated lodge in Maryland, but kept bank account, picked up guests, and bought supplies in Delaware, was required to be admitted in order to sue bank for dishonoring checks; less business is required for the admittance requirement than for liability to suit under long-arm statute).

Metric Steel Co. v. BLI Construction Co., 147 Ga.App. 380, 249 S.E.2d 121 (1978) (out-of-state corporation that contracted to supply steel for Georgia school building, and sent representatives into state to check plans and sign contract, was unable to sue on contract without being admitted in Georgia).

Amenability of corporation to suit:

Long-arm statutes and cases decided thereunder typically render out-of-state corporations amenable to suit based on sufficient contacts within the state, irrespective of registration.

Mann v. Frank Hrubetz Co., 361 So.2d 1021 (Ala.1978) (Oregon manufacturer of merry-go-round that was delivered to a carnival company in Wisconsin was liable to suit in Alabama for injuries occurring in Alabama).

cation Statutes: An Evaluation, 63 Colum. L.Rev. 117 (1963).

6. Note, Multiple Incorporation as a Form of Railroad Organization (1937) 46 Yale L.J. 1370.

7. Ibid. An additional reason may have been the absence of statutes permitting the routine admission of foreign corporations, such as are common today.

8. See Foley, Incorporation, Multiple Incorporation and the Conflict of Laws (1929) 42 Harv.L.Rev. 516.

9. Note, supra note 6, at 1372; Henn, Law of Corporations (1970) 236; Pa.Bus. Corp.L. § 1909, 15 Purdon Pa.Stat.Ann. § 1909 (1967).

10. E.g., Note, The Legal Consequences of Failure to Comply with Domestication Statutes (1961) 110 U.Pa.L.Rev. 241; Moore Golf, Inc. v. Shambley Wrecking Contractors, Inc., 22 N.C.App. 449, 206 S.E.2d 789 (1974).

Connelly v. Uniroyal, Inc., 75 Ill.2d 393, 27 Ill.Dec. 343, 389 N.E.2d 155 (1979) (Belgian tire manufacturer whose products were retailed in Illinois was amenable to suit in Illinois by injured purchaser of a car assembled in Belgium with defendant's tires).

Liability of directors, officers and agents:

Virginia Code § 13.1–119 (1973): "If a foreign corporation transacts business in this state without a certificate of authority, its directors, officers and agents doing such business shall be jointly and severally liable for any contracts made or to be performed in this State and any torts committed in this State between the time when it began to transact business in this State and the date when it obtains a certificate of authority."

Miller & Rhoads v. West, 442 F.Supp. 341 (E.D.Va.1977) (court applies Virginia Code § 13.1–119, above, only to officers and agents acting within the state).

Limited partnerships:

Note, Regulation of Foreign Limited Partnerships (1972) 52 Boston L.Rev. 64 (reviews laws requiring filing in foreign state under original ULPA).

Revised ULPA §§ 901–908 (subjects limited partnerships formed in another state to a regime similar to foreign corporations, using the term "registration" rather than "admission.").

Critiques:

Conard, Theses for a Corporate Reformation, 19 UC Davis L.Rev. 259, 272, 290 (1986).

Walker, Foreign Corporation Laws: the Loss of Reason (1968) 47 N.C.L.Rev. 1.

Walker, Foreign Corporation Laws: Source and Support for Reform, 1969 Duke L.J. 1145.

C. THE VIRTUES OF CORPORATE FORM

The attractions and detractions of corporate form were briefly summarized in an earlier section. However, the attentive attorney may find upon closer examination that what appear to be virtues of the corporate form are really not advantages for a particular enterprise. Let us suppose that the three shareholders of a closely-held family business, now a partnership, decide to incorporate. What advantages will they recognize? Although the corporation may be established with unlimited life, the family and business dislocations attendant upon the death of one of the shareholders will be virtually the same as those that would prevail were the business in partnership form. And while the shareholders will obtain limited liability, no bank is likely to extend the corporation credit without the individual guarantee of the principal shareholders. Of course, the shareholders will also obtain limitation of liability as to tort claims. But did they not already achieve that status through insurance, even in partnership form? Even the claimed tax advantages may disappear as the shareholders discover the impracticability of establishing stock options and pension plans in a corporation of this size; the corporation may even elect to be taxed under Subchapter S.

The preceding paragraph is not intended to be a brief against the corporate form, but rather a demonstration that the corporation may not be the best form for *every* business. It may safely be said that as the scale of the business increases and as its capital needs expand the corporate form becomes increasingly attractive. If you will review the virtues of corporate form, you will see that they increase in importance as the enterprise becomes larger.

WALKOVSZKY v. CARLTON
New York Court of Appeals, 1966.
18 N.Y.2d 414, 276 N.Y.S.2d 585, 223 N.E.2d 6.

FULD, JUDGE. This case involves what appears to be a rather common practice in the taxicab industry of vesting the ownership of a taxi fleet in many corporations, each owning only one or two cabs.

The complaint alleges that the plaintiff was severely injured four years ago in New York City when he was run down by a taxicab owned by the defendant Seon Cab Corporation and negligently operated at the time by the defendant Marchese. The individual defendant, Carlton, is claimed to be a stockholder of 10 corporations, including Seon, each of which has but two cabs registered in its name, and it is implied that only the minimum automobile liability insurance required by law (in the amount of $10,000) is carried on any one cab. Although seemingly independent of one another, these corporations are alleged to be "operated . . . as a single entity, unit and enterprise" with regard to financing, supplies, repairs, employees and garaging, and all are named as defendants. The plaintiff asserts that he is also entitled to hold their stockholders personally liable for the damages sought because the multiple corporate structure constitutes an unlawful attempt "to defraud members of the general public" who might be injured by the cabs.

The defendant Carlton has moved, pursuant to CPLR 3211(a) 7, to dismiss the complaint on the ground that as to him it "fails to state a cause of action". The court at Special Term granted the motion but the Appellate Division, by a divided vote, reversed, holding that a valid cause of action was sufficiently stated. The defendant Carlton appeals to us, from the nonfinal order, by leave of the Appellate Division on a certified question.

The law permits the incorporation of a business for the very purpose of enabling its proprietors to escape personal liability (see, e.g., Bartle v. Home Owners Co-op., 309 N.Y. 103, 106, 127 N.E.2d 832, 833) but, manifestly, the privilege is not without its limits. Broadly speaking, the courts will disregard the corporate form, or, to use accepted terminology, "pierce the corporate veil", whenever necessary "to prevent fraud or to achieve equity". . . .

In determining whether liability should be extended to reach assets beyond those belonging to the corporation, we are guided, as Judge Cardozo noted by "general rules of agency". (Berkey v. Third Ave. Ry. Co., 244 N.Y. 84, 95, 155 N.E. 58, 61, 50 A.L.R. 599.) In other words, whenever anyone uses control of the corporation to further his own rather than the corporation's business, he will be liable for the corporation's acts "upon the principle of *respondeat superior* applicable even where the agent is a natural person". . . . Such liability, moreover, extends not only to the corporation's commercial dealings. . . .

In the Mangan case (247 App.Div. 853, 286 N.Y.S. 666, mot. for lv. to app. den. 272 N.Y. 676, 286 N.Y.S. 666, supra), the plaintiff was injured as a result of the negligent operation of a cab owned and operated by one of four corporations affiliated with the defendant Terminal. Although the defendant was not a stockholder of any of the operating companies, both the defendant and the operating companies were owned, for the most part, by the same parties. The defendant's name (Terminal) was conspicuously displayed on the sides of all of the taxis used in the enterprise and, in point of fact, the defendant actually serviced, inspected, repaired and dispatched them. These facts were deemed to provide sufficient cause for piercing the corporate veil of the operating company—the nominal owner of the cab which injured the plaintiff—and holding the defendant liable. The operating companies were simply instrumentalities for carrying on the business of the defendant without imposing upon it financial and other liabilities incident to the actual ownership and operation of the cabs.

In the case before us, the plaintiff has explicitly alleged that none of the corporations "had a separate existence of their own" and, as indicated above, all are named as defendants. However, it is one thing to assert that a corporation is a fragment of a larger corporate combine which actually conducts the business. (See Berle, The Theory of Enterprise Entity, 47 Col.L.Rev. 343, 348–350). It is quite another to claim that the corporation is a "dummy" for its individual stockholders who are in reality carrying on the business in their personal capacities for purely personal rather than corporate ends. . . . Either circumstance would justify treating the corporation as an agent and piercing the corporate veil to reach the principal but a different result would follow in each case. In the first, only a larger *corporate* entity would be held financially responsible (see, e.g., Mangan v. Terminal Transp. System, 247 App.Div. 853, 286 N.Y.S. 666, mot. for lv. to app. den. 272 N.Y. 676, 286 N.Y.S. 666, supra) . . . while in the other, the stockholder would be personally liable. . . . Either the stockholder is conducting the business in his individual capacity or he is not. If he is, he will be liable; if he is not, then it does not matter—insofar as his personal liability is concerned—that the enterprise is actually being carried on by a larger "enterprise entity". (See Berle, The Theory of Enterprise Entity, 47 Col.L.Rev. 343). . . . Reading the complaint in this case most favorably and liberally, we do not believe that there can be gathered from its averments the allegations required to spell out a valid cause of action against the defendant Carlton.

The individual defendant is charged with having "organized, managed, dominated and controlled" a fragmented corporate entity but there are no allegations that he was conducting business in his individual capacity. Had the taxicab fleet been owned by a single corporation, it would be readily apparent that the plaintiff would face formidable barriers in attempting to establish personal liability on the part of the corporation's stockholders. The fact that the fleet ownership has been deliberately split up among many corporations does not ease the plaintiff's burden in that respect. The corporate form may not be disregarded merely because the assets of the corporation, together with the mandatory insurance coverage of the vehicle which struck the plaintiff, are insufficient to assure him the recovery sought. If Carlton were to be held individually liable on those facts alone, the decision would apply equally to the thousands of cabs which are owned by their individual drivers who conduct their businesses through corporations organized pursuant to section 401 of the Business Corporation Law, Consol.Laws, c. 4 and carry the minimum insurance required by subdivision 1 (par. [a]) of section 370 of the Vehicle and Traffic Law, Consol. Laws, c. 71. These taxi owner-operators are entitled to form such corporations . . . and we agree with the court at Special Term that, if the insurance coverage required by statute "is inadequate for the protection of the public, the remedy lies not with the courts but with the Legislature." It may very well be sound policy to require that certain corporations must take out liability insurance which will afford adequate compensation to their potential tort victims. However, the responsibility for imposing conditions on the privilege of incorporation has been committed by the Constitution to the Legislature (N.Y. Const., art. X, § 1) and it may not be fairly implied, from any statute, that the Legislature intended, without the slightest discussion or debate, to require of taxi corporations that they carry automobile liability insurance over and above that mandated by the Vehicle and Traffic Law.

. . .

In point of fact, the principle relied upon in the complaint to sustain the imposition of personal liability is not agency but fraud. Such a cause of action cannot withstand analysis. If it is not fraudulent for the owner-operator of a single cab corporation to take out only the minimum required liability insurance, the enterprise does not become either illicit or fraudulent merely because it consists of many such corporations. The plaintiff's injuries are the same regardless of whether the cab which strikes him is owned by a single corporation or part of a fleet with ownership fragmented among many corporations. Whatever rights he may be able to assert against parties other than the registered owner of the vehicle come into being not because he has been defrauded but because, under the principle of *respondeat superior,* he is entitled to hold the whole enterprise responsible for the acts of its agents.

In sum, then, the complaint falls short of adequately stating a cause of action against the defendant Carlton in his individual capacity.

The order of the Appellate Division should be reversed, with costs in this court and in the Appellate Division, the certified question answered in the negative and the order of the Supreme Court, Richmond County, reinstated, with leave to serve an amended complaint.

KEATING, JUDGE (dissenting). The defendant Carlton, the shareholder here sought to be held for the negligence of the driver of a taxicab, was a principal shareholder and organizer of the defendant corporation which owned the taxicab. The corporation was one of 10 organized by the defendant, each containing two cabs and each cab having the "minimum liability" insurance coverage mandated by section 370 of the Vehicle and Traffic Law. The sole assets of these operating corporations are the vehicles themselves and they are apparently subject to mortgages.

From their inception these corporations were intentionally undercapitalized for the purpose of avoiding responsibility for acts which were bound to arise as a result of the operation of a large taxi fleet having cars out on the street 24 hours a day and engaged in public transportation. And during the course of the corporations' existence all income was continually drained out of the corporations for the same purpose.

The issue presented by this action is whether the policy of this State, which affords those desiring to engage in a business enterprise the privilege of limited liability through the use of the corporate device, is so strong that it will permit that privilege to continue no matter how much it is abused, no matter how irresponsibly the corporation is operated, no matter what the cost to the public. I do not believe that it is.

Under the circumstances of this case the shareholders should all be held individually liable to this plaintiff for the injuries he suffered. . . . At least, the matter should not be disposed of on the pleadings by a dismissal of the complaint. "If a corporation is organized and carries on business without substantial capital in such a way that the corporation is likely to have no sufficient assets available to meet its debts, it is inequitable that shareholders should set up such a flimsy organization to escape personal liability. The attempt to do corporate business without providing any sufficient basis of financial responsibility to creditors is an abuse of the separate entity and will be ineffectual to exempt the shareholders from corporate debts. It is coming to be recognized as the policy of law that shareholders should in good faith put at the risk of the business unincumbered capital reasonably adequate for its prospective liabilities. If capital is illusory or trifling compared with the business to be done and the risks of loss, this is a ground for denying the separate entity privilege." (Ballantine, Corporations [rev. ed., 1946], § 129, pp. 302–303.)

In Minton v. Cavaney, 56 Cal.2d 576, 15 Cal.Rptr. 641, 364 P.2d 473, the Supreme Court of California had occasion to discuss this problem in a negligence case. The corporation of which the defendant was an organizer, director and officer operated a public swimming pool. One afternoon the plaintiffs' daughter drowned in the pool as a result of the alleged negligence of the corporation.

Justice Roger Traynor, speaking for the court, outlined the applicable law in this area. "The figurative terminology 'alter ego' and 'disregard of the corporate entity'", he wrote, "is generally used to refer to the various situations that are an abuse of the corporate privilege. . . . The equitable owners of a corporation, for example, are personally liable when they treat the assets of the corporation as their own and add or withdraw capital from the corporation at will . . .; when they hold themselves out as being personally liable for the debts of the corporation . . .; *or when they provide inadequate capitalization and actively participate in the conduct of corporate affairs*". (56 Cal.2d, p. 579, 15 Cal.Rptr., p. 643, 364 P.2d, p. 475; italics supplied.)

Examining the facts of the case in light of the legal principles just enumerated, he found that "[it was] undisputed that there was no attempt to provide adequate capitalization. [The corporation] never had any substantial assets. It leased the pool that it operated, and the lease was forfeited for failure to pay the rent. Its capital was 'trifling compared with the business to be done and the risks of loss' ". (56 Cal. 2d, p. 580, 15 Cal.Rptr., p. 643, 364 P.2d, p. 475.)

It seems obvious that one of "the risks of loss" referred to was the possibility of drownings due to the negligence of the corporation. And the defendant's failure to provide such assets or any fund for recovery resulted in his being held personally liable.

. . .

The defendant contends that a decision holding him personally liable would discourage people from engaging in corporate enterprise.

What I would merely hold is that a participating shareholder of a corporation vested with a public interest, organized with capital insufficient to meet liabilities which are certain to arise in the ordinary course of the corporation's business, may be held personally responsible for such liabilities. Where corporate income is not sufficient to cover the cost of insurance premiums above the statutory minimum or where initially adequate finances dwindle under the pressure of competition, bad times or extraordinary and unexpected liability, obviously the shareholder will not be held liable (Henn, Corporations, p. 208, n. 7).

The only types of corporate enterprises that will be discouraged as a result of a decision allowing the individual shareholder to be sued will be those such as the one in question, designed solely to abuse the corporate privilege at the expense of the public interest.

For these reasons I would vote to affirm the order of the Appellate Division.

DESMOND, C.J., and VAN VOORHIS, BURKE and SCILEPPI, JJ., concur with FULD, J.

KEATING, J., dissents and votes to affirm in an opinion in which BERGAN, J., concurs.

MINTON v. CAVANEY
Supreme Court of California, 1961.
56 Cal.2d 576, 15 Cal.Rptr. 641, 364 P.2d 473.

TRAYNOR, JUSTICE. The Seminole Hot Springs Corporation, hereinafter referred to as Seminole, was duly incorporated in California on

March 8, 1954. It conducted a public swimming pool that it leased from its owner. On June 24, 1954 plaintiffs' daughter drowned in the pool, and plaintiffs recovered a judgment for $10,000 against Seminole for her wrongful death. The judgment remains unsatisfied.

On January 30, 1957, plaintiffs brought the present action to hold defendant Cavaney personally liable for the judgment against Seminole. Cavaney died on May 28, 1958 and his widow, the executrix of his estate, was substituted as defendant. The trial court entered judgment for plaintiffs for $10,000. Defendant appeals.

Plaintiffs introduced evidence that Cavaney was a director and secretary and treasurer of Seminole and that on November 15, 1954, about five months after the drowning, Cavaney as secretary of Seminole and Edwin A. Kraft as president of Seminole applied for permission to issue three shares of Seminole stock, one share to be issued to Kraft, another to F.J. Wettrick and the third to Cavaney. The commissioner of corporations refused permission to issue these shares unless additional information was furnished. The application was then abandoned and no shares were ever issued. There was also evidence that for a time Seminole used Cavaney's office to keep records and to receive mail. Before his death Cavaney answered certain interrogatories. He was asked if Seminole "ever had any assets?" He stated that "insofar as my own personal knowledge and belief is concerned said corporation did not have any assets." Cavaney also stated in the return to an attempted execution that "[I]nsofar as I know, this corporation had no assets of any kind or character. The corporation was duly organized but never functioned as a corporation."

Defendant introduced evidence that Cavaney was an attorney at law, that he was approached by Kraft and Wettrick to form Seminole, and that he was the attorney for Seminole. Plaintiffs introduced Cavaney's answer to several interrogatories that he held the post of secretary and treasurer and director in a temporary capacity and as an accommodation to his client.

Defendant contends that the evidence does not support the court's determination that Cavaney is personally liable for Seminole's debts and that the "alter ego" doctrine is inapplicable because plaintiffs failed to show that there was " '(1) . . . such unity of interest and ownership that the separate personalities of the corporation and the individual no longer exist and (2) that, if the acts are treated as those of the corporation alone, an inequitable result will follow.' " Riddle v. Leuschner, 51 Cal.2d 574, 580, 335 P.2d 107.

. . .

The figurative terminology "alter ego" and "disregard of the corporate entity" is generally used to refer to the various situations that are an abuse of the corporate privilege. . . . The equitable owners of a corporation, for example, are personally liable when they treat the assets of the corporation as their own and add or withdraw capital from the corporation at will; . . . when they hold themselves out as being personally liable for the debts of the corporation; . . . or when they provide inadequate capitalization and actively participate in the conduct of corporate affairs.

. . .

In the instant case the evidence is undisputed that there was no attempt to provide adequate capitalization. Seminole never had any substantial assets. It leased the pool that it operated, and the lease was forfeited for failure to pay the rent. Its capital was " 'trifling compared with the business to be done and the risks of loss . . . .' " *Automotriz Del Golfo De California S.A. De C.V. v. Resnick, supra,* 47 Cal.2d 792, 797, 306 P.2d 1, 4. The evidence is also undisputed that Cavaney was not only the secretary and treasurer of the corporation but was also a director. The evidence that Cavaney was to receive one-third of the shares to be issued supports an inference that he was an equitable owner (see *Riddle v. Leuschner, supra,* 51 Cal.2d 574, 580, 335 P.2d 107), and the evidence that for a time the records of the corporation were kept in Cavaney's office supports an inference that he actively participated in the conduct of the business. . . .

There is no merit in defendant's contentions that the "alter ego" doctrine applies only to contractual debts and not to tort claims. . . .

In this action to hold defendant personally liable upon the judgment against Seminole plaintiffs did not allege or present any evidence on the issue of Seminole's negligence or on the amount of damages sustained by plaintiffs. They relied solely on the judgment against Seminole. Defendant correctly contends that Cavaney or his estate cannot be held liable for the debts of Seminole without an opportunity to relitigate these issues. . . .

The judgment is reversed.

GIBSON, C.J., and PETERS, WHITE and DOOLING, JJ., concur.

SCHAUER, JUSTICE (concurring and dissenting).

I concur in the judgment of reversal on the ground that (as stated in the majority opinion, 15 Cal.Rptr. 644,) "In this action to hold defendant personally liable upon the judgment against Seminole plaintiffs did not allege or present any evidence on the issue of Seminole's negligence or on the amount of damages sustained by plaintiffs. They relied solely on the judgment against Seminole. Defendant correctly contends that Cavaney or his estate cannot be held liable for the debts of Seminole without an opportunity to relitigate these issues. [Citations.] Cavaney was not a party to the action against the corporation, and the judgment in that action is therefore not binding upon him . . . ."

I dissent from any implication that *mere professional activity by an attorney at law, as such,* in the organization of a corporation, can constitute any basis for a finding that the corporation is the attorney's alter ego or that he is otherwise personally liable for *its* debts, whether based on contract or tort. That in such circumstances an attorney does not incur any personal liability for debts of the corporation remains true whether or not the attorney's professional services include the issuance to him of a qualifying share of stock, the attendance at and participation in an organization meeting or meetings, the holding and exercise for such preliminary purposes, in the course of his professional services, of an office or offices, whether secretary or treasurer or presiding officer or any combination of offices in the corporation.

. . .

REFERENCES

Contract liability:

Bartle v. Home Owners Co-operative, Inc., 309 N.Y. 103, 127 N.E.2d 832 (1955) (defendant organized a subsidiary, carefully observed all formalities of organization and operation, but so capitalized and operated the subsidiary that it could make no profit and was barely solvent. Held, defendant not liable for subsidiary's contract debts).

Zaist v. Olson, 154 Conn. 563, 227 A.2d 552 (1967) (on facts similar to *Bartle,* held that the subsidiary was but a conduit of the parent corporation, and therefore parent was liable for subsidiary's debts).

Automotriz Del Golfo De California S.A. De C.V. v. Resnick, 47 Cal.2d 792, 306 P.2d 1 (1957) (holding shareholder liability based on trifling capital and lack of formalities incident to corporate formation and operation).

Japan Petroleum Co. (Nigeria) Ltd. v. Ashland Oil Co., 456 F.Supp. 831 (D.C.Del.1978) (U.S. parent company not liable on contract made by wholly owned Nigerian subsidiary, although officers of subsidiary held identical offices in other subsidiaries, parent and subsidiary engaged together in joint ventures, and parent's annual report referred to Nigerian operations as its own).

Flynt Distributing Co. v. Harvey, 734 F.2d 1389 (9th Cir.1984) (evidence that shareholders converted corporate assets, leaving corporation undercapitalized, made prima facie case for shareholders' liability for contract debts).

Morgan Bros. v. Haskell Corp., 24 Wn.App. 773, 604 P.2d 1294 (1979) (parent of seller conducted in its own name negotiations with purchaser concerning defects in merchandise sold; court imposed liability for defects on parent).

Critiques:

Conard, Theses for a Corporate Reformation, 19 UC Davis L.Rev. 259, 269, 288 (1986).

Clark, The Duties of a Corporate Debtor to its Creditors, 90 Harv.L.Rev. 505 (1977).

Note, Should Shareholders be Personally Liable for the Torts of their Corporations? (1967) 76 Yale L.J. 1190.

Subordination:

Although officers, directors and majority shareholders of corporations may generally enforce claims as creditors of their own corporations, their claims are sometimes subordinated to those of other creditors—or sometimes, as in *Taylor* below—even subordinated to the claims of other shareholders. The grounds for subordination are similar to the grounds for imposing personal liability, although the emphasis is on inadequacy of capital.

Taylor v. Standard Gas & Electric Co., 306 U.S. 307, 59 S.Ct. 543, 83 L.Ed. 669 (1939) (claim of utility holding company against bankrupt subsidiary was subordinated to claims of other creditors and preferred stockholders because of fraudulent conveyances, inadequate capitalization and other factors). The name of the subsidiary, Deep Rock Oil Corp., became the name of the doctrine of subordination enunciated in this case: the "Deep Rock doctrine."

Matter of Multiponics, 622 F.2d 709 (5th Cir.1980) (director's claim against company subordinated when director had participated in several transactions impoverishing the company and benefitting the directors).

Clark, The Duties of a Corporate Debtor to its Creditors, 90 Harv.L.Rev. 505 (1977).

Professional corporation:

First Bank & Trust Co. v. Zagoria, 250 Ga. 844, 302 S.E.2d 674, 39 A.L.R. 4th 551 (1983) (shareholder of professional corporation who held self out as member of firm was liable for firm debts as matter of policy regardless of corporation law).

Reiner v. Kelley, 8 Ohio App.3d 390, 457 N.E.2d 946 (1983) (shareholder of professional corporation liable for corporate obligations by virtue of court's Rules of Practice).

SECTION 6. OTHER FORMS OF ORGANIZATION

The ingenuity of lawyers, and of enterprisers acting without lawyers, has created an infinite variety of organizational forms. Most of these can be subsumed under the categories of proprietorship, partnership, limited partnership and corporation, but some of them fit so oddly that they call for further explanation. There are others that do not fit at all, and survive as distinct forms of organization. Listed below are some forms of both kinds.

Joint venture. A few writers persist in viewing a joint venture as a separate form of unincorporated organization for business or (less often) pleasure, but twentieth century opinion has trended toward regarding joint ventures as a variety of partnership (if for business) or of association (if for other purposes). The term is also used, confusingly, to designate a corporation that is formed by two or three other corporations for a common purpose, such as producing a product needed by both; this type of organization is better characterized as a "joint venture corporation."

Joint stock company. In Great Britain, "joint stock company" generally designates an incorporated organization that would be called in the United States a "business corporation," although the term is usually shortened to "company." In the United States, the term was used in the nineteenth and early twentieth centuries to designated organizations that were formed with transferrable shares, like corporations, but without filing papers as required for corporations. They were generally employed to escape some of the restrictions that applied to corporations, such as limits on landholding and the requirement of obtaining admittance in each state in which they might want to do business. The liberalization of corporation laws appears to have led to the disappearance of joint stock companies in this sense.

Business trust; real estate investment trust (REIT). Another form of organization devised to escape the earlier restrictions of corporation laws was the business trust. Investors paid money to trustees, who invested it in property—typically real estate or securities—and paid the income to the investors, as in a corporation. The device was particularly popular in Massachusetts, and became known as a "Massachusetts trust." Eventually Massachusetts provided a law similar to a business corporations law to govern the business trust, so that the business trust became virtually an alternative form of corporation.

The liberalization of corporation laws eliminated most of the original reasons for forming business trusts, and they became rare except in Massachusetts. However, the use of the business trust elsewhere was revived by an amendment of the Internal Revenue Code in 1960 that created tax advantages for certain trusts formed to make and manage investments in real estate and some other forms of property.[1] The eligible form of organization was designated as a "real estate investment trust," generally abbreviated as REIT. The reasons for favoring real estate investments over other kinds of investment, and for favoring a trust form of organization over a corporate or limited partnership form are too obscure to be explained here, if explainable at all.

Cooperatives. Organizations that are formed for business, but primarily to benefit the people with whom they do business (customers or employees) as distinguished from investors, are called "cooperatives." Agricultural cooperatives are probably the most important class; they may be formed primarily to supply members with seed and fertilizer, or to buy and distribute agricultural products. Consumer cooperatives that retail groceries and household supplies are common. Residential cooperatives that own apartment houses and rent apartments to members are often met.

Some cooperatives—especially agricultural coops—are formed under special statutes designed for this type of organization. Others are formed under the laws of business corporations or of nonprofit corporations, and provide in their charters and bylaws for the practices that distinguish them as cooperatives. A few are unincorporated, occupying a no-man's-land between partnerships and associations. In short, "cooperative" does not designate a form of organization, but a purpose and mode of operation that is adaptable to various forms.

Affiliated groups. Most of the enterprises that we perceive as very large corporations (like General Motors and Exxon) are complex aggregations of scores of corporations, arranged pyramidally with a top holding company, subsidiaries and subsidiaries of subsidiaries. Although the subsidiaries are nominally separate entities, with their own officers, boards of directors, properties and shareholders, their principal policies are generally directed by the holding companies above them. Consequently the ordinary laws of corporate procedure, civil liability, and taxation become awkward or ineffective when applied to these groups.

A few rules of case law and statute law have been developed to deal with the phenomena of corporate groups. The case law on "disregarding the corporate entity," especially in regard to subordination of creditors' claims, resolves some of the problems presented by corporate groups. The federal Securities Act and Securities Exchange Act mak-

---

1. IRC §§ 860–862, 26 U.S.C. §§ 860–862.

ing "controlling persons" liable prima facie for securities violations [2] were probably designed primarily for corporate groups. The Internal Revenue Code requires consolidation of the tax returns of corporations of which eighty percent of the shares are held by members of the group.[3]

However, the rules of corporate governance take very little account of the group phenomenon. West Germany is apparently alone in establishing a statutory regime for relations among group members.[4]

REFERENCES

Corporate groups:

P.I. Blumberg, The Law of Corporate Groups: Procedural Law (1983).

P.I. Blumberg, The Megacorporation in American Society (1975).

M.A. Eisenberg, Megasubsidiaries: The Effect of Corporate Structure on Corporate Control, 84 Harv.L.Rev. 1577 (1977); adapted and reprinted in M.A. Eisenberg, The Structure of the Corporation 277–320 (1976).

2. Securities Act of 1933 § 15, 15 U.S.C. § 77o; Securities Exchange Act of 1937 § 20(a), 15 U.S.C. § 78r(a).

3. Internal Revenue Code §§ 1501–1505, 26 U.S.C. §§ 1501–1505.

4. The German Stock Corporation Law §§ 15–22, 291–338 (Mueller-Galbraith trans., 1976).

Chapter 2

VICARIOUS LIABILITY FOR INJURIES

Tort reform, which usually means reform of the tort compensation system rather than changes in standards of liability, is much in the news again. Legislative changes are being discussed in Congress and virtually every state legislature.

Most of this interest would not exist if it were not for the general acceptance of the concept of vicarious liability. The public concern would be minimal if the law of torts were left to an individualistic response: the person whose negligence caused the harm shall pay for the damage. Most of the people who operate the machines that do the harm are too poor to pay the losses they cause; at least they are too poor to be forced to pay very much under contemporary debtor-protection laws. What makes tort law worthwhile is the means of imposing the loss on somebody beyond the tort feasor—somebody anciently called the "master" and lately identified as the "enterprise". How and why we have moved progressively from individual to "enterprise liability" is the subject of this chapter as well as the one which follows.

SECTION 1. ORIGINS AND JUSTIFICATION

JONES v. HART

England, Court of King's Bench, 1698.
Holt, K.B. 642, 90 Eng.Rep. 1255.

A servant to a pawn-broker took in goods, and the party came and tendered the money to the servant, who said he had lost the goods. Upon this, action of trover was brought against the master; and the question was, whether it would lie or not?

HOLT, C.J.[1] The action well lies in this case: If the servants of A. with his cart run against another cart, wherein is a pipe of wine, and overturn the cart and spoil the wine, an action lieth against A. So where a carter's servant runs his cart over a boy, action lies against the master for the damage done by this negligence: and so it is if a smith's man pricks a horse in shoeing, the master is liable. For whoever employs another, is answerable for him, and undertakes for his care to all that make use of him.

---

1. Sir John Holt, Lord Chief Justice of England from 1689 to 1710, adapted the rules of the common law, framed in feudal times, to the needs of the emerging commercial society. In a series of cases he developed much of the law of negotiable instruments which has survived into the twentieth century. In the area of personal rights Holt was the first to hold that slavery could not exist in England, stating "As soon as a Negro comes to England, he is free; one may be a villein in England, but not a slave." Smith v. Brown (1706) 2 Salk. 666, 91 Eng.Rep. 566.

The act of a servant is the act of his master, where he acts by authority of the master.

REFERENCES

Other cases illustrating the development of vicarious liability in English law from 1401 to 1800 A.D. may be found in Wambaugh, Cases on Agency (3d ed. 1925) 79–104.

For analyses of these and other cases, see Holmes, Wigmore and Baty, cited below.

NOTE: JUSTIFICATION OF VICARIOUS LIABILITY

The rule of vicarious liability, announced by Chief Justice Holt in Jones v. Hart (above) has been an axiom of the common law for almost three centuries. There has been no split of authority, nor shifting back and forth; only the boundaries of its application have provoked judicial differences.

Doubts about vicarious liability first arose when legal scholarship of the Victorian era began to wash legal ideas in what Justice Holmes called "cynical acid." Holmes opened the door of doubt when he demonstrated that the judicial enunciators have generally derived the rule from a bare fiction, or from gross over-extension of the precedents. Holmes' philosophical queries became polemic denunciations in the hands of the apostles of individualism exemplified below by Thomas Baty. Others, including Wigmore and Laski, attempted to find new justifications for the beleaguered doctrine.

The most significant breakthrough seems to have been made by a professor who was not seeking to justify or to unjustify vicarious liability, but to decide how far it should be extended into zones of detour and frolic.

Aside from reading and understanding the viewpoints of the principal commentators on this evergreen controversy, it is useful to go behind the expressed contentions, and ask how Holmes would have responded to Smith or Calabresi. Are there important differences about their assumptions regarding the aims of law?

THE HISTORY OF AGENCY [1]
Oliver Wendell Holmes, Jr.[2], 1882.
4 Harv.L.Rev. 345, 5 Id. 1; reprinted in 3 Selected Essays on Anglo-American Legal History (1909) 368.

. . . The Roman law, it is true, developed no such universal doctrines of agency as have been worked out in England. Only innkeepers and shipowners (*nautae, caupones, stabularii*) were made answerable for the misconduct of their free servants by the praetor's edict. It was not generally possible to acquire rights or to incur obligations through the acts of free persons. But, so far as rights of property, possession, or contract could be acquired through others not slaves, the law undoubtedly started from slavery and the *patria potestas.*

1. This Essay originally formed two lectures delivered by the author in 1882 while professor in the Law School of Harvard University.

2. Oliver Wendell Holmes, Jr., was the famous justice of the Supreme Judicial Court of Massachusetts (1882–1902) and of the Supreme Court of the United States (1902–1932), and subject of the entertaining biography, Yankee from Olympus, by Catherine Drinker Bowen. The "Junior" distinguishes him from his father, the physician, essayist ("Autocrat of the Breakfast Table"), and poet ("Old Ironsides"; "Last Leaf on the Tree").

It will be easy to see how this tended toward a fictitious identification of agent with principal, although within the limits to which it confined agency the Roman law had little need and made little use of the fiction. . . .

Such a formula, of course, is only derivative. The fiction is merely a convenient way of expressing rules which were arrived at on other grounds. The Roman praetor did not make innkeepers answerable for their servants because "the act of the servant was the act of the master," any more than because they had been negligent in choosing them. He did so on substantive grounds of policy—because of the special confidence necessarily reposed in innkeepers. So when it was held that a slave's possession was his owner's possession, the practical fact of the master's power was at the bottom of the decision.

   . . .

At about the time of the Conquest, what was known as the *Frithborh,* or frankpledge, was either introduced or grew greatly in importance. Among other things, the master was made the pledge of his servants, to hand them over to justice or to pay the fine himself.

 . . .

I think I now have traced sufficiently the history of agency in torts. The evidence satisfies me that the common law has started from the *Patria potestas* and the *frithborh,*—whether following or simply helped by the Roman law it does not matter,—and that it has worked itself out to its limits through the formula of identity. It is true that liability for another as master or principal is not confined to family relations; but I have shown partly, and shall complete the proof later, that the whole doctrine has been worked out in terms of master and servant and on the analogies which those terms suggested. . . .

I assume that common sense is opposed to making one man pay for another man's wrong, unless he actually has brought the wrong to pass according to the ordinary canons of legal responsibility,—unless, that is to say, he has induced the immediate wrongdoer to do acts of which the wrong, or, at least, wrong, was the natural consequence under the circumstances known to the defendant. . . . I therefore assume that common sense is opposed to the fundamental theory of agency, although I have no doubt that the possible explanations of its various rules which I suggested at the beginning of this Essay, together with the fact that the most flagrant of them now-a-days often presents itself as a seemingly wholesome check on the indifference and negligence of great corporations, have done much to reconcile men's minds to that theory.

FROLIC AND DETOUR [1]

Young B. Smith,[2] 1923.
23 Col.L.Rev. 444, 456–460.

[After reviewing the arguments of Holmes and Baty, the author continues as follows:]

Why, then, should the master be responsible?

A reason which occurs to the writer is that which has been offered in justification of workmen's compensation statutes. In substance it is the belief that it is socially more expedient to spread or distribute among a large group of the community the losses which experience has taught are inevitable in the carrying on of industry, than to cast the loss upon a few.

. . .

A taxicab negligently runs into a pedestrian. If the injured person's sole remedy is against the negligent chauffeur, in most cases the loss will fall on the pedestrian. On the other hand if the person carrying on the taxicab business is held responsible, the loss will not fall on him alone. Like the employer under workmen's compensation statutes, it is feasible for him (through the medium of insurance) to spread the loss among others carrying on a similar business, and he can pass his proportionate part of the loss (the insurance premium) in the form of slightly higher charges to the hundreds and thousands of persons who use his cabs and thus "the shock of the accident may be borne by the community."

. . .

It is admitted that in the case of domestic servants there is less justification for applying the rule of *respondeat superior.* No doubt this is why most of the workmen's acts which have been passed do not include domestic servants. But like many other common law doctrines, the limits of *respondeat superior* have not been fixed with reference to any clearly defined policy. However, by far the greater number of servants in present times are not domestics but are engaged in industry, and their employers are in a position to distribute as well as spread the losses which they may cause. Furthermore, most of the cases of injuries to third persons are caused by servants engaged in business or industry. Practically the only type of domestic servant who injures others with any degree of frequency is the family chauffeur, and in this case the imposition of liability upon the employer is not as harsh as it might seem. The availability of insurance against such liability, and the common practice among owners of cars to carry indemnity insurance, actually result in spreading such losses among the group of

---

1. The selection above is an excerpt from a law review article bearing the same title.

2. Young B. Smith (b. 1889) joined the Columbia Law School faculty in 1916, served as its dean from 1928 to 1952, and was the co-editor of a widely used casebook on Torts. He served as chairman of the New York State Law Revision Commission and in many other public capacities, and died in 1960.

automobilists carrying such insurance which is by no means a small proportion of the community, and the proportionate part which a particular employer is made to bear (the insurance premium) is relatively small. Is it not better that all persons employing chauffeurs should pay a small amount annually into an insurance fund, than to cast severe losses upon the few victims of the chauffeurs' negligence?

Furthermore, through the agency of insurance it would be possible to effectuate a spreading of practically all forms of losses, and it is the opinion of the writer that within the next hundred years the possibilities of the principle of insurance will lead to very marked changes in the prevailing attitude towards the whole subject of legal responsibility.

Again let it be said, the writer does not claim that Holt and Kenyon declared the master responsible for his servants' unauthorized negligence because of any such conception of social policy as has been here suggested. What the writer believes is that the doctrine, whatever may have been the reasons for its origin, finds its justification as a rule of present-day law in the social policy above stated. If this be correct, the courts in applying the rule ought to bear in mind its justification and seek to reach conclusions which will further the policy upon which the justification rests.

VICARIOUS LIABILITY AND ADMINISTRATION OF RISK
William O. Douglas [1] (1929).
38 Yale Law Journal 584, 587.

. . . Why Holt, J. put his seal of approval on the doctrine of vicarious liability is still a riddle. From whence came the rule and a complete exposition of its pedigree are problems as yet unanswered. The learned attempts made are admittedly ineffectual. Similarly, whether the rules of vicarious liability made satisfactory and effective adjustments of the economic and social conflicts in the industrial society out of which they rose is highly significant and as yet unexplored. Each of these problems is of great importance to every legal historian, and of immeasurable interest to all who are concerned with the history of the science of jurisprudence. But one of more immediate significance to all legal scholars—teacher, practitioner and judge—and to all social scientists is, what rationale justifies the various rules of vicarious liability in modern society? The importance of the answer to that question is at once apparent when the first court is striving to phrase the rule, when the hundredth variation of the normal situation is up for decision and the court is seeking to delimit the rule, when bases for legislation are sought, and when the economic and social effects of these social regulatory rules are measured.

The necessary economic and social data are not at hand to attempt a complete statement of the rationale, but one major problem can be

1. This article by a law professor who later became a United States Supreme Court Justice, offers a functional analysis of the independent contractor problem in place of the doctrinal one of the cases; many later analyses of the problem owe much to this article.

analyzed. It is the problem of the administration of these risks. The delimiting factors of these various rules deny recovery against certain individuals and certain businesses at certain times. The reasons for making some delimitations would be more particularly concerned with the case of the person seeking to escape the legal duty, than with the case of him seeking to assert the right. The judgments enforcing these rules are saddled on the respective businesses involved. They become cost items, and the managers must pay them. Likewise, they will probably want to provide for them, and to attempt to absorb them. Their problems in administering these items of risk are therefore pertinent to any attempt either to delimit the rules of liability or to expand them. The efficiency with which business under modern society can administer these risks is not, to be sure, the whole problem. Compensation for an injured party comes first, but that cannot be considered separately from the capacities of the parties, to whom the loss is allocated, to bear it. Only when those capacities are measured, can the scope of the right of the injured party be intelligently determined. Otherwise the rule which is fashioned may be too lax or too burdensome. An analysis of these rules in light of the problems of an administrator of risk will therefore be undertaken. Though that analysis may do nothing more than to state succinctly one of the primary issues involved in the cases, if that issue is met, a basis for a rationale of these rules will be forthcoming. . . .

Administration of risk is so broad it has elements of vagueness. It properly includes four distinct and separate concepts—avoidance, prevention, shifting, and distribution.[2] M might have avoided this type of risk by refraining from entering business, or a business requiring delivery by truck, or by not making this particular delivery. M might have taken all steps known to man to lessen the likelihood of such injuries, those steps including the installation of four wheel brakes, extreme care in selection of truck drivers, etc. M might have contracted with T, whereby T agreed to assume the particular type of risk. Or M might have assumed the risk, and recouped by distributing the cost of assumption among the consumers of the product he sells. For purposes of convenience these four types of activity may be respectively called risk avoidance, risk prevention, risk shifting and risk distribution. Do the rules of frolic and detour when translated into these administrations of risk concepts make workable, understandable rules?

---

2. "He may avoid the uncertainty peculiar to a specific form of industrial activity by keeping out of the industry; he may reduce the degree of uncertainty by adopting devices that make the occurrence of the loss less probable; or he may assume the risk and endure the attendant uncertainty. The first form of activity may be called avoidance of risk, the second, prevention, and the last, assumption." WILLETT, The Economic Theory of Risk and Insurance (1901) note 6, at 88.

SOME THOUGHTS ON RISK DISTRIBUTION AND THE LAW OF TORTS

Guido Calabresi.
70 Yale Law Journal 499, 500–502, 543–544 (1961).

"Activities should bear the costs they engender"; "it is only fair that an industry should pay for the injuries it causes." "Enterprise liability"—the notion that losses should be borne by the doer, the enterprise, rather than distributed on the basis of fault—is usually explained in such terms. A statement of this kind is generally followed by an additional one which implies that the enterprise can pass the loss on to the consumers in price rises, and that therefore enterprise liability is really a form of "risk spreading." It is, of course, true that enterprise liability sometimes does spread losses; it is equally true, however, that sometimes it does not. In discussing risk spreading at a later point in this Article we will consider when enterprises can in fact, and when they cannot, spread losses. And since risk spreading is not always a valid justification for enterprise liability we are at the moment less concerned with the risk spreading potential of enterprise liability than with whether another, more general, justification exists for the "should" in the phrase "an enterprise should bear its costs."

. . .

. . . That justification can be called the "allocation of resources" justification. At its base are certain fundamental ethical postulates. One of these, perhaps the most important, is that by and large people know what is best for themselves. If people want television sets, society should produce television sets; if they want licorice drops, then licorice drops should be made. And, the theory continues, in order for people to know what they really want they must know the relative costs of producing different goods. The function of prices is to reflect the actual costs of competing goods, and thus to enable the buyer to cast an informed vote in making his purchases.

. . .

Respondeat superior—like workmen's compensation, to which it has often been analogized—was the forerunner of modern enterprise liability. As a result, both have been written about extensively, though usually with emphasis only on their "loss spreading" or "deep pocket" potentials. Both are based on the notion that no single employee deems the risk of injury arising out of his employment to be great enough to justify him either in insuring or in asking substantially higher wages because of it. The proposition is an empirical one which can be fairly readily accepted. Respondeat superior applies it to injuries to third parties, while workmen's compensation applies it to the worker himself.

The effect of this proposition in terms of the justifications for enterprise liability is clear. The master is the best insurer, both in the sense of being able to obtain insurance at the lower rates and in the sense of being most aware of the risk. Consequently, he is the best primary risk spreader. The cost of insurance is normally allocated in part to the cost of labor, and thereby spread backwards. It is in part spread forward to consumers, through adjustments of price and output. The remainder is—after a transition period now long past in every industry—spread forward in all industries except monopolistic ones. Thus, very broad spreading, both primary and secondary, is achieved. In addition, of course, what is not spread can be justified both on monopoly tax grounds and on the broader deep-pocket notions which emphasize the generally stronger financial position of masters than of servants.

Equally strong allocation-of-resources arguments can be made. Unless wages reflect the risk of injuries the true cost of labor in an industry is not shown. Similarly, the failure to show injury costs means that the prices of the goods the industry sells understate their true costs, and that too much is produced in that industry compared to those which are less accident prone. On the other hand, if workers were to insure themselves and to demand higher wages to pay for the insurance, the fact that insurance would probably cost them more than their employers would mean that injury costs in the industry would be overstated. Either way, workmen's compensation and respondeat superior would tend toward a better allocation of resources. Needless to say, contribution between master and servant, or reimbursement of the master by the servant tortfeasor—though possibly supported on "fault" grounds—runs directly counter to all the "risk distribution" justifications. As a result, one can understand the tendency of some courts to avoid such contributions and even to let a verdict against the master— based on the servant's negligence—stand together with a finding of no negligence in the suit against the servant.

. . .

AN ECONOMIC ANALYSIS OF THE CHOICE BETWEEN ENTERPRISE AND PERSONAL LIABILITY FOR ACCIDENTS

Lewis A. Kornhauser, 1982.
70 California Law Review 1345, 1349–1352.

This Article examines several potential "costs" that might lead to different levels of care under the two different legal regimes. The essential assumption of the model is that one such cost, which is always present, is the enterprise's inability to write and enforce employment contracts that condition the wage of the employee on a specific level of care. Employment contracts can, however, be conditioned on observable events that are proxies for the level of care taken. These proxies may be more or less "noisy"—that is, they are less than perfectly correlated with the agent's actual level of care. The assumption that employers cannot condition on a specific level of care is quite reasonable given that principals do not observe every act of their subordinates. Similarly, while courts resolve controversies, they do not, with certainty, ascertain the degree of care exercised by the agent. In fact, the model will restrict enterprises to a very narrow set of contracts defined by the proxy which may be used in employment contracts.

The other potential costs examined derive from arguments offered elsewhere in the legal literature. First, the agent may not have sufficient assets to cover the judgment, in which case his liability would be limited. If the agent has insufficient assets to cover the damage he causes, the assignment of liability to him arguably will not completely internalize the costs of his decisionmaking. Some of the loss will still fall on innocent third parties, and the agent will take too little care measured from a social perspective that seeks to minimize the sum of accident costs and accident prevention costs. To complete the argument, one must be able to conclude that assigning liability to the financially solvent enterprise will increase the care taken by the agent.

Second, employers may not screen their employees on the basis of carefulness. Unless the enterprise is liable it will be indifferent to the carefulness with which its agents undertake their tasks. It may therefore hire too many careless employees and again too many accidents may result. This argument assumes, of course, that the injury-causing activity is not related to the efficiency with which the agent achieves the goal of the enterprise. If more careless employees also produce more profit for the enterprise, this second justification would suggest that enterprises would hire far too many careless people. Conversely, if lack of care hindered productivity, enterprises would have some, but perhaps inadequate, incentive to screen applicants on the basis of care.

Third, failure to assign liability to the enterprise arguably leads to the provision of a work environment that is too dangerous to third parties. The danger may arise either from the inadequate supervision of workers or from the arrangement of the production process in a way that enhances profits at the cost of injuries to a third party and borne by the employee. Again this argument suggests that enterprise liability would induce higher care levels than agent liability.

Fourth, assignment of liability to the agent may be inadequate because most injuries result from a complicated combination of acts by various agents. Courts are unable to disentangle the event and hence many agents escape liability because the plaintiff cannot prove a particular agent was at fault. Thus, for reasons similar to those considered under the first rationale, too many accidents occur. Assignment of liability to the enterprise not only insures compensation of the victim but places responsibility on a party either better able than the court to identify the responsible individuals or with a wider range of sanctions available.

Fifth, there is a conflict of interest between agent and principal in which the agent prefers, if all else is equal, to take less care, while the principal cares only about her profit. This rationale assumes that the agent's exercise of care decreases productivity so that if he takes more care, enterprise profits fall. However, under a rule of law that assigns liability to the agent, the agent's interests conflict with those of the enterprise. Thus, in order to avoid liability, he might take more care than he otherwise would under enterprise liability. Consequently, from an economic standpoint, too few accidents and too little profit (or governmental service) would be produced under agent liability.

Sixth, for unspecified reasons, the entity cannot communicate incentives to the agent. Enterprise liability would then lead to more accidents than agent liability because the courts may provide incentives that the enterprise cannot.

The Article therefore examines seven factors that might potentially lead to different care levels prevailing under the two legal regimes: (1) limitations on contractual form that derive from imprecise monitoring of agent care; (2) conflicts of interest between principal and agent; (3) costs of screening employees on the basis of carefulness; (4) partial control by the enterprise of the probability of an accident; (5) limited liability of the agent; (6) additional non-labor market impediments to the contractual form; and (7) differences in court and enterprise ability to hold agents responsible. In every case examined, the limitations on contractual forms and the conflict of interest between agent and principal will exist. The precise meaning of each of these costs will be specified later in the Article.

. . .

D. Summary of Conclusions

The results of the analysis may be simply stated. Agent liability and enterprise liability induce the same level of care in the basic case in which the enterprise cannot condition wages on the exact level of care taken and in which the agent's interests diverge from the interests of the principal. In addition, the two legal regimes lead to the same levels of care when the problems of supervision and screening are added to the basic conflict of interest and to the limitation on contractual form. On the other hand, the legal regimes lead to different levels of care when the two basic costs are complicated by limited liability of the agent, a difference between court and enterprise ability to identify responsible agents, or some additional restriction in the enterprise's ability to condition its employment contract.

Under limited liability, the level of care under agent liability may be greater than, equal to, or less than the level of care induced by enterprise liability. Casual empiricism would suggest that when there is limited liability, less care is usually taken under agent liability. Generally, enterprises are more able than courts to identify responsible actors; consequently, this fact suggests that more care results from a system of enterprise liability. Similarly, differentials between court and enterprise ability to monitor care can lead to different levels of accidents. Which regime of liability induces greater care levels depends on which institution, court or enterprise, monitors better. Conversely, if for reasons unrelated to the labor market, the principal is restricted in her ability to condition wages even on noisy indicators of care, then agent liability leads to more care than enterprise liability. This latter result has special significance for the public employee case in which civil service regulations may restrict the government's ability to condition wages, broadly defined, on performance.

REFERENCES

Historical studies:

Further light on historical origins, casting some doubt on Holmes' analysis:

Pollock and Maitland, 2 History of English Law (2d ed. 1903) 528–534.

T.B. Smith, Master and Servant—Further Historical Outlines (1958) 1958 Juridical Review 215.

Wigmore, Responsibility for Tortious Acts: Its History. (1894) 7 Harv.L.Rev. 383. (Questions Holmes "history", and argues that it is reasonable to look to the party which can best prevent the risk).

Evaluation:

Further observations on the justification for vicarious liability:

Hackett: Why is a Master Liable for the Torts of his Servant? (1893) 7 Harv.L.Rev. 107 (an echo of Holmes).

T. Baty, Vicarious Liability (London, 1916). (A spirited attack on vicarious liability, charging it as a historical error, an indefensible grasp for the "deep pocket," and an injury to industry).

Laski, The Basis of Vicarious Liability (1916) 26 Yale L.J. 105 (The social distribution of profit and loss is least disturbed by placing liability on the employer).

Clarence Morris (Univ. of Pennsylvania law professor): The Torts of an Independent Contractor (1935) 29 Ill.L.Rev. 339–341 (developing the "deterrent" idea which Laski took from Bentham).

Warren A. Seavey (Harvard law professor, Reporter for the Restatement of Agency): Speculations as to Respondeat Superior (1934) Harvard Legal Studies 433, reprinted in Seavey, Studies in Agency (1949) 129 (comprehensive review of arguments pro and con).

Role of fictions in law:

Fuller, Legal Fictions (1930) 25 Ill.L.Rev. 363.

Palmer, Legal Fictions and Red Room Wine (1952) 38 A.B.A.J. 23.

Pollock and Maitland, 2 Hist.Eng.L. 558, 564 (2d ed. 1903)—fictional extension of common law forms of action.

Conflict of laws:

Ehrenzweig: Vicarious Liability in the Conflict of Laws, 69 Yale L.J. 978 (1960).

Laws on parental liability:

Note, 54 A.L.R.3d 974: Liability of parents for intentional acts. (Common law rejects such liability; note discusses several statutes imposing such liability).

Note, 8 A.L.R.3d 612: Validity and construction of statutes. (Constitutionality rarely tested; one case sustains constitutionality).

NOTE: VICARIOUS LIABILITY IN FOREIGN LAW

When we encounter a principle of law whose utility is disputed, we can often gain perspective by discovering whether foreign legal systems, coming at the problem from a different direction, have arrived at the same or at different conclusions; and, if the latter, whether they are happy with them.

It is usual to look first at France, because of the worldwide influence of French language and culture, of which the Napoleonic codes are a particular prominent part. The French law is not only like the common law in this matter, but arrived at its position by a surprisingly similar route. In almost the same year that Chief Justice Holt was announcing the English rule, a French writer named Domat was doing likewise in France; his views (with some variation) were codified in the Code Napoleon in 1804. Just as in the common law world, 19th century French scholars discovered that, through historical error, the rule had been formulated too broadly, but no one changed it. In the early twentieth century, French writers (like English and American) discovered that there were social justifications for the rule which had been adopted much earlier. In the many countries which have copied the Code Napoleon without substantial reexamination, the vicarious liability rule has been automatically adopted.

In those parts of the Western world where neither the common law nor the Code Napoleon prevail, there are a variety of statutory formulations of employers' liability. Nearly all of them express the idea that the employer is liable unless he has used due care to avoid accidents; in judicial application, the burden is placed on the employer to prove his freedom from fault in selection, instruction and supervision of the employee.

RESPONDEAT SUPERIOR IN THE LIGHT OF COMPARATIVE LAW
Robert Neuner.
4 Louisiana State Law Review 1, 2, 7–8 (1941).

Both the common law and the French law are in accord on the principle that the liability of an employer for the wrongful acts of his employees is in no way dependent on any fault of the employer. In marked contrast to this position German law has imposed a more limited liability upon the employer by connecting his liability with his personal fault; the master is liable only when he has engaged a servant whom he knew or should have known was unfit, or when he did not properly supervise the servant's activities.

. . .

Several conclusions can be drawn from the German experience. In the first place, a court, when faced with the facts of a concrete case, usually looks with disfavor upon the defense that the employer was not guilty of negligence or other personal fault. Only this can satisfactorily explain the restrictions in both scope and content which Section 831 of the German Civil code underwent in practice. A reading of the many hundreds of German decisions that deal with the master's liability leads to the further conclusion that a legal rule which makes the master's liability depend upon his own negligence introduces an element of unreality and uncertainty into the law beyond all tolerable limits. It is unrealistic to require a degree of care in selection and control which as a practical matter cannot be exercised. The servant often has a technical knowledge which the master does not possess; an effective supervision would involve an intolerable expense, and finally changes in the social position of the economically dependent classes make impossible many forms of interference which formerly may have been practical.

If the degree of care in supervision exacted by the courts is in fact illusory, still less can there be any certainty in the application of such an illusory concept. How can the courts work out standards of care in selection and supervision which will furnish employers a dependable guide for future conduct? The German Supreme Court has not been able to do it. The obvious conclusion is that a system of law which bases the employer's liability upon his own negligence does not recommend itself.

CODE NAPOLEON
Art. 1384, 1804

A person is responsible not only for the injury which is caused by his own act, but also for that which is caused by the act of persons for whom he is bound to answer, or by things which he has under his care.

The father, and the mother after the decease of her husband, are responsible for the injury caused by their minor children residing with them;

Masters and contractors, for the damages caused by their servants and employees in the functions for which they have employed them;

Teachers and artisans for the damage caused by their students and apprentices during the time that they are under their superintendance.

The foregoing responsibility is incurred unless the father and mother, the teachers and artisans can prove that they were not able to prevent the act which gives rise to such responsibility.

1937 Amendment:

The foregoing responsibility is incurred unless the father and mother and the artisans prove that they could not prevent the act which gives rise to the responsibility.

With respect to teachers, the offenses, imprudence or negligence charged against them as the cause of the harmful act must be proved by the plaintiff in the case according to general principles of law.

1970 Amendment:

The father and mother, in so far as they exercise their right of control [droit de garde] are jointly liable for the damage caused by their minor children living with them.

NOTE: CODE NAPOLEON

A number of statutes provide rules that deviate from the principles of article 1384 for specified categories of injuries, including those caused by automobiles, aircraft and aerial cable cars.

REFERENCES

Exposition:

Conant, Liability of Principals for Torts of Agents: A Comparative View (1968) 47 Neb.L.Rev. 42.

Fleming, Defective Automobiles: France and America (1925) 23 Am.J.Comp.L. 513.

Hellner, The New Swedish Tort Liability Act (1974) 22 Am.J.Comp.L. 1, 8–11 (introduction of vicarious liability in Swedish law by statute of 1972).

Planiol, Etudes sur la Responsabilite Civile (1909) 38 Rev.crit.Leg. & Jur. 282 (origins and justification of rule in France; role of Domat).

Riccobono, Reception of Forms of Agency in Roman Law (1932) 9 N.Y.U.L.Q. 271 (ancient Rome).

Savatier, 1 Traite de la Responsabilite (2d ed. 1951) no. 274–282b.

Surveyer, Comparison of Delictual Responsibility (1933) 8 Tulane L.Rev. 53 (survey of basic principles in Egypt, Germany, Italy, Japan, Panama, Spain).

Case:

Porto Rico Gas & Coke Co. v. Frank Rullan & Associates, 189 F.2d 397 (1st Cir.1951) (interpreting Puerto Rican Civil Code provisions).

NOTE: VICARIOUS CONTRIBUTORY NEGLIGENCE?

An intriguing question which sharply divides opinion is whether an employer is barred from recovering damages by the contributory negligence of his employee. Many reasons which lead to the same result regarding primary negligence indicate differing results when applied to contributory negligence.

The traditional view has been that an employee's negligence which would have made the employer liable to another bars the employer's claim against another.[1] The doctrine is known as "imputed contributory negligence." In 1966, a Minnesota court rejected the idea;[2] in 1968, a North Dakota court reaffirmed it.[3] Many law reviews got into the act.[4]

SECTION 2. VICARIOUS LIABILITY RELATIONSHIPS

For better or for worse, the principle of vicarious liability is established in the law of English-speaking countries. The difficulty remains of knowing to whom and to what it should be applied.

For Justice Holt, the answer was easy. The people who are responsible are the masters, and the people for whom they are responsible are their servants.

With a formula like this, the law might have gone in either of two directions. People who are described in common parlance as "servants" have become notoriously scarce, and those known as "masters" completely extinct. It is not only the words that have gone, but the

---

1. Prosser, Torts (5th ed. 1984) p. 529, fn. 3.

2. Weber v. Stokeley-Van Camp, 274 Minn. 482, 144 N.W.2d 540 (1966).

3. Wilson v. Great Northern Railway Co., 83 S.D. 207, 157 N.W.2d 19 (1968).

4. E.g., 19 Ala.L.Rev. 219, 9 Ariz.L.Rev. 122, 20 Ark.L.Rev. 380, 16 DePaul L.Rev. 478, 45 Tex.L.Rev. 364, 36 U.Cinc.L.Rev. 143, 39 U.Colo.L.Rev. 170, 27 Md.L.Rev. 387, 44 N.D.L.Rev. 105, 6 Washburn L.J. 508, 42 Wash.L.Rev. 662, 69 W.Va.L.Rev. 236.

institutions—involving the right to administer corporal punishment, and to recapture "runaway servants," of which there are ample evidences in early reports. As these rights faded away with the disappearance of "masters," vicarious liability might have done the same. On the contrary, it flourished while other aspects of baroque master-and-servant law were vanishing.

What are the criteria which cause the rule of vicarious liability to extend to some areas and to exclude others? Analysts have commonly identified three. First, the principal (the person whose putative liability is in question) must have assented in some way to the relationship with the actor. Second, the principal must expect to derive some "benefit"—i.e., something he wants—from the relationship. Third, he must have some element of "control." Since the third criterion gives by far the greatest difficulty in practice, we have concentrated our case selection on this area. We will deal summarily with the other issues.

In studying the application of these criteria, you may notice that they can be applied very narrowly or very broadly. In seeking clues to the ways in which criteria are applied, it is helpful to remember the disputes about the principle of vicarious liability itself. Some judges share the hostility toward it which was voiced by Holmes. Some accept it, but think it should be applied primarily to maximize the incentive to exercise care in supervision. Others probably accept, even if tacitly, the suppositions of Smith and Calabresi that the main thing is to spread the loss among participants in the loss-causing activity.

Another interesting variation in the literature of vicarious liability relates to the language in which the subject is discussed. Justice Holt spoke of "masters" and "servants," which were current coin in 17th century speech. These terms are perpetuated today in many judicial decisions, and in the Restatement of Agency. Students should be familiar with them but should not, we think, acquire the habit of using them. Defenders of the Restatement contend that these words, precisely because they are archaic, are neutral tokens of communication. It is clear, however, that the terms are still alive enough to be offensive to laborers and labor representatives. We suspect that those who consider them neutral are simply unaware of how much their own ideas are contaminated by archaic conceptions of employment relationships.

A. THE CONCEPT OF EMPLOYMENT

In the vast majority of cases involving vicarious liability the issue of whether or not there is a sufficient vicarious liability relationship is clearcut. The party committing the act is clearly identified as an employee of the principal. Questions of assent, benefit, and control are foreclosed by the existence of an employment contract. They become issues only in the relatively few cases where the employment relationship is informal.

Some problems with assent

The basis of the assent requirement is obvious enough. A baby (even a wealthy baby) should not be liable for the excessive force used by its nurse in repelling a noisy dog. Granted that this is true, where should we draw the line on the question of capacity to enter into a contract which can result in vicarious liability? In general terms the question of capacity in these cases follows basic contract law. This can lead to surprising results. In a leading case, a young man of 20 years and 8 months was held not liable for the negligence of a friend driving the young man's car, since the young man could not give a binding assent. Academics are generally critical of these decisions, but few judges have defied the weight of precedent.

Another distinction involving assent which should be obvious separates the volunteer helper who has been requested to perform a service from the good samaritan who becomes a self-appointed helper. A stalled motorist should not be liable for a misguided samaritan's errors which cause harm to others.

Some problems with benefit

The requirement for showing benefit should also be an obvious one. It arises principally with bailments. One can loan his dog, gun, or chainsaw without incurring liability for what the borrower does with it—even though the lender has certainly assented, and may well retain some rights of control over the object's use. The distinction between employment and loan seems to rest primarily in the fact that the loan in these cases is for the benefit of the borrower. It would be quite different if the "borrower" were taking the dog, gun, or chainsaw with the mission of bringing back food or firewood to the owner.

Difficulty with the question of benefit has arisen chiefly with regard to automobiles. There are various cases in which the employment concept has been extended to extreme and implausible lengths in order to impose liability nominally on the automobile owner, and factually on the liability insurer. The main surge in this direction has been in connection with a car owned by a parent and loaned to a child. Several courts tortured this situation into an "employment situation", on the theory that the child's pleasure was the parent's business; this theory was known as the family purpose doctrine. The family purpose doctrine has been rendered nearly obsolete since prevalent forms of liability insurance protect anyone driving with the consent of the owner. Since the same insurance company pays regardless of whether the owner is or is not vicariously liable it is seldom worth arguing about.

Parental liability

The Code Napoleon goes beyond concepts of employment and extends a rule of presumptive vicarious liability to parents for acts of their minor children.[1] No such general principle has arisen in the common law, and in all jurisdictions with the exception of Louisiana parents are not vicariously liable for the torts of their children. The family purpose doctrine mentioned above was one effort to fashion a protective remedy. In virtually every jurisdiction there are parental liability statutes which impose liability on parents for damage caused by a child, but in most the conduct must be willful, wanton, or malicious, and usually there is a limitation on damages (most commonly under $5,000). [2]

WHITE v. CONSUMERS FINANCE SERVICE, INC.

Pennsylvania Supreme Court, 1940.
339 Pa. 417, 15 A.2d 142.

Opinion by MR. JUSTICE BARNES:

The plaintiff was employed by the Republic Oil Company at its gasoline station in Kingston, Luzerne County. On the morning of September 7, 1937, he was engaged in fastening a gasoline pump to a concrete island on the station premises when an automobile driven by one Rex Huddy came over the curb and struck plaintiff in such manner that he sustained serious injuries.

The owner of the automobile was Michael Hanchulak, who resided in the borough of Edwardsville, which adjoins the city of Wilkes-Barre. The defendant, Consumers Finance Service, Inc., with its offices in the city of Wilkes-Barre, held an encumbrance upon the car, the payments of which were in default.

On the day in question the finance company instructed one of its employees, George T. Smith, to call at the residence of Hanchulak, repossess the car and deliver it to Sam Feldman, a dealer in used cars, doing business under the name of the Goodwin Auto Company, in the borough of Kingston, adjacent to Edwardsville. . . .

While enroute to take the car, Smith called at the Feldman place of business and requested Huddy, a salesman in the employ of Feldman, to accompany him to the Hanchulak home at Edwardsville, and assist him in repossessing the car. Feldman was not on the premises at the time, and knew nothing of Smith's request for assistance. Upon arrival at Hanchulak's residence the car was found in the driveway and Smith took possession of it. The two men were unable to get the engine started, and they pushed the car into the street. Huddy, who was in the driver's seat, steered the car, while Smith in his automobile pushed it a distance of about thirty feet, until the motor finally started. Huddy then drove the car along the main street of Edwardsville in the direction of Feldman's establishment, with Smith following in his

1. Marvin, Discerning the Parents Liability for the Harm Inflicted by a Non Discerning Child, 44 La.L.Rev. 1213 (1984) (Review of parental liability in Louisiana).

2. Parental Liability for Torts of Children 9 Nova L.J. 205 (1986) (a good summary of the current status of parental liability indicating some judicial movement in cases where a parent knew or should have known of a necessity to control a child's behavior).

automobile. When Huddy reached a point about opposite to the gasoline station in near-by Kingston, he suddenly swerved the car, went over the curb and sidewalk into the station, and there struck and injured the plaintiff.

The present action in trespass was instituted by the plaintiff against the Consumers Finance Service, Inc., alleging that it was the employer of Huddy at the time of the accident. . . . A verdict for the plaintiff in the sum of $9,500 was returned, and the motions of the original defendant for a new trial and for judgment non obstante veredicto were denied by the court in banc. The appeal is brought by the original defendant. . . .

The liability of the original defendant for the acts of Huddy depends upon the question whether Smith, its employee, had express or implied authority to obtain Huddy's assistance in the repossession of the car. The general rule applicable to situations of this type is stated in many of our decisions. We said in Corbin v. George, 308 Pa. 201, 162 A. 459, speaking by the present Chief Justice (p. 204): "The relation of master and servant cannot be imposed upon a person without his consent, express or implied. The exception to this rule is that a servant may engage an assistant in case of an emergency, where he is unable to perform the work alone." [Citing cases.]

In the present case we have searched the record in vain for evidence that Smith was instructed to engage an assistant. Certainly his authority to do so cannot be implied from the nature of the service which he was directed to perform. The repossession of the car was not such a task as "to require, as a necessary incident, the employment of outside help": See Tusko v. Lynett, supra (p. 452). In this respect, the present case is clearly distinguishable from Kirk v. Showell, Fryer & Co., Inc., 276 Pa. 587, 120 A. 670, where it appeared (p. 592): ". . . that the article carried by direction of the master, was of such size and weight as to require the aid of an assistant in handling, thus creating a necessity which justified the driver in securing aid."

It does not appear that the finance company or Smith himself had reason to anticipate that any difficulties would be encountered in obtaining the car. Plaintiff contends that Smith could not have been expected to drive both his own car and the one he was sent to repossess. But his employer had no knowledge so far as the record indicates, that Smith intended to use his automobile for this purpose, or that some other means of transportation was not available. Unquestionably, it served Smith's convenience to have Huddy accompany him, "but this comes far short of a necessity calling for assistance." [Citing cases.]

We fail to see that there was any emergency confronting Smith which made it essential that he entrust the operation of the repossessed car to Huddy. The fact that the automobile failed to start, and that

Smith, alone, was unable to push it, created a difficulty in the performance of his task, but did not constitute an emergency. Smith was in
possession of the keys to the car, and the situation was not one of such
urgency that he could not have requested further instructions from his
employer. It is only where "an unforeseen contingency arises making
it impracticable to communicate with the principal and making such an
appointment reasonably necessary for the protection of the interests of
the principal entrusted to the agent," that an agent may be said to have
implied authority to employ an assistant. See Restatement, Agency,
Section 79(d); Jacamino v. Harrison Motor Freight Co., 135 Pa.Super.
356, 5 A.2d 393.

We therefore conclude that there is no evidence in the present case
to justify a finding by the jury that Huddy was acting as the agent or
servant of the defendant finance company at the time when the
accident occurred, and that the court below should have directed a
verdict in its favor. The refusal of its motion for judgment non
obstante veredicto was error, and must be reversed. . . .

[In omitted portions of the opinion, the court also held Feldman not
liable, since he had not authorized Huddy to help Smith. Huddy's
liability was not discussed, since no suit was brought against him.]

NOTE ON WHITE v. CONSUMERS FINANCE SERVICE, INC.

The opposite result was reached in a somewhat similar case decided in the
same year by the Third Circuit Court of Appeals, applying Pennsylvania law:
Waggaman v. General Finance Co., 116 F.2d 254 (C.C.A.3d 1940). The finance
company had retained McWilliams to repossess cars, and he in turn hired
Houston, who was driving at the time of the accident in suit. Jones, Circuit
Judge, analyzed the facts as follows:

"It may be fairly said that the arrangement between the appellant and
McWilliams for the delivery of repossessed cars contemplated McWilliams'
hiring drivers to deliver them. It was not intended that McWilliams
should personally drive the repossessed cars to the appellant in Philadelphia. Indeed, it was not possible for him to make all of the deliveries, a
fact known to the appellant. The record shows the delivery to Philadelphia of a large number of automobiles which McWilliams had repossessed
for the appellant and it further shows that Houston's job with McWilliams
was exclusively to drive to Philadelphia the cars reclaimed for the appellant. McWilliams' authority to hire another to assist him in performing
his work for the appellant may be reasonably inferred from the evidence.
That only McWilliams paid Houston is not determinative that Houston was
not a co-servant for the appellant. Burns, et al. v. Elliott-Lewis Electrical
Co., 118 Pa.Super. 243, 248, 179 A. 47. In White v. Consumers Finance
Service, Inc., 339 Pa. 417, 15 A.2d 142, where the defendant's employee
asked a person to assist him in repossessing a car, the defendant knew
nothing of the assistance and there was no evidence that assistance was
required nor did the circumstances imply the employee's authority to
obtain assistance. Hence, liability was not visited upon the employer for

the negligence of the unauthorized assistant of the employee. The facts in this case are to the contrary. . . ."

REFERENCES

Employees' helpers ("subservants"):

Potter v. Golden Rule Grocery Co., 169 Tenn. 240, 84 S.W.2d 364 (1935) (grocer not liable for negligence of grocer's thirteen-year-old son whom regular driver permitted to drive truck).

Curran v. Dorchester Theatre Co., 308 Mass. 469, 32 N.E.2d 690 (1941) ("stooge" did odd jobs around theater in exchange for passes; owner liable for stooge's excessive force in evicting a customer).

Kosick v. Standard Properties, Inc., 13 N.J.Misc. 219, 177 A. 428 (1935) (defendant's janitor was helped by son who in turn was helped by friend; friend's negligence in handling shovel caused injury to plaintiff; defendant not liable).

Anglo-Chinese Shipping Co. v. United States, 130 Ct.Cl. 361, 127 F.Supp. 553 (1955) (United States and other occupying powers not liable for acts of Japanese government, although controlled by them, which were done for benefit of Japanese people).

Seavey, Subagents and Subservants (1955) 68 Harv.L.Rev. 658, 669.

Restatement of Agency 2d (1958) §§ 5 ("Subagents and subservants"), 221 ("Master's Consent to Service"), 255 ("Acts of Subservants and other Subagents").

Gratuitous helpers:

Heims v. Hanke, 5 Wis.2d 465, 93 N.W.2d 455 (1958) (car owner liable for negligence of nephew who, in helping to wash car, left water to freeze on sidewalk).

Moore v. El Paso Chamber of Commerce, 220 S.W.2d 327 (Tex.Civ.App.1949) (Chamber sponsored rodeo week, in which local citizens wore frontier costumes; liable for act of a participant in lassoing a resident who had not donned costume).

Malloy v. Fong, 37 Cal.2d 356, 232 P.2d 241 (1951) (church held liable for negligent driving of a divinity student who was helping transport children during church school).

Under-age employers:

Palmer v. Miller, 380 Ill. 256, 43 N.E.2d 973 (1942), noted in 21 Chi.U.L.Rev. 195, 31 Ill.Bar.J. 355 (20-year-old not liable for negligence of friend driving car for him).

Scott v. Schisler, 107 N.J.L. 397, 153 A. 395 (1931) (minor liable).

Covault v. Nevitt, 157 Wis. 113, 146 N.W. 1115 (1914) (minor owner of building not liable for janitor's negligence).

Gregory, Infant's Responsibility for his Agent's Tort (1930) 5 Wis.L.Rev. 453.

Reluctant employers:

Employer's Liability for Employee He was Compelled to Hire (1967) 16 Clev.Mar.L. Rev. 541.

Family purpose doctrine:

King v. Cann, 184 Wash. 554, 52 P.2d 900 (1935) (parent liable when son drove car to dance, and let negligent friend drive home).

White v. Seitz, 342 Ill. 266, 174 N.E. 371 (1930) (family purpose doctrine rejected); comment, 26 Ill.L.Rev. 439.

Fridman, The Doctrine of the "Family Car": A Study in Contrasts (1976) 8 Texas Tech.L.Rev. 323 (U.S.-British-Canadian comparative study).

Bailor's liability situations:

Weatherman v. Ramsey, 207 N.C. 270, 176 S.E. 568 (1934) (owner who lent car to friends to attend baseball game not liable for friends' negligence).

Gorton v. Doty, 57 Idaho 792, 69 P.2d 136 (1937) (schoolteacher who lent car to coach to take team to basketball game held liable).

Haring v. Myrick, 368 Mich. 420, 118 N.W.2d 260 (1962) (owner who lent car to friend known to be dangerous driver held liable).

Mitchell v. Resto, 157 Conn. 258, 253 A.2d 25 (1968) (owner of car not liable where she loaned car to nephew and wife to preserve their troubled marriage).

Loan to dangerous driver:

Perdue, Negligent Entrustment of Automobile (1968) 6 Houston L.Rev. 129.

Government subdivisions:

Martinez v. Reynolds, 398 So.2d 156 (La.App.1981) (Deputy sheriff an employee of state, but by statute plaintiff's recovery limit to suit against the Sheriff).

B. COMMON CAUSES

Justice Holt's dictum on vicarious liability referred clearly to organizational arrangements in which one man commanded another. The commander was responsible. This model of social structure, which characterized the monarchy and the papacy, was doubtless pervasive in commercial society. But the proprietorship—as we would call it—was already giving way to the partnership and the joint stock company, while political parliaments and religious congregations were taking over earlier functions of king and pope.

Scarcely blinking, the common law extended the single proprietor's liability to partners and made each partner liable not only for the negligence of the joint employees, but also for that of the other partners. The rules for partnerships have been applied, with equal insouciance, to the temporary business alliances or syndicates known to lawyers as "joint ventures."

When persons join their efforts for common purposes which are not designed to produce profits, but for pleasurable, social, charitable or political ends, the general approach is against liability for membership alone. Some direct participation, authorization or control over the party committing the tort is needed.[1]

With respect to partnerships, as we have already seen, the nexus is provided by sections 9, 13 and 15 of the Uniform Partnership Act, which you should review.[2] If no partnership can be found among the participants, the inquiry becomes much more difficult. Many cases have found evidence of "joint enterprise" or "joint adventure" among co-participants in a nonbusiness undertaking. For example, the passengers who shared the rental of an airplane for a fishing trip were all held liable for damage to the airplane caused by negligence of the pilot, on the basis that they were involved in a joint enterprise.[3] Similarly,

1. Review the cases in Ch. 1, section 4.

2. See generally Note, Partners' Liability for Tort (1946) 9 Ga.Bar J. 203; Note, Partners' Tort Liability (1948) 34 Va.L.Rev. 614.

3. Shook v. Beals, 96 Cal.App.2d 963, 217 P.2d 56 (1950).

three persons involved in target practice were deemed a joint venture, liable for the injuries caused by one.[4]

The automobile cases provide authority for nearly every conceivable proposition. Some find joint enterprise among family members,[5] and others find evidence of joint control sufficient to impose liability.[6] Still others reject the joint venture approach in the absence of evidence of pecuniary purpose.[7]

An interesting footnote concerns the possibility that a minor might incur vicarious liability by virtue of joint enterprise, despite his disability to become a principal or partner. Several cases have held in favor of such liability.[8]

C. INDEPENDENT OPERATIVES

A century after the vicarious liability principle was announced in English law, a difficult problem presented itself. A householder hired a tradesman to repair his house, and the tradesman hired various workmen to bring materials and do the work. A workman was careless, and a passerby was injured and sued the householder.

When this type of situation first appeared, the court saw no sufficient reason to except the case from the general rule of vicarious liability.[1] After all, the owner of the house was its "master" and the workmen were "servants." A half century later, the judges had changed their minds, and recognized an employer's immunity in this situation; over the years many other situations were analogized to it.[2] The term "independent contractor" was taken from the construction cases and extended to many other situations where the actor was independent of the defendant, although working pursuant to his orders. Thus cab drivers, physicians, traveling salesmen, and garage keepers came to be classified as "independent contractors."

A number of difficulties arose in connection with the independent contractor concept. First, there was the problem of identifying the true

4. Kuhn v. Bader, 89 Ohio App. 203, 101 N.E.2d 322 (1951).

5. E.g., Archer v. Chicago, Milwaukee, St. Paul & Pacific Railway Co., 215 Wis.2d 509, 255 N.W. 67, 95 A.L.R. 851 (1934); Straffus v. Barclay, 147 Tex. 600, 219 S.W.2d 65 (1949).

6. Howard v. Zimmerman, 120 Kan. 77, 242 P. 131 (1926).

7. E.g., Easter v. McNabb, 97 Idaho 180, 541 P.2d 604 (1975), Edlebeck v. Hooten, 20 Wis.2d 83, 121 N.W.2d 240 (1963).

8. Howard v. Zimmerman, 120 Kan. 77, 242 P. 131 (1926); Carroll v. Harrison, 49 F.Supp. 283 (D.C.Va.1943), affirmed on other grounds 139 F.2d 427 (C.C.A.4th).

1. Bush v. Steinman, 1 Bos. & Pul. 404, 126 Eng.Rep. 978 (Common Pleas 1799).

The case involved the repair of a house, rather than the construction of a new one, but the Chief Justice's opinion rejected the whole idea of obtaining immunity by delegating a job to a "contractor."

2. The first recognition of the independent contractor defense seems to have been in cases involving the hiring of horses and a driver from a liveryman. Laugher v. Pointer, 5 B. & C. 903, 108 Eng.Rep. 204 (King's Bench 1826). The doctrine was soon extended to the case of a railroad which let a contract to build a viaduct. Reedie v. London and North Western Railway Co., 4 Exch. 244, 154 Eng.Rep. 1201. (Exchequer 1849).

criterion by which independent workmen should be distinguished from dependent ones, or (in the argot of the courts) how "independent contractors" should be distinguished from "servants." The earlier cases suggested a number of tests, involving the expertise required for the job, the adherence of the workman to a separate craft, the repeated or occasional nature of the service, the control exercised. In the course of time, all these visible, factual elements became subordinated to a construct called "right of control." This "right," however, must be distinguished from actual exercise of control.

In the complexity of arrangements to divide labor which prevail today even in simple transactions, the "right to control" is a constant source of litigation. The fact that there is substantial evidence in a case from which a jury could reasonably find an independent contractor does not prevent a finding of liability if there is also substantial evidence from which a jury could find a "right to control". As will be seen, trial judges rule "as a matter of law" at their peril. There is a strong presumption in these cases that they should go to the jury.

Aside from the general difficulty of defining and ascertaining the right of control, the independent contractor concept ran into particular difficulties when workmen were temporarily "loaned" from one employer to another, under such conditions that the workmen would normally be responsive to either or both employers. Many courts found it quite unacceptable, and violative of moral principle, to recognize that a workman might be responding to mixed voices; they struggled against great odds to discern the "true master."

Finally, many judges rebelled against the generality of the independent contractor rule, and invented a series of exceptions to it, to which they attached such names as "inherent danger," "franchised activity," "non-delegable duty," and "estoppel."

The exceptions have become so large that one sometimes wonders whether there is something wrong with the independent contractor idea. It may be worthwhile to return for a few moments to the various reasons adduced to justify vicarious liability. Do they justify any "independent contractor" exception? If so, what criteria would be indicated by the various rationales?

REFERENCES

Ferson, The Meaning of "Independent Contractor," 3 Vand.L.Rev. 1 (1949).

Jacobs, Are Independent Contractors Really Independent? (1953) 3 De Paul L.Rev. 23 (contending that the original and best test of the independent contractor is an independent calling).

History and development:

The following articles trace independent contractor theory from its common law origins to twentieth century common law, and on into twentieth century social legislation:

Asia, Employment Relation—Common Law Concept and Legislative Definition (1943) 55 Yale L.J. 76.

Stevens, The Test of the Employment Relation (1939) 38 Mich.L.Rev. 188.

Wolfe, Determination of Employer-Employee Relationships in Social Legislation (1941) 41 Col.L.Rev. 1015.

Comment, Liability to Employees of Independent Contractors Engaged in Inherently Dangerous Work: A Workable Workers' Compensation Proposal (1980) 48 Fordham L.Rev. 1165.

Study, Liability of a Principal for Negligent Injuries Inflicted by Independent Contractors, 1939 N.Y.L.Rev.Comm.Rept. 409–684 (concluding that no statutory revision of law is necessary).

England:

Chapman, Liability for the Negligence of Independent Contractors (1934) 50 L.Q.Rev. 71 (finding "general rule" no longer general).

RESTATEMENT OF AGENCY 2d, SECTIONS 2, 220
American Law Institute, 1958.

Sec. 2. Master; Servant; Independent Contractor

(1) A master is a principal who employs an agent to perform service in his affairs and who controls or has the right to control the physical conduct of the other in the performance of the service.

(2) A servant is an agent employed by a master to perform service in his affairs whose physical conduct in the performance of the service is controlled or is subject to the right to control by the master.

(3) An independent contractor is a person who contracts with another to do something for him but who is not controlled by the other nor subject to the other's right to control with respect to his physical conduct in the performance of the undertaking. He may or may not be an agent.

Sec. 220. Definition [of servant]

(1) [Similar to sec. 2(2), above]

(2) In determining whether one acting for another is a servant or an independent contractor, the following matters of fact, among others, are considered:

(a) the extent of control which, by the agreement, the master may exercise over the details of the work;

(b) whether or not the one employed is engaged in a distinct occupation or business;

(c) the kind of occupation, with reference to whether, in the locality, the work is usually done under the direction of the employer or by a specialist without supervision;

(d) the skill required in the particular occupation;

(e) whether the employer or the workman supplies the instrumentalities, tools, and the place of work for the person doing the work;

(f) the length of time for which the person is employed;

(g) the method of payment, whether by the time or by the job;

(h) whether or not the work is a part of the regular business of the employer;

(i) whether or not the parties believe they are creating the relationship of master and servant; and

(j) whether the principal is or is not in business.

MURRELL v. GOERTZ
Court of Appeals of Oklahoma, 1979.
597 P.2d 1223.

REYNOLDS, JUDGE:

Mrs. C.L. Murrell, plaintiff in the trial court, appeals the order sustaining the motion for summary judgment in favor of co-defendant Oklahoma Publishing Company (appellee), in a suit for damages resulting from an alleged assault and battery by co-defendant Bruce Goertz.

On August 27, 1976, Bruce Goertz was making monthly collections for the delivery of appellant's morning newspaper, the Daily Oklahoman, which is published by appellee. Appellant questioned Goertz concerning damage to appellant's screen door caused by the newspaper carrier throwing the newspaper into it. An argument ensued culminating in appellant slapping Goertz who in turn struck appellant. As a result thereof, appellant was allegedly injured, requiring medical treatment and subsequent hospitalization. Appellant filed suit in the District Court of Oklahoma County seeking a total of $52,500 for past and future medical expenses, pain and suffering, and exemplary damages.

Appellant's petition contends that Goertz was a servant of appellee either by agreement between the co-defendants, or by appellee creating the apparent belief in appellant that Goertz was a servant by allowing Goertz to deliver the paper, advertise that product, and to collect for accounts due. Both appellee and Goertz answered denying that Goertz was appellee's servant.

Pursuant to District Court Rule 13, appellee filed a motion for summary judgment which was sustained by the trial court. The trial court then denied appellant's motion for new trial and this appeal was perfected.

. . .

The line of demarcation between an independent contractor and a servant is not clearly drawn. An independent contractor is one who engages to perform a certain service for another according to his own methods and manner, free from control and direction of his employer in all matters connected with the performance of the service except as to the result thereof. . . . The parties agree that the decisive test for determining whether a person is an employee or an independent contractor is the right to control the physical details of the work. . . .

Appellant contends that the distribution of papers and the collection of money therefor is an integral part of appellee's business.

Appellant cites the following factors as indicative of the high degree of control appellee possesses over the physical details of the work: ultimate control over the territorial boundaries of Goertz's route; appellee set a standard policy that paper deliveries be completed by 6 a.m.; appellee set policy that all papers were to be held by rubber bands; customers who were missed by the carrier called appellee to report it; complaints concerning the service were lodged with appellee; and new subscribers called appellee to initiate newspaper service.

Appellee submits that the affidavit of Russell Westbrook and Goertz's deposition reveal that Goertz had no contact with appellee. Westbrook stated that he was an independent newspaper distributor for appellee and that he employed Bruce Goertz as an independent carrier salesman. Westbrook further stated that Goertz was responsible only to him for the delivery of the newspapers and was in no way under the supervision, dominion, and control of appellee. By the terms of Westbrook's contract, he was an independent contractor and likewise not subject to the supervision, dominion, and control of appellee as to the manner and method of performing his job. Appellee further cites the statements of Westbrook and Goertz that Goertz was collecting money for Westbrook at the time of the incident with appellant, and that appellee received money only from Westbrook.

From a review of the record we conclude that the evidence is reasonably susceptible of but one inference. Bruce Goertz was hired as an independent carrier salesman by his friend Russell Westbrook, who was himself an independent contractor. Appellee had no input into the decision to hire Goertz and had no knowledge of his employment. Goertz had no direct contract with appellee in his business operations. While appellee established certain policies and standards to which all distributors and carriers were to adhere, such policies and standards do not rise to that level of supervision, dominion, and control over Goertz's day to day activities as to make him appellee's servant.

Affirmed.

ROMANG, P.J., and BOX, J., concur.

REFERENCES

Construction workers:

Bonenberger v. Sears, Roebuck and Co., 449 S.W.2d 385 (Mo.App.1969) (worker hired to remove furnace; jury could properly find a right to control although it was not exercised, and worker was not reported as an employee to the Internal Revenue Service).

Pasko v. Commonwealth Edison Co., 14 Ill.App.3d 481, 302 N.E.2d 642 (1973) (employer who reserved some control over safety aspects of construction contract was liable for negligent failure to maintain safety).

Lee v. Junkans, 18 Wis.2d 56, 117 N.W.2d 614 (1962) (husband and wife contracted for a carpenter and his crew to "rough in" a house. A plumber's helper doing other work on the house was injured when he fell from a defective scaffold built by the carpenter's crew. The husband was held liable because he had worked along with the workmen and thus had not turned over complete control of the premises to his independent contractor. The wife was relieved of liability).

Prisoners:

What is the relation to the state of a convict utilized for labor who injures someone by his negligence? Alliance Co. v. State Hospital, 241 N.C. 329, 85 S.E.2d 386 (1955) (state not liable); Washington v. State, 277 App.Div. 1079, 100 N.Y.S.2d 620 (1950) (state liable).

Inspection and supervision:

What is the relationship to workmen of an employer who lets a contract expressly reserving right to supervise performance, prescribe safety measures, regulate minimum wages and maximum hours, forbid discrimination, and terminate without notice? Strangi v. United States, 211 F.2d 305 (5th Cir.1954) (contractor held "independent"). Compare (with same result) Dougall v. Spokane, Portland & Seattle Railway Co., 207 F.2d 843 (9th Cir.1953); Gallagher v. United States Lines Co., 206 F.2d 177 (2d Cir.1953).

Jones v. Indianapolis Power & Light Co., 158 Ind.App. 676, 304 N.E.2d 337 (1973) (power company not liable for negligence of contractor installing generator, where it reserved control solely for purposes of ascertaining fulfillment of contract).

Flight Kitchen, Inc. v. Chicago Seven-Up Bottling Co., 22 Ill.App.3d 558, 317 N.E.2d 663 (1974) (client liable for lawyer's directing sheriff to make improper levy on plaintiff's goods).

Public relations officer:

Carmin v. Port of Seattle, 10 Wn.2d 139, 116 P.2d 338 (1941) (salaried employee travelled about making speeches, etc.; employer liable).

Oil and Gas Broker:

Soderback v. Townsend, 57 Or.App. 366, 644 P.2d 640 (1982) (gas company not liable for auto accident of broker paid per diem to negotiate oil leases).

Proof of employment relationship:

Peetz v. Masek Auto Supply Co., 160 Neb. 410, 70 N.W.2d 482 (1955) (payment of Social Security Tax as evidence of employment relation imposing vicarious tort liability on employer). Noted 54 Mich.L.Rev. 436 (1956).

Detective service:

King v. Loessin, 572 S.W.2d 87 (Tex.Civ.App.1978) (merchant employed "protective service" to find out who was selling competitive merchandise below usual prices; protective service burglarized competitor's office to obtain evidence; merchant liable because illegal methods were impliedly contemplated in the employment).

ROCKWELL v. KAPLAN

Pennsylvania Supreme Court, 1961.
404 Pa. 574, 173 A.2d 54.

[Mr. Rockwell submitted to surgery to remove a small bursa from his right elbow. In the surgical preparation room, the anesthesiologist administered a sodium pentothal hypodermic to the plaintiff's left arm in such a way as to cause a cutting off of blood in the arm. The anesthesiologist did not tell the surgeon of the mistake and the surgeon did not discover it until the arm had been so damaged that it had to be amputated. The patient recovered judgments against Stone, the chief anesthesiologist, and Kaplan, the surgeon. In a separate opinion, the Supreme Court sustained the judgment against Stone on the basis of personal negligence and vicarious liability (404 Pa. 561, 173 A.2d 48). The opinion below relates to the appeal of the surgeon.]

BOK, JUSTICE. The facts need not be repeated here, since they have been fully set forth in Mr. Justice Benjamin R. Jones's opinion in Rockwell v. Stone, Pa.1961, 173 A.2d 48. Suffice it to say that plaintiff recovered a verdict against both doctors, who have separately appealed. Dr. Kaplan, the subject of this opinion, asks judgment n.o.v. or, if he may not have it, a new trial. Both requests were refused below and this appeal is from the ensuing judgment (for $70,000).

. . .

The following facts appear in the record: Dr. Kaplan said that he was "the boss of the surgical end of it and that the plaintiff was his patient; he chose the hospital and arranged the plaintiff's admission; he chose to use a minor elective surgical procedure to remove the bursa from plaintiff's right arm, which procedure could be postponed or done at the patient's convenience; he overruled his patient, who wanted local anesthesia, and ordered a general one; if he did not choose Dr. Stone, who was the chief of the hospital's anesthesiology department, he chose Dr. Stone's hospital and was satisfied with him and with his choice of sodium pentothal as the induction agent and a gas for the general anesthesia; . . .

There is no dispute that the misuse of sodium pentothal caused the condition of plaintiff's arm, which in turn caused its amputation. . . .

As for Dr. Kaplan's responsibility for Dr. Stone's negligence, Dr. Stone testified that a surgeon could use the hospital's anesthesiologist or bring in his own. Dr. Kaplan testified that he was "the boss of the surgical end of it", and that "as long as Dr. Stone had anything to do with the anesthesia I was perfectly satisfied." He chose the hospital in which Dr. Stone worked and chose a general rather than a local anesthetic. Dr. Stone testified that Dr. Kaplan had the authority to ask or tell him what sort of anesthesia he wanted, although it was not the practice at the Graduate Hospital to do so. Dr. Kaplan said that if it was best for his patient's safety he could discontinue the operation and tell the anesthesiologist to stop giving anesthetic, particularly in minor elective surgical procedure. His words were, on the latter point:

"Q. Suppose you felt that anesthesia should stop and the anesthetist felt that it should continue, and you felt that continuation would create a critical condition for your patient? A. I would stop immediately, regardless of what he had to say, if I felt strongly that this should stop, I would stop it.

"Q. And you would tell the anesthetist to stop it, wouldn't you? A. I would.

"Q. And he would stop, wouldn't he? A. I think he would have to."

The foregoing is very different from the independent contractor-like language of Dr. Kaplan's brief. We think it points clearly to the language concerning borrowed employes in Mature v. Angelo, 1953, 373 Pa. 593, 97 A.2d 59, 60: "A servant is the employe of the person who has the *right* of controlling the manner of his performance of the work, irrespective of whether he actually *exercises* that control or not."

.   .   .

Nor was there a conflict of evidence on the question of right of control. Dr. Kaplan and Dr. Stone did not disagree in their testimony as it has been condensed above, nor can there be doubt based on common sense that Dr. Stone acted on Dr. Kaplan's business: he had to or the surgeon could not operate. The undisputed evidence clearly shores up the instruction of the trial judge. "And in the eyes of the law, in this case, Dr. Stone was the agent for a step in the operative procedure, the anesthesia step. He was the agent of Dr. Kaplan."

It is clear, under Yorston v. Pennell, 1959, 397 Pa. 28, 153 A.2d 255, that doctors are subject to the law of agency and may at the same time be agent both of another physician and of a hospital, even though the employment is not joint.

This establishes the theory of respondeat superior and also answers the heart of defendant's motion for a new trial. We have carefully read the charge and see no error in it when looked at in the round. We have also examined defendant's make-weight arguments and find them without merit.

Judgment affirmed.

BENJAMIN R. JONES, J., files a dissenting opinion in which BELL, J., joins.

Although alleged, the case at bar in my opinion presents no evidence of any *direct* negligence on the part of Dr. Kaplan, and Dr. Kaplan's liability, if any, must be premised on the theory of vicarious liability. Stated otherwise, is Dr. Kaplan liable for malpractice under the doctrine of respondeat superior for an act of negligence which occurred, outside his presence and without his knowledge, during the preoperative procedure involved in the administration of an anesthesia?

Certain factual circumstances must be noted. Dr. Kaplan neither requested nor exercised any choice in the selection of any particular anesthesiologist to administer the anesthesia. Although Dr. Kaplan, as any other surgeon, was at liberty to select any anesthesiologist he so desired, he simply indicated to Dr. Stone, the Chief of the Department of Anesthesiology, that he wanted a general anesthesia administered and relied upon Dr. Stone's professional competency for selection of the type of anesthesia and the person or persons to administer it. Such service was provided by the hospital and the compensation for such service would be billed by the hospital to the patient and would be paid by the latter directly to the hospital. The personnel of the Department were employed by, paid by and under the general control and direction of the hospital which had the sole power to dismiss such personnel.

When the incident occurred, as previously stated, Dr. Kaplan was not present nor was his presence required at that time and, while the

injection and ensuing incident took place at approximately 9:45 a.m.,
Dr. Kaplan was unaware of it until approximately noon.

. . .

In the case at bar, Dr. Kaplan neither prescribed nor was he
advised of the use of sodium pentothal; he did not administer it, was
not present when it was administered and, in fact, did not know of it
until hours later.   Moreover, he exercised no direction, control or
authority over Drs. Stone and Jiminez, or Molnar, while in the induction room and he did not request any of them to administer this drug.
Dr. Kaplan was simply using the hospital facilities and its personnel, a
service for which Rockwell would be billed directly.

The sodium pentothal was administered, outside of Dr. Kaplan's
presence, in the induction room over which, to employ the language of
McConnell, he was not the "captain of the ship": over the personnel in
that room—all hospital regularly employed persons—at that time *only*
Dr. Stone was in command.

. . .

The surgery performed by Dr. Kaplan on November 11, 1955 was
successful and entirely free of any negligent conduct on his part.
There is not a scintilla of evidence of any direct negligence on Dr.
Kaplan's part sufficient to subject him to liability.   On the other hand,
neither Dr. Stone, nor Dr. Jiminez, nor Molnar were acting in an
agency capacity for Dr. Kaplan at the time of the injection of the
sodium pentothal.   Under such circumstances, in my opinion, Dr.
Kaplan could not be held liable upon any theory of respondeat superior
and the judgment as to Dr. Kaplan should be reversed and judgment
n.o.v. entered in his favor.

BELL, J., joins in this dissenting opinion.

NOTE ON ROCKWELL v. STONE

In the companion case of Rockwell v. Stone, 404 Pa. 561, 173 A.2d 48 (1961),
which was concerned with the liability of the anesthesiologist, the facts concerning the injury to Mr. Rockwell were more fully elaborated:

. . . In the induction room, Rockwell was prepared for an injection of
sodium pentothal to be followed by a general anesthesia of cyclopropane
gas, ether and oxygen.   The initial preparation was by Mr. Molnar, a
registered nurse doing graduate work in anesthesiology who was employed
and paid by the hospital.   When Rockwell was prepared for the injection of
sodium pentothal, Molnar notified his superior, Dr. Stone.   Dr. Stone, busy
at the time, directed a Dr. Jiminez, a resident physician and a hospital
employee in the Anesthesiology Department, to administer sodium
pentothal.

Dr. Jiminez had injected the needle in Rockwell's left arm and was
proceeding with the sodium pentothal injection when Rockwell instantane-
ously cried out with pain in his left forearm and hand.   Dr. Jiminez then
either removed the needle or it slipped out and he went to summon Dr.
Stone.   When Dr. Stone arrived, Rockwell, although under the effects of
the sodium pentothal, could be aroused.   Rockwell's left arm was then

blanched and he had very little pulse. After some deliberation, Drs. Stone and Jiminez, together with Molnar, proceeded to administer the general anesthesia.

Rockwell was then removed to the operating room for the surgery on his right arm. *Dr. Kaplan was not told by Dr. Stone or anyone else of what had taken place in the induction room.* The surgery on the right arm, successful in nature, was concluded within thirty to thirty-five minutes. Over two hours after the sodium pentothal injection, Dr. Kaplan learned of the incident which had taken place in the induction room.

Rockwell was taken from the operating room to the recovery room and Dr. Stone consulted with other staff physicians concerning the condition of Rockwell's left arm. Numerous measures were taken by Dr. Stone, Dr. Kaplan—after he learned of the incident—and others to counteract the effects of the sodium pentothal in Rockwell's left arm, but such were of no avail. Three days later Rockwell's left arm had to be amputated.

.   .   .

REFERENCES

"Captain of the ship" doctrine:

The "captain of the ship" doctrine imposes liability on the surgeon in charge when the employees—nurses, anesthesiologists, etc.—are technically under his "control", even though they may be independent contractors or employees of the hospital. In addition to Rockwell v. Kaplan, the following is a leading case: Thomas v. Hutchinson, 442 Pa. 118, 275 A.2d 23 (1971).

Doctrine rejected:

In a number of jurisdictions, the doctrine has been rejected as inconsistent with the facts and illogical. Leading cases include:

Sparger v. Worley Hospital, Inc., 547 S.W.2d 582 (Tex.1977); comments, 9 Texas Tech.L.Rev. 199 (1977), 9 St. Mary's L.Rev. 159 (1977).

Sesselman v. Muhlenberg Hospital, 124 N.J.Super. 285, 306 A.2d 474 (1973).

Borrowed servant rule applied:

In other cases, the "captain of the ship" doctrine has been distinguished or rejected, and traditional application of the borrowed servant doctrine has resulted in liability on the part of the party exercising detailed control.

Marvuli v. Elshire, 27 Cal.App.3d 180, 103 Cal.Rptr. 461 (1972) (surgeon not liable, since nurse was under control of anesthesiologist).

Burns v. Owens, 459 S.W.2d 303 (Mo.1970) (surgeon not liable for negligent injection by nurse, which he did not supervise).

Commentaries:

Morris, The Negligent Nurse—The Physician and the Hospital (1981) 33 Baylor L.Rev. 109.

Note, Surgeons and Anesthesiologists, Vicarious Liability 9 Ohio N.V.L. 437 (1982) (reviews Borrowed Servant and Captain of the Ship theories of Liability).

PARK NORTH GENERAL HOSPITAL v. HICKMAN

Texas Court of Appeals, 1985.
703 S.W.2d 262.

COLEMAN, ASSIGNED JUSTICE.

Lydia G. Hickman sued Nathaniel G. Tippit, M.D., for medical malpractice and fraud and joined as a defendant Park North General Hospital. She alleged that the hospital was negligent in granting Tippit hospital privileges. Judgment was rendered on a jury verdict against Tippit and the hospital, jointly and severally, for the sum of $38,250.00 for actual damages. Exemplary damages were awarded the plaintiff in the sum of $500,000.00 against Dr. Tippit and in the sum of $375,000.00 against Park North General Hospital. Only the hospital has appealed. . . .

The hospital contends that the trial court erred in overruling its motion for instructed verdict and its motion for judgment *non obstante veredicto* because the plaintiff failed to prove that there was an employer-employee, principal-agent, partnership, or joint venture relationship between the hospital and Dr. Tippit. Basically its contention is that a hospital is not liable for the granting or continuing surgical privileges to a doctor where a patient has chosen the physician and the hospital is not otherwise liable. The hospital's position is based upon the case of Jeffcoat v. Phillips, 534 S.W.2d 168 (Tex.Civ.App.—Houston [14th Dist.] 1976, writ ref'd n.r.e.).

We assume that in *Jeffcoat* the plaintiff alleged a cause of action against the hospital based upon its negligence in granting hospital privileges to Dr. Phillips. The hospital was granted an interlocutory summary judgment which was affirmed. The testimony established that the patient chose Dr. Phillips as her physician prior to his admission into the hospital. In affirming the summary judgment the court relied upon the general rule that no *respondeat superior* liability attaches where the physician is an independent contractor and not an employee or servant of the hospital.

In making this decision the court distinguished the case of Purcell v. Zimbelman, 18 Ariz.App. 75, 500 P.2d 335 (1972), on the basis that the American Osteopathic Association has established accreditation requirements which imposed an obligation on governing authorities of accredited hospitals to screen those who are granted privileges to use the hospital, and that it was a practice among these hospitals to set up committees to carry out that purpose.

The court also distinguished the case of Darling v. Charleston Community Memorial Hospital, 50 Ill.App.2d 253, 200 N.E.2d 149 (1964), affirmed 33 Ill.2d 326, 211 N.E.2d 253 (1965), cert. denied 383 U.S. 946, 86 S.Ct. 1204, 16 L.Ed.2d 209 (1966) upon the basis that the hospital's bylaws required consultation and review of staff physicians' work.

Mrs. Hickman introduced into evidence the bylaws, rules and regulations of the medical staff of Park North General Hospital which set out in detail the procedure for the appointment of physicians to the hospital staff. The rules required an investigation by the hospital Credentials Committee to examine the character, professional competence, qualifications and ethical standing of the practitioner through information contained in references given by the practitioner and from other sources available to the committee, including an appraisal from the clinical department in which privileges are sought, whether the practitioner has established and meets all the necessary qualifications for the category of staff membership and clinical privileges requested by him.

The rules also required an annual reappointment process which required a report from the Credentials Committee based upon such member's professional competence and clinical judgment in the treatment of patients, his ethics and conduct, and other matters. Evidence was also introduced to the effect that the standard adopted by Park North General Hospital in its rules was the same general standard employed by other hospitals in the community.

These facts furnish a significant distinction between the case under review and *Jeffcoat*. Since *Jeffcoat* was decided, a number of states have adopted the doctrine of corporate responsibility for the quality of medical care. That is, the doctrine that a hospital owes a duty to its patients to exercise reasonable care in the selection of its medical staff and in granting specialized privileges. . . .

We hold that Park North General Hospital had a duty to Mrs. Hickman to exercise reasonable care in the selection of its medical staff and in granting specialized privileges to them. It also has a duty to periodically monitor and review their competency. . . .

[The Court found there was no evidence the hospital was negligent in its "care and treatment" of Mrs. Hickman, and remanded to determine whether reasonable care was used in allowing staff privileges to the doctor who performed the negligent surgery.]

NOTE: LIABILITY OF HOSPITALS

In Bing v. Thunig, 2 N.Y.2d 656, 163 N.Y.S.2d 3, 143 N.E.2d 3 (1957), the Court of Appeals reversed a long line of decisions on the liability of hospitals for torts of doctors and nurses. One reason for the old rule was the doctors and nurses were considered independent contractors because of their skill and the lack of control exercised over them. The Court said that the special skill of other employees "(such as airplane pilots, locomotive engineers, chemists, to mention a few)" has never been the basis to deny the application of respondeat superior. Since this decision a large number of jurisdictions have specifically held hospitals liable under a theory of vicarious liability.

Darling v. Charleston Community Memorial Hospital, 33 Ill.2d 326, 211 N.E.2d 253 (1965), certiorari denied 383 U.S. 946, 86 S.Ct. 1204, 16 L.Ed.2d 209, was the first case to hold a hospital liable for faulty medical care based on a theory of direct negligence. Specifically, the Court noted that a jury verdict of negligence would be supported on allegations that the hospital failed to have a sufficient number of trained nurses for bedside care of patients capable of recognizing the progressive gangrenous condition of the plaintiff's right leg, and the hospital failed to require consultation with or examination by members of the hospital surgical staff to review the treatment rendered to the plaintiff.

Under each of these theories there is a recognition that the hospital or medical facility itself is responsible for the delivery of health care. Identification of the hospital as the most appropriate party to exercise quality control over doctors and nurses is an important policy factor in these cases.

REFERENCES

Cases following Darling v. Charleston Community Memorial Hospital:

Mitchell County Hospital Authority v. Joiner, 229 Ga. 140, 189 S.E.2d 412 (1972).

Purcell v. Zimbelman, 18 Ariz.App. 75, 500 P.3d 335 (1972).

Articles and comments:

Lisko, Hospital Liability Under Theories of Respondeat Superior and Corporate Negligence (1978) 47 UMKC L.Rev. 171.

Morris, The Negligent Nurse—The Physician and the Hospital (1981) 33 Baylor L.Rev. 109 (reviews alternative theories, including direct liability, respondeat superior and "captain of the ship").

Cases recognizing duty of Hospital to exercise care in selection of staff:

Johnson v. Misericordia Community Hospital, 99 Wis.2d 708, 301 N.W.2d 156 (1981).

Pedroza v. Bryant, 101 Wn.2d 226, 677 P.2d 166 (1984).

Ferguson v. Gonyaw, 64 Mich.App. 685, 236 N.W.2d 543 (1975).

Mitchell County Hospital Authority v. Joiner, 229 Ga. 140, 189 S.E.2d 412 (1972).

Purcell v. Zimbelman, 18 Ariz.App. 75, 500 P.3d 335 (1972).

Beeck v. Tuscon General Hospital, 18 Ariz.App. 165, 500 P.2d 1153 (1972).

Comment, Patient Recovery—A Poor Prognosis for Hospitals? The Expanding Scope of Hospital Liability, 10 Ohio N.U.L.Rev. 519 (1983) (good review of recent cases and current theories of Hospital Liability).

Comment, Corporate Negligence of Hospitals and the Duty to Monitor and Oversee Medical Treatment, 17 Wake Forest L.Rev. 309 (1981) (extensive discussion of origins and implications of direct liability).

ALUMINUM CO. OF AMERICA v. WARD

United States Court of Appeals, Sixth Circuit, 1956.
231 F.2d 376.
Noted: 14 Wash. & Lee Law Rev. 40 (1957), 19 Georgia Bar J. 99 (1956).

SIMONS, CHIEF JUDGE. For the death of her husband, William A. Ward, the appellee sought and obtained a judgment against the appellant based upon negligence. A first trial of the issues involved having proved abortive because of failure of the jury to agree, the case was retried resulting in the presently challenged judgment. The appellant's motion for judgment in its favor notwithstanding the verdict, having been denied, it appealed.

Ward was a truck driver for the Dixie-Ohio Express Company, (D.O.X.) a common carrier by motor vehicle. His equipment was a tractor and trailer. With it on the day of the accident he was transporting a load of aluminum from the appellant's plant at Alcoa, Tennessee, to points in Ohio and New York. While making a left turn from one street to another, in Knoxville, both tractor and trailer overturned, resulting in Ward's death. There is substantial and cumulative evidence that the accident was caused by the shifting of the load on the trailer and this the appellant appears to concede, for it suggests no negligence of Ward in respect to speed or carelessness in making the turn. The theory upon which the appellant was sought to be held was that the Aluminum Company undertook to load the trailer, as it did with the many trailers employed by it for delivery of its product, that it had negligently loaded and braced its cargo and that, as a result, the tractor and trailer overturned and killed the decedent.

The principle upon which the Aluminum Company seeks to defeat liability is that it did not load and brace the cargo; that such work was being performed solely by the carrier; that although the loading and bracing was done by the Aluminum Company's general employees they were loaned to the carrier for that purpose and, so, came within the loaned servant doctrine. . . .

The proofs show that Davis, a fellow employee of Ward, had towed the trailer from the Aluminum Company plant where it had been partially loaded to a cafe where he had stopped for coffee; that the decedent there joined him, having arrived towing an empty trailer; that they there exchanged trailers; . . .

Davis said he was not only a truck driver but for a year prior to the accident had been a supervisor for the carrier, supervising the loading of all of its trailers at the Aluminum Company's Alcoa plant, and had supervised the loading of the trailer here involved. Although the Aluminum Company paid the loading crew, furnished the wood, timbers, nails and steel bands used in bracing the cargo and performed this work with its own equipment, it was under his direction and supervision, the loaders doing only the actual mechanical work. . . .

Davis further testified that the procedure followed in the loading and bracing of the aluminum in the trailer was in accordance with the method pursued in the loading of all D.O.X. trailers at Alcoa. He always backed his trailer into the dock, told the company checker what and how he wanted it done, and the trailers were loaded according to his instructions; that on occasions, when the loading or bracing was not done as instructed, he refused to move the trailer until it was loaded and braced as he had directed; that sometimes he would not require boxes of aluminum to be braced, where in his judgment it was unnecessary; that no one but he at any time gave any directions for loading D.O.X. trailers and that on the occasions when he thought a load was not braced safely he went to the loading or bracing crew and told them what to do. Occasionally, however, he went to the Aluminum Company foreman, if this was more convenient, and told him what changes were to be made and had no trouble in getting the crew to follow his instructions. Davis' evidence, in this respect, was in part corroborated by other supervisors, by the Assistant Business Agent in Knoxville for the Teamsters' Union and some of the members of the loading crew.

On the basis of this evidence, the Aluminum Company insists a legal conclusion follows that the responsibility for the loading and bracing was upon the trucker because the employees who performed the loading and bracing became servants of the trucker, and if such employees were negligent the Aluminum Company was not responsible. This leads us to a consideration of the loaned servant doctrine as it may be spelled out from relevant decisions. In Charles v. Barrett, 233 N.Y. 127, 135 N.E. 199, 200, Chief Judge Cardozo stated the general principle in these words: "The rule now is that, as long as the employee is furthering the business of his general employer by the service rendered to another, there will be no inference of a new relation unless command has been surrendered, and no inference of its surrender from the mere fact of its division." In an illuminating opinion of Mr. Justice Christianson of the Minnesota Supreme Court in Nepstad v. Lambert, 235 Minn. 1, 50 N.W.2d 614, 620, it was pointed out that the courts have relied principally on two tests, in determining when a worker becomes a loaned servant. The first of these is the " 'whose business' test" but this test is practically valueless where the general employer's business consists of furnishing men to perform work for the special employer because by doing his job the worker is necessarily furthering and doing the business of both employers. A second test is the so-called "control" test but one danger in using this test is failing to define sufficiently the scope and meaning of the term. In a general sense, both employers frequently have powers over the employee which may be considered elements of control. He comes to the conclusion, however, that "the orders of the borrowing employer must be commands and not requests if the worker is to be found to be a loaned servant. . . . The right to discharge is one element in measuring the authoritativeness of the order, but it should not be made decisive. . . . Authority to designate only the result to be reached is not sufficient under the control test. There must be the authority to exercise detailed authoritative control over the manner in which the work is to be done."

Tennessee law is in accord. In Chamberlain v. Lee, 148 Tenn. 637, 642, 257 S.W. 415, 417, the court said: "In order to escape responsibility for the negligence of his servant on the theory that the servant has been loaned, the original master must resign full control of the servant for the time being. It is not sufficient that the servant is partially under the control of a third person." The Aluminum Company places great reliance upon the United States Supreme Court's decision in Denton v. Yazoo & M. Valley R. Co., 284 U.S. 305, 52 S.Ct. 141, 142, 76 L.Ed. 310, wherein the loaned servant rule was stated as follows: "When one person puts his servant at the disposal and under the control of another for the performance of a particular service for the latter, the servant, in respect of his acts in that service, is to be dealt with as the servant of the latter and not of the former." But in distinguishing the Denton case from Standard Oil Co. v. Anderson, 212 U.S. 215, 29 S.Ct. 252, 53 L.Ed. 480, and Driscoll v. Towle, 181 Mass. 416, 63 N.E. 922, Mr. Justice Sutherland, in the Denton case, said, 284

U.S. at page 311, 52 S.Ct. at page 143: "In each of these cases, the facts plainly demonstrated that the work was that of the general master, and that in doing it, the servant had not passed under the direction and control of the person for whom the immediate work was being done; the latter being looked to not for commands, but for information." The commands in Denton were found to reside in a Federal statute.

With these observations, we turn to the record to determine whether complete control over the loading force was placed in the trucking company, having in mind that upon a contested issue of fact we are bound by the verdict, if substantial evidence supports it. Hubert Payne was a driver for another carrier and also Assistant Business Agent of the local Teamsters' Union. He testified as to the general practices of the Aluminum Company, in respect to loading, and was asked this question: "Did you ever attempt to tell the workmen what to do or did the foreman pass the work to them?" to which his reply was: "I would tell the foreman and he normally would ask me what I thought was wrong with it and he in turn would instruct the people." To the question: "Did you ever attempt to boss or supervise workmen in their work or did their own foreman do that?" his reply was: "I did not supervise, no sir." The supervisor Davis, hereinbefore referred to, was asked this question: "But you didn't feel like you had direct control over the employees yourself?" and his answer was: "I didn't have any control over the employees." Burnett, a checker for D.O.X. testifying for the appellee, was asked whether the Aluminum Company had a head man there, said that it had both a checker and a foreman; that the checker checks the net weight and gross weight and the number of the boxes; then was asked this question: "And who else do you say the Aluminum Company has there?" his reply was: "They have, I would imagine, a superintendent." And when asked what he did the answer was: "He is the boss over the whole thing, the shipping department." Asked whether the Dixie-Ohio employees do anything at all in actually loading the aluminum in the trailer and in bracing it, he testified: "No, that's one thing you can't do it. You strike the Aluminum Company if you do their work. They should strike. They do their own work."

In view of this evidence, even though controverted, the jury was warranted in drawing the inference that the Aluminum Company had not surrendered complete control of its employees to the trucking company. It had its own foreman or superintendent on the job. This was fully recognized by the trucking company supervisors who, on occasion, transmitted their instructions to the loading crew through the foreman or superintendent. The most that can be said on the subject of control is that there was divided authority and this falls short of that power to command which is the necessary element in the determination of a surrender of complete control by the general employer to the temporary employer under the loaned servant doctrine.

. . .

Affirmed.

NOTE: OBSERVATIONS OF JUDGE CARDOZO [1]

In "A Ministry of Justice," Judge Cardozo urged the scholarly study of law improvement, and is widely believed to have struck the spark which led to formation of the law revision commissions of New York and other states. He gave a number of instances of legal problems which deserve study, including the following:

> "The law that defines or seeks to define the distinction between general and special employers is beset with distinctions so delicate that chaos is the consequence. No lawyer can say with any assurance in any given situation when one employment ends and the other begins. The wrong choice of defendants is often made, with instances, all too many, in which justice has miscarried." [2]

The next year Judge Cardozo sat on Charles v. Barrett, cited on page 135, in which an injury victim had sued an express company which loaded and unloaded vans by its own workmen, but hired its vans with drivers from a trucker. The van had injured the plaintiff while being driven, and he had recovered a verdict.

The trial judge ruled as a matter of law that the express company was liable. The appellate division reversed, dismissing the complaint, and Judge Cardozo in the opinion of the Court of Appeals affirmed the dismissal. Immediately preceding the "rule" quoted in the principal case above, he wrote:

> "We think that truck and driver were in the service of the general employer. . . . Where to go and when might be determined for the driver by the commands of the defendant. The duty of going carefully for the safety of the van, as well as for that of wayfarers, remained a duty to the master at whose hands he had received possession. Neither the contract nor its performance shows a change of control so radical as to disturb that duty or its incidence. . . . We do not say that in every case the line of division has been accurately drawn. The principle declared by the decisions remains unquestioned. At most the application is corrected."

REFERENCES

Articles:

Talbot Smith, Scope of the Business: The Borrowed Servant Problem (1940) 38 Mich. L.Rev. 1222 (advocating criterion of scope of business instead of control). For a dual employment case in which the author, having become a Supreme Court Justice, concurred in result only, see White v. Bye, 342 Mich. 654, 70 N.W.2d 780 (1955).

Power, It's Time to Bury the Borrowed Servant Doctrine (1973) 17 St. Louis Univ.L.J. 464–474 (author proposes statutory solution—to place liability on general employer).

History:

For the earliest judicial brush with this quandary, in which the judges came off no better nor worse than in the contemporary cases, see Laugher v. Pointer, 5 B. & C. 547, 108 Eng.Repr. 204 (King's Bench 1826).

1. Judge of the New York Court of Appeals, 1918–1932; Justice of the United States Supreme Court, 1932–1938. Best known to law students for the tort cases of Palsgraf v. Long Island R., Hynes v. New York Central R., and the contract case of De Cicco v. Schweizer.

2. Cardozo, A Ministry of Justice (1921) 35 Harv.L.Rev. 113, 121.

Supply of equipment with operator:

Harvey v. C.W. Matthews Contracting Co., 114 Ga.App. 866, 152 S.E.2d 809 (1966) (contracting agency hiring truck with driver not liable for driver's negligence).

Stone v. Bigley Brothers Inc., 309 N.Y. 132, 127 N.E.2d 913 (1955) (supplier of truck liable for negligence of driver while he was unloading under direction of borrower), noted 9 Vand.L.Rev. 574 (1956).

Hand signals to operator:

Scharf v. Gardner Cartage Co., 95 Ohio App. 153, 113 N.E.2d 717 (1953) (supplier not liable where operator following another's signals).

White v. Bye, 342 Mich. 654, 70 N.W.2d 780 (1955) (supplier liable although operator following another's signals).

Loans to or by government:

Maryland v. United States, 381 U.S. 41, 85 S.Ct. 1293, 14 L.Ed.2d 205 (1965), reversed United States v. Maryland, 116 U.S.App.D.C. 259, 322 F.2d 1009 (D.C.Cir.1963) (held members of state national guard and civilian "caretakers" of guard property are not employees of the Federal Government for Tort Claims Act purposes, but are employees of the states.)

Fries v. United States, 170 F.2d 726 (6th Cir.1948) (United States not liable for acts of driver furnished with auto to county for disease survey).

Carnes v. Department of Economic Security, 435 S.W.2d 758 (Ky.1968) (state paid and supplied under antipoverty program to city which directed them in clean-up work; some of them negligently set fire to loading platform; state not liable because it had relinquished entire control to city).

McFarland v. Dixie Machinery & Equipment Co., 348 Mo. 341, 153 S.W.2d 67 (1941) (defendant's tractor and driver rented to WPA project injured workman; defendant not liable on holding that at time of injury driver was "doing business" of government).

Marino v. Trawler Emil C., Inc., 350 Mass. 88, 213 N.E.2d 238 (1966), certiorari denied 384 U.S. 960, 86 S.Ct. 1587, 16 L.Ed.2d 673 (fishing ship owner liable for negligence of crew of plane hired to spot fish because of (1) inherent danger of activity and (2) detailed directions given from ship to plane on where to fly).

STRAIT v. HALE CONSTRUCTION CO.

California Court of Appeals, Fourth District, 1972.
26 Cal.App.3d 941, 103 Cal.Rptr. 487.
Comment, 5 St. Mary's L.J. 196 (1973)

KERRIGAN, ASSOCIATE JUSTICE.

Two lawsuits were filed against three defendants as a result of a collision between a tractor (earthmover) and a truck on September 6, 1966, at the intersection of Route 115 and Allbright Street in the County of Imperial. The truck driver (Oliver Strait) was seriously injured in the collision and sued to recover damages for his injuries. The truck owner (Topham & Sons, a corporation) sued for the property damage to its truck. The earthmover was owned by a farmer (William E. Young, Jr.) and was being operated by his employee (Miguel Hurtado). Young had let the tractor and the operator (Hurtado) to a road construction firm (Hale Construction Company, a copartnership). At the time of the accident, the road builder (Hale) was converting Allbright Street from a dirt road to a paved street.

The two actions against the farmer, the tractor operator and road builder (Young, Hurtado and Hale) were consolidated for trial. The jury awarded the truck driver $225,700 and the truck owner $8,603 against all defendants. This appeal ensued.

. . .

Hale Construction Company is a firm specializing in road and airport work. It entered into a contract with the county of Imperial and the federal government to do the work on Allbright Street. . . . Someone told Hale that Young owned a 50–10 tractor. To accelerate construction, Hale contacted Young about letting the rig with an operator.

. . .

Inasmuch as the machine was not then being utilized in farming operations, he agreed to rent the rig and supply Hurtado as the operator for $18.00 an hour. Young was to pay Hurtado $5.00 an hour to operate the rig from the $18.00 hourly rental.

. . .

In addition to a construction superintendent, the Allbright Street job was under the direct supervision of Raymond Hale, a general partner and officer of Hale Construction Company. Hale had a grade checker located at the place where the dirt was to be removed by the various tractor operators, as well as a dump boy at the site where the dirt was to be deposited by them. . . .

In hauling dirt from a removal point west of the intersection to the dumpsite at a point east of the intersection, Hurtado collided with the truck being driven by Strait and owned by Topham & Sons which was proceeding north on Route 115. . . .

The difficulty in determining the issue as to whether the general employer or the special employer, or both, should be liable for the tort of the loaned servant arose out of the test governing its application. In determining the vicarious liability issue, the courts have uniformly applied the *test of control*, i.e., which employer had actual control or the right of control—the power to direct the borrowed servant in the details of the work at the time the tort occurred? In adopting the control theory and in weighing the elements of control, courts were inexorably driven to the expedience of making and accepting disparate refinements, ethereal in substance and revolting in reason, in order to reach any semblance of reconciliation of the results flowing from the borrowed servant cases. (See Smith, Scope of the Business: The Borrowed Servant Problem, [1940] 38 Mich.L.Rev. 1222, 1253.)

As in other jurisdictions, California courts applied the control test with varying results. . . .

As early as 1947, the California Supreme Court defined the public policy factors underlying an employer's vicarious liability in the following terms: "The principal justification for the application of the doctrine of *respondeat superior* in any case is the fact that the employer may spread the risk through insurance and carry the cost thereof as part of his costs of doing business." (Johnston v. Long, 30 Cal.2d 54, 64, 181 P.2d 645, 651.) Twenty-three years later, the same court amplified the policy factors underlying the doctrine imposing liability without fault in Hinman v. Westinghouse Elec. Co., 2 Cal.3d 956, 959–960, 88 Cal.Rptr. 188, 190, 471 P.2d 988, in the following language: "Although earlier authorities sought to justify the *respondeat superior* doctrine on such theories as 'control' by the master of the servant, the master's 'privilege' in being permitted to employ another, the third party's innocence in comparison to the master's selection of the servant, or the master's 'deep pocket' to pay for the loss, the modern justification for vicarious liability is a rule of policy, a deliberate allocation of a risk. The losses caused by the torts of employees, which as a practical matter are sure to occur in the conduct of the employer's enterprise, are placed upon that enterprise itself, as a required cost of doing business. . . ."

In an expert critique, a legal source points out why the *control* justification for liability should be discarded in the dual employer situation just as it has been abandoned in the single employer situation. In the case of a borrowed servant, both the general employer and special employer share control; while the general employer can fire the employee, the special employer can dismiss him from the particular job; while the general employer can direct the borrowed servant in the general use of the instrumentality, the special employer directs him on the particular aspects of the job at hand; control is thus actually *split* and it is a test without meaning. (Borrowed Servants and the Theory of Enterprise Liability, [1967] 76 Yale L.J. 807; see also Smith, Scope of the Business: The Borrowed Servant Problem [1940] 38 Mich.L.Rev. 1222, 1228–1231.)

Liability in borrowed servant cases involves the exact public policy considerations found in sole employer cases. Liability should be on the persons or firms which can best insure against the risk, which can best guard against the risk, which can most accurately predict the cost of the risk and allocate the cost directly to the consumers, thus reflecting in its prices the enterprise's true cost of doing business.

Control, then, at least in the narrow sense suggested by Hale, is not dispositive of this case. The theory having greater integrity in *respondeat superior* cases is allocation of risk.

In light of the policy factors underlying *respondeat superior,* it is inconceivable that Hale should escape liability. A special employment relationship with Hurtado was conclusively established. Obviously, the resurfacing work being accomplished was within the regular scope of Hale's business. Hale was to profit from this job. Hale understood the risks inherent in construction work and was in a position to guard against, and insure against, such risks. Consequently, Hale was not at all prejudiced by the trial court's ruling allowing the question of its liability to go to the jury. To the contrary, the court could have instructed the jury, in view of the foregoing policy factors, that the road builder was vicariously liable for Hurtado's negligence as a matter of law.

. . . an employee can have more than one employer, both of whom may be simultaneously liable for a negligent act of the employee. . . .

This is just such a case. Young owned the tractor and was profiting from the renting of the rig, as well as Hurtado's employment with Hale. Young reserved the right to dismiss Hurtado. This analysis of Young's liability does not contradict the earlier discussion holding Hale liable. . . .

In conclusion, it should be parenthetically noted that Hale (special employer) and Young (general employer) have filed cross-complaints against the other based on implied indemnity. In any future trial, the joint tortfeasors will then be accorded the opportunity to show, on equitable principles, why the other should be held primarily liable for Hurtado's negligence. . . .

The judgment is affirmed.

GARDNER, P.J., and GABBERT, J., concur.

REFERENCES

Liability of two employers for single act:

Gordon v. S.M. Byers Motor Car Co., 309 Pa. 453, 164 A. 334 (1932) (supplier of truck and driver and renter both held liable).

Railroad lease:

Wilson v. Terminal Railroad Association, 333 Ill.App. 256, 77 N.E.2d 429 (1948) (where one railroad leases tracks to another, both companies liable for acts of employees on leased tracks).

Embezzlement:

Seavey, Embezzlement by Agent of Two Principals (1951) 64 Harv.L.Rev. 431 (problem of who bears loss when embezzler holds offices in both corporations involved).

Note, Agency and Escrow (1951) 26 Wash.L.Rev. 46 (problem of who bears loss when escrow holder embezzles; criticism of assumption that holder must be agent of one of parties, not of both).

Nurse:

Dickerson v. American Sugar Refining Co., 211 F.2d 200 (3d Cir.1954) (court applied Pennsylvania law and held both the company which employed the nurse, and the doctor who worked part time for the company and directed the nurse's activity when he was present could be liable for negligence of the nurse).

Supply of truck and driver:

Keitz v. National Paving & Contracting Co., 214 Md. 479, 134 A.2d 296 (1957), noted (1958) 18 Md.L.Rev. 345 (court determines that jury could find both the supplier of truck and the borrower liable for negligence of driver while on a delivery).

NOTE: INDEPENDENT CONTRACTOR—HAZARDOUS ACTIVITY AND NON–DELEGABLE DUTIES

As we have seen, the general rule of non-liability for the negligence of one engaged as an independent contractor is fraught with difficulties. These difficulties do not end even if one has a clearly identified independent contractor. If the work contracted for can be classified as "inherently dangerous" there may still be liability. This "exception" to non-liability for acts of an independent contractor is stated as follows in Two Restatement of Torts Second, (1965) Sec. 416.

> One who employs an independent contractor to do work which the employer should recognize as likely to create during its progress a peculiar risk of physical harm to others unless special precautions are taken, is subject to liability for physical harm caused to them by the failure of the contractor to exercise reasonable care to take such precautions, even though the employer has provided for such precautions in the contract or otherwise.

This exception is frequently used in cases where one employs another to perform work on his premises which endangers passersby. The argument was succinctly stated in the case of McHarge v. M.M. Newcomber & Co., 117 Tenn. 595, 100 S.W. 700 (1907), which involved injury by the fall of an awning overhanging a public street while being repaired by an independent contractor, "to argue that this was not a thing intrinsically dangerous to the public would be to assert the perfection of mankind and deny the laws of gravity."

Some jurisdictions have codified the exceptions as in Georgia, but this does not prevent courts from adding others. In Peachtree-Cain Co. v. McBee, 254 Ga. 91, 327 S.E.2d 188 (1985) the court determined the statutory list was not exclusive, and found liability of property owners for the intentional torts of personnel of a security agency which was hired by a Management Company of the property owners.

GEORGIA CODE ANN. § 51–2–5
(Michie 1982).

Liability for negligence of contractor

An employer is liable for the negligence of a contractor:

(1) When the work is wrongful in itself or, if done in the ordinary manner, would result in a nuisance;

(2) If, according to the employer's previous knowledge and experience, the work to be done is in its nature dangerous to others however carefully performed;

(3) If the wrongful act is the violation of a duty imposed by express contract upon the employer;

(4) If the wrongful act is the violation of a duty imposed by statute;

(5) If the employer retains the right to direct or control the time and manner of executing the work or interferes and assumes control so as to create the relation of master and servant or so that an injury results which is traceable to his interference; or

(6) If the employer ratifies the unauthorized wrong of the independent contractor.

REFERENCES

Contractee liable—inherent danger:

Bleeda v. Hickman-Williams & Co., 44 Mich.App. 29, 205 N.W.2d 85 (1973) (coke dealer who bought coke and employed Korno to sort coke into different sizes and ship to customers on Korno's premises was liable for dust nuisance caused by Korno's operations).

Person v. Cauldwell-Wingate Co., 176 F.2d 237 (2d Cir.1949) (army camp builder liable for negligence of electrical sub-contractor, because work was "inherently dangerous").

Lamb v. South Unit Jehovah's Witnesses, 232 Minn. 259, 45 N.W.2d 403, 33 A.L.R.2d 1 (1950) (excavation between sidewalk and street, reopened by sinking of fill dirt); see annotation, 33 A.L.R.2d 7.

Richman Brothers v. Miller, 131 Oh.St. 424, 3 N.E.2d 360 (1936) (retail store owners liable for negligence of independent painter hired by independent sign contractor to maintain sign projecting over public sidewalk).

Szymanski v. The Great Atlantic & Pacific Tea Co., 79 Ohio App. 407, 74 N.E.2d 205 (1947) (detective agency's acts "too personal" to be delegated); comment, 38 Ohio App. 116.

Contractee not liable—danger not inherent:

Williams v. Wometco Enterprises Inc., 287 So.2d 353 (Fla.App.1973) (theater company not liable for shooting by security guard hired and supervised by detective agency corporation).

Bowyer & Johnson Construction Co. v. White, 255 F.2d 482 (5th Cir.1958) (use of fire to clear way for highway construction).

Brien v. 18925 Collins Avenue Corp., 233 So.2d 847 (Fla.App.1970) (real estate corporation employed security service to guard property; security service employee injured plaintiff with firearm; real estate corporation not liable because security service was independent contractor, and activity not inherently dangerous).

Cary v. Thomas, 345 Mich. 616, 76 N.W.2d 817 (1956) (use of cyanide gas to fumigate home).

Dekle v. Southern Bell Telegraph & Telephone Co., 208 Ga. 254, 66 S.E.2d 218 (1951) (unguarded excavation in street); comment, 14 Ga.Bar J. 229.

Mercer v. Ohio Fuel Gas Co., 80 N.E.2d 635 (Ohio Ct.Com.Pl.1947) (where defendant employed contractor to replace gas mains through farm land, defendant not liable for injury to farmer's hogs); affirmed and approved 79 N.E.2d 685, 80 N.E.2d 441 (Ohio Ct. App.1947).

Non-Delegable Duty:

Westby v. Itasca County, 290 N.W.2d 437, (Minn.1980) (county held liable for negligence of state officer in blowing up a beaver dam; road maintenance held a non-delegable duty.)

Hodges v. Johnson, 52 F.Supp. 488 (D.C.Va.1943) (franchise-holding lessee liable to public).

Hall v. Gallagher, 50 Del. 148, 125 A.2d 507 (1956) (one-way lease—accident on return trip and holder of franchise not liable—result of this and similar cases criticised in 10 Vand.L.Rev. 600 (1957)).

Berry v. Golden Light Coffee Co., 160 Tex. 128, 327 S.W.2d 436 (1959) (lessee held liable under conspiracy theory as neither he nor the trucker had permit required).

Spongenberg, Agency Problems in Motor Carrier Cases, 6 Clev.-Mar.L.Rev. 130 (1957).

Utility maintenance:

Williamson v. Southwestern Bell Telephone Co., 265 S.W.2d 354 (Mo.1954) (telephone company not liable for accident caused by brush-clearing contractor while transporting equipment on highway).

NOTE: LIABILITY TO EMPLOYEES OF INDEPENDENT CONTRACTORS

Concepts of Enterprise Liability have spread in a few cases to provide compensation to employees of Independent Contractors who are injured on the job.

McDonough v. General Motors Corp., 388 Mich. 430, 201 N.W.2d 609 (1972) found a cause of action against General Motors for the death of an employee of an independent construction company while erecting a structural steel addition to an assembly plant. The Court extended the inherent danger exception to cover this situation as well as injuries to third parties.

Becker v. Interstate Properties, 569 F.2d 1203 (3d Cir.1977) cert. denied 436 U.S. 906, 98 S.Ct. 2237, 56 L.Ed.2d 404 (1978) held a general contractor could be liable for the injuries of an employee of a sub-subcontractor hired by one of his sub-contractors. The court imposed the duty when the contractor failed to require his subcontractor be financially responsible.

Touscher v. Puget Sound Power and Light Co., 96 Wn.2d 274, 635 P.2d 426 (1981). The public utility was found to have no liability to an employee of an independent contractor under either the inherent danger or non-delegable duty exception.

Katapodis v. Koppers Co. Inc., 770 F.2d 655 (7th Cir.1985) relied on a state Safety Code to find a non delegable duty on the prime contractor for injuries to an employee of a subcontractor.

CHEVRON OIL CO. v. SUTTON
Supreme Court of New Mexico, 1973.
85 N.M. 679, 515 P.2d 1283.

McMANUS, CHIEF JUSTICE.

This suit began in the District Court of Bernalillo County. Sutton, respondent, sought damages for death by wrongful act pursuant to § 22–20–1 et seq., N.M.S.A.1953, against petitioner, Chevron Oil Company (Chevron), Lee Sharp (lessee for Chevron) and Herbert R. Buss (Sharp's employee). Sutton's wife had died from injuries sustained in a car accident when a wheel of a car repaired by Buss came off the vehicle. The district court granted Chevron's motion for a summary judgment. On appeal to the Court of Appeals, the summary judgment was reversed. Sutton v. Chevron Oil Co., 85 N.M. 604, 514 P.2d 1301 (Ct.App., June 6, 1973). The matter is now before this court on certiorari to the Court of Appeals.

.   .   .

The main issue before this court is whether Chevron asserted enough control over its lessee to constitute a master-servant relationship. If such relationship is present then Chevron could be found liable under the doctrine of respondeat superior. The district court granted

Chevron a summary judgment on this issue and the Court of Appeals reversed on grounds that there were sufficient indicia of control to warrant the submission of the issue to a jury.

In the present case, there are two important contract provisions which must be considered. The first provided that Sharp was ". . . engaged in an independent business, and nothing herein contained shall be construed as granting to [Chevron] any right to control [Sharp's] business or operations, or the manner in which the same shall be conducted." This agreement, on its face, tends to show that there was no master-servant relationship present, but that Sharp was merely an independent contractor. However, the majority rule is that the manner in which the parties designate a relationship is not controlling, and if an act done by one person on behalf of another is in its essential nature one of agency, the one is the agent of the other, notwithstanding he is not so called. . . .

Furthermore, it has long been the rule that a third person who deals with an agent is not bound by any secret or private instructions given to an agent by the principal. . . .

When such agreements do not control, "whether a station operator is an employee of an oil company or an independent contractor depends on *the facts of each case,* the principal consideration being the control, or right to control, of the operation of the station." . . .

In the present case, there is a substantial dispute as to a material fact, and this should foreclose summary judgment. The fact in dispute is whether or not Chevron exercised such control over Sharp as to bring the doctrine of respondeat superior into play. Independent stations of the appellant were required to: (1) diligently promote the sale of Chevron's brand products; (2) remain open for certain hours and days and "meet the operating hours of competitors"; (3) keep the premises, restrooms and equipment in a "clean and orderly condition"; (4) present a "good appearance"; and (5) promote Chevron's image to the motoring public. In addition, Sharp also (6) sold Chevron products and dispensed gasoline and oil provided by the Chevron organization; (7) received the benefit of Chevron advertising; (8) wore uniforms containing the Chevron emblem; (9) used calling cards which billed the station as "Lee Sharp Chevron and Four Wheel Drive Equipment" (apparently with Chevron's consent); and (10) the customers of the Sharp station were permitted to charge purchases of *both* products and repairs on Chevron credit cards. No one of these factors is controlling, but all are useful in determining whether or not control was present. By using all of these factors, there is a sufficient factual question as to whether or not there was an actual master-servant relationship.

Even if there were not a material issue as to whether or not Chevron asserted enough control as to create an actual master-servant relationship, there still exists a material issue as to whether or not Chevron had clothed the lessee with apparent authority.

. . .

Here, Chevron knew of and allowed Sharp to conduct his Four Wheel Drive Fixit Shop and it would be reasonable to assume that if Chevron did not want Sharp to continue such a business, it should have forbidden such activities or at least have put the *public* on notice that Sharp did not have the authority to make repairs and that it would not be responsible for such repair activities. Instead of putting the public on notice that Sharp did not have the authority to make such repairs, Chevron advertised in the telephone directory that its stations performed auto repairs, and that its repairmen were skillful. Sutton relied on such statements, in addition to relying on signs, uniforms and credit card privileges which indicated to the public that Sharp was under the control of and was an agent of Chevron. See Gizzi v. Texaco, Inc., supra, for similar facts. Thus, because Sutton relied on such statements and indicia of authority, there is a material question of fact present as to whether or not Sharp had been clothed with apparent authority by Chevron to act as Chevron's agent.

The second contractual provision is to the effect that Chevron ". . . has no right to exercise any control over any of [Sharp's] employees, all of whom are entirely under the control and direction of [Sharp] who shall be responsible for their actions and omissions."

The general rule is that a principal is not liable for the wrongful act of an assistant who has been procured by his agent unless the latter can be said to have been clothed with authority to employ help. . . .

Such authority may, however, be implied from the nature of the work to be performed. As stated in Monetti v. Standard Oil Co., 195 So. 89 (La.App.1940):

> "We find that . . . where the work for the performance of which the contract is entered into is such as to indicate the necessity of the employment of a subagent, there is liability in the principal for the acts of the subagent. . . ."

Here, the record shows that it would be quite impracticable for Sharp to have operated the Chevron gas station by himself. In fact, various clauses in the contract show clearly that the parties contemplated that such an assistant, or possibly more, should be employed. Furthermore, Gulf Refining Co. v. Brown, 93 F.2d 870, 116 A.L.R. 449 (4th Cir.1938) states:

> "It is clear that a principal may not escape liability to third persons for the torts of a subagent, appointed by his agent with his consent, merely by entering into a contract with his agent under which the latter assumes sole responsibility for the subagent's conduct."

Therefore, if a master-servant relationship in fact existed, the liability of the subagent may be imputed to Chevron regardless of the language in the written contract to the contrary.

The cause is reversed and remanded to the District Court of Bernalillo County for action consistent with this opinion.

It is so ordered.

OMAN, MONTOYA and MARTINEZ, JJ., concur.

STEPHENSON, J., not participating.

NOTE: "HOLDING OUT"

The "holding out" or "apparent agent" argument is gaining increasing acceptance particularly in franchise cases. This is in spite of concern with the use of the term "apparent authority" in tort cases.

Drexel v. Union Prescription Centers, 582 F.2d 781 (3d Cir.1978) which involved a wrongful death action against a drugstore franchisor contains a lengthy discussion of this approach with extensive citation of recent cases. The court quoted with approval § 267 of the restatement of agency (2d 1958) as follows:

> "One who represents that another is his servant or other agent and thereby causes a third person justifiable to rely on the care or skill of such apparent agent is subject to liability to the third person for harm caused by the lack of care or skill of the one appearing to be a servant or other agent as if he were such."

The court approved the proposition that a finding of the franchisee to be an "independent contractor" in respect to his relationship with the franchisor, would not prevent the franchisee from being an "employee" in respect to this particular plaintiff in a tort action. The franchisee is treated like an "employee" in this case because of findings that the franchisor held him out to be an employee and the plaintiff relied thereon.

REFERENCES

Franchise operations:

Oil company liable:

Gizzi v. Texaco, Inc., 437 F.2d 308 (3d Cir.1971), cert. denied 404 U.S. 829, 92 S.Ct. 65, 30 L.Ed.2d 57 (1972) (oil company liable to customer injured by defective repair of brakes by station operator, because signs and uniform insignia gave apparent authority to warrant merchandise and services).

Aweida v. Kientz, 536 P.2d 1138 (Colo.App.1975) (plaintiff injured in car accident when tire recently purchased from station ruptured; company held liable under control test).

Jackson v. Standard Oil Co. of California, 8 Wn.App. 83, 505 P.2d 139 (1972) (welder killed when fuel tank exploded; court held there is only need to show control of that part of the operation of station which caused the injury to get the question of liability to the jury).

Oil company not liable:

Huffmann v. Gulf Oil Corp., 26 N.C.App. 376, 216 S.E.2d 383 (1975) (oil company not liable for injuries to child attacked by dog kept by station operator where dog was guarding separate business).

Manis v. Gulf Oil Co., 124 Ga.App. 638, 185 S.E.2d 589 (1971) (claim that diesel truck damaged when filled with regular gas; oil company not liable on theory of apparent authority merely because Gulf products marketed at gas station).

Greenberg v. Mobil Oil Corporations, 318 F.Supp. 1025 (D.Tex.1970) (service station lessee was "independent contractor"; oil company not liable for attendant's shooting customer).

Iowa National Mutual Insurance Co. v. Backens, 51 Wis.2d 26, 186 N.W.2d 196 (1971) (Goodyear Tire Co. not liable for negligence of independent tire recapper who displayed Goodyear insignia and was authorized Goodyear dealer).

Apple v. Standard Oil Division, 307 F.Supp. 107 (D.Cal.1969) (oil company whose signs dominated service station was not estopped to assert that station operator was independent lessee).

Distributors:

Peterson v. Sinclair Refining Co., 20 Wis.2d 576, 123 N.W.2d 479 (1963) (the Court found the oil company had an implied duty of safe delivery).

Reaching opposite result: Still v. Union Circulation Co., 101 F.2d 11 (C.C.A.2d 1939) (driver for crew of magazine salesmen; thorough but subtle opinion by L. Hand, J.).

Gulf Refining v. Brown, 93 F.2d 870 (C.C.A.4th 1938) (oil company liable for negligence of distributor in mixing gasoline in kerosene tank).

Department store cases:

Augusta Friedman's Shop v. Yeates, 216 Ala. 434, 113 So. 299 (1927) (department store liable for scorching of plaintiff's hair by beauty salon lessee).

Manning v. Leavitt Co., 90 N.H. 167, 5 A.2d 667, 122 A.L.R. 248 (1939) (similar to Augusta case, above).

Santise v. Martins, Inc., 258 App.Div. 663, 17 N.Y.S.2d 741 (1940) (department store liable for injury caused by a faulty shoe sold by shoe department lessee).

Hotels:

Billops v. Magness Construction Co., 391 A.2d 196 (Del.1978) (court refuses to dismiss action against Hilton Hotels and Hilton International for tort of banquet manager of franchised motel).

Sapp v. City of Tallahassee, 348 So.2d 363 (Fla.App.1977) (motel franchisor sued as principal of negligent motel; remanded to determine whether franchisor is liable by reason of control or estoppel).

Wood v. Holiday Inns, Inc., 508 F.2d 167 (5th Cir.1975) (franchisor held liable for action of employee of franchisee on "holding out" theory).

Miscellaneous:

Singleton v. International Dairy Queen, Inc., 332 A.2d 160 (Del.Super.1975) (cause of action exists against an ice-cream franchisor for injury to a child who fell through a store door based on the "concept of apparent agent.")

Eckerle v. Twenty Grand Corp., 8 Mich.App. 1, 153 N.W.2d 369 (1967) (night club liable for negligence of employee of next-door parking lot overhung by sign of night club).

Christian v. Elden, 107 N.H. 229, 221 A.2d 784 (1966) (owner of stable liable for negligence of riding master who operated school under name of stable owner).

Note, You Can Trust Your Car to the Man Who Wears the Star—Or Can You? The Use of Apparent Authority to Establish A Principal's Tort Liability. (1971–72) 33 U.Pitt. L.Rev. 257–270 (the author is critical of the extension of liability of oil companies based on apparent authority).

Monica, Franchisor Liability to Third Parties, 49 Missouri L.Rev. 309 (1984).

THE TORTS OF AN INDEPENDENT CONTRACTOR
Clarence Morris [1] (1935).
29 Illinois Law Review [2] 339, 341–345.

At first glance, the policies which underlie *respondeat superior* seem inapplicable when the employer of an independent contractor, rather than the employer of a servant, is considered. Independent contractors, as a class, are not judgment proof. If the contractor is at fault, without the concurrence of fault on the part of the contractee, he deserves admonition and should suffer the sting of tort liability by being made to compensate for the injuries which result from his wrongful conduct. He is not able to avoid the discharge of his liabilities which the servant ordinarily escapes through being judgment proof. Further, should the contractor happen to be a man without means, the contractee is not in a particularly good position to punish him. Indirect punishment by the contractees, such as servants receive at the hands of their masters, usually would not result from holding contractees responsible for the torts of their contractors. Independent contractors are usually employed for an occasional, rather than for a continuous service, and they are rarely dependent on any particular contractee for future employment. A contractee cannot refuse a contractor advancement, dock his wages, or lay him off, and the refusal of any one contractee to recommend a contractor to others may do him little harm. If the tort is committed by the servant of an independent contractor, then the reasons supporting the rule of *respondeat superior* indicate that the contractor should be held, rather than the contractee. It is in the prosecution of the contractor's business that a tort is committed, and the loss should be treated as a cost of his business. The contractor has the selection and control of his servants to the exclusion of the contractee, and only the contractor can select servants carefully and punish those who commit torts for their misdeeds.

Still, all independent contractors are not financially responsible, and none of these ends which are effected by holding the contractor can be accomplished when he is unable to discharge the liability imposed on him. Obviously, then, it is important that independent contractors be financially responsible; or, to put it inversely, it is important that those who have insufficient means to discharge tort obligations which may arise during the prosecution of an enterprise be prevented from undertaking such an enterprise as independent contractors. This proposition competes with the democratic value placed on opportunity for all men to make a living as they see fit, but the competition is not necessarily fatal to it. If a man cannot get sufficient money or credit to set up a retail store, he is not deserving of a subsidy merely because he happens

1. Clarence Morris is a Professor of Law at the University of Pennsylvania, and author of the book "How Lawyers Think," as well as of numerous law review articles.

2. Name since changed to Northwestern University Law Review.

to prefer that business to other ways of making a living. Similarly, if a man cannot meet the recognized obligations of an independent contractor, it is perhaps better that he be kept out of that business, instead of being allowed to conduct it at the expense of those unfortunates who are injured by his torts. But without attempting to argue the matter with any finality at this time, let us assume for the purposes of discussion that, by and large, the value of excluding people with insufficient means from the field outweighs the value of freedom of opportunity which would be promoted by the absence of such restrictions. This blanket assumption will need some modification later on.

How is it possible to separate the sheep from the goats, the responsible from the irresponsible candidates? . . . If contractees were held to be guarantors of the financial responsibility of their contractors to those who are injured by the contractor's torts committed in the prosecution of the enterprise, very few irresponsible persons could find this sort of employment. For contractees would protect themselves by employing persons whom they knew to be responsible or by demanding indemnity bonds which are not available to those without funds. This is not entirely Utopian. It is probably a fairly accurate picture of what happens now when a contractee who knows the law employs an independent contractor to prosecute an enterprise which falls within one of the exceptions to the rule of insulation from liability. . . .

These considerations have led the writer to conclude that, while it is usually desirable that a contractor be ultimately liable for his torts, in general, the contractee should be responsible to third persons. It is believed that the apparently expanding exceptions to the traditional rule of insulation indicate that the law is headed in that direction. But the term "independent contractor" is a loose one. It includes seamstresses and railroad builders, messenger boys and owners of hydroelectric plants; and it would be surprising if the problems of responsibility for torts committed in disparate enterprises could be well solved by one simple rule. It would seem that insulation of the contractee, rather than responsibility, needs special explanation. . . .

REFERENCES

Analysis:

Harper, The Basis of the Immunity of an Employer of an Independent Contractor (1935) 10 Ind.L.J. 494 (finding rule corresponds to a "crude notion of a fair distribution of loss").

Steffen, Independent Contractor and the Good Life (1935) 2 U.Chi.L.Rev. 501 (finding basis of rules in implicit tenets of economic philosophy).

Note, Borrowed Servants and the Theory of Enterprise Liability (1967) 76 Yale L.J. 807 (applying reasoning of Professor Calabresi).

Communication and Study Relating to Liability of a Principal for Negligent Injuries Inflicted by Independent Contractors, 1939 N.Y.L.Rev.Rep. 409–684 (exhaustive review of New York law on independent contractors, with conclusion that the law is so uncertain that it is difficult to tell what if anything needs to be changed).

NOTE: THE RELATIONSHIP OF PRODUCTS LIABILITY TO VICARIOUS LIABILITY

The recent expansion of concepts of products liability has provided an alternate or additional basis for liability in some cases.

In Harris v. Aluminum Company of America, 550 F.Supp. 1024 (W.D.Va. 1982) the plaintiff lost an eye when a twist-off aluminum cap blew from a Coca-Cola bottle. She sued among others the local Coca-Cola bottling company (the franchisee) and the Coca-Cola Company (the franchisor). The Coca-Cola Company argued they only sold syrup to the franchisee, and it was the franchisee which made all decisions on the type of bottle and cap. The court held that the implied warranties of merchantability applied to the franchisor, and it would be a fact question if the packaging was unreasonably dangerous for ordinary use, and if that condition existed when the bottling requirements were under the franchisor's control. The court quoted with approval from Kosters v. Seven-Up Co., 595 F.2d 347, 353 (6th Cir.1979) which held the franchisor liable when a bottle slipped out of a defective paper carton which had been manufactured by a third party and sold to the franchisee bottling company. The Seven-Up Corporation claimed its only "control" of the carton was to insure that its trade-mark was properly displayed. The court of appeals stated that the obligation of the franchisor:

> "[A]rises from several factors in combination:
>
> (1) The risks created by approving for distribution an unsafe product likely to cause injury,
>
> (2) The franchisor's ability and opportunity to eliminate the unsafe character of the product and prevent the loss,
>
> (3) The consumer's lack of knowledge of the danger, and
>
> (4) The consumer's reliance on the trade name which gives the intended impression that the franchisor is responsible and stands behind the product. The liability is based on the franchisor's control and the public's assumption induced by the franchisor's conduct, that it does in fact control and vouch for the product."

SECTION 3. THE SCOPE OF ENTERPRISE

INTRODUCTORY NOTE

The outer boundaries of the vicarious liability principle ran into additional trouble with regard to the acts of disobedient and erring employees. In the classic decision which first delineated the problem sharply, a gentleman's servant had apparently struck the plaintiff while driving his master's cart a mile or so away from any place where he had a right to be.[1] (This would probably be the equivalent of a ten-mile joyride in an automobile.) Should vicarious liability extend so far?

Possibly this problem could have been solved under the control test by asking whether the master still had a right to control his servant when so far away. But the control test was hardly formulated at this

---

1. Joel v. Morison, 6 Car. & P. 501, 172 Eng.Rep. 1338 (Nisi Prius, Exch.1934).

time, and independent contractors were more likely to be distinguished by their "independent calling." In any event, the judge took a new tack, and distinguished between a mere "detour," which would not interrupt vicarious liability, and "a frolic of his own," for which the master should not be made to pay. He told the jury, "If the servants, being on their master's business, took a detour to call upon a friend, the master will be responsible. . . . [I]f you think the young man who was driving took the cart surreptitiously, and was not at the time employed on his master's business, the defendant will not be liable." The paired terms, "frolic and detour," have attained immortality as opposite poles in the law of "scope of employment."

In some ways this problem is just like so many other problems of degree—what is negligence?—when is a contractor independent? In some ways it is more baffling. Although we are not quite sure how much care is required, we are fairly sure of our objective, which is to impel people to keep up to the average in regarding the safety of others. We are not quite sure how much control destroys independence, but we have some plausible theories about what we are trying to achieve, which is to induce employers to enforce safety standards when they can.

In the area of the scope of employment, the big difficulty is that we are not sure what purpose we are trying to serve by the test we apply. This was the enigma which inspired the immortal essay of Dean Young B. Smith on the functions of vicarious liability, and a further inquiry by a bright young Yale professor, later to become a Supreme Court Justice—William O. Douglas.

RESTATEMENT OF AGENCY 2d
American Law Institute, 1958.

§ 228. General Statement

(1) Conduct of a servant is within the scope of employment if, but only if:

(a) it is of the kind he is employed to perform;

(b) it occurs substantially within the authorized time and space limits;

(c) it is actuated, at least in part, by a purpose to serve the master, and

(d) if force is intentionally used by the servant against another, the use of force is not unexpectable by the master.

(2) Conduct of a servant is not within the scope of employment if it is different in kind from that authorized, far beyond the authorized time or space limits, or too little actuated by a purpose to serve the master.

§ 229. Kind of Conduct Within Scope of Employment

(1) To be within the scope of the employment, conduct must be of the same general nature as that authorized, or incidental to the conduct authorized.

(2) In determining whether or not the conduct, although not authorized, is nevertheless so similar to or incidental to the conduct authorized as to be within the scope of employment, the following matters of fact are to be considered:

(a) whether or not the act is one commonly done by such servants;

(b) the time, place and purpose of the act;

(c) the previous relations between the master and the servant;

(d) the extent to which the business of the master is apportioned between different servants;

(e) whether the act is outside the enterprise of the master or, if within the enterprise, has not been entrusted to any servant;

(f) whether or not the master has reason to expect that such an act will be done;

(g) the similarity in quality of the act done to the act authorized;

(h) whether or not the instrumentality by which the harm is done has been furnished by the master to the servant;

(i) the extent of departure from the normal method of accomplishing an authorized result; and

(j) whether or not the act is seriously criminal.

RIVIELLO v. WALDRON
New York Court of Appeals, 1979.
47 N.Y.2d 297, 418 N.Y.S.2d 300, 391 N.E.2d 1278.

FUCHSBERG, JUDGE.

Plaintiff Donald Riviello, a patron of the Pot Belly Pub, a Bronx bar and grill operated by the defendant Raybele Tavern, Inc., lost the use of an eye because of what was found to be negligence on the part of Joseph Waldron, a Raybele employee. The jury having decided for the plaintiff, in due course the trial court entered a judgment in his favor for $200,000 plus costs and interest from the date of the verdict. . . .

As was customary, on the Friday evening on which Riviello sustained his injuries, only two employees manned the Pot Belly. One was the bartender. The other was Waldron, who, in this modest-sized tavern, wore several hats, primarily that of short-order cook but also the ones that went with waiting on tables and spelling the bartender. Though his services had been engaged by Raybele's corporate president in the main to improve business by introducing the sale of food, his testimony showed that the fact that, as a local resident, he was known to most of the customers in this neighborhood bar figured in his hiring as well. There was also proof that, in the time he had been there, when not preparing or serving food or relieving the bartender, he would follow the practice of mingling with the patrons.

Nor was Riviello a stranger when he entered the premises that night. Living nearby, he had frequented the establishment regularly for some years. The two men knew one another and, after a while, Riviello gravitated to the end of the bar near the kitchen, where, during an interval when he had no food orders to fill, Waldron and another patron and mutual friend, one Bannon, were chatting. Riviello joined in the discussion, which turned to street crime in the neighborhood. In the course of the conversation, Waldron exhibited a knife, variously described as a pocketknife or, according to Bannon, a boy scout knife, containing a small blade and screwdriver attachment, which he said he carried for protection. At this point Waldron broke away to go to the kitchen to fill a food order for another patron. Several minutes later, while Waldron was returning from his chore to rejoin Bannon and Riviello, the latter suddenly turned and, as he did so, his eye unexpectedly came in contact with the blade of the knife which Waldron still had in his hand. On defendant's case, Waldron largely confirmed these facts, but added that he was "flipping" the knife, presumably as one might flip a coin, as he was coming from the direction of the kitchen and inadvertently struck the plaintiff. No one else so testified.

Applying the pertinent legal precepts to this factual framework, we first note what is hornbook law: the doctrine of *respondeat superior* renders a master vicariously liable for a tort committed by his servant while acting within the scope of his employment. . . . The definition of "scope of employment", however, has not been an unchanging one.

Originally defined narrowly on the theory that the employer could exercise close control over his employees during the period of their service, as in other tort law contexts . . . social policy has wrought a measure of relaxation of the traditional confines of the doctrine (see Restatement, Agency 2d, § 219, Comment *[a]*). Among motivating considerations are the escalation of employee-produced injury, concern that the average innocent victim, when relegated to the pursuit of his claim against the employee, most often will face a defendant too impecunious to meet the claim, and that modern economic devices, such as cost accounting and insurance coverage, permit most employers to spread the impact of such costs (see Prosser, Torts [4th ed], § 69; Seavey, Agency, § 83).

So no longer is an employer necessarily excused merely because his employees, acting in furtherance of his interests, exhibit human failings and perform negligently or otherwise than in an authorized manner. Instead, the test has come to be " 'whether the act was done while the servant was doing his master's work, no matter how irregularly, or with what disregard of instructions' " . . .

Surely, the fact that Waldron, at the precise instant of the occurrence, was not plying his skills as a cook, waiter or bartender did not take him beyond the range of things commonly done by such an employee. The intermittent demands of his work meant that there would be intervals in which his function was only to stand by awaiting a customer's order. Indeed, except perhaps in a world of complete automation, as portrayed for instance in Charlie Chaplin's classic film "Modern Times", the busiest of employees may be expected to take pauses and, when they do, engage in casual conversation, even punctuated, as here, by the exhibition to others of objects they wear or carry on their persons.

.   .   .

Indeed, where the element of general foreseeability exists, even intentional tort situations have been found to fall within the scope of employment (see, e.g., Sims v. Bergamo, 3 N.Y.2d 531, 534–535, 169 N.Y.S.2d 449, 450–451, 147 N.E.2d 1, 2–3 [assault of unruly patron by bartender to protect employer's property and to maintain order on premises]; De Wald v. Seidenberg, 297 N.Y. 335, 337–338, 79 N.E.2d 430, 431–432, supra [assault of tenant by building superintendent during attempted enforcement of occupancy rules]).

Given all this, it was permissible to find as a fact that Raybele could have anticipated that in the course of Waldron's varied activities in the pursuit of his job, he might, through carelessness, do some injury. The specifics of the act, though it was not essential that they be envisaged, could be, as here, the product of an inattentive handling of the pocketknife he had described to Riviello and Bannon, or a similar mishandling of a paring knife he could have had in his hand as he left the kitchen, or perhaps a steak knife with which he was on his way to set a table. Or, perchance, instead of a knife, with equal nonmalevolence it could in similar fashion have been a pen, a comb, a nail file, a pencil, a scissors, a letter opener, a screwdriver or some other everyday object that he was displaying. In any of these cases, an instant of inattention could render each an instrument of injury.

Further, since, as a result of our decision, this case will return to the Appellate Division for consideration of the facts, it is not amiss to add the following observations: Waldron's own testimony that he had "flipped" the knife (though not intending any injury) was no part of plaintiff's case. If it had been, it is not to be assumed that this kind of motion, any more than would the twirling of a chain containing sharp-pointed keys or the tossing of a coin, or some other gesture, whether used as an aid to communication or an outlet for nervous energy, would be beyond the broad ambit of the employer's general expectation. For one employing men and women takes them subject to the kind of conduct normal to such beings.

JONES, JUDGE (concurring).

I concur in result in this case but cannot accept what appears to me to be the overbreadth of the majority opinion, addressing as it does matters which are not necessary for the resolution of this appeal.

COOKE, C.J., and GABRIELLI and WACHTLER, JJ., concur with FUCHS-BERG, J.; JONES, J., concurs in result in a separate memorandum; JASEN, J., dissents and votes to affirm for the reasons stated in the concurring memorandum by Mr. Justice Vincent A. LuPiano at the Appellate Division (63 A.D.2d 593, 404 N.Y.S.2d 859). . . .

LUPIANO, J., dissenting

As the record fails to provide a reasonable predicate for the conclusion that the negligent act was within the scope of Waldron's employment, it must be viewed as having occurred outside that employment as a matter of law. Waldron's unexpected knife flipping was not actuated by a purpose to serve Raybele. Assuming Waldron was available to prepare food for bar patrons at the time the accident occurred, he was not engaged in preparing or serving food when he flipped his own knife accidentally in plaintiff's eye. Indeed, Waldron was satisfying a personal desire to converse with friends. There is no explanation of his knife play which in any manner connects it with furthering the duties entrusted to him by his employer. Not only was this act dissimilar to any act he was authorized to perform, it was an act not commonly done by food preparers or foreseeable by his employer. . . .

NOTE: FROLIC AND DETOUR

In Riley v. Standard Oil Co., 231 N.Y. 301, 132 N.E. 97 (1921) a driver stopped at his sister's house which was four blocks off his assigned route, dropped off some material and was headed back towards his assigned destination when an accident occurred. The trial court ruled that the accident was not in the scope of the employer's business. Reversing, the Court of Appeals held that the employee was not "going on a frolic of his own" but at most there had been a "temporary abandonment" and a "re-entry".

One year later the same New York court decided Fiocco v. Carver, 234 N.Y. 219, 137 N.E. 309 (1922), in which a driver after making his assigned delivery visited his mother's home and went to a neighborhood carnival. An injury took place as the driver was starting the truck, presumably to return to the garage. The court held the lower court was in error in allowing this case to go to the jury, because there was not enough evidence there had been a "re-entry". In making the determination the court stated as follows:

> "Location in time and space are circumstances that may guide the judgment, but will not be suffered to control it, divorced from other circumstances that may characterize the intent of the transaction. The dominate purpose must be proved to be the performance of the master's business. Until then there can be no resumption of a relation which has been broken and suspended."

WRIGHT v. SOUTHERN BELL TELEPHONE COMPANY
United States Court of Appeals, 5th Circuit (1979).
605 F.2d 156.

Before SIMPSON, TJOFLAT and HILL, CIRCUIT JUDGES.

JAMES C. HILL, CIRCUIT JUDGE:

This appeal involves the tragic death of a homeowner who was killed when the temporary blocks supporting his mobile home gave way and the home collapsed upon him. Specifically, we are asked to decide whether the telephone company may be held liable for this death, assuming that the homeowner was under the house at the request of the telephone company's employee. After careful consideration of this question, we reach the conclusion that there is no legal basis for recovery against the phone company. Accordingly, we reverse the judgment entered in favor of the plaintiff. . . .

In preparing to move into the mobile home, Mr. Wright contacted Southern Bell and asked that three telephones be installed. On the morning of May 19, 1975, Southern Bell's employee, Vivian Cox, arrived at the Wright's home and was instructed by Mr. Wright where each phone was to be placed.

The Wrights requested that one of the phones be installed in an inner wall in the kitchen. In order to install this phone, Cox drilled a hole through the kitchen floor, inserted a wire into the hole, and went underneath the mobile home to pull it through. She was unable to pull the wire through, so she returned to the kitchen and repeated the procedure a second time, but was again unsuccessful in pulling the wire through.

At this point, Mr. Wright crawled underneath the home to assist Cox by attempting to pull the wire through the hole while she pushed it through from the kitchen. While Mr. Wright was under the mobile home, the concrete block which was underneath the tongue and jack at the front of the home broke or cracked, and the mobile home fell upon him causing his death. . . .

The thrust of Ms. Wright's case is relatively simple. She alleges that Cox, by virtue of her vast experience in installing telephones in mobile homes, was fully aware of the dangers inherent in working under mobile homes that were only temporarily secured. Thus, because of Cox' superior knowledge in such matters, she owed a duty to the decedent to warn him of the dangers of going underneath his mobile home. By asking Mr. Wright to go under the home without warning him of the danger of doing so, Ms. Wright contends, Cox was negligent and her negligence proximately caused Mr. Wright's death.

Southern Bell advances several persuasive arguments to support its contention that it cannot, as a matter of law, be liable for the death of Mr. Wright. We need look no further than the first one to conclude that Southern Bell cannot be liable in this case.

As we have already illustrated by our synopsis of the plaintiff's case, she attempts to impose liability on Southern Bell under the doctrine of *respondeat superior*. A review of the complaint, pre-trial order and evidence presented at trial shows that the only acts or omissions complained of are those of Cox. Under Georgia law, before a master may be held liable for the negligent acts of its servants, the servant must have been acting both within the scope of his employment and in the prosecution of the master's business. . . .

Southern Bell is willing to concede that Cox' request for assistance may have been in the prosecution of Southern Bell's business, but it vigorously denies that Cox acted within the scope of her employment in enlisting the aid of Mr. Wright. . . .

> No employee has power to employ another to assist him in his work without express authority; and if he does so, he is acting without the scope of his authority.

In *Burke* [Huddle House Inc. v. Burke, 133 Ga.App. 643, 647, 211 S.E.2d 903, 907 (1974)] the employee had enlisted the help of a customer, a young boy, who was injured as he was removing ice from the storage area of an ice machine. The Georgia Court of Appeals held, *inter alia,* that the employer could not be liable for the acts of its servants in enlisting the help of the customer since they acted outside the scope of their employment in doing so. Southern Bell argues that a similar conclusion is especially appropriate in this case because Southern Bell's own regulations specifically forbid employees from requesting the assistance of customers in the performance of company work. In view of this controlling authority, we must agree with Southern Bell that it cannot be responsible for the negligent acts of Cox because she acted outside the scope of her employment in asking the decedent to assist her. . . . Under the plaintiff's theory of the case, Southern Bell can only be liable for any negligence of Cox if she were acting within the scope of her employment and, as we have already seen, Cox was acting outside the scope of her employment in enlisting the aid of Mr. Wright.

The result we reach is not at odds with the established rule in Georgia that the fact that a servant disobeys the instructions of his master does not insulate the master from liability for the servant's negligence. See Porter v. Jack's Cookie Co., 106 Ga.App. 497, 127 S.E. 2d 313 (1962); Evans v. Caldwell, 52 Ga.App. 475, 184 S.E. 440 (1936), aff'd, 184 Ga. 203, 190 S.E. 582 (1937). As the court in *Porter* specifically recognized, a violation of instructions may constitute a departure from the scope of employment. 106 Ga.App. at 501, 127 S.E.2d 313.

Because we conclude that Southern Bell cannot be liable for the negligence of Cox, we reverse the district court's decision to overrule Southern Bell's motion for judgment notwithstanding the verdict. Accordingly, judgment should be entered for Southern Bell.

Reversed.

REFERENCES

Departure with permission:

If the employee is permitted by the employer to leave the route dictated by the task, he will still be outside the employment if serving his private purposes exclusively. The border line seems no easier to draw than when the departure is forbidden:

Rhude v. Ed. G. Koehl, Inc., 85 Ohio App. 223, 88 N.E.2d 269 (1948) (using employer's car to go to and from home, and possibly solicit order; employer liable); comment, 11 Ohio St.L.J. 283.

Senn v. Lackner, 91 Ohio App. 83, 100 N.E.2d 419, 432 (1951) (using employer's car to come to work, employer not liable).

Smoking:

Herr v. Simplex Paper Box Corp., 330 Pa. 129, 198 A. 309 (1938) (defendant not liable for accident caused by employee's smoking while taking gasoline delivery; 2 dissents); comment, 18 Or.L.Rev. 261.

Kelly v. Louisiana Oil Refining Co., 167 Tenn. 101, 66 S.W.2d 997 (1933) (employee tossed match which ignited cotton lint on plaintiff's clothing; employer not liable).

Maloney Tank Manufacturing Co. v. Mid-Continent Petroleum Corp., 49 F.2d 146 (10th Cir.1931) (defendant contracted to repair oil tanks; because of "inherent danger," liable for employee's carelessness with match).

George v. Bekins Van & Storage Co., 33 Cal.2d 834, 205 P.2d 1037 (1949) (storage company liable for negligence of employees smoking in warehouse).

Note, Imputation of Employee's Negligent Smoking to Employer (1950) 4 Ark.L.Rev. 217.

Restatement of Agency 2d, § 235, Illus. 5 and 6.

The leading English case on the employer's non-liability for accidents caused by employees' smoking is Williams v. Jones, 3 H. & C. 602, 159 Eng.Rep. 668 (1865). The court reasoned that the lighting of a pipe was not within the scope of employment because not done for the employer's benefit. Two justices dissented.

The employer was, however, held liable for a smoking accident, and Williams v. Jones overruled, in Century Insurance Co. v. North Ireland &c. Board [1942] 1 All Eng. Rep. 491 (House of Lords). Lord Wright observed, "I think that what plausibility the contrary argument might seem to possess results from treating the act of lighting the cigarette in abstraction from the circumstances as a separate act. This was the line taken by the majority judgment in Williams v. Jones, from which Mellor and Blackburn, JJ., as I think rightly dissented."

Washroom:

J.C. Penney v. McLaughlin, 137 Fla. 594, 188 So. 785 (1939) (employer liable for negligence of clerk opening restroom door so quickly that it knocked down plaintiff).

Restatement of Agency 2d (1958) § 229, Illus. 10: P furnishes a lavatory in which employees may wash, if they wish, before or after working hours, P retaining no control over it except in regard to keeping it clean. An employee turns on the water to wash his hands after hours and fails to turn it off. The act is not within the scope of employment.

Use of Employee's Car:

Boynton v. McKales, 139 Cal.App.2d 777, 294 P.2d 733 (1953) (employer held for negligence of employee driving home in his own car after a company party—this within the "special errand rule" as employee was expected to attend).

Brinkley v. Farmers Elevator Mutual Ins. Co., 485 F.2d 1283 (10th Cir.1973) (client held not liable for negligence of attorney who drove home in intoxicated condition four hours after close of trial).

Employee Ability to Expand Scope:

Kinnard v. Rock City Const. Co., 39 Tenn.App. 547, 286 S.W.2d 352 (1956) (injury caused when worker moved car at the direction of his foreman—employer liable).

Oganaso v. Mellow, 356 Mo. 228, 201 S.W.2d 365 (1947) (injury caused when worker moved his car at direction of and for benefit of employer—no liability on employer).

Scottsdale Jaycees v. Superior Court, 17 Ariz.App. 571, 499 P.2d 185 (1972) (Jaycee corporation held not liable when one Jaycee drove others to state board meeting, and negligently injured them).

Drunken Employee:

Otis Engineering Corp. v. Clark, 668 S.W.2d 307 (Tex.1983) (employer liable for negligence for sending an intoxicated employee home in his own car.)

Pinkham v. Apple Computer, Inc., 699 S.W.2d 387, (Tex.App.1985) (no liability on employer for accident by drunken employee after a company party absent evidence of affirmative action by supervisory personnel to control the employee.)

Davis v. Sam Goody, Inc., 195 N.J.Super. 423, 480 A.2d 212 (1984) (commercial hosts as well as social hosts can be held liable for the foreseeable consequences to third parties that result from a guest (employee's) drunken driving.)

Government Employees:

Daugherty v. United States, 427 F.Supp. 222 (W.D.Pa.1977) (employee of Federal Home Loan Bank Board driving own car home from a bank inspection—United States not liable for accident.)

Kemerer v. United States, 330 F.Supp. 731 (W.D.Pa.1971) (employee of Rural Electrification Administration driving own car home from a business conference and had an official letter to mail—United States liable for accident.)

Erwin v. United States, 445 F.2d 1035 (10th Cir.1971) (United States not liable for negligence of "Vista Volunteer" driving in car owned by agency to catch an airplane for a vacation.)

Theory and function of scope of employment rules:

Laski, The Basis of Vicarious Liability (1916) 26 Yale L.J. 105, 115–126.

Smith (Young B.), Frolic and Detour (1923) 23 Col.L.Rev. 444 (a classic analysis).

Douglas, Vicarious Liability and Administration of Risk (1929) 38 Yale L.J. 584, 585–594.

Neuner, Respondeat Superior in the Light of Comparative Law (1941) 4 La.L.Rev. 1, 33.

Small, The Effect of Workmen's Compensation Trends on Agency-Tort Concepts of Scope of Employment (1953) 12 NACCA L.J. 21.

Calabresi, Some Thoughts on Risk Distribution and the Law of Torts (1961) 70 Yale L.Rev. 499.

C.R. Morris, Jr., Enterprise Liability and the Actuarial Process—The Insignificance of Foresight (1961) 70 Yale L.Rev. 554.

NELSON v. AMERICAN–WEST AFRICAN LINE, INC.

United States Circuit Court of Appeals, Second Circuit, 1936.
86 F.2d 730.

L. HAND, CIRCUIT JUDGE. This is an appeal from a judgment dismissing the complaint at the close of the plaintiff's evidence in an action to recover for personal injuries under section 33 of the Merchant Marine Act of 1920, U.S.Code, title 46, section 688 (46 U.S.C.A. sec. 688). The plaintiff was an able seaman upon the defendant's steamer,

"West Irmo," on a voyage from New York to West Africa; and while the ship was lying in a port on the Congo River at between eleven-thirty and twelve o'clock at night, the ship's boatswain entered the crew's quarters and struck him a blow across the face with a wooden bench while he lay in his bunk. The theory of the action was that the boatswain was acting within the scope of his authority, and that the statute created a cause of action against the owner under the doctrine of Jamison v. Encarnacion, 281 U.S. 635, 50 S.Ct. 440, 74 L.Ed. 1082, and Alpha S.S. Corp'n v. Cain, 281 U.S. 642, 50 S.Ct. 443, 74 L.Ed. 1086. In the light of those decisions no issue remains except whether the boatswain was so acting, as to which the evidence is as follows. The "West Irmo" had but one boatswain; he had been off duty ashore, where he got roaring drunk, and came aboard at night with much noise, disorder and violence. He first chased the carpenter into the lavatory, and tried to break through the door to get at him; he then went back into the mess room, where he furiously raged about for a while, until the notion seized him to go into the crew's quarters, where the plaintiff was trying to sleep. It was still a half hour before midnight when the plaintiff was to go on watch, but the boatswain apparently had a mad idea that the plaintiff should get up and go on deck at once, for as he struck him, he cried out to him, "Get up, you big son of a bitch, and turn to." Having roused him by the first blow, he engaged in a fight with him in which the plaintiff was further injured. The boatswain kept no watches, but worked as occasion required; he had authority to call out all hands when he thought best, and did so, for example, on leaving port, or in stress of weather. Like other boatswains, he was foreman, so to say, of the crew. The judge thought that at the time of the assault he was not acting for the ship and dismissed the complaint. The plaintiff appeals. . . .

A principal is not chargeable with willful acts, intended by the agent only to further his own interest, not done for the principal at all. . . . But motives may be mixed; men may vent their spleen upon others and yet mean to further their master's business; that meaning, that intention is the test. . . . In the case at bar the boatswain may indeed have had no other purpose than to do violence to anyone who fell in his way; unless there was some evidence that he supposed himself engaged upon the ship's business, the ship was not liable. In support of the conclusion that he did not so suppose, the ship argues that there was no occasion for him to intervene at all; that the plaintiff had nothing to do till he went on watch which was half an hour off; and that there was every reason to suppose that he would do his duty when his turn came. In truth it was at best an act of wanton tyranny to get him out of his bunk at that time, to say nothing of the violence used in effecting it. But the boatswain was blind drunk, and through his clouded mind all sorts of vague ideas may have been passing; the fact that he had made himself incompetent to further the ship's business was immaterial, the owner had selected him to command, whatever his defects and his addictions. If he really meant to rouse the plaintiff and send him upon duty, if he really meant to act as boatswain and for the ship, however imbecile his conduct it was his master's. We are disposed to think that when he told him not only to get up, but to "turn to," that order was some evidence that he meant to act for the ship, and not alone to satisfy his vindictive passions. Normally when an officer, drunk or sober, tells a man to go to his duty, it is not for the mere show of authority, but at least in part because he supposes that some work should be done. The best that an owner can ask in such a case is that if the jury believes that the order, though in form in the ship's behalf was given only in vainglory, he shall not be charged. The result does not depend upon the scope of the boatswain's authority in the ordinary sense; we have not to say whether an act, for example forbidden by the master, should nevertheless be imputed to him. There is here no doubt that if the boatswain intended to act for the ship at all, his command was within his powers; he had been authorized to order any seaman to work at any time; the order was within not only his apparent authority—whatever that phrase may mean—but within his express authority. The inquiry into the tangled mazes of a drunken boatswain's mind may be beyond the powers of a jury, but it is the fact upon which the case turns, and there was enough to justify them in finding that he supposed that he was acting as boatswain and not wholly as a petty tyrant. It does not indeed follow that the subsequent affray was in the same class as the original blow, but that is a matter to be dealt with when the judge charges the jury.

Judgment reversed.

IRA S. BUSHEY & SONS, INC. v. UNITED STATES
United States Court of Appeals, Second Circuit, 1968.
398 F.2d 167.

FRIENDLY, CIRCUIT JUDGE. While the United States Coast Guard vessel Tamaroa was being overhauled in a floating drydock located in Brooklyn's Gowanus Canal, a seaman returning from shore leave late at night, in the condition for which seamen are famed, turned some wheels on the drydock wall. He thus opened valves that controlled the flooding of the tanks on one side of the drydock. Soon the ship listed, slid off the blocks and fell against the wall. Parts of the drydock sank, and the ship partially did—fortunately without loss of life or personal injury. The drydock owner sought and was granted compensation by the District Court for the Eastern District of New York in an amount to be determined, 276 F.Supp. 518; the United States appeals.

. . .

The Government attacks imposition of liability on the ground that Lane's acts were not within the scope of his employment. It relies heavily on § 228(1) of the Restatement of Agency 2d which says that "conduct of a servant is within the scope of employment if, but only if: . . . (c) it is actuated, at least in part by a purpose to serve the master." Courts have gone to considerable lengths to find such a purpose, as witness a well-known opinion in which Judge Learned Hand concluded that a drunken boatswain who routed the plaintiff out of his bunk with a blow, saying "Get up, you big son of a bitch, and turn to," and then continued to fight, might have thought he was acting in the interest of the ship. . . .

It would be going too far to find such a purpose here; while Lane's return to the Tamaroa was to serve his employer, no one has suggested how he could have thought turning the wheels to be, even if—which is by no means clear—he was unaware of the consequences.

In light of the highly artificial way in which the motive test has been applied, the district judge believed himself obliged to test the doctrine's continuing vitality by referring to the larger purposes *respondeat superior* is supposed to serve. He concluded that the old formulation failed this test. We do not find his analysis so compelling, however, as to constitute a sufficient basis in itself for discarding the old doctrine. It is not at all clear, as the court below suggested, that expansion of liability in the manner here suggested will lead to a more efficient allocation of resources. As the most astute exponent of this theory has emphasized, a more efficient allocation can only be expected if there is some reason to believe that imposing a particular cost on the enterprise will lead it to consider whether steps should be taken to prevent a recurrence of the accident. Calabresi, The Decision for Accidents: An Approach to Non-fault Allocation of Costs, 78 Harv.L. Rev. 713, 725–34 (1965). And the suggestion that imposition of liability here will lead to more intensive screening of employees rests on highly questionable premises, see Comment, Assessment of Punitive Damages Against an Entrepreneur for the Malicious Torts of His Employees, 70 Yale L.J. 1296, 1301–04 (1961). The unsatisfactory quality of the allocation of resource rationale is especially striking on the facts of this case. It could well be that application of the traditional rule might induce drydock owners, prodded by their insurance companies, to install locks on their valves to avoid similar incidents in the future, while placing the burden on shipowners is much less likely to lead to accident prevention.[7] It is true, of course, that in many cases the plaintiff will not be in a position to insure, and so expansion of liability will, at the very least, serve *respondeat superior*'s loss spreading function. See Smith, Frolic and Detour, 23 Colum.L.Rev. 444, 456 (1923). But the fact that the defendant is better able to afford damages is not alone sufficient to justify legal responsibility, see Blum & Kalven, Public Law Perspectives on a Private Law Problem (1965), and this overarching principle must be taken into account in deciding whether to expand the reach of *respondeat superior*.

A policy analysis thus is not sufficient to justify this proposed expansion of vicarious liability. This is not surprising since *respondeat superior*, even within its traditional limits, rests not so much on policy

---

7. Although it is theoretically possible that shipowners would demand that drydock owners take appropriate action, see Coase, The Problem of Social Cost, 3 J.L. & Economics 1 (1960), this would seem unlikely to occur in real life.

grounds consistent with the governing principles of tort law as in a deeply rooted sentiment that a business enterprise cannot justly disclaim responsibility for accidents which may fairly be said to be characteristic of its activities. It is in this light that the inadequacy of the motive test becomes apparent. Whatever may have been the case in the past, a doctrine that would create such drastically different consequences for the actions of the drunken boatswain in *Nelson* and those of the drunken seaman here reflects a wholly unrealistic attitude toward the risks characteristically attendant upon the operation of a ship.

. . .

Put another way, Lane's conduct was not so "unforeseeable" as to make it unfair to charge the Government with responsibility. We agree with a leading treatise that "what is reasonably foreseeable in this context [of *respondeat superior*] . . . is quite a different thing from the foreseeably unreasonable risk of harm that spells negligence . . .. The foresight that should impel the prudent man to take precautions is not the same measure as that by which he should perceive the harm likely to flow from his long-run activity in spite of all reasonable precautions on his own part. The proper test here bears far more resemblance to that which limits liability for workmen's compensation than to the test for negligence. . . ." 2 Harper & James, The Law of Torts 1377–78 (1956).

. . . Consequently, we can no longer accept our past decisions that have refused to move beyond the *Nelson* rule, Brailas v. Shepard S.S. Co., 152 F.2d 849 (2d Cir.1945), cert. denied, 327 U.S. 807, 66 S.Ct. 970, 90 L.Ed. 1032 (1946); Kable v. United States, 169 F.2d 90, 92 (2 Cir. 1948) since they do not accord with modern understanding as to when it is fair for an enterprise to disclaim the actions of its employees.

One can readily think of cases that fall on the other side of the line. If Lane had set fire to the bar where he had been imbibing or had caused an accident on the street while returning to the drydock, the Government would not be liable; the activities of the "enterprise" do not reach into areas where the servant does not create risks different from those attendant on the activities of the community in general.

. . .

Affirmed.

REFERENCES

General discussion:

Brill, Liability of an Employer for the Wilful Torts of his Servant within the Scope of Employment (1968) 45 Chi.-Kent L.Rev. 1.

Rose, Liability for an Employee's Assaults (1977) 40 Modern L.Rev. 420 (more restrictive view of liability in commonwealth cases).

Comment, Respondeat Superior and the Intentional Tort: A Short Discourse on How to Make Assault and Battery a Part of the Job (1976) 45 U.Cinc.L.Rev. 235.

Note, Agency: Liability of the Master to Third Persons For Intentional Torts of the Servant (1976) 29 Okl.L.Rev. 946 (discusses Oklahoma cases).

Note, The Assessment of Punitive Damages Against an Entrepreneur for the Malicious Torts of His Employee (1961) 70 Yale L.J. 1296.

Seamen and seaworthiness:

Boudoin v. Lykes Brothers Steamship Co., 348 U.S. 336, 75 S.Ct. 382, 99 L.Ed. 354 (1955) (employer liable to seaman assaulted by another of known unruliness, because keeping of such sailor aboard violates "warranty of seaworthiness").

Scope of partnership:

Phillips v. Cook, 239 Md. 215, 210 A.2d 743 (1965) (partnership liable for negligence of partner driving partnership car home to dinner, since partner was "on call" and did business at all hours); comment, 26 Md.L.Rev. 161.

Kelsey-Seybold Clinic v. Maclay, 466 S.W.2d 716 (Tex.1971) (medical partnership liable for acts of partner in seducing client).

Attempted murder:

Miller v. Keating, 349 So.2d 265 (La.1977) (corporate president attempted to murder plaintiff in order to collect life insurance proceeds for the corporation. Held, action with within scope of employment). Discussed and criticized (1978) 52 Tulane L.Rev. 443.

Defamation:

Jones v. Sears, Roebuck & Co., 459 F.2d 584 (6th Cir.1972) (employer liable for employee's accusations of shoplifting, although procedure manual said only higher supervisors should address suspects).

Gerald v. Ameron Automotive Centers, 145 Ga.App. 200, 243 S.E.2d 565 (1978) (corporation not liable for store supervisor's accusing customer of theft, without actual authorization).

Assaults:

Rodgers v. Kemper Construction Co., 50 Cal.App.3d 608, 124 Cal.Rptr. 143 (1975) (employer liable for assault by construction workers while drunk on weekend).

Serman v. Unigard Mutual Insurance Co., 504 F.2d 33 (10th Cir.1974) (apartment manager outside of scope of his employment in shooting prowler).

Jones v. City of Hialeah, 368 So.2d 398 (Fla.App.1979) (paid police informant who tried unsuccessfully to produce an illegal drug sale was acting outside scope of his employment when he got into argument with drug dealer and shot him).

Williams v. Community Drive-In Theater, Inc., 214 Kan. 359, 520 P.2d 1296 (1974) (theatre company was liable for act of business office assistant who threatened troublesome customer with shot gun and accidentally shot him).

Employer's liability for hiring violent employees:

Kendall v. Gore Properties, 98 U.S.App.D.C. 378, 236 F.2d 673 (1956) (landlord liable for failure to investigate before hiring a maintenance man who strangled a tenant), noted 45 Geo.L.J. 310 (1956).

Comment, The Responsibility of Employers for the Actions of Their Employees: The Negligent Hiring Theory of Liability (1977) 53 Chi.Kent L.Rev. 717.

Pontica's v. K.M.S. Investments, 331 N.W.2d 907 (Minn.1983) (Landlord liable for negligent hiring of manager who raped a tenant.)

Insurance coverage:

An insurance policy against liability for "accidents" will not, of course, protect the insured against his liability for intentionally assaulting some one. Will it protect the insured against liability for the intentional torts of his employees?

Woodhead, Insurance Against the Consequences of Wilful Acts (1948) Ins.L.J. 867 (modern view: policy covers; older cases divided).

Dart Industries, Inc. v. Liberty Mutual Insurance Co., 484 F.2d 1295 (9th Cir.1973) (although California statute made liability insurer nonliable for wilful wrongs, it did not exclude insurance against vicarious liability for wilful wrongs within scope of employment, including libel by president of company that was insured).

Security law violations:

Fitzpatrick and Carman, Respondeat Superior and the Federal Securities Laws: A Round Peg in a Square Hole, 12 Hofstra L.Rev. 1 (1983) (discusses the split in the federal circuits on the use of vicarious liability as an additional basis for holding employers liable for violations of the security acts by employees.)

Disciplinary sanctions:

United States v. Lane, 34 Court Martial Reports 744 (1964) (seaman Lane, who opened the valves, was sentenced to 9 months confinement and suspension of pay, and reduced to seaman recruit).

Union activity:

United Mine Workers of America v. Patton 211 F.2d 742 (4th Cir.1954) (Held national organization for acts of field representatives following common law rules).

Carbon Fuel Co. v. United Mine Workers, 444 U.S. 212, 100 S.Ct. 410, 62 L.Ed.2d 394 (1979) (international union not liable for wildcat strikes of locals, absent proof that strikes were "in accordance with the fundamental agreement of association"; held error to charge jury that international is liable unless it did all in its power to stop wildcat strikes).

Navios Corp. v. National Maritime Union, 359 F.2d 853 (3d Cir.1966) certiorari denied 385 U.S. 900, 87 S.Ct. 205, 17 L.Ed.2d 132 (foreign shipping line can enforce union's vicarious liability under Taft-Hartley Act, which is designed to protect only U.S. employers).

National Labor Relations Bd. v. P.R. Mallory & Co., 237 F.2d 437 (7th Cir.1956) (Union not responsible for acts of stewards who were elected by employees, and not appointed).

NOTE: RATIFICATION OF TORT

HOLMES, J., in DEMPSEY v. CHAMBERS, 154 Mass. 330, 28 N.E. 279 (1891):

"If we were contriving a new code today, we might hesitate to say that a man could make himself a party to a bare tort, in any case, merely by assenting to it after it had been committed. But we are not at liberty to refuse to carry out to its consequences any principle which we believe to have been part of the common law, simply because the grounds of policy on which it might be justified seem to us to be hard to find, and probably to have belonged to a different state of society.

"It is hard to explain why a master is liable to the extent that he is for the negligent acts of one who at the time really is his servant, acting within the general scope of his employment. Probably master and servant are 'fained to be all one person' by a fiction which is an echo of the *patria potestas* and of the English frankpledge. . . . Possibly the doctrine of ratification is another aspect of the same tradition. . . .

"Doubts have been expressed, which we need not consider, whether this doctrine applied to a case of a bare personal tort. . . . If a man assaulted another in the street out of his own head, it would seem rather strong to say that, if he merely called himself my servant, and I afterwards assented, without more, our mere words would make me a party to the assault, although in such cases the canon law excommunicated the principal if the assault was upon a clerk. . . .

"But the language used by judges and textwriters, and such decisions as we have been able to find, is broad enough to cover a case like the present. . . ."

[The "present case" was one in which a member of the household of the defendant, who had no authority to work about the defendant's business, filled a customer's order for coal, and in delivering it broke the customer's window; the defendant, with full knowledge of the circumstances, sent the customer a bill for the coal.]

REFERENCES ON RATIFICATION OF TORT

Assault:

Novick v. Gouldsberry, 173 F.2d 496 (9th Cir.1949) (employer ratified assault by oral statement of approval of employee's acts.)

Jameson v. Gavett, 22 Cal.App.2d 646, 71 P.2d 937 (1937) (employer ratifies assault by failure to express disapproval to employee, and by retaining him).

McChristian v. Popkin, 75 Cal.App.2d 249, 171 P.2d 85 (1946) (retention of employee after assault constitutes some evidence of approval and ratification).

Caldwell v. Farley, 134 Cal.App.2d 84, 285 P.2d 294 (1955) (union local ratified shop steward's assault on member by secretary's threat to bust in some more heads).

State ex rel. K.C.P.S. Co. v. Shain, 345 Mo. 543, 134 S.W.2d 58 (1939) (employer supplied counsel to defend employee against criminal prosecution; held this was some evidence of ratification of assault); comment, 6 Mo.L.Rev. 99.

Shandor v. Lischer, 349 Mich. 556, 84 N.W.2d 810 (1957) (employer held when assault by bartender took place in her presence) Comment, 4 Wayne L.Rev. 172.

Defamation:

Rosenberg v. J.C. Penney Co., 30 Cal.App. 609, 86 P.2d 696 (1939) (slander ratified by retaining employee, and pleading truth of statement in defense of suit).

Edwards v. Kentucky Utilities Co., 289 Ky. 375, 158 S.W.2d 935, 139 A.L.R. 1063 (1942) (slander not ratified by retention of employee, and pleading truth of statement in defense of suit).

Annotation, 139 A.L.R. 1066.

Abuse of process:

Addair v. Huffman, 156 W.Va. 592, 195 S.E.2d 739 (1973) (hospital through accounting error thought paid bill was still owing and had it sent to collection agent; collection agent attached supposed debtor's wages; held, collection agent and hospital liable for compensatory and punitive damages).

Azar v. General Motors Acceptance Corp., 134 Ga.App. 176, 213 S.E.2d 500 (1975) (finance company which retained car repossessed by independent contractor was liable by ratification for contractor's unlawful acts in repossession).

Negligence:

Ernshaw v. Roberge, 86 N.H. 451, 170 A. 7 (1934) (property owner ratifies negligence of manager by approving manager's conduct in repairing house, in course of which negligence occurred).

Jones v. Mutual Creamery Co., 81 Utah 223, 17 P.2d 256, 85 A.L.R. 908 (1932) (volunteer gathered country eggs for defendant, injuring plaintiff on the way; defendant kept and paid for the eggs; held, defendant did not ratify negligence, distinguishing but also disapproving Dempsey v. Chambers).

Annotation, 85 A.L.R. 915.

FROLIC AND DETOUR

Young B. Smith, 1923.
23 Columbia Law Review 444, 716.

. . . . As already stated, the employer should be made responsible for injuries caused others by his employees not merely because the employer is better able to pay, but because he is in a better position than the employee to effectuate the spreading and distribution of the loss. Consequently it would seem that in every enterprise in which two or more persons are participants, responsibility for resulting injuries to others should be cast upon him who is best able to effectuate the spreading and distribution of the loss (p. 460).

Granted, however, that it is both desirable and expedient to make the entrepreneur responsible for injuries to third persons, as well as to his employees, incidental to the undertaking, it does not follow that he should be made responsible for any and every tortious act which his servant may commit. To make the entrepreneur responsible for acts of his employees in no way connected with the enterprise would be undesirable because it would result in including in the cost of production an item which economically does not belong there. Moreover, there is at present no available machinery for insuring against such losses. . . . (p. 461).

This problem is not one easy of solution. In view of the suggested justification for *respondeat superior*, it may be argued that it is a matter of common knowledge that servants employed to drive automobiles frequently do make short excursions on errands of their own which they would not have made but for the fact that they had been sent on an errand for the master. Such conduct on the part of servants must, therefore, be regarded as a probable result of employing servants to drive automobiles: just as probable as that they will drive at a reckless speed. Accordingly the undertaking of an enterprise involving the employment of chauffeurs must necessarily expose third parties to a risk of injury from such excursions as well as expressly authorized acts and should therefore, be borne by the enterprise which caused the risk. Had the courts taken this view of the problem, many of the subtle distinctions between "frolics" and "detours" would not exist. In deciding whether the master is responsible in a particular case, the court should consider first, whether the conduct of the master's business was a contributing cause of the servant's act in starting the car. If not, the master is not liable. If so, the court should next inquire whether, in view of what the servant was actually employed to do, it was probable that he would do what he did, instead of inquiring into the servant's immediate motive in doing the act, or considering whether the particular act, when separated from its setting, was an act done in furtherance of the particular work the servant was employed to do. It seems to the writer that such an approach to the problem of the master's responsibility would more nearly accomplish the objects which have heretofore been pointed out as the only justification for making the master liable in any case, than the approach which many courts have taken. Furthermore, this approach will harmonize most of the deviation cases. . . . (p. 724)

The limits of the zone of risk will, of course, vary with the particular case. A chauffeur who is told to drive ten miles is more apt to deviate a mile or two from the direct route than a chauffeur who is told to drive ten blocks. But in every case, there is a zone within which there may fairly be said to exist a risk of injury to others in view of what the servant was employed to do. In a particular case the servant, at the moment of the accident, may so clearly have been within or without the limits of such a zone that a court may rule that the master is liable or not liable. On the other hand, the circumstances may be such that men may reasonably differ as to whether the servant was within or without the zone of risk. In such a case, the question should be submitted to the jury to decide. But whether the question be decided by the court or the jury, injuries occurring within the zone should be borne by the enterprise which caused the risk where it appears that the affairs of the enterprise were a contributing cause of the chauffeur's act in driving the car (p. 728).

ENTERPRISE LIABILITY AND THE ACTUARIAL PROCESS—THE INSIGNIFICANCE OF FORESIGHT
C. Robert Morris, Jr., 1961.
70 Yale Law Journal 554.

. . . If the enterprise is uninsured and has no cash reserve, a judgment may ruin the business or may leave a family with only its exempt assets. The same result, of course, is possible if a judgment exceeds the maximum of the insurance policy or the reserve. Can the entrepreneur theory justify the harsh results in such cases? The answer given is that the entrepreneur should have adequately funded or insured. The entrepreneur must make provision for the costs of his enterprise or suffer financial failure. The law makes the risk of enterprise liability a cost of the enterprise. The entrepreneur who does not make provision for this cost should fail, just as one who does not provide for his labor cost or for interest on his borrowed capital will be put out of business. As Professor Ehrenzweig puts it, the law should not concern itself with the uninsured entrepreneur, but should decree liability in areas where "the defendant could reasonably be expected to carry such insurance. Not insurance, itself, obligates, but 'Assurabilite Oblige.'" (p. 556).

It is from this point that the zone-of-risk analysis proceeds. If the law requires an entrepreneur to insure the risks of his enterprise at his peril, then the law must take care to limit liability to those risks against which the entrepreneur can reasonably be expected to insure.

In general, then, the actuarial process produces a generalized measure of risk. The actuary deduces this figure from data concerning a large number of recent events, which he projects into the future. The risk allocated to a unit of exposure or to the usual enterprise is merely a fraction of that general risk. Furthermore, the actuary does not analyze all of the risk-causing factors. . . . A very fine analysis is not attempted (p. 574).

Dean Smith hypothesized a business near Wall Street in Manhattan with customers in the Times Square area and a truck for making deliveries to them. Though the entrepreneur orders his truck driver to stay on Broadway and to avoid personal errands, he can foresee that the truck will occasionally return south by way of Seventh Avenue for reasons personal to the driver. He can even foresee that the driver may deviate as far north as Columbus Circle. He cannot foresee a trip to the Bronx or to Staten Island, so the zone-of-risk does not include upper Manhattan, the Bronx, or Staten Island. The entrepreneur, then, should not be liable for accidents in those places.

But, again, the entrepreneur's *personal* estimate of his zone of risk is irrelevant. The rate territory for commercial vehicles in lower Manhattan includes all of Manhattan, plus the Bronx and Brooklyn. In other words, the Wall Street entrepreneur pays his share of the total risk incurred by trucks garaged in those three boroughs. . . . Assume that each entrepreneur within the rating territory has formulated an idea of his enterprise's zone of risk. Occasionally a truck will stray beyond its zone and have an accident. Will this happen so infrequently that liability in such cases will not affect insurance rates? If so, the zone-of-risk concept is irrelevant. If, on the other hand, it happens frequently enough to affect insurance rates this extra-zone risk is insurable (p. 576–77).

There is also a logical fallacy in the zone-of-risk approach. This theory would have the law decide which losses should be charged to the entrepreneur by discovering what losses he has provided for. But the entrepreneur provides for the losses the law dictates he must bear. The theory, then, is tautological (p. 581).

The entrepreneur theory also attempts to gain credence by invoking the concept of commutative justice. Though the entrepreneur himself is relatively blameless, his enterprise entails a certain amount of risk, and it is proper to place the burden of this risk upon him in the first instance, because he can pass it on to his customers. . . . [But] it is probable that customers will not suffer the entire burden of enterprise liability. Prices, after all, are determined by the interaction of supply and demand. If demand remains stable, an industry cannot raise its prices without also decreasing its sales (p. 584).

SOME THOUGHTS ON RISK DISTRIBUTION AND THE LAW OF TORTS

Guido Calabresi, 1961.
70 Yale Law Journal 499.

We are now in a better position to understand what may be meant when it is said that masters "should" be liable for the torts of their servants, but should "only" be liable for them if they occur in the scope of the servants' employment. Similarly, we can now understand the "arising out of or in the course of employment" limitation on workmen's compensation. . . . [I]t is not difficult to see that whatever the other elements of risk distribution will show, allocation of resources gives quite substantial support to doctrines which rely essentially on an enterprise concept of scope of liability.

Proper resource allocation militates strongly against allocating to an enterprise costs not closely associated with it—"liability should be limited to injuries arising out of or in the course of employment." But it also militates for allocating to an enterprise all costs that are within the scope of that enterprise. "The enterprise is held liable for the injuries even though no fault on its part can be shown." Not charging an enterprise with a cost which arises from it leads to an understatement of the true cost of producing its goods; the result is that people purchase more of those goods than they would want if their true cost were reflected in price. On the other hand, placing a cost not related to the scope of an enterprise on that enterprise results in an overstatement of the cost of those goods, and leads to their underproduction. Either way the postulate that people are by and large best off if they can choose what they want, on the basis of what it costs our economy to produce it, would be violated.

In view of the weaknesses of resource allocations as an exact theory there is no need for a rigid relation between losses and the scope of the enterprise. No serious misallocations are likely to occur if the scope of an enterprise is broadly or narrowly interpreted. Reasons for a broad or narrow interpretation will perhaps appear from the other justifications of risk distribution. But insofar as the allocation-of-resources justification is concerned, there are too many minor misallocations for it to matter at all if we don't have a perfect system for deciding what enterprise is exactly responsible for what injury. Nonetheless, it is equally clear that if people are to have any intelligent role in deciding what is to be produced, liability must finally be limited by some criterion connected with the scope of the activity charged (p. 514–15).

RESPONDEAT SUPERIOR IN THE LIGHT OF COMPARATIVE LAW
Robert Neuner, 1941.
4 Louisiana Law Review 1, 33–39.

Under all legal systems the master is not liable for the torts committed by a servant unless the latter's wrong bears a relationship of some sort to his employment. It would hardly be contended, for example, that an employer should be held for injuries inflicted in an affray which takes place over domestic difficulties in the employee's own residence. The function of the concept "within the scope of the employment" is to separate such cases from others where the employer is responsible. That this function must be fulfilled, and through the

means of a concept of some sort, is beyond question. But the concept
employed may be well adapted to its purpose or not. The latter is the
case if the concept when applied to the factual situations which are
brought before the court give rise to considerable doubt and uncertainty. If we are to judge from the enormous amount of litigation arising
out of question whether a servant's tort was committed "within the
scope of his employment," we are tempted to conclude that the device
adopted by the common law judges is not a happy one. Doubts grow
stronger as we observe that civil law jurisdictions have been able to
solve this same problem with much less litigation, although the task is
the same, and similar notions are in use. . . . The only explanation
this writer can offer is that different methods of interpretation have
been adopted under the several systems. From the very beginning the
French and German courts have given their concepts a very broad
meaning and left their application to the lower courts which have to
decide the questions of fact. The German Supreme Court does not
require more than that there be a connection between the servant's tort
and the work incumbent upon him, while the French Supreme Court
has gone still further and states that the master is liable even for torts
committed *a l'occasion du travail.* Under so broad a definition only a
few situations, such as, for example, the "smoking cases" and some of
the cases involving an agent's fraud, have remained really doubtful. In
contrast to this approach the common law courts have attempted to
work out a variety of tests to ascertain whether a tort was or was not
committed "within the scope of employment"; but the experience of
more than a century has proved all these tests unsatisfactory. . . .

It is not difficult to understand why the effort to establish criteria
distinguishing acts within the scope of employment from those outside
it has been unsuccessful. The different criteria proposed did not refer
to easily distinguishable facts, but to notions which are quite as fluid as
the notion of scope of employment itself: furtherance of the master's
business, compact of duties, et cetera. One uncertain notion has been
supplanted by other notions of equal uncertainty. However the notion
may be defined, the decision is based upon value judgments which it
seems impossible to make more specific, but which, at the same time,
appear to have a solid base in common sense.

BRINER v. HYSLOP
Supreme Court of Iowa, 1983.
337 N.W.2d 858.

SCHULTZ, JUSTICE.

On November 7, 1979, Hyslop left Colorado and drove a McLane
truck loaded with cattle to Sioux Center, Iowa. Another of McLane's
employees, Leo Scowden, notified McLane at approximately 2:00 p.m.
on November 8 that Hyslop had arrived in Sioux Center. McLane told
Scowden that he and Hyslop were to begin driving to Waterloo. Later
that evening Scowden and Hyslop stopped in Fort Dodge to allow

Scowden to call McLane. McLane instructed them to go to Rowley, Iowa, to pick up a load of cattle early in the morning of November 9. While stopped in Fort Dodge Hyslop consumed several double scotches. He then got back in his truck and began driving to Rowley. Unfortunately, he fell asleep while driving and his truck drifted over the center line and collided with the oncoming Briner automobile. . . .

After the trial the jury returned a joint verdict for compensatory damages for $116,846.08 against both defendants and separate verdicts for punitive damages against Hyslop for $100,000 and against McLane for $150,000. The court subsequently granted a judgment notwithstanding the verdict for McLane on the punitive damage award and entered judgment for the plaintiff in conformance with the other verdicts.

Punitive damage award against McLane. . . .

Those authorities that have considered the issue are divided into two groups. One group holds the corporate employer liable for punitive damages whenever the employee's actions within the scope of employment make the employee liable. . . . These authorities generally term their analysis as the liberal approach or the course of employment rule. . . . The other group of authorities finds the corporate employer liable for punitive damages only when the corporate employer wrongfully authorized, contributed to, or ratified the outrageous conduct which caused plaintiff's injury. . . . This rule is termed the complicity rule. . . . It is expressed by the Restatement (Second) of Agency § 217C and the nearly identical Restatement (Second) of Torts § 909, which states:

> Punitive damages can properly be awarded against a master or other principal because of an act by an agent if, but only if:
>
> (a) the principal authorized the doing and the manner of the act, or
>
> (b) the agent was unfit and the principal was reckless in employing him, or
>
> (c) the agent was employed in a managerial capacity and was acting in the scope of employment, or
>
> (d) the principal or the managerial agent of the principal ratified or approved the act.

Restatement (Second) of Torts § 909 (1979). . . .

Of the fifty states and the District of Columbia, twenty-two states follow either the Restatement or a more restrictive rule; twenty states follow the course of employment rule; four states do not allow punitive damages; four states have not addressed the issue; and the rule in Iowa is in question. [case citations given for each state]

Summarizing our research, we find that the jurisdictions are nearly evenly split between the two rules; we find no basis for the assertions that the course of employment rule is the prevailing rule. Consequently, the justifications for either rule assume a more dominant feature in our determination. . . .

Punishment is a valid justification for punitive damages where the corporation is at fault, but with the course of employment rule, the one punished may be without fault and would be held liable merely on the basis of its role as employer. Thus, the major justification for the course of employment rule must be deterrence. . . . It is obvious, however, that there can be no effective deterrence unless there is some conduct which can be deterred. Thus, if an employer is only vicariously liable and could have done nothing to prevent the misconduct of its employee, it seems of little value to award punitive damages against the employer. In many instances there is probably little that an employer can do to prevent the employee from committing outrageous torts. . . .

Plaintiff also claims justification for the more liberal rule because of the difficulty experienced in proving authorization or ratification on the part of the corporate employer. Plaintiff cites *Embrey v. Holly,* 293 Md. 128, 442 A.2d 966, 970–71 (App.1982), which quotes colorful language from *Goddard v. Grand Trunk Railway,* 57 Me. 202, 222–23 (1869), one of the first judicial considerations of the issue:

> A corporation is an imaginary being. It has no mind but the mind of its servants; it has no voice but the voice of its servants; and it has no hands with which to act but the hands of its servants. All its schemes of mischief, as well as its schemes of public enterprise, are conceived by human minds and executed by human hands; and these minds and hands are its servants' minds and hands. All attempts, therefore, to distinguish between the guilt of the servant and the guilt of the corporation; or the malice of the servant and the malice of the corporation; or the punishment of the servant and the punishment of the corporation, is sheer nonsense; and only tends to confuse the mind and confound the judgment. Neither guilt, malice, nor suffering is predicable of this ideal existence, called a corporation. And yet under cover of its name and authority, there is in fact as much wickedness, and as much that is deserving of punishment, as can be found anywhere else. And since these ideal existences can neither be hung, imprisoned, whipped, or put in the stocks,—since in fact no corrective influence can be brought to bear upon them except that of pecuniary loss,—it does seem to us that the doctrine of exemplary damages is more beneficial in its application to them, than in its application to natural persons.

We find this argument more appropriate for claims that corporations should be held liable for punitive damages than for the rule that defines when a corporation is liable. . . .

Furthermore, while the complicity rule may be a more conservative approach, it is still a wide-ranging rule. We have little doubt that jury questions will be made and that juries will find verdicts that punish employers. The complicity rule is not limited solely to employee conduct that is expressly authorized by the corporation. Instead, the complicity rule extends employer liability to employee conduct which it would be difficult to show was authorized, but for which the employer is at least partially blamesworthy because he employed an unfit person. . . .

II. *Substantial evidence.* McLane maintains that there is insufficient evidence to present a fact issue to allow the issue of punitive damages to go to the jury under either the Restatement or course of employment rules. We determine that although there is sufficient evidence to provide a factual issue under either rule, we need only discuss this issue under the Restatement rule. . . . No argument was made that Hyslop was in a managerial capacity, nor was there any evidence that McLane was reckless in hiring or retaining Hyslop, or that it ratified or approved of his acts. The remaining issue is whether under subparagraph a of section 909 McLane authorized the doing and the manner of Hyslop's acts.

McLane attempts to narrow the issue concerning the employee's wrongful acts to Hyslop's intoxication. It then contends that the undisputed evidence is that McLane did not authorize this intoxication. . . .

It is also apparent that McLane or its managing agents were fully aware of the habits of their drivers, including Hyslop. McLane's utter lack of supervision and training, coupled with the disregard for the action of the employees, is sufficient evidence to make a jury question of whether it authorized the doing and the manner of the driving in question.

We conclude that a jury question was engendered as to whether McLane should have punitive damages awarded against it under the Restatement rule, . . .

Affirmed in Part; Reversed and Remanded in Part.

All Justices concur except UHLENHOPP, CARTER and WOLLE, JJ., who concur in part and dissent in part, and REYNOLDSON, C.J., who concurs in the result.

UHLENHOPP, JUSTICE (concurring in part, dissenting in part).

I concur in all of the majority opinion except division II and the result. I would adopt the complicity rule as the majority does, but I would affirm the judgment.

To me, absent the element of driving while intoxicated this would be a negligence case, although a strong one. The added intoxicated driving permits an award of punitive damages against *Hyslop. Sebastian v. Wood*, 246 Iowa 94, 106, 66 N.W.2d 841, 847 (1954). The intoxicated driving, however, does not permit an award of punitive damages against *McLane* without substantial evidence of complicity *regarding the intoxicated driving* in at least one of the respects stated in the Restatement, and such evidence does not appear. Substantial evidence of McLane's complicity regarding Hyslop's *negligence* does appear, but punitive damages are not awarded for negligence only. *Restatement (Second) of Torts* § 908 comment *b* (1977).

We see punitive damage awards in more and more cases; they are becoming commonplace rather than extraordinary. I view this trend with alarm. I think we should allow compensatory damages liberally to compensate prevailing claimants fully for their actual injuries, but we should restrict punitive damages to the truly extraordinary situations in which they are appropriate. *Id.* comment *f.* I agree with the District Judge that as to McLane, this is not a punitive damage case.

CARTER and WOLLE, JJ., concur in this partial concurrence and dissent.

COMMONWEALTH v. BENEFICIAL FINANCE CO.
Supreme Judicial Court of Massachusetts, 1971.
360 Mass. 188, 275 N.E.2d 33.

SPIEGEL, JUSTICE.　We have before us appeals emanating from 2 separate series of indictments and 2 separate jury trials of various individual and corporate defendants.

　．　．　．

These cases have become generally known as the "small loans" cases. In each case the defendants were charged with various offences under numerous indictments returned in 1964 by a special grand jury. The offences charged were offering or paying, or soliciting or receiving, bribes, or conspiring to do so. . . .

The evidence in the first trial, pertinent portions of which we summarize in detail later in this opinion, is here synopsized. This evidence tends to show that during the year 1962, several licensed small loans companies (corporate defendants), together with certain of their officers and employees (some of whom are defendants), conspired to bribe Hanley and Garfinkle in their capacities as public officials. The purpose of the alleged conspiracy and the payment of the bribe money was to insure the maintenance of a maximum interest rate which companies licensed to do business in the Commonwealth were permitted to charge. . . .

The evidence in the second trial, set out in detail in the subsequent portion of this opinion, tends to show that over a period of some 7 years (1957–1963) a number of small loans companies (including the corporate defendants), together with a number of their officers and employees (including the individual defendants named in the conspiracy indictment), allegedly conspired to bribe Hanley. His office as a public official clothed him with extensive powers to approve or disapprove the activities of small loans companies doing business in the Commonwealth. The bribes were alleged to have been paid to Hanley over this period to induce Hanley (1) to approve various requests pertaining to routine matters; (2) to refrain from taking action adverse to certain of

the defendants and co-conspirators at rate hearings held during 1957; and (3) to obtain approval of various changes in small loans regulations.
          . . .

Having concluded that the evidence was sufficient to establish that the defendants Pratt and Woodcock were part of a conspiracy joined in by Farrell, Glynn and Barber to bribe Hanley and Garfinkle, we turn to the question of whether there was sufficient evidence to support a finding that Beneficial, Household, and Liberty were parties to the conspiracy. . . .

With this in mind, perhaps it would be helpful at this point to briefly summarize the relationships between the various corporate defendants and individual defendants: (1) Household was held criminally responsible, in part, for the criminal conduct of Barber and Pratt. Barber and Pratt were employees of Household, but were neither directors nor officers. (2) Liberty was held liable, in part, for the criminal acts of Woodcock, who was 1 of Liberty's 2 executive vice-presidents and 1 of its 11 directors. (3) Beneficial was held criminally responsible, in part, for the conduct of Farrell and Glynn who were neither directors, officers nor employees of that corporation. . . .

. . . The defendants argue that a corporation should not be held criminally liable for the conduct of its servants or agents unless such conduct was performed, authorized, ratified, adopted or tolerated by the corporations' directors, officers or other "high managerial agents" who are sufficiently high in the corporate hierarchy to warrant the assumption that their acts in some substantial sense reflect corporate policy. This standard is that adopted by the American Law Institute Model Penal Code, approved in May, 1962. [Section 2:07] . . . The section proceeds to define "high managerial agent" as "an officer of a corporation . . . or any other agent . . . having duties of such responsibility that his conduct may fairly be assumed to represent the policy of the corporation."

The Commonwealth, on the other hand, argues that the standard applied by the judge in his instructions to the jury was correct. These instructions, which prescribe a somewhat more flexible standard than that delineated in the Model Penal Code, state in part, as follows: "[T]he Commonwealth must prove beyond a reasonable doubt that there existed between the guilty individual or individuals and the corporation which is being charged with the conduct of the individuals, such *a relationship that the acts and the intent of the individuals were the acts and intent of the corporation.* . . .

"How is that to be shown? How is the jury to determine whether the Commonwealth has proved that? . . . *It does not mean that the Commonwealth must prove that the individual who acted criminally was a member of the corporation's board of directors, or that he was a high officer in the corporation, or that he held any office at all.* . . . The Commonwealth must prove that the individual for whose conduct it seeks to charge *the corporation criminally was placed in a position by the corporation where he had enough power, duty, responsibility and authority to act for and in behalf of the corporation to handle the particular business or operation or project of the corporation in which he was engaged at the time that he committed the criminal act, with power of decision as to what he would or would not do while acting for the corporation, and that he was acting for and in behalf of the corporation in the accomplishment of that particular business or operation or project, and that he committed a criminal act while so acting.*

. . .

It may also be observed that the judge's standard is somewhat similar to the traditional common law rule of respondeat superior. However, in applying this rule to a criminal case, the judge added certain requirements not generally associated with that common law doctrine. He further qualified the rule of respondeat superior by requiring that the conduct for which the corporation is being held accountable be performed *on behalf of the corporation*. This factor is noted as important in the commentary to § 2.07(1) of the Model Penal Code. It may well be that there is often little distinction between an act done *on behalf of a principal* and an act done *within the scope of* *employment*, which is the traditional requirement of the doctrine of respondeat superior. Nevertheless, in the circumstances of this case it might reasonably be concluded that the explicit instruction of the judge that the jury look to the authority vested in the agent by the corporation to act within the particular sphere of corporate affairs relating to the criminal act, together with the explicit instruction that such act be performed on behalf of the corporation, required, in effect, the type of evidence which would support an inference that the criminal act was done as a matter of corporate policy. . . .

The foregoing is especially true in view of the particular circumstances of this case. In order to commit the crimes charged in these indictments, the defendant corporations either had to offer to pay money to a public official or conspire to do so. The disbursal of funds is an act peculiarly within the ambit of corporate activity. These corporations by the very nature of their business are constantly dealing with the expenditure and collection of moneys. It could hardly be expected that any of the individual defendants would conspire to pay, or would pay, the substantial amount of money here involved, namely $25,000, out of his own pocket. The jury would be warranted in finding that the disbursal of such an amount of money would come from the corporate treasury. A reasonable inference could therefore be drawn that the payment of such money by the corporations was done as a matter of corporate policy and as a reflection of corporate intent, thus comporting with the underlying rationale of the Model Penal Code, and probably with its specific requirements.

. . .

To permit corporations to conceal the nefarious acts of their underlings by using the shield of corporate armor to deflect corporate responsibility, and to separate the subordinate from the executive, would be to permit "endocratic" corporations to inflict widespread public harm without hope of redress. It would merely serve to ignore the scramble and realities of the market place.[58] This we decline to do. We believe that stringent standards must be adopted to discourage any attempt by "endocratic" corporations' executives to place the sole responsibility for criminal acts on the shoulders of their subordinates.

. . .

All judgments affirmed.

NOTE ON CORPORATE CRIMINAL LIABILITY

Recent disclosures concerning illegal campaign contributions by corporations and bribes of foreign government officials have raised in sharp focus the question of criminal liability for corporate action. There is currently a variety of legislation before Congress dealing with these and other aspects of corporate behavior, including new sanctions for pollution of the environment and participating in the Israeli boycott.

The difficulty in approaching this question is based both on a theoretical difficulty in arguing that a criminal act of an agent is within his "scope of employment", and in determining an appropriate sanction and, if that hurdle is overcome, in determining an appropriate sanction against a corporation. Commonwealth v. Beneficial Finance Co. offers a reasonable argument in respect to scope of employment when we are dealing with illegal contributions or bribes. We are still left, however, with the question of an appropriate sanction when a publicly-held corporation is involved. Even the strongest advocates of the entity concept of corporations recognize the difficulty of putting a corporation in jail. A monetary fine, on the other hand, serves only to hurt the shareholders.

These difficulties have led to an emphasis on a personal criminal liability for the officers and even directors. To what extent does this approach raise questions of an agent being in conflict with his principal? Is there a danger of moving only against employees who are a considerable way down the ladder?

REFERENCES

Principal held liable for criminal act of agents:

West Valley Estates, Inc. v. State, 286 So.2d 208 (Fla.App.1973) (corporation was liable for illegal dredging ordered by vice-president who was in charge of dredging operation; Com. v. Beneficial Finance was cited and followed).

Principal not held criminally liable for act of agents:

United States v. Kemble, 198 F.2d 889 (3d Cir.1952), certiorari denied 344 U.S. 893, 73 S.Ct. 211, 97 L.Ed. 690 (union charged with violation of Hobbs Act—obstruction of commerce by extortion—acquitted because of lack of showing that Union authorized or ratified action by members).

State v. Weiner, 41 N.J. 21, 194 A.2d 467 (1963) (doctor charged with involuntary manslaughter for deaths caused by faulty injections by his nurse; held no liability for criminal act of nurse).

58. The term "endocratic" was coined by Dean Rostow and means a "large, publicly-held corporation, whose stock is scattered in small fractions among thousands of stockholders." Note, Increasing Community Control Over Corporate Crime—A Problem in the Law of Sanctions, 71 Yale L.J. 280, 281, n. 3.

Jail sentence for vicarious criminal liability:

In re Marley, 29 Cal.2d 525, 175 P.2d 832 (1946) (employee sold short weight while owner was out of store; owner convicted of short weight statute and sentenced to 90 days in jail).

Commonwealth v. Koczwara, 397 Pa. 575, 155 A.2d 825 (1959), certiorari denied 363 U.S. 848, 80 S.Ct. 1624, 4 L.Ed.2d 1731 (employees sold liquor to minors, owner convicted for violation of statute but jail sentence held deprivation of due process when crime vicarious) noted 7 Utah L.Rev. 132 (1960); 5 Vill.L.Rev. 682 (1960).

Articles and notes:

Coleman, Is Corporate Criminal Liability Really Necessary (1975–76) 29 S.W.L.J. 908 (the author answers "no", advocates prosecution of the agents responsible).

Note, Corporate Crime: Regulating Corporate Behavior through Criminal Sanctions (1979) 92 Harv.L.Rev. 1227 (at pp. 1251–1258 criticizes defense in § 2.07(5) of due diligence in supervision).

Comparative Law:

Venandet, La responsabilite penale des personnes morale dans lavant projet de code penal, J. trim. dr. com. 31 (1978), 731.

Analogous reasoning: vicarious punitive liability:

Merlo v. Standard Life & Accident Insurance Co., 59 Cal.App.3d 5, 130 Cal.Rptr. 416 (1976) (principal said to be liable for punitive damages only for personal fault in authorizing or employing, or for ratification, or for act of managerial employee).

Comment, Liability of Employers for Punitive Damages Resulting From Acts of Employees (1978) 54 Chi.Kent L.Rev. 829.

SECTION 4.   LIABILITY OF THE EMPLOYEE; INDEMNIFICATION

While a battle of words is waged over the liability of employers, little is said about the liabilities of the persons employed. Since the employer generally has the deeper pocket, injury victims have little interest in pursuing the operatives. We have noticed that students sometimes slip into the fallacious assumption that because the employer is liable, the employee is not. This idea is wholly false. The law of agency, which makes employers liable, does not repeal the law of torts, which makes negligent individuals liable.[1] Both are liable in typical situations. Indeed, a whole series of persons may be liable—a negligent operative, his negligent supervisor, his immediate employer, a general contractor who retained extensive control over the means of performance, and a contractee who let the contract for an inherently dangerous or a franchised activity.[2]

1. Seavey, Liability of an Agent in Tort (1916) 11 So.L.Q. 16, reprinted in Seavey, Studies in Agency (1949) 1.

2. If an employer is liable for failure to make premises and equipment safe, can injury victim sue the employee who had the primary responsibility to provide safety? See Johnson v. Schneider, 271 So.2d 579 (La.App.1973) (employee is liable if plaintiff can identify the one who had the primary responsibility).

McFeeters v. Renollet, 210 Kan. 158, 500 P.2d 47 (1972) (corporation president was liable along with corporation for negligence in building homes without ascertaining that basements were above water table).

Liability to Injury Victims. A few questions of interest arise in connection with the liability of employees to injury victims. For example, there is an old tort rule that a converter of property is liable regardless of fault. Should this apply to a broker who innocently receives stolen property while acting as a mere agent for someone else? [3] There is also the rule known as "res judicata," according to which a matter once adjudged cannot be sued on again. If an injury victim has sued a tort-feasor's employer, and won or lost, can he later maintain action against the tort-feasor himself for the same tort? [4] If the victim has settled out of court with the employer, can he thereafter maintain action against the employee? [5]

Some special problems have arisen with regard to government agents, chiefly because of the doctrine of governmental immunity.[6] If the government is immune from suit in a particular area, does the employee who carries out the government's policies share the same immunity? [7] Where a corporation undertakes to operate ships as an

---

3. Note, Liability for Innocent Conversion under Packers and Stockyards Act (1951), 24 So.Cal.L.Rev. 202.

Birmingham v. Rice Brothers, 238 Iowa 410, 26 N.W.2d 39, 2 A.L.R.2d 1108 (1947) (agent liable); comments, 47 Col.L.Rev. 861, 32 Iowa L.Rev. 755, 31 Marq.L.Rev. 103, 32 Minn.L.Rev. 86, 14 U.Chi.L.Rev. 713.

Sullivan Co. v. Wells, 89 F.Supp. 317 (D.C.Neb.1950) (broker not liable); comment, 24 So.Cal.L.Rev. 202.

Note, Sale of Negotiable Instrument by Agent without Notice that Principal is not Bona Fide Holder (1941) 16 Minn.L.Rev. 133.

4. Caldwell v. Kelly, 202 Tenn. 104, 302 S.W.2d 815 (1957) (only the employer sought certiorari from decision granting new trial against both employee and employer; when Supreme Court reversed and dismissed action as to employer the trial court also dismissed as to employee) noted 26 Tenn.L.Rev. 549 (1959).

Davis v. Perryman, 225 Ark. 963, 286 S.W.2d 844 (1956) (after unsuccessful action against employer, plaintiff barred from later action against employee) noted 10 Ark.L.Rev. 506 (1956).

Note—Master and Servant—Respondeat Superior—Joinder in Same Action (1957) 11 South Western L.J. 378.

Note, The Private Agent's Liability after a Suit by the Third Party has been Brought against the Principal (1948) 36 Georgetown L.J. 238.

5. Gavin v. Malherbe, 264 N.Y. 403, 191 N.E. 486 (1934) (release of employer acted to release employee).

Hamm v. Thompson, 143 Colo. 298, 353 P.2d 73 (1960) (release of employer held not to effect liability of employee) noted 6 Vill. L.Rev. 245 (1960–61); 13 Ala.L.Rev. 469 (1961).

Covenant not to sue employer, releases employee: Holmstad v. Abbott G.M. Diesel, Inc., 27 Utah 2d 109, 493 P.2d 625 (1972).

Note, The Private Agent's Liability after a Suit by the Third Party has been brought for or against the Principal (1948) 36 Geo. L.J. 238.

6. On the reverse question—whether an employer can be sued after a suit against the employee has failed, see Missouri, Kansas & Texas Railroad Co. v. Stanley, 372 P.2d 852 (Okl.1962); comment, 17 Okla.L. Rev. 432.

On the effect upon the employer's liability of a covenant not to sue the employee, see Holcom v. Flavin, 34 Ill.2d 558, 216 N.E.2d 811 (1966) (employee released); comments, 43 Ch.K.L.Rev. 201, 28 Oh.St. L.J. 537.

Release of agent releases employer: Drinkard v. Wm. J. Pulte Inc., 48 Mich. App. 67, 210 N.W.2d 137 (1973).

Stewart v. Craig-Morris Glass Co., 208 Tenn. 212, 344 S.W.2d 761 (1961) (covenant not to sue given to employee operates as a release of his employer) noted 28 Tenn.L. Rev. 579 (1961).

Harris v. Aluminum Company of America, 550 F.Supp. 1004 (W.D.Vir.1982) (covenant not to sue employee does not release employer).

7. See Larson v. Domestic & Foreign Commerce Corp., 337 U.S. 682, 69 S.Ct. 1457, 93 L.Ed. 1628 (1949) (court refuses to

"agent" of the government, does it become liable as an employer for the seamen's negligent acts? This question awakened a flurry of litigation in the late forties,[8] but has since subsided, probably because of the lapse of the war-time practice of making corporations into "agents" of the government, and because the enactment in 1950 of the Federal Tort Claims Act provided injury victims with an even deeper pocket from which to seek reparation.

With respect to motor vehicles, operators who occasion injuries in the course of their employment by the United States are expressly exempted by a provision which was added in 1961 to the Federal Tort Claims Act of 1948.[9] This provision was adopted in order to relieve federal employees from the necessity of buying liability insurance at their own expense.[10]

Liability to Indemnify Employer. Of greater practical importance are questions involving the liability of the employee to indemnify the employer who has been made vicariously liable through the employee's fault. The principle of liability in such cases is generally acknowledged, and codified in the Restatement.[11]

In order to examine the radiations of this principle in human behavior, we should first separate the employee who is an individual wage or salary earner from the enterprise (whether individual or corporate) which undertakes jobs for a price, although both are governed, in the law's majestic equality, by the same blackletter.

—liability of wage earners. With regard to the indemnification liability of individual wage earners, it is obvious that payments from their own pockets are not likely to make a significant contribution to the aggregate losses of injury victims; wage earners seldom have the resources to satisfy large tort judgments. Their liability may yet be

enjoin government officer from breaking government contract with plaintiff; dissent from Frankfurter, Douglas, Jackson and Burton). In Malone v. Bowdoin, 369 U.S. 643, 82 S.Ct. 980, 8 L.Ed.2d 168 (1962), a divided Supreme Court, through Mr. Justice Douglas, relied upon Larson v. Domestic & Foreign Commerce Corp. to dismiss an ejectment action against a Forest Service Officer since he had not exceeded his statutory authority. The Court reasoned that the action was therefore one against the United States. For a criticism of both of these cases, see Note, The Supreme Court, 1961 Term, 76 Harv.L.Rev. 54, at 220–222 (1962).

8. Hust v. Moore-McCormack Lines, 328 U.S. 707, 66 S.Ct. 1218, 90 L.Ed. 1000 (1946) (managing agent liable).

Caldarola v. Eckert, 332 U.S. 155, 67 S.Ct. 1569, 91 L.Ed. 1968 (1947) (agent not liable, distinguishing Hust case).

Cosmopolitan Shipping Co. v. McAllister, 337 U.S. 783, 69 S.Ct. 1317, 93 L.Ed. 1692

(1949) (managing agent not liable to seaman under Jones Act, overruling Hust case; 4 justices dissenting).

Fink v. Shepard Steamship Co., 337 U.S. 810, 69 S.Ct. 1330, 93 L.Ed. 1709 (1949) (managing agent not liable to seaman under admiralty law; 4 justices dissenting).

Weade v. Dichmann, Wright & Pugh, 337 U.S. 801, 69 S.Ct. 1326, 93 L.Ed. 1704 (1949) (managing agent not liable to passenger for act of seaman; 4 justices dissenting).

9. 28 U.S.Code § 2679, making the remedy against the U.S. "exclusive of any other civil action . . . against the employee or his estate. . . ."

10. See Senate Rept. No. 736, 87th Cong., U.S.Cong. & Adm.News, 1961, vol. 2, pp. 2784, 2789.

11. Restatement of Agency 2d, § 401.

significant in several ways. In the first place, it may be disastrous for the wage earner. Although his small resources may not do much for a victim, their loss may be tragic for him.

Although the probability of wage earners' having to indemnify their employers may be small, it may have significant side effects.[12] For one thing, the fear of it may be a useful incentive to employees to use care about their work—if we are prepared to believe that workmen contemplate legal principles as they brandish their tools. More plausibly, the possibility that a friendly workman might be held liable would lead a plaintiff to press his claim less aggressively (or witnesses to testify less positively) than if they thought that only the employer would have to pay. This hypothesis is suggested by a celebrated English decision which provoked an unusual flood of law review comment. A bus driver had run the bus into his own father, who sued the bus company. The bus company's insurer impleaded the son to indemnify it for any amount it might be obliged to pay the father.[13] Still another consequence of the employee's liability to indemnify might be to cause the employer to include in his liability insurance policies clauses covering employees' liabilities as well. With respect to motor vehicles in American practice, the liability insurance of employers usually covers the employees, thus nullifying whatever due-care-incentive might be supplied by the principle of employee's liability to indemnify.

—liability of contractors and subcontractors. The cases in which indemnification most frequently presents itself in litigation are cases in which a business enterprise (individual, partnership or corporate) has contracted to do a job, and has somehow brought liability upon the contractee. For instance, a railroad company has let a contract to build a tunnel, the construction contractor has let a subcontract to blast out the rock, and a careless blaster has caused damage to neighbors. Although the blasting subcontractor would be, prima facie, an "independent contractor," the railroad company or the general contractor might be held liable by reason of pervasive control, or because of "inherent danger" or other exception to the independent contractor rule.

In these situations, unlike those involving individual wage earners, there is quite likely to be insurance covering all parties; the immediately interested parties are the insurance companies. If there is no

---

12. See Isbrandtsen Co. v. Johnson, 343 U.S. 779, 72 S.Ct. 1011, 96 L.Ed. 1294 (1952) (employer attempted to set off, against employee's wage claim, employee's duty to indemnify employer for damages paid on account of employee's assault on a fellow worker).

13. Lister v. Romford [1957] 1 All.E.R. 125, 2 W.L.R. 158, in which the House of Lords (Denning L.J. dissenting) affirmed the Court of Appeal, decision reported in [1956] 2 Q.B. 180 [1955] 3 All.E.R. 460

[1955] 3 W.L.R. 631. The case inspired comments in 1957 Camb.L.J. 21, 10 Ind. L.J. 247, 11 id. 18 (1956), 72 L.Q.R. 7, 73 id. 283, 20 Mod.L.Rev. 220 (1957), 35 N.Z.L.J. 129, 161 (1959), 73 S.A.L.J. 328 (1956), 2 Sydney L.Rev. 577 (1958).

Most commentators applauded the justices' steady adherence to liability for fault, but Glanville Williams in the Modern Law Journal thought it better to let the insurer bear the loss rather than the negligent wage earner.

insurance, or inadequate insurance, the indemnification liability may be quite disastrous for the enterprise involved, and the question may be which enterprise is to be bankrupted by failure to insure. Well drawn contracts frequently resolve these questions in advance, but situations which the draftsman failed to foresee are bound to arise.[14]

Effect of Employee's Release on Liability of Employer.

An injury victim will often settle quickly with the employee—either because the employee cannot be expected to pay much anyway, or because the victim thinks an unworried employee will make a less hostile witness—but continue to prosecute his action against the employer. Against this pursuit, the employer will contend (on a conceptual level) that if the victim is satisfied with respect to the wrongdoer, he should not continue to make claim against another, whose fault is purely vicarious. In favor of the claim, the victim will contend (on a functional level) that his only practical way of getting compensation is to settle separately with each person liable, on the best terms he can get. Judges and theorists have often propounded a specious reconciliation of these conflicting arguments by saying that a "release" of one releases all, but a "covenant not to sue" one preserves the remedy against others. The argument is then continued as a dispute over the categorization of the settlement as a "release" or "covenant not to sue." [15]

HEARINGS ON FEDERAL TORT CLAIMS ACT

Hearings before the House Committee on the Judiciary on H.R. 5373
and H.R. 6463, 77th Cong., 2d Sess., pp. 9–10. Quoted in
United States v. Gilman (1954).
347 U.S. 507, 74 S.Ct. 695, 98 L.Ed. 898.

[Mr. Shea, the witness in the following passage, was then Assistant Attorney General, appearing in favor of the proposed bill. The provision in question provided that if the injured person recovered judgment against the United States, he could not thereafter maintain a claim against the employee who caused his injury.]

"Mr. Springer. I would like to direct your attention, Mr. Shea, to line 19. Why do you provide this acceptance of the award as constituting a bar to the claim against the employee? Is that the intention of the provision, and what is the ultimate purpose of it?

"Mr. Shea. . . . It has been found that the Government, through the Department of Justice, is constantly being called on by the heads of the various agencies to go in and defend, we will say, a person

---

14. See Parsons v. Amerada Hess Corp., 422 F.2d 610 (10th Cir.1970) (under contract making contractor liable for losses arising out of operation, contractor was liable for contractee's costs of legal defense, even though contractee escaped liability).

Cf. Brda v. Chrysler Corp., 50 Mich.App. 332, 213 N.W.2d 295 (1973) (contractor's promise to indemnify contractee was unenforceable with respect to loss caused by negligence of contractee's employees).

15. See References fn. 6; Note, A Master's Liability when an Injured Party Covenants not to Sue his Servant (1967) 28 Oh. St.L.J. 537.

who is driving a mail truck when suit is brought against him for damages or injuries caused while he was operating the truck within the scope of his duties. Allegations of negligence are usually made. It has been found, over long years of experience, that unless the Government is willing to go in and defend such persons the consequence is a very real attack upon the morale of the services. Most of these persons are not in a position to stand or defend large damage suits, and they are of course not generally in a position to secure the kind of insurance which one would if one were driving for himself.

"If the Government has satisfied a claim which is made on account of a collision between a truck carrying mail and a private car, that should, in our judgment, be the end of it. After the claimant has obtained satisfaction of his claim from the Government, either by a judgment or by an administrative award, he should not be able to turn around and sue the driver of the truck. If he could sue the driver of the truck, we should have to go in and defend the driver in the suit brought against him, and there will thus be continued a very substantial burden which the Government has had to bear in conducting the defense of postoffice drivers and other Government employees.

"Mr. McLaughlin. Have you considered the practice followed by large corporations and railway companies with respect to defense of employees who are joined as defendants in negligence actions?

"Mr. Shea. I should think that what ordinarily happens in the case of an accident caused by a driver for a big corporation is that suit is brought jointly against the two, and usually it is satisfied by the corporation, and then ordinarily the corporation's remedy against the driver is to fire him if he is negligent too often. Ordinarily the corporations cover such risks by insurance, which is paid for by the employer, I think.

"The Chairman. Mr. Shea, you are discussing and directing your remarks to the matter where, if a person is injured and files a claim against the Government and the Government satisfies that claim, that is the end of the claim against anybody?

"Mr. Shea. That is right.

"The Chairman. What is the arrangement when the Government has an employee who is guilty of gross negligence and injury results? Is there any requirement that that employee should in any way respond to the Government if it has to pay for the injury, in the event of gross negligence?

"Mr. Shea. Not if he is a Government employee. Under those circumstances, the remedy is to fire the employee.

"Mr. McLaughlin. No right of subrogation is set up? . . .

"Mr. Shea. Not against the employee.

REFERENCES

Sweden: Hellner, The New Swedish Tort Liability Act (1974) 22 Am.J.Comp.L. 1, 10–11 (statute exonerates employee from liability for ordinary negligence within the scope of employment).

FIREMAN'S FUND AMERICAN INSURANCE COMPANIES v. TURNER

Supreme Court of Oregon, 1971.
260 Or. 30, 488 P.2d 429, 53 A.L.R.3d 620.
Comment, 53 Or.L.Rev. 366 (1974).

TONGUE, JUSTICE.

This is an action for indemnity brought by the insurer of an employer against an employee. The purpose of the action is to recover from insurer of the employee the defense costs and amount paid by the insurer of the employer in satisfaction of a judgment against both employer and employee in favor of a third party injured by an automobile owned by the employee and negligently driven by him in the course of his employment. Plaintiff appeals from a judgment in favor of defendant as entered by the court, sitting without a jury.

. . .

Plaintiff issued to Oregon Sign & Neon Corporation (Oregon Sign) a policy of liability insurance with limits for personal injury in the sum of $100,000. That policy covered Oregon Sign against liability arising from the operation of vehicles owned by certain employees, including defendant, but did not cover the employees against liability. The policy also contained a subrogation clause in general form, under which plaintiff, as the insurer, was subrogated to the rights of Oregon Sign in the event that plaintiff, as its insurer, made payments under the terms of the policy.

Defendant was the manager of Oregon Sign and carried his own liability insurance under a policy with limits of $10,000 for injury to one person. He was paid a monthly "car allowance" by Oregon Sign for expenses incurred in the operation of his car for business purposes.

While operating his automobile in the course of his employer's business defendant rear-ended another automobile. The party injured in that accident brought an action for personal injuries and recovered judgment in the sum of $9,177.23 and $75 in costs against both Oregon Sign and defendant, based solely upon negligent driving by defendant. The recovery against Oregon Sign was based solely on the doctrine of respondeat superior, without claim of negligence by it as employer.

Plaintiff insurer paid $7,401.76 in satisfaction of that judgment (or $^{10}/_{11}$th of that judgment), and expended an additional $1,186 in defending the action. Defendant's insurer contributed the balance (or $^{1}/_{11}$th), in satisfaction of that same judgment.

. . .

The trial court also made the following conclusions of law:

"That no recovery may be had by an employer against an employee even though such employee is guilty of negligence constituting a mere inadvertence [sic] or mistake where the employee is at the time complained of rendering good and faithful service to his employer.

"That plaintiff's action may not be maintained because it is against public policy to permit subrogation of a personal injury award.

"That each carrier having discharged its prorata share of the judgment, and each having received a premium therefor no recovery can be had by the one against the other."

. . .

Plaintiff, as appellant contends that it has long been recognized at common law and by most courts, including this court, that an employer held vicariously liable to a third person injured by the negligence of an employee, without negligence on the part of the employer, may seek indemnity against the employee.

. . .

Defendant, while recognizing the authorities cited by plaintiff, contends that "considerations of public policy . . . [are] of greater importance than recognition of an out-dated rule of law exercised without regard to its effect." Thus, defendant contends that Oregon Sign, as an employer, knew that it was inevitable that defendant in driving from 24,000 to 36,000 miles each year would have an accident; that defendant obtained insurance coverage to protect it against such accidents and that where, as in this case, there was no drinking or gross negligence, but no more than "mere inadvertent negligence which was within the contemplation of the parties," the employer should not, as a matter of public policy, be entitled to "pass the economic loss off on to the employee when it is foreseeable at the outset."

We may agree that this contention may have considerable merit as a matter of abstract justice, depending upon the circumstances of the particular case. Indeed, the common law rule of indemnity by an employer against his employees has been strongly criticized for much the same reasons.[4] Defendant has cited no cases, however, in which the courts have undertaken to abolish that rule by judicial decision, and perhaps for good reason.

The "fault concept"—that all persons should be held responsible for the consequences of their wrongful acts, including "inadvertent negligence,"—while subject to criticism, is still firmly established as the foundation of tort liability. Exceptions to and modifications of that rule, such as the requirement of gross negligence, rather than simple

---

4. See Steffan, The Employer's "Indemnity" Action, 25 U.Chi.L.Rev. 465, 489–494 (1958); James, Indemnity, Subrogation, and Contribution and the Efficient Distri-bution of Accident Losses, 21 NACCA L.J. 360, 362, 368–370, 374 (1958). See also Prosser, supra note 3, at 313.

negligence, as the basis for liability of the driver of an automobile to a guest passenger, have usually been adopted as the result of statute, rather than court decision. And while the legislatures, rather than the courts, are ordinarily considered to have the primary responsibility for changes in the law for reasons of public policy, legislation which undertakes to relieve persons from responsibility for their wrongful acts is also usually subject to strong criticism. (Witness the current controversy over proposals for "no-fault" insurance legislation.)

It has been contended that to permit employers to seek such indemnity against their employees would "thwart efficient loss distribution in pursuit of perfecting the fault principle" and that "if this doctrine were carried to its logical conclusion most of our accident loss would ultimately be paid for by the operators of machines or other workmen." [5]

In considering this contention, however, it must be kept in mind that, as a practical matter, few employers seek to exercise such a right of indemnity against their individual employees, and for three good reasons: (a) the adverse effect upon employee morale; (b) the inability of most employees to pay such indemnity, and (c) the opposition of unions. And while in cases involving automobile accidents the insurers of employers may not be inhibited by these considerations, most employees today also carry automobile liability insurance, as in this case. In addition, in this case, defendant was paid a monthly "car allowance" to cover the cost of expenses incurred in the operation of his car for business purposes. This, of course, raises the problem of the exercise by the insurer of an employer of its rights of subrogation and the problem of whether the insurance companies for both employer and employee should contribute to the loss in a case such as this, as considered separately below.

It must also be kept in mind that the rule of vicarious liability of employers, although a court-made rule, is a rule under which persons injured by the wrongful acts of employees may seek recovery against the employer as the one best able to pay and to distribute the resulting loss—all in the absence of any negligence or "fault" on part of the employer. Thus, it is contended, and with some merit, that if such liability without fault is imposed on the employer, it is not contrary to public policy to permit him to seek indemnity against the person at fault, despite the fact that such person may be his employee.

In any event, it is our view that the right of an employer held vicariously liable to a third person injured by the wrongful act of an employee to seek indemnity against the employee is too well established to be abolished at this time by decision of this court as contrary to public policy, at least under the facts and circumstances of this case.

5. See James, supra note 4, at pp. 369–370. See also Steffan, supra note 4, at 489–490.

For all of these reasons, the judgment of the trial court must be reversed and the case remanded for proceedings not inconsistent with this opinion.

Reversed and remanded.

McLEOD v. DEAN

United States District Court, Southern District of New York, 1967.
270 F.Supp. 855.

MOTLEY, DISTRICT JUDGE.

Cross-Claim

Findings of Fact and Conclusions of Law

Defendant Raymond Dean (Dean) is the owner of a protective service which orally agreed with defendant Daitch Crystal Dairies (Daitch) to furnish a Dean guard to protect the merchandise in a Daitch store from pilferage by customers. Defendant Canty is the guard furnished pursuant to this agreement. Before he was assigned to stores by Dean, Canty had undergone a two-week period of training and orientation as a store guard. Upon reporting to the Daitch store in question, the manager directed Canty where to stand and which counters to guard with especial care. The Daitch store manager instructed Canty to inform him should Canty detect any shoplifting. The manager also directed Canty where to station himself when the manager was out to lunch. Canty punched two time cards each morning when he arrived at the Daitch store—one for Daitch and one for Dean. Daitch paid Dean who in turn paid Canty.

The plaintiff, Mary McLeod, recovered a judgment in the amount of $3,000 for slander against Dean, Daitch and Canty upon which this cross-claim by Daitch is based. The plaintiff's action for slander arose out of questions directed by Canty to plaintiff, a female customer of the Daitch store involved, in the course of a conversation with the plaintiff about the disposition of a certain article of merchandise which Canty erroneously believed he saw her put into her tote bag.

In the first instance, we are faced with the question of the relationship between Daitch and defendants Dean and Canty. Was the protective service an independent contractor or the agent of Daitch? To determine this question we must look to the surrounding facts and circumstances. This contract was to be performed in the Daitch store. A Daitch store manager on the premises could and did give directions to the Dean employee on how to carry out his function of protecting the Daitch merchandise from pilferage by customers of Daitch. In addition, there is the important consideration that the contract could be terminated by either Dean or Daitch at will. . . .

When defendant Canty inquired of the Daitch customer as to the disposition of goods he thought he had seen the customer handle, he was acting to further the interest of Daitch and under Daitch authori-

ty—expressed and implied. For such an authorized act Daitch is liable
in damages. . . .

. . .

The jury verdict having been returned against all three defendants,
the question of defendants' rights as between themselves remains.
This is not a simple case of negligence by an agent or servant where the
established doctrines of active and passive tortfeasors come into play.
What we have here is a case where the very act in question is an act
which was authorized by Daitch, done at the direction of Daitch, and in
the furtherance of the interests of Daitch. The fact that this was an
authorized act makes it an exception to the general rule that an agent
who subjects a principal to liability because of his wrongful act is
subject to liability to the principal for the loss which results therefrom.
Restatement (Second), Agency § 401d (1958).

Exception

To these exceptional cases, a different rule applies. Where a
person, acting at the direction of and on account of another, does an
authorized act because of which both are liable in tort, the person who
did the act is entitled to indemnity from the other for expenditures
properly made in the discharge of such liability—providing the actor
acted in good faith and the act is not apparently illegal. . . .

Rule

Provided the act was within the scope of his authority, the agent
has a right to indemnity from the principal even though the act was
wrongful and the agent lost a suit brought by the third party against
him. . . .

Therefore, in the case before the court, though plaintiff has a valid
judgment against all three defendants, as between the defendants,
Dean and Canty have a right to be indemnified by Daitch for any
expenditures they have made or may make in discharge of this liability.

This result is dictated by and rests upon a decisional law. However, as Adams v. F.W. Woolworth, supra, has pointed out, there are, in
addition, strong policy considerations raised by a case of this nature.

The owner of a store, if he so chooses, is entitled to take certain
measures to protect his merchandise from pilferage—including the
hiring of store guards. It should be contemplated that authorized
guards in carrying out their authority to protect the merchandise may
speak to customers and that such speech in some instances may give
rise to an action for slander. This should be a risk that the store owner
assumes in electing to use certain measures to protect his merchandise.
Without guards or other devices a store owner runs all the risks of
pilferage.

Foreseeability

He should not merely by placing guards in his store be able to
escape all risks and responsibility. He has a right to protect his
merchandise but as with the exercise of many rights, there must be
attendant risks. Guards placed in a store are viewed by the public as
working and acting for the store. Their primary reason for being there
is to protect and advance the store owner's economic interest. In such

circumstances, ultimate accountability for the guards' authorized acts should rest with the party who is exercising control over the store and enjoying the fruits of protection.

Defendants Dean and Canty are entitled to be indemnified by Daitch for any expenditures they have made or may make as a result of plaintiff Mary McLeod's action for slander against them.

Based on the foregoing findings of fact and conclusions of law, defendant Daitch's cross claim for judgment over against defendants Dean and Canty, and for costs, disbursements and expenses incurred in the defense of this action by Daitch is denied.

REFERENCES

Walker v. Fontenot, 329 So.2d 762 (La.App.1976) (insurance company liable for unfaithful act of agent in failing to obtain insurance policy entitled to indemnification from agent).

McLouth Steel Corp. v. A.E. Anderson Construction Corp., 48 Mich.App. 424, 210 N.W.2d 448 (1973) (in prior suit by injured workmen against McLouth as employer and Anderson as contractor, jury found both guilty of negligence; this did not preclude McLouth from obtaining indemnification from Anderson, since jury in indemnification suit found that McLouth's negligence was not proximate cause of injury).

Ayala v. Bailey Electric Co., Inc., 318 So.2d 645 (La.App.1975) (employer not allowed indemnification against employee who started fire while cleaning a building, because employer found to be independently negligent in the instructions he gave the employee).

Provencal v. Parker, 66 Mich.App. 431, 239 N.W.2d 623 (1976) (indemnification not allowed against employer by automobile owner who was held liable under owner's liability statute for injury to third party caused by employee who had borrowed the auto).

Liability of supervisory officers:

Craven v. Oggero, 213 N.W.2d 678 (Iowa 1973) (supervisory employees who had personal duty to inspect machinery and failed to do so were liable to injured worker).

Kerrigan v. Errett, 256 N.W.2d 394 (Iowa 1977) (executive in charge of medical matters, plant safety, plant protection, plant newspaper, public relations, group insurance, food services, training, and suggestions was not liable for failure to make periodic inspections of machinery).

United States v. Park, 421 U.S. 658, 95 S.Ct. 1903, 44 L.Ed.2d 489 (1975) (president of corporation that sold contaminated food due to lack of plant inspections, liable on proof that president had authority and responsibility for entire operation; no requirement of "awareness of some wrongdoing.").

Donsco, Inc. v. Casper Corp., 587 F.2d 602 (3d Cir.1978) (president of corporation who participated in planning a copy of another seller's product and publicity was personally liable, with corporation, for unfair competition).

Note, Decisionmaking Models and Corporate Crime (1976) 85 Yale L.J. 1091.

Chapter 3

THE EMPLOYMENT RELATIONSHIP
UNDER SOCIAL LEGISLATION

INTRODUCTORY NOTE

Although vicarious liability for injuries imposes significant costs on every enterprise that employs labor, it is probably the least of the legal worries of a vice-president in charge of personnel. He buys liability insurance and forgets about it. There are many other juridical ramifications of employment which impose equal or greater burdens, and more frequent dilemmas. Unlike vicarious liability, which common law judges developed through brilliant intuition or perhaps blind luck, these other ramifications are largely the result of legislative activity that overruled or supplemented judicial perceptions of justice.

Some of the programs were designed to affect the employment relation itself, by changing the terms of employment in favor of employees. In this category may be placed industrial accident legislation (employers' liability and workmen's compensation), wage and hours laws, and unionization laws. Some of the other programs do not directly affect the terms of employment; rather, they seize on the payroll as a convenient base for a tax, and on the employer as a surrogate tax collector. This is the essence of unemployment taxes, federal insurance contributions, and withholding taxes.

In this chapter, we attempt to give to prospective business counselors a speaking acquaintance with some of the principal legislative programs which impose financial and administrative responsibility on enterprise managers. We provide them with a partial checklist, with an awareness that these programs exist, and with some clues about where he can get further information when he needs it.

The costs of these legally mandated programs are commonly grouped with benefits conferred voluntarily or through collective bargaining under the name of "fringe benefits." The following tables, compiled by the U.S. Chamber of Commerce, indicate the magnitude of total fringe benefits, and the legally mandated share of the total.

Five Levels of Employee Benefits, 1978

Item	As percent of payroll	Cents per payroll hour	Dollars per year per employee
10% of firms paid more than	48.7%	360.6¢	$7,548
25% of firms paid more than	42.1	300.5	6,205
50% of firms paid more than	35.9	238.0	4,917
75% of firms paid more than	30.9	188.1	3,889
90% of firms paid more than	25.6	139.5	2,954
Mean or average payment	36.9%	247.14	$5,138

Employee Benefits, by Type of Benefit, 1978

Type of benefit	Total, all companies
Total employee benefits as percent of payroll..................	36.9
1. Legally required payments (employer's share only)............	9.0
a. Old-Age, Survivors, Disability, and Health Insurance (FICA taxes)	5.6
b. Unemployment Compensation.........................	1.7
c. Workers' compensation (including estimated cost of self-insured)	1.6
d. Railroad Retirement Tax, Railroad Unemployment and Cash Sickness Insurance, state sickness benefits insurance, etc.	0.1
2. Pension, insurance, and other agreed-upon payments (employer's share only)	12.2
3. Paid rest periods, lunch periods, wash-up time, travel time, clothes-change time, get-ready time, etc.	3.6
4. Payments for time not worked	9.7
5. Other items	2.4

One of the most conspicuous legislative trends of the twentieth century has been the proliferation of statutes imposing obligations on employers. The following list, with dates indicating the year of first enactment, indicate the variety of federal legislation, some of which is accompanied by parallel regulation in the states. The sections cited are those containing definitions of "employer," "employee" or "employment."

Age Discrimination Act, 29 U.S.C. (1974) § 630(f).

Civil Rights Act, Title VII, (1964) 42 U.S.C. § 2000e(f).

Employee Retirement Income Security Act "ERISA" (1974), 29 U.S.C. § 1002(6).

Fair Labor Standards Act (1938) 29 U.S.C. § 203(e).

Income Tax—Withholding (1954) 26 U.S.C. § 3401.

Insurance Contributions Act (1935) 26 U.S.C. § 3121.

Longshoremen's & Harbor Workers' Compensation Act (1927) 33 U.S.C. § 902(3).

National Labor Relations Act (1935) 29 U.S.C. § 152(3).

Occupational Safety & Health Act "OSHA" (1970) 29 U.S.C. § 652(6).

Social Security Act (1935), 42 U.S.C. § 410(j).

Unemployment Tax Act (1935) 26 U.S.C. § 3306.

Many of these acts contain limits of coverage based on such factors as participation in interstate commerce, or number of employees, or line of business. As originally enacted, however, most of them left open the question of what is an employment relation. Most judges assumed without much debate that the criteria of an employment relation that have been developed to solve problems of vicarious liability should be applied likewise to problems under legislative enactments. A few argued for some other criterion which, they contended, would better serve the purposes of the legislation. In the federal sphere, Congress reacted by instructing the judges to be guided under certain acts by "common law" standards. Even then, they did not specify what part of the common law was intended; they are generally assumed to have referred to the law of vicarious liability for tortious injuries. Under a larger number of statutes, the criteria of an employment relationship have remained undefined.

OILFIELD SAFETY & MACHINE SPECIALTIES v. HARMAN UNLIMITED

United States Court of Appeals, Fifth Circuit, 1980.
625 F.2d 1248.

Before GOLDBERG, TATE and SAM D. JOHNSON, CIRCUIT JUDGES.

SAM D. JOHNSON, CIRCUIT JUDGE:

. . . Charles Hansen was injured while making a safety inspection of an oil drilling platform in the Gulf of Mexico. Hansen's two employers, Oilfield Safety, Inc., and Harman Unlimited, Inc., each denied being his employer at the time of the injury and instead pointed their finger at the other party. The Administrative Law Judge (ALJ) and the Benefits Review Board (Board) held that both Oilfield Safety and Harman Unlimited were Hansen's employers at the time of the accident, and that both were jointly and severally liable for his worker's compensation benefits under the Longshoremen's and Harbor Workers' Compensation Act, (LHWCA). Additionally, the ALJ and the Board awarded attorney's fees to Hansen's counsel. Both employers appeal. We affirm.

. . .

The central issue on appeal is whether an employee-employer relationship existed between Clarence Hansen and Harman Unlimited, Oilfield Safety, or both. Harman Unlimited and Oilfield Safety contend that the Board erred in holding Hansen was their employee. In order to resolve this dispute this Court must first determine the standard for deciding whether an individual is an employee. Second, we must decide whether the Board correctly held that the ALJ's finding of dual employment is supported by substantial evidence on the record as a whole and is in accordance with the law. Finally, if both Harman Unlimited and Oilfield Safety are found to have been Hansen's employers at the time of the injury, this Court must determine which of them is liable.

A. The Appropriate Standard

The initial step in resolving the employment question is to ascertain the standard to be applied in deciding whether an individual is an employee. . . .

Both Oilfield Safety and Harman Unlimited urge that this Court adopt the "right to control" test. They contend that only if a party has the right to control the details of another's work does an employee-employer relationship exist. Two other courts that have considered this issue have adopted this standard. *Cardillo v. Mockabee,* 102 F.2d 620 (D.C.Cir.1939); *Yellow Cab Co. v. Magruder,* 49 F.Supp. 605 (D.Md. 1943), *affirmed* 141 F.2d 324 (4th Cir.1944). Both the ALJ and the Board used the "relative nature of the work" test. That test requires examining the nature of a claimant's work and the relation of that work to an employer's regular business. In deciding which test should be incorporated into LHWCA jurisprudence, this Court must examine the background and policies underlying the two standards. The test that best promotes the purposes and policies of the LHWCA should be used in determining the existence of an employer-employee relationship.

The "right to control" test comes from common law. It serves one main function in common law: to limit the scope of an employer's vicarious tort liability. 1C A. Larson, *Workmen's Compensation Law* § 43.42 (1980). Within the context of *respondeat superior* the focus on control is proper, because only if an employer controlled the details of an employee's work should the employer be liable for the employee's negligence. The principles underlying worker's compensation, however, are completely different from those that animate *respondeat superior.*

> The theory of compensation legislation is that the cost of all industrial accidents should be borne by the consumer as part of the cost of the product. It follows that any worker whose services form a regular and continuing part of the cost of that product, and whose method of operation is not such an independent business that it forms in itself a separate route through which his own cost of industrial accidents can be channeled, is within the presumptive area of intended protection.

Id. at § 43.51. In short, the basic purpose for which the employee-employer relationship is used in compensation law is completely different from the basic purpose for which that relationship is used in the doctrine of *respondeat superior*. In the area of worker's compensation, the employee-employer test should be inclusive. . . .

The test that best suits the principles of the LHWCA is the one applied by the ALJ and the Board, the relative nature of the work test. In determining the existence of an employee-employer relationship pursuant to this test, one examines the nature of the claimant's work in relation to the regular business of the employer. This examination must focus on two distinct areas: the nature of the claimant's work and the relation of that work to the alleged employer's regular business. In evaluating the character of a claimant's work, a court should focus on various factors, including the skill required to do the work, the degree to which the work constitutes a separate calling or enterprise, and the extent to which the work might be expected to carry its own accident burden. *Id.* at § 43.52. In analyzing the relationship of the claimant's work to the employer's business the factors to be examined include, among others, whether the claimant's work is a regular part of the employer's regular work, whether the claimant's work is continuous or intermittent, and whether the duration of claimant's work is sufficient to amount to the hiring of continuing services as distinguished from the contracting for the completion of a particular job. *Id.*

. . .

This is not to say that the various factors composing the right to control test are irrelevant. The factors should be used in determining the existence of an employee-employer relationship. Indeed, in many cases, the traditional right to control test will produce a result that is appropriate in the LHWCA context. There will be cases, however, where the right to control test simply produces an inappropriate conclusion. Given the nature of the LHWCA and workers' compensation statutes in general, this Court holds that the proper test to be used in determining whether an employer-employee relationship exists is the relative nature of the work test.

B. The Employment Relationship with Oilfield Services

The evidence offered at the hearing before the ALJ established that Hansen was a one-half owner of Oilfield Services. His job entailed obtaining contracts and performing safety inspections on behalf of Oilfield Safety. On October 30, 1976, Hansen went offshore to an Amoco Production oilfield complex to conduct safety inspections. On that trip he wore coveralls bearing the Oilfield Safety emblem. The helicopter pilot responsible for transporting Hansen to the offshore rigs logged him in as an employee of Oilfield Safety. On November 2, the date of the accident, Michael Brien, the other half-owner of Oilfield Safety, went to the hospital and admitted Hansen as an employee of Oilfield Safety. On December 6, 1976, over one month after the injury, Oilfield Safety paid Hansen $550 for salary. Finally, and perhaps most importantly, Hansen testified at the hearing that, on the date of his injury, he was doing safety inspection work for Oilfield Safety.

. . .

C. The Employment Relationship with Harman Unlimited

Billy Harman was vice president and chief executive officer of Harman Unlimited, a firm whose primary business was furnishing welding and sandblasting services. The record indicates that in early October 1976, Billy Harman contacted Clarence Hansen and sought help from Hansen in obtaining new business for Harman Unlimited. Hansen agreed to do what he could for Harman Unlimited. In return, Billy Harman agreed to pay Hansen an unspecified commission for any new work that Hansen brought into the office. During the month of October Hansen contacted several companies on behalf of Harman Unlimited and was instrumental in getting Harman Unlimited included on Amoco Production's approved list of contractors. When Hansen went offshore in late October to conduct the safety inspections on the Amoco Production oil rigs, he continued to promote Harman Unlimited. While on the offshore platforms he distributed Harman Unlimited cards and literature. His efforts on behalf of Harman Unlimited were apparently quite extensive, since Amoco Production's platform foreman listed Hansen as an employee of Harman Unlimited on the meal and bunk rosters, in the production reports, and on the accident report.

. . .

Once again, there is conflicting evidence about the existence of an employment relationship. Indeed, an analysis of the relationship under the common-law right to control test might lead to the conclusion that Hansen was not an employee of Harman Unlimited. An examination of the relationship pursuant to the relative nature of the work test, however, convinces us that the ALJ and Benefits Review Board did not err in holding that Hansen was a Harman Unlimited employee. In October 1976 Harman Unlimited was in dire financial straights. Billy Harman, the executive officer, turned to Clarence Hansen, an individual he knew would be able to obtain business for Harman Unlimited. He asked Clarence Hansen to use his contacts in the oil industry to promote Harman Unlimited and attract new customers. The nature of such a job virtually prohibits a supervisor from controlling the details of the work. That does not mean, however, that there should not be an employment relationship for the purposes of the LHWCA. Promotional activities were certainly a regular part of Harman Unlimited's business and had to be continuous in nature in order to ensure financial success. Further, this Court is unwilling to characterize Hansen's salesmanship as a separate calling typically expected to carry its own accident burden. There is substantial evidence to support the finding that the nature of Clarence Hansen's work in relation to the regular business of Harman Unlimited made him an employee.

D. Liability

There is substantial evidence to support the finding that Hansen was an employee of both Oilfield Safety and Harman Unlimited. . . . We affirm the order of the Benefits Review Board holding Oilfield Safety and Harman Unlimited jointly and severally liable for compensation benefits.

. . .

REFERENCES

Employment relation:

Stover Bedding Co. v. Industrial Commission, 99 Utah 423, 107 P.2d 1027 (1940) (salesman traveling in own car was not "employee" under workers' compensation law; dissent urging opposite result either by use of "independent calling" test or by applying "loss-shifting" criterion).

Luby v. Industrial Commission, 82 Ill.2d 353, 45 Ill.Dec. 88, 412 N.E.2d 439 (1980) (ice cream vendor who used pedal-cart provided by supplier was employee for workers' compensation).

Arthur Larson, Workmen's Compensation §§ 43–56 (1980 & supp.). A comprehensive treatment of relations covered.

Relation to employment:

Applied Plastics, Inc. v. Labor & Industrial Review Commission, 121 Wis.2d 271, 359 N.W.2d 168 (Ct.App.1984) (supervisor who was murdered by employee to whom he gave a ride to work was injured "in the course of employment").

Gaines v. Monsanto Co., 655 S.W.2d 568 (Mo.App.1983) (employee who was murdered in her apartment by fellow employee who learned her address through his service as mail clerk was not injured "in the course of employment").

College athletes as employees:

Note, The Status of the College Scholarship Athlete—Employee or Student? 13 Capital U.L.Rev. 87 (1983).

Note, Workers' Compensation and College Athletics: Should Universities be Responsible for Athletes Who Incur Serious Injuries? 10 J.College & Univ.L. 197 (1983).

UNITED STATES v. SILK

United States Supreme Court, 1947.
331 U.S. 704, 67 S.Ct. 1463, 91 L.Ed. 1757.
Comments, 16 Geo.Wash.L.Rev. 586, 32 Minn.L.Rev. 414.

MR. JUSTICE REED delivered the opinion of the Court.

We consider together the above two cases. Both involve suits to recover sums exacted from businesses by the Commissioner of Internal Revenue as employment taxes on employers under the Social Security Act. In both instances the taxes were collected on assessments made administratively by the Commissioner because he concluded the persons here involved were employees of the taxpayers. Both cases turn on a determination as to whether the workers involved were employees under that Act or whether they were independent contractors. . . . Varying standards have been applied in the federal courts [citing cases].

Respondent in No. 312, Albert Silk, doing business as the Albert Silk Coal Co., sued the United States, petitioner, to recover taxes alleged to have been illegally assessed and collected from respondent for the years 1936 through 1939 under the Social Security Act. The taxes were levied on respondent as an employer of certain workmen some of whom were engaged in unloading railway coal cars and the others in making retail deliveries of coal by truck.

Respondent sells coal at retail in the city of Topeka, Kansas. His coal-yard consists of two buildings, one for an office and the other a gathering place for workers, railroad tracks upon which carloads of coal are delivered by the railroad, and bins for the different types of coal. Respondent pays those who work as unloaders an agreed price per ton to unload coal from the railroad cars. These men come to the yard when and as they please and are assigned a car to unload and a place to put the coal. They furnish their own tools, work when they wish and work for others at will. One of these unloaders testified that he worked as regularly "as a man has to when he has to eat" but there was also testimony that some of the unloaders were floaters who came to the yard only intermittently.

Respondent owns no trucks himself but contracts with workers who own their own trucks to deliver coal at a uniform price per ton. This is paid to the trucker by the respondent out of the price he receives for the coal from the customer. When an order for coal is taken in the company office, a bell is rung which rings in the building used by the truckers. The truckers have voluntarily adopted a call list upon which their names come up in turn, and the top man on the list has an opportunity to deliver the coal ordered. The truckers are not instructed how to do their jobs, but are merely given a ticket telling them where the coal is to be delivered and whether the charge is to be collected or not. Any damage caused by them is paid for by the company. The District Court found that the truckers could and often did refuse to make a delivery without penalty. Further, the court found that the truckers may come and go as they please and frequently did leave the premises without permission. They may and did haul for others when they pleased. They pay all the expenses of operating their trucks, and furnish extra help necessary to the delivery of the coal and all equipment except the yard storage bins. No record is kept of their time. They are paid after each trip, at the end of the day or at the end of the week, as they request.

The Collector ruled that the unloaders and truckers were employees of the respondent during the years 1936 through 1939 within the meaning of the Social Security Act and he accordingly assessed additional taxes under Titles VIII and IX of the Social Security Act and Subchapters A and C of Chapter 9 of the Internal Revenue Code. Respondent filed a claim for a refund which was denied. He then brought this action. Both the District Court and the Circuit Court of Appeals [1] thought that the truckers and unloaders were independent contractors and allowed the recovery.

1. 155 F.2d 356.

Respondent in No. 673, Greyvan Lines, Inc., a common carrier by motor truck, sued the petitioner, a Collector of Internal Revenue, to recover employment taxes alleged to have been illegally assessed and collected from it under similar provisions of the Social Security Act involved in Silk's case for the years or parts of years 1937 through the first quarter of 1942. From a holding for the respondent in the District Court petitioner appealed. The Circuit Court of Appeals affirmed. The chief question in this case is whether truckmen who perform the actual service of carrying the goods shipped by the public are employees of the respondent. Both the District Court and the Circuit Court of Appeals [2] thought that the truckmen were independent contractors.

The respondent operates its trucking business under a permit issued by the Interstate Commerce Commission under the "grandfather clause" of the Motor Carrier Act, 49 U.S.C.A. section 301 et seq., 32 M.C.C. 719, 723. It operated throughout thirty-eight states and parts of Canada, carrying largely household furniture. While its principal office is in Chicago, it maintains agencies to solicit business in many of the larger cities of the areas it serves, from which it contracts to move goods. As early as 1930, before the passage of the Social Security Act, the respondent adopted the system of relations with the truckmen here concerned, which gives rise to the present issue. The system was based on contracts with the truckmen under which the truckmen were required to haul exclusively for the respondent and to furnish their own trucks and all equipment and labor necessary to pick up, handle and deliver shipments, to pay all expenses of operation, to furnish all fire, theft, and collision insurance which the respondent might specify, to pay for all loss or damage to shipments and to indemnify the company for any loss caused it by the acts of the truckmen, their servants and employees, to paint the designation "Greyvan Lines" on their trucks, to collect all money due the company from shippers or consignees, and to turn in such moneys at the office to which they report after delivering a shipment, to post bonds with the company in the amount of $1,000 and cash deposits of $250 pending final settlement of accounts, to personally drive their trucks at all times or be present on the truck when a competent relief driver was driving (except in emergencies, when a substitute might be employed with the approval of the company), and to follow all rules, regulations, and instructions of the company. All contracts or bills of lading for the shipment of goods were to be between the respondent and the shipper. The company's instructions covered directions to the truckmen as to where and when to load freight. If freight was tendered the truckmen, they were under obligation to notify the company so that it could complete the contract for shipment in its own name. As remuneration, the truckmen were to receive from the company a percentage of the tariff charged by the company varying between 50 and 52% and a bonus up to 3% for satisfactory performance of the service. The contract was terminable at any time by either party. These truckmen were required to take a

2. 156 F.2d 412.

short course of instruction in the company's methods of doing business before carrying out their contractual obligations to haul. The company maintained a staff of dispatchers who issued orders for the truckmen's movements, although not the routes to be used, and to which the truckmen, at intervals, reported their positions. Cargo insurance was carried by the company. All permits, certificates and franchises "necessary to the operation of the vehicle in the service of the company as a motor carrier under any Federal or State Law" were to be obtained at the company's expense.

. . .

The problem of differentiating between an employee and an independent contractor or between an agent and an independent contractor has given difficulty through the years before social legislation multiplied its importance. When the matter arose in the administration of the National Labor Relations Act, 29 U.S.C.A. section 151 et seq., we pointed out that the legal standards to fix responsibility for acts of servants, employees or agents had not been reduced to such certainty that it could be said there was "some simple, uniform and easily applicable test." The word "employee," we said, was not there used as a word of art, and its content in its context was a federal problem to be construed " 'in the light of the mischief to be corrected and the end to be attained.' " We concluded that, since that end was the elimination of labor disputes and industrial strife, "employees" included workers who were such as a matter of economic reality. The aim of the Act was to remedy the inequality of bargaining power in controversies over wages, hours and working conditions. We rejected the test of the " 'technical concepts pertinent to an employer's legal responsibility to third persons for the acts of his servants.' " This is often referred to as power of control, whether exercised or not, over the manner of performing service to the industry. Restatement of the Law, Agency, section 220. We approved the statement of the National Labor Relations Board that " 'the primary consideration in the determination of the applicability of the statutory definition is whether effectuation of the declared policy and purposes of the Act comprehend securing to the individual the rights guaranteed and protection afforded by the Act.' " National Labor Relations Board v. Hearst Publications, 322 U.S. 111, 120, 123, 124, 128, 131, 64 S.Ct. 851, 855, 856, 857, 859, 860, 88 L.Ed. 1170.

Application of the social security legislation should follow the same rule that we applied to the National Labor Relations Act in the Hearst case. This, of course, does not leave courts free to determine the employer-employee relationship without regard to the provisions of the Act. The taxpayer must be an "employer" and the man who receives wages an "employee." There is no indication that Congress intended to change normal business relationships through which one business organization obtained the services of another to perform a portion of production or distribution. Few businesses are so completely integrated that they can themselves produce the raw material, manufacture and distribute the finished product to the ultimate consumer without assistance from independent contractors. The Social Security Act was drawn with this industrial situation as a part of the surroundings in which it was to be enforced. Where a part of an industrial process is in the hands of independent contractors, they are the ones who should pay the social security taxes. . . .

Giving full consideration to the concurrence of the two lower courts in a contrary result, we cannot agree that the unloaders in the Silk case were independent contractors. [Citations omitted.] They provided only picks and shovels. They had no opportunity to gain or lose except from the work of their hands and these simple tools. That the unloaders did not work regularly is not significant. They did work in the course of the employer's trade or business. This brings them under the coverage of the Act. [Citations omitted.] They are of the group that the Social Security Act was intended to aid. Silk was in a position to exercise all necessary supervision over their simple tasks. Unloaders have often been held to be employees in tort cases. [Citations omitted.]

There are cases, too, where driver-owners of trucks or wagons have been held employees [citations omitted] in accident suits at tort or under workmen's compensation laws. But we agree with the decisions below in Silk and Greyvan that where the arrangements leave the driver-owners so much responsibility for investment and management as here, they must be held to be independent contractors. [Citations omitted.] These driver-owners are small businessmen. They own their own trucks. They hire their own helpers. In one instance they haul for a single business, in the other for any customer. The distinction, though important, is not controlling. It is the total situation, including the risk undertaken, the control exercised, the opportunity for profit from sound management, that marks these driver-owners as independent contractors.

No. 312, United States v. Silk, is affirmed in part and reversed in part.

No. 673, Harrison v. Greyvan Lines, Inc., is affirmed.

MR. JUSTICE BLACK, MR. JUSTICE DOUGLAS and MR. JUSTICE MURPHY are of the view that the applicable principles of law, stated by the Court and with which they agree, require reversal of both judgments in their entirety.

[Mr. Justice Rutledge dissented in a separate opinion.]

UNITED STATES v. W.M. WEBB, INC.
United States Supreme Court, 1969.
397 U.S. 179, 90 S.Ct. 850, 25 L.Ed.2d 207.

MR. JUSTICE HARLAN delivered the opinion of the Court.

The respondents in this case, which was consolidated below, own boats that are used in commercial fishing in the Atlantic Ocean and the Gulf of Mexico. Their fishing is carried out through contractual arrangements, shaped by established custom, with boat captains, who man the boats and manage their day-to-day operation. The question before the Court is whether the captains and crewmen of the boats are the "employees" of the respondents within the provisions of the Federal Insurance Contributions Act (FICA) and the Federal Unemployment Tax Act (FUTA), which impose taxes on employers to finance government benefits for employees.

I

During the taxable periods involved here, the respondents' vessels were engaged in fishing for menhaden, a nonedible fish that is processed and used for various industrial purposes. The owner of each vessel equipped the vessel and secured the services of an experienced fisherman to be captain. The captain then assembled a crew. The captain customarily served on the same vessel for a full season, and occasionally for several consecutive seasons, although the oral arrangements between owners and captains permitted either to terminate the relationship at the end of any fishing trip. The fishing trips lasted from one to several days.

The vessels were operated from docking facilities owned by fish-processing plants, and discharged their catch at these plants upon the completion of each trip. The plants paid respondents for the fish according to the volume of the catch, and respondents paid the captains and crews on the same basis, following terms that had been negotiated in advance. Neither captains nor crews were guaranteed any earnings if they failed to catch fish. While respondents determined the plant to which the vessels would report and generally where and when the fishing would take place, the captains managed the details of the operation of the boats and the manner of fishing.

Respondents filed tax returns as employers under the FICA and the FUTA, and paid the employer's share of the taxes due on the earnings of the captains and crews. After making the appropriate claims for refunds, they sued for refunds in the District Court for the Eastern District of Louisiana. The District Court, sitting without a jury, determined after trial that the captains and crews were not respondents' employees for the purposes of these tax statutes. The trial court noted that both the FICA and the FUTA define "employee" as any individual who has employee status under "the usual common law rules" applicable to a determination of the master-servant relationship. It found "without merit" the Government's contention "that the common-law governing the relationship of the taxpayer and the fishermen in pursuing fishing ventures in the Gulf of Mexico and the Atlantic Ocean is the general maritime law." 271 F.Supp. 249, 257 (1967). The court found further that the degree of control exercised by respondents over these fishing activities was not sufficient, under the common-law standards governing land-based occupations, to create the relationship of employer and employee between respondents and the captains and crews. Respondents were thus held entitled to their refunds.

On appeal, the Court of Appeals for the Fifth Circuit affirmed. It reviewed the facts and observed that "it is clear that under maritime law the captain is the agent of the owner . . . and the crew hands are employees," and that "[i]f we were free to apply maritime law as a test of the employer-employee relationship, we would reverse the decision of the district court." 402 F.2d 956, 959 (1968).[4] However, the Court of Appeals agreed with the District Court that the statutes' prescription of "common law rules" barred application of maritime standards.

This conclusion conflicts with the approach of the Court of Claims in Cape Shore Fish Co. v. United States, 165 Ct.Cl. 630, 330 F.2d 961 (1964). In that decision the court found scallop fishermen, operating under arrangements similar to those here, to be employees of the shipowner for the purposes of these statutes. It reached this conclusion by applying to the facts the standards of maritime law. We granted certiorari in this case, 394 U.S. 996 (1969), to resolve this conflict, and to clarify the application to maritime workers of these important federal statutes.

II

The parties agree that both the FICA and the FUTA impose taxes on employers measured by the compensation paid to employees, and that in terms of this case the two statutes define "employee" identically. In the FICA "employee" is defined to include "any individual who, under the usual common law rules applicable in determining the employer-employee relationship, has the status of an employee," and the language of the FUTA is to the same effect.[5] These definitions were not included in the original Social Security Act as it was adopted in 1935, which defined "employee" merely by specifying that it "includes an officer of a corporation," [6] but were added by amendment in 1948. We must consider the events that prompted the amendment.

4. We are not called upon to, and do not, intimate any view on the correctness of the Court of Appeals' statement on this score.

5. The definitions provide:

"For purposes of [the FICA], the term 'employee' means—(1) any officer of a corporation; or (2) any individual who, under the usual common law rules applicable in determining the employer-employee relationship, has the status of an employee; or (3) [any member of several specific occupations, not including fishing, when certain conditions are satisfied]." 26 U.S.C. § 3121(d).

"For purposes of [the FUTA], the term 'employee' includes an officer of a corporation, but such term does not include— (1) any individual who, under the usual common law rules applicable in determining the employer-employee relationship, has the status of an independent contractor, or (2) any individual (except an officer of a corporation) who is not an employee under such common law rules." 26 U.S.C. § 3306(i).

6. Social Security Act § 1101(a)(6), 49 Stat. 647. The language of § 1101(a)(6) was carried over to §§ 1426(c) and 1607(h) of the Internal Revenue Code of 1939, the predecessors of present §§ 3121(d) and 3306(i) of Title 26, respectively. See 53 Stat. 178, 188.

In 1935 the draftsmen of the Social Security Act apparently thought it unnecessary to elucidate the meaning of "employee" because they assumed that the term, as it was applied to varying factual situations, would be given the "usual" meaning it bore at common law. See S.Rep. No. 1255, 80th Cong., 2d Sess., 3–4 (1948). However, over the years of applying the Act to a myriad of work relationships, the lower federal courts developed somewhat varying approaches, certain courts relying more heavily on common-law precedents and others attempting to discern a special meaning for the term from the purposes of the legislation. In addition, the courts tended to look to local precedents to determine the common-law standards, producing different results for similar factual situations in various parts of the country. This divergence of views led this Court in 1947, to render two decisions in an attempt to clarify the governing standards. United States v. Silk, 331 U.S. 704; Bartels v. Birmingham, 332 U.S. 126.

In *Silk*, the Court upheld the lower courts' determination that certain truck drivers were, under the circumstances, independent contractors rather than employees, but it upset a similar ruling with respect to a group of men who unloaded coal from railroad cars. In *Bartels* the Court, reversing the Court of Appeals, held that the members of certain dance bands were not employees of the owners of the dance halls at which they were engaged, despite contractual provisions characterizing them as employees. While the Court's opinions in these cases stressed many of the factors that had been important in common-law determinations of employee status, they also contained language that could be read to detach the question of statutory coverage from the common-law tests. The Court stated, in *Bartels*, that "in the application of social legislation employees are those who as a matter of economic reality are dependent upon the business to which they render service." 332 U.S., at 130.

Acting upon this language, the executive agencies set about replacing their original regulation, which had defined the employment relation in terms of the incidents of employment at common law, with a new regulation that would embody the test of "economic reality." However, the proposed new regulation never took effect. Within two months of its announcement, a resolution was introduced in both the House of Representatives and the Senate calling for "a reassertion of congressional intent regarding the application of the act." S.Rep. No. 1255, supra, at 7. This resolution, which was finally passed over the President's veto, added to the statutes the present definitions of "employee."

The report of the Senate Finance Committee on the resolution makes clear a congressional purpose to disapprove the proposed regulation and to reaffirm that determinations of employee status were to be based on the traditional legal tests. The Committee seems to have thought that the *Silk* and *Bartels* decisions had applied traditional common-law standards, despite the language in the opinions suggesting a less constrictive approach. However, noting that the Treasury Department claimed support in those decisions for its contemplated new departure, the Committee declared: "But if it be contended that the Supreme Court has invented new law for determining an 'employee' under the social-security system in these cases, then the purpose of this resolution is to reestablish the usual common-law rules, realistically applied." Id., at 2.

The causes of congressional dissatisfaction with the proposed regulation were twofold. As a fiscal matter, the Committee cited testimony that the new regulation would extend social security benefits to between 500,000 and 750,000 new workers, who had not been covered previously and had not contributed to the trust fund from which benefits would be paid, thus endangering the integrity of the fund. More generally, the Committee was fearful of the uncertainty that would be created by the new regulation, and the discretion it would give to the executive agencies in determining the applicability of the statutes. The report stated:

> "In a word, by unbounded and shifting criteria, [the proposed regulation] would confer in those administering the Social Security Act full discretion to include, or to exclude, from the coverage of the act any person whom they might decide to be, or might decide not to be, an 'employee'; and like discretion to fasten tax liabilities and the administrative duties and costs of compliance with the act upon any person whom they might decide to be an 'employer.'

> . . .

> "The *proposed* regulation discards the common-law rules for distinguishing the employer-employee relationship distilled from many decisions by many courts out of many insights of real situations, for a new rule of nebulous character.

> "Under the *proposed* regulation an 'employee' is 'an individual in a service relationship who is dependent as a matter of economic reality upon the business to which he renders service and not upon his own business as an independent contractor.'

> "The rule, obviously, will not serve to make the necessary distinctions. Who, in this whole world engaged in any sort of service relationship, is not dependent as a matter of economic reality on some other person? . . .

> . . .

> "[T]he *proposed* regulation concerns itself mainly, as was stated to your committee by a witness at the hearings: '. . . with making it abundantly clear that on virtually no state of facts may anyone be certain whether or not he has a tax liability until the Commissioner has made up his mind about it.'" Id., at 7, 10, 11.

The Committee stated that, in contrast to the proposed regulation, whose "basic principle . . . is a dimensionless and amorphous abstraction," the existing regulation was "not devoid of uncertainty, but its basis is in established standards of law which frame and limit its application." Id., at 12. The conclusions stated in the House Report were similar. H.R.Rep. No. 1319, 80th Cong., 2d Sess. (1948). By the resolution, Congress unequivocally tied the coverage of these tax provisions to the body of decisional law defining the employer-employee relationship in various occupations.

In none of the discussions of the 1948 resolution was there any discussion of maritime employees. The respondents argue that, by failing to make specific provision for the application of maritime law to seagoing occupations, Congress impliedly decreed that those occupations should be gauged by the standards of the "common law" applicable to land-based activities. They rely in part on the fact that the phrase "common law" is sometimes used in contradistinction to the "maritime law" traditionally applied in courts of admiralty, and they also point to the fact that the Senate Report stressed the degree of the employer's control over the employee's work as central to the Committee's understanding of the common-law tests of employment. The Senate Report quoted with approval the then-existing regulation, substantially identical to the one now in effect, which stated:

> "Every individual is an employee if the relationship between him and the person for whom he performs services is the legal relationship of employer and employee.

> "Generally such relationship exists when the person for whom services are performed has the right to control and direct the individual who performs the services, not only as to the result to be accomplished by the work but also as to the details and means by which that result is accomplished. That is, an employee is subject to the will and control of the employer not only as to what shall be done but how it shall be done." S.Rep. No. 1255, supra, at 3.

Respondents argue that this language indicates a congressional intent that, where the maritime nature of a vocation makes impracticable the degree of control generally exercised by land-based employers over their employees, the land-based standards must nevertheless be applied, with the result that no "employment" exists for the purposes of those statutes.

III

We do not think Congress intended the anomalous result of having maritime activities subject to standards, for social security tax purposes, other than those that are relevant to seafaring enterprises. Such a result is not necessary to accomplish the dual concerns underlying the 1948 amendment. Application of maritime standards to determine the status of members of fishing ventures will not open brand new areas of social security coverage. To the contrary, the employee status of captains and crewmen engaged in fishing operations similar to these is supported by a Treasury Department interpretation, applying maritime standards, that was issued in 1940, immediately after maritime employees were first brought within the coverage of the Social Security Act by amendment in 1939. S.S.T. 387, 1940–1 Cum.Bull. 192; see Social Security Act Amendments of 1939, §§ 606, 614, 53 Stat. 1383, 1392, as amended, 26 U.S.C. §§ 3121(b), 3306(c). This ruling, which the Social Security Administration has accepted for purposes of paying benefits to claimants, had existed for eight years before Congress added the present definitions of "employee" to the statutes. It was not mentioned at the time of the 1948 amendment. Since the ruling represented the accepted view of both the taxing and paying agencies, Congress could have had no concern that payment of benefits to maritime employees would constitute an uncompensated drain on the social security fund.[15]

More important, the chief concern behind the 1948 amendment— avoiding the uncertainty of the proposed "economic reality" test—is wholly satisfied if seafaring work relationships are tested against the standards of maritime, rather than land-based, decisional law. Congress' fearfulness of the "nebulous" nature of the proposed regulation indicates that it used the phrase "usual common law rules" in a generic sense, to mean the standards developed by the courts through years of adjudication, rather than in a technical sense to mean those standards developed by "common law" courts as opposed to courts of admiralty. Maritime law, the common law of seafaring men, provides an established network of rules and distinctions that are practically suited to the necessities of the sea, just as land-based decisional law provides a body of rules adapted to the various forms of domestic employment. The goal of minimizing uncertainty can be accomplished, in the maritime field, by resort to the "usual" rules of maritime jurisprudence.[16]

This conclusion is not weakened by the emphasis given, both in the Senate Report and in the regulation, to the factor of control. Control is probably the most important factor under maritime law,[17] just as it is

---

15. Subsequent amendments to the social security laws make it now even clearer that classification of some maritime workers as employees will not threaten the social security fund. The Social Security Act Amendments of 1950 extended benefits coverage to the self-employed for the first time, 64 Stat. 502, 540; see H.R.Rep. No. 1300, 81st Cong., 1st Sess., 9–10 (1949). Benefits for the self-employed are financed by taxes paid by them under the Self-Employment Contributions Act, 26 U.S.C. § 1401 et seq.; see H.R.Rep. No. 1300, supra, at 135–145; S.Rep. No. 1669, 81st Cong., 2d Sess., 153–166 (1950). Therefore, the captains and crewmen are eligible for social security benefits whether they are considered employees or self-employed.

16. A conclusion that maritime standards could not be applied might frustrate Congress' evident expectation that the FICA and FUTA legislation would apply to seamen, and specifically to fishermen. As

noted above, the 1939 amendments extended the statutes to cover maritime employees. Additionally, 26 U.S.C. § 3121(b)(4) provides an exemption for service by aliens on foreign vessels, and § 3306(c)(17) exempts fishermen on vessels that do not exceed 10 tons in displacement. These provisions raise the inference that fishermen on larger vessels were expected to be covered, under the general "common law rules" provision. However, if shipowners were relieved of the employers' tax liabilities unless their relationship with the captains and crews were of the sort that would constitute an employer-employee relationship in a land-based activity, application of the statutes to fishermen might be seriously limited.

17. See, e.g., Cape Shore Fish Co. v. United States, 165 Ct.Cl. 630, 637–641, 330 F.2d 961, 965–968 (1964); G. Gilmore & C. Black, The Law of Admiralty § 4–21 (1957).

under the tests of land-based employment. It may be true that, in most maritime relationships, the workers enjoy discretion that is unusually broad if measured by land-based standards—a discretion dictated by the seafaring nature of the activity. However, except where there is nearly total relinquishment of control through a bareboat, or demise, charter the owner may nevertheless be considered, under maritime law, to have sufficient control to be charged with the duties of an employer. See e.g., The Norland, 101 F.2d 967 (C.A.9th Cir.1939); G. Gilmore & C. Black, The Law of Admiralty § 4–23 (1957). Congress' stress on the importance of control reflects the primacy of that factor in the rules governing the most common, land-based vocations,[18] which were certainly foremost in the congressional mind at the time of the 1948 amendment. It does not preclude the application, in different areas, of decisional rules that vary in the precise degree of control that is required. Cf. Deecy Products Co. v. Welch, 124 F.2d 592, 598–599 (C.A.1st Cir.1941); McGuire v. United States, 349 F.2d 644 (C.A.9th Cir. 1965).[19]

The guidelines in the regulation also allow for such flexibility, as is attested by the existence, for nearly 30 years, of the Treasury ruling, S.S.T. 387, confirming the employee status of fishermen such as those involved here. Now, as in 1948, the regulation proceeds, after the language already quoted, to elaborate some of the factors other than control that may be important:

> "The right to discharge is also an important factor indicating that the person possessing that right is an employer. Other factors characteristic of an employer, but not necessarily present in every case, are the furnishing of tools and the furnishing of a place to work, to the individual who performs the services." 26 CFR § 31.3121(d)–1(c)(2).

It is clear that this brief sketch of relevant factors cannot be intended to provide a workable test, complete in itself, displacing the complex of common-law rules Congress so carefully tried to preserve. Rather, the regulation provides a summary of the principles of the common law, intended as an initial guide for the determination, required by the first sentence of the regulation, whether a relationship "is the legal relation-

---

18. See, e.g., Radio City Music Hall Corp. v. United States, 135 F.2d 715, 717–718 (C.A.2d Cir.1943).

19. See H.R.Rep. No. 2168, supra, n. 13, at 9–10:

"Ample flexibility is possible under [the common-law] rule to accommodate peculiar or unusual employment relationships so frequently found in our complex economic system.

. . .

"The common-law concept of master and servant, of course, is no more fixed and immutable than the common law

itself. Hence it will produce in practice varying results under varying circumstances and in different jurisdictions. But such variations will not offend the common-law rule itself. . . .

". . . There is nothing to fear from differences in the application of the common-law tests, but there is much to fear from the abandonment of recognized common-law principles in resolving such questions of fact. Such abandonment would simply amount to reliance upon no recognized body of legal principles."

ship of employer and employee." The thrust of both statute and regulation is that the standards that are to govern in any field are those that the courts customarily apply to define this "legal relationship."

We conclude that the Court of Appeals erred in declining to judge the status of the captains and crewmen against the standards of maritime law. Accordingly, the judgment is reversed, and the case is remanded to that court for proceedings consistent with this opinion.

It is so ordered. [1]

EQUAL EMPLOYMENT OPPORTUNITY COMMISSION v. ZIPPO MANUFACTURING CO.

United States Court of Appeals, Third Circuit, 1983.
713 F.2d 32.

A. LEON HIGGINBOTHAM, JR., CIRCUIT JUDGE.

J. Gordon Matheny and the Equal Employment Opportunity Commission ("EEOC"), on behalf of Jack A. Schelling, Arthur H. Schulte and Raymond J. Weinberg, appeal the district court's order granting Zippo Manufacturing Company's ("Zippo") summary judgment motion. Appellants claim that Zippo violated the Age Discrimination in Employment Act ("ADEA"), 29 U.S.C. § 623(a)(1), because it terminated them as District Managers ("DM") when they turned 65. The ADEA only covers employees. The district court found the appellant DMs to be independent contractors, not employees, outside the purview of ADEA. Thus, the critical issue raised by this appeal is whether the district court erred in its determination that DMs under contract with Zippo were independent contractors who are not covered by ADEA rather than employees within the meaning of ADEA. . . .

. . .

Zippo exercises virtually no control over the DMs in their sale of Zippo products. Retaining only experienced salespersons, Zippo has no need to train or to direct DMs about how to sell its products. DMs set their own working hours and days as well as vacation time without consultation with or accountability to Zippo. Moreover, DMs may freely operate under the business form of their choice whether it be a sole proprietorship, as most DMs are, a partnership or a corporation. They may hire employees without regard to Zippo. DMs provide and finance their own work facilities, such as office space, office furniture, secretarial assistance, telephone and automobile. Zippo does, however, offer to and furnishes DMs with Zippo stationery, business cards, order blanks and samples, but DMs are not required to use these materials.

The only significant accountability DMs provide to Zippo involves their volume of sales. Zippo's decision to renew a DM's contract

1. On remand, the district court was ordered to dismiss the taxpayers' complaints. United States v. W.M. Webb, Inc., 424 F.2d 1070 (1970).

depends upon the DM maintaining a volume of sales that Zippo considers satisfactory.

Appellants Schelling, Schultz, Weinberg and Matheny served as Zippo DMs for periods ranging from ten to over twenty years before being terminated pursuant to a clause contained in all DM agreements calling for the termination of an agreement when a DM reaches the age of 65. Zippo terminated appellants on thirty days written notice shortly after they turned 65.

. . .

Although the Age Discrimination in Employment Act has such a laudable title that might induce laymen to infer that the statute was designed to prevent *all* age discrimination against those who work for a living, its congressional purpose was far less extensive since it prohibits only some types of age discrimination. Although some people who discriminate against the aged might offend an increasingly shared social value which condemns such discrimination, such discrimination would not thereby violate any federal law unless it was specifically prohibited by Congress.

In this case, we are concerned with 29 U.S.C. § 623(a)(1) of ADEA which provides:

(a) It shall be unlawful for an employer—

(1) to fail or refuse to hire or to discharge any individual or otherwise discriminate against any individual with respect to his compensation, terms, conditions, or privileges of employment, because of such individual's age. . . .

In addition to its language, the legislative history of this statute, 1967 U.S.Code Cong. & Ad.News 2214–27, evinces the clear legislative intent to prohibit "age discrimination by employers against employees and applicants for employment." *Levine v. Fairleigh Dickinson University,* 646 F.2d 825, 828 (3d Cir.1981). Therefore, if appellants were not Zippo employees, ADEA is not applicable to their cause and their allegation that Zippo violated ADEA in terminating them because they reached the age of 65 must be rejected.

. . .

Even before courts assess the facts, they must first decide upon the proper method of assessment. Thus, in order to decide whether appellants were Zippo employees, we must first determine how employee status is shown for purposes of ADEA. For this purpose, we are not without some guidance.

Prior to 1947, courts distinguished an employee from an independent contractor by using a common law test of the degree of control over the individual's work performance exercised by the alleged employer over the individual whose status was in dispute. If the alleged employer had the right to determine not only what work should be done but also how it should be done, then the worker was deemed to be an employee. *See United States v. Silk,* 331 U.S. 704, 714 n. 8, 67 S.Ct. 1463, 1468 n. 8, 91 L.Ed. 1757 (1947).

In 1947, however, the United States Supreme Court held that the common law "right to control" test was too narrow for use in deciding employee status for the purposes of far reaching social legislation such as the Social Security Act. *Bartels v. Birmingham,* 332 U.S. 126, 130, 67 S.Ct. 1547, 1549–1550, 91 L.Ed. 1947 (1947). Accordingly, the court enunciated what has come to be known as the "economic realities" test. The Court declared:

> Obviously control is characteristically associated with the employ-er-employee relationship, but in the application of social legislation employees are those who as a matter of economic reality are dependent upon the business to which they render service. In *Silk,* we pointed out that permanency of the relation, the skill required, the investment in the facilities for work, and opportunities for profit or loss from the activities were *also factors* that should enter into judicial determination as to the coverage of the Social Security Act. It is the total situation that controls.

Id. (emphasis added.) The Supreme Court's language and its reliance on *Silk, supra,* suggest that it did not intend to displace control as a factor in determining an individual's status as an employee. . . .

In the wake of these three decisions courts evolved two different standards to determine employee status for purposes of social legisla-tion. The standard used depends upon the legislation involved. The "economic realities" standard is generally used in cases involving the Fair Labor Standards Act ("FLSA"), 29 U.S.C. § 201 *et seq. Donovan v. Sureway Cleaners,* 656 F.2d 1368, 1370 (9th Cir.1981); *Usery v. Pilgrim Equipment Company, Inc.,* 527 F.2d 1308, 1311 (5th Cir.1976), *cert. denied,* 429 U.S. 826, 97 S.Ct. 82, 50 L.Ed.2d 89 (1976). In these cases, it is the "degree of [economic] dependence of alleged employees on the business with which they are connected . . . that indicates employee status." *Usery v. Pilgrim Equipment Company, Inc.,* 527 F.2d at 1311. The courts based their determinations of the individuals' economic dependence upon the factors listed in *Bartels, supra,* and *Silk, supra,* and added others such as the importance of the service to the alleged employer's business. *Donovan v. Sureway Cleaners,* 656 F.2d at 1370.

Other courts have applied a hybrid of the common law "right to control" standard and the "economic realities" standard to determine employee status for purposes of Title VII, 42 U.S.C. § 2000e *et seq. Cobb v. Sun Papers, Inc.,* 673 F.2d 337, 341 (11th Cir.1982); *Unger v. Consolidated Foods Corporation,* 657 F.2d 909, 915 n. 8 (7th Cir.1981); *Spirides v. Reinhardt,* 613 F.2d 826, 831–32 (D.C.Cir.1979). These cases hold that "it is the economic realities of the relationship viewed in light of the common law principles of agency and the right of the employer to control the employee that are determinative." *Cobb v. Sun Papers, Inc.,* 673 F.2d at 341. . . .

Courts have thus refrained from using the broader "economic realities" test in Title VII cases. The reason given for the use of the narrower hybrid standard is

> that there is no statement in the [Civil Rights] Act or legislative history of Title VII comparable to one made by Senator Hugo Black (later Justice Black), during the debates on the Fair Labor Standards Act, that the term 'employee' in the FLSA was given 'the broadest definition that has ever been included in any one act.' (citations omitted.)

Cobb v. Sun Paper, Inc., 673 F.2d at 340. In addition, while expressing the desirability of eliminating discrimination in all business enterprises, the court concluded that Congress had a more limited objective in enacting Title VII, namely, to eliminate discrimination in employment only. *Id.* Finding that "Congress [did not intend] the words of the statute to have anything but their ordinary meaning as commonly understood," *id.,* the court concluded that "the term 'employee' in cases under Title VII is to be construed in light of general common law concepts." *Id.* at 340–41. Consequently, the hybrid "right to control/economic realities" standard is the proper test of employee status for the purposes of Title VII.

What we must decide now is whether the "economic realities" standard used in FLSA cases or the hybrid "right to control/economic realities" standard is the proper test to determine whether an individual is an employee for purposes of ADEA.

The question of which standard of employee status is applicable to ADEA cases is one of first impression. Appellants argue that the proper standard in ADEA cases such as this one is the economic realities standard. They insist that under the economic realities standard they must be deemed employees for ADEA purposes because of their economic dependence upon Zippo. We disagree with both of appellants' contentions.

The Supreme Court has observed that ADEA is a hybrid of both FLSA and Title VII. *Lorillard v. Pons,* 434 U.S. 575, 578, 98 S.Ct. 866, 868–869, 55 L.Ed.2d 40 (1978). The Court found that Congress "intended to incorporate fully the remedies and procedures of the FLSA." *Id.* at 582, 98 S.Ct. at 871. Thus, ADEA's scope for purposes of procedure and remedies is determined by FLSA. However, the substantive "prohibitions of the ADEA were derived *in haec verba* from Title VII." *Id.* at 584, 98 S.Ct. at 872. Therefore, the scope of its substantive prohibition of discrimination in employment is determined by Title VII. The determination of employee status is a question relating to the substantive prohibitions of ADEA and not to its remedies and procedures. Consequently, the hybrid standard that combines the common law "right to control" with the "economic realities" as applied in Title VII cases is the correct standard for determining employee status under ADEA.

. . .

In this case, only the length of time appellants worked as DMs points toward their status of employees. Therefore, even if appellants were required to sell only Zippo products, and even if they were economically dependent on the income they earned as Zippo DMs, these factors are not sufficient to establish that they were employees when balanced against the other factors that tend to establish their status as independent contractors. In any event, we believe that appellants were independent contractors even under the more liberal "economic realities" standard as applied in FLSA cases. . . .

REFERENCES

National Labor Relations Acts:

Yeshiva University Faculty Association v. NLRB, 444 U.S. 672, 100 S.Ct. 856, 63 L.Ed.2d 115 (1980) (faculty of Yeshiva University were not "employees" because of significant participation in university's decision-making).

NLRB v. Sure-Tan, Inc., 583 F.2d 355 (7th Cir.1978) (illegal aliens were "employees" entitled to vote in election of bargaining agent).

Fair Labor Standards Act:

Walling v. General Industries Co., 330 U.S. 545, 67 S.Ct. 883, 91 L.Ed. 1088 (1947) (engineers in charge of power plant subject to Act; 3 justices dissenting).

Weisel v. Singapore Joint Venture, Inc., 602 F.2d 1185 (5th Cir.1979) (parking valet compensated only by tips was covered by FLSA).

Real v. Driscoll Strawberry Associates, 603 F.2d 748 (9th Cir.1979) (farm workers who bought strawberry plants under agreement to resell strawberries produced under conditions regulated by seller may be "employees' for purposes of minimum wage requirements; summary dismissal reversed).

Federal Insurance Contributions Act:

Mednick v. Albert Enterprises, Inc., 508 F.2d 297 (5th Cir.1975) (cardroom operator held to be employee although sole compensation from tips, he hired and fired his own sub-employees, received no benefits from hotel and little supervision, and he filed self-employed tax returns).

Avis Rent A Car Systems, Inc. v. United States, 503 F.2d 423 (2d Cir.1972) (car shuttlers held to be employees although hired only for single job, and they frequently worked for other car companies. The court describes the present statutory definition of employee under the act as serving to codify the result in *Silk.*)

Federal Health Insurance Benefits:

Coddens v. Weinberger, 505 F.2d 765 (10th Cir.1974) (determination of employee or independent contractor for purposes of allowing hospital benefits rests on economic realities, citing *Silk.*)

Under shareholders' liability law:

Addicott v. Upton, 26 Mich.App. 523, 182 N.W.2d 790 (1970) (under statute making shareholder liable for "labor debts" of insolvent corporation, salaried draftsmen could claim; act not confined to hourly manual laborers).

Under consumer protection laws:

Kugler v. Romain, 110 N.J.Super. 470, 266 A.2d 144 (1970) (proprietor of book selling operation through home solicitation was "employer" of salesmen even though their hours and methods were unsupervised, so as to be liable to injunction, restitution and statutory penalties under consumer protection act).

Occupational Safety and Health Act:

Brennan v. Gilles and Cotting, Inc., 504 F.2d 1255 (4th Cir.1974) (court should look to the purposes of the statute and not "technical distinctions of common law" in determining definition of employer and employee).

Employment discrimination:

Armbruster v. Quinn, 711 F.2d 1332 (6th Cir.1983) (in sex discrimination, salesperson characterized in contract as "manufacturer's representative" was "employee"; parent and subsidiary corporations were treated as one for purpose of attaining threshold of fifteen employees; "economic reality" tests applied).

Note, The Test of Employee Status: Economic Realities and Title VII, 26 W. & M.L. Rev. 75 (1984).

Note, Definition of Employee under Title VII: Distinguishing Employees and Independent Contractors, 53 U.Cin.L.Rev. 203 (1984).

Income tax withholding:

Roberts and Sullivan, Recent Developments in the Employee-Independent Contractor Controversy, 8 Rev.Tax.Ind. 148 (1984).

Chapter 4

AGENCY IN CONSENSUAL TRANSACTIONS

INTRODUCTION

A "representative relationship" is one that enables a person to acquire rights and duties by consensual transactions on behalf of somebody else. A dime store clerk selling a tube of toothpaste, a corporation purchasing agent contracting for a million dollars' worth of steel, and a lawyer litigating a claim are all acting in representative relationships.

This relationship is so familiar to us that we are likely to regard it as inherent in an ordered society. Yet the magnificent legal system of ancient Rome got along without recognizing it, except in rare cases. It seems to have gained recognition in the later middle ages or renaissance, paralleling the development of the law of merchants. But its development was not confined to that law; it grew simultaneously in the civil law system.

There are obvious similarities between the legal recognition of the representative relation and the acceptance of vicarious liability; both were unknown to Roman law, and both are taken for granted today. Probably both are indispensable to the exchange of goods and services in a society of free men (in contrast to the slavery-based world of ancient Rome), and both were equally destined to prevail. But their legal formulations have been quite independent, and the reactions of legal scholars quite different.

The representative relationship appears in the earliest yearbooks, while vicarious liability does not show up until about 1700. Most of the law about the representative relationship is classified under "Principal and Agent," and deals with what we could now call "white collar employees." Most of the law about vicarious liability corresponds with the earlier correlatives of "blue collar workers" and clustered around the title of "Master and Servant." The 19th century rationalists (led by Holmes) who found vicarious liability nonsensical accepted representation without even noting its deviation from their individualistic axioms.

In broad terms, this chapter is concerned with finding the outer boundaries of representation in contractual situations. The chapter continues the study of circumstances which subject the inactive participant (principal) to the dealings of the active one (the agent). It is similar to the study of the relationship which leads to vicarious liabilities for tort, but you should be alert for differences in the tests.

You will find a great variety of circumstances leading to liability. First, you will see cases in which the principal's liability commends itself immediately to your common sense, because he has in fact told the agent to make the very contract he has made. In these cases, you will find it natural to say that the principal has "authorized" the agent, or has given him "authority".

Beyond the cases of simple "authority", you will encounter cases in which the principal who is bound had told the agent not to enter the transaction in question. The principal may be liable under a variety of rationales if justice seems to require this result. One group of cases rests liability on the particular kind of agent involved (e.g., the attorney, the corporate officer, or the partner). Other cases involve concepts of "apparent authority" and "estoppel" which are more controversial, and more difficult to limit in their application.

You will also find cases where the principal was not bound by the agent's act at first, but because of something that happened later, the principal became liable on the contract already made. Here, you will find again the concept of "ratification" entering into the decision.

Throughout the chapter the question is raised on how authority relations once created are terminated.

Two other important problem areas exist. They both involve situations where the presence of the agency relationship adds or subtracts from what has been the intent of parties of a contract. The first of these involves the nondisclosure of the agency relationship by the agent at the time the contract was made. The second concerns agents who act beyond their authority or who misrepresent that authority.

The dilemma presented by many of the cases in this chapter may be seen as an attempt to balance two basic goals: First, the desire to protect the property of the principal and, second, the need to ensure smooth functioning of the commercial markets which requires that the third parties be able to rely on agents with a minimum of inquiry as to their authority.

LEGAL RELATIONS IN THE LAW OF AGENCY: POWER OF AGENCY AND COMMERCIAL CERTAINTY

Wolfram Müller-Freienfels,[*] 1964.
13 American Journal of Comparative Law 193–196 (excerpts).

The principle of agency includes a number of complicated legal relations. Its development is closely related to the changing needs for division of labor, which call for the delegation or distribution of various functions among assistants, clerks, managers, etc. According to

[*] Wolfram Müller-Freienfels is professor of law at the University of Freiburg, Baden, West Germany. He has written a comprehensive analysis of agency law in German, Die Vertretung beim Rechtsgeschäft (1955) in addition to articles in English and American law reviews.

Hauriou, it is a *"chose surprenante,"* that a stranger to a contract may participate in its formation. The complications which arise from the introduction of a third person affect fundamental principles of private law relating to self-determination; hence, the development of agency presupposes an advanced stage of legal thinking and a developed economic and institutional background. It is no mere coincidence that the first rules of agency, in the sense understood today, are not reported earlier than from the twelfth and the thirteenth centuries onwards: a phenomenon that occurred simultaneously in the civil law and the common law countries, even though the original roots of this institution were developed independently in the two legal systems. According to Rabel, full development of the principle of representation "was absolutely nowhere reached before the time of the Reception." It was not until the nineteenth century that the rules of agency came to be organized and collected from the various fields over which they were distributed.

At first sight, it may seem surprising that Roman law, in spite of its high scientific level, never developed a complete theory of agency. This is especially true of their contract law. The Romans never acknowledged a general rule in their private law which declared that a person, acting as an intermediary, should be capable of creating valid contractual or commercial relations between the principal and a third party.

Various legal explanations have been offered for this deficiency. Primarily, it appears that in Rome agency was considered an undesirable invasion into the private autonomy of the Roman citizen because it would confer powers on one person to affect the rights and duties of another. In addition, Roman adherence to legal formalism, similarly to the Anglo-Saxon bent for formal contracts, which bound only those parties who actually participated in a legal transaction, was an obstacle to the development of the agency doctrine. Moreover, the concept of the Roman obligation, which was conceived of as a strictly personal tie between the parties to a contract, added an unsurmountable obstacle to the outright recognition of agency. On the other hand, economic needs did not create any compulsion for such recognition, and the legal effects given to transactions concluded by slaves and family members helped to fill this gap. Nevertheless, Roman law developed a few exceptions to the general nonrecognition of agency in the form of fairly cumbrous substitutes, for instance, by attributing to a servant's act in taking physical possession the same legal effect as to the taking of possession by his master. In the Middle Ages, due to the pressure of mercantile needs, the Glossators and Postglossators expanded these exceptions in very roundabout ways.

The canon law went further in developing principles of agency. . . .

This development of the canon law was not without effect on the secular law. . . .

In the civil law sphere, it remained for natural law to develop systematically agency law to its maturity. Hugo Grotius explained in his *De Jure Belli ac Pacis* (II, 11, 18) that a procurator acquires rights directly for his principal, his acts being based on the principal's mandate. . . .

This complicated development explains why, in spite of the needs of commerce, representation, as a homogeneous, generally accepted legal institution was acknowledged at such a relatively late date in the civil law. For this same reason, a clear and systematic treatment of representation as an autonomous legal category was still later in coming, a phenomenon that is felt in its repercussions even today.

. . .

REFERENCES

Theory and Terminology in General:

Abbott, Of the Nature of Agency (1896) 9 Harv.L.Rev. 507 (suggests rather vaguely that problems be analyzed as tripartite transactions, among principal, agent, and third persons, rather than as bipartite, with agent fictionally representing principal).

American Law Institute Proceedings (1926) vol. 4, pp. 147–164 (1933) vol. 11, pp. 79, 100 (showing difficulties in arriving at definitions, and conflict of ideas among advisers and members).

Corbin, The "Authority" of an Agent—Definition (1925) 34 Yale L.J. 788 (plea for defining "authority" as an operative fact, distinguished from "power," a legal relation).

Hohfeld, Some Fundamental Legal Conceptions as Applied in Judicial Reasoning (1913) 23 Yale L.J. 16, 46 reprinted in Fundamental Legal Conceptions (1923) 23, 52 (classic distinction between agent's legal relation of "power," as against facts creating the power).

Holmes, History of Agency (1891) 4 Harv.L.Rev. 345, 5 id. 1, reprinted in 3 Select Essays in Anglo-American Legal History 368, 390 (1909).

Seavey, The Rationale of Agency (1920) 29 Yale L.J. 859, reprinted in Studies in Agency (1949) 65 (the clearest and fullest statement of the elements of agency and authority in contractual relations; theories later incorporated, with slight modification, in Restatement).

Seavey, Problems in Restatement of the Law of Agency (1930) 16 A.B.A.J. 117 (difficulties of definition).

Seavey, Agency Powers (1948) 1 U.Okla.L.Rev. 3, reprinted in Studies in Agency (1949) 181.

Restatement of Agency 2d, (1958) §§ 6–8, 141–142 (definitions of terms used in Restatement; no discussion of alternative theories).

Conant, M. "The Objective Theory of Agency: Apparent Authority and the Estoppel of Apparent Ownership" (1968) 47 Neb.L.Rev. 678 (the author attempts to create a general theory of "authority". He argues that since objective, mutual assent is the basis for a contract, this assent should also be the basis for holding a principal liable for contractual obligations entered into by his agent).

"Estoppel" or "Apparent Authority":

Walter Wheeler Cook, Agency by Estoppel (1905) 5 Col.L.Rev. 36 (criticizing use of estoppel concept in agency cases).

Ewart, Agency by Estoppel (1905) 5 Col.L.Rev. 354 (defending estoppel concept).

Walter Wheeler Cook, Agency by Estoppel—A Reply (1906) 6 Col.L.Rev. 34.

Ferson, Bases for Master's Liability and for Principal's Liability to Third Persons (1951) 4 Vand.L.Rev. 260, 274–286 (simplified comparison of real and apparent authority, and estoppel).

What law governs:

Pfeifer, The Hague Convention on the Law Applicable to Agency (1978) 26 Am.J. Comp.L. 434. Text and comments of a proposed international treaty specifying which country's law shall govern the law of an agency having impacts in more than one country.

Hay and Müller-Freienfels, Agency in the Conflict of Laws and the 1978 Hague Convention (1979) 27 Am.J.Comp.L. 1.

SECTION 1. DOCUMENTARY AUTHORITY

An agent's power to bind his principal in contractual dealings does not usually depend on any particular form of communication by the principal. As the cases will show, power may be given by a great variety of expressions, actions, and failures to act.

But there are a limited number of situations in which the law requires that certain formalities be observed. In each instance, the need of formality between principal and agent is closely connected with a similar requirement in the main transaction. Hence, these requirements are better studied in detail in connection with the transactions themselves—in courses on contracts, conveyances, negotiable instruments, or mortgages. Only the general principles are set out below, with some references to further authorities on special problems.

The legal requirements of formality are, of course, a very different matter from the formalities required by good practice, or by prevailing custom. Comments and forms at the end of the section supply some information on certain formalities widely used (whether necessary or not) in agency transactions.

REFERENCE

Restatement of Agency 2d, (1958) §§ 26, 27.

POWER TO EXECUTE WRITTEN INSTRUMENTS

General rules regarding the power to execute written instruments are stated in the selection below from the Restatement. You will notice that its application depends upon the requirements of particular statutes. Illustrative statutory provisions are therefore supplied, following the statement of general rules.

Statutes which require written evidence are generally called "statutes of frauds," a term derived from the English prototype of 1676, which was known as the "Statute of Frauds and Perjuries." The New York statutes chosen for illustration are fairly typical in their enumeration of the kinds of transactions which must be established by writing and signature. Another statute of frauds is contained in the Uniform Commercial Code which is reproduced below.

The power to execute sealed instruments is a separate and additional problem. Ancient authorities declared that an instrument under seal could be executed only by the party himself or by an agent authorized under seal. The guarded language of the Restatement section, quoted below, indicates how little is left of this ancient doctrine. The present rule, it will be noted, only prevents the sealed instrument from operating "as such," and in no way precludes it from doing as much as can be done without any seal. Thus the rule is presumably without effect wherever statutes have made seals unnecessary, even though they have not entirely deprived them of their "efficacy."

RESTATEMENT OF AGENCY, 2d
American Law Institute, 1958.

§ 30. Authority to Execute Written Contracts

(1) Unless so provided by statute, a written authorization is not necessary for the execution of a writing.

(2) A statutory requirement that a memorandum of a transaction be signed by the parties in order to make it effective does not thereby impose a requirement of written authorization to execute such a memorandum.

NEW YORK "STATUTE OF FRAUDS" N.Y. GENERAL OBLIGATIONS LAW
(McKinney's Consolidated Law of New York, Book 23A)

§ 5–701. Agreements Required to be in Writing

Every agreement, promise or undertaking is void, unless it or some note or memorandum thereof be in writing, and subscribed by the party to be charged therewith, or by his lawful agent, if such agreement, promise or undertaking:

1. By its terms is not to be performed within one year from the making thereof or the performance of which is not to be completed before the end of a lifetime;

2. Is a special promise to answer for the debt, default or miscarriage of another person;

3. Is made in consideration of marriage, except mutual promises to marry;

4. Is a conveyance or assignment of a trust in personal property;

5. Is a subsequent or new promise to pay a debt discharged in bankruptcy;

6. Notwithstanding section 2–201 of the uniform commercial code, if the goods be sold at public auction, and the auctioneer at the time of the sale, enters in a sale book, a memorandum specifying the nature and price of the property sold, the terms of the sale, the name of the purchaser, and the name of the person on whose account the sale was

made, such memorandum is equivalent in effect to a note of the contract or sale, subscribed by the party to be charged therewith;

7. Is a contract to bequeath property or make a testamentary provision of any kind;

8. Is a contract to establish a trust;

9. Is a contract to assign or an assignment, with or without consideration to the promisor, of a life or health or accident insurance policy, or a promise, with or without consideration to the promisor, to name a beneficiary of any such policy. This provision shall not apply to a policy of industrial life or health or accident insurance.

10. Is a contract to pay compensation for services rendered in negotiating a loan, or in negotiating the purchase, sale, exchange, renting or leasing of any real estate or interest therein, or of a business opportunity, business, its good will, inventory, fixtures or an interest therein, including a majority of the voting stock interest in a corporation and including the creating of a partnership interest. This provision shall not apply to a contract to pay compensation to an auctioneer, an attorney at law, or a duly licensed real estate broker or real estate salesman.

[Subsections 4, 7 and 8 were repealed from § 5–701 in 1967, and at the same time the following section was enacted in the Estates, Powers and Trusts Code.]

§ 13–2.1   Agreements Involving a Contract to Establish a Trust, to Make a Testamentary Provision of Any Kind, and by a Personal Representative to Answer for the Debt or Default of a Decedent, Required to be in Writing

(a) Every agreement, promise or undertaking is unenforceable unless it or some note or memorandum thereof is in writing and subscribed by the party to be charged therewith, or by his lawful agent, if such agreement, promise or undertaking:

(1) Is a contract to establish a trust.

(2) Is a contract to make a testamentary provision of any kind.

(3) Is a promise by a personal representative to answer for the debt or default of his decedent. L.1966, c. 952, eff. Sept. 1, 1967.

§ 5–703.   Conveyances and Contracts Concerning Real Property Required to be in Writing

1. An estate or interest in real property, other than a lease for a term not exceeding one year, or any trust or power, over or concerning real property, or in any manner relating thereto, cannot be created, granted, assigned, surrendered or declared, unless by act or operation of law, or by a deed or conveyance in writing, subscribed by the person creating, granting, assigning, surrendering or declaring the same, or by his lawful agent, thereunto authorized by writing. But this subdivision does not affect the power of a testator in the disposition of his real

property by will; nor prevent any trust from arising or being extinguished by implication or operation of law, nor any declaration of trust from being proved by a writing subscribed by the person declaring the same.

2.   A contract for the leasing for a longer period than one year, or for the sale, of any real property, or an interest therein, is void unless the contract or some note or memorandum thereof, expressing the consideration, is in writing, subscribed by the party to be charged, or by his lawful agent thereunto authorized by writing.

3.   A contract to devise real property or establish a trust of real property, or any interest therein or right with reference thereto, is void unless the contract or some note or memorandum thereof is in writing and subscribed by the party to be charged therewith, or by his lawfully authorized agent.

4.   Nothing contained in this section abridges the powers of courts of equity to compel the specific performance of agreements in cases of part performance.

UNIFORM COMMERCIAL CODE

Section 2–201. Formal Requirements; Statute of Frauds

(1) Except as otherwise provided in this section a contract for the sale of goods for the price of $500 or more is not enforceable by way of action or defense unless there is some writing sufficient to indicate that a contract for sale has been made between the parties and signed by the party against whom enforcement is sought or by his authorized agent or broker. A writing is not insufficient because it omits or incorrectly states a term agreed upon but the contract is not enforceable under this paragraph beyond the quantity of goods shown in such writing.

[Subsections (2) and (3) contain exceptions covering a merchant's acquiescence to a written proposition, goods specially manufactured, contracts admitted in court and acceptance of goods in partial fulfillment of contract.]

CALIFORNIA CIVIL CODE
West's Ann.Cal.Civ.Code § 2309.

§ 2309. Form of Authority

An oral authorization is sufficient for any purpose, except that an authority to enter into a contract required by law to be in writing can only be given by an instrument in writing.

NOTE ON CALIFORNIA CIVIL CODE § 2309

California Civil Code § 2309, unchanged since its original enactment in 1872, was based on Field's draft of a New York commercial code. Very few jurisdictions have such a provision in effect, and even in California, it appears that the courts have attempted to mitigate its harsh results. In one major decision, the California Supreme Court held that the section does not bar an action for indemnification by an agent against the principal, despite the absence of a written agency agreement.[1] Neither, apparently, does the section bar direct enforcement against the principal when the agent executes a written contract in the presence, and with the concurrence, of the principal.[2] It was but a short step from these decisions to the holding that the statutory rule is inapplicable to agents who are executive officers of corporations.[3]

NOTE ON AGENCY PROVISIONS IN STATUTES OF FRAUDS

The original English Statute of Frauds, passed in 1676, dealt with conveyances of lands in section 1, and with contracts for the sale of lands in section 4, which also governed promises by executors, promises to pay the debts of another, promises in consideration of marriage, and promises not to be performed within one year. Under section 1, conveyances had to be signed by the person to be charged, or by his agent "thereunto lawfully authorized by writing"; under section 4, contracts had to be signed by the person to be charged or by an agent "thereunto lawfully authorized." Stat. 29 Car. II, c. 3, §§ 1, 4 (1676).

In most of the modern statutes that we have examined, contracts for the sale of land have been separated from other contracts and subjected to the same requirements as conveyances—both requiring any authorization, as well as the principal instrument, to be in writing and signed. In other contracts, the laws continue to require a writing only for the principal contract.

There are occasional variations. In Florida, for instance, land contracts continue to be treated as other contracts, without a requirement of written authorization. More surprisingly, the requirement of written authorization has been eliminated from the section on conveyances. Fla.Stat.Ann. §§ 689.01, 725.01 (1969).

RESTATEMENT OF AGENCY, 2d
American Law Institute, 1958.

§ 28. Authority to Execute Sealed Instruments

(1) Except as stated in Subsection (2), an instrument executed by an agent as a sealed instrument does not operate as such unless authority or apparent authority to execute it has been conferred by an instrument under seal.

(2) Sealed authority is not necessary to execute an instrument under seal where:

(a) the instrument is executed in the principal's presence and by his direction;

1. Sunset-Sternau Food Co. v. Bonzi, 60 Cal.2d 834, 36 Cal.Rptr. 741, 389 P.2d 133 (1964); Comment, 49 Minn.L.Rev. 302 (1964).

2. Lathrop v. Gauger, 127 Cal.App.2d 754, 274 P.2d 730 (1954) (alternative holding).

3. Ripani v. Liberty Loan Corp., 95 Cal. App.3d 603, 157 Cal.Rptr. 272 (1979); Monteleone v. Southern California Vending, Inc., 264 Cal.App.2d 798, 70 Cal.Rptr. 703 (1968).

(b) the instrument is authorized by a corporation or partnership in accordance with the rules relating to the authorization of such instruments by such associations; or

(c) a statute deprives seals of their legal significance.

REFERENCES

Digests:

See any Key Number Digest: Frauds, Statute of ☞116; Principal and Agent ☞117(1).

Power to fill in blanks:

If a deed to real estate is signed by the owner and delivered to an agent with certain blanks remaining to be filled in, is the deed valid after blanks are filled in by an agent who lacks written or sealed authority? The answer is usually yes; the problem is frequently analyzed as involving the requisites of delivery of deeds, rather than as involving agency problems.

Durbin v. Bennett, 31 F.Supp. 24 (D.C.Ill.1939); comment, 18 Tex.L.Rev. 498.

Sirois v. Sirois, 308 Ill. 453, 139 N.E. 874 (1923).

Prosser v. Nickolay, 249 Wis. 75, 23 N.W.2d 403 (1946); comment, 30 Marq.L.Rev. 202.

Bretta v. Meltzer, 280 Mass. 573, 182 N.E. 827 (1932) (query).

Restatement of Agency 2d, § 28, comment c (valid as to "non-essentials" only).

Signature by agent for partially disclosed principal:

If an agent signs a memorandum required by statute to be in writing, purporting to act as agent but withholding the name of the principal, does the memorandum fulfill the statutory requirement? Authority is divided.

Dodge v. Blood, 299 Mich. 364, 300 N.W. 121, 138 A.L.R. 322 (1941); comments, 42 Col.L.Rev. 475, 40 Mich.L.Rev. 900 (memorandum sufficient; extensive review of authorities).

Jaynes v. Petoskey, 309 Mich. 32, 14 N.W.2d 566 (1944) (memorandum not sufficient; limiting doctrine of Dodge v. Blood).

Statute of Frauds—signature by corporation:

Bayless Building Materials Co. v. Peerless Land Co., 509 S.W.2d 206 (Mo.App.1974) (minute of directors' resolution to buy land satisfied requirement of statute of frauds; no discussion of how "signature" requirement was met).

Written authority:

Lee v. Stroman, 470 S.W.2d 783 (Tex.Civ.App.1971) (purchaser not liable for breach of real estate contract when agent of the seller accepted but failed to disclose written authority.)

Articles and comments:

Brown, Statute of Frauds and Land Transactions (1964) 13 Clev.-Mar.L.Rev. 205.

Statute of Frauds Under Article 2 of the U.C.C. (1964) 15 Syracuse L.Rev. 532.

Changes Effected in the Statute of Frauds by the enactment of the U.C.C. in Pennsylvania (1962) 36 Temp.L.Q. 75.

U.C.C. § 1–206, A New Departure in the Statute of Frauds (1961) 70 Yale L.J. 603.

The Authority to Sign for Another in Conveying Immovable Property (1965) 25 La.L. Rev. 977 (in Louisiana an agent may transfer real property on oral authority as long as the principal is in the agent's presence when the signing takes place. This occurs most often when a notary public signs for an illiterate).

NOTE: POWERS OF ATTORNEY

Written authorizations may be in many forms; some of them are simply letters of instructions. More formal authorizations are usually called "powers of attorney." In this expression, the word "power" is used to describe a document, rather than a legal relation. The word "attorney" also requires some explanation, since the person who receives the power is not usually an attorney-at-law. The usage derives from the early common law, when any agent might be called an "attorney," and when a portion of the law of agents was called the law of "attorneys." The holder of a documentary "power" is frequently called an "attorney-in-fact." "Fact" is also used in a sense now unfamiliar, and corresponds to the old legal term "factum" (an act), as used in the term "fraud in the factum," or in the plea "non est factum." Thus we may translate "attorney in fact" as "agent in transacting."

Some powers of attorney are separate documents, containing nothing but an authorization. Others are conferred in language incidental to some other instrument, such as an assignment or promissory note.

CHICAGO TITLE INS. CO. v. PROGRESSIVE HOUSING, INC.

United States District Court, District of Colorado, 1978.
453 F.Supp. 1103.

FINDINGS OF FACT, CONCLUSIONS OF LAW AND ORDER

KANE, DISTRICT JUDGE.

Plaintiff Chicago Title Insurance Company brings this action for damages it incurred as a result of a default by Progressive Housing, Inc., the general contractor, in a construction project of ninety-one (91) low-income housing units in Denver, Colorado. Trial has been bifurcated and we are concerned here only with the claims against three of the defendants. Plaintiff bases its claim against these defendants [Hayne, Goreham and Willis] on an alleged guaranty of Progressive's performance. The circumstances under which the guaranty was prepared and presented form the basis of the instant controversy.

The issues are limited to three. Many others related to liability and damages are reserved. . . . Since I resolve the first issue in favor of these defendants and hold that they did not in fact guarantee anyone's performance for the benefit of plaintiff, it is not necessary to decide the remaining two issues. . . .

The series of transactions involving this construction project which preceded the alleged guaranty of performance now at issue began in the spring of 1973. At that time Progressive contracted with the Housing Authority of the City and County of Denver to construct the low-income housing units. In July, 1973, Progressive obtained a written commitment from Realty and Mortgage Investors of the Pacific (RAMPAC) to provide interim construction financing for the project in the amount of $2,304,000. This commitment was contingent upon two material conditions: that Progressive obtain the personal guaranties of defendants

Hayne, Goreham and Willis and William Nemour, President of Progressive; and that RAMPAC and CTI reach an agreement whereby CTI would act as disbursement agent of the loan funds.

In order to meet the first of these conditions to the RAMPAC loan commitment, Progressive and these three individual defendants entered into an agreement for the sales of their personal guaranties of the loan to the construction lender. Under the terms of this agreement, defendants Hayne, Goreham and Willis agreed to provide their guarantees of the construction loan in exchange for a $75,000 fee to be paid by Progressive. On July 26, 1973 this loan guaranty was executed by defendants to Colorado National Mortgage Company which had become a participant lender with RAMPAC in the construction loan. The terms of the guaranty were carefully detailed in an instrument over two printed pages in length and the document was personally signed by defendants and their spouses in their resident state of California.

The other condition to the RAMPAC financing commitment was fulfilled at the loan closing on August 7, 1973 when Progressive agreed to participate in CTI's construction disbursing program. By this program CTI undertook to disburse the construction funds and to issue title insurance policies on the various sites, insuring title free and clear of mechanic's and materialmen's liens. Reciprocally, Progressive agreed to complete the construction of the project according to plans and specifications by July 29, 1974. CTI agreed that in the event of Progressive's default, at its option CTI would either purchase the note from the lender or complete the project.

During the August 7, 1973 closing a single typed sentence was added to CTI's construction disbursement agreements. A few days prior to the closing a CTI employee in Chicago recommended that an additional guaranty by Hayne, Goreham and Willis of Progressive's performance to CTI was needed. The evidence shows that defendants Hayne, Goreham and Willis were never informed of this additional performance guaranty requirement by CTI. In fact, a blank copy of the agreements to be signed at the closing without the guaranty language had been sent to the defendants for their review. Even though CTI had drafted all the construction disbursement agreements for this type of project on standard forms that did not include a guaranty of performance provision, the recommendation to amend the standard agreements for this transaction was not acted upon by CTI personnel in Denver until the morning of the closing. At the eleventh hour the additional guaranty of Progressive's performance was hastily typed on the bottom of the preprinted agreement between CTI and Progressive by an employee of CTI. . . .

CTI argues that Pawlek had authority to bind defendants under the general power of attorney given to him for the purpose of representing them at the loan closing. . . .

Plaintiff contends that the language of the powers of attorney is broad enough to authorize Pawlek's execution of the performance guaranty and relies on subsection (f) of these instruments which includes this litany of authorized transactions:

> To transact business of any kind or class and any act and deed to sign, execute, acknowledge and deliver any deed, lease, assignment of lease, covenant, indenture, indemnity, agreement, mortgage, deed of trust, assignment of mortgage or of the beneficial interest under deed of trust, extension or renewal of any obligation, subordination or waiver of priority, hypothecation, bottomry, charterparty, bill of lading, bill of sale, bill, bond, note, whether negotiable or non-negotiable, receipt, evidence of debt, full or partial release or satisfaction of mortgage, judgment and other debt, requests for partial or full reconveyance of deed of trust and such other instruments in writing of any kind or class as may be necessary or proper in the premises.

Significantly, the word "guaranty" is absent from the list.

CTI claims that the authority to sign an agreement is broad enough to include guaranties. Courts have recognized that a guaranty agreement imposes serious obligations upon a guarantor and have generally required evidence of specific authorization before finding that an agent has the authority to bind his principal in a guaranty agreement. . . .

When courts have applied rules of construction to powers of attorney, they have held that such a grant of authority must be strictly construed when determining the scope of authority it vests in an agent, *Von Wedel v. McGrath*, 180 F.2d 716 (3rd Cir.1950), *cert. denied* 340 U.S. 816, 71 S.Ct. 45, 95 L.Ed. 600. . . . Since Pawlek's powers of attorney lacked a specific grant of authority to bind his principals to a guaranty agreement, he lacked actual authority to effectuate the guaranty.

The question next arises whether Pawlek had implied authority to enter into this agreement. CTI presented the testimony of its closing officer at trial who stated that he read the general powers of attorney at the closing and assumed that each vested Pawlek with authority to sign the guaranty. Case law is well-settled that when a third party knows that an agent's authority is contained in a power of attorney, that party has the duty to read the instrument carefully for limitations of such authority. . . . The closing officer for CTI was an experienced employee who was well acquainted with closing procedures. He testified that he examined the powers of attorney at the closing. This examination should have revealed that nowhere in the powers was the express authority to enter into guaranty agreements stated. Normal care in the closing of a transaction involving in excess of two million dollars should have been taken by CTI when it belatedly decided to require an additional guaranty of performance from these defendants. CTI knew well in advance of the closing that these defendants would not personally be attending. No conduct on the part of defendants contributed in any way to plaintiff's insouciance. CTI representatives, as persons of ordinary prudence in business matters, should have perused the instruments granting Pawlek a general power of attorney and should have insisted upon more than was furnished by him as evidence of his authority to enter into the specific transaction. In order for there to be a finding of implied authority some facts must exist upon which the implication can adhere. The mere presence of an agent armed with general powers of attorney at a multi-party financial closing is not sufficient in law or in fact to bind absent principals to a guaranty added to a prepared document after submission of the document to the principals for their inspection when the powers of attorney do not specifically delegate the power to make guaranties. . . .

[The court then decided that the elements for ratification were not present.]

IT IS ORDERED that the complaint of Chicago Title Insurance Company against defendants Willard W. Hayne, William B. Goreham and Andrew Willis, defendants is dismissed with prejudice. Said defendants shall have judgment for their costs expended herein upon the filing of a bill of costs with the Clerk of the Court within ten (10) days from the date hereof.

REFERENCES

Power to make gifts:

If a power of attorney permits the holder to "convey, transfer, assign," etc., does the holder have power to make gratuitous gifts? Most cases answer "no."

Johnson v. Fraccatera, 348 So.2d 570 (Fla.App.1977) (power of attorney to "bargain, sell, release, convey and mortgage lands" did not authorize agent's conveyance from principal to principal and husband as joint tenants with right of survivorship).

Hudges v. Surratt, 366 So.2d 768 (Fla.App.1978) (power of attorney "to act with full power and authority" did not confer power to donate principal's property to agent's husband).

Bloom v. Weiser, 348 So.2d 651 (Fla.App.1977) (power of attorney granted "full power and authority to do and perform all and every act . . . in and about the premises." Held, no power to make gift of condominium).

Power to buy and to sell:

Restatement of Agency 2d, §§ 52–66.

Article:

Stultz, Construction of Written Powers of Attorney (1957) 18 Ohio State L.J. 129.

Soders v. Armstrong, 172 Okl. 50, 44 P.2d 868 (1935) (parol evidence used to determine that power to sell was also power to convey).

Lacey v. Cardwell, 216 Va. 212, 217 S.E.2d 835 (1975) (authority "to offer the entire property" resulted in a contract upon acceptance by third party).

Eitel v. Schmidlapp, 459 F.2d 609 (4th Cir.1972) (conveyance with agent's authority "to sell" not valid because "implicit" was concept that real consideration would be present and available to the principal).

Scope of authority:

Crane v. Kangas, 53 Mich.App. 653, 220 N.W.2d 172 (1974) (power of attorney of wife to collect on husband's bank accounts and draw on bank accounts gave no authority to convey real estate).

U.S. v. Sanches, 521 F.2d 244 (5th Cir.1975) (surety company supplied agent with powers of attorney containing limit of $5,000, for deposit in court; agent altered to permit $50,000, and signed a bond for $20,000; company liable).

Culbertson v. Cook, 308 Pa. 557, 162 A. 803 (1932) (strict interpretation held power to postpone lien not included in other general powers).

First Nat. Bank in Dallas v. Kinabrew, 589 S.W.2d 137 (Tex.Civ.App.1979) (power to convey mineral or royalty interest includes power to convey an overriding oil interest to settle a debt).

NOTE: ALTERNATIVE TO STRICT CONSTRUCTION OF POWERS OF ATTORNEY

The strict construction of powers of attorney illustrated in the Chicago Title Ins. Co. case presents problems to both parties. It places on the third party a burden of comparing meticulously the authority granted with the transaction made, and of demanding additional documentation if any discrepancy is discovered. It places on the principal the burden of foreseeing and naming every kind of transaction that might possibly be useful, or of executing a new authority for each novel transaction.

A possible escape from this dilemma is offered in New York by the Statutory Short Form of Power of Attorney, General Obligations Law §§ 5–1501 through 5–1508. This law provides that a power of attorney may specify any of a list of categories of transactions for which the agent is authorized; this list includes "real estate transactions," "chattel and goods transactions," "banking transactions," and so on. The statute provides a list of transactions that is authorized by virtue of naming the category. This provision relieves the principal of the need of foreseeing each type of transaction, if it is one that the legislature has foreseen, but does not relieve the third party of the need of ascertaining whether the particular transaction is within the legislative list. Annotations indicate that the act has seldom come into litigation, which may mean either that it is seldom used, or that it works so well that no controversies arise from it.

A radically different approach to documentary authority is illustrated by the German law of the "procura" [*Prokura*]. The procura is an authorization given by a commercial employer (individual or incorporated) to an individual. It must contain the technical word *Prokura;* otherwise it does not invoke the special statutory provisions applicable to it. It should be recorded in the Commercial Register, but may take effect without recording if its existence has been announced to the agent. The agent to whom a procura has been granted is called a "procurist" [*Prokurist*].

The distinctive feature about the procura is that the holder of it has power to bind the principal in all transactions except transfer of real estate; the text of the documentary procura has nothing to do with the matter! The procurist is not even restricted to the "usual" scope of the business. There are only two limitations on this broad power. One is that the procura may be given only for a particular branch of the business, located in a separate city; the other is that the third party cannot hold the principal if he dealt in bad faith with the procurist, knowing that the procurist was acting disloyally. This is much more than having mere reason to know of limitations on authority, or having insufficient reason to rely on the procurist's authority.

It is perhaps surprising that German employers grant procuras, in view of the dangers involved. Nevertheless, it appears to be a general practice, and apparently German business men in large transactions expect to deal with some one who is able to sign, "Schmidt, Prokurist."

REFERENCES

R.R. Powell, Powers of Attorney, in Report of the New York State Law Revision Commission for 1947, 679–728 (review of New York case law on powers of attorney, and basis for recommendation of commission which led to enactment of the N.Y. statutory short form of general power of attorney).

Ernest C. Steefel, Trading under the Laws of Germany 46–48 (2nd ed., 1956, New York: German American Trade Promotion Office).

Handelsgesetzbuch, 1897, §§ 48–53.

MORGAN v. HARPER
Texas Commission of Appeals, 1922.
236 S.W. 71.

[Action for specific performance of a contract to convey land to the plaintiff. The contract was made in the defendant's name, by Simmons. A verdict was directed and judgment rendered for the defendant. This was affirmed by the Court of Civil Appeals, 219 S.W. 888, from which the plaintiff appealed to this court.]

HAMILTON, J. . . . In this case Harper supplied his agent with written authority, the empowering paragraph of which reads:

"I hereby authorize H.H. Simmons, of Hillsboro, Texas, as my sole agent to sell or trade the property described on reverse side hereof at the price and upon the terms above named or upon any other price or terms that I may agree to, from this date to 12/1/17 and I authorize him to close trade by written contract in accordance with above terms and conditions, upon purchaser paying to him a sum, either in money or by note, satisfactory to said H.H. Simmons as my agent, and I obligate myself in an amount equal to the obligation put up by purchaser to place at an early date, at the convenience of H.H. Simmons, who is to prepare same, deed executed by myself and wife, with said obligation and contract held in connection with sale, in accordance with terms of same."

He afterwards sent his son to Simmons with this instruction:

"Tell Mr. Simmons and Real Estate Company that the land has advanced so much that I couldn't afford to sell it at that price and to not sell it for that. . . . My son came back and told me he delivered that message to Simmons, or at his office."

Simmons testified:

"At the time I signed the contract binding, or attempting to bind, Mr. Harper to convey the land, I had received notice from him or had been notified to withdraw the land from the market. I learned it through F.W. Simmons."

This was sufficient to revoke his authority. The authority of an agent, when revocable, may be revoked "by a simple and private declaration." 1 Mechem on Agency, s. 613.

A principal has the power to revoke the authority of such an agent at any time, with or without reason therefor. Mechem on Agency, s. 561 et seq. But when Harper revoked the agency he left the contract authorizing the agency in Simmons' hands. This showed on its face that Simmons was authorized to sell the land "to December 1, 1917." Plaintiff in error would have testified, if he had been permitted by the court to do so, that he knew of the agency contract at the time he signed the sales contract, and that he "contracted with reference thereto."

Plaintiff in error assigns as error the action of the court in excluding this testimony. The assignment must be sustained. If plaintiff in error saw the written contract authorizing Simmons to sell the land to December 1, 1917, at the time he made the contract of purchase, and in reliance on that authority he bought the land from Simmons, believing him to be the agent of Harper, we think Harper is estopped from showing the revocation of Simmons' authority, and that he is bound by the contract of sale.

No attempt to give notice of the revocation of agency to third persons was made by Harper. While, ordinarily, notice of the revocation of the authority of a special agent is not required to be given, except to the agent, where the principal seeks to revoke the authority before its execution, "he must do whatever he reasonably should, if anything, to prevent third persons who are charged with the duty of protecting themselves, in dealing with agents, from being misled by acting upon a power withdrawn." Mechem on Agency, s. 630. Harper should have withdrawn from Simmons the written authority so that he might not lead third persons to believe he was authorized to December 1, 1917, to sell the land. If Simmons refused to give it up, Harper was under the duty to give notice of his revocation of the purported authority shown on its face to exist to that date. Since he did neither, if the agent used the instrument left in his hands to mislead Morgan by exhibiting it to him, Harper must suffer the injury, if any. Where one of two equally innocent parties must suffer by reason of the fraud of another, the loss should fall upon him whose negligent act or omission has enabled the wrongdoer to commit the fraud.

. . .

If Morgan merely depended on Simmons' representation, made after the revocation of the agency, that he was authorized by the contract to sell the land, we think Morgan was negligent and remiss in trusting to such representations because "a party dealing with the agent must not rely on what the agent alone may say or do . . . but he must be able to trace the authority on which he relies back to some word or deed of the principal," 1 Mechem on Agency, s. 750.

If, on another trial, it should develop that Morgan "knew of the existence of the contract" merely from such representations of the agent, he is not entitled to judgment.

We recommend that the judgment of the Court of Civil Appeals be reversed, and that the cause be remanded to the district court for a new trial.   . . .

RESTATEMENT OF AGENCY, 2d
American Law Institute, 1958

§ 120. Death of Principal

(1) The death of the principal terminates the authority of the agent without notice to him, except as stated in subsections (2) and (3) and in the caveat.

(2) Until notice of a depositor's death, a bank has authority to pay checks drawn by him or by agents authorized by him before death.

(3) Until notice of the death of the holder of a check deposited for collection, the bank in which it is deposited and those to which the check is sent for collection have authority to go forward with the process of collection.

Caveat:

No inference is to be drawn from the rule stated in this Section that an agent does not have power to bind the estate of a deceased principal in transactions dependent upon a special relation between the agent and the principal, such as trustee and beneficiary, or in transactions in which special rules are applicable, as in dealings with negotiable instruments.

§ 121. Death of Agent

The death of the agent terminates the authority.

§ 122. Loss of Capacity of Principal or Agent

(1) Except as stated in the caveat, the loss of capacity by the principal has the same effect upon the authority of the agent during the period of incapacity as has the principal's death.

(2) The agent's loss of capacity to do an act for the principal terminates or suspends his authority.

Caveat:

The Institute expresses no opinion as to the effect of the principal's temporary incapacity due to a mental disease.

§ 133. Incapacity of Parties or Other Impossibility

The apparent authority of an agent terminates upon the happening of an event which destroys the capacity of the principal to give the power, or an event which otherwise makes the authorized transaction impossible.

PROCEEDINGS OF THE AMERICAN LAW INSTITUTE
11 Proc.Am.L.Inst. 86, 87, 90, 94, 1933.

MR. WICKERSHAM [presiding]: We turn to Section 120—Death of Principal.

"Sec. 120. Death of Principal . . .

"The death of the principal terminates the authority of the agent."

MR. SEAVEY: Here is one thing I think you ought to argue about anyway. The bald statement, "The death of the principal terminates the authority of the agent," indicates that when the principal dies, the agent's power to bind the estate of the principal thereby terminates, and after that he cannot bind the estate of the principal to third persons. This, it seems to us, is a very shocking result. . . . It may be quite true that fictitiously speaking the death of the principal is notorious; that everybody in the world knows about it all at once. But that is true only fictitiously. . . .

It would seem to be very much more equitable if a result could be reached stating that the authority of the agent does not terminate until the agent has notice of the principal's death, bearing in mind that notice means either that the agent knows or has reason to know or should know or has received a notification and if, under those conditions, of course the agent has notice of the principal's death, he would have to take his chance. . . .

Nevertheless, two years ago when the group asked the advice of the Council . . . as to what should be stated as the law I think it was pretty nearly unanimously agreed that since we are not a body of reformers and since we are stating the law as it is and not as we should like to have it, we should have to state it in this way.

. . .

MR. ROSE: . . . It is perfectly true that the overwhelming weight of authority supports the Blackletter, but we know that that Blackletter is a relic of remote barbarism. . . .

. . .

MR. WICKERSHAM: All we can say is that the law ought to be changed in our opinion. We cannot say that this is not the law, except in particular cases. . . . The motion is we adopt the Restatement with the caveat.

(Motion seconded and carried.)

UNIFORM PROBATE CODE, Part 5
National Conference of Commissioners on Uniform State Laws, 1979.
8 U.L.A., Supp. (1980) pp. 180–185.

§ 5–504. [Power of Attorney Not Revoked Until Notice]

(a) The death of a principal who has executed a written power of attorney, durable or otherwise, does not revoke or terminate the agency as to the attorney in fact or other person, who, without actual knowledge of the death of the principal, acts in good faith under the power. Any action so taken, unless otherwise invalid or unenforceable, binds successors in interest of the principal.

(b) The disability or incapacity of a principal who has previously executed a written power of attorney that is not a durable power does not revoke or terminate the agency as to the attorney in fact or other person, who, without actual knowledge of the disability or incapacity of the principal, acts in good faith under the power. Any action so taken, unless otherwise invalid or unenforceable, binds the principal and his successors in interest.

.   .   .

NOTE: MODIFICATIONS OF THE RULES OF TERMINATION BY DEATH AND DISABILITY

Termination by Death

Starting in the 1800s, a number of states modified by statute the rule of automatic termination by death. Some of them preserved the agent's power only until the agent had notice; others preserved it until the third party had notice. During World War II a large number of states adopted rules preserving the power of agents of soldiers and sailors until some kind of notice had been received. In 1979, the National Conference of Commissioners on Uniform State Laws promulgated a proposal to extend the powers of the agents of all kinds of principals with respect to persons who had no notice of death. Their proposal was framed as a revision of Uniform Probate Code § 504, and as section 4 of a new Uniform Durable Powers of Attorney Act. This provision had been adopted by 1986 in fourteen states.

A related problem with regard to the authority of the surviving partners of a deceased partner had been solved by case law in a provision codified by UPA § 35. Please examine this provision, and consider why the law treated a partner's death differently from the death of a sole proprietor.

Termination by Incapacity

Parallel to the rule of automatic termination of agency powers by death of the principal, the common law contained a rule that powers were also terminated, regardless of notice, by the principal's loss of capacity. The Uniform Probate Code and the Uniform Durable Powers of Attorney Act modify this rule in two ways. (1) As in the case of death, the power does not terminate with respect to parties who lack notice. (2) The power persists with respect to third parties who know about the incapacity, if the document creating the power states that intention. Such powers are denominated "durable." The purpose is to permit trusted friends and relatives to handle a sick patient's affairs without resort to a court-appointed guardian.

Although only fourteen states had, by 1986, adopted the Uniform Probate Code all fifty states had adopted some sort of Durable Power of Attorney legislation authorizing powers of attorney that would survive disability. Three states, Delaware, California, and Virginia, explicitly authorize appointing an agent to make medical decisions in the event the principal becomes incapacitated. These statutes are intended to provide the terminally ill with some decision-making power, and to remove any doubt that Durable Power of Attorney Statutes can be used for medical decisions.

Powers coupled with an interest

An earlier judicial effort to escape some of the consequences of the rules on termination by death or disability appeared in cases in which a property-owner granted authority to deal with the property as an incident of a contract. The typical case was that of a borrower who granted to a money-lender the power to sell property of the borrower in order to repay the loan in case of default. If a power of attorney of this kind was found to be "coupled with an interest," it would not only survive death and incapacity, but would also survive any effort of the principal to recall it. It would be "irrevocable," regardless of notice to the agent or third party. The leading U.S. case is Hunt v. Rousmanier's Administrators, 21 U.S. (8 Wheat.) 174 (1823), which declared that the grantee's power is not "coupled with an interest" unless the grant of authority is accompanied by the grant of an ownership interest in the property that is the subject of the power. The doctrine is still alive, but occasions recurrent difficulties in determining what is a sufficient ownership interest, and how closely it must be "coupled" with the power.

REFERENCES

Beane, Terminating an Agent's Authority—Is Notice Required? 19 Wake Forest Law Rev. 181 (1983) (a short review of the type of notice required in various situations).

Note—Appointing an Agent to Make Medical Treatment Choices, 84 Columbia L.Rev. 985 (1984) (an excellent review of agency issues in medical cases; citation to all states Durable Power of Attorney Statutes.)

Meiklejohn, Incompetent Principals, Competent Third Parties and the Law of Agency, 61 Ind.L.J. 115 (1986). (reviews Cambell v. United States, 657 F.2d 1174 (Ct.Cl.1981) which allowed agent (son) to purchase "Flower Bond" after parent became incompetent, and argues that court should look to issues of fairness in determining whether incompetence should terminate an agent's power to act.)

NOTE: TERMINATION OF AGENCY POWERS IN FOREIGN LAW

The wrestling of Anglo-American law with the problems of termination of authority finds little if any counterpart in European law, which has reached sensible and satisfactory solutions without difficulty. The rule that a power once given cannot be voluntarily revoked without notice to the third party was expressly set out in the Code Napoleon, and faithfully copied in other codes.[1] In this regard, the codes accord with Anglo-American law; the remarkable point is that here they give the recognition to the protection of third party expectations which is so signally lacking in their other provisions on mandate.

Termination by death also occasions few problems. There is no conceptual difficulty about an agent's representing a man's heirs under an authorization to represent the ancestor, if there was an appropriate intent. The French Civil Code expressly directs the agent to continue his uncompleted tasks after the mandatary's death if there is any danger of loss by delay of completion.[2]

The French Civil Code also provides that the agent's authority continues to exist until the agent knows about the principal's death, but does not provide for continuation until the *third party* has notice. This does not seem to be a serious gap, perhaps because of the freely admitted freedom to provide by

---

1. Code Civil, art. 2005; BGB, arts. 170–172; Codice Civile, art. 1396.

2. Code Civil, art. 1991, par. 2; BGB, art. 672; Codice Civile, art. 1728.

contract for survival of the power.[3]   However, the German and Italian civil codes provide expressly for continuation of power after a principal's death until the *third party* has knowledge or reason to know of it.[4]

SECTION 2.   POWERS OF POSITION

INTRODUCTORY NOTE

In the voluminous flow of judicial opinion about the powers of some persons to impose obligations on others, one encounters a large number of generalizations about what can or cannot be done by a wife to bind her husband, by an attorney to bind his client, by a partner to bind his partnership, by a corporate officer to bind his corporation, and by a salesman, secretary, or truck driver to bind his employer.   A productive penman could probably find material for a chapter, if not a treatise, on the agency power of each of these categories, and many more.[1]   For those who are more interested in condensing the volume of law which they must learn than in inflating it, it would be helpful to know whether the rules enunciated about these various kinds of agents are significantly different, or whether they are mere applications to specific cases of the same principles enunciated elsewhere.

A partner is one category of agent with respect to whom the rule of agency has been codified, by section 9 of the Uniform Partnership Act.

Corporate officers are another group about whom rules seem to crystallize, although there is a good deal of diversity in the rules.   One can find judicial pronouncements that a corporate president has by virtue of his office no authority, or presumptive authority, or apparent authority, or inherent or implied authority.

Under a rule of common law which has often been codified, a married woman has power to bind her husband by purchases of necessaries; this is a power which exists even if the husband attempts to repudiate it, and obviously rests on somewhat different grounds than the authority of a partner or corporate president.[2]   For this reason, the American Law Institute prefers to say that the relation is not one of agency, but of "the holding of a power to create restitutional rights." [3] Obviously it becomes entangled in living situations with "true" agencies, so that the distinction in terminology is difficult to maintain.[4]   In

3.   Planiol, Traite Elementaire de Droit Civil, English translation, 1959, art. 2263.

4.   BGB § 169; Codice Civile, art. 1396, par. 2.

1.   The two-volume treatise on agency by Floyd Mechem (2nd ed., 1914) first expounds the general principles applicable to any kind of agents, then devotes about four hundred pages to separate treatments of "particular classes of agents"—attorneys at law, auctioneers, brokers and factors.

2.   Madden, Persons and Domestic Relations (1931) sec. 60; Vernier, American Family Laws (1935) 47; For a routine application of the rule, see Daggett v. Neiman-Marcus Co., 348 S.W.2d 796 (Tex.Civ. App.1961); comment, 13 Baylor L.Rev. 291 (1961).

3.   Restatement of Agency, 2d (1958) § 14–I.

4.   See Daggett v. Neiman-Marcus Co., supra, note 2; Jordan Marsh Co. v. Hedtler, 238 Mass. 43, 130 N.E. 78 (1921) (wife by bigamous marriage bound husband by purchases; husband created "implied agency" by living with her and introducing her to his friends as a wife).

todays world a husband could probably claim power to bind his wife by purchases of necessities as well.

THOMAS v. AMERICAN NATIONAL BANK

Texas Court of Appeals, 1985.
694 S.W.2d 543.

KEITH, JUSTICE (RETIRED).

This is an appeal from a summary judgment granted against appellants, Charles F. Thomas (Thomas) and B.J. McCombs (McCombs) and in favor of appellee, American National Bank (American Bank).

American Bank brought suit against Southwestern Cinema, A Joint Venture (Southwestern Cinema) to collect on a $360,000.00 promissory note executed by Celso Gonzalez (Gonzalez) on behalf of Southwestern Cinema [on May 21, 1982]. American Bank also sued the individual partners of Southwestern Cinema: Thomas; McCombs; and PGR Investment Company (PGR), a partnership composed of Charles R. Porter, Jr. (Porter), Rick Rogers (Rogers), Terrell W. Dahlman (Dahlman) and Gonzalez. The trial court granted the Bank's Motion for Summary Judgment against Southwestern Cinema, McCombs, Thomas, PGR, Porter, Gonzalez, Rogers and Dahlman, jointly and severally, for the sum of $430,544.08, together with attorney's fees of $9,325.00.

Appellants McCombs and Thomas challenge the summary judgment on their position that they had transferred their partnership interests in Southwestern Cinema and, thus, ceased to be partners prior to the time Gonzalez executed the note to American Bank. . . .

The material facts are not in dispute. Southwestern Cinema is a joint venture organized by the above parties for the purpose of purchasing and distributing two motion pictures. Pursuant to the Joint Venture Agreement, Gonzalez was designated as the "Managing Venturer" with express authority to borrow up to $500,000.00 to finance the venture. The distributive shares of the venturers are as follows: McCombs—33⅓%; Thomas—33⅓%; and PGR owning the remaining 33⅓% collectively. All profits and losses for each fiscal year of the joint venture were allocated among the venturers in proportion to their respective distributive shares. The initial funding for the joint venture was ultimately consolidated into a loan of $360,000.00 from Parkdale State Bank (Parkdale Bank) in Corpus Christi, Texas. Thomas and McCombs acknowledged that they were individually liable as partners for the Parkdale Bank indebtedness. In fact, in May of 1982, Thomas and McCombs each paid $5,125.48 to Southwestern Cinema as their share of an interest payment of $15,376.00 made to Parkdale Bank on Southwestern Cinema's note.

When the Parkdale Bank note became due, the partnership "preferred to continue financing." Accordingly, on May 21, 1982, Gonzalez, acting as the "Managing Venturer," negotiated the subject loan from American Bank for the continued financing of Southwestern Cinema. The proceeds of the loan (i.e., $360,000.00) were deposited in Southwestern Cinema's Bank account at American Bank, and a check was in turn issued to discharge the partnership's debt to Parkdale Bank (i.e., $367,101.37). . . .

In their response to the Bank's motion for summary judgment, Thomas and McCombs contended that they were not obligated to repay any part of the loan because Thomas had entered into an agreement with Gonzalez in which he (Gonzalez) agreed to personally assume their partnership indebtedness in return for their partnership interests in the assets of Southwestern Cinema. . . .

Thomas and McCombs contend that American Bank has failed to meet its burden of proof to establish as a matter of law that they were partners . . . It is undisputed that all the participants intended to establish and maintain a joint venture for the purchase and distribution of two motion pictures. Further, the summary judgment proof clearly established that Thomas and McCombs were original partners to the Southwestern Cinema Joint Venture. By their own testimony, Thomas and McCombs were jointly and severally liable for the partnership debts incurred prior to May 21, 1982.

A partnership, once proved, presumptively continues until the contrary appears. . . . The determinative issue in this appeal, then, is whether the appellee Bank has established as a matter of law that, on May 21, 1982, when Southwestern Cinema borrowed $360,000.00 from American Bank, Thomas and McCombs had neither dissolved the partnership nor terminated their participation by an effective transfer of their interests to Gonzalez.

There is no doubt that the joint venture agreement gave Gonzalez the express authority to execute the promissory note to American Bank on behalf of Southwestern Cinema. Even assuming that Thomas and McCombs had no prior knowledge of the American Bank loan, Gonzalez was acting within the scope of and in furtherance of the partnership. Every partner is an agent of the partnership and his actions bind the partnership. . . .

The summary judgment proof establishes that American Bank relied on Thomas' and McCombs' continued participation in Southwestern Cinema as represented in the Joint Venture Agreement in making the loan to the partnership. Adams testified that he relied on the representations of Gonzalez, who was authorized to act on behalf of the partnership according to the written agreement. Adams further testified that the Bank received the requested financial information (i.e., financial statements) from Thomas and McCombs.

It is undisputed that there was no observance by McCombs and Thomas of the provision of Article XI A of the Joint Venture Agreement which provided that . . . "no venturer shall sell, transfer, assign, mortgage or convey any of his or its interests in the Venture and/or his share of distributions of the Venture as set forth in Article VI without the express written consent of the other venturers. . . ."

It is also undisputed that, as of May 21, 1982, neither McCombs nor Thomas had communicated with or given notice to any of the remaining partners of PGR or American Bank that they had sold or transferred their interest in the partnership to Gonzalez. Further, there had been no publication of such a change in ownership of the partnership in Nueces County, Texas.

The summary judgment proof clearly shows that Thomas and McCombs had not effectively withdrawn or terminated their participation in Southwestern Cinema before May 21, 1982. In this respect, we agree with the Bank's contention that any such agreement between Thomas and Gonzalez concerning the transfer of interests in the partnership, without the express consent of the other partners, merely amounted to an executory agreement.

Reading the summary judgment proof of both parties in light of the standard previously set out, we now hold that American Bank, as movant, has conclusively established that no genuine issue of material fact exists that McCombs and Thomas, as partners in Southwestern Cinema, were jointly and severally liable for the partnership indebtedness to American Bank.

.　.　.

Appellants' point of error is overruled, and the judgment of the trial court is Affirmed.

THOMAS v. AMERICAN NATIONAL BANK
Supreme Court of Texas, 1986.
704 S.W.2d 321.

McGee, Justice.

This is an appeal from a summary judgment granted in favor of American National Bank. . . .

The court of appeals affirmed the trial court judgment, holding that Thomas and McCombs had not effectively withdrawn their participation in Southwestern Cinema and, therefore, were liable on the note to American National Bank. 694 S.W.2d 543. We reverse the judgment of the court of appeals and remand the cause to the trial court. An issue of fact exists whether Thomas and McCombs effectively withdrew from the joint venture and dissolved the partnership prior to American National Bank's loan to Southwestern Cinema. . . .

In their depositions, both Thomas and McCombs state that they came to a mutual agreement early in 1982 to get out of the venture because of their inability to obtain information from Gonzalez with regard to their interests in the joint venture. Thomas and McCombs contend they dissolved the joint venture when Thomas told Gonzalez, the managing partner of PGR Investment Company and the managing venturer of Southwestern Cinema, prior to May 21, 1982, that he and McCombs wanted out of the joint venture. Tex.Rev.Civ.Stat.Ann. art. 6132b, § 31 (Vernon 1970). They further contend that subsequent to

Thomas telling Gonzalez that he and McCombs wanted out, it was agreed that Thomas and McCombs would assign their interest in the joint venture to Gonzalez in his individual capacity.

American National Bank, however, does not characterize that conversation as including a notice of dissolution. Rather, American National Bank characterizes it simply as an assignment of Thomas's and McCombs's interest in the joint venture to Gonzalez in his individual capacity. By characterizing the conversation simply as an assignment, the Bank reaches the conclusion that a dissolution did not occur. Tex.Rev.Civ.Stat.Ann. art. 6132b, § 27(1) (Vernon 1970).

While it is true that an assignment of interest in a partnership by a partner will not cause a dissolution of the partnership itself, American Bank's reliance on section 27 is misplaced. . . . In contrast, section 29 of the UPA provides that dissolution of a partnership is the change in relation of the partners caused by any partner ceasing to be associated in the carrying on of the business. This section is consistent with the concept expressed in section 31 of the UPA, upon which Thomas and McCombs rely, which provides that dissolution is caused by "the express will of any partner. . . ." Tex.Rev.Civ.Stat.Ann. art. 6132b, §§ 29, 31 (Vernon 1970). Thus, no party is compelled to continue as a partner when, by his express will, he chooses to withdraw.

In his deposition, Thomas states he informed Gonalez, prior to May 21, 1982, of his and McCombs's desire to "get out" of Southwestern Cinema; that Gonzalez agreed; and that Gonzalez told him he and McCombs could consider themselves "out of the deal." For summary judgment purposes, the court must accept this statement as true. *Wilcox v. St. Mary's University of San Antonio,* 531 S.W.2d 589 (Tex.1975). . . .

However, American National Bank asserts that even assuming that Thomas told Gonzalez of his and McCombs's intent to get out of Southwestern Cinema, notice to Gonzalez was insufficient to constitute notice to PGR Investment Company. American National Bank contends that because Thomas's assignment of his and McCombs's interest in Southwestern Cinema to Gonzalez was in Gonzalez's personal capacity, then any notice of dissolution he received was also in his personal capacity and, therefore, does not operate as notice to the joint venture. Rather, American National Bank argues that Thomas and McCombs were required to give notice to each member of PGR Investment Company before there could be an effective dissolution.

Section 12 of the UPA, however, provides that "notice to any partner of any matter relating to partnership affairs . . . operates as notice to or knowledge of the partnership." Tex.Rev.Civ.Stat.Ann. art. 6132b, § 12 (Vernon 1970). Notice of dissolution is a matter relating to partnership affairs. In this case, Gonzalez was a partner at the time he received notice, if any, of the dissolution. If Thomas told Gonzalez that he and McCombs no longer wanted to be involved in the venture and wanted out, this was notice to PGR Investment Company. There is no requirement that notice of dissolution be communicated to each and every member of a joint venture. But even if there were, the only partner left in Southwestern Cinema was PGR Investment Company. Notice to one of the members of PGR Investment Company is sufficient to constitute notice to that partnership of the dissolution of Southwestern Cinema.

In *Green v. Waco State Bank*, 78 Tex. 2, 14 S.W. 252 (Tex.1890), this court considered what was required for an effective dissolution and held it was not necessary that there be a distinct agreement between all the members at the same time that a dissolution shall take place at a certain time. Rather, this court held that any of the partners in the firm could have dissolved it at any time and that the notice to the other partners could be in any manner. The Uniform Partnership Act, which has been adopted by 48 states, including Texas, allows dissolution of a partnership by the express will of a partner. Other states have held this to mean that dissolution is accomplished by giving notice to the other partners and that no particular form of notice is required. *See,* e.g., *Wester & Co. v. Nestle,* 669 P.2d 1046 (Colo.App.1983) (withdrawal of partner); *Babray v. Carlino,* 2 Ill.App.3d 241, 276 N.E.2d 435 (1971) (verbal agreement to dissolve); *Cave v. Cave,* 81 N.M. 797, 474 P.2d 480 (1970) (mutual consent to dissolve evidenced by acts); *Nicholes v. Hunt,* 273 Or. 255, 541 P.2d 820 (1975) (telephone call advising partner that business relationship was at an end was sufficient notice of dissolution); *Timmermann v. Timmermann,* 272 Or. 613, 538 P.2d 1254 (1975) (oral notice).

Therefore, we conclude that Thomas's deposition testimony raised a question of fact whether dissolution had occurred prior to May 21, 1982. Finding that a fact issue does exist which would preclude a summary judgment on behalf of American National Bank, we reverse the judgment of the court of appeals and remand the cause to the trial court.

COMMENTS ON GENERAL AND SPECIAL AGENTS

Richard R.B. Powell,[1] in Tiffany on Agency (2d ed., 1924), sec. 18.
(Author's footnotes omitted).

It is submitted that the attempted division of agents into general agents and special agents is meaningless and confusing. It is usually said that a general agent is one authorized to transact the business generally of his principal, or the business of his principal of a particular kind, or the business of his principal in a particular place. Those who thus define "general agent" say that a special agent is one given power to do individual acts only. Other courts apply the term "general agent" to any professional or customary agent, such as an attorney, broker, factor, or auctioneer, although he may be employed only in a

---

1. Richard R.B. Powell (born 1890) has been known in recent years chiefly for his work in the Property field. He has edited casebooks on Possessory Estates, Trust and Future Interests, and was Reporter for the major part of the Restatement of Property. Since 1921 he has been a member of the Columbia Law School faculty.

single transaction. It is now quite frequently admitted that the distinction is unsatisfactory and lacking in precision. What the courts are seeking to do is to point out that some agents have more power to bind their principals than other agents. This is true. But the determination of that power, in a given case, does not turn upon whether A. was a general or special agent, but rather upon whether the act of A. was within or without the authority or power conferred by P. upon A. in his dealings with others. If the act of A. is within that authority or power, P. is bound, regardless of what special instructions P. may have given A."

FLOYD R. MECHEM, in colloquy over definition of a "general agent," 4 Proc.Am.L.Inst., 1926, p. 154 [2].

"It is hard to define what is general. I have tried for many years to minimize the distinction between general and special agents, but, when it came to this Restatement, it seemed to me that they were still in our law, and that I could not safely omit them. Some of my learned associates have suggested that we say nothing about the distinction at all, and perhaps that would be a better way."

REFERENCES

General and special agents:

Pollitt, Agency—General and Special (1932) 17 Minn.L.Rev. 17 (1933), 21 Ky.L.J. 369, 22 Ky.L.J. 11 (collects comments criticizing the classification, defends classification as useful, and offers careful collection and analysis of cases employing the distinction).

UNIFORM PARTNERSHIP ACT, SECTION 9

Read text of the section.

COURTNEY v. G.A. LINAKER CO.
Arkansas Supreme Court, 1927.
173 Ark. 777, 293 S.W. 723.

HART, C.J. (after stating the facts). The record shows that the business was first owned by the defendant, Mrs. E.E. Courtney, and that she subsequently sold it to her two sons, who moved the store from one part of the town of McGehee to another part of it. According to the evidence for the plaintiff, it had no notice that Mrs. Courtney had sold the business to her sons and that they were operating it as their own when the bill of goods in question was purchased. It is true that the goods were purchased after the bill of sale had been executed, but, according to the evidence for the plaintiff, it had no notice that Mrs. Courtney had sold the business to her sons, and it sold the goods to the sons believing that they were the agents of their mother and were purchasing the goods for her. While the testimony of the plaintiff on this point was contradicted by that of the defendant, the finding of the circuit court in favor of the plaintiff is conclusive upon us upon appeal.

---

2. Reprinted by permission of the American Law Institute.

The case then stands here as if the plaintiff, not being notified of the sale of the store to C.A. Courtney and his brother, and consequently not being notified of the revocation of his authority as the agent of his mother, was justified in acting upon the presumption of its continuance. On its face the agency of C.A. Courtney as the representative of his mother in operating the store was a continuing authority, on which the plaintiff had a right to rely until its revocation. Persons who deal with an agent before notice of the recall of his powers are not affected by the recall. Hatch v. Coddington, 95 U.S. 48, 24 L.Ed. 339; Insurance Co. v. McCain, 96 U.S. 84; Johnson v. Christian, 128 U.S. 374, 9 S.Ct. 87, 32 L.Ed. 412; 2 C.J. ss. 650(3), page 920, and 21 R.C.L. ss. 37, page 860.

In a note to 41 L.R.A.,N.S., at page 664, it is said that it is settled that the acts of an agent, after his authority has been revoked, bind a principal as against third persons who, in the absence of notice of the revocation of the agent's authority, rely upon its continued existence. It is also said that the cases are practically unanimous on this general rule, and most of them summarily state it as if it were an axiom. Many cases are cited in support of the rule. The cases hold that the duty of the principal to notify third persons of the termination of the agency is of the same character and requires the same degree of certainty as that which the law imposes upon the members of a partnership in the case of dissolution as a measure of protection against liability by reason of the subsequent acts of the former members of the dissolved firm.

This court is committed to the rule that the retiring members of a dissolved partnership continue liable to creditors who deal with the remaining members upon the faith of its continued existence without notice of its dissolution. Bluff City Lumber Co. v. Bank of Clarksville, 95 Ark. 1, 128 S.W. 58, and cases cited.

It is next insisted that the testimony of C.A. Courtney to the effect that notice was published in a newspaper in McGehee, stating that the business would be operated thereafter in the name of C.A. Courtney, grocer, was notice to the creditors that the sale had been made. The court properly sustained an objection to this testimony because proof of publication of the notice itself would have been the best evidence, and no foundation was laid for admitting secondary evidence of the publication of the notice. Moreover, if primary evidence of the publication of the notice had been introduced, it would only have been evidence of the fact of the sale and consequent revocation of the authority of C.A. Courtney to act as agent for his mother as between themselves. Under the authorities cited above, after a principal has appointed an agent in a particular business, parties dealing with him in that business have a right to rely upon the continuance of his authority until in some way informed of its revocation.

It follows that the judgment must be affirmed.

REFERENCES

Scope of the partnership:

Matanuska Valley Bank v. Arnold, 15 Alaska 557, 223 F.2d 778 (9th Cir.1955) (partner not liable for debts made outside the scope of the partnership).

Notice of termination:

Anderson, Clayton & Co., Inc. v. Swallows, 84 N.Mex. 486, 505 P.2d 431 (1973) (partners who bought from plaintiff before incorporation were liable for purchases after incorporation, in the absence of notification; payment by corporate checks was not notice of dissolution of partnership).

Meggs v. Central Supply Co., 159 Ind.App. 431, 307 N.E.2d 288 (1974) (seller of business, expressly including business name, was liable for goods bought by buyers of business from former supplier between date of sale and date of notification of supplier).

UNIFORM PARTNERSHIP ACT, SECTION 35

Read text of the section.

VIRGINIA CONCRETE CO. v. BOARD OF SUPERVISORS

Virginia Supreme Court of Appeals, 1956.
197 Va. 821, 91 S.E.2d 415, 56 A.L.R.2d 1283.

[The Board of Supervisors filed suit for an injunction against the concrete company; while the suit was pending, it adopted a resolution looking toward the repeal of the ordinance involved in the suit; when this was brought to the attention of their attorneys, in the course of the trial, the attorneys consented to a dismissal with prejudice. Later the Board rescinded its resolution for repeal of the ordinance, and moved to set aside the dismissal of the injunction proceeding; the lower court granted the motion.]

BUCHANAN, J. . . . It is clear that there was a voluntary dismissal of the injunction suit by the Board's attorneys, accompanied by their consent that it be done with prejudice. It is in order to inquire first what is the effect of the decree, and second whether the Board's attorneys possessed authority to agree to make that disposition of the case.

[The court concluded that the effect of the dismissal, if authorized, would be to adjudicate finally all rights of the plaintiff in the subject matter].

The next question presented is whether the attorneys for the Board had authority to agree to the entry of that decree.

It is not questioned and it is plain from the record that the attorneys for the Board acted in good faith and in the belief that they had the authority which they undertook to exercise. The minutes of the Board show that Mr. McCandlish was "requested to assist" the Commonwealth's attorney, Mr. Marsh, in the prosecution of the suit. He testified that he believed he had authority to dismiss under his general retainer. Mr. Marsh thought he had the authority to handle the case as it should be handled by virtue of his office as Commonwealth's attorney and the customary way of his handling legal matters for the Board, but he stated, "this is the first time a case of that type has been handled by us." Neither claimed any express authority from the Board to dismiss the case with prejudice and it is clear that none was given.

. . .

In Harris v. Diamond Const. Co., 184 Va. 711, 721–722, 36 S.E.2d 573, 578, this court said it was settled that an attorney at law, by virtue of his employment as such, has no authority to compromise his client's claim or surrender any of his substantial rights without his consent, but the attorney has full authority to act on behalf of his client in the conduct of litigation before the court, and by virtue of such authority he may make admissions and stipulations as to facts, the effect of which is to dispense with proof of such facts. 5 Am.Jur., Attorneys at Law, § 98, p. 318; 1955 Cum.Supp. at 39; Annotation, 30 A.L.R.2d 944.

. . . It would be wholly illogical to say that an attorney must have special authority in order to compromise his client's suit and accept less than his client claims, but has sufficient authority under his general employment as attorney to dismiss his client's case so as to bar him from any recovery both then and thereafter.

The prevailing rule is well stated in 7 C.J.S. Attorney and Client § 87, p. 908:

> "In the absence of statute, an attorney can enter a dismissal, discontinuance, or retraxit, which terminates the case on its merits, only where he has been expressly authorized to do so; but it is generally held that an attorney has implied authority to enter or take a dismissal, discontinuance, or nonsuit, which does not bar the bringing of another suit on the same cause of action."

The rule applies to attorneys for municipalities as well as to attorneys for private individuals, and particularly where such a decree or order would have the effect of preventing the enforcement of a valid ordinance or the exercise of governmental powers. West v. Bank of Commerce & Trusts, 4 Cir., 167 F.2d 664, 666; United States v. Beebe, 180 U.S. 343, 21 S.Ct. 371, 45 L.Ed. 563.

. . .

In the absence of express authority from the Board the consent of its attorneys did not bind it or deprive it of a right to have the "with prejudice" feature of the decree set aside. The decree appealed from which set aside the dismissal with prejudice and adjudged that the dismissal should be without prejudice is, therefore,

Affirmed.

REFERENCES

Lipp v. National Screen Corp., 290 F.2d 321 (3d Cir.1961) (client bound by attorney stipulation that conspiracy and monopoly issues in his case be determined in a companion case brought by a different plaintiff).

Cusimano's Will, 174 Misc. 1068, 22 N.Y.S.2d 677 (1940) (client bound by attorney's release of client's right to contest will, where client got full amount which he claimed).

Yarnall v. Yorkshire Worsted Mills, 370 Pa. 93, 87 A.2d 192, 30 A.L.R.2d 939 (1952) (client bound by attorney's consent to order, where client did not promptly repudiate).

Mungin v. Florida East Coast Railway Co., 318 F.Supp. 720 (D.Fla.1970) (where attorney entered into unauthorized settlement principals deemed to have ratified it since they did not protest within a reasonable time).

Cohen v. Goldman, 85 R.I. 434, 132 A.2d 414 (1957) (client bound by compromise to which attorney forged client's signature); comment (1958) 56 Mich.L.Rev. 437.

Bursten v. Green, 172 So.2d 472 (Fla.App.1965) (written authorization to attorney "to act in the matter as fully as he could act for himself, including the right to file any proceedings deemed advisable and to negotiate settlement thereof" did not authorize attorney to stipulate final settlement of case).

Castell v. United States, 98 F.2d 88 (2d Cir.1938) (power of attorney to "settle on such terms as he may deem proper" authorized final settlement of suit).

Quintero v. Jim Walter Homes, Inc., 709 S.W.2d 225 (Tex.App.1985) (knowledge of a prior judgment which attorney should have known with due diligence is imputed to client).

Annotation, Authority of attorney to compromise action (1953) 30 A.L.R.2d 944.

ITALO–PETROLEUM CORP. v. HANNIGAN
Delaware Supreme Court, 1940.
40 Del. 534, 14 A.2d 401.

The plaintiff below sued upon two promissory notes under seal payable on demand, alleged to have been executed and delivered in the State of California by the defendant corporation to Fred Shingle, syndicate manager. The notes were signed by the corporation's president and attested by its assistant secretary. . . .

Proof was made of certain by-laws of the corporation. Section 2 of Article 3, was, in part, as follows: "The president shall be the chief executive officer of the corporation and shall exercise general supervision and administration over its affairs, and over all of its other officers. . . . He shall sign and execute all authorized contracts, obligations, conveyances, papers, and writings requiring the corporate name . . . ." Section 4, of the Article, relating to the duties of the secretary, was, in part, as follows: "He shall provide and keep in safe custody the corporate seal, and when authorized or directed by the Board of Directors shall affix the same to any instrument requiring such seal and shall attest the same by his signature". Section 1, of Article 7, relating to checks, drafts, etc., was as follows: "All checks, drafts or orders for the payment of moneys and all notes and acceptances shall be signed by the President, Vice-President or Manager, and also by the Secretary or Assistant Secretary, unless the power to sign the same shall have been duly delegated by the Board of Directors to some other officer or officers of the corporation".

. . .

At the close of the plaintiff's testimony, a motion for a non-suit was refused. At the close of the testimony, on motion of the plaintiff, a verdict was directed, and entered in the sum of $70,332.87, being the full amount of the notes with interest. A motion for a new trial was made, argued and refused.

LAYTON, C.J.

. . .

The second question is whether there was sufficient proof of authority for the execution of the notes sued on to entitle them to be admitted in evidence, having regard for the affidavit denying signature filed by the defendant, and the plea of non est factum.

. . .

The plaintiff proved the identity and signatures of the president and assistant secretary, and proved the corporate seal. In Conine v. J. & B.R.R. Co., 3 Houst. 288, 89 Am.Dec. 230, the former Court of Errors and Appeals laid down the rule thus: "When the common seal of a corporation appears to be affixed to an instrument and the signature of a proper officer is proved or admitted, the Court is bound to presume that the officer did not exceed his authority, and the seal itself is prima facie evidence that it was affixed by proper authority; and the burden of showing that it is wrongfully there rests upon the party objecting to it". Stated otherwise, it is implied from the seal that the corporation, through its directors or those empowered to conduct the corporate business, authorized the president, secretary or other official acting in the particular case to make the contract evidenced by the instrument on which the seal is placed; and the instrument thus sealed, in the absence of opposing proof, is to be regarded as the binding act and deed of the corporation. 6 Fletcher, § 2471. This evidence is merely presumptive. It is not conclusive of the assent and act of the corporation. The presumption of due execution raised by the corporate seal may always be overcome. But, in the ordinary case, on such proof, the instrument is admissible in evidence, and, presumptively binds the corporation.

The defendant, however, contends that the question whether its president had authority to bind the corporation by executing the notes should have been left to the jury. This is, of course, true if evidence to overcome the presumption was, in fact, introduced. In this respect the record is somewhat confusing. It is not clear whether the defendant was in a position to show that its officers acted without authority, but was prevented by a preliminary adverse ruling of the court. However that may be, it is entirely clear that the court found express authority for the acts of the corporation's officers in Section 1 of Article 7 of the by-laws. "The question before me", said the court, "being the construction of Article Seven of the by-laws of the corporation, was clearly a legal one which should never be left to the jury".

Properly construed, the by-law may not be regarded as a grant of power. It is unreasonable to suppose that it was intended to lodge the power to bind the corporation by notes and acceptances indiscriminately in the president, vice-president and manager. Reasonably interpreted, the by-law merely designates the officer who may perform the ministerial act necessary to carry into execution the order of the board of directors. Clearly, the authority relates to the formalities of execution.

The defendant, on the other hand, contends that Sections 2 and 4 of Article 3 of the by-laws relating, respectively, to the powers and duties of the president and secretary, clearly show that these officers had no power to bind the corporation by the execution of the notes in the absence of express authority from the board of directors. This contention is not acceptable. The word, "authorized", appearing in each of the sections of the by-laws referred to, does not have the restricted meaning of authority expressly conferred. Implied authority is, nevertheless, authority. Apparent authority is authority, if it be shown that the board of directors has knowingly permitted the officers of the corporation to exercise authority in the particular matters, or has held them out as possessing authority. See Greenspon's Sons Iron & Steel Co. v. Pecos Valley Gas Co., 4 W.W.Harr. 567, 156 A. 350. However arising, authority is power. The sections of the by-laws, relied on by the defendant as being restrictive in nature, do no more than designate the officers who shall attend to the formalities of execution if authority to act in the particular matter has proceeded, either expressly or by implication, from the board of directors.

The direction of a verdict for the plaintiff for the reason that under Section 1 of Article 7 of the by-laws, the president was expressly authorized to bind the corporation by executing the notes sued on was error; and as a retrial of the cause will be ordered, it has seemed advisable to express an opinion with respect to questions that may arise.

The strict rule that the president of a private corporation has little or no authority to bind the corporation by virtue of his office is slowly but certainly giving place to the more reasonable and practical view that he is presumed to have, by virtue of his office, certain more or less limited powers in the transaction of the usual and ordinary business of the corporation. See Atlantic Refining Co. v. Ingalls & Co. Inc., 7 W.W. Harr. 503, 185 A. 885.

It is not unreasonable to presume that the president has the authority to bind the corporation by executing and transferring negotiable paper to pay the debts of the corporation; and the more reasonable view, proceeding from realistic considerations, is that presumption should be indulged that the president has the authority to bind the corporation by the execution and transfer of negotiable paper in the ordinary course of the corporation's business. 2 Fletcher, supra, § 599. The power to bind the principal by making, accepting or endorsing negotiable paper is, of course, an important power, susceptible to abuse, and dangerous in its consequences to corporations; but there seems to be no sufficient reason to conclude that corporations will suffer such consequences by recognizing presumptive authority in the president to bind the corporation by the execution and transfer of negotiable paper in the ordinary course of its business. A defendant corporation is in a better position, perhaps, than the plaintiff to show want of express authority for the act of its president, or that his authority was definitely restricted. It is in an equally favorable position with the plaintiff to show that no implied power existed, or no apparent authority arising out of a course of conduct. The opportunity is open for it to show that the transaction was unusual or extraordinary; that it was not in the ordinary course of its business; that the president was serving his own interests; that the plaintiff had knowledge of want of authority; or other facts and circumstances sufficient to overcome the presumption. And, where a plaintiff in an action against a corporation on promissory notes, purporting to have been executed by its authority, relies on the presumption of authority arising from the presence of the corporate seal on the instrument sued on or on the presumptive authority of the president to execute or transfer the instrument, the character of the transaction, the course of conduct on the part of the president, or other officer executing the instrument, and the corporation with respect to like matters, ratification or acceptance of benefits by the corporation, or other facts in the nature of an estoppel sufficient to overcome the defense of want of authority, are all proper subjects of inquiry. A reasonable latitude should be permitted in the development of the evidence on behalf of either party.

. . .

The court below erred in directing a verdict in favor of the plaintiff. The judgment is reversed, with a venire de novo.

IN RE WESTEC CORP.

WALKER v. CARPENTER

United States Court of Appeals, Fifth Circuit, 1970.
434 F.2d 195.

WISDOM, CIRCUIT JUDGE. This case tangentially relates to the collapse of Westec Corporation, a Texas corporation now in proceedings for reorganization under Chapter X of the Bankruptcy Act. The facts out of which it arises constitute a prescription for corporate collapse: loose stock transactions, a corporate acquisition made to placate and benefit a subsidiary's principal officer and, allegedly, double payment for an officer's activities.

Garland Walker asserts a claim of $383,000 against the Trustee in Bankruptcy based on an alleged contract with Westec. The district court disallowed the claim on the ground that no binding contract was entered into between Westec and Walker. . . .

[Walker had performed various services for Westec on a vague understanding with Westec's president for compensation or reimbursement. He claims that the president finally agreed to issue him 7,000 Westec shares in compensation. These shares multiplied in value six times between the dates of the alleged promise and the breach; the sum of $383,000 was their value at date of breach. At the time of this litigation, they were probably worth little or nothing.]

A. The first point urged by Walker is that the trial court erred in finding that Hall had no authority to contract for the issuance of Westec's capital stock. Walker asserts that the actions of a corporate president are presumed to be within the scope of his authority absent contrary proof. But Texas law is clearly to the contrary. As to actual authority,

> . . . one who seeks to hold a corporation liable upon a contract made by an agent has the burden of proof, not only the execution of the contract for the corporation, but the authority of the agent through whom it is claimed the corporation acted.

Adkins-Polk Co. v. Pate, Tex.Civ.App.1928, 11 S.W.2d 654. See Perper v. Sonnabend, 5 Cir.1955, 221 F.2d 142, 144. As to apparent authority, the plaintiff had the burden of proving

> . . . such conduct on the part of the principal as would lead a reasonably prudent person, using diligence and discretion, to suppose that the agent has the authority he purports to exercise.

Chastain v. Cooper & Reed, 152 Tex. 322, 331, 257 S.W.2d 422, 427 (1953).

The record supports the trial court's findings of neither real nor apparent authority. Walker made no showing with respect to Hall's actual authority. In fact, the law generally on this point is that the president has "no authority to bind the company by a contract for the issuance of its capital stock". 2 Fletcher Cyclopedia Corporations § 604 (1969 rev.). As to apparent authority, Walker asserted only that Hall had in the past fulfilled promises of stock. But a finding of apparent authority depends on the standard of the reasonable man using diligence and discretion. An *insider,* such as Walker, has no license to rely on such authority. Additionally, Walker indicates in his testimony that he knew that it was the board's responsibility to issue stock. He knew that the stock option promised at the same time as the shares outright had to be submitted to the board. He also knew that he would have to wait for the board meeting to get his 7,000 shares; it was the date of the directors' meeting that Walker later set up as the date of default by calculating damages on the basis of the day's stock prices.

B. Walker next asserts that the rule that knowledge of the president is imputed to the corporation somehow overcomes Hall's lack of authority. If this were the rule, there would be no effective limitations on the contracting authority of corporate officers. The cases do not support Walker's claim. Rather, they hold only that imputation of officers' knowledge to the corporation works together with the rule that a corporation is estopped to deny its officers' authority to make a contract when the corporation accepts the benefits of the contract knowing of the concomitant contractual burdens. See Vogel v. Zipp, Tex.Civ.App.1936, 90 S.W.2d 668.

. . .

The Court's findings of fact are not clearly erroneous. We agree with its conclusion of law that no binding and enforceable legal contract was entered into obligating Westec to pay Walker anything of value over his salary for the services (if any) rendered in Seismic's acquisition of Continental Rubber.

. . .

NOTE: POWERS OF CORPORATION PRESIDENTS

There is the greatest diversity in the statements made by various courts about the power of a corporation president. In L.A. Wood & Co. v. Taylor the majority opinion declared, "It is well settled under the law of Georgia that the president of a corporation is its alter ego . . .."[1] In the same case, a dissenting judge said, "According to the general law, the president, by virtue of his office, has no authority save to preside at corporate meetings and to represent the corporation in court proceedings."[2]

The breadth of the apparent gap between these two views narrows somewhat when the facts of the cases are examined. The "alter ego" doctrine, when tracked to its lair, is found to flourish chiefly in cases involving the admissibility in evidence against the corporation of statements made by the corporation president.[3] The stricter statement is most commonly applied when the corporation is sued on a contract made by the president in the corporation's behalf.[4] The conflicting statements quoted above were made in a case involving the corporation's tort liability caused by the negligence of a guest in the corporation's automobile, of which the president was in charge. If there is a difference between the president's power to bind the corporation procedurally, and his power to bind it to contractual obligations, where should the line be drawn on his power to make it liable for tort?

If we confine our attention to contractual cases, we find many of the conflicts resolved by separating those instances in which the president has been actually instructed or permitted to run the company's business, and those in which he has not been.[5] But we can hardly eliminate all conflict, even by the closest analysis. Some courts evidently indulge a presumption that the president is in charge of the business, putting the burden on the company to show that he is not.[6] Others evidently require the third party to bear the initial

1. L.A. Wood & Co. v. Taylor, 154 F.2d 548, 550 (C.C.A.5th 1946).

2. Id., 551.

3. For example, Franklin Savings & Loan Co. v. Branan, 54 Ga.App. 363, 188 S.E. 67 (1936) (case relied on by majority in L.A. Wood Co. case; and see dissent in L.A. Wood Co., at 551. The dissent states that the doctrine is also applicable where process against the corporation is served on the president; usually statutes authorize such service).

4. Kelly v. Citizens Finance, 306 Mass. 531, 28 N.E.2d 1005 (1940), comments 29 Calif.L.Rev. 422, 89 U.Pa.L.Rev. 386 (president who was one of two directors of corporation had no authority to hire attorney to defend action for dissolution of the corporation); Stoneman v. Fox Film Corp., 295 Mass. 419, 4 N.E.2d 63, 107 A.L.R. 989 (1936); comment, 17 Boston U.L.Rev. 176; Horowitz v. S. Slater & Sons, 265 Mass. 143, 164 N.E. 72 (1928).

5. In addition to cases reprinted above, and those cited in note 4, see St. John v. Fulton Market Corp., 248 N.Y. 636, 162 N.E. 555 (1928) (president, in charge of business, had power to hire real estate broker to sell land); Twyeffort v. Unexcelled Manufacturing Co., 263 N.Y. 6, 188 N.E. 138 (1933) (president, in charge of business, had power to hire attorney); Oakes v. Cattaraugus Water Co., 143 N.Y. 430, 38 N.E. 461, 26 L.R.A. 544 (1894).

6. Canister Co. v. National Can Corp., 63 F.Supp. 361 (D.C.Del.1945); In re Henry Harrison Co., 40 F.Supp. 733 (D.C.N.Y. 1941).

burden of showing that the president is in fact in the position of a manager.[7] The former presumption leads quite naturally to the view that the third party is entitled to make the same presumption which the courts make, thus giving the president a wide "apparent authority." [8]

When the president of the company completely controls the company, courts usually will "expand" his authority to act. In Renault v. L.N. Renault & Sons, 188 F.2d 317 (3d Cir.1950), the company was being sued on a promise of the president to pay a debt that was barred by the statute of limitations. In allowing the claim the court stated:

> Defendant also urges that John D'Agostino lacked the authority to bind defendant by the alleged renewal promise. A study of the record discloses no evidence of express authority in John D'Agostino. Further, the law of both New Jersey and Pennsylvania limits the scope of a corporate president's implied authority to acts within the ordinary course of business. A promise to pay a stale debt has usually been designated an extraordinary promise not within the president's implied authority. Reuter Organ Co. v. First Methodist Episcopal Church, 1941, 7 Wash.2d 310 109 P.2d 798, 802; Salt Lake Valley Loan & T. Co. v. St. Joseph Land Co., 1928, 73 Utah 256, 273 P. 507. Where one man completely controls a corporation, however, a necessary and logical exception has been carved out of the above rule. In such situation, the one man achieving unrestrained control is held prima facie to have power to do all acts which the Board of Directors could have authorized. Chestnut Street Trust & Savings Fund Co. v. Record Pub. Co., 1910, 227 Pa. 235, 75 A. 1067; C.L. McClain Fuel Corp. v. Lineinger, 1941, 341 Pa. 364, 19 A.2d 478. We shall consider appellant's contention that the case at bar falls within this exception.

The court then noted that at the time the president made the promise he owned all of the stock in the company.

REFERENCES

In general, see citations in footnotes to preceding note.

One person domination:

Plains Builders, Inc. v. Pride Transport Co., 554 S.W.2d 59 (Tex.Civ.App.1977) (evidence that Wardlaw was principal shareholder, chief operating officer and president of Wardlaw Transport Express, Inc., was sufficient to establish authority to sign promissory note).

Moore v. Phillips, 176 Cal.App.2d 702, 1 Cal.Rptr. 508 (1959) (corporation liable for obligation incurred in own name by president who mingled his affairs with those of corporation).

20th Century Coal Co. v. Taylor, 275 S.W.2d 72 (Ky.1954) (corporation liable where president handled all affairs of corporation).

Pettit v. Doeskin Products, Inc., 270 F.2d 95 (2d Cir.1959) rehearing denied 270 F.2d 669 (2d Cir.1959), certiorari denied 362 U.S. 910, 80 S.Ct. 660, 4 L.Ed.2d 618 (1960) (corporation not bound by act of its president done dishonestly and without board approval although president dominated corporation and made or unmade directors at will). This case involved the Birrell frauds.

7. See Massachusetts cases, cited in note 4 above.

8. See cases cited above, note 6.

Scope of activities:

Lee v. Jenkins Brothers, 156 F.Supp. 858 (D.Conn.1957), affirmed 268 F.2d 357 (2d Cir.1959), certiorari denied 361 U.S. 913, 80 S.Ct. 257, 4 L.Ed.2d 183 (1959) (chief executive not authorized to promise employee life employment and pension).

Liebermann v. Princeway Realty Corp., 13 N.Y.2d 999, 245 N.Y.S.2d 390, 195 N.E.2d 57 (1963) (president not authorized to promise to pay large bonus to employee).

Aimonetto v. Rapid Gas, Inc., 80 S.D. 453, 126 N.W.2d 116 (1964) (evidence sustained inference that directors had authorized president to write check).

Home Savings Bank v. Gertenbach, 270 Wis. 386, 71 N.W.2d 347 (1955) (president of bank had no authority to release a guarantee of a loan).

Formalities required:

Lockwood v. Wolf Corp., 629 F.2d 603 (9th Cir.1980) (settlement agreement signed by corporate president, who warranted his authority, and attested by assistant secretary, held binding upon corporation despite absence of formal approval by board of directors).

Stewart Capital Corp. v. Andrus, 468 F.Supp. 1261 (S.D.N.Y.1979) (bid submitted at auction of offshore drilling rights, signed by president, was binding on company and was therefore in compliance with rules of auction even though not attested by secretary as prescribed by directors' resolution).

Village Creations v. Crawfordsville Enterprises, 232 Ga. 131, 206 S.E.2d 3 (1974) (trust deed of corporation not presumed valid when signed by president and attested by secretary, but lacking corporate seal).

Shareholders' approval:

Some corporate actions, such as a sale or mortgage of a major portion of the property, may require a specific vote by shareholders, who cannot delegate general authority to the president or anyone else. In such cases, whether the corporation is bound may depend upon whether third parties have "notice" of the lack of shareholder action.

Matter of Itemlab, Inc., 197 F.Supp. 5 (D.N.Y.1961) (mortgagee had notice of possible defect from fact that corporation was mortgaging property for another's benefit).

Roxbury State Bank v. The Clarendon, 123 N.J.Super. 400, 303 A.2d 340 (1973) *modified* 129 N.J.Super. 358, 324 A.2d 24 (corporation not liable on mortgage loans made for benefit of shareholders, who received entire proceeds, where lender had notice of improper purposes).

SEC v. First Securities Co., 463 F.2d 981 (7th Cir.1972) (corporation was liable to customers for frauds of president who owned 92 percent of stock, and had been permitted for years to handle accounts without supervision).

Corporate litigation:

Goebel, The Authority of the President over Corporate Litigation: A Study in Inherent Agency (1962) 37 St. John's L.Rev. 29.

Authority of general manager:

Willsey v. W.C. Porter Farms Co., 522 S.W.2d 29 (Mo.App.1975) (founder, principal shareholder, president and general manager of farming corporation did not have implied or apparent authority to sell 35 percent of the corporation's land).

Apex Financial Corp. v. Decker, 245 Pa.Super. 439, 369 A.2d 483 (1976) (manager of finance company, scope of whose duties was not shown, has no implied or apparent authority to subordinate lien of finance company gratuitously).

Crawford Savings & Loan Association v. Dvorak, 40 Ill.App.3d 288, 352 N.E.2d 261 (1976) (daughter of restaurant owner who managed all its business for seven years did not have implied or apparent authority to mortgage real estate; no discussion of statute of frauds or ratification).

NOTE: POWERS OF POSITION IN FOREIGN LAW [1]

The German conception of an agent's external power (Vollmacht) led quite naturally to rules conferring definite powers in commercial matters on certain office-holders. The German Code of Commerce of 1897 provides that a person in charge of a business has power to make all transactions usual in the type of business, (Art. 54) and that a clerk in a store has inherent authority to sell goods and to receive payment (Art. 56). Although partners may allot authority in the business to different areas of activity, these limitations have no effect on third persons (Art. 126). Similarly broad powers are given to the management in stock companies (Aktiengesetz, art. 74(2)) and limited liability companies (GmbH Gesetz, art. 37).

A literal reading of these German laws would lead to the conclusion that the principal is bound even though the third party had reason to doubt that the principal intended to incur such an obligation. Apparently this is correct, but the German courts have imposed some limits on the third party's opportunism. When the third party conspired with the agent to defeat the principal's intentions, the principal is not liable; and this exception probably extends to all other cases in which the third party can be said to have lacked "good faith." [2]

The Scandinavian states have moved one step beyond the German Code of Commerce, and have codified the general principle that when a person holds a position to which certain authority is attached by usage, he shall have corresponding powers. "This type of power was by no means unknown before the codification. . . ." Professor Grönfors observes. "What was new was the idea of forming an express provision on the matter, phrased in such a general and all embracing way." [3]

The Scandinavian provisions are said to have served as models for provisions of an international uniform law on agency, proposed by the Rome Institute for the Unification of Private Law.[4] The draft contains these provisions:

Article 4.—*Implied Authorization.* The authority of a person to act in the name of another may arise from some position which that person occupies with the consent of the other, and from which the power to act in the name of that other arises according to the law and usages applicable.

Article 8.—*Scope of Authorization Implied from a Position.* In the case of authorization implied from a position, the agent shall be authorized to perform in the name of his principal all those acts normally implied by his position.

If a person shall be entrusted by another with the management of his business, then by that fact he shall be authorized to perform all acts required by the normal running of the business.

1. See Kurt Grönfors, Powers of Position in the Swedish Law of Agency, in 6 Scandinavian Studies in Law 97 (1962).

2. W. Müller-Freienfels, Legal Relations in the Law of Agency: Power of Agency and Commercial Certainty, 13 Am. J.Comp.L. 193 (Spring, 1964).

3. K. Grönfors, supra note 1, at pp. 98–99.

4. Preliminary Draft of a Uniform Law on Agency (1955, Rome: Editions Unidroit).

EBASCO SERVICES, INC. v. PENNSYLVANIA POWER & LIGHT CO.

United States District Court, E.D. Pennsylvania, 1978.
460 F.Supp. 163.

[In a complex suit involving installation of a power plant, one question was whether Ebasco, which was Pennsylvania Power & Light Company's agent to negotiate construction of a power plant, had power to modify the master contract by the terms of an agreement designated "Supplement 16."]

EDWARD R. BECKER, DISTRICT JUDGE.

. . .

C. *Did Ebasco Possess Authority to Issue Supplement 16 (or, Did PP & L Ratify it)?*

1. *Introduction*

We commence with the authority question because, even if PP & L had somehow previously acquired contract rights greater than those conferred by Supplement 16, Supplement 16 is valid so long as Ebasco had authority to negotiate and issue it on PP & L's behalf. In *Ebasco I,* see 402 F.Supp. at 445–52, we analyzed the authority question in terms of four potential kinds of authority—express, implied, apparent and inherent—and in terms of the notion of ratification. We shall do so again, in the wake of our findings of fact. We discussed in *Ebasco I* the meaning of those legal concepts and will not repeat their description now. For the reasons that follow, our conclusion is that, under the facts as we have found them, Ebasco possessed express, implied, apparent, and inherent authority to issue Supplement 16.

2. *Express Authority*

We note preliminarily that, if there were no claim of intervening acquisition of greater contract rights, there could be no colorable assertion by PP & L that Ebasco lacked authority to enter into Supplement 16. Ebasco's express authority to purchase permanent project equipment and to negotiate commercial terms and conditions in connection therewith would then plainly prevail. However, given the intervening acquisition claim, it cannot be said that Ebasco possessed *express* authority to negotiate downward and thereby to dilute rights won for PP & L either via U.C.C. § 2–207 or on the theory that, even in the absence of § 2–207, there was a threshold contract for the steam turbine generator on Ebasco terms.

There is, however, the matter of "quid pro quo," which we have found to attend Supplement 16. In light of our finding that Supplement 16 represented a negotiating trade-off in which PP & L both won and lost certain contract advantages and considering the extremely broad authority conferred by PP & L upon Ebasco under the turnkey concept, we believe that Ebasco did possess express authority to negotiate and issue Supplement 16. The Supplement 16 negotiations fall within the continuum of Ebasco authority and responsibility for purchasing permanent project equipment and for negotiating commercial terms and conditions in connection therewith. We do not believe that an analysis of the advantages and disadvantages of Supplement 16 can be applied to alter this conclusion any more than PP & L could avoid what it deemed to be unfavorable terms of earlier Supplements on the ground that they were detrimental. We add only a reference to our finding that at no point in the PP & L-Ebasco dealings was Ebasco divested of its broad authority by a direction from PP & L to secure protection against the cost of replacement power. To the contrary, in accordance with the GE-Ebasco course of dealing and general trade custom, PP & L did not expect that cost of replacement power could be recovered.

3. *Implied Authority*

We have found that Ebasco's extremely broad turnkey authority to get Brunner # 3 built included, among the acts incidental to or that usually accompany or are reasonably necessary to accomplish such a task, negotiating and issuing Supplement 16. The quid pro quo finding, of course, supports this conclusion, but it would in any event be supported by the finding that it was customary for engineer-constructors to have authority even to negotiate "downward." It is also important to note in this regard that Supplement 16 cannot be deemed to stand apart from the general process of contract negotiations for, as we have found, it was customary within the power generation industry for a formal contract, with all the essential terms and conditions, not to be finally executed until years after the order was placed. Moreover, PP & L knew that before October 1967 there was no final contract, but only a letter of intent subject to further negotiations; thus, final negotiations were in fact anticipated by PP & L. In connection with implied authority, we referred in *Ebasco I* to § 33 of the Restatement (Second) of Agency and to Comment b thereto:

> An agent is authorized to do, and to do only, what it is reasonable for him to infer that the principal desires him to do *in the light of the principal's manifestations and the facts as he knows or should know them at the time he acts.* (emphasis added).

> Comment b. Authority distinct from contract of agency. An agent is a fiduciary under a duty to obey the will of the principal as he knows it or should know it. This will may change, either with or without a change in events. Whatever it is at any given time, if the agent has reason to know it, his duty is not to act contrary to it. The fact that in changing his mind the principal is violating his contract with the agent does not diminish the agent's duty of obedience to it. Hence the rule applicable to the interpretation of authority must be as flexible as the will of the principal may be. Thus, whether or not the agent is authorized to do a particular act at a particular time depends, not only on what the principal told

the agent, but upon a great variety of other factors, including changes in the situation after the instructions were given. The interpretation of authority, therefore, differs in this respect from the interpretation of a contract, even the contract of agency.

We then observed:

> When PP & L and Ebasco first negotiated the agency contract, they did not cover the situation that arose when Ebasco and GE were unable to agree on the terms of the sale of the turbine generator unit. In such a situation, Comment *b* indicates that Ebasco's authority should be measured in light of the circumstances prevailing at the time difficulties in negotiating Supplement 16 were encountered. As we indicated previously, it is difficult to determine when viewed ten years later whether a § 2–207 contract existed while the Supplement 16 negotiations were proceeding. Whether Ebasco could reasonably have determined that one did exist, and whether, if one did, Ebasco could reasonably have been led to believe that PP & L would therefore have forbade the negotiation of Supplement 16 is a question for the trier of fact. Further, the fact finder would also have to take into account GE's forceful contentions that Supplement 16 was not a "downward" negotiation for PP & L but, rather, a quid pro quo.

402 F.Supp. at 448–49.

We have already resolved the quid pro quo question in GE's favor. We add here that we do not believe that Ebasco could reasonably have determined that a § 2–207 contract existed. Even if it could have so determined, we do not think that it could have reasonably believed that PP & L would, under all the circumstances, have forbidden this negotiation of Supplement 16. In short, under the facts as they existed at the time of the Supplement 16 negotiations and given Ebasco's broad turnkey authority (and, additionally, the quid pro quo that was negotiated), we are satisfied that Ebasco was doing what it was reasonable for it to believe PP & L would have wished it to do, in light of PP & L's manifestations and the facts as Ebasco knew them at the time (including PP & L's failure to give specific instructions on replacement power in the face of its knowledge of the negotiations leading to Supplement 16).

4. *Apparent Authority*

We have found that PP & L held out or manifested to GE that Ebasco was authorized to negotiate Supplement 16 (as well as do everything else reasonably necessary in connection with Brunner # 3). PP & L put Ebasco in the traditional architect/engineer/constructor role, which included purchase of equipment and negotiation of commercial terms and conditions, but never advised GE of any limitations on Ebasco's authority, even in the presence of what it knew to be final negotiations to resolve a dispute about limitation of liability. GE, on the other hand, observed that PP & L had given Ebasco a completely free hand in the negotiation of commercial terms, even in the face of a veritable "blow up" over those terms in the summer of 1967. GE saw the PP & L-Ebasco relationship as tracking the conventional "all authority to the engineer" pattern prevalent in the trade. Under these circumstances, GE was, in our view, both led and entitled to believe that Ebasco was authorized to negotiate Supplement 16.[47]

5. *Inherent Authority*

Inherent agency power refers to the power of an agent, derived not from authority, apparent authority, or estoppel, but solely from the agency relationship. It exists for the protection of persons harmed by or dealing with a servant or other agent. Restatement (Second) of Agency § 8A. Moreover:

> A general agent for a disclosed or partially disclosed principal subjects his principal to liability for acts done on his account which usually accompany or are incidental to transactions which the agent is authorized to conduct if, although they are forbidden by the principal, *the other party reasonably believes that the agent is authorized to do them* and has no notice that he is not so authorized. (emphasis added).

Restatement, *supra*, § 161.

Our findings of fact compel the conclusion that what Ebasco did for PP & L (even if without express or implied authority, see *Ebasco I*, 402 F.Supp. at 446), was what usually is done in connection with the transactions Ebasco was employed to conduct. Additionally, we have found that, in the trade, turnkey contractors have plenary negotiating power, even to negotiate downward—though, we reiterate, here there was a quid pro quo. Based upon its many years of experience dealing with Ebasco (and other architect/engineer/constructors) GE reasonably believed that Ebasco had the usual broad authority in connection with the turbine generator and Supplement 16. Given the stress laid by the Restatement upon promoting regularity in mercantile affairs by protecting the reasonable expectations of third parties who deal with the agents of known principals, we believe that it would be improper to deprive GE of the benefits of its good faith reliance.[48] We conclude that Ebasco also possessed inherent authority to execute Supplement 16.

6. *Ratification*

Ratification is defined by the Restatement (Second) of Agency § 82 as:

---

47. In addition to the cases cited in *Ebasco I*, see *Continental-Wirt Electronics Corp. v. Sprague Electric Co.*, 329 F.Supp. 959 (E.D.Pa.1971); *East Girard S & L v. Houlihan*, 373 Pa. 578 (1973); *Roth v. Ducks Hockey Club*, 52 Misc.2d 533, 276 N.Y.S.2d 246 (1966); Restatement (Second) of Agency, §§ 8, 27, & 49.

48. We reaffirm our reliance in this regard on *Diuguid v. Bethel A.M.E. Church*, 119 Pa.Super. 493, 180 A. 737 (1935). Pennsylvania law may well govern the PP & L-Ebasco agency relationship but the result would, in our view, be no different under New York law. *See Ebasco I*, 402 F.Supp. at 446 n. 41.

the affirmance by a person of a prior act which did not bind him but which was done or professedly done on his account, whereby the act, as to some or all persons, is given effect as if originally authorized by him.

Section 94 of the Restatement states: "An affirmance of an unauthorized transaction can be inferred from a failure to repudiate it." However, in order to find ratification from failure to repudiate the agent's unauthorized actions, it is necessary that the principal have full knowledge of the material facts and circumstances attending the transaction to be ratified. *Schwartz v. Mahoning Valley Country Club,* 382 Pa. 138, 142, 114 A.2d 78, 80 (1965).

We have found as facts that after the October 26, 1967 meeting, Salerno phoned Baum and related the negotiations with GE on commercial terms and conditions covering the topics of technical direction of installation, warranty, limitations of liability, and patents, and that Salerno's statements gave an accurate picture as to what had transpired at the meeting. We have made findings on certain ensuing discussions and correspondence between PP & L and Ebasco and noted that PP & L received a copy of Supplement 16 on December 7, 1967, and yet made no objection and, while receiving later supplements, neither took action with regard to it until filing this lawsuit nor attempted to rescind any of Ebasco's authority.

During the course of our findings of fact, we have also commented upon PP & L's arguments against a finding of ratification, which are founded on the contention that Ebasco did not keep PP & L fully advised of what was going on and particularly of the nature of its prior relationship with GE. We observed:

> While Ebasco doubtless did not relate every detail of the complex evolving GE/Ebasco scenario to PP & L, we know of no *material* thing that PP & L needed to know that was withheld. The basic and salient features were communicated, and, after all, PP & L was no novice in the field. Insofar as the alleged failure to detail the history of the GE-Ebasco relationship is concerned, PP & L is really saying that Ebasco did not relate that history according to the tenor of PP & L's version thereof. But we have, in our findings, rejected the PP & L version. In any event, we have drawn different inferences than PP & L as to the import of that relationship. For example, we have found that cost of replacement power was not recoverable even under the Ebasco standard terms. Under our findings, the history of Ebasco's relationship with GE would have been immaterial.

Text *supra* at 196.

PP & L thus had knowledge of the *material* facts concerning the negotiations leading up to Supplement 16. Even after receiving a copy of Supplement 16 PP & L did nothing that would suggest rejection. Furthermore, PP & L manifested approval of Ebasco's acts by allowing Ebasco to continue to negotiate and issue Supplements 18–22, as late as

June 1969. Under these circumstances, we hold that PP & L ratified Supplement 16. . . .

LIND v. SCHENLEY INDUSTRIES, INC.

United States Court of Appeals, Third Circuit, 1960.
278 F.2d 79.

Before BIGGS, CHIEF JUDGE, and GOODRICH, MCLAUGHLIN, KALODNER, STALEY, HASTIE and FORMAN, CIRCUIT JUDGES.

BIGGS, CHIEF JUDGE. This is a diversity case. Lind, the plaintiff-appellant, sued Park & Tilford Distiller's Corp.,[1] the defendant-appellee, for compensation that he asserts is due him by virtue of a contract expressed by a written memorandum supplemented by oral conversations as set out hereinafter. . . . The evidence, including Lind's own testimony, taking the inferences most favorable to Lind, shows the following. Lind had been employed for some years by Park & Tilford. In July 1950, Lind was informed by Herrfeldt, then Park & Tilford's vice-president and general sales-manager, that he would be appointed assistant to Kaufman, Park & Tilford's sales-manager for metropolitan New York. Herrfeldt told Lind to see Kaufman to ascertain what his new duties and his salary would be. Lind embarked on his new duties with Kaufman and was informed in October 1950, that some "raises" had come through and that Lind should get official word from his "boss", Kaufman. Subsequently, Lind received a communication, dated April 19, 1951, signed by Kaufman, informing Lind that he would assume the title of "District Manager". The letter went on to state: "I wish to inform you of the fact that you have as much responsibility as a State Manager and that you should consider yourself to be of the same status." The letter concluded with the statement: "An incentive plan is being worked out so that you will not only be responsible for increased sales in your district, but will benefit substantially in a monetary way." . . . In July 1951, Kaufman informed Lind that he was to receive 1% commission on the gross sales of the men under him. This was an oral communication and was completely corroborated by Mrs. Kennan, Kaufman's former secretary, who was present. On subsequent occasions Lind was assured by Kaufman that he would get his money. Lind was also informed by Herrfeldt in the autumn of 1952 that he would get a 1% commission on the sales of the men under him. Early in 1955, Lind negotiated with Brown, then president of Park & Tilford, for the sale of Park & Tilford's New Jersey Wholesale House, and Brown agreed to apply the money owed to Lind by reason of the 1% commission against the value of the goodwill of the Wholesale House. The proposed sale of the New Jersey Wholesale House was not consummated.

---

1. Park & Tilford Distiller's Corp. was merged into Schenley Industries, Inc., a Delaware corporation, before the commencement of this action, with Schenley assuming all of Park & Tilford's obligations. Schenley was substituted in this action on March 31, 1958, by order of Judge Wortendyke.

Notice to produce various records of Lind's employment was served on Park & Tilford but one slip dealing with Lind's appointment as district manager was not produced and is presumed to have been lost. The evidence was conflicting as to the character of the "incentive compensation" to be offered Lind in connection with his services as a district manager. Herrfeldt designated the incentive an "added incentive plan with a percentage arrangement". Kaufman characterized the plan as "bonuses and contests". Weiner, Park & Tilford's Secretary, said that the incentive was a "pension plan." Kaufman testified, however, that the pension plan had nothing to do with the bonus incentive he referred to.

The record also shows that Lind commenced his employment with Park & Tilford in 1941, that from 1942 to 1950 he worked on a commission basis, that on August 31, 1950, he became an assistant sales manager for the New York metropolitan area at $125 a week, which was raised to $150 a week on October 1, 1950, plus certain allowances. After Lind became district manager on April 19, 1951, he continued to receive the same salary of $150 a week but this was increased to $175 in January 1952. On February 1, 1952, Lind was transferred from New York to New Jersey to become state manager of Park & Tilford's business in New Jersey. He retained that position until January 31, 1957, when he was transferred back to New York.

Park & Tilford moved for but was denied a directed verdict at the close of all the evidence under Rule 50, Fed.R.Civ.Proc., 28 U.S.C. However the court below invoked Rule 50(b) [2] and submitted the case to the jury subject to a later determination of the legal questions raised by Park & Tilford's motion to dismiss. The court then requested the jury to answer the following five questions: "1. Did Kaufman offer plaintiff one percent of gross sales effected by the salesmen under plaintiff?" "2. If the answer to question 1 is yes, when was plaintiff to commence such commissions?" "3. If the answer to question 1 is yes, when was the commission arrangement to terminate?" "4. Did defendant cause the plaintiff to believe that Kaufman had authority to make the offer to plaintiff referred to in question 1?" "5. Was plaintiff justified in presuming that Kaufman had the authority to make the offer?"

---

2. Rule 50(b) provides as follows: "Whenever a motion for a directed verdict made at the close of all the evidence is denied or for any reason is not granted, the court is deemed to have submitted the action to the jury subject to a later determination of the legal questions raised by the motion. Within 10 days after the reception of a verdict, a party who has moved for a directed verdict may move to have the verdict and any judgment entered thereon set aside and to have judgment entered in accordance with his motion for a directed verdict; or if a verdict was not returned such party, within 10 days after the jury has been discharged, may move for judgment in accordance with his motion for a directed verdict. A motion for a new trial may be joined with this motion, or a new trial may be prayed for in the alternative. If a verdict was returned the court may allow the judgment to stand or may reopen the judgment and either order a new trial or direct the entry of judgment as if the requested verdict had been directed. If no verdict was returned the court may direct the entry of judgment as if the requested verdict had been directed or may order a new trial."

[The jury's answers to these questions were essentially affirmative.]

. . .

The jury did not give a dollar award for the commission deemed owing but the court "molded" the verdict in accordance with the jury's findings and judgment was rendered in favor of Lind against Schenley for $36,953.10 plus interest for the commission and $353.00 for the moving expenses. However, the judgment was nullified by the court's decision to enter a verdict for the defendant under Rule 50(b) in accordance with Schenley's first motion. The court, also under Rule 50(b), granted a new trial in the event that the judgment in favor of the defendant was subsequently reversed. See D.C.N.J.1958, 167 F.Supp. 590.

The decision to reverse the verdict for Lind with respect to the 1% commission was based on two alternative grounds. First, the court found that Lind had failed to prove a case of apparent authority in that the evidence did not disclose that Park & Tilford acted in such a manner as to induce Lind to believe that Kaufman had been authorized to offer him the 1% commission. . . .

The jury clearly found that Kaufman had apparent agency power to offer Lind the 1% commission and this verdict may be reversed only if there is no substantial evidence which could support the verdict.

. . .

The problems of "authority" are probably the most difficult in that segment of law loosely termed, "Agency". Two main classifications of authority are generally recognized, "actual authority", and "apparent authority". The term "implied authority" is often seen but most authorities consider "implied authority" to be merely a subgroup of "actual" authority. Mechem, Agency, §§ 51–60 (4th ed. 1952). An additional kind of authority has been designated by the Restatement, Agency 2d, §§ 8A and 161(b) as "inherent agency". Actually this new term is employed to designate a meaning frequently ascribed to "implied authority."

"Actual authority" means, as the words connote, authority that the principal, expressly or implicitly, gave the agent. "Apparent authority" arises when a principal acts in such a manner as to convey the impression to a third party that an agent has certain powers which he may or may not actually possess. "Implied authority" has been variously defined. It has been held to be actual authority given implicitly by a principal to his agent. Another definition of "implied authority" is that it is a kind of authority arising solely from the designation by the principal of a kind of agent who ordinarily possesses certain powers. It is this concept that is called "inherent authority" by the Restatement. In many cases the same facts will support a finding of "inherent" or "apparent agency". Usually it is not necessary for a third party attempting to hold a principal to specify which type of authority he relies upon, general proof of agency being sufficient. Pacific Mut.

Life Ins. Co. of California v. Barton, 5 Cir., 1931, 50 F.2d 362, certiorari denied 1931, 284 U.S. 647, 52 S.Ct. 29, 76 L.Ed. 550.

In the case at bar Lind attempted to prove all three kinds of agency; actual, apparent, and inherent, although most of his evidence was directed to proof of "inherent" or "apparent" authority. From the evidence it is clear that Park & Tilford can be held accountable for Kaufman's action on the principle of "inherent authority". Kaufman was Lind's direct superior, and was the man to transfer communications from the upper executives to the lower. Moreover, there was testimony tending to prove that Herrfeldt the vice-president in charge of sales, had told Lind to see Kaufman for information about his salary and that Herrfeldt himself had confirmed the 1% commission arrangement. Thus Kaufman, so far as Lind was concerned was the spokesman for the company.

It is not necessary to determine the status of the New York law in respect to "inherent agency," for substantially the same testimony that would establish "inherent" agency under the circumstances at bar proves conventional "apparent" agency. . . . There is some uncertainty as to whether or not the third person must change his position in reliance upon these manifestations of authority, but this is of no consequence in the case at bar since Lind clearly changed his position when he accepted the job of district manager with its admittedly increased responsibilities. . . .

The opinion of the court below and the argument of the appellee here rely heavily on Gumpert v. Bon Ami Corporation, 2 Cir., 1958, 251 F.2d 735, a diversity case decided under New York law, upholding the lower court's reversal of a jury verdict for the plaintiff. The facts in that case showed that Gumpert had been hired by Rosenberg, a director and member of the executive board of the Bon Ami company for a salary of $25,000 in cash plus $25,000 worth of the company's common stock. The Court of Appeals found that the jury could not properly find that the Bon Ami company had clothed Rosenberg with apparent authority to offer Gumpert $25,000 in common stock. This decision is inapposite for here we deal with an offer made by an employee's immediate superior, the man who represented the company to those under him, not a contract offered by one not an officer of a corporation to prospective employee. Furthermore a salary of $25,000 in cash and $25,000 in common stock might well be deemed unusual enough to put the prospective employee on notice as to a possible lack of authority in the director to make the offer but the same may not be said of an offer of a commission to a salesman who had been habitually working on that basis, in a corporation that confined itself to selling others' products. It should be borne in mind also that a director, even if he be a member of the executive board, does not ordinarily hire employees. Moreover in the case at bar there was evidence by an employee of Schenley that at least some state managers received 1% commissions.

Testimony was adduced by Schenley tending to prove that Kaufman had no authority to set salaries, that power being exercisable solely by the president of the corporation, and that the president had not authorized Kaufman to offer Lind a commission of the kind under consideration here. However, this testimony, even if fully accepted, would only prove lack of actual or implied authority in Kaufman but is irrelevant to the issue of apparent authority.

The opinion below seems to agree with the conception of the New York agency law as set out above but the court reversed the jury's verdict and the judgment based on it on the conclusion, as a matter of law, that Lind could not reasonably have believed that Kaufman was authorized to offer him a commission that would, in the trial judge's words "have almost quadrupled Lind's then salary". But Lind testified that before he had become Kaufman's assistant in September 1950, the latter position named being that which he had held before being "promoted" to district manager in April 1951, he had earned $9,000 for the period from January 1, 1950 to August 31, 1950, that figure allegedly representing half of his expected earnings for the year. Lind testified that a liquor salesman can expect to make 50% of his salary in the last four months of the year owing to holiday sales. Thus Lind's salary two years before his appointment as district manager could have been estimated by the jury at $18,000 per year and his alleged earnings, as district manager, a position of greater responsibility, do not appear disproportionate. On the basis of the foregoing it appears that there was sufficient evidence to authorize a jury finding that Park & Tilford had given Kaufman apparent authority to offer Lind 1% commission of gross sales of the salesmen under him and that Lind reasonably had relied upon Kaufman's offer. . . .

The judgment of the court below will be reversed and the case will be remanded with the direction to the court below to reinstate the verdict and judgment in favor of Lind.

HASTIE, CIRCUIT JUDGE, with whom KALODNER, CIRCUIT JUDGE, joins (dissenting).

I agree that the order granting judgment for the defendant notwithstanding the verdict for the plaintiff, must be set aside. However, I think the majority make a serious mistake when they take the extraordinary additional step of reversing the alternative order of the trial judge, granting a new trial because he considered the verdict against the weight of the evidence. . . .

The majority think the trial judge usurped the function of the jury. I think it is we who are impinging upon the function and discretion of the trial judge in a way that is serious, regrettable and without precedent in this court.

KIDD v. THOMAS A. EDISON, INC.

United States District Court, Southern District of New York, 1917.
239 Fed. 405.

At Law. Action by Mary Carson Kidd against Thomas A. Edison, Incorporated. On defendant's motion to set aside, on exceptions, a verdict for plaintiff. Motion denied.

This is a motion by the defendant to set aside a verdict for the plaintiff on exceptions. The action was in contract, and depended upon the authority of one Fuller to make a contract with the plaintiff, engaging her without condition to sing for the defendant in a series of "tone test" recitals, designed to show the accuracy with which her voice was reproduced by the defendant's records. The defendant contended that Fuller's only authority was to engage the plaintiff for such recitals as he could later persuade dealers in the records to book her for all over the United States. The dealers, the defendant said, were to agree to pay her for the recitals, and the defendant would then guarantee her the dealers' performance. The plaintiff said the contract was an unconditional engagement for a singing tour, and the jury so found.

LEARNED HAND, DISTRICT JUDGE (after stating the facts as above).

The point involved is the scope of Fuller's "apparent authority," as distinct from the actual authority limited by the instructions which Maxwell gave him. The phrase "apparent authority," though it occurs repeatedly in the Reports, has been often criticized (Mechem, Law of Agency, §§ 720–726), and its use is by no means free from ambiguity. The scope of any authority must, of course, in the first place be measured, not alone by the words in which it is created, but by the whole setting in which those words are used, including the customary powers of such agents. Lowenstein v. Lombard, Ayres & Co. (1900) 164 N.Y. 324, 58 N.E. 44; Lamon v. Speer Hardware Co. (1912, 10th Cir.) 119 C.C.A. 1, 198 F. 453. This is, however, no more than to regard the whole of the communication between the principal and agent before assigning its meaning, and does not differ in method from any other interpretation of verbal acts. In considering what was Fuller's actual implied authority by custom, while it is fair to remember that the "tone test" recitals were new, in the sense that no one had ever before employed singers for just this purpose of comparing their voices with their mechanical reproduction, they were not new merely as musical recitals; for it was, of course, a common thing to engage singers for such recitals. When, therefore, an agent is selected, as was Fuller, to engage singers for musical recitals, the customary implication would seem to have been that his authority was without limitation of the kind here imposed, which was unheard of in the circumstances. The mere fact that the purpose of the recitals was advertisement, instead of entrance fees, gave no intimation to a singer dealing with him that the defendant's promise would be conditional upon so unusual a condition as that actually imposed. Being concerned to sell its records, the venture might rightly be regarded as undertaken on its own account, and like similar enterprises, at its own cost. The natural surmise would certainly be that such an undertaking was a part of the advertising expenses of the business, and that therefore Fuller might engage singers, upon similar terms to those upon which singers for recitals are generally engaged, where the manager expects a profit, direct or indirect.

Therefore it is enough for the decision to say that the customary extent of such an authority as was actually conferred comprised such a contract. If estoppel be, therefore, the basis of all "apparent authority," it existed here. Yet the argument involves a misunderstanding of the true significance of the doctrine, both historically (Responsibility for Tortious Acts: Its History, Wigmore, 7 Harv.L.Rev. 315, 383) and actually. The responsibility of a master for his servant's act is not at bottom a matter of consent to the express act, or of an estoppel to deny that consent, but it is a survival from ideas of status, and the imputed responsibility congenial to earlier times, preserved now from motives of policy. While we have substituted for the archaic status a test based upon consent, i.e., the general scope of the business, within that sphere the master is held by principles quite independent of his actual consent, and indeed in the face of his own instructions. Of federal cases the following are illustrative: Union Mutual Life Ins. Co. v. Wilkinson (1871) 80 U.S. (13 Wall.) 222, 20 L.Ed. 617; Southern Life Ins. Co. v. McCain (1877) 96 U.S. 84, 24 L.Ed. 653; Great Northern Ry. v. O'Connor (1914) 232 U.S. 508, 34 S.Ct. 380, 58 L.Ed. 703; Butler v. Maples (1869) 76 U.S. (9 Wall.) 766, 19 L.Ed. 822 (obiter); Dysart v. Missouri, K. & T. Ry. (1903) 58 C.C.A. 592, 122 F. 228; Lamon v. Speer Hardware Co. (1912) 119 C.C.A. 1, 198 F. 453; Foster v. Cleveland, C., C. & St. L. Ry. Co. (1893) 56 F. 434. These were, it is true, all cases in which the third person took some action upon the faith of the agent's authority, and it is possible to speak of them as though they were cases of estoppel, but in truth they are not. It is only a fiction to say that the principal is estopped when he has not communicated with the third person and thus misled him. There are, indeed, the cases of customary authority, which perhaps come within the range of a true estoppel; but in other cases the principal may properly say that the authority which he delegated must be judged by his directions, taken together, and that it is unfair to charge him with misleading the public, because his agent, in executing that authority, has neither observed, nor communicated, an important part of them. Certainly it begs the question to assume that the principal has authorized his agent to communicate a part of his authority and not to disclose the rest. Hence, even in contract, there are many cases in which the principle of estoppel is a factitious effort to impose the rationale of a later time upon archaic ideas, which, it is true, owe their survival to convenience, but to a very different from the putative convenience attributed to them.

However it may be of contracts, all color of plausibility falls away in the case of torts, where indeed the doctrine first arose, and where it still thrives. It makes no difference that the agent may be disregarding his principal's directions, secret or otherwise, so long as he continues in that larger field measured by the general scope of the business intrusted to his care. Blumenthal v. Shaw (1897) 23 C.C.A. 590, 77 F. 954; Palmeri v. Manhattan R. (1892) 133 N.Y. 261, 30 N.E. 1001; Quinn v. Power, 87 N.Y. 535.

The considerations which have made the rule survive are apparent. If a man select another to act for him with some discretion, he has by that fact vouched to some extent for his reliability. While it may not be fair to impose upon him the results of a total departure from the general subject of his confidence, the detailed execution of his mandate stands on a different footing. The very purpose of delegated authority is to avoid constant recourse by third persons to the principal, which would be a corollary of denying the agent any latitude beyond his exact instructions. Once a third person has assured himself widely of the character of the agent's mandate, the very purpose of the relation demands the possibility of the principal's being bound through the agent's minor deviations. Thus, as so often happens, archaic ideas continue to serve good, though novel, purposes.

In the case at bar there was no question of fact for the jury touching the scope of Fuller's authority. His general business covered the whole tone test recitals; upon him was charged the duty of doing everything necessary in the premises, without recourse to Maxwell or anyone else. It would certainly have been quite contrary to the expectations of the defendant, if any of the prospective performers at the recitals had insisted upon verifying directly with Maxwell the terms of her contract. It was precisely to delegate such negotiations to a competent substitute that they chose Fuller at all.

The exception is without merit; the motion is denied.

SECTION 3. CIRCUMSTANTIAL AUTHORITY

INTRODUCTORY NOTE

In the last section you examined cases in which contracts were enforced in situations where there was no express authority for the agent's action. The transactions involved agents of particular types, and the rationale for liability was based on their implied powers. In this section are examined other theories to justify the enforcement of contracts when express authority does not exist.

In the course of modern society, most goods are sold, workers hired, and money paid or received by employees who exhibit no power of attorney, and who have none to exhibit. These employees are trusted by other people because such acts of agency are normal usage, and the proper exercise of authority is a normal expectation. The exercise of discretion in business affairs by employees who carried no documentary certification showed up in English cases involving mercantile transactions around 1700.[1]

As time went on, the simple assumption that an agent's power is as broad as would be indicated by normal usage and expectation ran into increasing difficulties. Perhaps the judges were alarmed by the financial risks to which this view exposed an employer. More visibly, they were troubled by the developing concept of contract as an expression of consent freely given, which conflicted with making the employer a "party" to a contract against the employer's will. This difficulty was enhanced by early treatises on agency, by Livermore (Boston, 1811), Paley (London, 1811) and United States Supreme Court Justice Joseph Story (Boston, 1830).[2] These works tended to conceptualize "authority" as the result of a consensual transaction between the principal and the agent.[3] In Livermore and Story, this conception was reinforced by their knowledge of Roman and French law, in which the law of mandate (the nearest analogue of agency) is largely concerned with the contract between the principal and agent; relations between the principal and third party, when recognized at all, are treated as mere derivatives of the principal-agent contract.[4]

Under this conception of agency, any rule by which the principal became bound against his will was an anomaly, which called for explanation to reconcile it with the "general principle."

One type of case which lent itself to rationalization under the consensual theory was one in which the principal imposed limits on the agent which the agent must not disclose; for example, telling him to buy a horse for up to £5, but not (of course) to reveal the price limit to the seller. This formula proved to be readily expansible and contractible; since the details of authorization are rarely communicated to the

---

1. Wambaugh's Cases on Agency (1896) trace the origins of a principal's contractual liability from Boulton v. Arlsden, 3 Salk. 234, 91 Eng.Rep. 797 (1967) (liability for purchases of merchandise), Anon., 12 Mod. 514, 88 Eng.Rep. 1486 (1701) (power of a factor to sell principal's goods on credit), Ward v. Evans, (1702–3) 2 Salk. 442, 91 Eng.Rep. 383 (1702–3) (servant's acceptance of draft in lieu of cash), Thorold v. Smith, 11 Mod. 71, 87, 88 Eng.Rep. 896, 912 (1706) (same as Ward v. Evans), and Nickson v. Brohan, 10 Mod. 109, 88 Eng. Rep. 649 (1712) (same).

2. Samuel Livermore, a Treatise on the Law relative to Principals, Agents, Factors, Auctioneers and Brokers (Boston, 1811). William Paley, A Treatise on the Law of Principal and Agent, chiefly with reference to Mercantile Transactions, (London, 1812; a "second" American edition was published at Exeter, N.H., in 1822).

Joseph Story, Commentaries of the Law of Agency as a Branch of Commercial and Maritime Jurisprudence, with Occasional Illustrations from the Civil and Foreign Law (Boston, 1839).

3. For an exposition of the contrast between the Roman law concept of mandate as a relation between principal and agent, and the modern commercial concept of agency as an incident of the relation between the principal and the third party, see Müller-Freienfels, Legal Relations in the Law of Agency: Power of Agency and Commercial Certainty (1964) 13 Am.J. Comp.L. 193.

4. These works also contain many observations, derived from the cases, which do not fit the consensual conception. Paley for instance offers the unorthodox observation that "As the law of master and servant in the basis of this branch of the law of agency [i.e., implied authority], it may be proper to refer to that source of authorities." 2nd Am. ed., 1822, p. 137.

third party, almost any negative element can be found (at the court's discretion) to be a "secret limitation" of the authority.[5]

A further step along this line was to say that if the agent was a "general agent" who had received "general authority" in a line of business, no limitations would be valid; the only problem was to distinguish the limits of the line of business from the limitations on authority within the line of business.[6]

Another rationale for a principal's liability, was the "distribution of loss" theory. According to this view, if the agent makes a contract with the third party which the principal has not authorized, a situation arises in which the court must place the loss on one of two innocent parties—the principal or the third party—on some basis of comparative merit or demerit.[7] Various enunciations of the theory state that the loss should fall on him "who made it possible," or "whose negligence made it possible," or "who reposed confidence in the wrongdoer." These formulations usually led to weighing whether the plaintiff or defendant had the better chance to avoid the misunderstanding by more efficient management of his affairs.

Another concept which judges found useful in rationalizing their agency judgments employed the concept of "apparent authority," which meant the power which the agent appeared to an outsider to have, in contrast to the power which his principal had intended or purported to give him. This concept was given a powerful boost by Lord Ellenborough, who in 1812 uttered the paradox, that "the apparent authority is the real authority."[8] By "apparent authority" was meant, of course, the authority which appeared to third persons, in contradistinction to that which appeared to the principal himself, or to the agent. The "apparent authority" idea has had great success, and occupies a commanding position in twentieth century thinking about agency, as indicated by the American Law Institute's Restatement of the Subject.[9]

Alongside these rationalizations there arose another called "estoppel." This was the concept that even if the agent lacked authority, the lack could be excluded from consideration if the principal were "estopped" to assert it. The principal was said to be "estopped" if he had deceived the third party, or permitted him to be deceived by the agent, and precluded from asserting in court a fact which was unknown to the third party at the time of the transaction.[10] Some of the judges who

---

5. A classic disquisition in these slippery terms is Hatch v. Taylor, 10 N.H. 538 (1840), citing the treatise of Story which had just been published in the preceding year.

6. Butler v. Maples, 76 U.S. (9 Wall.) 766, 19 L.Ed. 822 (1869); Thurber & Co. v. Anderson, 88 Ill. 167 (1878).

7. This rationale was enunciated by Chief Justice Parsons to impose liability of a principal on an endorsement of a note as early as 1808 in Putnam v. Sullivan, 4

Mass. 45. A well known recent invocation of the theory appears in Charleston & Western Carolina Railway Co. v. Lassiter & Co., 207 N.C. 408, 177 S.E. 9 (1934).

8. See Pickering v. Busk, 15 East 38, 43, 104 Eng.Rep. 758 (1812).

9. Restatement of Agency, 2d (1958) §§ 8, 159.

10. The word "estoppel" was not commonly applied to agency situations before the middle of the 19th century. It does not

employ this doctrine seem to revel in the paradox of deliberately averting the eyes of Justice from a relevant fact; it is said that he who remained silent when he should have spoken will not be permitted to speak when he should remain silent.[11]

There is at least one other interesting situation for which the law has developed a theory of agency based on a desire to benefit a class of persons regardless of whether a reasonable third person would suppose that authority has been given. That is the situation in which an employee is seriously injured, and a superior employee engages medical services. Some nineteenth century cases discovered an "implied agency" for this purpose.[12] Such cases are now rare, probably because workmen's compensation laws oblige the employers to pay for medical services to injured workmen, and also because improved communications permit direct consultation of authorized superior officers.[13]

Another situation which lends itself to a treatment distinct from the general principles of apparent authority is the one in which the actor does not appear to be anyone's agent, but to be himself the owner. Here one certainly cannot speak of "apparent agency" since no agency appears; some writers find it equally impossible to speak of "apparent authority," since authority means to them a power and privilege conferred by someone else.[14] But in another sense "authority" is even more apparent than in the apparent agency cases, for an owner has complete authority over his own property and affairs.

Two general classes of cases involving apparent ownership can be usefully distinguished. The first class involves people in possession of chattels or documents or both who sell or encumber them; the question arises whether the true owner's title is impaired. These cases invite interesting applications of agency principles, and could usefully be explored here if space permitted. The student would discover that separate bodies of law have grown up and been codified for the different kinds of property—chattels, bills and notes, bills of lading and ware-

---

appear in Story's treatise until inserted in the index of the ninth edition (1882). Bigelow, in his Treatise on Estoppel published in 1872, regarded it as applicable to apparent ownership cases, but not apparently to other agency situations (p. 468). But Ewart's Treatise of Estoppel, published in 1900, contended that estoppel was the key to all cases of agents' acts not intentionally authorized by principals, superseding especially the rules about secret instructions, and general and special agents (p. 473 ff.)

11. See Strauss Brothers v. Denton, 140 Miss. 745, at 752, 106 So. 257, 45 A.L.R. 341 (1925). Another paradox was noted in White v. Duggan, 140 Mass. 18, at 20, 2 N.E. 110 (1885), where the court held the principal to be estopped to deny authority to execute a sealed instrument, although "A specialty deriving its validity from an estoppel *in pais* is perhaps somewhat like

Nebuchadnezzar's image with a head of gold supported by feet of clay".

12. Hutchins, Liability of Railroad Companies for Medical Services Rendered to Injured Employees and Others (1903) 2 Mich.L.Rev. 1 (thorough examination of authorities, whether based on agency principles or other grounds); Annotation, Implied or Ostensible Authority of Officer or Agent to Engage Medical Services, 71 A.L.R. 638; see any Key Number Digest, Principal and Agent ⬅102(3).

13. For an unsuccessful modern attempt to invoke the doctrine see Sheehan v. Elliott Manufacturing Co., 83 N.H. 542, 145 A. 139, 71 A.L.R. 633 (1929); comment, 78 U.Pa.L.Rev. 101.

14. Restatement of Agency 2d, (1958) § 194, comment a.

house receipts, and investment security certificates. The rules are found in various chapters of the Uniform Commercial Code. It seems advantageous in the contemporary curriculum to leave these problems to the courses on Sales, Bills and Notes, Commercial Transactions, and Corporations or Investment Securities.

The other class of apparent ownership case involves a person who is the apparent owner of a business establishment, and who makes purchases or borrows money as the owner. Suppose that instead of following instructions, the apparent owner deliberately disregards them. In what sense is he now the agent of the owner? How far should the latter be bound? If the owner is bound, what is the rationale for this result?

In the interest of brevity, the development and rejection of these various rationales is not traced through the nineteenth century cases; a few twentieth century cases are presented to suggest the spectrum of approaches currently in use. The student should of course identify the various theory elements which seem to be at work, and might ask himself whether in fact the theories are in conflict, or are merely alternative ways of articulating the same factors of decision.

On a more practical plane, the reader may properly ask himself these questions: What are the kinds of conduct by the principal which will expose him to liability by the act of an agent in violation of instructions? To what extent is it necessary that he should have any reason to foresee the liability incurred? Also, what kinds of conduct by a third party will permit him to enforce a contract made by an agent in violation of his instructions? Is he protected when he failed to make diligent inquiry, if the diligent inquiry would not have disclosed the lack of "actual" authority? What sort of "change of position" is implicit in the "reliance" requirement?

REFERENCES

Theories of agency:

Mearns, Vicarious Liability for Agency Contracts (1962) 48 Va.L.Rev. 50 (contention that modern business practice demands a scope of agency more like the "scope of employment" applied in tort cases than the traditional "authority" and "apparent authority" analysis).

Runbenstein, Apparent Authority: An Examination of a Legal Problem (1958) 44 A.B.A.J. 849 (compares theories of apparent authority and estoppel).

Conant, The Objective Theory of Agency: Apparent Authority and the Estoppel of Apparent Ownership (1968) 46 Neb.L.Rev. 678 (argues for a contract approach to apparent authority with a need to show a manifested assent by the principal).

Hetherington, Trend in Enterprise Liability: Law and the Unauthorized Agent (1966) 19 Stan.L.Rev. 76 (argues that market functioning is of primary importance and that recent cases in apparent authority field are part of a broader trend toward enterprise liability.

Fridman, Establishing Agency (1968) 84 L.Q.Rev. 224 (a discussion of whether courts will infer consent from conduct and attendant circumstances).

HOLMES, HISTORY OF AGENCY (1881), 5 Harv.L.Rev. 1, 3 Select Essays in Anglo-American Legal History 390: "The history of agency as applied to contract is next to be dealt with. In this branch of the law there is less of anomaly and a smaller field in which to look for traces of fiction than the last [i.e., torts]. A man is not bound by his servant's contracts unless they are made on his behalf and by his authority, and that he should be bound is plain common sense. It is true that in determining how far authority extends, the question is of ostensible authority and not of secret order. But this merely illustrates the general rule which governs a man's responsibility for his acts throughout the law. If, under the circumstances known to him, the obvious consequence of the principal's own conduct in employing the agent is that the public understand him to have given the agent certain powers, he gives the agent those powers. And he gives them just as truly when he forbids their exercise as when he commands it. It seems always to have been recognized that an agent's ostensible powers were his real powers; and on the other hand it always has been the law that an agent could not bind his principal beyond the powers given in the sense just explained."

KARAVOS COMPANIA NAVIERA, S.A. v. ATLANTICA EXPORT CORP.

United States Court of Appeals, Second Circuit, 1978.
588 F.2d 1.

Before WATERMAN, FRIENDLY and MULLIGAN, CIRCUIT JUDGES.

FRIENDLY, CIRCUIT JUDGE:

This is an appeal from an order of the District Court for the Southern District of New York under §§ 4 and 5 of the Federal Arbitration Act, 9 U.S.C. §§ 4, 5 (1976), directing Atlantica Export Corporation to submit to arbitration of a claim by Karavos Compania Naviera, S.A. (Karavos), for breach of an alleged agreement to charter its vessel M/V Swede Tonia. The agreement, never signed but alleged to have resulted from telephone and telex exchanges by various ship brokers described below, would have incorporated the New York Produce Exchange Form Time Charter which provides for arbitration of disputes between "Owners and Charterers." Atlantica's defense was that it had not authorized anyone to charter the Swede Tonia on its behalf and hence was not a "party" to any written agreement to arbitrate within § 4. It is agreed that this issue was one for determination by the court.

The *dramatis personae*, in addition to the petitioner Karavos, are as follows:

(1) *Atlantica Export Corporation (Atlantica)*, a "branch" of a Philippine corporation called Atlantica Corporation, is a California corporation headquartered in San Francisco. It is a trading company owned by John Lim, its president, and his family.

(2) *Atlantica Export Suppliers Corporation (Suppliers)*, with an office in New York City, is a sales affiliate of Atlantica whose prime function is to take care of the Middle East market. Half

its stock is owned by Jose Grajo, Jr., its president, Jessie Coronel, its executive vice-president, and Luis Uranza, Jr., a vice-president and director; the other half is owned by John Lim, Domingo Yao and Carlos Tejuco, the last being vice-president and secretary-treasurer of Atlantica.

(3) *International Resources Exchange, Inc. (Resources),* a New York corporation, also with an office in New York City. It is a trading company represented in the transaction here at issue by Raymond Kenard and Alfred Repetti.

(4) *Ottar Grundvig,* president of Grundvig Chartering, Inc., a New York ship broker, alleged by petitioner to have been acting on behalf of Atlantica.

(5) *Edward Licho,* an employee of Federal Motorship Corporation, also a New York ship broker, who fixed the charter with the agent of the shipowner upon instruction from Grundvig.

(6) *John Vatis,* an employee of Trans-Ocean Steamship Agency, Inc., a New York ship broker acting on behalf of the ship-owner.

The line of authority relied on by Karavos runs:

Atlantica >   Resources   Grundvig >   Licho <   Vatis
                 (or Repetti)   <

<Karavos

The dispute is over the existence of the link between Atlantica and Resources (or Repetti) necessary to bind Atlantica. . . .

The imbroglio that brought this case to court began about the middle of September, 1976, when, according to Grundvig, he "was introduced to a Mr. Raymond Kenard of International Resources Exchange Corporation of New York City through a friend . . . .." During an ensuing luncheon Kenard explained to Grundvig "that his company represented various European cement manufacturers and that within a short time his clients, to whom he sold the cement, would require transportation ships, ships to transport the cement to the destinations and that he would keep in touch with me." At the start therefore the buyer was to be the charterer. Grundvig continued that around September 20 Kenard called to explain that Atlantica was about to conclude a contract to ship cement, starting with about 160,000 metric tons, from Spain to Saudi Arabia and that Kenard would call him back as soon as all formalities and letters of credit were in order. Grundvig may still have believed that Detrick Corporation, the ultimate buyer of the cement for use in Saudi Arabia, would be the charterer; in any event there is nothing to indicate that he clearly ascertained what Atlantica's role in the transaction was to be.

Grundvig next testified that about September 27 or 28 Kenard called again and said he should now telephone Atlantica in San Francisco and "speak with a Mr. Repetti, who would give me all details of the shipping requirements." According to Grundvig, Kenard told

him that Repetti, who in fact was Kenard's associate in Resources, was
"part of the Atlantica Export Corporation organization" and Grundvig
thought until mid-October that Repetti was an Atlantica employee.
However, he made no endeavor to find out anything about this from
Atlantica, although shipment of 160,000 metric tons would have involved very large charter hire.   On September 29 Grundvig called
Repetti at Atlantica's office in San Francisco. Repetti told him that
Atlantica would require ships to transport 160,000 tons of cement from
Spain to Saudi Arabia, with loading of the first ship to start not later
than October 15 but preferably October 10, and authorized him to find
a vessel for this.   While the record is not altogether clear how much
the first shipment was to be, apparently Repetti talked in terms of
15,000 metric tons. According to Grundvig, Repetti told him that the
charterer would be Atlantica and that they were "first-class charterers." Grundvig then called Licho who shortly came up with the Swede
Tonia. Grundvig thereupon sent a telex to Repetti in Atlantica's San
Francisco office "confirming our discussions with Mr. Kenard" that
"our owners friends will nominate a vessel tomorrow" that would meet
the time and place requirements.   The telex promised that the full
terms and conditions including required references would then be
telexed but that these were expected to be the same "as per discussions
with Mr. Kenard." Grundvig's notes show many discussions of the
terms of the charter with Mr. Kenard, which at least show Grundvig's
awareness that Resources had a substantial interest in the charter.
. . .

Grundvig's testimony, if the judge credited it as he was entitled to
do, showed that Repetti had authorized him to charter the Swede Tonia
on Atlantica's behalf. What it did not do was to provide any evidence,
except for the presence of Repetti in Atlantica's office and his receipt of
telex' and his receiving and making telephone calls there, that Atlantica had authorized this or sufficiently created an appearance of authorization to warrant Grundvig in assuming that it had.

Tejuco began his testimony by flatly stating that prior to October 2,
1976, Atlantica had never chartered a vessel. He denied that he or
anyone else at Atlantica had ever heard of or spoken to Grundvig,
Licho, Vatis, the shipowner or any representative of it. He specifically
denied having received a phone call from Licho and had no knowledge
that any employee of Atlantica had done so. With respect to the
telephone talk of October 6, he testified that Coronel and Uranza had
called to say that Repetti and others were at Suppliers' office and
wanted to know if he would be willing to sign a charter party on behalf
of Atlantica. Tejuco said "No." He elaborated that he was "entering
into no charter party agreements" and had not authorized anyone to
obtain one.

Cross-examination put some, although not much, flesh on these
bones. Repetti had come to Atlantica's San Francisco office with
Coronel and Grajo. Repetti "is the one who put together the supplies

[sic] and the shipment of cement which Atlantica Export is selling to Detrick Corporation" at a price of $45.75 per metric ton c. & f. Tejuco's version of the transaction was that Resources would obtain the cement; that Resources would then sell it to Atlantica on a c. & f. basis; that Atlantica would sell to Detrick on the basis stated; that Repetti "has the vessel"; that the anticipated cost of shipment would be $15 per metric ton; and that the profit, namely, the excess of $45.75 per metric ton over the sum of the price to Repetti, insurance, and the freight would be divided equally between Atlantica and Resources. According to Tejuco, the Detrick deal fell through because "Repetti was not able to come up with the supplier of the cement." Tejuco was willing to pay shipping costs of $15 per metric ton and let Repetti keep, in addition to his equal share of the profits, any excess of that over the actual costs but would not have Atlantica enter into a charter party. He denied that, during the telephone talk, anyone told him that Atlantica was already committed. There is no evidence to the contrary.

Appellee's contention that "the existence of an agency relationship is a question of fact" the decision of which by a district judge must stand unless clearly erroneous, F.R.Civ.P. 52(a), flies in the face of this court's long-held position, reiterated as recently as in *Kennecott Copper Corp. v. Curtiss-Wright Corp.*, 584 F.2d 1195, 1200 n. 3, decided September 28, 1978, that "[t]he application of a legal standard to the facts is not a 'finding of fact' within the rule," citing *In re Hygrade Envelope Corp.*, 366 F.2d 584, 588 n. 4 (2 Cir.1966). The soundness of this view could hardly be better illustrated than by the instant case where the judge's decision of the "fact" of agency rested heavily on citations to the Restatement of Agency 2d which Atlantica argues to have been misapplied. . . .

On the question of actual authority we perceive no sufficient basis for the court's statement, "Based on Tejuco's testimony alone, it appears that Repetti had actual authority to obtain shipping," if this is read, as it must be in order to have legal significance, to mean "to obtain shipping for Atlantica". Tejuco's denial of this was as straightforward as could be imagined, and the judge never found that he was not a truthful witness. . . .

The court's finding of apparent authority was based largely on Atlantica's having permitted Repetti to work in its San Francisco office and to receive telex' and receive and make telephone calls. We do not follow the court in concluding that this alone justified Grundvig in believing that Repetti was authorized to commit Atlantica to a costly charter, with many more to come, and relieved him of the duty of reasonable inquiry. Restatement of Agency 2d § 8, comments a & c, § 27, comment a; 2 Mechem, Agency § 1721, at 1307 (1914 ed.); Mechem, Outlines of the Law of Agency ¶ 94, at 61–62 (1952 ed.). Grundvig had had no previous dealings with Atlantica; indeed had never heard of it. Neither had he had any previous dealings with Resources. Prior to Repetti's trip to California, he had been told that the buyer would be the charterer. Apart from Repetti's presence in Atlantica's office and use of its communication facilities, his sole bases for thinking that Repetti had authority to bind Atlantica were that Kenard allegedly told him that Repetti was an Atlantica employee—a statement which, as indicated above, was not corroborated by Kenard— and that Repetti told him he had authority to act. Neither of these afforded any ground for holding Atlantica. Professor Mechem stated many years ago that "[t]he authority of an agent, and its nature and extent . . . ., can only be established by tracing it to its source in some word or act of the alleged principal. The agent cannot confer authority upon himself or make himself agent merely by saying that he is one." 1 Mechem, Agency § 285, at 205 (1914 ed.). See also Restatement of Agency 2d § 27, comment a, § 285; *Edwards v. Dooley,* 120 N.Y. 540, 551, 24 N.E. 827 (1890); *National Surety Corp. v. Inland Properties, Inc.,* 286 F.Supp. 173, 180 (E.D.Ark.1968), *aff'd,* 416 F.2d 457 (8 Cir.1969). As Judge Levet shrewdly observed in *Dr. Beck & Co. v. General Electric Co.,* 210 F.Supp. 86, 90 (S.D.N.Y.1962), *aff'd,* 317 F.2d 538 (2 Cir.1963):

> While agents are often successful in creating an appearance of authority by their own acts and statements, such an appearance does not create apparent authority. Mechem, Agency 61 (4 ed. 1952).

Moreover, even if Grundvig had been justified in believing that Repetti was an Atlantica employee, he was bound to inquire what his authority was; not every employee of a trading company has authority to fix a time charter, let alone a series of such charters. . . .

We likewise can find no sufficient basis to support the conclusion that Atlantica is estopped from denying Repetti's authority. An essential element of such an estoppel is a finding that the person sought to be charged intentionally or carelessly caused the plaintiff to believe in the authority of the purported agent or that "knowing of such belief and that others might change their positions because of it, he did not take reasonable. steps to notify them of the facts." Restatement of Agency 2d § 8B(1). There is no evidence that Atlantica intentionally caused a belief that Repetti had authority to bind it. While Atlantica may be charged with knowledge that Repetti was receiving telex' and making and receiving telephone calls at its San Francisco office, this does not suffice to show that it carelessly caused others to believe he had authority to execute a charter on its behalf or knew that they had such a belief. On Atlantica's theory that Repetti was to provide the ship, it was altogether normal that he should be communicating with New York, and there is not a scintilla of evidence that Atlantica knew the content of the telex' or the telephone calls. Moreover, reasonableness of reliance is as essential an element for establishing liability on the basis of estoppel as of apparent authority. *Berns & Koppstein, Inc. v. Orion Ins. Co.,* 170 F.Supp. 707, 715 (S.D.N.Y.1959), *aff'd,* 273 F.2d 415 (2 Cir.1960). Finally the court neglected another essential element of estoppel, namely, a change of position by the plaintiff. Restatement of Agency 2d § 8B(1) and (3). The Restatement defines this as "payment of money, expenditure of labor, suffering a loss or subjection to legal liability." A comment adds, *id.* at 42:

It is arguable that there is no change of position merely by entering into what is believed to be an executory contract with the principal.

There is nothing in the record to indicate that Karavos suffered anything more than the loss of a presumably profitable bargain.

It may be that a fuller presentation of the facts by Karavos would have demonstrated actual or apparent authority or estoppel. It may also be that a fuller presentation would have demonstrated the opposite. We do not know, or care, whether the meagreness of the presentation was due to inability to produce anything more, to trial strategy or to overconfidence. It suffices that, having had its day in court, petitioner clearly failed to carry its burden of persuasion.

The order is reversed, with instructions to dismiss the petition.

SOUTHWESTERN PORTLAND CEMENT v. BEAVERS
Supreme Court of New Mexico, 1970.
82 N.M. 218, 478 P.2d 546.

McKENNA, JUSTICE. Appellee Southwestern Portland Cement brought this suit to collect payment on an account in the amount of $1,647.00, plus costs and attorney fees, against appellants Beavers and Glasgow, doing business as Plains Sand and Gravel, and defendant Adams. Judgment was entered against all three jointly and severally for the sum sued for, plus costs and attorney fees of $549.31. Only Beavers and Glasgow appealed.

In February of 1968, the appellants formed a partnership known as Plains Sand and Gravel to provide concrete for a construction project at Cannon Air Force Base. The general contractor for the project was Wilkerson-Webb. Defendant Adams had no proprietary interest in the partnership. In March, 1968, the partnership entered into an oral agreement with Adams to use his ready-mix concrete batching plant and delivery trucks to mix and deliver concrete to the project. The partnership made arrangements with appellee Southwestern to furnish bulk cement to Adams at his plant. The method of payment for the delivered concrete was for Wilkerson-Webb to issue their check payable jointly to Plains Sand and Gravel and to Southwestern.

On March 20, 1968, and again on April 30, 1968, Southwestern delivered cement to Adams' plant for the partnership account. Adams received these deliveries at his plant and signed truck tickets for the cement on behalf of Plains Sand and Gravel for the Cannon Air Force job. These two deliveries of cement were paid for by Wilkerson-Webb's joint check in the amount of $1,052.70.

On July 10, 13 and 16, Adams ordered cement from Southwestern telling it that the order was for Plains Sand and Gravel. Similarly, Adams received the three deliveries at his plant, signed truck tickets for receipt of the cement on behalf of Plains Sand and Gravel for the Cannon Air Force job.

It was established during trial that prior to the last three deliveries by Southwestern, Adams' equipment broke down and he was unable to deliver the concrete to the job site and Plains Sand and Gravel made other arrangements with another firm to deliver the concrete. However the appellants did not inform Southwestern of this prior to the last three deliveries. . . . Wilkerson-Webb refused to issue a joint check for the delivered cement. Thereupon, Southwestern called one of the appellant partners who denied that Adams had authority to order the cement.

Southwestern then sued Beavers, Glasgow and Adams for the last three loads delivered.

. . .

Obviously, the course of dealing was not lengthy, and was limited, in terms of time span and deliveries, but this must be viewed in light of the limited business relationship which was involved—it was for only one project at Cannon Air Force Base. It is equally obvious that the component acts in the course of dealing were identical and reflected a common pattern. See Ulen v. Knecttle, 50 Wyo. 94, 58 P.2d 446, 111 A.L.R. 565 (1936). Each of the deliveries made to Adams by Wilkerson-Webb was for the account of Plains Sand and Gravel for use on the particular project in accordance with the pre-arranged procedure. Each delivery was made to the same location; each was receipted for by Adams for the partnership. If Southwestern had not been paid for the first two loads, it would have been warned or alerted—at least the law would so view it (Malia v. Giles, 100 Utah 562, 114 P.2d 208 [1941])—but having been paid for the first two loads by the very procedure agreed upon, Southwestern could reasonably construe this as ratification of the previous course of business. We cannot say that under these circumstances Southwestern acted in bad faith or without reasonable prudence in delivering the last three shipments. As between Southwestern and the partners it is the latter's conduct which fails to meet the test of reasonable prudence, for not only did they have the responsibility for the relationship, they neglected to notify Southwestern that they had made different arrangements for delivery of the concrete when Adams' equipment broke down. If they had done this, Southwestern's delivery of the last three shipments would have been at its peril.

An agent's scope of authority embraces not only his actual authority but also that apparently delegated. A settled course of conduct does serve to create apparent authority in the agent binding upon the principal where the acts are not timely disavowed and a third party is thereby induced to rely on the ostensible authority of the agent and does so in good faith and with reasonable prudence. The doctrine is based upon an estoppel: the principal will not be permitted to establish that the agent's authority was less than what was apparent from the

course of dealing for when one of two innocent parties must suffer, the loss must fall upon the party who created the enabling circumstances.
. . .

. . . It is the appellants who should bear the loss since they are responsible for a course of business with the necessary apparent authority and are now estopped to deny that authority, the appellant having reasonably relied upon it. Furthermore, balancing the positions of both sides, the appellants fall short for they could have easily averted their loss by advising Southwestern that they had made other arrangements for the concrete because of Adams' equipment failure. . . .

The appellants claim that Southwestern *did not know* who placed the first orders for cement and accordingly it could not rely on a settled "course of conduct" as to the last three shipments. Southwestern's evidence did not cover this point specifically, but we believe it immaterial. The district court's uncontested finding No. 8, supra, is that the partnership made arrangements with Southwestern to furnish cement to Adams on behalf of the partnership for use on the project and deliveries were made to Adams in accordance with the agreed procedure for which payment was made and received. We think this sufficient to establish a course of dealing for which appellants should be held responsible. The primary test for determining the scope of apparent authority is not the acts of the agent but the principal's conduct.
. . .

REFERENCES

Reliance reasonable:

Southwest Motor Leasing Inc. v. Matthews Lumber Co., 325 So.2d 870 (La.App.1976) (principal created apparent authority in agent to receive full year's payment in advance when he gave actual authority to deliver leased car and documents, and to collect first month payment).

Miller & Miller Auctioneers, Inc. v. Mersch, 442 F.Supp. 570 (W.D.Okl.1977) (verifying existence of agency by telephone was reasonable diligence to hold principal liable for unauthorized signature).

Patrick v. Miss New Mexico, 490 F.Supp. 833 (W.D.Tex.1980) (pageant contestant reasonable in relying on statements of eligibility of local pageant representative).

Apparent Authority and the Joint Venture, 13 Davis L.R. 831–867 (1980) (argues that partnership standard with respect to apparent authority should not apply to joint ventures.)

Reliance unreasonable:

Jacobson v. Leonard, 406 F.Supp. 515 (E.D.Pa.1976) (prospective faculty member not reasonable in belief that chairperson of department had authority to make final appointment since he was aware of an appointments committee).

GENERAL REFRIGERATION & PLUMBING CO. v. GOODWILL INDUSTRIES

Appellate Court of Illinois, Fifth District, 1975.
30 Ill.App.3d 1081, 333 N.E.2d 607.

JONES, PRESIDING JUSTICE:

Plaintiff General Refrigeration and Plumbing Company, brought an action to recover the value of services rendered and materials supplied in the amount of $634.59. Judgment was rendered in favor of plaintiff with respect to defendant Seidel Company, Inc. and against plaintiff with respect to Goodwill Industries of St. Louis, Missouri and Marjorie Wonnacott. Plaintiff appeals from the judgment only with respect to Goodwill Industries.

In the spring of 1973 Seidel Company owned a building located in Alton, Illinois which it had leased to Goodwill Industries. Goodwill Industries used the building for operation of a branch store which at that time was managed by Mrs. Wonnacott. As a result of flood conditions along the Mississippi River, flood waters entered the building and caused damage to the heating equipment. In order to have the equipment repaired Mrs. Wonnacott telephoned General Refrigeration, which had done maintenance or repair work previously in the Alton Goodwill store at the request of Mrs. Wonnacott.

After examining the damage and determining that major repairs were required, a representative of General Refrigeration advised Mrs. Wonnacott that she should contact the St. Louis Office of Goodwill Industries for permission to proceed with the repairs. Shortly thereafter Mrs. Wonnacott again contacted General Refrigeration and stated that they should undertake the repairs as she had the necessary authority. General Refrigeration then completed the repairs and submitted its invoices to the Alton Goodwill store in the amount of $634.59.

. . .

Irrespective of any lease considerations, plaintiff contends that Goodwill Industries should be bound either because Mrs. Wonnacott was an agent acting with apparent authority to bind Goodwill Industries or because Goodwill Industries acted as the agent of an undisclosed principal (Seidel Company). Pointing out once again that we are not herein dealing with liabilities under the lease, we feel that General Refrigeration is not entitled to judgment against Goodwill Industries on the basis of the issues brought before this court.

Plaintiff first contends that Mrs. Wonnacott was clothed with apparent authority to bind Goodwill Industries for the services rendered by plaintiff either because she was the general agent of Goodwill Industries or because of an established course of dealing between the parties.

. . .

Plaintiff asserts that Mrs. Wonnacott, as manager of the Alton Goodwill store, was the general agent of Goodwill Industries and, as such, had apparent authority to bind Goodwill Industries. Plaintiff cites Hodges v. Bankers Surety Company, 152 Ill.App. 372. However, the evidence clearly shows that plaintiff did not in fact believe that Mrs. Wonnacott's authority, as manager of the Alton store, extended to repairs such as are herein involved. Mr. Thomas DeClew, vice-president of General Refrigeration, testified at the trial and made numerous references to the fact that he knew Mrs. Wonnacott did not have authority to authorize repairs which would require a substantial expenditure of money on the part of Goodwill Industries. Some of these references are as follows:

> "Except that I did have our people to call and tell them it was going to run quite a bit of money and they better get the okay from the St. Louis office.
>
> . . . Our dealing was with the Goodwill people on Third Street [the Alton store]. I told our people to tell her it was up to her to get the okay from whoever, whether it was the main office in St. Louis or who.
>
> . . .

The record in the instant case, particularly the testimony of Mrs. Wonnacott and of Mr. DeClew, clearly shows that General Refrigeration made no efforts to determine whether Mrs. Wonnacott was acting within the scope of her authority as an agent of Goodwill Industries. Instead General Refrigeration relied exclusively on the statements of Mrs. Wonnacott that she had authority to order the repairs even though Mrs. Wonnacott at no time stated that Goodwill Industries had given her authority. The relevant portions of Mr. DeClew's testimony are as follows:

> "Q. You don't know where the actual authority came from for the job?
>
> A. Unless we got it from Mrs. Wonnacott.
>
> . . .
>
> I told our people to tell her *it was up to her to get the okay* from whoever, whether it was the main office in St. Louis or who. (emphasis added)
>
> . . .
>
> I knew she had to deal with the St. Louis office and I instructed my people to tell her it would be quite expensive and *then I don't know who she called.* (emphasis added)
>
> Q. You don't know from whom she got authority?
>
> A. Right."
>
> . . .

General Refrigeration knew that Mrs. Wonnacott did not have authority on her own to order repairs of the type herein involved. A reasonable inquiry by General Refrigeration would have disclosed the true state of Mrs. Wonnacott's powers. However, instead of calling the St. Louis office of Goodwill Industries or making some other effort to determine whether Goodwill Industries would accept responsibility for payment, General Refrigeration relied totally on the statement of Mrs. Wonnacott that she had authority. Under these circumstances we do not feel that General Refrigeration exercised reasonable diligence and prudence in determining the extent of Mrs. Wonnacott's apparent authority. Goodwill Industries cannot, therefore, be held to have been bound merely on the basis of apparent authority of its agent.

. . .

For the foregoing reasons, the judgment against General Refrigeration with respect to Goodwill Industries is hereby affirmed.

EBERSPACHER and GEORGE J. MORAN, JJ., concur.

BOGUE ELECTRIC MANUFACTURING CO. v. COCONUT GROVE BANK

United States Court of Appeals, Fifth Circuit, 1959.
269 F.2d 1.

JONES, CIRCUIT JUDGE. The appellant is the successor in interest through merger of its one-time subsidiary, Belco Industrial Equipment Division, Inc. In 1950 Belco, by a written agreement, made an appointment of Florida Industrial Equipment Division, Inc., as its exclusive agent in Florida for the sale of electrical and filtration equipment for swimming pools, for the period of a year. The agreement was extended from year to year through 1956. George H. Neubauer was the president, principal stockholder and the directing head of Florida Industrial. Until 1952 Belco sold equipment to Florida Industrial on open account. . . . In 1952 Belco learned that Florida Industrial had failed to remit to Belco after the collection of funds from a customer, McCann Plumbing Company. Belco then terminated the open account arrangement. Equipment was thereafter sold under written contracts, negotiated by Neubauer, between Belco and the customers. These contracts contained a clause providing, "All remittances are to be made direct to Belco Industrial Equipment Division, Inc., Patterson, 3 N.J." . . .

In most instances, during the 1952–1956 period, payments of customers were made by their checks payable to Belco and transmitted to it either directly or through Florida Industrial. In some instances payments were made to Belco through the medium of bank drafts or cashier's checks. Florida Industrial, from time to time, purchased for its own account materials and supplies from Belco for which payments were made by checks of Florida Industrial drawn on the appellee bank. Neubauer testified that checks were sometimes received by him, of which some were payable to Belco, some to Florida Industrial and some to Neubauer personally. . . .

Between June 12, 1955, and November 27, 1956, Neubauer received from contract customers seven checks payable to Belco in an aggregate amount exceeding $17,000. These were indorsed by Neubauer with a rubber stamp indorsement bearing Belco's name and Florida Industrial's name, directing payment to the appellee for deposit to the account of Florida Industrial. . . . The appellee bank credited the account of Florida Industrial with the proceeds of the seven checks. In course of time Florida Industrial withdrew the funds. Approximately $10,000 was sent by cashier's checks to Belco. When Belco discovered that Neubauer had diverted its funds to Florida Industrial it made a demand on the bank and followed its demand with a suit. The case was tried to the court without a jury.

The district court concluded that although Florida Industrial had no actual authority to indorse checks payable to Belco and deposit them in the appellee bank to the credit of Florida Industrial, there was an ostensible authority so to do with which Belco had clothed Florida Industrial by a long continued course of conduct in permitting such practice. . . .

The burden of proving agency is on the party asserting it. Miller v. Chase & Company, 88 Fla. 500, 102 So. 553; 3 C.J.S. Agency § 315b, p. 253. Whether or not acts are within the scope of an agent's apparent authority is to be determined, under the applicable rules, as a question of fact. Bush Grocery Co. v. Conely, supra. Since findings of fact are not to be set aside unless clearly erroneous, Rule 52(a), Fed.Rules Civ. Proc., 28 U.S.C.A., we look to the record to see whether the evidence is insufficient to sustain the findings or if the findings were induced by an erroneous view of the law. Robey v. Sun Record Co., 5 Cir., 1957, 242 F.2d 684, certiorari denied 355 U.S. 816, 78 S.Ct. 20, 2 L.Ed.2d 33. It is only by evidence of acts and conduct of Belco which were known to and relied upon by the Coconut Grove Bank that the bank can prove an apparent authority in Florida Industrial to indorse checks payable to Belco and deposit them in the bank to the credit of Florida Industrial.

Belco had knowledge that Florida Industrial used a stationery with the word "Belco" at the top along with Florida Industrial's name, address, telephone numbers and cable address, and a legend at the bottom reciting "Exclusive Agent and Distributor for Belco Equipment in Florida" etc. A letter on this stationery had been written to the Bank. In 1951, Neubauer wrote Belco saying, among other things, that "in this part of the country" Belco, Florida Industrial and Neubauer "are synonymous as far as the persons with whom I deal are concerned." An officer of the Bank testified that Neubauer was even known as "Mr. Belco" in many instances. While these facts show that Florida Industrial had a connection with Belco they are not of evidentiary value in establishing an apparent authority of Florida Industrial or Neubauer to indorse Belco's checks. . . .

There was a finding that the Bank knew that Florida Industrial was a sales agent of Belco. Its knowledge of this uncontroverted fact is not persuasive on the question at issue. It was also found that the Bank knew that Florida Industrial was remitting checks on its account in the Bank to Belco. This does not have any bearing upon the question of apparent authority to indorse and deposit.

It was found by the district court that Florida Industrial, between 1952 and 1956, remitted to Belco collections made by Florida Industrial by its checks or by cashier's checks and not by the checks of customers, and that Belco made no objection either to Florida Industrial or the Bank to this manner of remittances. These findings and the evidence which supports them would be material if Belco was asserting a claim against a contract purchaser who had made payment by a check issued to Florida Industrial in violation of the contract provision that "All remittances are to be made direct to Belco Industrial Equipment Division, Inc." No such question is here presented and we think these matters are not relevant to the question that is present in this case.

There is a finding that other collections were made by Neubauer in the form of checks payable to Belco which were deposited in the account of Florida Industrial and remitted to Belco by checks of Florida Industrial. Coupled with this is the finding that Belco had knowledge that it was receiving payments on its contracts by checks of Florida Industrial and not the checks of its customers. On these findings, primarily, is based the court's conclusion that Belco knew or should have known that Florida Industrial was depositing in its bank account checks payable to Belco. We think the court's inference is not warranted. Eight checks of Florida Industrial to Belco subsequent to 1952 were in evidence. Some of these were shown not to have been remittances of collections from customers on Belco contracts. Others might have been remittances of such collections but there was no proof of the fact. It was established that two, possibly three, of the checks were in payment of customers' obligations on Belco contracts. There was no evidence that Florida Industrial had received payment from any of these customers by a check payable to Belco. In any event a course of dealings is necessary to establish apparent authority. Isolated or occasional transactions are not enough. 2 C.J.S. Agency § 112, a(1), p. 1301. . . .

REFERENCES

Fairfield Lease Corp. v. Radio Shack Corp., 5 Conn.Cir. 460, 256 A.2d 690 (1968) (store manager's authority to sign lease for food vending machine was not proved by series of rent payments and other circumstances).

Liberty Mutual Insurance Co. v. Enjay Chemical Co. (Now Exxon), 316 A.2d 219 (Del. Super.1974) (checks for duPont were sent for nine years to department head, who embezzled some of them; duPont's failure to complain gave apparent authority for receipt of checks).

Bill Terry's, Inc. v. Westside Auto Radio, 376 So.2d 890 (Fla.App.1979) (customer who allowed various individual employees to buy from plaintiff on its purchase orders, without verifying authority, was liable for purchases made by non-employees on stolen purchase orders).

Jackson v. First National Bank of Memphis, Inc., 55 Tenn.App. 545, 403 S.W.2d 109 (1966) (bank should bear loss of forged checks of an unfaithful servant of a church. Endorsement by a dog track should have put bank on notice to make inquiry).

Ames v. Great Southern Bank, 672 S.W.2d 447 (Tex.1984) (bank liable for allowing bookkeeper who had authority to handle banking transactions for corporation to make withdrawal from personal account of president and sole shareholder of the Corporation).

SAUBER v. NORTHLAND INSURANCE CO.

Minnesota Supreme Court, 1958.
251 Minn. 237, 87 N.W.2d 591.

KNUTSON, JUSTICE. On June 18, 1953, R.J. McDonald was the owner of a 1952 Hudson automobile. On that date he procured a policy of insurance on the car from defendant. Among other things, the policy covered damages caused by collision or upset. The policy ran for two years, and the premium was paid for that length of time.

On November 20, 1953, McDonald sold the car to his brother-in-law, John E. Sauber. The transfer was completed in a bank at Farmington. After transferring the title card to Sauber, McDonald handed him an envelope containing the insurance policy. Sauber then called Northland Insurance Company, defendant herein, on the telephone about the insurance. His testimony is that a woman answered the telephone. She inquired whether she could help him, and his testimony in that regard was as follows:

"I was informed, naturally, it was the Northland Insurance Company; I didn't know her name or whether she said this was the Northland Insurance Company, but she knew I was talking to the right place; the purpose was, I told her I had purchased the car and it was transferred to me and I was the new owner of the car and I had the insurance policy and I wanted to know if it was all right I would drive the car with this insurance and she said it is perfectly all right, go ahead and that is about the summary of the whole deal; I was the new owner of the car and it was insured by them people."

One of defendant's employees, Helen Serres, was called as a witness by defendant. She testified that on November 20, 1953, she answered a telephone call at the company office. She said that the call came from a man, but she did not remember whether he identified himself or not; he did tell her, however, that he was calling in regard to insurance issued to McDonald on the 1952 Hudson; and she checked the files in the office and found the policy. She denied that she told the person calling that it would be all right to drive or that the policy would be transferred. She said: "He only asked if it could be done." It was her testimony that she informed the person calling that the policy could not be transferred until the Industrial Credit Company, which carried a finance contract on the car, had been paid. At the time of the call she made a memo on a pad. A portion of it, written in ink, reads:

"11/20 sold to

"J.E. Sauber

Farmington, Minn.

"Employed

Plumbing &

    Heating

    Self.

"Age—58."

. . .

When McDonald sold the car to Sauber he reserved the right to use it when he wished and to buy it back if he chose to do so. He did borrow the car on two occasions, and on the last occasion, March 24,

1954, he was forced off the highway by another automobile, and the Hudson was badly wrecked. A joint action originally was commenced by McDonald and Sauber to collect on the collision insurance coverage of the policy involved. The action brought by McDonald was dismissed by the trial court, and the jury returned a verdict in favor of Sauber in his action. . . . Defendant appeals from the order denying its motion for judgment notwithstanding the verdict, and plaintiff appeals from the order granting a new trial.

. . .

Defendant's argument is based largely on the proposition that plaintiff has failed to identify the person with whom he talked on the telephone and that he has failed to establish the authority of such person to act for defendant. . . .

On the issue of identification, it is always sufficient if it can be shown that the person calling can identify the voice of the person speaking at the other end of the line. But it is not always essential that identity be so established. It may be established by other surrounding facts and circumstances.[1] Circumstances preceding or following the conversation or the subject matter itself may serve to establish the identity of the party.[2]

A slightly different situation arises when a person calls an established place of business listed in a telephone directory. That is the type of case we are dealing with here. In such case, we long ago indicated that we favored the so-called liberal view, followed by a majority of the courts,[3] that, where a place of business installs a telephone and invites the public to use it in the transaction of business by listing its name in the telephone directory, one who answers a call at such place of business and undertakes to respond as the agent of the business establishment is presumed to have authority to speak in respect to matters of the general business carried on at such establishment.[4] Here, identification of a particular person who answers the telephone is not essential. In a truer sense, we are concerned with the identity of the place of business rather than with a certain individual. In order for the conversation to be admissible, all that is necessary is to show that the place of business was called and that someone at that place

---

1. Merchants Nat. Bank of St. Paul v. State Bank, 172 Minn. 24, 214 N.W. 750.

2. Katzmarek v. Weber Brokerage Co., 214 Minn. 580, 8 N.W.2d 822. For Annotations on the entire subject, see 71 A.L.R. 5 and 105 A.L.R. 326; see, also, 20 Am.Jur., Evidence, §§ 365, 366.

3. 20 Am.Jur., Evidence, § 367; 31 C.J.S. Evidence § 188; 7 Wigmore, Evidence (3d Ed.) § 2155, p. 620; McCormick, Evidence, § 193, note 8; Annotations, 71 A.L.R. 13 and 105 A.L.R. 330.

4. Gardner v. Hermann, 116 Minn. 161, 133 N.W. 558; Wetmore v. Hudson, 149

Minn. 332, 183 N.W. 672; Merchants Nat. Bank of St. Paul v. State Bank, 172 Minn. 24, 214 N.W. 750; Gilliland & Gaffney v. Southern Ry., 85 S.C. 26, 67 S.E. 20, 27 L.R.A.,N.S., 1106, 137 Am.St.R. 861 (which case was followed by us in Gardner v. Hermann, supra); Stein v. Jasculca, 165 Wis. 317, 162 N.W. 182; Kiviniemi v. American Mutual Lia. Ins. Co., 201 Wis. 619, 231 N.W. 252; Zurich General Accident & Liability Ins. Co. Ltd. v. Baum, 159 Va. 404, 165 S.E. 518.

answered and purported to act for the business establishment. Here, again, proof subsequent to the conversation may be sufficient to establish the identity of the business, and in this case it was admitted in the pretrial deposition and by her testimony at the trial that Mrs. Serres actually did receive a call which the jury could well find was that made by plaintiff.

When the conversation becomes admissible, the authority of the person who answers to speak for the business establishment becomes important. Here, again, we have indicated that we favor the rule that, when an employee of the business place answers the telephone at such established place of business and purports to act for such concern, a presumption arises that such person has authority to act. As a result of this presumption, the burden rests on the business establishment to rebut the presumption. In the absence of such rebutting evidence, the presumption controls as a matter of law. In Gardner v. Hermann, 116 Minn. 161, 165, 133 N.W. 558, 560, we said:

> ". . . Business concerns, by installing a telephone in their places of business to be used in the transaction of affairs there conducted, impliedly invite the public to make use of that medium of communication. It is thereby made an agency for the transaction of business, and there are forcible reasons for the position that persons thus dealing have the right to assume that one answering his telephone call, who asserts a right to speak for his principal or employer, is authorized to do so and to transact the business there conducted."

. . .

This presumption rests on the apparent authority of an agent and is based on the law that a principal is bound by the acts of his agent within the apparent authority which he knowingly or negligently permits the agent to assume or which he holds the agent out as possessing. . . .

Apparent authority in cases of this kind arises by virtue of the fact that: (1) The business has invited the public to use the telephone to transact business with it; (2) the business has permitted an employee to answer the telephone; (3) such person has purported to act for the business with authority; and (4) the person calling the place of business had a right to assume that the person permitted to answer the telephone had authority to act. The presumption is not conclusive, but, once the basic facts giving rise to the presumption are proven, it is incumbent upon the defendant to produce evidence to rebut it. It might be rebutted, for instance, by showing plaintiff was not acting in good faith or had no reason to believe that defendant's employee had authority to act. But, in the absence of evidence rebutting the presumption, it controls as a matter of law. Once evidence competent to rebut the presumption is introduced, it becomes a question of fact whether plaintiff had good reason to rely on the apparent authority.

Defendant offered to prove by Mrs. Serres that she had no actual authority. It was not error to reject the offer of proof. We are not here concerned with actual or express authority. Apparent authority exists by virtue of conduct on the part of the principal which warrants a finding that a third party acting in good faith, was justified in relying on the assumption that the agent had authority to act.

We think that any other rule, in these days of modern business when so much business is transacted over the telephone, would not only be unjust but unrealistic. It would make it possible for a business concern to escape liability on agreements made in good faith simply by requiring the party doing business with it over the telephone to identify a person whom he has never seen or met or to prove the authority of that person to act for the establishment. When an employee of a business establishment is authorized to answer calls coming over the telephone, we think that it is only right that the burden of proving lack of authority should rest on the one who has placed such employee in a position where others dealing with the place of business would be apt to rely on his apparent authority.

It follows in this case that, when Sauber testified that he called defendant's office and someone answered and it was later shown that Mrs. Serres had a conversation with someone about the same subject, the jury could well find that plaintiff's conversation was had with her and that she answered in behalf of defendant company. Thereupon the presumption arose that she had authority to act for defendant in that matter. No proof was offered to rebut this presumption so it follows as a matter of law that authority to act has been established.

Defendant argues that the above rules do not apply where it must be shown that a conversation was with a particular person. It is true that, if it must be established that the conversation was had with some particular individual, there must be proof that the person who answered the telephone was such person. Even in such case, however, proof of identity at the time of the conversation is not essential. The identity of the person answering the call may be established by means of surrounding facts and circumstances preceding or following the conversation or it may be established from the subject matter itself. However, the exception to the general rule does not apply here. In this case it is obvious that the call was made to an established place of business, and the identity of the particular person answering the telephone need not be established. The important question is the identity of the place of business and the fact that someone at that place answered and purported to act for it. So much has been established here.

. . .

The order denying defendant's motion for judgment notwithstanding the verdict is affirmed, and the order granting a new trial for errors of law is reversed with instructions to reinstate the verdict.

REFERENCES

Persons receiving mail and telephone calls:

Fielding Home for Funerals v. Public Savings Life Insurance Co., 271 S.C. 117, 245 S.E.2d 238 (1978) (insurance company liable to policy assignee who was assured by telephone operator that policy was in effect).

Devers v. Prudential Property & Casualty Co., 86 Ill.App.3d 542, 42 Ill.Dec. 84, 408 N.E.2d 462 (1980) (person answering telephone for insurance company had apparent or implied authority to bind company on insurance policy).

Long v. Atlantic Freight Lines, 47 Ohio Op. 283, 64 Ohio L.Abs. 173, 103 N.E.2d 799 (Com.Pl.1952) (trucking company liable to filling station which supplied gasoline on credit to driver of truck bearing company name, in reliance on advice received by telephoning company's dispatcher).

Note, Telephone Response by Unidentified Party (1950) 12 Pitts.L.Rev. 112 (discussing presumption that person answering telephone is authorized to take messages).

Persons "in charge":

Regal Shop Co. v. Legum Distributing Co., 206 Md. 267, 111 A.2d 613, 50 A.L.R.2d 323 (1955) (wholesaler was bound by receipt of returned merchandise by men in charge of warehouse). Comment (1956) 16 Md.L.Rev. 154.

White v. Sorenson, 141 Mont. 318, 377 P.2d 364 (1963) (man in charge of used car lot for 15 days had "authority" to sell for a trade-in).

Finnegan Construction Co. v. Robino-Ladd Co., 354 A.2d 142 (Del.Super.1976) (apparent authority present for individual at the "office of the registered agent" to accept service of process from a deputy sheriff).

Oral Representation by Insurance Agent:

General Ins. Co. v. Truly Nolen of America, 136 Ariz. 142, 664 P.2d 686 (App.1983) (insurance company estopped from denying coverage by oral representation of agent when loss occurred prior to insured receiving written contract).

DULUTH HERALD AND NEWS TRIBUNE v. PLYMOUTH OPTICAL CO.

Supreme Court of Minnesota, 1970.
286 Minn. 495, 176 N.W.2d 552.

THEODORE B. KNUDSON, JUSTICE. Appeal by defendant Plymouth Optical Company, from a judgment awarding plaintiff recovery in the sum of $2,470.10.

In 1964, Paul McJames and Dr. Warren Reyburn (an optometrist who lived near Duluth and who at the time of this action was employed by defendant) organized Paul's Opticians, Inc., a Minnesota corporation (hereinafter referred to as Paul's). Paul's entered into a franchise agreement with Plymouth Optical Company whereby the former was authorized by the latter to use the Plymouth Optical Company trade name in connection with the operation of Paul's Duluth store.

McJames as president and general manager of "Plymouth Optical Company" entered into a contract with plaintiff which provided that plaintiff would print advertisements in its papers at specified rates for "Plymouth Optical Company" located in Duluth. This contract was executed on November 22, 1964. It was renewed by McJames and William R. Srnec, store manager, in the name of "Plymouth Optical Company" on November 1, 1965, and renewed again by Srnec as store manager in the name of "Plymouth Optical Company" on November 1, 1966.

Under the 1966 renewal, plaintiff provided advertising services in the sum of $2,470.10 which Paul's failed to pay. Plaintiff sued defendant on the theory of apparent authority of Paul's representatives to bind defendant.

Not only did Paul's Duluth store use the name Plymouth Optical Company in executing the contract with plaintiff, but it paid plaintiff with checks imprinted with the name "Plymouth Optical Company." Its advertisements in plaintiff's papers were in the name "Plymouth Optical Company"; it had that name on its office sign and door; and it was listed in the telephone and city directories as "Plymouth Optical Company."

Paul's Duluth store, in fact, was merely a franchise holder of defendant with no actual or implied authority, at least at the outset, to bind defendant.　.　.　.

The trial court determined by its findings that the business conducted at 8 East Superior Street in Duluth was held out as being "Plymouth Optical Company"; that, implicitly, such holding out, as to this plaintiff at least, continued for a period of 3 years; that the same was over such an extended period of time that if Paul's authority was exceeded by its representatives, it should have been discovered by defendant Plymouth Optical Company, which had all the facts concerning the relationship and either knew or should have known of its operations. From these findings, the trial court concluded that the plaintiff was entitled to rely upon the apparent authority of Paul McJames and William R. Srnec to bind Plymouth Optical Company.

Plaintiff relies principally on Lindstrom v. Minnesota Liquid Fertilizer Co., 264 Minn. 485, 119 N.W.2d 855, and Restatement, Agency (2d) § 27.　.　.　.

In Lindstrom defendant leased its Farmington branch to one Weaver. Weaver operated as if he were the agent of defendant; that is, defendant's name was printed on the buildings, tanks, and equipment with nothing to indicate Weaver was actually a lessee. Plaintiff, who supplied materials to Weaver, was allowed recovery from defendant under the rule of apparent authority quoted above. The trial court found that defendant by its actions had created a situation in which third parties could be misled into thinking that Weaver was defendant's agent or employee and therefore was liable.

In a further discussion of estoppel in the Lindstrom case, we quoted the following from a strikingly similar case on the facts:

"In Manning v. The Leavitt Co., 90 N.H. 167, 5 A.2d 667, 122 A.L.R. 249, a department store leased a portion of the store to another for use as a beauty parlor and authorized the use of its name in advertisements of the tenant. Plaintiff who had sustained burns from an electrical apparatus while undergoing hair treatment in the beauty parlor sued the store owner for damages. She testified that she had patronized the beauty parlor because defendant had 'always advertised very extensively . . . I thought it was a good store and I went in there.' There, in holding the defendant might be liable, the court stated (90 N.H. 170, 5 A.2d 670):

" 'The evidence was sufficient to establish all of the necessary elements of an estoppel; (1) a representation made with the authority of the defendant that it conducted a beauty parlor, under such circumstances that the defendant could foresee that women might act upon it to their possible prejudice, thus imposing upon the defendant a duty to avoid the misapprehension, (2) a belief in the mind of the plaintiff that the fact was as thus misrepresented, and a submission to the care of the shop and its employees in reliance upon that belief, and (3) consequent prejudice to the plaintiff.
. . .

" ' . . . if the defendant wished to avoid the duty to act in reference to the situation this apparently created, it should have refused to be a party to the misrepresentation and have taken steps reasonably calculated to remove misapprehension from the public mind.' " 264 Minn. 495, 119 N.W.2d 862. . . .

To this point, in Lindstrom, we said:

" . . . [C]ontractual provisions to the effect that a party to a contract shall not be considered as agent or employee of the other have repeatedly been held not to foreclose findings that nevertheless the former was the agent or employee of the latter." 264 Minn. 494, 119 N.W.2d 861.

See, Annotation, 116 A.L.R. 457, 461.

Applying the rule of apparent authority to the findings of the trial court, we conclude that the conduct of defendant franchiser in authorizing and permitting the franchisee in this case to use the name "Plymouth Optical Company" for 3 years under the circumstances disclosed by the findings and the limited record created an apparent authority in the franchisee to bind defendant franchiser, and accordingly defendant is liable as principal for the advertising services furnished it by plaintiff.

Defendant contends that franchising is a new way of business life which will be disrupted by the imposition of liability under the circumstances of this case. We are not impressed that this will be the effect of our decision. Franchisers can protect themselves from liability by insuring that their franchisee outlets make it clear to their customers and creditors that they are not dealing with a franchiser but with an independent business as a franchisee.[3] This can be accomplished in the

3. In Lindstrom v. Minnesota Liquid Fertilizer Co., 264 Minn. 485, 496, 119 N.W.2d 855, 862, we met this contention as follows: "In Annotation, 116 A.L.R. 457, 462, the editor comments as follows:

name it employs and in advertising which candidly discloses the relationship which exists.[4]

REFERENCES

Franchise:

Wood v. Holiday Inns, Inc., 508 F.2d 167 (5th Cir.1975) (on contract theory, employer liable for act of employee's clerk in retaining and canceling guest's credit card).

Nichols v. Arthur Murray, Inc., 248 Cal.App.2d 610, 56 Cal.Rptr. 728 (1967) (franchisor liable for franchisee's failure to furnish lessons for which customer prepaid).

Porter v. Arthur Murray, Inc., 249 Cal.App.2d 410, 57 Cal.Rptr. 554 (1967) (liable for franchisee's failure to furnish lessons by reason of bankruptcy).

Vowels v. Arthur Murray, Inc., 12 Mich.App. 359, 163 N.W.2d 35 (1968) (same; contract made on stationery bearing name of franchisor).

Butler v. Colorado International Pancakes, Inc., 510 P.2d 443 (Colo.App.1973) (franchisor liable on franchisee's contract to buy assets of a subfranchisee, where principal franchisee was acting on instructions of franchisor).

McLaughlin v. Chicken Delight, 164 Conn. 317, 321 A.2d 456 (1973) (franchisor not liable for negligent driving by franchisee's employee delivering merchandise).

Murphy v. Holiday Inns, Inc., 216 Va. 490, 219 S.E.2d 874, 1 A.L.R. 756 (1975) (franchisor not liable for defective maintenance, causing plaintiff to slip and fall).

Oberlin v. Marlin American Corp., 596 F.2d 1322 (7th Cir.1979) (SCM franchised Marlin American Corporation to distribute phones; Marlin sold franchise to Oberlin, without disclosing material obstacles to distribution; SCM not liable to Oberlin; SCM's control over contract forms and use of trademark did not make Marlin a mere agent).

Subsidiary company:

A–A–A Foundations Inc. v. Elite Homes, 217 So.2d 666 (La.App.1969) (where affairs of three corporations are interwoven and president of one purports to act as agent of another the burden is on the corporations to make clear which is the contracting party).

UNIFORM PARTNERSHIP ACT, SECTION 16

Read the text of the section in the Statutory Supplement.

COMMISSIONERS' NOTE

This section clears several doubts and confusions of our existing case law. It has been held that a person is liable if he has been held out as a partner and knows that he is being held out, unless he prevents such a holding out, even if to do so he has to take legal action. (Fletcher v. Pullen (1889) 70 Md. 205, 16 A. 887, 14 Am.St.Rep. 355;

" '. . . In addition, these agreements [between oil producing corporations and local distributors of their products] commonly provide . . . that the company's signs, trademarks, etc, shall be placed on the buildings, trucks, tank wagons, etc.; that the "agent" and his employees shall not be deemed employees of the company, which shall not in any event be liable for the negligence of the "agent" or his employees . . . ,' and cites numerous decisions holding that under such circumstances there may be a finding of ostensible agency as between the producer and its local distributor. As indicated above, to avoid liability in such situations the corporate producer may display its properties in such a way as 'to remove misapprehension from the public's mind' as to the actual ownership of the local business involved."

4. Many franchise operations in the form of retail chain outlets employ names such as Gamble's "Authorized Dealer" or other names to indicate to customers and creditors alike that the outlet is not operated by the franchiser.

Tanner, etc., Engine Co. v. Hall (1888) 86 Ala. 305, 5 So. 584; Ritten-
house v. Leigh (1850) 57 Miss. 697; Speer v. Bishop (1874) 24 Ohio St.
598; Prof. Burdick in 30 Cyc. 393.) On the other hand, the weight of
authority is to the effect that to be held as a partner he must consent to
the holding and that consent is a matter of fact. The act as drafted
follows this weight of authority and better reasoning. Morgan v. Farrel
(1890) 58 Conn. 413, 20 A. 614; Bishop v. Georgeson (1871) 60 Ill. 484;
Thompson v. Nat. Bank of Toledo (1884) 4 S.Ct. 689, 111 U.S. 529, 28
L.Ed. 507; Fisher v. A.Y. McDonald Co. (1899) 85 Ill.App. 653; Ihmsen
v. Lathrop (1883) 104 Pa. 365, 42 L.I. 28, 32 P.L.J. 417.

REFERENCES

Partnership by estoppel:

Boone v. General Shoe Corp., 219 Ark. 340, 242 S.W.2d 138 (1951) (store owner bound
by purchases of lessee who appeared to be part of same operation).

Wisconsin Tel. Co. v. Lehmann, 274 Wis. 331, 80 N.W.2d 267 (1957) (defendant not
bound as partner by estoppel because plaintiff did not prove it would have refused credit
in absence of belief of partnership).

Anderson Hay & Grain Co. v. Dunn, 81 N.M. 339, 467 P.2d 5 (1970) (consent to being
held out as partner implied by conduct and failure to deny).

NOTE: USAGE AND EXPECTATION IN EUROPEAN LAW

The derivation of agency powers from third party expectations, when in
conflict with the principal's expressed intentions, has had even harder going in
Europe than in the United States. The Code Napoleon seems to exclude it
categorically: "The mandator is bound to perform the contracts entered into by
the mandatary in accordance with the authority which the mandatary has been
given. Beyond this, the mandator is not bound by anything that has been done,
unless he has ratified it expressly or by silence." (Art. 1998). The German
Civil Code is to the same effect (Art. 177). Even the Italian Civil Code of 1942,
which reflects many other elements of twentieth century legal thinking, gives
no express recognition to the expectation element in measuring authority (see
Arts. 1387–1400, 1703–1730).

However, under the pressure of hard cases, European judges have found
means of holding the principal liable by inventing a doctrine that the scope of
the authority should be judged by its exterior appearance (*apparence* or
Schein).[1] But this doctrine is rather lightly touched on in the treatises—
seemingly much less than in the United States.[2]

On the other hand, the proposed international uniform law of agency,
drafted by a European committee and published in 1955 gives express recognition to the reasonable-expectation idea in a limited area:

1. J. Hemard, Le Mandat Commercial,
a chapter in J. Escarra et al., 2 Traite de
Droit Commercial (1955) § 654; W. Müeller-Freienfels, Die Vertretung beim Recht-
sgeschaft (1955) 77; Planiol et Ripert, 11
Traite Pratique de Droit Commercial Fran-
cais § 1500 (2d ed., 1954).

2. The matter of apparent authority
does not appear to be treated at all in

Planiol, Traite Elementaire de Droit Civil
(11th ed. 1939, translated into English,
1959, Louisiana State Law Institute),
§§ 2231–2264. The treatments in Hemard,
Müeller-Freienfels and Planiol-Ripert (supra, note 1) are relatively brief.

"Any restriction on the scope of the agent's authorization may only be set up against a third party if such third party knew or ought to have known of it at the time the agent carried out the act. If, however, a third party only knows of the agent's authorization as a result of a statement by the agent, the principal shall not be bound by an act carried out by the agent which exceeds the scope of that authorization." [3]

SECTION 4. RATIFICATION: SUBSEQUENT AFFIRMATION AND RETENTION OF BENEFITS

INTRODUCTORY NOTE

The cases you have been studying showed how a man could, by prior actions, empower another to bind him. Whether the principal gave this power by written document, or by entering into a business association, or assenting to similar past incidents, the conduct you looked at was always *prior* to the transaction on which liability was directly based.

In some of the cases you studied, the principal escaped liability because nothing he had done, before the transaction, was enough to enable the agent to bind him. In those same cases, could the principal have become liable if he had done something more, *after* the agent negotiated his transaction?

The contrast between the two problems may be put this way. A plumber says to a houseowner, "I am going to buy you some pipe." If the houseowner, in the presence of a pipe-dealer, says "okay," or stands silent, we have a problem of authority, apparent authority, or estoppel to deny authority.

Suppose that the plumber first broaches the subject after he has bought the pipe, and then says, "I bought you some pipe." Again the houseowner may say "okay," or may stand silent. What are the consequences? The following cases are designed to give some indications.

As the focal word in the prior cases was "authority," here again there is a word on which debate tends to center. It is "ratification." Some authorities—notably the Restatement—like to restrict this word to the clearest-cut cases of liability by subsequent conduct. Others will be found using "ratification" in a much broader sense, to include any form of adherence to a previously negotiated transaction.

The main object of your search, however, will not be terminology. You will want to find out what kinds of conduct will, or will not, render a principal liable on a previously negotiated contract. In analyzing the cases, it may be helpful to distinguish three general classes of facts. First, there is the measure of the principal's assent to the contract,

---

3. International Institute for the Unification of Private Law, Preliminary Draft of a Uniform Law on Agency in International Relations Concerning Private Law Matters of a Patrimonial Character (1955, Rome: Editions "Unidroit"), Art. 10, par. 2.

which may be express, or merely suggested by his failure to repudiate; or there may be outright dissent. Second, there is the measure of the third party's understanding—whether he thought the principal had agreed, or merely hoped so, or knew he had not. Third, there is the measure of consideration, which may be purely past consideration (if affirmance follows the third party's performance), or the receipt of benefits by the principal, or the incurring of expenses or losses by the third party. These elements concur in varying mixtures; will more of one make up for less of another?

In this section as in other sections of the book cases may be logically classified in different areas depending on the emphasis desired. Cases involving ancillary promises are included in this section since they relate to ratification. They also usually involve misrepresentation or other fraudulent acts by the agent, and relate to issues raised in the following section. On the other hand forgery cases are not included here, but are in the following section, although they may be analyzed as involving ratification.

REFERENCES ON RATIFICATION IN GENERAL

Seavey, The Rationale of Agency (1920) 29 Yale L.J. 859, 886–892 (brief analysis), reprinted in Studies in Agency (1949) 65, 98–105.

Breckenridge, Ratification in North Carolina (1940) 18 N.C.L.Rev. 308 (incisive analysis, not confined in usefulness to North Carolina).

Wambaugh,[1] A Problem as to Ratification (1895) 9 Harv.L.Rev. 60 (discussing five possible theories, or analogies, as to effect of ratification).

Philip Mechem, Rationale of Ratification (1952) 100 U.Penn.L.Rev. 649.

Twerski, Independent Doctrine of Ratification v. The Restatement and Mr. Seavey, (1968) 42 Temp.L.Q. 1 (an attempt to justify ratification as a separate agency concept that is beneficial to commercial operations).

EVANS v. RUTH

Pennsylvania Superior Court, 1937.
129 Pa.Super. 192, 195 A. 163.

BALDRIDGE, J. James S. Evans brought an action in assumpsit against Homer Ruth, trading as the Ruth Lumber and Supply Company, to recover $131.11 alleged to be due for hauling stone under an oral contract. It was agreed upon the record at the time of the trial that the disposition of this case shall govern four other actions against the defendant, brought by Roy W. Stafford, Fred M. Schwartz, W.M. Keown, and A.M. Kaldusan.

It appears from the evidence that in the fall of 1933, Ruth was awarded by the State Department of Property and Supplies two purchase orders under which he was to furnish crushed stone to certain state highways being constructed. Evans, having learned that there was work to be obtained at Bradford Woods stone quarry, applied there

---

1. Eugene Wambaugh, long a member of the Harvard law faculty, published the second American casebook on Agency (1896). This was the first casebook to de- velop Agency along the lines projected by Holmes—including the law of "Master and Servant," and emphasizing the role of legal fictions.

to an unidentified foreman, and was employed to haul stone. In answer to his inquiries, Evans was told that the Ruth Lumber and Supply Company of Scottdale had charge of the work and that he would be paid 40 cents per ton. Each load of stone was weighed and slips bearing the name of the Ruth Lumber Company, admittedly furnished by Ruth, were made out, in triplicate, containing the weight and other necessary data. Ruth acknowledged that one of these slips was then given to him, one was delivered to the State Highway Department, and the third was retained by Evans.

From October 30th to November 23, 1933, the plaintiff hauled stone, and it is conceded that there was due him the sum for which he sued.

On December 5th, after the work was completed, the plaintiff together with four or five other truckers, went to Ruth's place of business in Scottdale and presented him with their bills. After examining these accounts, Ruth said: "Well, I see you finished the work for me . . . If you will have a sworn affidavit to that statement, I will pay you. I have the money right in the safe there." Ruth was furnished this affidavit, but Evans was not paid. Later, at a squire's office in Warrendale, Ruth offered to pay, and did pay, 53 per cent of the claims to some of the claimants, but Evans refused to accept that proposition.

Ruth denied any liability to Evans, alleging that he had never entered into a contract of employment with him. He offered in evidence a written contract between himself and George Darr, subletting all the work allotted to him under the purchase orders to Darr as an independent contractor. He stated that he, personally, was never on the job, or had anything to do with it, other than to furnish two trucks on one occasion to hasten delivery of the stone. Darr testified to the existence of the contract, that he had two foremen on the job who kept the records, and that he was in complete control of the work. There was no evidence that Evans knew or had any way of knowing that Darr had this subcontract. Darr got into financial difficulty and whatever money may have been due him from Ruth was attached by one of Darr's creditors.

The plaintiff obtained a judgment. This appeal followed.

The plaintiff relied primarily upon an oral contract with an agent, subsequently ratified by the principal. Affirming agency, the burden rested upon him to prove it: Lewis v. Matias et ux., 300 Pa. 238, 150 A. 636. The agency could not be established by the declaration of the agent alone: Lawall v. Groman, 180 Pa. 532, 37 A. 98, 57 Am.St.Rep. 662; Yubas Ex. v. Makransky, 300 Pa. 507, 150 A. 900; Van Pelt v. Spotz, 92 Pa.Superior Ct. 213. If plaintiff's case depended solely on the statements of the unidentified foreman, admitted in evidence without objection, the position of the appellant that the agent's authority was not shown would be well taken. But the proof that Ruth furnished the weigh slips and received a copy after each load of stone hauled by the plaintiff had been weighed, which was the basis upon which Ruth was paid by the state, and Ruth's failure to disavow the contract, instead of affirming it by stating that the work was done for him, and that he would pay for it provided an affidavit was furnished, were sufficient for the jury's consideration.

It is a well-recognized rule of law that, if A assumes to act for B without precedent authority, and B subsequently affirms A's act, it is a ratification which relates back and supplies original authority for the act. B is bound then to the same extent as if previous authority had been granted A: 21 R.C.L. p. 919, sec. 99.

Ruth could have previously authorized the plaintiff's employment, and it follows that he could subsequently ratify it. "Ratification is the affirmance by a person of a prior act which did not bind him but which was done or professedly done on his account, whereby the act, as to some or all persons, is given effect as of originally authorized by him:" Restatement, Agency, sec. 82, p. 197. "Affirmance is a manifestation of an election by the one on whose account an unauthorized act has been performed to treat the act as authorized, or conduct by him justifiable only if there is such an election": Restatement, Agency, sec. 83, p. 198. Our own cases are in accord with this pronouncement of the law: Palmer v. General Flooring & Mfg. Co., 62 Pa.Superior Ct. 598; Bell et al. v. Scranton Trust Co., 282 Pa. 562, 128 A. 494.

The verbal agreement of Ruth to pay Evans did not fail for consideration, as appellant argues, as ratification does not require a new consideration: Garrett v. Gonter, 42 Pa. 143. The proof of the written contract Ruth had with Darr was evidence entitled to a careful consideration by the jury. In an impartial and entirely adequate charge, to which no exceptions were taken, that important factor in defendant's case was specifically referred to, as well as the burden that was on the plaintiff to establish by the fair weight of the evidence the essential facts upon which he relied.

We find no error in this record.

Judgment in each of the five appeals is affirmed.

REFERENCES

Analogous case:

Linn v. Kendall, 213 Iowa 33, 238 N.W. 547 (1931) (contractor engaged to build for P asked architect to draw plans; P later approved; P liable to architect).

Formality of ratification:

Where the agent's act is one which could not be authorized in advance without a written or sealed power of attorney, can P incur liability by subsequent conduct which lacks the same degree of formality?

Restatement of Agency 2d, sec. 93(2): "Where formalities are requisite for the authorization of an act, its affirmance must be by the same formalities to constitute a ratification."

Same, sec. 103: "A person who untruthfully manifests to a third person that an act purported to be done on his account was authorized or ratified in a manner sufficient for authorization or ratification, or that an act done by another who impersonates him was done by him, knowing or having reason to know that the third person is likely to act in reliance upon such manifestation, is subject to liability as if such act were authorized or ratified or had been done by him, if the third person so changes his position in reasonable reliance upon such manifestation that it would be inequitable not to impose such liability."

Ferguson v. Carter, 208 Ga. 143, 65 S.E.2d 600 (1951) (principal estopped by receipt of benefits, and third party's reliance, to deny agent's authority to execute sealed agreement); comment, 14 Ga.Bar.J. 227.

Note, Ratification of an Unauthorized Act (1967) 19 S.C.L.Rev. 788 (a discussion of the factual elements necessary to prove ratification).

Communication of affirmance:

If the third party does not learn of the principal's affirmance until after the principal has repudiated it, is it effective? Case authority is scant. For an affirmative answer, see Restatement of Agency 2d, secs. 95, 102.

Retention of benefits:

Wilkins v. Waldo Lumber Co., 130 Me. 5, 153 A. 191 (1931) (retaining benefits from part of a lumber contract served to ratify the total contract).

Land Title Co. of Dallas v. F.M. Stigler, Inc., 609 S.W.2d 754 (Tex.1980) (vendor ratified unauthorized subordination of lien by retaining down payment of sales agreement after learning the down payment came from the second—not first—lien.

Knapp v. Baldwin, 213 Iowa 24, 238 N.W. 542 (1931) (failure to repudiate contract for improvements ratifies unauthorized action by vendee of a land contract).

Contract requiring confirmation by principal:

Rodewald v. Randolph Mutual Insurance Co., 333 Ill.App. 271, 77 N.E.2d 443 (1948) (insurance adjuster and insured signed agreement settling claim "subject to approval of the Board of Directors"; company took no action confirming or rejecting for several months; held, company bound).

Hirzel Funeral Homes v. Equitable Trust Co., 7 Terry (46 Del.) 334, 83 A.2d 700 (1951) (principal not bound by later affirmation, where agent had not purported to have prior authorization); comments, 56 Dick.L.Rev. 263, 21 U.Chi.L.Rev. 248 (by Warren A. Seavey).

Failure to act as ratification:

Watson v. Schmidt, 173 La. 92, 136 So. 99 (1931) (retention of sale price for three months ratified unauthorized sale of a race horse.)

David v. Serges, 373 Mich. 442, 129 N.W.2d 882 (1964) (principal can be held to have ratified loan without any showing of benefits received).

Covington v. Butler, 242 So.2d 444 (Miss.1970) (agent executed written deed after his power had expired; principal held to have ratified the transfer because he had later recognized the grantee's interest).

Deveny v. Cranpsey, 1 Ont.R. 647, 62 Dom.L.R. 244 (1967) (where 3 or 4 joint tenants of certain land, upon learning of an agreement between the fourth tenant and another to sell the property, do nothing for over six months, they are estopped from denying agency and authority of the selling joint tenant); comment, 46 Can.B.Rev. 293 (1968).

Tyson v. Robinson, 329 So.2d 781 (La.App.1976) (accepting checks not marked "in full settlement" or "payment in full" does not ratify unauthorized price on sales contract).

Restatement of Agency 2d, § 94—Failure to Act as affirmance. The Reporter's Notes to this section contains an excellent discussion to the problem.

CHARTRAND v. BARNEY'S CLUB, INC.
United States Court of Appeals, Ninth Circuit, 1967.
380 F.2d 97.

HAMLEY, CIRCUIT JUDGE. This is a diversity action arising out of a counterclaim by Richard L. Chartrand to compel Barney's Club, Inc., a Nevada corporation, to issue to Chartrand fifteen shares of its capital stock or, in the alternative, to pay damages in the sum of $25,000. After a trial without a jury, judgment was entered for defendant corporation. Chartrand appeals.

We first summarize the district court's findings of fact. In the summer of 1960, Chartrand and Barney E. O'Malia (O'Malia), entered into an agreement in contemplation of incorporating Barney's Club, Inc. In this contract, Chartrand and O'Malia each agreed to contribute $80,000 as an investment in a proposed operation of a casino at Stateline, Nevada, to be known as Barney's Club. In consideration of this contribution, each was to receive an equal interest in fifty-one percent or more of the corporation. Therefore, under the terms of the pre-incorporation agreement, Chartrand was to have a $25\frac{1}{2}$ percent or more interest in the business.

Both O'Malia and Chartrand contributed their respective $80,000, either in cash, services, or by making expenditures on behalf of the corporation. All of Chartrand's contribution was made in cash, but the final $30,000 of his share was not paid until April, 1961, which was after some of the events described below.

Upon the incorporation of Barney's Club, Inc., in August, 1960, capital stock in the amount of $500,000 was authorized, divided into one thousand shares having a par value of five hundred dollars each. . . .

On March 20, 1961, the board of directors of Barney's Club, Inc., adopted a resolution approving the issuance of capital stock of Barney's Club, Inc., as follows: O'Malia, 240 shares; Chartrand, 240 shares; Frances O'Malia, fifteen shares; William F. O'Malia, fifteen shares.

Capital stock of Barney's Club, Inc. was issued in accordance with the resolution of March 20, 1961. Since June, 1961, Chartrand has repeatedly demanded an additional fifteen shares of the capital stock of Barney's Club, Inc. This would have given Chartrand a total of 255 shares, representing $25\frac{1}{2}$ percent of the total authorized stock in accordance with the pre-incorporation agreement.

On the basis of these findings, the trial court found and concluded that the knowledge of O'Malia concerning the terms of the pre-incorporation agreement should be imputed to Barney's Club, Inc., and that the corporation, at all times pertinent, had knowledge of such agreement. The court further concluded, however, that the evidence created a substantial uncertainty whether Barney's Club, Inc. adopted the pre-incorporation agreement. Finally, the court concluded that the credible evidence refuted the inference of adoption which would otherwise be justified from acceptance of benefits with knowledge of the agreement, and Chartrand therefore did not sustain the burden of proving such adoption.

On this appeal Chartrand argues, in effect, that since the trial court found and concluded that Barney's Club, Inc. accepted the benefits of the pre-incorporation agreement by receiving Chartrand's $80,000 contribution, and assertedly did so with imputed knowledge of that agreement, the court erred in further concluding that Chartrand had failed to sustain the burden of proving that the corporation had adopted the pre-incorporation agreement.

Under Nevada law, if a pre-incorporation contract made by promoters is within the corporate powers, the corporation may, when organized, expressly or impliedly ratify the contract and thus make it a valid obligation of the corporation. This is especially true if the agreement appears to be a reasonable means of carrying out any of the corporate powers or authorized purposes. Alexander v. Winters, 23 Nev. 475, 49 P. 116, rehearing denied, 24 Nev. 143, 50 P. 798.

The pre-incorporation agreement here in question is of a kind which is within the corporate powers of Barney's Club, Inc., and appellee does not contend otherwise. Nor does appellee assert that the pre-incorporation agreement entered into by O'Malia and Chartrand was not a reasonable means of carrying out the corporate powers and authorized purpose of that corporation.

Consistent with this Nevada rule, which accords with the weight of authority, it is generally held that if a corporation, with full knowledge of a contract that was formulated before the corporation came into existence, accepts the benefits thereof, it will be required to perform the contract obligations.

. . .

Courts in other jurisdictions are not consistent in their interpretation of this rule, but it is generally held that knowledge of a promoter, without more, is not imputed to a corporation. Most courts, however, recognize an exception which allows a promoter's knowledge to be imputed to the corporation where a promoter becomes a director and stockholder in the corporation or is the controlling stockholder. . . .

In the case now before this court, the benefit accruing to Barney's Club, Inc., was the $80,000 invested by Chartrand. Having accepted the entire $80,000 as part of the capital of the new corporation, with full knowledge of the burdens which would accompany such a contract, Barney's Club, Inc. did adopt the pre-incorporation contract and is now obliged to perform its side of the pre-incorporation agreement, unless it can show that the terms of this agreement were ambiguous, which does not appear to be the case here, or were changed or modified by some subsequent agreement.

It may very well be that there are circumstances which would warrant a conclusion, upon some such theory as contract modification, abrogation, or equitable estoppel, that Barney's Club, Inc., was relieved of what would otherwise be its obligation to issue 255 shares of Barney's Club, Inc. stock to Chartrand. Absent findings of fact which reveal such circumstances, however we are of the opinion that the ultimate conclusion drawn by the trial court cannot stand. Moreover, it is apparent that the trial court did not base its holding upon any of these theories.

Reversed and remanded for further proceedings consistent with this opinion.

NOTE: LIABILITY OF CORPORATION ON CONTRACTS MADE FOR IT BEFORE INCORPORATION

Closely allied with the requirement that the agreement ratified be made on behalf of the principal is an alleged requirement that the principal must have been capable of making the original agreement.[1] This point often comes up when promoters have negotiated agreements between a corporation to be formed, and a third person.

On this problem the Supreme Court of Minnesota observed in 1892:

"There is a line of cases which hold that where a contract is made in behalf of, and for the benefit of, a projected corporation, the corporation, after its organization cannot become a party to the contract, either by adoption or ratification of it. . . . This, however, seems to be more a question of name than of substance; that is, whether the liability of the corporation in such cases is to be placed on the grounds of its adoption of the contract of its promoters, or upon some other ground, such as equitable estoppel. This court, in accordance with what we deem sound reason, as well as the weight of authority, has held that, while a corporation is not bound by engagements made on its behalf by promoters before its organization, it may, after its organization, make such engagements its own contracts. . . ."[2]

Discussing the same matter, the Fourth Circuit Court of Appeals observed:

"While there are many decisions holding corporations liable in such cases, the courts have had great difficulty in finding a scientific or rational basis for sustaining such liability. The usual grounds that have been suggested are ratification, adoption, novation, and that the proposition made to the promoters is a continuing offer to be accepted or rejected by the corporation when it comes into being; and upon acceptance becomes an original contract on its part; and the liability has also been sustained on the ground that the corporation, by accepting the benefits of a contract, takes it cum onere, and is estopped to deny its liability on the contract. . . . This is really based upon the theory of implied ratification."[3]

SEIFERT v. UNION BRASS & METAL MANUFACTURING CO.

Minnesota Supreme Court, 1934.
191 Minn. 362, 254 N.W. 273.
Comment: 19 Minn.L.Rev. 318.

STONE, JUSTICE. After trial without a jury and decision for plaintiff, defendant appeals from the order denying its motion for amended findings or a new trial.

1. Restatement of Agency 2d, sec. 84.

2. McArthur v. Times Printing Co., 48 Minn. 319, 51 N.W. 216, 31 Am.St.Rep. 653 (1892).

3. Clifton v. Tomb, 21 F.2d 893 (C.C.A.4th 1927).

January 2, 1930, plaintiff closed the purchase of 25 shares of defendant's preferred stock. He was dealing with C.B. Michel, defendant's president and general manager. As part of the transaction and a condition of the contract of purchase, Mr. Michel gave him a letter signed for defendant by himself wherein "in consideration of this purchase" defendant, in terms, promised plaintiff a monthly bonus of $25, and that, in the event plaintiff desired to sell the stock, defendant would, upon 30 days' notice, repurchase it at $100 per share. The agreement also reserved to defendant the option to repurchase the stock at $100 per share plus accrued dividends at any time after five years.

Plaintiff declared originally upon the express contract of repurchase, suing for his $2,500 and interest. He duly tendered surrender of the stock certificate. Upon resting, he was met by motion to dismiss, the difficulty being, apparently, that he had not shown to the satisfaction of the court that Mr. Michel had authority to bind defendant on the promise to repurchase. (Without such showing, suit on the contract was futile.) Thereupon he was given leave to amend his complaint. The trial was adjourned ten days and then proceeded after plaintiff had come in with an amended complaint declaring, not upon the express contract to repurchase or any other, but in *quasi* contract for money had and received. Upon that theory the decision below went for plaintiff. . . .

1. The findings establish that Mr. Michel had no authority to bind defendant by offer of monthly bonus or to repurchase. But, nevertheless, that agreement was both term and condition of the supposed contract under which plaintiff parted with his money. Defendant cannot affirm in part and repudiate in part. Failure of the agreement to bind defendant according to its terms makes a clear case of no contract. Plaintiff did not get what he paid for; there was failure of consideration for his payment, and so he is entitled to recover it in order to prevent the unjust enrichment of defendant which otherwise would result. One of the long recognized heads for such recovery is "where the money was paid under a mistake as to the creation, existence, or extent of an obligation." Keener, Quasi-Contracts, 112. This is just such a case.

There was no mutual assent to the supposed contract. Defendant never assented to it because Mr. Michel had no authority to bind it as he attempted to. Plaintiff never assented to any other agreement. In McDonald v. Lynch, 59 Mo. 350, the plaintiff was awarded recovery of money paid in the belief that a contract had been created between himself and the defendant when in fact there was no contract because of mutual misunderstanding of a material term. In Gruesner v. Thatcher, 158 Minn. 470, 197 N.W. 968, the defendant counterclaimed for money he had paid under an agreement for the purchase of real estate. It was not a contract because it left open a material term. A recovery was had, *quasi ex contractu,* of the money paid. . . .

2. Of course there can be no recovery *quasi ex contractu* unless otherwise there will be unjust enrichment. But, without recovery, there would be such unconscionable enrichment of the party who gets money, property, or service from another in exchange for an apparently binding contractual promise which is not binding in fact and successfully repudiated by the promisor. In such case there is an obviously unlawful and unconscionable acquisition, attended by the obligation to disgorge the proceeds. That is the obligation enforced as it would be if bottomed on contract (which it is not), and hence called for convenience a *quasi* contract. Burleson v. Langdon, 174 Minn. 264, 268, 219 N.W. 155. See also Todd v. Bettingen, 109 Minn. 493, 124 N.W. 443, and Town of Balkan v. Village of Buhl, 158 Minn. 271, 197 N.W. 266, 35 A.L.R. 470.

Order affirmed. . . .

NOTE: ANCILLARY PROMISES

Ratification questions become more complicated when they involve contracts in which the primary provisions have been authorized but other important provisions have not.

An example involves an agent authorized to sell stock in a company, who on his own adds an unauthorized provision promising that the company will repurchase the stock at the original sale price any time within three years. If there is no authority for the repurchase provision—actual, inherent, or apparent—it would appear that the company should be able to enforce the authorized part of the contract and repudiate the unauthorized part. But if the company seeks to enforce its purchase contract it may be held to be ratifying the repurchase provisions.[1] On the other hand if the buyer attempts specific enforcement of the repurchase agreement he will probably fail.[2]

In this situation it may be possible, however, to argue for a rescission of the basic contract based on mutual mistake. The company believed it was simply selling stock for cash, while the buyer believed it was paying cash for stock coupled with a repurchase agreement. If both parties were reasonable in believing the contract was on their terms, rescission is an appropriate remedy. The *Seifert* case presents this approach.

NOTE: RATIFICATION OF FORGERY

In the matter of terminology there are authorities which take the position that there can be neither "ratification" nor "adoption," in a forgery situation since the signer of the check does not purport to act for the principal, but purports to be himself the principal. They concede, however, that the principal may become liable because he is "estopped." As you have already seen, other courts use the term "ratification" to cover cases of estoppel as well as cases of express affirmance.

1. Independent Harvester Co. v. Malzohn, 147 Minn. 145, 179 N.W. 727 (1920) (Company cannot collect on promissory note for sale of stock without ratifying an unauthorized provision promising employment to the buyer.)

2. Murray v. Standard Pecan Co., 309 Ill. 226, 140 N.E. 834 (1923) (Company that received payment for stock sale without knowledge of repurchase agreement is not bound by unauthorized repurchase provision.)

In the matter of substance, there is no doubt that the principal may become liable on a forged instrument under some circumstances. From the statement quoted below from the Reporter's Notes to Restatement of Agency, 2d, § 85 you can see that the critical question concerns what circumstances will "preclude" the principal from setting up forgery as a defense. At one extreme one could require that the principal mislead the third party before the latter pays the check. At the other extreme the principal could be precluded by only an unreasonable delay.

RESTATEMENT OF AGENCY, 2d

American Law Institute, 1958.

§ 85. Purporting to Act as Agent as a Requisite for Ratification

REPORTER'S NOTES

Forgery and personification. There was no general agreement in the early cases as to possibility of ratification of a forgery. The courts of Illinois, Maine, Massachusetts and New Hampshire indicated that in the absence of an illegal agreement, there could be; denying the possibility of ratification (but not of estoppel) were the courts of England, Kentucky, Ohio and Pennsylvania. See cases cited in 150 A.L.R. 978. With the advent of the Uniform Negotiable Instruments Act, which denied ratification, the states accepted the plain statement in § 23 of the act, which denied the possibility of ratification, except where a party is "precluded". In most courts "precluded" has been interpreted as meaning estopped, as in Home Credit Co. v. Fouch, 155 Md. 384, 142 A. 515 (1928). But it has also been held that one who had accepted the proceeds of the forgery, ratified it, a rational cutting of legal obstacles. Strader v. Haley, 216 Minn. 315, 12 N.W.2d 608, 150 A.L.R. 970 (1943). The New Uniform Commercial Code (§§ 3–404) provides: "(1) Any unauthorized signature is wholly inoperative as that of the person whose name is signed unless he ratifies it or is precluded from denying it; but it operates as the signature of the unauthorized signer in favor of any person who in good faith pays the instrument or takes it for value. (2) Any unauthorized signature may be ratified for all purposes of this Article. Such ratification does not of itself affect any rights of the person ratifying against the actual signer." Although the Code covers only negotiable instruments, it is a reasonable assumption that in states accepting the Code, the courts will tend to follow its implications into other forms of transactions and permit the affirmance of forged documents to have the normal effect of ratification. Where the affirmance occurs without overtones of an illegal agreement there is no reason to distinguish the forgery cases from the normal purporting cases.

. . .

SECTION 5. NONDISCLOSURE OF AGENCY

INTRODUCTORY NOTE

Jurists for centuries (even millenia) have been prone to assume that people who exchange promises in commercial transactions intend to incur legal obligations, and acquire the legal obligations of others. For better or for worse, these concepts of right and duty have small place in the cerebrations of the men who buy and sell lumber, labor or building lots. The buyer thinks, "I will have those 2×4s on the premises by Wednesday morning," and the seller thinks, "I will get cash for that stuff by the tenth of next month."

Consequently, they frequently neglect to specify for whose benefit purchases and sales are being made. Sometimes their neglect results from mere haste or confusion causing them to forget their usual precautions. Sometimes they neglect to specify because this "paperwork" is left to others; a builder may leave it to his bookkeeper to allocate the bills to different jobs, undertaken in different capacities. In some businesses—notably stock brokerage—brokers have found it more convenient to pay to and collect from each other than clients; by association rules they can be assured of one another's solvency, and can often set off reciprocal balances of cash or securities so as to minimize the inflows and outflows of assets. In other areas, buyers or sellers often affirmatively desire secrecy. This is most frequently encountered in purchases of real estate, where a barren range may suddenly leap in price if its purchase is known to be sought by an oil or mining company. The case law has seldom distinguished between causes of non-disclosure.

Anglo-American case law is quite clear that non-disclosure is no obstacle to the liability of a principal; the difficulty is in distinguishing a principal from a customer. A merchant buys everything for the benefit of his customers, but they are not all his principals. There is also a problem about the liability of the agent who reveals he has been acting for someone else, and whether he is released by the promisee's pursuit of the principal.

Separate attention should be given to the questions which arise when the undisclosed principal is the plaintiff. Are the equities different than when he is the defendant?

LUBBOCK FEED LOTS, INC. v. IOWA BEEF PROCESSORS
United Court of Appeals, Fifth Circuit, 1980.
630 F.2d 250.

Before MORGAN, CHARLES CLARK and TATE, CIRCUIT JUDGES.

TATE, CIRCUIT JUDGE:

The defendant packer appeals from judgment holding it liable to the plaintiffs, feedlot operators, for the unpaid price of cattle purchased by a buyer found to be its agent. . . .

The plaintiffs, two Texas feedlot operators, sold their customers' cattle to one Louie Heller. Heller, in his turn, passed the cattle on to the defendant out-of-state meat packer in purportedly a sales transaction. The packer paid Heller in full, but Heller's checks to the feedlot operators were dishonored because of his insolvency. In response to special verdict instructions, the jury found that the relationship between Heller and the meat packer was one of agency and not of dealer-purchaser. On that basis the feedlot operators were awarded some $512,000 plus six percent prejudgment interest. . . .

Factual Context

The plaintiff-appellees in this action, Lubbock Feed Lots, Inc. (Lubbock) and Lockney Cooperative Gin, Inc. (Lockney), are custom feedlots. Their function in the cattle industry is dual. They serve both a "hotel" and sales function: There, cattle are fed and cared for to fatten them and render them suitable for slaughter; there also prospective buyers visit to inspect the cattle and to negotiate terms of sale with the feedlot operators. When a prospective buyer makes an offer for the cattle, the feedlot operator—depending upon his agreement with the cattle owners—either communicates the offer to the owner and obtains the owner's response or counter-offer, or exercises his authority to accept or reject the offer himself. The sales price is on a "live-weight" basis—the total weight of the animals sold multiplied by the negotiated price per pound. When the terms of the sale are agreed upon, the cattle are weighed; as they cross the scales, delivery is effected and the cattle become the property of the buyer. The feedlots send an invoice along with the cattle, and it is usual that the buyer mails his check in payment to the feedlots upon receipt of that invoice. The manner in which remittance of the purchase price is made by the feedlots to the cattle owners is not entirely clear from the record—Lockney, it appears, would deduct any unpaid balance due on the owner's feed bill or other charges and then forward the proceeds to the owners.

The defendant-appellant in this action, Iowa Beef Processors, Inc. (IBP), is a large meat packer that purchases cattle for slaughter, processing, and packaging. Its purchases, generally conducted through an intermediary, are on a "dressed-weight" basis—the weight of the dressed carcasses of the purchased cattle multiplied by the agreed upon price per pound. Thus, the packer does not know the exact price he will pay for a given shipment of cattle until he has received delivery and slaughtered, dressed, and weighed the cold carcasses. At that point, the packer is obliged to remit payment to his seller.

Louie Heller, the bankrupt whose insolvency has precipitated this action, was IBP's intermediary in the sales/purchases that are the focus of this case. The cattle industry recognizes three basic categories of cattle buyers who act as intermediaries between the selling feedlots and the purchasing meat packers:

(1) Packer buyers, who are salaried employees of the packer;

(2) Order buyers, who buy for various packers either on a commission basis or for a fixed price from the packers, and who may purchase cattle (a) in their own name, (b) for the packer, or (c) both; and

(3) Dealers, who are independent purchasers buying in their own name in the hope of reselling at a profit, and who bear the risk of market price fluctuations.

Between January 14, 1974, and February 4, 1974, Heller made six purchases from Lubbock and four purchases from Lockney—transactions involving some 1700 head of cattle. All the cattle purchased in these transactions ultimately found their way to IBP. Upon receipt of the cattle from Heller, IBP advanced money to him against the ultimate price. These advances never exceeded the final price to be paid. Upon dressing and weighing the carcasses, either the same day or the day following delivery, IBP paid over to Heller the difference between the advances and the exact purchase price. It is undisputed that IBP paid Heller in full for all of the purchases in question. Heller's payment to the feedlots, however, was not so promptly made—as a rule, seven to ten days elapsed between Heller's receipt of delivery and the issuance of his checks—and in the interim between IBP's payment to Heller and the feedlots' attempts to cash Heller's checks, Heller became insolvent and his checks were ultimately dishonored. . . .

The expert testimony of Eugene Redd

Eugene Redd, a livestock order buyer and cattle dealer, was called as an expert witness by the feedlots.

After lengthy testimony, Redd was asked about Louie Heller's reputation in the South Plains cattle industry. Over IBP's objections, Redd testified that in January and February of 1974 Heller was considered by "most of the people in the [South Plains cattle] industry" to be an order buyer for IBP. Redd was then asked on what facts he based his knowledge of Heller's reputation, and he responded that the bulk of Heller's cattle went to IBP. After a flurry of objections, Redd testified that he was closely associated with Heller's activities, buying from the same feedlots, dealing with the same people, and watching the movements of the cattle Heller procured. . . .

As to the fact of actual agency, the composite out-of-court utterances of the cattle industry recounted by Eugene Redd clearly constitutes hearsay, and is inadmissible under both the hearsay rule and the rule embodied in *Deaton & Son v. Miller Well Servicing Co., supra.* As to the issue of apparent agency, however, evidence of reputation is not barred by the *Deaton* rule; further, being offered to prove elements of *apparent* agency, as opposed to the fact of actual agency, it is clearly not hearsay. Thus, it is admissible for that purpose, which was an issue in the present case, although not admissible to prove *actual agency.*

In determining the existence of an agency relationship in the context of the present case, where the alleged agent purchases property that it subsequently passed on to the alleged principal, the courts of Texas have adopted the rules set out in the Restatement (Second) of Agency:

> One who contracts to acquire property from a third person and convey it to another is the agent of the other only if it is agreed that he is to act primarily for the benefit of the other and not for himself.

Restatement (Second) of Agency § 14K (1957).

Factors indicating that the one who is to acquire the property and transfer it to the other is selling to, and not acting as agent for, the other are: (1) That he is to receive a fixed price for the property, irrespective of the price paid by him. This is the most important. (2) That he acts in his own name and receives the title to the property which he thereafter is to transfer. (3) That he has an independent business in buying and selling similar property. None of these factors is conclusive.

The evidence shows a long and well-established relationship between Heller and IBP. They had been trading with each other for some eight years prior to the sales in question here. Heller was in daily contact with IBP, obtaining such information as the number and quality of the cattle desired by IBP, the price IBP would pay therefor, and the price Heller himself should pay. As between IBP and Heller, Heller had a fixed, exclusive territory to which he was restricted and within which he suffered no competition for the favor of IBP. The great bulk of the total number of cattle purchased by Heller found their way to IBP. Heller's buying practices fluctuated according to the expressed needs of IBP and not according to the fluctuation of market price. Although his operations were not free from risk, the risk was not that normally associated with the independent speculator who buys low in the hope of later selling high—Heller knew what he would get before he bought. Heller received large advances from IBP, an unusual practice between packers and independent cattle buyers. Heller had railroad cars on lease for the purpose of shipping cattle to IBP's Emporia, Kansas, plant—again, an unusual practice for an independent dealer. During the 1973 price freeze, Heller appears to have sold his cattle directly to IBP's customers at IBP's request or direction. Also during that price freeze, an IBP employee, Pat Henry, appears to have been "loaned" to Louie Heller. Heller had left instructions with some feedyards to call IBP with information concerning each day's purchases.

There is also evidence tending to counter that from which an agency relationship might be inferred. It is clear that the feedlots in question here dealt directly with Heller, and never with IBP. They expected, and (when they received payment at all) they received, their payment from Heller rather than IBP. All the documents generated during the sales name Heller, not IBP, as the purchaser. The feedlots first sought redress from Heller alone, and only upon their inability to collect from him did they turn to IBP. Heller always received a fixed price from IBP, regardless of the price he paid for the cattle. There is some evidence that the feedlots viewed Heller as an independent cattle buyer and not as IBP's agent. And finally, Heller did conduct, at least as to packers other than IBP, an independent business in buying and selling cattle. . . .

Our task here is to determine whether the evidence, taken as a whole and in the light most favorable to the feedlots, is such that reasonable persons might reach a conclusion contrary to that urged by the party seeking to avoid the jury's verdict. . . . we cannot say that the facts and inferences point so strongly in favor of IBP that reasonable jurors could not reach a contrary conclusion.

For these reasons, we affirm the district court's denial of IBP's motions for judgment n.o.v. and for a new trial.

REFERENCES

For a similar decision see: A. Gay Jenson Farms Co. v. Cargill, Inc., 309 N.W.2d 285 (Minn.1981).

For two decisions reaching opposite results compare:

Farmers Elevator Co. of Reserve v. Pheister, 153 Mont. 152, 455 P.2d 325 (1969) (holding no principal-agent relationship).

Butler v. Bunge Corp., 329 F.Supp. 47 (N.D.Miss.1971) (finding principal-agent relationship).

Discharge of principal by payment to agent:

According to one view, commonly called the "majority rule," the principal is discharged by the payment: Fradley v. Hyland, 37 F. 49, 2 L.R.A. 749 (D.C.N.Y.1888); West's Ann.Cal.Civ.Code, § 2335; Ga.Code, § 4-305.

According to another rule, sometimes called the "English" or "minority" rule, the principal is not discharged unless the third party has in some way led him to believe that the agent has paid or settled the account: Restatement of Agency 2d, § 208 and Reporter's Notes to § 208.

For a thorough review of authorities, see Note (1947) 18 Miss.L.J. 436. In view of the small number of cases, and their ancient vintage, it would be difficult to predict the result today in a state which does not have an applicable statute.

Stecher, The Doctrine of Election as Applied to Undisclosed Principal and Agent (1935) 7 Miss.L.J. 466 (criticizing rule that principal may discharge self by paying agent).

THE LIABILITY OF AN UNDISCLOSED PRINCIPAL
Floyd R. Mechem, 1910.
23 Harvard Law Review 413–414.

It is ordinarily to the interest, as it is usually the duty, of an agent in making contracts for his principal fully to disclose the fact of the agency and to make the contract in the name and on the account of the principal. It often happens, however, that the agent will either intentionally or unintentionally omit to do this. He may (1) disclose that he has a principal but conceal his name and identity; or he may (2) wholly conceal the fact that he is an agent and contract as though he were himself the principal in the transaction. In either of these cases the agent usually makes himself personally liable upon the contract. In the second case the liability of the agent is ordinarily clear, because no other person being known in the transaction, the agent is the one upon whom the liability directly rests. In the first case also the agent may be liable because, though disclosing the fact that he has a principal, but concealing his name, he may be held to have pledged his own responsibility.

Conceding that the agent thus is, or may be, liable upon the contract, the question arises whether the principal, if discovered, may be held liable upon it also. In favor of such a liability it may be urged that inasmuch as there is a principal in the transaction who has authorized the contract to be made and who is entitled to its benefits, the principal should be held liable upon the contract when he is discovered. Against such a liability it may be urged that it is contrary to the general principles of contract to permit a person to be bound upon a contract who does not appear to be a party to it, and that in the case where no principal was known to exist the effect of such a rule is to give to the other party the benefit of a liability which he did not contemplate at the time of making the contract and for which he did not stipulate. A right to hold the undisclosed principal in such a case would, as was pointed out by a distinguished English judge, come to the other party as a mere "God-send."

Whatever may be thought where the contract is informal and oral, it is certain that where the contract is in writing, and especially where it contains no intimation of the existence of a principal, a rational theory for the principal's liability is not easy to discover. The contract is in the name and over the signature of the agent. How can that name and signature be treated as the name and signature of the principal? If the agent also could not be held upon it, it might then be said that the agent's name had, for the time being, been adopted as the business name of the principal, and was therefore, in this case, the name of the principal. But if the agent is to be held liable also because it is his name, how can the principal be held upon the theory that the name used is not the agent's name but the business name of the principal? May the name be, at the same time, the actual name of the agent and the trade name of the principal?

A theory of the legal identification of the principal with the agent leads to the same result. If the principal and the agent are legally one and that one the principal, it may not be difficult to see that the contract is the principal's contract, but it is not easy to see how the contract is also the contract of the agent.

. . .

THE LIABILITY OF THE UNDISCLOSED PRINCIPAL IN CONTRACT
William Draper Lewis, 1909.
9 Col.L.Rev. 116, 133–134.[1]

[In an action of assumpsit] it is not the defendant's promise to the plaintiff on which the plaintiff recovers, but the fact that the defendant caused the plaintiff to do an act (though that act is merely a promise

1. The quotation is excerpted from an article of the same name. William Draper Lewis (1867–1949) was dean of the Department of Law of the University of Pennsylvania from 1896 to 1914, when he resigned to run for Governor of Pennsylvania on the Progressive ticket. He was drafts-man (after Ames' resignation) of the Uniform Partnership Act (completed 1914). But he is likely to be best remembered as the organizer of the American Law Institute, of which he was director from 1923 to 1947, and through which he fathered the Restatements of the Law.

with the intent of being legally bound), which he would not have done had not the defendant acted. . . .

Where the agent acts openly in his principal's name the usual explanation of the principal's liability on the promise is the fiction that the principal has made the promise. But if the thought just expressed is correct, the fiction is an unnecessary invention,—the principal is liable on the contract because he has so acted as to induce the plaintiff to change his position for a stipulated reward. . . .

Where the principal is disclosed and the contract is made in his name, he has so acted as to induce the plaintiff to change his position. But the same is equally true in the case of the undisclosed principal; he has also moved his agent in the same way. To no greater and to no less extent than the disclosed principal has he caused the plaintiff to alter his position. To permit the person who has dealt with the undisclosed principal's agent in such a way as to raise a contract on which the action of assumpsit could be brought, on discovery of the principal, to elect whether he shall regard the contract as with the agent or with the principal, instead of being an anomaly and contrary to the fundamental common law idea of the reason for the obligation of the contract, would appear to fit in as perfectly with the fundamental idea lying at the foundation of the liability, as the denial of such a right to one who has made a formal contract under seal with agent of the undisclosed principal, fits in with the fundamental idea lying at the foundation of liability on formal contracts. . . .

THE UNDISCLOSED PRINCIPAL
W. Müller-Freienfels, 1953.
16 Modern L.Rev. 299.

"A prophet is not without honour, save in his own country"—this biblical truth is nowadays again illustrated in the field of legal institutions by "undisclosed agency." While Germany and France are admiring it more and more, it is losing favour in its own mother country and in the U.S.A.

The present appreciation of undisclosed agency in England is well known. No decision and no textbook omits to call it expressly "an anomaly in the law of contracts," out of harmony with basic legal principles. . . .

On the other hand, Continental jurisprudence esteems the institution of undisclosed agency very highly.

. . . Undoubtedly no theory of contract based on the liberal idea of mutual assent can explain how the third party can make a contract with a person of whose existence he does not even know. But is it a conceptual necessity in any case that a person acting in his own name can bind and entitle only himself personally? Is not the real problem of the law of contracts to settle the various mutual interests in the most fair, reasonable, simple and speedy way, without laying an unjust burden upon one party? . . . Legal rights and obligations are acquired in the first instance through the exercise not of the will of parties but of legal officials. Viewed in this light there is no obstacle to an undisclosed principal suing and being sued by the third party.

However, it is remarkable that it is the English common law which reached this solution of creating direct relationship between an undisclosed principal and the third party. For English common law insists so strongly, by its principle of "privity of contract," upon the limitation of the contractual effects to the contracting parties. . . .

REFERENCES ON UNDISCLOSED PRINCIPALS

Articles:

Sir Frederick Pollock, editorial note (1887) 3 L.Q.Rev. 358–359 (denouncing rights of undisclosed principal).

Holmes, History of Agency (1882) 4 Harv.L.Rev. 345, 5 id. 1, reprinted in 3 Select Essays in Anglo-American Legal History (1909) 368; see especially 3 Select Essays 390–395, 410.

Ames, Undisclosed Principal—His Rights and Liabilities (1909) 18 Yale L.J. 443 (advancing the "trust" theory, whereby the agent of an undisclosed principal should be regarded as a trustee for the principal; pointing out that European law does not recognize undisclosed principals). Ames (1846–1910) distinguished himself as a scholar by his pioneering in the making of casebooks when that art was new, and his historical studies, particularly of some of the common law forms of action. He was a member of the Harvard law school faculty from 1873 to 1909, and its dean from 1895 to 1909.

Ferson, Undisclosed Principals (1953) 22 U.Cin.L.Rev. 131.

Ferson, Fiction v. Reality re Contracts (1954) 7 Vand.L.Rev. 325, 336 (attributing objections to undisclosed principal's liability to the fiction that a breach of promise is a tortious deceit).

Schiff, The Undisclosed Principal: An Anomaly in the Laws of Agency and Contract, 88 Com.L.J. 229–237 (1983) (a brief comparison of the approach to liability in various disclosed and undisclosed principal situations).

Seavey (in colloquy), 7 A.L.I.Proc. (1929) 259.

England and Canada:

Higgins, The Equity of the Undisclosed Principal (1965) 28 Mod.L.Rev. 167 (reviews English cases, finds equitable basis for undisclosed principal's liability).

Comment, The Undisclosed Principle of Undisclosed Principals, (1975) 212 McGill L.J. 298–306 (an exploration of English and Canadian cases dealing with the separate relationship of undisclosed principal to third party, and agent to third party).

Europe:

Müeller-Freienfels, Comparative Aspects of Undisclosed Agency (1955) 18 Mod.L.Rev. 33 (comparing rules in France, Germany, Scandinavia, Switzerland and England).

Note, Apparent Authority and Undisclosed Principal under German Law (1974) 4 Cal.West.L.Rev. 340.

GRINDER v. BRYANS ROAD BUILDING & SUPPLY CO.

Maryland Court of Appeals, 1981.
290 Md. 687, 432 A.2d 453.

RODOWSKY, JUDGE.

The liability of an undisclosed principal has been called an "anomaly" from the standpoint of the law of contracts. Here we focus on a particular aspect of the anomaly. Where the creditor obtains a final judgment against one of the parties to the agency relationship, after learning of the existence and identity of the principal, the creditor is precluded from obtaining judgment against the other party. This is so even if the first judgment is unsatisfied. Reexamination of this rule of law convinces us that it is unsound and should no longer be followed. We adopt the rule that, absent other defenses, the third party may ordinarily proceed against the agent, or the previously undisclosed principal, or both, until the performance is satisfied.

This appeal arises out of a common business situation. G. Elvin Grinder (Grinder) of Marbury, Maryland is a building contractor. He did business as an individual and traded as "Grinder Construction." Grinder maintained an open account, on his individual credit, with Bryans Road Building & Supply Co., Inc. (the Plaintiff). On May 1, 1973 G. Elvin Grinder Construction Inc., a Maryland corporation (the Company), was formed. Grinder owned 52% of the stock.

[Plaintiff sued Grinder and the Company on certain purchases. Summary judgment was entered against the Company for $5,912.68. On trial of the action against Grinder personally, the Trial Court held that the summary judgment against the Company did not preclude judgment against Grinder. Judgment was so entered.]

. . .

Three days thereafter, Grinder filed a "motion to strike and enter judgment" which the court in effect treated as a motion for new trial under Md. Rule 567 by deferring entry of final judgment. Grinder's supporting statement of authorities referred to E.J. Codd Company v. Parker, 97 Md. 319, 55 A. 623 (1903) and thereby, for the first time, injected the concept of election into the case. In *Codd* the creditor, upon finding that it had been dealing with an agent, made claim against the principal in a proceeding in equity where an auditor's account was finally stated and ratified but under which no dividends were paid to the creditor. In a subsequent action by the creditor against the agent, in which the agent by special plea had set up the defense of election based upon the prior judgment against the principal, judgment went for the agent and was affirmed on appeal. This Court said (97 Md. at 325, 55 A. at 624):

> And the general principle appears to be established that where an agent contracts in his own name, without disclosing his interest, though in fact for the exclusive benefit of another person, who is afterwards discovered, the creditor may sue either, but after he has elected whom to sue and has sued either the agent or the principal to *final judgment,* he cannot after that sue the other, whether the first suit has been successful or not. [Emphasis in text.]

[In a hearing on the motion, the Trial Court reversed the judgment against Grinder personally. The intermediate appeals court remanded, without affirmance or reversal, to permit plaintiff to make an election.]

. . .

This disposition by the Court of Special Appeals leaves the Plaintiff with a judgment either against Grinder or against the corporation, but not against both. But, in its cross-petition for certiorari, which we granted, the Plaintiff argues that it should be entitled to a judgment against both. That was, of course, the original decision by the trial court. . . .

. . .

[The Court reviewed Maryland's decisions, which hold that the doctrine of election bars the entry of final judgment against both principal and agent except when the creditor takes judgment against the agent before knowing the identity of the principal.]

On the foregoing review of the Maryland precedents, we could dismiss the Plaintiff's request for reexamination of the election rule because it is too deeply embedded in our law to change. But a reading of these cases makes plain that we are not dealing with a rule in reliance on which people order their affairs or structure their business transactions. It is not a rule with respect to which predictability of the result of its application should remain stable in order to protect past transactions. Indeed, from the standpoint of the principal and agent, the rule predicts only that an election must be made, but because the election is that of the creditor, the result of the election is not necessarily predictable. As Grinder would urge in the instant matter, the election could occur by operation of law and unintentionally from the creditor's standpoint. . . . In any event, prevention of vexatious double litigation against the principal as an explanation for the election rule is greatly undercut by modern practice. If the agent is sued first, he may implead the principal as a third party defendant on the indemnification claim. If the parties are sued jointly, the agent may cross-claim for indemnity.

The one contract-no windfall rationale for the election rule was well stated in Tabloid Lithographers, Inc. v. Israel, 87 N.J.Super. 358, 365, 209 A.2d 364, 368–69 (1965) as follows:

> There is no reasonable basis for giving plaintiff a cause of action against both the agent and the principal when plaintiff contracted for only one. Giving plaintiff an alternative right to go directly against the principal is an additional advantage to the creditor. It permits the creditor to reach directly the agent's right to exoneration or indemnification. It puts the parties in the same position as if the agent had disclosed that he was acting for another. But since the creditor did not extend credit to the principal, he has the option of insisting on his original debtor or accepting the substitution of the principal for the agent. Before doing so, he can draw credit reports on both the agent and the principal. After suit had been started he can explore the facts in discovery proceedings. He need not elect even up to the trial. But the entry of judgment against either one is a recorded public act of

election and should be binding. It is neither unjust nor unreasonable to treat it so.

The leading decision espousing the opposite, but minority, view is Beymer v. Bonsall, 79 Pa. 298 (1875). There the buyer, with knowledge of the principal, had taken judgment against the agent for breach of a contract to sell petroleum. When the judgment remained unsatisfied, the buyer sued the principal and obtained judgment. In affirming, the Supreme Court of Pennsylvania, without citation of any authority, concluded (id. at 300):

> Undoubtedly an agent who makes a contract in his own name without disclosing his agency is liable to the other party. The latter acts upon his credit and is not bound to yield up his right to hold the former personally, merely because he discloses a principal who is also liable. The principal is liable because the contract was for his benefit, and the agent is benefited by his being presumedly the creditor, for there can be but one satisfaction. But it does not follow that the agent can afterwards discharge himself by putting the creditor to his election. Being already liable by his contract, he can be discharged only by satisfaction of it, by himself or another. So the principal has no right to compel the creditor to elect his action, or to discharge either himself or his agent, but can defend his agent only by making satisfaction for him.

Under the Pennsylvania rule, the liability of the agent and previously undisclosed principal is joint and several. Joseph Melnick Building & Loan Ass'n v. Melnick, 361 Pa. 328, 335, 64 A.2d 773, 777 (1949).

The Restatement of Agency has adopted the position that an undisclosed principal is discharged if, with knowledge of his identity, the creditor recovers judgment against the agent, but that the principal is not discharged if judgment against the agent is taken without knowledge of the principal's identity. Restatement (Second) of Agency §§ 210, 337 (1957); Restatement of Judgments § 100 (1942). Comment *a* to § 210 frankly acknowledges the inconsistency of the theories. It recognizes that the rule of discharge "cannot properly rest upon a normal doctrine of election—that is, a definitive choice between alternatives—since only a judgment against the agent destroys the claim. . . ." It acknowledges that the exception for lack of knowledge seems to reject merger by judgment or that the contract is one by which the creditor is to have the liability of the principal or agent but not of both. Discharge of the principal is stated to be apparently inconsistent with "the basic reason underlying the liability of the undisclosed principal," namely that he is liable because of the agency relation, while the agent is liable because of his promise. "From this it is not possible to find a joint promise," but because of the lack of knowledge exception "it is difficult to conceive of a promise in the alternative." Discharge by judgment, however, "represents the prevailing judicial viewpoint. . . ."

How the American Law Institute arrived at the position stated in the Restatement is set forth in the explanatory notes, found in Temporary Draft No. 4 of March 1929, to § 435 of Restatement of Agency, for which Professor Seavey was Reporter. We quote liberally therefrom.

> The majority of cases is in accordance with the rule as stated in this Section. The minority view is that a judgment against the agent, although with knowledge of the principal's identity, should not discharge the principal from liability. The Reporter, his Advisors, and some members of the Council, believe that the minority is correct, and should be recognized as law because more consistent, more just and more desirable from a business standpoint, if the state of the authorities permits. The undisclosed principal is made liable originally upon the transaction, because he initiated it; because he profits by it; because it is his business, conducted under his control. Policy requiring that he be liable, he should be discharged only if the debt is paid. There is doubt, however, as to the advisability of a statement contrary to the decisions of a number of very strong courts.

> .   .   .

The American Law Institute's position was almost immediately attacked by Professor Maurice H. Merrill in his article, Election Between Agent and Undisclosed Principal: Shall We Follow the Restatement?, 12 Neb.L.Bull. 100 (1933). He reviewed the decisions state by state. He recognized that what one considered to be the numerical majority rule depended very much on the interpretation given to the then existing decisions. His reading of the cases for their holdings found five jurisdictions supporting the Restatement position and four in which satisfaction of the obligation was the decisive test. If *obiter dicta* were included in the examination, Merrill would add ten additional states as supporting election by judgment. On the other hand, if "those courts which treat the recovery of judgment against both principal and agent in the same action as a problem of procedure rather than of substance are properly to be aligned with the opponents of the Restatement rule," then Merrill would count eleven as favoring the Pennsylvania rule and four as favoring the Restatement rule. 12 Neb.L. Bull., supra, at 117.

.   .   .

The commentators appear to be nearly unanimous in their support of the minority, i.e., satisfaction, rule. Justice Story, in his Commentaries on the Law of Agency § 295, at 378 (3d ed. 1846), speaking of shipowner and master, expressed the opinion that, under the common law, a creditor was not precluded by judgment against one "from maintaining another action against the party not sued, unless, in the first action, he has obtained a complete satisfaction of the claim." (Priestly v. Fernie, supra, rejected Story's position and questioned his supporting authority.) F. Wharton, A Commentary on the Law of Agency and Agents § 473, at 307–08 (1876), opines that there is "much reason" for the satisfaction rule and refers to Justice Story's opinion to that effect, but notes that *Priestly* rejected that conclusion. E. Huffcut, The Law of Agency § 126, at 169 (2d ed. 1901) took the position that "[i]t is generally held that an unsatisfied judgment is not conclusive proof of an election [citing, inter alia, Beymer v. Bonsall, supra] though the ruling is otherwise in England and some of our States." 2 F. Mechem, A Treatise on the Law of Agency § 1759 (2d ed. 1914), wrote that "it cannot well be said that changing the form of the agent's obligation, or putting it into a condition in which it can be more readily enforced, is inconsistent with an intention to proceed against the principal also. Nothing short of satisfaction of the judgment against the agent would then release the principal as a matter of law, and some cases have so held." W. Seavey, Studies in Agency § 210 (1949) states that the American Law Institute "decided that it was coerced by the cases." He acknowledges that most of the cases which he has noticed since publication of the Restatement have been in accord with its position, but he then sets forth in his work the same analysis which appeared in the Restatement explanatory note, supra. P. Mechem, in his fourth edition of F. Mechem, Outlines of the Law of Agency § 159, at 105 (1952), refers to the "illogicality and unfairness of the conventional rule." He expresses the hope that the Pennsylvania view "will ultimately still prevail." Id. at 106.

Some highly respected judges share the same view. Judge Augustus Hand has said "that anything less than a complete satisfaction or an estoppel in pais affords no logical basis for barring a remedy against both agent and undisclosed principal. . . ." Johnson & Higgins v. Charles F. Garrigues Co., 30 F.2d 251, 254 (2d Cir.1929) (dissenting opinion). Judge Clarke, writing for Judges Swann and Frank as well, has called the election rule a "harsh doctrine, resting at most on a rather barren logic. . . ." Ore Steamship Corporation v. D/S A/S Hassel, 137 F.2d 326, 330 (2d Cir.1943).

Ferson, Undisclosed Principals, 22 U.Cin.L.Rev. 131, 142–44 (1953) presents an analysis and proposed solution in modern terms to the many anomalies which plague this problem. He states:

> [T]he third party can hold an undisclosed principal; he can also hold the agent, and, yet, he is entitled to only one performance. What is the theory of the situation? It seems clear that when the agent of an undisclosed principal makes a contractual promise to a third person the result is not *one* obligation. It is *two* obligations. The agent is bound because he makes a contract that in terms is binding on him. The principal is bound owing to a different set of facts, viz. he assented—i.e., offered to be bound if and when the agent should make such a contract. The condition is met when the agent makes his contract. The principal and agent each consented to assume, and thus created, his own obligation. The obligations are not of identical origin, and they bind different obligors even though each obligation would be broken or satisfied according to

whether the obligee gets what is coming to him. "It would seem," says Professor Seavey, "that there are two groups of liabilities—one running between the third person and the agent and the other between the third person and the principal."

It should not be necessary to argue at this late date that a principal and his agent are not identical. But it was approved learning in earlier days. . . . Out of the false assumption that only one obligation was created by the agent's contract, has come a century of confusion and disagreement with regard to the liabilities of principal and agent.

When it is recognized that the third person acquires several rights against the principal and agent, there does not seem to be any reason of logic, justice or expediency why he should not have every advantage that accrues to anyone else who has more than one right. Specifically his attempt to hold one obligor should not exonerate another obligor.

. . .

The foregoing reasoning is unassailable on every ground other than its lack of strict adherence to the precedents. . . .

. . .

We deal here with a question of whether a judge made legal theory has become outmoded. This is traditionally a matter for a state court of highest resort. Modern practitioners have no difficulty in viewing the liability of the undisclosed principal to the creditor as founded in a policy of the law which looks to the reality that the undisclosed principal, for his business purposes, has authorized the contract through his agent, even though the creditor may have intended to form a contract only with the agent.

The rule of election first enunciated by this Court in *Codd* is overruled. We hold that a creditor who contracts with the agent for an undisclosed principal does not obtain alternative liability, that he may proceed to judgment against both, but that he is limited to one satisfaction.

. . .

REFERENCES

Old Ben Coal Co. v. Universal Coal Co., 248 Mich. 486, 227 N.W. 794 (1929) (states the "majority" rule that an election is binding if a judgment is obtained after notice of an undisclosed principal).

Richmond, Scraping Some Moss from the Old Oaken Doctrine; Election Between Undisclosed Principals and Agents and Discovery of their Net Worth, 66 Marq.L.Rev. 745 (1983) (reviews election cases in every state and argues: (1) election in contract cases is no more logical than in tort cases, and (2) where election is required the discovery of net worth of the two possible parties by the plaintiff should be permitted).

NOTE: SUITS BY UNDISCLOSED PRINCIPALS

The legitimate business reasons for a principal to remain undisclosed are occasionally challenged by a surprised third party, who might argue that it would not have done business if it had known the real party in interest. Perhaps the undisclosed principal is a competitor, or there is some personal or business animosity between the parties. The contract price may be lower than if there were full disclosure at the time of the contract.

Generally, the undisclosed principal may enforce the contract. The analysis is patterned on the law of assignments in contract. If the rights to a contract could have been assigned, then an undisclosed principal may enforce, and the burden is on the third party to prove that enforcement would be unfair. Evidence of false statements or fraud by the agent may preclude enforcement.

A further analogy to assignments is that the third party can retain all claims he may have against the agent even though the undisclosed principal receives the benefits of the contract. In addition to the right of election of the third party to collect from the agent, any set-off available against the agent can also be applied against the principal.

Even the demonstrated use of strawmen will not automatically prevent enforcement by an undisclosed principal. Straw parties may be used when law or custom requires a formal document, but the principal wishes to remain undisclosed. Straw parties are real people—often law office secretaries or law clerks—who have no real interest in the transaction, and little financial responsibility. In a Missouri case where the straw party was a barman at a beerhall, Judge Lamm was moved to observe:

> "In this condition of the record the case does not call for judicial comment on the business morality of the secret and deceptive use of a 'man of straw' in real estate contracts—a questionable practice, the product of insincerity and mere sharp commercialism. By the term 'man of straw' we understand one of no substance, one in name only, an irresponsible person having no property to respond in damages, who loans himself out to others to sign contracts as a purchaser knowing he is acting a lie—an office no honorable man should fill, and no honorable man should ask another to fill. When a case comes here in which a litigant, innocent of the deception practiced on him, is fraudulently misled and injured by the man-of-straw method, and raises such issue by his pleading, we can deal with it." [1]

In this case, specific performance was denied, primarily because the name of the straw party was affixed without his authorization (i.e., forged), although later ratified. The same result occurred in a pair of Illinois cases involving the combination of a straw party and an unauthorized signature.[2]

On the other hand, the explicit and admitted use of a straw party did not prevent specific performance in a Pennsylvania case.[3]

Again, the test turns on proof that the arrangement worked a fraud on the third party.

1. Houtz v. Hellman, 228 Mo. 655, 128 S.W. 1001 (1910).

2. Cowan v. Curran, 216 Ill. 598, 75 N.E. 322 (1905); Wloczewski v. Kozlowski, 395 Ill. 402, 70 N.E.2d 560 (1947); comments, 32 Iowa L.Rev. 790, 15 U.Chi.L.Rev. 143.

3. Warner Co. v. MacMullen, 381 Pa. 22, 112 A.2d 74 (1955) (broker explained that nominal buyer was straw party for real purchaser; specific performance granted).

REFERENCES

Enforcement by undisclosed principal

Kelly Asphalt Block Co. v. Barker Asphalt Paving Co., 211 N.Y. 68, 105 N.E. 88 (1914) (undisclosed competitor allowed to enforce contract absent any showing of fraud).

Specific performance denied:

New York Brokerage Co. v. Wharton, 143 Iowa 61, 119 N.W. 969 (1909) (contract to sell stock of goods to man who represented himself as purchaser, but was actually managing agent of business owned by others; specific performance refused).

Gloede v. Socha, 199 Wis. 503, 226 N.W. 950 (1929) (contract to sell land to person claiming to represent a man "in Chicago," but actually representing a nearby competitor of seller; specific performance refused).

Said v. Butt, [1920] 3 K.B. 497 (plaintiff, to whom theater manager had refused to sell ticket, had someone buy a ticket for him, but was refused admittance at the theater door; held, he was not entitled to damages beyond the refund of the price of the ticket because no "equitable right" acquired).

In the following cases specific performance was denied partly on the ground that the plaintiff was an undisclosed principal, and partly on the ground that the undisclosed principal was not bound at the making of the contract, which therefore lacked "mutuality":

Cowan v. Curran, 216 Ill. 598, 75 N.E. 322 (1905).

Wloczewski v. Kozlowski, 395 Ill. 402, 70 N.E.2d 560 (1947); comments, 32 Iowa L.Rev. 790, 15 U.Chi.L.Rev. 143.

Houtz v. Hellman, 228 Mo. 655, 128 S.W. 1001 (1910).

Specific performance granted:

Standard Steel Car Co. v. Stamm, 207 Pa. 419, 56 A. 954 (1904) (manufacturing company employed representatives to buy in own names, and they purchased as if for themselves; specific performance granted).

Warner Co. v. MacMullen, 381 Pa. 22, 112 A.2d 74 (1955) (broker explained that nominal buyer was straw party for real purchaser; specific performance granted).

Cole v. Hunter, 61 Wash. 365, 112 P. 368, 32 L.R.A.,N.S., 125, Ann.Cas.1912C, 749 (1910) (real estate purchased in name of man who was, unknown to seller, a Negro; specific performance granted at suit of Negro).

Specific performance or damages:

In most of the cases denying specific performance, it is not clear whether the contract is wholly unenforceable, or merely too inequitable for the remedy of specific performance. However, in Miller v. Fulmer, 25 Pa.Super. 106 (1904) the court affirmed only that part of the trial court's decree which denied specific performance, and reversed the portion which decreed cancellation of the contract.

Annotation:

Concealment of identity of purchaser, 121 A.L.R. 1162.

Set-off by third party:

Hamman v. Paine, 56 F.2d 19 (1st Cir.1932) (third party can set off obligation owed by agent in an enforcement action brought by an undisclosed principal.)

Restatement, Agency 2d (1958) § 306.

Illegal sale:

Under state law, it was unlawful to sell certain stocks to a private individual, but lawful to sell them to a bank. An individual caused a bank to purchase them, in its own name, for her. Becoming dissatisfied later, she sued the seller under her statutory right to rescind the illegal sale. Held, for defendant, because undisclosed principal is bound by any defenses which would have been available against the agent. Howell v. First of Boston Corp., 309 Mass. 194, 34 N.E.2d 633 (1941).

Set-off against partnerships:

When partners sue, may the defendant counterclaim for wrongs done to him by some or all of the partners?

Ruzicka v. Rager, 305 N.Y. 191, 111 N.E.2d 878 (1953) (limited partnership sues attorney for withholding funds; attorney's counterclaim for conspiracy of partners to destroy his professional standing disallowed). Noted (1953) 28 St.Johns L.Rev. 123.

England:

Ivamy, Right of Set-off against Undisclosed Principal (1950) 17 Sol. 271.

Annotation:

Defenses against an undisclosed principal, 53 A.L.R. 414.

Strawmen:

Fiechter, Are Straw Men Worth Crowing About? (1938) 12 Temple L.Q. 361. Cook, Straw Men in Real Estate Transactions (1940) 25 Wash.U.L.Q. 232 (comments on honest and dishonest uses of straw men).

HERKERT–MEISEL TRUNK CO. v. DUNCAN

Kansas Supreme Court, 1935.
141 Kan. 564, 42 P.2d 587.
Comment, 1 Mo.L.Rev. 343.

HARVEY, J. This was an action on an account for merchandise sold. . . . The defendants named were L.E. Smith and W.H. Hollis, Jr., partners as Smith & Hollis. By an amended bill of particulars Joseph Duncan was made a party defendant, and the action later was dismissed as to Smith & Hollis. There was a judgment for plaintiff, from which Duncan appealed to the district court. He died while the action was pending and it was revived in the name of his executor. The trial of this and two allied cases was by the court, which made findings of fact and conclusions of law and rendered judgment for plaintiff. The defendant has appealed. The principal question presented is whether there is any evidence to sustain the judgment of the trial court, on any theory.

There is no serious conflict in the evidence. The record discloses that on January 1, 1930, Joseph Duncan was the owner of a certain store building in Salina. He was also the owner of the stock of goods, furniture, fixtures and equipment belonging to a mercantile business there being conducted which he desired to sell to Smith & Hollis, and on that date they entered into a written contract which recited these facts. In that contract Duncan was referred to as the first party and Smith and Hollis as the second parties. Shortly stated, it provided that in consideration of the sum of $3,087.01, to be paid to the first party by second parties at the times and in the manner therein stated, with eight per cent interest on deferred payments, the first party "agrees to sell and deliver said stock of goods, furniture, fixtures and equipment to said second parties upon full payment therefor as hereinafter set forth." The second parties agreed "to conduct the business . . . as the agents of the said party of the first part, and out of the proceeds arising from said business to pay said first party": *First,* $120 per month rent for the building; *second,* $100 per month to apply upon the purchase price, with interest. . . . It further was agreed that until the payment had been fully made, as provided in the contract, "The title and the right to possession to said stock of goods, . . . and any and all other goods that may at any time be purchased and added to said stock of goods shall remain in the said party of the first part." The contract contained this paragraph:

> "It is further agreed by and between the parties hereto that any merchandise, furniture or equipment that may be purchased by the said second parties shall be purchased for cash only, and paid for at the time of purchase, and that the said second parties shall have no authority of any kind to purchase any goods upon credit except upon the written consent of said party of the first part."

It further provided that if second parties should fail to make the payments provided therein, or, if the first party deemed himself insecure, the first party had the right to take immediate possession of the stock of goods, furniture, fixtures and equipment and to sell the same as though they had been taken upon a chattel mortgage, and after deducting the expense of the sale and the amount due first party to pay any surplus to the second parties. It further was agreed that upon full payment and compliance with the contract by second parties the stock of goods, furniture, fixtures and equipment then belonging to the stock of merchandise should become the absolute property of the second parties.

Smith & Hollis took possession of the stock of merchandise under this contract with Duncan and conducted a retail mercantile business in the building for more than a year before this action was brought. In fact, they had conducted the same line of business in the same location for many years under the name of Smith & Hollis Furniture Company, handling new and used furniture. Some months before making this contract with Duncan it appears they became financially involved, and through a credit association made an assignment for creditors, as a result of which the assignee sold the stock of merchandise. Duncan bought the stock at that sale. That is how he came to own it on January 1, 1930. Sometime in 1930, while Smith & Hollis were conducting the business of the store under their contract with Duncan, plaintiff's traveling salesman called upon Smith & Hollis and took their order for a bill of merchandise to be purchased on account on customary terms as to discount and time of payment. This was sent to plaintiff's headquarters at St. Louis, where the credit man O.K.'d the order, and the goods were shipped. They were received by Smith & Hollis and placed in the stock of merchandise. This account was not paid, and this action was brought in January, 1931. Soon after this action was brought Joseph Duncan filed a replevin action in the district court against Smith & Hollis for the recovery of the possession of the stock of merchandise then on hand, alleging that he had a special ownership to the amount of $2,000 in such merchandise by reason of the contract hereinbefore set out. Duncan succeeded in getting possession of the merchandise by that replevin action, and thereafter advertised the goods and sold them as sales would be conducted under a chattel mortgage. Soon after the replevin action was brought plaintiff filed its amended bill of particulars in the city court making Duncan a party defendant. . . .

The rule of law, applicable to the situation is well stated in 21 R.C.L. 890, as follows:

"For most purposes the contract of an agent, who deals in his own name without disclosing that of his principal, is the contract of the principal. When discovered the principal may be held liable. . . . For example, where a broker or agent purchases goods, without disclosing his principal, the principal, when discovered, is nevertheless liable for the price."

To the same effect, see 2 C.J. 840. The courts of various states many times have followed with approval what was said in Hubbard v. Tenbrook, 124 Pa. 291, 16 A. 817, 2 L.R.A. 823, 10 Am.St.Rep. 585 where it was held:

"Where one is put forward to conduct a separate business in his own name, but with the property and as the agent of an undisclosed principal, the latter may not escape liability for goods sold to the agent in the course of the business, by a limitation upon the agent's authority to purchase." (Syl. par. 1.) . . .

In Restatement, Agency, § 195, the rule is thus stated:

"An undisclosed principal who intrusts an agent with the management of his business is subject to liability to third persons with whom the agent enters into transactions usual in such business and on the principal's account, although contrary to the directions of the principal."

See, also, sections 161, 194, and comments on each of them.

Apparently appellant concedes Smith & Hollis could do all they did do except to buy on credit without his consent. Under the rule as above stated Duncan would be liable even though the goods were purchased on credit without the written consent of Duncan. That is a common method for retail merchants to use in buying goods. Since plaintiff had no knowledge of the limitations of Smith & Hollis with respect to buying goods on credit, and conducted business with them in the manner in which such business ordinarily is conducted, they are not bound by such limitation of authority. The trial court correctly held Duncan to be the undisclosed principal of Smith & Hollis, his agents to conduct a retail mercantile business for him, and to be bound by their acts in purchasing from plaintiff merchandise on account, as such merchandise ordinarily is purchased by retail merchants. . . .

We find no material error in the case. The judgment of the court below is affirmed.

NOTE: AN ALTERNATIVE SOLUTION—LIABILITY OF GOODS

As you read the Herkert-Meisel case, it may have occurred to you that the court should never have allowed Duncan (in the prior replevin action) to recover his goods. Since Smith and Hollis had appeared to be the owners, their creditors should be able to levy on the goods. If this line had been taken, there would have been no need for Herkert-Meisel to sue Duncan.

This result may be reached under statutes of a few states, sometimes called "Traders Acts." Although sometimes treated as a phase of agency law, this result is distinctly different in that it does not make the principal personally liable, but only renders certain of his goods liable to seizure for another man's debt. Hence, its further investigation is left to courses on "Creditors' Rights" or "Debtors' Estates." If the subject is pursued in treatises, encyclopedias, or digests, it will be found most fully treated under the title "Fraudulent Conveyances."

REFERENCES

Armstrong Music Co. v. Boysen, 77 Okl. 55, 185 P. 828 (1919) (case 1) (where local piano dealer, handling pianos on consignment, engaged drayman to haul them, owner held not liable for drayage).

Associated Creditors' Agency v. Davis, 13 Cal.3d 374, 118 Cal.Rptr. 772, 530 P.2d 1084, (1975) (owners of bar obtained license in their own names, but leased the whole operation to a party that exercised complete control; owners could be liable on "ostensible agency" to any liquor wholesaler who could show he relied on the owner's names on the license as a basis for extending credit).

Ferson, Undisclosed Principals (1953) 22 U.Cin.L.Rev. 131 (proposing theory that undisclosed principal is liable as the employer of an independent contract, for inherently dangerous activities).

Brooks v. Shaw, 197 Mass. 376, 84 N.E. 110 (1908) (manager appeared to be owner of business; owner liable on manager's promise to pay a claim; court treats as ordinary case of "ostensible authority," citing Holmes).

Senor v. Bangor Mills, Inc., 211 F.2d 685 (3d Cir.1954) (supplying funds to jobber not enough to hold ultimate purchaser where no actual authority existed).

MOORE v. CONSOLIDATED PRODUCTS CO.
United States Circuit Court of Appeals, Eighth Circuit, 1926.
10 F.2d 319.

[Plaintiff sued defendant company to recover compensation for services rendered in compromising a patent infringement suit which had been brought against the defendant. A.P. Hunt, president of the company, had signed an agreement, stating, among other things, "In consideration of the services rendered by John F. Moore . . . I hereby agree . . . to pay to said Moore one-half of the proceeds . . . (Signed) A.P. Hunt." The trial court dismissed the plaintiff's petition, and the plaintiff appeals.]

PHILLIPS, DISTRICT JUDGE. . . . In passing upon the demurrer and motion, the court held that the plaintiff, by the written agreement purporting to have been entered into between him and Hunt, released his right to recover under the oral agreement theretofore entered into with the defendant company, and that the plaintiff could not show by oral evidence that Hunt entered into the written agreement for and in behalf of the defendant as its agent, because to do so would violate the rule that parol evidence is not admissible to vary or contradict a written instrument. . . .

The written agreement was a simple contract, and not one under seal. To permit the plaintiff to show that Hunt entered into the written contract in behalf of the defendant company, as its agent, would not violate the rule that a written instrument may not be varied or contradicted by parol evidence. Ford v. Williams, 21 How. (62 U.S.) 287, 16 L.Ed. 36; the Salmon Falls Mfg. Co. v. Goddard, 14 How. (55 U.S.) 446, 454, 14 L.Ed. 493.

In the case of Ford v. Williams, supra, the court said:

"The contract of the agent is the contract of the principal, and he may sue or be sued thereon, though not named therein; and, notwithstanding the rule of law that an agreement reduced to writing may not be contradicted or varied by parol, it is well settled that the principal may show that the agent who made the contract in his own name was acting for him. This proof does not contradict the writing; it only explains the transaction. But the agent, who binds himself, will not be allowed to contradict the writing by proving that he was contracting only as agent, while the same evidence will be admitted to charge the principal. 'Such evidence (says Baron Parke) does not deny that the contract binds those whom on its face it purports to bid, but shows that it also binds another, by reason that the act of the agent is the act of the principal.' See Higgins v. Senior, (8 Meeson & Welsby, 834). . . ."

Counsel for defendant contend, however, that the above rule applies only in the case of an undisclosed principal, and cannot be invoked against or in behalf of a principal known to the other party to the contract at the time the contract was made. They say that where a person, with knowledge of the agency, enters into a contract with the agent in the agent's name, his election to deal with the agent as an individual conclusively appears.

The question, after all, is one of fact. Was the contract made for and in behalf of a principal? If it was, the act of the agent was the act of the principal, and the principal may sue or be sued thereon. The great weight of modern authority applies the rule, both where the principal is known and where the principal is undisclosed, to the other party to the contract. New York & C.S.S. Co. v. Harbison (C.C.) 16 F. 688, 692; Exchange Bank v. Hubbard et al. (C.C.A.2d) 62 F. 112, 10 C.C.A. 295; Byington et al. v. Simpson, 134 Mass. 169, 45 Am.Rep. 314.

. . .

In Byington v. Simpson, supra, Mr. Chief Justice Holmes then judge of the Supreme Judicial Court of Massachusetts, said:

". . . We are of opinion that the plaintiff's knowledge does not make their case any weaker than it would have been without it. Whatever the original merits of the rule, that a party not mentioned in a simple contract in writing may be charged as a principal upon oral evidence, even where the writing gives no indication of an intent to bind any other person than the signer, we cannot reopen it, for it is as well settled as any part of the law of agency. Huntington v. Knox, 7 Cush. [Mass.] 371, 374 . . . Higgins v. Senior, 8 M. & W. 834, 844. And it is evident that words which are sufficient on their face, by established law, to bind a principal, if one exists, cannot be deprived of their force by the circumstance that the other party relied upon their sufficiency for that purpose. Yet that is what the defendant's argument comes to. For the same parol evidence that shows the plaintiff's knowledge of the agency may warrant the inference that the plaintiffs meant to have the benefit of it and to bind the principal.

     . . .

"The most that could fairly be argued in any case would be that, under some circumstances, proof that the other party knew of the agency, and yet accepted a writing which did not refer to it, and which in its natural sense bound the agent alone, might tend to show that the contract was not made with any one but the party whose name was signed; that the agent did not sign as agent, and was not understood to do so, but was himself the principal. But these are questions of fact."

     . . .

It follows that the court erred in sustaining the demurrer to the first cause of action and the motion to strike the second cause of action. The cause is therefore reversed and remanded.

NORTHERN PROPANE GAS CO. v. COLE
United States Court of Appeals, Fifth Circuit, 1968.
395 F.2d 1.

JOHN R. BROWN, CHIEF JUDGE. This is a sort of man-bites-dog situation. Instead of the usual situation in which the author, confector and instigator of a boiler plate adhesion-type contract seeks to hold the weaker, pliant, submissive, unequal acceptor to the literal pound of flesh, the reverse is here claimed. Asserting with dead earnestness that its own form contract, filed in by its own responsible and presumably articulate representative of considerable responsibility, is ambiguous in its reference to the identity of all the parties to be bound by it, the contention is made that the Trial Court erroneously granted summary judgment since a question of fact existed as to the intention of the parties on which extrinsic evidence was admissible. In this setting in which there is not a single identifiable new question of law, or for that matter, much of a dispute as to what the law is, we agree with the Trial Court and affirm.

What is specifically at issue is the covenant not to compete contained in a buy-out contract between the acquirer, Northern,[1] and Economy,[2] the local dealer being bought out. More specifically the question is whether in addition to binding Economy, the corporation, the covenant also bound Mike Cole, its President and $99^{44}/_{100}\%$ sole stock holder. What launched the controversy was the unabashed reentrance into the LP-gas business in the trade territory prescribed by Mike Cole within a couple of months after the execution of the contract, triggered presumably because Northern decided to terminate the employment of Mike Cole's wife. To make an ambiguity takes a lot of doing in this simple contract.[3]

AGREEMENT OF SALE

THIS AGREEMENT, made this *1st* day of *August,* 1964, between *Economy Gas & Supply Co.*
(hereinafter referred to as "Seller"), and NORTHERN PROPANE GAS COMPANY, a corporation having its principal offices in Omaha, Nebraska, (hereinafter referred to as "Buyer"), WITNESSETH THAT:

In consideration of the mutual promises, covenants and agreements of the parties herein contained, it is agreed as follows:

1. That Seller, in consideration of the sums herein agreed to be paid by the Buyer, has granted, sold and conveyed, and by these presents does grant, sell and convey into the Buyer, the following described property to-wit:

[Here follows description of tank trucks,

propane storage tanks and accounts

receivable]

2. Buyer agrees to pay for all of the foregoing a total of Twenty-one Thousand, Three Hundred and Twenty Dollars ($21,320.00), receipt of which is acknowledged by Seller's signature to this Agreement.

3. Seller, for himself and for his heirs, successors and assigns, does hereby covenant with Buyer and its assigns, that he is the true and lawful owner of the goods described above and has full power and authority to sell and convey the same; that the title conveyed hereby is clear, free and unencumbered; and that he does hereby warrant and will defend the same against the claims of all persons whomsoever.

4. Seller further agrees, in consideration of the payment of those sums of money to be paid by the buyer hereunder, not to reestablish or in any manner become interested, directly or indirectly, in any LP-Gas business within twenty-five (25) miles of Beaumont, Texas, within five (5) years from the date hereof without the express consent of Northern Propane Gas company.

IN WITNESS WHEREOF, the parties have executed this Agreement this *1st* day of *August,* 1964.

"SELLER"	"Buyer"
Economy Gas & Supply Co.	NORTHERN PROPANE GAS COMPANY
/S/ MIKE COLE	/S/ M.V. STAFFORD
President	

---

1. Northern Propane Gas Company, the Appellant, a Delaware corporation with its principal offices in Omaha, Nebraska.

2. Economy Gas & Supply Company, a Texas corporation.

3. This contract form was on a typewritten form. The matter interlined by typewriter is shown in italics. Handwritten signatures are shown as "/S/ Mike Cole," etc.

In its formidable undertaking Northern insists that there was a genuine material issue of fact as to the intention of the parties concerning whether Mike Cole intended to bind himself in his individual capacity as well as in his capacity as agent (President) for the corporate transferor. Its attack is anchored on Cavaness v. General Corp., 1955, 155 Tex. 69, 283 S.W.2d 33, principally because the Supreme Court there approved § 323 of the Restatement of the Law of Agency. Subdivision (1) of that section provides in substance that if it appears *unambiguously* in a contract that a party who executes a contract as an agent is or is not a party to the contract, extrinsic evidence is not admissible to show a contrary intent, except for the purpose of reforming the contract. On the other hand, subdivision (2) permits extrinsic evidence where "there is no unambiguous expression of an intention." These not surprising principles find general acceptance in Texas and elsewhere. These principles, Northern asserts, have been given application by the Texas Courts in cases which call for a reversal here.

The problem under this boiler plate contract boils down to the simple question of whether there is really any doubt on the face of this contract that the party sought to be bound by the covenant not to compete (paragraph 4) was other than the admitted corporate transferor. To overcome the surface tension against extrinsic evidence stress is laid, not on the obligation in dispute (paragraph 4), but rather it is directed toward paragraph 3 covering a matter nowhere in dispute. Thus Northern insists that where, in the warranty of title and ownership, paragraph 3 speaks in terms of "Seller, for himself and for his heirs, successors and assigns, ..." this indicates either as a matter of law that it was the purpose of the corporate agent to bind himself in his individual capacity or at least to raise a substantial question of fact on which extrinsic evidence would be admissible.[7]

But to us this asserted ambiguity of paragraph 3 is but a ripple, considering that it is uncontradicted that Northern knew the business being acquired was conducted in the form of a corporation, which the formal contract (note 3 supra) very precisely reflected. The contract gave its own definition of "Seller." Typed into the form contract was the corporate name "Economy Gas & Supply Co." It was this concern, and no other that the contract declared was "(hereinafter referred to as 'Seller')." That this was no inadvertent slip of the typist's finger is reflected further by the repetition of the corporate title "Economy Gas & Supply Co." Immediately below the contract term "Seller" in the

---

7. Once sufficient uncertainty on the face of the contract is established Northern urges two principal pieces of extrinsic evidence pointing toward assumption of personal liability by Mike Cole. The first is the letter proposal July 24, 1964, on the stationery of Economy Gas & Supply signed by Mike Cole, President, addressed to Northern in which the first person is repeatedly used (e.g., "I will sell . . ." and "I will sign a noncompetitive agreement" and "I will furnish a resolution from my Board of Directors authorizing me to sell . . . ."). Second, Stafford's pretrial deposition quoting Cole as saying "I will sign any kind of non-competitive agreement, I have no intention of going back in business."
. . .

signature clause. And to cap it all there was typed in under the line for signature the significant corporate title. "President." Moreover, although one can imagine that this was wholly accidental and just one of the perils that comes from form agreements that reflect the likelihood that the first and only time the writing came close to a lawyer was in the litigation seeking to enforce or defend it, when Northern intended to depart from the structured definition of "Seller" it did so in precise terms by adding, for example, "for himself and for his heirs, successors and assigns" in paragraph 3. Elsewhere, in paragraph 1, paragraph 2, and paragraph 4 the contract definition of "Seller" was thought to be adequate. Structured as the contract was with the purposeful typewritten insertion of the corporate name and the corporate title of the signatory agent there is no basis whatsoever for holding that there was either an intention to hold Mike Cole personally responsible or any basis for any genuine doubt thereon. This makes it unnecessary for us to discuss in detail the cases stressed by Northern, none of which require a different result here.

Only a tag end remains, Langford v. Shamburger, 5 Cir., 1968, 392 F.2d 939 (1968). Northern insists that Mike Cole is bound personally because he is the alter ego of the wholly-owned corporation which may be disregarded. No possible showing of a question of fact under accepted Texas principles appears in this record to rescue Northern from its undeniable knowledge that the enterprise was in a corporate form being transferred to it in the corporate name through a corporate officer.

Affirmed.

REFERENCES ON PAROL EVIDENCE RULE

Compare the following case with the principal case:

Schnucks Twenty-Five, Inc. v. Bettendorf, 595 S.W.2d 279 (Mo.App.1980) (individual's covenant not to compete was violated by competition of corporation that was formed and wholly owned by the individual).

Contract exonerating principal:

The principal case states that proof of a principal's existence does not contradict the writing. Ordinarily this is true. But it is possible to have a writing which states expressly that the named party is the principal. A line of English cases has held that in this situation, parol evidence to hold the true principal is inadmissible. There is, however, some conflict of opinion as to what sort of language in the contract will have this effect. See, Note, Parol Evidence and Undisclosed Principals (1945) 61 L.Q.R. 130.

Liability of undisclosed principal:

Jolles v. Holiday Builders, 222 Ga. 358, 149 S.E.2d 814 (1966) (president signed contract in name of corporation to convey land which president owned individually; court refuses to order specific performance either by corporation—which can't convey—or by president—who didn't promise to; no discussion of damage remedy).

Liability of agent:

G.E. Conkey Co. v. Bochmann, 220 F.Supp. 284 (D.Iowa 1963) (agent who signed notes in own name to raise money for principal because principal's credit was not acceptable was liable; dictum, he would have been liable even if intention of parties was that principal should pay, since parol evidence rule would bind agent).

Yellow Manufacturing Acceptance Corp. v. Britz, 8 Wis.2d 666, 100 N.W.2d 305, 80 A.L.R.2d 1134 (1960) (where contract was signed "George P. Britz" by George P. Britz, Sr. latter could introduce in defense evidence that intent of parties was to bind his son, George P. Britz, Jr.).

Undisclosed principal's suit against third party:

Heart of America Lumber Co. v. Belove, 111 F.2d 535 (C.C.A.8th 1940) (corporation not permitted to sue on lease signed individually by its president).

Looman Realty Corp. v. Broad Street National Bank of Trenton, 32 N.J. 461, 161 A.2d 247 (1960) (where broker submitted written offer on behalf of "a company owned by" two named individuals, both of whom signed the letter, there was a sufficient memorandum to satisfy statute of frauds; whether corporation or individuals are the proper plaintiffs depends on intention to be shown by parol evidence).

Analysis:

Note, Partially Disclosed Agency and its Significance (1951) 39 Ky.L.J. 208.

Note, The Agent Signs a Paper (1949) 29 Boston U.L.Rev. 375 (integrated contracts and sealed instruments in Massachusetts).

F.M.B. Reynolds, Personal Liability of an Agent (1969) 85 L.Q.Rev. 92 (review of English cases on transactions on behalf of corporation not formally identified as principal).

THE PARADOXES OF LEGAL SCIENCE [1]
Benjamin N. Cardozo, 1927.

The tendency of principle and rule to conform to moral standards, which is a true avenue of growth for law, is not to be confounded with the suspension of all principle and rule and the substitution of sentiment or unregulated benevolence, which, pushed to an extreme, is the negation of all law. . . .

Two cases recently determined in my own court will illustrate my thought. The rule was settled at common law that an undisclosed principal might not be held to liability upon a contract which had been executed under seal. Much of the law as to seals has small relation in society as now organized to present-day realities. The question came up whether we would adhere to the rule that I have mentioned, or hold it to have faded away with the fading significance of seals. The decision was that the old rule would be enforced. Precedents of recent date made departure difficult if *stare decisis* was not to be abandoned altogether, but there were other and deeper grounds of policy. Contracts had been made and transactions closed on the faith of the law as it had been theretofore declared. Men had taken title in the names of "dummies," and through them executed deeds and mortgages with the understanding, shared by the covenantees, that liability on the covenant would be confined to the apparent principal. They had done this honestly and without concealment. Something might be said, too, in favor of the social utility of a device by which the liability of the apparent principal could be substituted without elaborate forms for the

1. The selection above is a part of a lecture delivered at Columbia University in 1927, and may be found in context at pages 68–71 of Cardozo's Paradoxes of Legal Science (1928).

liability of another back of him who was to reap the profits of the transaction. The law has like devices for limiting liability in other situations, as, e.g., in joint stock associations, corporations, and limited partnerships. In any event retrospective change would be unjust. The evil, if it was one, was to be eradicated by statute.

[JUDGE CARDOZO proceeded to discuss another situation in which he believed that the historical rule of law should have been abandoned. He had been overruled, however, by a majority of the court.]

NOTE: STATUTES MODIFYING OR ABOLISHING EFFECTS OF SEALS

A great many states now have laws which purport to eliminate the seal as a factor in legal controversies—completely, or in broad areas. One widely used formula is illustrated by the Minnesota statute, which provides,

> "Private seals are abolished, and all written instruments formerly required by law to be sealed shall be equally effective for all purposes without a seal. . . ."

Another formula, copied in several other states, is the California one, which states,

> "All distinctions between sealed and unsealed instruments are abolished."

One of the latest formulations of the same purpose is New York's, which says,

> ". . . the presence or absence of a seal upon a written instrument hereafter executed shall be without legal effect."

In all these statutes, there is an apparent clarity, and a subtle ambiguity. What is clear is that henceforth the rules applied to the sealed instruments are to be the same as those henceforth applied to the unsealed instruments. But the question remains, which set of rules are to be applied to both? Courts could comply with the mandate of the statute either by applying to all instruments the rules formerly applied to the sealed, or the rules formerly applied to the unsealed.

With respect to ordinary contracts, the courts seem to have assumed, without argument or dissent, that the rules formerly applied to unsealed contracts are henceforth to apply to all.

With respect to deeds, this solution will hardly do. Formerly, unsealed deeds were legally invalid; they did not convey legal title, and might at most serve as memoranda of a contract. If we apply henceforth to deeds the rules formerly applied to unsealed deeds, we will have no valid deeds. The other horn of the dilemma seems better—to treat all deeds as we formerly treated sealed deeds. This leads to preserving, in reference to deeds, all the common law rules on sealed instruments which the legislators probably intended to abolish.

REFERENCES

C.B. McMullen v. J.T. McMullen, 145 So.2d 568 (Fla.App.1962) (undisclosed principal not liable on sealed instrument even though Florida Statute abolished necessity of seal).

Vigdor v. Nelson, 322 Mass. 670, 79 N.E.2d 288 (1948) (undisclosed principal liable on sealed instrument, where necessity of seal had been removed by statute); comments, 28 Boston U.L.Rev. 496, 29 Boston U.L.Rev. 388, 12 U.Detroit L.J. 89.

Crowley v. Lewis, 239 N.Y. 264, 146 N.E. 374 (1925) (this is case referred to by Judge Cardozo below) comments, 13 Geo.L.J. 400, 9 Minn.L.Rev. 580, 34 Yale L.J. 782.

Toll v. Pioneer Sample Book Co., 373 Pa. 127, 94 A.2d 764 (1953) (lists four exceptions to the "general rule" that a principal is not bound when a contract is made by an agent in his own name and under seal).

Harris v. McKay, 138 Va. 448, 122 S.E. 137, 33 A.L.R. 156 (1924) (undisclosed principal liable on sealed instrument, where necessity of seal removed by statute).

In re Childs Co., 163 F.2d 379 (C.C.A.2d 1947) (bidder at judicial sale released by court's confirmation of contract with bidder's straw party).

Most of the discussion of the effects of the seal, and of statutes modifying it, are concerned primarily with the seal as a substitute for consideration. Citations on this aspect are more fully supplied in casebooks on Contracts.

New York Law Revision Commission, Report (1936) 287–373 (a superb comprehensive study).

R. Braucher, Status of the Seal Today (1963) 9 Prac.Law., No. 5, p. 97.

Note, Present Status of the Sealed Obligation (1939) 34 Ill.L.Rev. 457.

Note, The Seal in Present American Law (1936) 5 Fordham L.Rev. 144.

COLONIAL BAKING CO. OF DES MOINES v. DOWIE
Iowa Supreme Court, 1983.
330 N.W.2d 279.

Considered by LeGRAND, P.J., and McCORMICK, McGIVERIN, LARSON, and SCHULTZ, JJ.

SCHULTZ, JUSTICE.

The events leading to this appeal began when Frederick J. Dowie, president and sole stockholder of Fred Dowie Enterprises, Inc. (corporation), a catering corporation, obtained the opportunity to operate concession stands at the Living History Farms during the Pope's visit to Des Moines in 1979. With high expectations Dowie ordered 325,000 hotdog buns from the Colonial Baking Company (Colonial). Before the buns were delivered he presented to Colonial a postdated check in the amount of $28,640. This check shows the name of the corporation and its address in the upper lefthand corner. The signature on the check is in the form "Frederick J. Dowie" and there are no other words of explanation. Unfortunately, dreams of riches often turn to dust and so it was in this case; only 300 buns were sold. Following a dispute over the ownership and responsibility for the remaining buns, payment was stopped on the check.

Colonial then sued Dowie in his personal capacity as signer of the check. . . .

To have shown an issue of fact in the summary judgment proceedings, it was necessary for Dowie to have pleaded and provided evidence that there was an agreement, understanding, or course of dealing between the parties that when Dowie signed the check he did so in a representative capacity and was not to be personally liable on the check. Iowa Code section 554.3403(2) assesses liability to a person whose signature is affixed to commercial papers as follows:

An authorized representative who signs his own name to an instrument

a. is personally obligated if the instrument neither names the person represented nor shows that the representative signed in a representative capacity;

b. except as otherwise established between the immediate parties, is personally obligated if the instrument names the person represented but does not show that the representative signed in a representative capacity. . . .

If Dowie wished to avail himself of the exception from liability provided by the phrase "except as otherwise established," it was necessary for him to plead and prove that he fell within the exception. Although we have not previously interpreted the language of section 554.3403(2)(b), we now hold that this section provides liability against the drawer of a check if there is no evidence that the check was signed in a representative capacity. Other courts have held that the fact that a corporate name is imprinted on the check is not alone sufficient evidence that the drawer, who signs his own name to the instrument, has otherwise established that he is not personally liable. *See Miller & Miller Auctioneers, Inc. v. Mersch,* 442 F.Supp. 570, 573, n. 2 (W.D.Okla. 1977) (defendant's failure to show title of his office results in personal liability); *American Exchange Bank v. Cessna,* 386 F.Supp. 494, 495 (M.D.Okla.1974) (although check bore corporate name and address, signer of check is liable because he put only his personal signature and not title on check); *Casey v. Carrollton Ford Co.,* 152 Ga.App. 105, 107, 262 S.E.2d 255, 257 (1979) (individual signer liable); *Leahy v. McManus,* 237 Md. 450, 454, 206 A.2d 688, 691 (1965) (a person who signs a note made by a corporation is prima facie liable to the payee unless he affirmatively shows an understanding between him and the payee); *Carleton Ford Inc. v. Oste,* 1 Mass.App. 819, 819, 295 N.E.2d 402, 402 (1973) (check imprinted with company name that was signed by the defendant with nothing to indicate a representative capacity placed on the signer the burden to disprove personal liability); *Financial Associates v. Impact Marketing, Inc.,* 90 Misc.2d 545, 546, 394 N.Y.S.2d 814, 815 (1977) (although checks contain a printed corporate name the drawer is personally liable as he failed to show he signed the note in a representative capacity); *Griffin v. Ellinger,* 538 S.W.2d 97, 100 (Tex. 1976) (burden is on drawer to disclose his representative capacity). *Cf. Speer v. Friedland,* 276 So.2d 84, 86 (Fla.App.1973) (presumption that defendant signs an instrument in a personal capacity was overcome by the manifest weight of parol evidence). *Contra Southeastern Financial Corp. v. Smith,* 397 F.Supp. 649, 653 (N.D.Ala.1975) (statute inapplicable as improbable that anyone would be confused where the corporation was listed and although the signature did not designate capacity it was proceeded by "By"), *but see Legg v. Kelly,* 412 So.2d 1202, 1205 (Ala.

1982) (holding signer liable where signature preceded by "by"); *Pollin v. Mindy Manufacturing Co.*, 211 Pa.Super. 87, 236 A.2d 542 (1967) (corporate payroll check signed by president without indication of representative capacity held obligation of the corporation); J. White & R. Summers *Uniform Commercial Code* § 13–4 (representative capacity should be more easily found on checks than corporate notes). . . .

A motion for summary judgment was a proper method of arriving at a judgment when there was no genuine issue of fact indicating that defendant acted in a representative capacity. *Rotuba Extruders, Inc.*, 46 N.Y.2d at 231, 413 N.Y.S.2d at 145, 385 N.E.2d at 1072. On the basis of the record at the time the trial court ruled, it erred when it denied the motion and failed to enter judgment for the amount of the check.

REFERENCES:

Failure to show representative capacity:

Individual liability:

Casey v. Carrollton Ford Co., 152 Ga.App. 105, 262 S.E.2d 255 (1979) (individual liable on corporate check drawn on corporate account when signature lacked representative capacity, and evidence showed check was for a personal not corporate purpose).

Financial Associates v. Impact Marketing Inc., 90 Misc.2d 545, 394 N.Y.S.2d 814 (1977) (no parole evidence allowed to show representative capacity on a corporate check when payee had sold checks to third party).

Robin Seafood Co., Inc. v. Duggar, 485 So.2d 593 (La.App.1986) (individual liable on corporate check signed without representative capacity in spite of evidence that previous payments had been made with corporate checks).

Norman v. Beling, 58 N.J.Super. 575, 157 A.2d 17 (1959) (president and treasurer of corporation signed under corporation name but without their titles or other showing of representative capacity; in action by holder in due course, parol evidence inadmissible to show intent that only corporation be bound).

Seale v. Nichols, 505 S.W.2d 251 (Tex.1974) (note signed "The Fashion Beauty Salon, Carl V. Nichols"; Nichols personally liable although he intended to sign for a corporation named "Mr. Carl's Fashion Inc." and doing business as "The Fashion Beauty Salon").

No individual liability:

Valley Nat. Bank, Sunnymead v. Cook, 136 Ariz. 232, 665 P.2d 576 (App.1983) (court states it adopts "minority rule" in denying liability on corporate check even though signature lacked representative capacity).

Highfield v. Lang, 182 Ind.App. 77, 394 N.E.2d 204 (1979) (signature on corporate check lacked representative capacity, but court allowed parol evidence to show payee knew or should have known signer was working for a corporation).

First National Bank of Elgin v. Achilli, 14 Ill.App.3d 1, 301 N.E.2d 739 (1973) (heirs of sole proprietor of Highland Motor Sales signed renewal note "Highland Motor Sales, Ruth Achilli, Howard Achilli"; heirs entitled to introduce parol evidence to show bank's understanding that only estate of decedent was to be held liable).

Michigan National Bank v. Hardman Aerospace, 36 Cal.App.3d 196, 111 Cal.Rptr. 514 (1974) (signer of note not liable when payee understood that it was made on behalf of another corporation, which was intended to pay).

UNIFORM COMMERCIAL CODE
Article 3—Commercial Paper

Section 3–401. Signature

(1) No person is liable on an instrument unless his signature appears thereon.

(2) A signature is made by use of any name, including any trade or assumed name, upon an instrument, or by any word or mark used in lieu of a written signature.

COMMENT

1. No one is liable on an instrument unless and until he has signed it. The chief application of the rule has been in cases holding that a principal whose name does not appear on an instrument signed by his agent is not liable on the instrument even though the payee knew when it was issued that it was intended to be the obligation of one who did not sign. . . .

Nothing in this section is intended to prevent any liability arising apart from the instrument itself. The party who does not sign may still be liable on the original obligation for which the instrument was given, or for breach of any agreement to sign, or in tort for misrepresentation, or even on an oral guaranty of payment where the statute of frauds is satisfied. He may of course be liable under any separate writing. The provision is not intended to prevent an estoppel to deny that the party has signed, as where the instrument is purchased in good faith reliance upon his assurance that a forged signature is genuine.

. . .

Section 3–403. Signature by Authorized Representative

(1) A signature may be made by an agent or other representative, and his authority to make it may be established as in other cases of representation. No particular form of appointment is necessary to establish such authority.

(2) An authorized representative who signs his own name to an instrument

    (a) is personally obligated if the instrument neither names the person represented nor shows that the representative signed in a representative capacity;

    (b) except as otherwise established between the immediate parties, is personally obligated if the instrument names the person represented but does not show that the representative signed in a representative capacity, or if the instrument does not name the person represented but does show that the representative signed in a representative capacity.

(3) Except as otherwise established the name of an organization preceded or followed by the name and office of an authorized individual is a signature made in a representative capacity.

COMMENT

Prior Uniform Statutory Provision: Sections 19, 20 and 21, Uniform Negotiable Instruments Law.

Changes: Combined and reworded; original Section 21 omitted.

Purposes of Changes:

1. The definition of "representative" in this Act (Section 1–201) includes an officer of a corporation or association, a trustee, an executor or administrator of an estate, or any person empowered to act for another. It is not intended to mean that a trust or an estate is necessarily a legal entity with the capacity to issue negotiable instruments, but merely that if it can issue them they may be signed by the representative.

The power to sign for another may be an express authority, or it may be implied in law or in fact, or it may rest merely upon apparent authority. It may be established as in other cases of representation, and when relevant parol evidence is admissible to prove or to deny it.

2. Subsection (2) applies only to the signature of a representative whose authority to sign for another is established. If he is not authorized his signature has the effect of an unauthorized signature (Section 3–404). Even though he is authorized the principal is not liable on the instrument, under the provisions (Section 3–401) relating to signatures, unless the instrument names him and clearly shows that the signature is made on his behalf.

3. Assuming that Peter Pringle is a principal and Arthur Adams is his agent, an instrument might, for example, bear the following signatures affixed by the agent—

   (a) "Peter Pringle", or

   (b) "Arthur Adams", or

   (c) "Peter Pringle by Arthur Adams, Agent", or

   (d) "Arthur Adams, Agent", or

   (e) "Peter Pringle

       Arthur Adams", or

   (f) "Peter Pringle Corporation

       Arthur Adams".

A signature in form (a) does not bind Adams if authorized (Sections 3–401 and 3–404).

A signature as in (b) personally obligates the agent and parol evidence is inadmissible under subsection (2)(a) to disestablish his obligation.

The unambiguous way to make the representation clear is to sign as in (c). Any other definite indication is sufficient, as where the instrument reads "Peter Pringle promises to pay" and it is signed "Arthur Adams, Agent." Adams is not bound if he is authorized (Section 3–404).

Subsection 2(b) adopts the New York (minority) rule of Megowan v. Peterson, 173 N.Y. 1 (1902), in such a case as (d); and adopts the majority rule in such a case as (e). In both cases the section admits parol evidence in litigation between the immediate parties to prove signature by the agent in his representative capacity. Case (f) is subject to the same rule. . . .

REFERENCES ON UNDISCLOSED PRINCIPALS IN NEGOTIABLE INSTRUMENTS

Undisclosed principal not held "on the note":

Lady v. Thomas, 38 Cal.App.2d 688, 102 P.2d 396 (1940) (contains good statement of policy behind the rule, and dicta that recovery possible in quasi-contract).

Cases holding principal on quasi-contractual theory:

Johnson v. Maddock, 119 Fla. 777, 161 So. 842 (1935).

Bride v. Stormer, 368 Ill. 524, 15 N.E.2d 282 (1938).

Lincoln Joint Stock Land Bank v. Bexten, 129 Neb. 422, 261 N.W. 845 (1935); Comment, 14 Neb.L.Bull. 310.

Is it significant, or coincidental, that the principal held in each of the above cases was a bank? The same result was reached in the following non-bank case:

Schwaegler Co. v. Marchesotti, 88 Cal.App.2d 738, 199 P.2d 331 (1948).

Quasi-contractual recovery denied:

Opelika Production Credit Association, Inc. v. Lamb, 361 So.2d 95 (Ala.1978) (farm owner not liable for debt embodied in manager's note for unauthorized purchases of cattle from which he received no benefit).

Naas v. Peters, 388 Ill. 505, 58 N.E.2d 530 (1944) (no showing that principal received any actual benefits in the transaction). Comment, 40 Ill.L.Rev. 133.

Assumed or business name:

Schwaegler Co. v. Marchesotti, 88 Cal.App.2d 738, 199 P.2d 331 (1948) (undisclosed partner liable, where note signed in firm name, on theory of quasi-contract).

NOTE: AGENT'S RIGHTS AGAINST THIRD PARTY

Litigation over an agent's right to maintain suit on a contract made on behalf of a principal is rare. Presumably few agents have had any desire to bring such suits. Moreover, if the contract is the principal's, in fact and in form, it seems obvious that the agent's suit will fail on the simple ground that he is not the owner of the cause of action.[1] Where an agent purports to represent a principal, but is actually dealing for himself, recovery by the agent has been denied.[2]

The question takes on significance chiefly in those cases where the third party thought the agent was the principal, the true principal being undisclosed.

1. See Farjeon v. Fulton Securities Co., 225 App.Div. 541, 233 N.Y.S. 577 (1929), where an agent to collect notes sought unsuccessfully to bring suit upon them.

2. Van Hall v. Gehrke, 117 Colo. 223, 185 P.2d 1016 (1947).

In many such cases, the principal probably remains undisclosed throughout the proceedings, and the third party remains ignorant of any defense he may have. The question can only arise where the third party discovers the existence of the principal before trial.

As a matter of common law, there is no objection to the suit's being brought in the agent's name rather than in his employer's. Applying the tests of common law pleading, an English judge ruled more than a century ago, ". . . the plaintiff's appear [in the contract] as principals. The rest of the facts are dehors the question." [3]

The solution is no different under reformed procedure, despite the "real party in interest" laws. Most of them contain provisions such as that of the New York Civil Practice Act, which declares,

"Every action must be prosecuted in the name of the real party in interest, *except that* an executor or administrator, a trustee of an express trust, *a person with whom or in whose name a contract is made for the benefit of another,* or a person expressly authorized by statute, *may sue* without joining with him the person for whose benefit the action is prosecuted." (Italics supplied.) [4]

Under this and similar statutes, agents have generally been permitted to maintain actions on contracts made in their names on behalf of others.[5]

In equity pleading, where unaffected by statute, there is some evidence that a suit could be defeated on the ground that the plaintiff was not the real owner of the cause of action, even though the contract was made in his name.[6]

How do these tenets apply to the case of a partner and his partnership? We have found no authorities directly in point. It is, of course, a general rule that on a cause of action of the partnership, all partners must be joined as plaintiffs.[7] Paradoxically, this rule is not applied to "dormant partners" that is, partners who never participate in management, and never appear on behalf of the firm.[8]

SECTION 6. LACK OF AUTHORITY AND MISREPRESENTATION

You have been observing various ways in which well-meaning intermediaries, intending to state the reciprocal undertakings of others, become personally obligated because they have not said (or have not said in the right place and form) who was to perform the indicated

3. Short v. Spackman, 2 B. & Ad. 962, 109 Eng.Rep. 1400 (King's Bench 1831).

4. New York Civil Practice Act, § 210.

5. For some casual applications of this rule, made without discussion, see Chase v. Van Camp Sea Food Co., 109 Cal.App. 38, 292 P. 179 (1930); City and County of Denver v. Morrison, 88 Colo. 67, 291 P. 1023 (1930); Sheppard v. Jackson, 198 N.C. 627, 152 S.E. 801 (1930).

6. Cowan v. Kane, 211 Ill. 572, 71 N.E. 1097 (1904). In Wloczewski v. Kozlowski,

395 Ill. 402, 70 N.E.2d 560 (1947), it appears that the action had been commenced in the name of the agent, but was amended to one in the name of the principal.

7. Thomas v. Benson, 264 Mass. 555, 163 N.E. 181 (1928).

8. Kassly Undertaking Co. v. Fixible Co., 313 Ill.App. 653, 40 N.E.2d 621 (1942) (abstract).

obligation. These cases have taught you how an agent should denote the identity of his principal, and the limited role of himself.

However, an agent who observes all these precautions may still entangle himself in liabilities, if the principal whom he denotes does not become legally bound. This may happen because the indicated principal has never given the requisite assent, or appearance of assent; or if, even if he has assented, his assent is somehow inoperative, for one of the reasons which may be enclosed in the term "incapacity."

GRISWOLD v. HAAS

Missouri Supreme Court, 1919.
227 Mo. 255, 210 S.W. 356.
Comment: 25 Yale L.J. 156.

[Griswold, respondent in this appeal, sued Haas, appellant, who had refused to pay for bonds on which he entered a bid at a sale.]

BLAIR, P.J. . . . In 1907, respondent was, by the Circuit Court of the City of St. Louis, appointed commissioner to make a sale of certain bonds involved in litigation pending in that court. He duly offered the bonds for sale, and, appellant making the highest bid, they were knocked down to him at a price of $276, fifteen dollars of which was paid at the time. When respondent asked him who was the purchaser, appellant stated that he bought them for George F. McLain. Respondent, as commissioner, reported to the court the sale of the bonds to McLain, and that sale was duly approved. Later, respondent tendered the bonds to McLain and demanded the balance of the sale price $261. McLain refused to accept the bonds or pay the balance. This was reported to the circuit court, and respondent ordered to bring suit. Respondent had the bonds in his possession. He sued appellant Haas on the contract of sale [and received judgment]. The case reached the Court of Appeals. Griswold v. Haas, 145 Mo.App. 578, 122 S.W. 781. The statement averred a sale to Haas, and the suit was one to recover the purchase price. The court held there was "a fatal departure from the allegations of the petition." It held that respondent Griswold's testimony in that case disclosed "a sale to McLain, a report to the court of the fact of a sale to McLain, and an approval and confirmation by the court of a sale to McLain." The court said Haas had not, in that case, been "sued as agent, nor for deceit in pretending to be an agent, when in fact he was principal." The court held, citing authorities, that the suit was one for goods sold and delivered, and that Haas could not be held in such an action; that "where one acts professedly for another, but without authority, he renders himself individually liable;" that the remedy is "for deceit, or in assumpsit upon the express or implied warranty of authority. If he knowingly and falsely represents that he had authority to act, the former remedy is the appropriate one. If he makes the representation in good faith, then the latter remedy should be pursued." The court thereupon reversed the judgment outright.

Subsequently, respondent brought this suit. . . .

The court rendered judgment against appellant for $261. An appeal took the case to the Court of Appeals. The majority opinion holds that the measure of damages was the difference between the amount bid and the sum paid; that the value of the bonds was immaterial; and that the judgment was for the right party and should be affirmed.

It is to be kept in mind that respondent now has the bonds and, also, a judgment exactly equivalent to the unpaid portion of the bid made at the sale. . . .

The general rule, subject to exceptions not here involved, which is supported by reason and the weight of authority, is that if one represents himself as the agent of a disclosed principal and attempts to contract in the name of such principal without authority or in excess of his authority, he becomes liable to the third party. Not on the contract, unless it contains apt words to bind him, but for breach of the express or implied covenant of authority or, in a proper case, in an action of fraud and deceit. The decisions in this State are in accord with this rule. . . .

II. In a case like this the measure of recovery is the damage suffered by breach of the warranty of authority. . . .

If there was a valid contract of sale, this action for damages cannot be sustained at all. If there was no such contract, then respondent did not lose title to the bonds. There was no showing the bonds were worth less than the bid. If the bonds are worth anything, a recovery, under the statement, of the full difference between the bid and the amount paid is wrong. There was no evidence of damage, and, consequently, no evidence to support any judgment against appellant.

III. Appellant urges that the evidence establishes as a matter of law that McLain ratified the contract. One may ratify the act of another who undertook, without proper authority, to act as his agent, and such ratification is retroactive. . . . The contention of appellant is that an express ratification was conclusively shown. This contention is founded upon the testimony of McLain who was offered as a witness by respondent. His testimony is not entirely consistent with itself. The trier of the fact was not bound to find all that he said was true. The fact that respondent offered him did not necessarily require the court to believe him. He was not a party to the suit. Apparently the court did not believe part of his testimony.

. . . The judgment is reversed and the cause remanded. . . .

NOTE: ANALYSIS OF THE WARRANTY

An interesting analysis of the "warranty of authority" was made by Judge Lehman of the New York Court of Appeals in the case of Moore v. Maddock, 251 N.Y. 420, 167 N.E. 572, 64 A.L.R. 1189 (1929). The unauthorized act of the agent had been committed more than six years before suit was brought, although the principal's repudiation was less than six years before. Six years were the limitation period applicable to a breach of warranty suit in New York.

The court therefore had to determine at what time the breach of warranty should be considered to have occurred. In holding that the cause of action could be dated from the principal's repudiation, Judge Lehman declared:

"Before we can determine when a warranty or promise is broken, the terms of the warranty or promise must be formulated. The defendant did not, in fact, make any promise or warranty. . . . The only promise or warranty on the part of the defendant . . . is implied by law regardless of the defendant's actual intent. If the defendant attempted to make a contract on behalf of the corporation without authority, it is but just that the loss, occasioned by there being no contract with the principal, should be borne by the agent who acted without authority. As a device by which that loss may be placed upon the agent, the courts have held that a promise or warranty must be implied. . . .

"The doctrine of an implied warranty is based upon a fiction, and there is need of caution in determining the final consequences of a fiction. Much might be said in favor of and against the various possible views of the nature of the warranty implied in law. These cases are of importance because they show a tendency in the courts to extend the implied promise till it gives protection against all damages which naturally flow from continued reliance upon the agent's assertion of authority. . . ."

REFERENCES

Liability on warranty:

Robinson v. Pattee, 359 Mo. 584, 222 S.W.2d 786 (1949) (error to instruct jury that agent is liable "on contract"); comment, 16 Mo.L.Rev. 59.

Levey v. Orcuto, 73 N.Y.S.2d 202 (1947) (partners who signed for firm without authority not liable on contract).

.   Notes on Moore v. Maddock (above, in text): 43 Harv.L.Rev. 324, 7 N.Y.U.L.Q.Rev. 541, 16 Va.L.Rev. 164.

Liability on contract:

Early cases (mostly before 1900) in many states took the view that the agent who signed without authority was liable "on the contract." In some states, there has been no repudiation of these cases, but neither have there been recent decisions following them. For a dictum that the early view is still adhered to, see Medlin v. Ebenezer Methodist Church, 132 S.C. 498, 129 S.E. 830 (1925).

For an exhaustive survey of the evolution of opinion on this subject, and of the diversity of opinion still prevailing, see Abel, Some Spadework on the Implied Warranty of Authority (1942) 48 W.Va.L.Q. 96.

Note, Implied Warranty (1951) 16 Mo.L.Rev. 59 (reviewing older authorities for liability on contract).

Liability in deceit:

Most cases, like Griswold v. Haas, appear to allow the third party to sue either on an implied warranty, or in tort for deceit. For the view that the suit must be in tort for deceit, see Henry W. Savage, Inc. v. Friedberg, 322 Mass. 321, 77 N.E.2d 213 (1948).

Effect of apparent authority:

Suppose that the principal becomes bound by the unauthorized act of the agent by virtue of apparent authority. Will the agent be liable to the third party? For a negative answer, see Fryar v. Employers Insurance of Wausau, 94 N.M. 77, 607 P.2d 615 (1980).

Effect of ratification:

If the principal, although not originally bound by the contract, subsequently becomes liable by ratification, is the agent's liability terminated? Most cases say yes. See, for example, Henry W. Savage, Inc. v. Friedberg, 322 Mass. 321, 77 N.E.2d 213 (1948).

Annotations:

42 A.L.R. 1310, 60 A.L.R. 1348.

Joinder of agent with principal:

Snider v. Dunn, 33 Mich.App. 619, 190 N.W.2d 299 (1971) (suit against principal and agent for specific performance "on the contract" was lost on a finding the agent lacked authority; a second suit charging the agent with breach of implied warranty was dismissed because res judicata applied for issues that could have been raised but were not).

Campbell v. Murdock, 90 F.Supp. 297 (D.Ohio 1950) (plaintiff joined agent with disclosed principal in suit on contract; action dismissed as to agent); comment, 49 Mich. L.Rev. 438.

Gracie Square Realty Corp. v. Choice Realty Corp., 305 N.Y. 271, 113 N.E.2d 416 (1953) (agent not liable for unauthorized oral contract, since contract would not have bound principal even if authorized).

CALIFORNIA CIVIL CODE
West's Ann.Cal.Civ.Code §§ 2342, 2343.

§ 2342. Warranty of Authority

One who assumes to act as an agent thereby warrants, to all who deal with him in that capacity, that he has the authority which he assumes.

§ 2343. Agent's Responsibility to Third Persons

One who assumes to act as an agent is responsible to third persons as a principal for his acts in the course of his agency, in any of the following cases, and in no others:

(1) When, with his consent, credit is given to him personally in the transaction:

(2) When he enters into a written contract in the name of his principal, without believing, in good faith, that he has authority to do so; or,

(3) When his acts are wrongful in their nature.

REFERENCES

The California Civil Code provision was drawn from §§ 1255, 1256 of Field's Civil Code, and was enacted in 1872. It has remained unchanged to this day. At least three other states adopted the same provisions in the late 19th century; as presently in effect, they are:

Montana Code Ann. (1979) §§ 28–10–701, 28–10–702.

North Dakota Century Code (1975) §§ 3–0401, 3–0402.

South Dakota Codified Laws (1978) §§ 59–5–1, 59–5–2.

Cases:

Jeppi v. Brockman Holding Co., 206 P.2d 847, 34 Cal.2d 11, 9 A.L.R.2d 1297 (1949) (agent liable for breach of warranty, or if action was in bad faith, as principal).

Borton v. Barnes, 48 Cal.App. 589, 192 P. 307 (1920) (agent liable as principal).

Note:

Liability of Agent Who Signs Without Authority (1929) 3 So.Cal.L.Rev. 59.

UNIFORM COMMERCIAL CODE

Section 3–404. Unauthorized Signatures

(1) Any unauthorized signature is wholly inoperative as that of the person whose name is signed unless he ratifies it or is precluded from denying it; but it operates as the signature of the unauthorized signer in favor of any person who in good faith pays the instrument or takes it for value.

(2) Any unauthorized signature may be ratified for all purposes of this Article. Such ratification does not of itself affect any rights of the person ratifying against the actual signer.

COMMENT

Prior Uniform Statutory Provision: Section 23, Uniform Negotiable Instruments Law.

Changes: Reworded; new provisions.

Purpose of Changes and New Matter: The changes are intended to remove uncertainties arising under the original section:

1. "Unauthorized signature" is a defined term (Section 1–201). It includes both a forgery and a signature made by an agent exceeding his actual or apparent authority.

2. The final clause of subsection (1) is new. It states the generally accepted rule that the unauthorized signature, while it is wholly inoperative as that of the person whose name is signed, is effective to impose liability upon the actual signer or to transfer any rights that he may have in the instrument. His liability is not in damages for breach of a warranty of his authority, but is full liability on the instrument in the capacity in which he has signed. It is, however, limited to parties who take or pay the instrument in good faith; and one who knows that the signature is unauthorized cannot recover from the signer on the instrument.

3. Subsection (2) is new. It settles the conflict which has existed in the decisions as to whether a forgery may be ratified. A forged signature may at least be adopted; and the word "ratified" is used in order to make it clear that the adoption is retroactive, and that it may be found from conduct as well as from express statements. Thus it may be found from the retention of benefits received in the transaction with knowledge of the unauthorized signature; and although the forger is

not an agent, the ratification is governed by the same rules and principles as if he were.

This provision makes ratification effective only for the purposes of this Article. The unauthorized signature becomes valid so far as its effect as a signature is concerned. The ratification relieves the actual signer from liability on the signature. It does not of itself relieve him from liability to the person whose name is signed. It does not in any way affect the criminal law. No policy of the criminal law requires that the person whose name is forged shall not assume liability to others on the instrument; but he cannot affect the rights of the state. While the ratification may be taken into account with other relevant facts in determining punishment, it does not relieve the signer of criminal liability.

4. The words "or is precluded from denying it" are retained in subsection (1) to recognize the possibility of an estoppel against the person whose name is signed, as where he expressly or tacitly represents to an innocent purchaser that the signature is genuine; and to recognize the negligence which precludes a denial of the signature.

STANLEY J. HOW & ASSOCIATES, INC. v. BOSS

United States District Court, S.D.Iowa, 1963.
222 F.Supp. 936.

HANSON, DISTRICT JUDGE. The plaintiff claims that on or about April 20, 1961, the plaintiff and defendant entered into a contract for the performance of architectural services by the plaintiff for the defendant; . . .

. . . On or about April 20, 1961, the defendant together with Mr. Hunter and representatives of the owners of Southdale Shopping Center met in the offices of Southdale at Edina for the purpose of entering into a lease between the promoters of a new corporation to be formed by the defendant and his associates and owners of Southdale Shopping Center. The plaintiff was also present at that meeting and the architectural agreement now being sued on was signed during that meeting.

. . .

The plaintiff had secured blank copies of the standard form of agreement between owner and architect on forms prepared and printed by the American Institute of Architects. He took these forms to the Southdale Offices and penciled in the appropriate blanks and gave the forms to a secretary to be typed. The first page of such contract stated that it was between Boss Hotels Co., Inc. and Stanley J. How & Associates, Inc., and places for signature in this manner were typed on the third page.

After completion of the signing of the lease the defendant, Mr. Boss, and his associate, Mr. Hunter, took the prepared contract to a back room out of the hearing of the plaintiff and discussed it between themselves. At that time the defendant erased the words "Boss Hotels

Co., Inc." from the place for signature and below the line typed the words "By: Edwin A. Boss, Agent for a Minnesota Corporation to be formed, who will be the Obligor."

The defendant and Edwin R. Hunter then took the contract back to Stanley J. How and showed it to him. Mr. Boss then said, "Is this all right?" or "Is this acceptable, this manner of signing?" or words to that effect. Stanley How said "Yes," and the contracts were then signed by the defendant and Stanley J. How.

Plaintiff returned to Omaha and complete plans, working drawing, and specifications for the construction of the motel were prepared by his offices, and sums were expended by the plaintiff for engineering and consultation services.

The defendant and his associates caused an Iowa corporation to be formed by the name of Minneapolis-Hunter Hotel Co. . . .

In July, 1961, the plaintiff received an amount of $7,500.00 as partial payment on the contract. In May, 1962, the defendant was already in default upon his lease with Southdale and he requested the plaintiff to furnish preliminary sketches for a building with a budget of $600,000.00. The plaintiff informed Boss that he would proceed no further without some further payment on its fee. Consequently, the defendant forwarded to the plaintiff an amount of $7,000.00.

The plans for the motel were finally completely abandoned by the promoters. . . . They apparently organized the Minneapolis-Hunter Hotel Co. as a corporation. To what extent it actually came into being is not clear in the record. No corporate charter, by-laws, or resolutions were offered into evidence. At any rate, if this new corporation exists, there are no assets in it to pay the amount due on the contract.

There really is not much debate as to what the law is on the questions raised. Both parties cite King Features Syndicate, Dept. of Hearst Corp. International News Service Division v. Courrier (1950) 241 Iowa 870, 43 N.W.2d 718, 41 A.L.R.2d 467, for the proposition that a promoter, though he may assume to act on behalf of the projected corporation and not for himself, will be personally liable on his contract unless the other party agreed to look to some other person or fund for payment.

Comment b under Section 326 of the R.S. of Agency sets out the three possible understandings that the parties may have when the agreement is made on behalf of a corporation to be formed by one of the parties. These are as follows:

(One) An offer or option to the corporation to be formed which will result in a contract if it is accepted when the corporation is formed. The correlative promise for the continuing offer or option is the promoter's promise to organize the corporation and give it the opportunity to pay the debt. Cases on this type of understanding are cited in 41 A.L.R.2d p. 517. This type of situation was in the Restatement treated as two different types of situations but for purposes of this case can be treated as one type of situation.

The second type of situation is where the parties agree to a present contract by which the promoter is bound, but with an agreement that his liability terminates if the corporation is formed and manifests its willingness to become a party. This is an agreement for a future novation best illustrated by the recent Iowa decision, Decker v. Juzwik (1963) 255 Iowa 358, 121 N.W.2d 652.

This second possible interpretation is not very important in this case because a novation was not pleaded or argued. Cases holding that a novation must be pleaded are: First & American Nat. Bank of Duluth v. Whiteside (1940) 207 Minn. 537, 292 N.W. 770; Dintenfass v. Wirkman, 14 Pa.Dist. & Co.R. 798; Benton v. Morningside College (1926) 202 Iowa 15, 209 N.W. 516; Tuttle v. Nichols Poultry & Egg Co. (1949) 240 Iowa 199, 35 N.W.2d 875; Glover v. First Universalist Parish of Dowagiac (1882) 48 Mich. 595, 12 N.W. 867.

The third type of understanding is where the parties have agreed to a present contract upon which, even though the corporation later becomes a party, the promoter remains liable either primarily or as surety for the performance of the corporation's obligation. There are many cases cited in A.L.R.2d annotations to King Features Syndicate, Dept. of Hearst Corp. International News Service Division v. Courrier, supra, wherein the courts have sustained this proposition. See also Randolph Foods, Inc. v. McLaughlin (1962) 253 Iowa 1258, 115 N.W.2d 868.

In the present case, the contract was signed: "Edwin A. Boss, agent for a Minnesota corporation to be formed who will be the obligor." The defendant argues that this is an agreement that the new corporation is solely liable. The problem here is what is the import of the words "who will be the obligor." It says nothing about the present obligor. The words "will be" connote something which will take place in the future. It was held in Muirhead v. Johnson (1951) 232 Minn. 408, 46 N.W.2d 502, that the words "will be" when used in the third person ordinarily denote simple futurity. It contemplates future and further action. While that case is not factually the same as the present one, it is indicative of the ordinary meaning of these words. In Bass v. Ring (1943) 215 Minn. 11, 9 N.W.2d 234, the court said words are always to be given the meaning they have in common use unless there are very strong reasons to the contrary. This is the general rule.

. . .

In this case, the defendant was the principal promoter, acting for himself personally and as President of Boss Hotels, Inc. The promoters abandoned their purpose of forming the corporation. This would make the promoter liable to the plaintiff unless the contract be construed to mean: (1) that the plaintiff agreed to look solely to the new corporation for payment, and (2) that the promoter did not have any duty toward the plaintiff to form the corporation and give the corporation the opportunity to assume and pay the liability.

. . .

Whether the duty not to abandon the project exists is a matter of interpretation of the agreement. . . . In all situations wherein the promoter is not personally bound, the contracting party is agreeing that the new corporation should assume the liability. The phrase "content to take the risk of the ultimate incorporation and assumption of his claim" is the key to the distinction. In some cases, the promoters do not agree that this assumption will take place.

Applying this law to the present case, the court would have to hold that even if the plaintiff had agreed to look to the credit of the new corporation, the defendant would be liable. The defendant was the key promoter and as such would be a primary factor in abandoning the project. This would make the defendant liable.

. . .

At the time the specifications and drawings were completed, the amount owed the plaintiff was 75% of 6% of $850,000.00 (the reasonable cost estimate). This would amount to $38,250.00. $14,500.00 of this amount has been paid leaving an amount of $23,750.00 due to the plaintiff.

Accordingly the court concludes that the plaintiff, Stanley J. How & Associates, Inc. should have and recover judgment against the defendant, Edwin A. Boss, in the sum of $23,750.00, with interest and costs, and, accordingly, a judgment will be entered.

It is ordered that the foregoing shall constitute the findings of fact, conclusions of law, and order for judgment in this case. Rule 52(a) of the Federal Rules of Civil Procedure.

REFERENCES

Liability of corporate officers and promoters:

Johnson v. Sams, 296 Minn. 112, 206 N.W.2d 925 (1973) (signers in corporate name personally liable where corporation did not exist, and jury finds intention to bind defendants individually).

H.F. Philipsborn & Co. v. Suson, 14 Ill.App.3d 775, 303 N.E.2d 259 (1973) (promoter who signed contract in name of corporation which was formed later, and which adopted promoter's contracts, was not personally liable on contract).

Vodopich v. Collier County Developers, Inc., 319 So.2d 43 (Fla.App.1975) (promoters of corporation to be formed promised broker to give him exclusive agency for sale of company properties; corporation was formed, but repudiated promise; promoters are personally liable).

Jones v. Hartmann, 541 P.2d 123 (Colo.App.1975) (promoters of corporation to be formed liable to architect who started work before incorporation, even though after incorporation he billed corporation for services.).

Sandleitner v. Sadur & Pelland, 66 Md.App. 428, 504 A.2d 672 (1986) (attorney who performed services for Corporation during time its charter was forfeited for failure to pay taxes—1980 to 1984,—can only look to the corporation for payment once the charter is revised).

HALDEMAN v. ADDISON

Iowa Supreme Court, 1936.
221 Iowa 218, 265 N.W. 358.

This is an action at law in two counts for the recovery of the purchase price of a piano. In count I judgment is asked against the defendant on a promissory note . . . . Defendant claimed that he signed said note in a representative capacity only as superintendent of the league, and asked that the cause be transferred to equity for the purpose of reforming the note to show such fact. . . . The case was tried to the court without a jury, resulting in a judgment dismissing plaintiff's petition at plaintiff's costs. . . .

HAMILTON, J. . . . The action was against W.D. Addison, personally. Addison was the superintendent of the Pleasantville Epworth League at the time the note in question was executed. The signature on the note appeared as follows:

"Pleasantville Epworth League,

"E.L. Supt. W.D. Addison."

The purpose of the reformation was to show that Addison signed the note in a representative capacity only. The trial court made no specific finding on the question of reformation, but the result reached is equivalent to a finding in favor of the defendant on this issue. As we view the law applicable to the situation disclosed by the record in this case, the question of whether or not the defendant signed in a representative capacity is not controlling, the real question being, even though he signed in a representative capacity only, the Pleasantville Epworth League being an unincorporated association without legal entity, is the defendant bound, notwithstanding he executed the note as an officer of said association? . . .

As we understand the general rule of law to be, where a member of an unincorporated association, such as the Epworth League in this case is conceded to be, contracts in the name of such supposed principal, which has no legal existence and cannot sue or be sued, that such member is himself personally bound. In the case of Lewis v. Tilton et al., 64 Iowa 220, 19 N.W. 911, 52 Am.Rep. 436, the contract was made in the name of the Ottumwa Temperance Reform Club and was signed, "Executive Committee of the Ottumwa Temperance Reform Club," and under this appeared the individual names of the committee. It was insisted in that case that the contract showed that credit was extended to the club, and that the contract was made with the club, that the principal was named and therefore the individual members of the committee could not be made individually liable. The court said:

"This line of argument, possibly, would be conclusive if there was a principal. But there is none. The club is a myth. It has no legal existence and never had. It cannot sue or be sued. The defendants contracted in the name of a supposed principal; that is they claimed there was a principal for whom they were acting, but it now appears there was no principal known to the law."

The court further said in reference to the liability of the members of the committee:

". . . They certainly represented they had a principal for whom they had authority to contract. They, for or on behalf of an alleged principal, contracted that such principal would do and perform certain things. As we have said, there is no principal, and it seems to us the defendants should be held liable, and that it is immaterial whether they be so held because they held themselves out as agents for a principal that had no existence, or on the ground that they must, under the contract, be regarded as principals, for the simple reason that there is no other principal in existence."   . . .

There can be no dispute about this principle of law, which is well settled by the above authorities in this state.

It is equally as well settled that in order to avoid personal liability, one who has contracted in the name of such a principal has the burden of showing that there was an agreement with the person with whom the contract was made that he was not to be personally bound. In the case of Comfort v. Graham, 87 Iowa 295, 54 N.W. 242, 243, this court said:

"If the defendant sought, as he did, to shield himself from personal liability because the contract for services was made in a representative capacity, it was incumbent on him to establish that fact."

The case of Andrew v. Pella Golf Club, 217 Iowa 577, 579, 250 N.W. 709, 710, is squarely in point on his question. In that case, Andrew brought suit against the Pella Golf Club, an unincorporated association, on a note which was signed, "Pella Gulf Club, C. Smorenburg, Treas." Plaintiff sued the golf club and also Smorenburg. In that case the evidence shows without dispute that Smorenburg *refused* to sign the note until assured by the cashier of the bank to which the note was given that his execution of the note in the manner in which it was executed should impose *no personal liability upon him.* The court said:

"In this situation there was no liability on the part of Smorenburg on account of the fact that the club was not a legal entity. Codding v. Munson, 52 Neb. 580, 72 N.W. 846, 66 Am.St. Rep. 524."   . . .

We have carefully read and considered the evidence in the light of the foregoing pronouncements of our court and of other courts upon this subject, and we are unable to find from the evidence proof of any facts that takes this case out of the general rule. In other words, it does not appear from the evidence that there was any agreement whatsoever that the defendant was not to be personally bound. It is not enough to show that the plaintiff knew the piano was being

purchased for the Epworth League or that defendant said to the plaintiff that the league expected to pay for the piano out of funds to be raised by socials, etc. The very fact that the contract is executed in the name of the association connotes all this. Neither does the fact that plaintiff in good faith attempted to collect the note from the association, or the church of which the league is an auxiliary society, establish such agreement. . . . Both plaintiff and defendant testified that there was nothing said either pro or con as to whether defendant was or was not to be held personally. In the absence of any statement on the subject, how can it be said that the minds of the parties met on an agreement or understanding that defendant was not to be held personally? In the absence of such proof, the law steps in and settles the matter for the parties. It may be conceded that both of these parties had the thought in their minds at the time this piano was purchased and this note given that it was the obligation of the league and not the obligation of the defendant, but neither of them uttered his thoughts.
. . .

The case is reversed and remanded, with instructions to enter judgment in accordance with this opinion.

REFERENCES

Analogous cases:

Hagan v. Asa G. Candler, Inc., 189 Ga. 250, 5 S.E.2d 739, 126 A.L.R. 108 (1939) (defendant signed lease with corporate name, although corporation did not exist; liable on lease); comment, 53 Harv.L.Rev. 1042.

Medlin v. Ebenezer Methodist Church, 132 S.C. 498, 129 S.E. 830 (1925) (agents of unincorporated church liable).

Forsberg v. Zehm, 150 Va. 756, 143 S.E. 284, 61 A.L.R. 232 (1928) (officials of unincorporated church liable on contract employing organist); comment, 15 Va.L.Rev. 98.

Robbins Co. v. Cook, 42 S.D. 136, 173 N.W. 445, 7 A.L.R. 218 (1919) (members of "commission" appointed by governor with no statutory authority, to raise funds for a state entry at an exposition, liable on purchases in name of commission; dissent).

Vader v. Ballou, 151 Wis. 577, 139 N.W. 413, 7 A.L.R. 216 (1913) (members of political committee held liable for stationery ordered by committee decision, although purchased in name of chairman only).

Contra:

Roller v. Smith, 88 N.M. 572, 544 P.2d 287 (1975) (defendant who signed auto purchase agreement as "agent for the Committee to Save Black Mesa", not bound on the contract unless the plaintiff proved the agent lacked authority).

Greenlee v. Beaver, 334 Ill.App. 572, 79 N.E.2d 822 (1948) (third party held to have contractual knowledge that village officials lacked authority to sign promissory notes).

RESTATEMENT OF AGENCY, 2d
American Law Institute, 1958.

§ 326. Principal Known to be Nonexistent or Incompetent

Unless otherwise agreed, a person who, in dealing with another, purports to act as agent for a principal whom both know to be nonexistent or wholly incompetent, becomes a party to such a contract.

§ 332.   Agent of Partially Incompetent Principal

An agent making a contract for a disclosed principal whose contracts are voidable because of lack of full capacity, or for a principal who, although having capacity to contract generally, is incompetent to enter into the particular transaction, is not thereby liable to the other party. He does not become liable by reason of the failure of the principal to perform, unless he contracts or represents that the principal has capacity or unless he has reason to know of the principal's lack of capacity and of the other party's ignorance thereof.

NOTE: MISREPRESENTATION AND FRAUDULENT AGENTS

Nineteenth century doubts about whether the principal should be liable at all for an agent's fraud or misrepresentation are now of merely historical interest. There does remain a worry about what the theory of liability should be. Since misrepresentation is commonly classified as a "tort" in the law school curriculum and in common law pleading, it has been argued that liability should be based on the rules of other tort liability, including the doctrines of "independent contractor" and "scope of employment."

Few vestiges of this controversy remain in the modern cases, which seem to discuss agency to commit fraud in much the same way in which they discuss agency to make promises. Perhaps identification arises more by inadvertence than by intention, but it is not hard to justify. Misrepresentations, like promises, are made to people who deal with each other; they generally do not occur, as automobile accidents do, between total strangers. Misrepresentations, like promises, do harm chiefly to those who rely upon them. In most cases involving vicarious liability for misrepresentations the misrepresentation is made in the context of a contract. The lawsuit involves not only the liability of the principal for damages, but also the third party's right to rescind the agreement.

If the court approaches these cases in terms of inherent or apparent authority to make the misrepresentation then the remedies can include expectation damages on the contract. If the analysis is based on vicarious liability then only the usual tort remedies should be available. In this regard, however, the Restatement of Torts, 2d, § 910 (1979) allows for expectation damages for a business tort.

In some cases of this type the courts resort to imputed knowledge as a rational for holding the principal. Imputed knowledge is an ambiguous concept, and it is difficult to define limits.

REFERENCES

Ferson, Agency to Make Representations (1948) 2 Vanderbilt L.Rev. 1 (a synthesis of cases involving different kinds of representations—a watchman's representation that it is safe to cross a railroad track, a freight agent's representation that goods have arrived, a defamatory representation on someone's character, and representations inducing contracts); Liability of Employers For Misrepresentations Made by "Independent Contractors" (1949) 3 Vand.L.Rev. 1.

Mearns, Vicarious Liability for Agency Contracts (1962) 48 Va.L.Rev. 50 (concludes that a principal should be liable for frauds of employees so long as they are acting in the principal's business).

Contract Analysis:

Johnson v. Harrigan—Peach Land Development Co., 79 Wn.2d 745, 489 P.2d 923 (1971) (principal liable for expectation damages on the contract, including the representations made by the salesman).

Loma Vista Development Co. v. Johnson, 142 Tex. 686, 180 S.W.2d 922 (1944) (court found agent had no authority for misrepresentation and denied damages on the contract; rescission of contract still possible, as is tort action against agent).

Friedman v. New York Telephone Co., 256 N.Y. 392, 176 N.E. 543 (1931) (vendor not liable for real estate broker's misrepresentations).

Jensen v. Manila Corp., 565 P.2d 63 (Utah 1977) (real estate broker had implied authority to represent boundaries of lot sold).

Note, Liability of Innocent Principal for Misrepresentation of Real Estate Agent (1933) 1 U.Chi.L.Rev. 137 (stating that broker binds principal by representations of quantity and location of land, although not by representations of "quality").

Tort Analysis:

Allen v. Morgan Drive Away, Inc., 273 Or. 614, 542 P.2d 896 (1975) (court determined agent was within scope of employment when he lied about moving costs, and allowed compensatory and punitive damages against principal).

RESTATEMENT OF AGENCY, 2d
American Law Institute, 1958.

§ 162. Unauthorized Representations

Except as to statements with relation to the agent's authority, in actions brought upon a contract or to rescind a contract, a disclosed or partially disclosed principal is responsible for unauthorized representations of the agent made incidental to it, if the contract is otherwise authorized and if true representations as to the same matter are within the authority or the apparent authority of the agent, unless the other party thereto has notice that the representations are untrue or unauthorized.

NOTE: AGENT'S FRAUD IN SECURITIES CASES

The Federal Securities Act of 1933 (§ 15), and the Securities and Exchange Act of 1934 (§ 20(a)) contain specific statutory provisions relating to the liability principals who are controlling persons as defined in the acts. A statutory defense is provided if the principal had "no knowledge or reasonable grounds to believe" the agent was involved in illegal fraudulent activity. The Federal Circuit Courts are split on the question whether the statutory remedies are exclusive, and some have allowed a common law action based on vicarious liability even though a statutory defense was proved. The Supreme Court has not yet spoken on the question. The following are some representative decisions.

REFERENCES

Vicarious liability not limited by statute:

Holloway v. Howerdd, 536 F.2d 690 (6th Cir.1976).

Henricksen v. Henricksen, 640 F.2d 880 (7th Cir.1981), certiorari denied 454 U.S. 1097, 102 S.Ct. 85, 70 L.Ed.2d 79 (1981).

Carras v. Burns, 516 F.2d 251 (4th Cir.1975).

Fey v. Walston & Co., Inc., 493 F.2d 1036 (7th Cir.1974).

Statutory liability exclusive:

Zweig v. Hearst Corp., 521 F.2d 1129 (9th Cir.1975), certiorari denied 423 U.S. 1025, 96 S.Ct. 469, 46 L.Ed.2d 399 (1975).

Rochez Brothers, Inc. v. Rhoades, 527 F.2d 880 (3d Cir.1975).

Comments:

"Control" Person Liability Under Section 20(a) of the Exchange Act (1980) 33 Okl.L. Rev. 665.

A Comparison of Control Person Liability and Respondeat Superior: Section 20(a) of the Securities Exchange Act (1979) 15 Cal.West.L.Rev. 152.

Secondary Liability of Controlling Persons Under the Securities Acts: Toward an Improved Analysis (1978) 126 U.Pa.L.Rev. 1345.

Vicarious Liability of Controlling Persons Under the Securities Acts (1977) 11 Loyola L.A.L.Rev. 151.

Compare, American Law Institute, Federal Securities Code § 1724.

Application of Common Law Agency Principles to Actions Under Securities Acts (1981) 32 Mercer L.Rev. 1283.

HARNISCHFEGER SALES CORP. v. COATS

California Supreme Court, 1935.
4 Cal.2d 319, 48 P.2d 662.

LANGDON, J. This is an action by plaintiff to recover the balance due on a conditional sale contract for the sale of a power shovel. Defendant answered and counterclaimed, setting up the defense of fraud. The jury brought in a verdict in favor of defendant on his counterclaim, in the sum of $2,500. The court, however, gave judgment for plaintiff notwithstanding the verdict, for the entire balance due on the contract. Defendant appealed.

The contract in this case was entered into after negotiations by defendant with plaintiff's agent, and it is the false representations of this agent which constitute the defense of fraud. After being signed by defendant and plaintiff's agent, the contract was sent to the eastern office of plaintiff, where it was approved, executed and a copy returned to defendant. The contract contained the following provision: "This agreement shall not be considered as executed, and shall not become effective until accepted by the vendee, and executed and approved by the president, or vice-president, or secretary of the vendor, and it is hereby further declared agreed and understood that there are no prior writings, verbal negotiations, understandings, representations or agreements between the parties not herein expressed."

It seems clear that this stipulation limits the authority of the agent to make representations, and purports to absolve the principal from all responsibility therefor. The question is whether such a stipulation may be given effect.

This problem was the subject of conflicting decisions in California until recently, when this court, in Speck v. Wylie, 1 Cal.2d 625, 36 P.2d

618, 95 A.L.R. 760, announced the governing rule. It was there held that an innocent principal might by such a stipulation protect himself from liability in a tort action for damages for fraud and deceit, but that the third party would nevertheless be entitled to rescind the contract. This is the rule declared in the Restatement of the Law of Agency, sections 259 and 260. See, also Lozier v. Janss Investment Co., 1 Cal.2d 666, 36 P.2d 620; Greenberg v. DuBain Realty Corp., 2 Cal.2d 628, 42 P.2d 628; Graham v. Los Angeles First Nat. T. & S. Bank, 3 Cal.2d 37, 43 P.2d 543. The distinction between the two situations is a sound one. The principal would normally be liable in tort for misrepresentations by an agent acting within the scope of his actual or ostensible authority, and by stipulating in the contract that the agent has no such authority, the principal has done all that is reasonably possible to give notice thereof to the third party. Under such circumstances the innocent principal may justly be relieved of liability for the agent's wrong. But where the principal sues to recover on the contract, he is seeking to benefit through the agent's fraud. This he cannot be permitted to do. His personal liability may be avoided, but the fraudulently procured contract is subject to rescission.

In the instant case, the counterclaim, which seeks the affirmative relief of damages, is objectionable for the same reason that an independent tort action would be. However, the principle followed in Speck v. Wylie, supra, warrants relief for fraud whether the injured party sets it up in an affirmative action for rescission, or as defensive relief in an action by the other party to enforce the contract; that is to say, the right of the aggrieved buyer to rescission exists regardless of which party initiates the proceedings on the contract. That the buyer may set up a claim for rescission in the seller's action has recently been held by the District Court of Appeal. California Mutual Co. v. Voigt, 5 Cal. App.2d 204, 42 P.2d 353. The defensive relief must not be such as to subject the plaintiff to affirmative liability for damages; nor would it be proper, under the rule just discussed, to permit an award of damages to offset liability for the balance of the purchase price. The defendant's relief is limited to rescission of the contract. Hence the affirmative verdict in favor of defendant on his counterclaim for damages is improper; but defendant may be entitled, because of the fraud to be placed in statu quo, by restoration of the consideration or its equivalent by both parties. See Curtis v. Title Guarantee & Trust Co., 3 Cal.App. 2d 612, 40 P.2d 562, 42 P.2d 323. The failure to demand the specific remedy of rescission is not, of course, fatal to the right, where the facts pleaded justify it. The fraud, and not the remedy therefor, constitutes the cause of action, the present judgment must be reversed and the case retried, with amended pleadings it defendant desires to offer them, to set forth such facts as may warrant rescission. If, upon a retrial of the cause, it appears that the requirements of rescission are satisfied, defendant should have judgment.

The judgment is reversed. . . . .

DANANN REALTY CORP. v. HARRIS

New York Court of Appeals, 1959.
5 N.Y.2d 317, 184 N.Y.S.2d 599, 157 N.E.2d 597.

[This case, which did not involve problems of agency, is interesting for the breadth of the disclaimer, in the following terms]:

The Purchaser has examined the premises agreed to be sold and is familiar with the physical condition thereof. The Seller has not made and does not make any representations as to the physical condition, rents, leases, expenses, operation or any other matter or thing affecting or related to the aforesaid premises, except as herein specifically set forth, and the Purchaser hereby expressly acknowledges that no such representations have been made, and the Purchaser further acknowledges that it has inspected the premises and agrees to take the premises "as is" . . . It is understood and agreed that all understandings and agreements heretofore had between the parties hereto are merged in this contract, which alone fully and completely expresses their agreement, and that the same is entered into after full investigation, neither party relying upon any statement or representation, not embodied in this contract, made by the other. The Purchaser has inspected the buildings standing on said premises and is thoroughly acquainted with their condition.

[The majority held that it was impossible for the buyer to have "reasonable reliance" in the face of such a disclaimer, and dismissed a damage action. The alleged misrepresentations were oral statements of rental income. The argument for the opposite conclusion was stated with unusual force in the dissenting opinion excerpted below.]

FULD, JUDGE (dissenting).

If the party has actually induced another to enter into a contract by means of fraud—and so the complaint before us alleges—I conceive that language may not be devised to shield him from the consequences of such fraud. The law does not temporize with trickery or duplicity, and this court, after having weighed the advantages of certainty in contractual relations against the harm and injustice which result from fraud, long ago unequivocally declared that "a party who has perpetrated a fraud upon his neighbor may [not] contract with him, in the very instrument by means by which it was perpetrated, for immunity against its consequences, close his mouth from complaining of it, and bind him never to seek redress. Public policy and morality are both ignored if such an agreement can be given effect in a court of justice. The maxim that fraud vitiates every transaction would no longer be the rule, but the exception." Bridger v. Goldsmith, 143 N.Y. 424, 428, 38 N.E. 458, 459. . . .

Contrary to the intimation in the court's opinion . . ., the nonreliance clause cannot possibly operate as an estoppel against the plaintiff. Essentially equitable in nature, the principle of estoppel is to be invoked to prevent fraud and injustice, not to further them. The statement that the representations in question were not made was, according to the complaint, false to the defendant's knowledge. Surely, the perpetrator of a fraud cannot close the lips of his victim and deny him the right to state the facts as they actually exist. . . .

The rule heretofore applied by this court presents no obstacle to honest business dealings, and dishonest transactions ought not to receive judicial protection. The clause in the contract before us may lend support to the defense and render the plaintiff's task of establishing its claim more difficult, but it should not be held to bar institution of an action for fraud. Whether the defendants made the statements attributed to them, and if they did, whether the plaintiff relied upon them, whether, in other words, the defendants were guilty of fraud, are questions of fact not capable of determination on the pleadings alone. The plaintiff is entitled to its day in court.

WITTENBERG v. ROBINOV

New York Court of Appeals, 1961.
9 N.Y.2d 261, 213 N.Y.S.2d 430, 173 N.E.2d 868.

FROESSEL, JUDGE. Plaintiff's action against defendant Robinov for fraudulently inducing a contract for the sale of real property will not lie. Under the authority of our decision in Danann Realty Corp. v. Harris, . . . the alleged misrepresentations here were disclaimed with sufficient specificity—except the alleged misrepresentation as to ownership of the kitchen ranges, which could not reasonably be said to come within the ambit of "physical condition or services." That alleged misrepresentation, however, in view of the bill of particulars limiting plaintiff's proof, was not material. Lack of ownership of a single range having a claimed value of $100 could hardly have induced this $32,375 sale.

With regard to defendant Feinberg, the real estate broker, however, he was not a party to the contract of sale, and the disclaimer provision by its express language did not inure to his benefit. The disclaimer provision in the contract constituted, in effect, a limitation upon the agent's authority to bind his principal. . . .. This case, therefore, assumes the posture of a third party allegedly suffering a loss as a result of an agent's unauthorized acts. Recourse, if any, in such case, by way of damages to recoup the loss sustained, may be sought against the agent. . . .

Our statement in the Danann case, supra, that the legal consequence of the disclaimer provision was to negate reliance was, in essence, only a concise way of saying that as to the seller in that case—the only party involved—no representations ever existed. That being so, there could be no reliance. There was nothing upon which to rely.

In the instant case, the representations—which plaintiff in his complaint alleges were made by the agent—were similarly declared nonexistent by the seller; and the purchaser expressly agreed to consummate the transaction on those terms. Such a declaration in the agency context here presented means, from the seller's point of view, that any agent's representations were unauthorized. An unauthorized representation of an agent does not exist insofar as a principal is concerned. As to the agent, however, the noncontracting party, any unauthorized representation remains real and existent—and if fraudulent he may be subjected to liability.

Accordingly, the order insofar as appealed from by defendant Robinov should be reversed, and the motion for judgment on the pleadings and dismissal of the complaint made on her behalf should be granted. In all other respects, the order appealed from should be affirmed, without costs. The question certified is answered in the negative.

[The concurring opinion of Judge Fuld is omitted].

Van Voorhis, J. (Dissenting in part).

The judgment entered upon the order of the Appellate Division should, in my view, be reversed so as to dismiss the complaint against the vendor's broker as well as against the vendor. I agree with Judge Fuld that "the distinction drawn between the liability of the owner and that of the agent" is "thoroughly unreal and unreasonable." I would have voted the other way in the Danann case if I had considered that such a distinction was compelled by it. Actually, however, instead of this distinction being inherent in the Danann decision, it is inconsistent with it. The point is that where, as here, a purchaser makes a representation in this contract of purchase that he has made his own investigation in regard to specific features of the property and relies on no representations concerning them made by or on behalf of the vendor, he cannot sue anybody in fraud under the ruling in Danann for the reason that he has disclaimed reliance upon any such representation. Absent reliance upon the misrepresentations, there can be no cause of action sounding in fraud against the maker of the misrepresentation or anyone else (Sager v. Friedman, 270 N.Y. 472, 1 N.E.2d 971). In that case, the court said through Lehman, J. (270 N.Y. at page 479, 1 N.E.2d at page 973): "A false representation does not, without more, give rise to a cause of action, either at law or in equity, in favor of the person to whom it is addressed. To give rise, under any circumstances, to a cause of action, either in law or equity, reliance on the false representation must result in injury."

The Danann decision was not based upon contracting away a cause of action in fraud by promises or covenants which are charged with having been given as a result of fraud. If that had been its rationale, Judge Fuld's dissenting opinion would have prevailed. The fraud cause of action was defeated, not on the basis that it was contracted out of existence, but that the purchaser had, beyond contradiction, disclaimed reliance upon any representation of the existence of the very facts concerning which he later claimed to have been deceived to his injury.

That this was the theory of Danann appears from the following statement in Judge Burke's opinion at pages 320–321 of 5 N.Y.2d at page 602 of 184 N.Y.S.2d, at page 599 of 157 N.E.2d: "Here, however plaintiff has in the plainest language announced and stipulated that it is not relying on any representations as to the very matter as to which it now claims it was defrauded. Such a specific disclaimer destroys the allegations in plaintiff's complaint that the agreement was executed in reliance upon these contrary oral representations (Cohen v. Cohen [1 A.D.2d 586, 151 N.Y.S.2d 949, affirmed 3 N.Y.2d 813, 166 N.Y.S.2d 10, 144 N.E.2d 649], supra)."

If, under the rationale of the Danann decision, a plaintiff is defeated for the reason that he did not rely upon the factual misrepresentations alleged, it can make no difference whether the misrepresentations were voiced by the principal or by his agent. Under familiar principles, no cause of action lies in fraud without reliance on the misrepresentations, even in an action against the person by whom they were uttered. I do not understand how plaintiff can be heard to assert that he did not rely upon these representations in his dealings with the vendor, from whom he bought the property, but that he did rely on them as against the vendor's broker.

The judgment appealed from should be reversed and the complaint dismissed, with costs to appellant in this court and in the Appellate Division.

NOTE: RETENTION OF BENEFITS OF TRANSACTION INDUCED BY AGENT'S FRAUD

The conflict and confusion in cases involving an agent's fraud is very marked. The cases have been analyzed in various ways, none of which disclose a consistent pattern. As one means of breaking the problem into its component parts the following classification is suggested:

1. *Where no disclaimer of authority is involved, and—*

(a) *Third party sues for damages for deceit:* If the agent's representations were within the scope of his actual or apparent authority to represent, the principal is of course liable. The principal in such cases may be a party to the fraudulently induced bargain, or an outsider whose agent induced the third party to make a deal with someone else.

If the agent's representations were not within his actual or apparent authority, the principal is not liable (see Loma Vista Co. v. Johnson). In the cases where the principal is a party to the transaction, it might be argued that his retention of benefits after knowledge of the agent's misconduct affirms the entire transaction, and ratifies the fraud. This argument, similar to the one made and rejected in such cases as Murray v. Standard Pecan, seems not even to be made in most of the fraud cases.

(b) *Third party sues for rescission:* It seems to be widely acknowledged by the contemporary decisions that the third party may rescind a transaction induced by fraud, even though the fraud was committed without shadow of authority by the other party's agent (Loma Vista v. Johnson).

2. *Where there is a disclaimer* of liability for any statements other than those in a printed contract, the cases are in greater conflict.

(a) *Where third party sues for damages for deceit:* Cases are in sharp conflict over the effectiveness of a disclaimer, where the other circumstances are such as to cause the third party to rely on the agent's authority. The California court refers in Harnischfeger to earlier conflicts in that court's decisions. Similar conflict has existed among decisions in the other states.[1] Further, some states have statutes which nullify such clauses if in small type (see Virginia Code, 1942, sec. 5562a).

If the agent would have no power to bind the principal even in the absence of a disclaimer, the disclaimer should not, of course, increase the principal's danger of liability. This point is seldom noticed in the cases, since disclaimers are naturally most used where, in their absence, the principal would surely be bound.

(b) *Where third party sues for rescission and restitution:* Again, conflict is encountered. On behalf of the principal, it is argued that he has warned the third party that the agreement consists solely of its written provisions, and that the third party should not be permitted to take back his money, and return the merchandise on the basis of oral evidence which contradicts the contract. To strengthen this argument, many contracts provide that they are not effective until accepted by the principal, *after* being signed by the third party; the third party, by the terms of these contracts, warrants to the principal that he has relied on nothing outside the contract itself.

REFERENCES ON DISCLAIMERS

Anderson v. Tri-State Home Improvement Co., 268 Wis. 455, 67 N.W.2d 853 (1955), rehearing denied 268 Wis. 455, 68 N.W.2d 705 (damages allowed for fraudulent misstatements by president of corporation in spite of presence of disclaimer clause in the contract).

Hall v. Crow, 240 Iowa 81, 34 N.W.2d 195 (1948) (defrauded buyer entitled to damages despite disclaimer of representations); criticized, 35 Iowa L.Rev. 105.

United States Fidelity & Guaranty Co. v. Dixie Parking Service, Inc., 262 La. 45, 262 So.2d 365 (1972) (garage liable for loss of luggage and fur stole left in car, as plaintiff was reasonable in relying on attendant's statement that goods would be safe, in spite of disclaimer on parking ticket, and on sign in parking lot).

Note, Apparent Authority in a Civil Law Jurisdiction (1973) 33 La.L.Rev. 735 (discusses United States Fidelity & Guaranty Co. v. Dixie Parking Service, Inc.).

HERZOG v. CAPITAL CO.

California Supreme Court, 1945.
27 Cal.2d 349, 164 P.2d 8.
Comment: 34 Cal.L.Rev. 751.

GIBSON, C.J. In June, 1938, defendants, acting through their local agent, Yakel, sold plaintiff a house in San Diego for $9,500, representing that it was in "sound condition" and "perfectly intact." The house began to leak badly during a heavy rain in January, 1940, and a subsequent inspection disclosed that the leakage was due to the use of

---

1. Compare the following Illinois cases: Zalapi v. Holcomb Co., 241 Ill.App. 102 (1926) (rescission denied, where sale contract excluded representations by agent); Ginsburg v. Bartlett, 262 Ill.App. 14 (1931) (damages allowed for real estate salesman's fraud, despite disclaimer in sale contract).

defective materials and improper bracing. This action for damages for alleged fraud in the sale of the house resulted in a judgment in favor of plaintiff in the sum of $3,500. . . .

The complaint alleged that when plaintiff inspected the house, it had been freshly painted thereby concealing from him, or anyone else making a reasonable inspection of the premises, the defective condition which caused the leaks, and that since there were no heavy rains until January, 1940, he did not sooner discover that the house leaked. . . .

It is claimed, however, that the trial court erred in holding defendants liable because the agreement of sale expressly provided that there were no promises, representations, verbal understandings or agreements except those contained therein.

A defrauded purchaser is not precluded by a provision of this kind from rescinding and pursuing the innocent seller far enough to secure a return of the consideration paid [citing cases]. Such a provision, however, will relieve an honest seller from liability for *damages* arising from the fraudulent representations of his negotiating agent [citing cases].[1] This rule, of course, applies only to recovery of damages based upon the misrepresentations of the agent, and it does not exempt the principal from liability for his own conduct.

Although plaintiff was notified by the contract provision that Yakel had no authority to make representations or enter into verbal understandings in connection with the sale of the property, it is clear that Yakel knew of the defective condition of the house and that he was acting within the scope of his authority when he caused it to be refinished and newly painted, thereby effectually concealing the structural defects. The knowledge of an agent, which he is under a duty to disclose to his principal, is to be imputed to the principal (Rest., Agency, § 275), and, accordingly, defendants are charged with Yakel's knowledge. Under these circumstances they had a duty to reveal the hidden and material facts concealed by their agent and of which they had knowledge, and their failure to disclose them constituted fraud [citing cases]. With respect to this positive duty of disclosure plaintiff could rely on Yakel's actual as well as ostensible authority, for the provision in the contract related only to the exclusion of liability for representations and verbal understandings. A principal under a positive duty to make a disclosure cannot escape liability for failure to do so by relying on a contract provision to the effect that there are no other representations except those contained in the written agreement. . . .

The judgment is affirmed.

REFERENCES ON IMPUTED KNOWLEDGE

Continental Casualty Co. v. United States, 337 F.2d 602 (1st Cir.1964) (surety held on bail bond even though agent executing the bond had no knowledge that the court had

1. The "local agent" was a full-time employee of the defendant; hence the need for the disclaimer. For a full discussion of this phase of the case, see the previous appeal, (1944, Cal.App.) 150 P.2d 218.

allowed the defendant to leave the country; a second agent of the surety had this knowledge and it was "imputed" to the surety).

If one agent states Blackacre is dry (believing it is), and the principal knows it is wet (but does not know what the agent is saying), can the court find falsity by imputing the agent's knowledge to the principal? This has been debated in an interesting series of English authorities, in which a law review writer had the rare privilege of correcting, as a judge, the error which he had criticized as a writer.

Patrick Devlin, Fraudulent Misrepresentation—Division of Responsibility between Principal and Agent (1937) 53 L.Q.R. 344 (criticizing the imputation).

Armstrong v. Strain [1952] 1 All.Eng.Rep. 139 (affirming lower court decision of Devlin in favor of principal). Comment, 1953 Wash.U.L.Q. 91 (finding no American cases).

Gower, Agency and Fraud (1952), 15 Mod.L.Rev. 232 (criticizing Armstrong case).

Unger, Agency and Fraud—Further Comment (1952), 15 Mod.L.Rev. 508 (a reply to Gower).

Chapter 5

FIDUCIARY RELATIONSHIPS

SECTION 1. FIDUCIARY CONCEPTS

THE FIDUCIARY PRINCIPLE
Austin W. Scott.[*]
Excerpts from an article of the same name in 37 California Law Review 539, at
540–541 and 555 (1949).[**]

The question arises at the outset, Who is a fiduciary? A fiduciary is a person who undertakes to act in the interest of another person. It is immaterial whether the undertaking is in the form of a contract. It is immaterial that the undertaking is gratuitous. Indeed, in England, where the courts of equity have always been strict in the enforcement of fiduciary obligations of a trustee, a trustee is ordinarily entitled to no compensation for his services unless it is otherwise provided by the terms of the trust.

What are the usual fiduciary relations? They include the relation of trustee and beneficiary, guardian and ward, agent and principal, attorney and client, executor or administrator and legatees and next of kin of the decedent. The directors and officers of a corporation are in a fiduciary relation to the corporation, and to some extent at least to the shareholders. In a partnership each partner is in a fiduciary relation to the others, since, although he has his own interests to look after, he also has the power and the duty to look after the interests of the others. So too, as Mr. Justice Jackson pointed out in a case decided just before the close of the last term, a stockholder who brings suit on a cause of action derived from the corporation is a fiduciary, since he volunteers to sue, not for himself alone, but as representative of the corporation.

Some fiduciary relationships are undoubtedly more intense than others. The greater the independent authority to be exercised by the fiduciary, the greater the scope of his fiduciary duty. Thus, a trustee is under a stricter duty of loyalty than is an agent upon whom limited authority is conferred or a corporate director who can act only as a member of the board of directors or a promoter acting for investors in a new corporation. All of these, however, are fiduciaries and are subject to the fiduciary principle of loyalty, although not to the same extent.

. . .

[*] Professor, Harvard Law School, 1909–1954; editor of Cases on Trusts, author of Law of Trusts, and Reporter for Restatement of the Law of Trusts.

[**] © Regents of the University of California, 1949. Reprinted by permission.

Let me conclude by quoting from the two great judges to whom I have referred from time to time; two judges who I think were most clearly conscious of the vital importance of the fiduciary principle.

Fifteen years ago, Mr. Justice (later Chief Justice) Stone, in a notable address on The Public Influence of the Bar said:

I venture to assert that when the history of the financial era which has just drawn to a close comes to be written, most of its mistakes and its major faults will be ascribed to the failure to observe the fiduciary principle, the precept as old as holy writ, that 'a man cannot serve two masters.' More than a century ago equity gave a hospitable reception to that principle and the common law was not slow to follow in giving it recognition. No thinking man can believe that an economy built upon a business foundation can permanently endure without some loyalty to that principle.[29]

In the famous case of *Meinhard v. Salmon,* to which I have already referred, Chief Justice Cardozo (later Mr. Justice Cardozo) said:

Many forms of conduct permissible in a workaday world for those acting at arm's length, are forbidden to those bound by fiduciary ties. A trustee is held to something stricter than the morals of the market place. Not honesty alone, but the punctilio of an honor the most sensitive, is then the standard of behavior. As to this there has developed a tradition that is unbending and inveterate. Uncompromising rigidity has been the attitude of courts of equity when petitioned to undermine the rule of undivided loyalty by the 'disintegrating erosion' of particular exceptions. Only thus has the level of conduct for fiduciaries been kept at a level higher than that trodden by the crowd. It will not consciously be lowered by any judgment of this court.[30]

CONFLICTS OF INTEREST: EFFICIENCY, FAIRNESS AND CORPORATE STRUCTURE

Alison Grey Anderson.*
25 UCLA L.Rev. 738, 1978.[1]

There is very little general writing which analyzes why fiduciaries as a group are subject to special regulation. It is possible, however, to suggest some general characteristics of fiduciaries which are related to the need to grant such persons discretion over the interests of others. Fiduciaries are typically decisionmakers; their specialized function is that of recommending or making decisions of a discretionary nature

29. Stone, The Public Influence of the Bar (1934) 48 Harv.L.Rev. 1, at 8.

30. Meinhard v. Salmon, 249 N.Y. 458 at 464, 164 N.E. 545 at 546. That such "uncompromising rigidity" with respect to trustees may not be followed in case of directors of corporations see Ballantine, Corporations (1946) 167, 203, 209; Note (1948) 61 Harv.L.Rev. 335. These writers suggest that in regard to the fiduciary duty of a director the policy of facilitating business has prevailed over the older policy of removal of temptation.

* Professor of Law, UCLA Law School.

1. © 1978, Regents of the University of California. Reprinted by permission. Footnotes selectively omitted.

about the management or investment of the property of others. Such decisions cannot easily be subjected to detailed standards or guidelines; instead, they require educated judgment about uncertain, problematical issues. In addition such decisions frequently require the use of specialized financial or business information. The inherent uncertainty involved in business and investment decisions make it difficult to evaluate such decisions or to characterize them as "good" or "bad" or "right" or "wrong." Because fiduciaries manage or have some control over very substantial property interests of others, they have the potential power to inflict great losses on those property owners. Finally, the economic interests of fiduciaries are frequently substantially affected by the discretionary decisions they make on behalf of others, since, as will be discussed, the magnitude of their own compensation for their services often depends to an unusual degree on decisions which they themselves make. As a result of all these characteristics, fiduciaries have unusually great opportunities to cheat without detection and they have unusually great incentives to do so. Moreover, the relative costs which their cheating may impose on those whose property they manage are frequently much greater than the relative costs that can be imposed without detection or remedy in simpler contractual exchanges.

As in the case of other exchange conflicts of interest, the conflict of interest problem affecting fiduciaries is one of maximizing the efficiency gains from specialization and minimizing the transaction costs associated with defining and enforcing the duties of fiduciaries while limiting any resulting cheating by fiduciaries to an acceptable level. In order to obtain a net benefit from fiduciary services, the property owner must grant discretion to the fiduciary, and yet avoid incurring high transaction costs in attempting to control the fiduciary.[61] Because of the greater information costs and uncertainty associated with fiduciary services, greater discretion is necessarily granted to most fiduciaries than to the typical seller of goods and services. Fiduciaries have correspondingly greater opportunities to cheat. Moreover, a fiduciary, like any party to an exchange, will be motivated to maximize his own wealth, not that of the property owner. If the fiduciary manages the property well, the owner will receive much of the benefit, while if the fiduciary manages poorly or diverts assets to himself, he can increase his own welfare while imposing much of the costs of his actions on the owner. The result is a "separation of ownership and control."

This separation of ownership and control is the source of legal conflicts of interest. While such separation and such conflicts of interest are inevitable if we rely on specialized property management, the absence of fully effective market controls gives fiduciaries opportunities and incentives to cheat. Fiduciary duties and conflict of interest regulation both provide standardized terms to minimize transaction costs and impose unwaivable quality requirements which prevent fidu-

---

61. Cf. Jensen & Meckling, Theory of the Firm: Managerial Behavior, Agency Costs and Ownership Structure, 3 J. Financial Econ. 305, 337–38 (1976) (costs of contractual constraints on corporate managers).

ciaries from taking unfair advantage of the superior bargaining power resulting from their specialized information and skills.

In most contractual exchanges, each party knows what his own best interests are. In a fiduciary relationship, the client or beneficiary depends on the fiduciary to an unusual degree to determine for the client what his best interests are. Given this disparity of expertise, it would be extremely difficult and costly for the client to draft a detailed contract defining the duties of the fiduciary.

Fiduciary duties economize on transaction costs by simply obliging the fiduciary to act in the best interests of his client or beneficiary and to refrain from self-interested behavior not specifically allowed by the employment contract. They codify the reasonable expectations of the client, by obliging the fiduciary to do what the client would tell him to do if the client had the same expertise as the fiduciary. They are thus more efficient than detailed contracts or detailed regulation since they restrict the fiduciary's opportunity to cheat without the costly drafting of elaborate rules while leaving him free to use his special skills in the client's interest.

As in the case of contract and warranty law, fiduciary duties are waivable when they perform only an efficiency function. Where bargaining power is roughly equal, specific fiduciary duties can be waived by the parties on the basis of full disclosure to and consent by the client. Because informational disparities so often mean that bargaining power is unequal, however, all fiduciaries have an unwaivable obligation of fairness toward the other party. Moreover, when fiduciary duties are waived, the waiver may be closely scrutinized to make sure it is valid. The ease with which fiduciary duties can be waived will be a function of the likelihood of unfairness; the greater the inequality in bargaining power, the greater the difficulty of waiver.

Fiduciary duties alone are not an adequate safeguard of fairness, since violations of fiduciary duty are frequently very difficult to detect. Special conflict of interest rules therefore apply to fiduciaries in situations in which the likelihood of cheating is regarded as particularly great. All such special rules are designed to protect the process of fiduciary decisionmaking from being affected by self-interest, since it is so difficult to detect the impact of self-interest by evaluating the decision itself.

Fiduciary duties and conflict of interest rules reflect a compromise between efficiency and fairness. The rules are efficient because they are a substitute for more costly contracts or regulation; they are fair because they restrict cheating to some extent. Elaborate direct regulation by government or by contract might be more fair; it might detect or deter more cheating.[69] Less stringent fiduciary duties and conflict of interest regulation might be more efficient in the sense of permitting

---

69. See Marsh, Are Directors Trustees?, 22 Bus.Law. 35, 73 (1966), proposing administrative review of interested transactions of corporate directors by the SEC in order to provide greater protection for investors.

more advantageous exchanges to take place at a lower cost. The rules
that exist sacrifice some fairness for efficiency and some efficiency for
fairness. In criticizing or analyzing such rules, therefore, one must
always keep in mind both the costs and the benefits.

THE MORAL THEME IN FIDUCIARY REGULATION
Tamar Frankel.*
Excerpt from "Fiduciary Law," 71 California Law Review 795,
at 829–832 (1983).**

Courts regulate fiduciaries by imposing a high standard of morality
upon them. This moral theme is an important part of fiduciary law.
Loyalty, fidelity, faith, and honor form its basic vocabulary.

Two aspects of moral behavior are important to understanding the
moral dimensions of fiduciary law. First, moral behavior is altruistic.
The moral person serves other members of the society and contributes
to society generally. He treats his own interests in a way that benefits
others, and he prefers the community to the self. Second, moral
behavior is voluntary. Thus, the more self-enforcing the altruistic
behavior is, the more it is considered moral. Self-enforcement reduces
risk and uncertainty in human relations, avoids enforcement costs and
the need for a strong enforcement organization, precludes deception,
and allays the fear that the actor will succumb to temptation.

The moral theme in fiduciary law contrasts with the role of
morality in contract law. It is true that the law of contract has moved
away from Holmes's view that a party may break his contract upon
payment of damages, and some writers have even stated that there is a
moral duty to perform a contract. Nevertheless, contract law does not
go beyond the morals of the marketplace. Each party may distinguish
his interests from those of the other and act for his own benefit. In the
world of contract, self-interest is the norm, and restraint must be
imposed by others. In contrast, the altruistic posture of fiduciary law
requires that once an individual undertakes to act as a fiduciary, he
should act to further the interests of another in preference to his own.

The law does not impose any obligation to act on the fiduciary
except to the extent that he has assumed fiduciary power. A person
may agree or refuse to serve as a fiduciary out of purely selfish reasons.
On this point, fiduciary law is as individualistic as contract. But
because the law gives the fiduciary the choice between avoiding conflicts of interest with another or refraining from acting altogether, the
law may be viewed as encouraging altruistic and moral behavior.
Thus, once a person becomes a fiduciary, the law places him in the role
of a moral person and pressures him to behave in a selfless fashion, to
think and act for others. In addition, the moral standard is not left to
the fiduciary or to custom. The courts do consider the parties' expecta-

* Professor, Boston University School of
Law.

** © Regents of the University of California. Reprinted by permission. Footnotes omitted.

tions and professional customs; but in the last analysis, it is the courts that determine the standards.

One can offer a number of reasons and justifications for the judicial incorporation of morality into fiduciary law. First, courts may have resorted to this high standard because of the historical jurisdictional authority over fiduciaries in the ecclesiastical and equity courts. Those courts imposed sanctions based on religion and morality, and not merely on force.

Second, the prevention of fiduciary abuse of power can pose serious problems. The moral theme of the law exerts pressure on the fiduciary to fulfill his obligations once he has agreed to enter into the relation. Morality is useful as an adjunct to law, because a sense of moral obligation will help bring about the desired behavior. Furthermore, an appeal to the fiduciary's conscience may in fact present a disguised threat.

Third, the emphasis of fiduciary law on morality resulted in elevating the purpose for which the fiduciary's power is granted to a position of priority over other values which may guide the fiduciary. For example, the corporate director's primary duty is to profit for the shareholders; the duty of the attorney is to represent his client's interests; and the duty of the physician is to heal and prolong life. These duties assume a greater moral stature than other, conflicting moral values. For example, the physician's duty to prolong life may take precedence over mitigation of the patient's suffering and his consideration of the family's impoverishment. But because fiduciaries must use the power entrusted to them for only one purpose, to perform services to the entrustor, ascribing the highest moral value to that purpose encourages the fiduciary's voluntary adherence to it. On the other hand, the moral emphasis on the purpose of the relation is not free from difficulties and criticism as is evidenced by the arguments for social responsibility of corporations and the competing claims on attorneys' fidelity to law enforcement, among others.

A fourth reason for viewing the fiduciary as a moral actor and distinguishing him from a selfish, profit-seeking individual is that the entrustor may refrain from entering into fiduciary relations unless he perceives the fiduciary as one who will pursue the entrustor's interests. By characterizing the fiduciary as an altruistic person, the courts emphasize and highlight the substitution aspect of the fiduciary relation, reassuring the entrustor that the fiduciary will act in the entrustor's interest.

Fifth, the moral posture of fiduciaries is related to the vulnerability of the entrustor. It is wrong to injure anyone. But it is more reprehensible to injure someone who cannot protect himself, as an entrustor in a fiduciary relation is. Thus, the degree of moral culpability of the fiduciary is positively related to the extent of the entrustor's helplessness.

Finally, the moral feature of fiduciary law forms a bridge between altruism and individualism by focusing on the objectives toward which the fiduciary must aim.   These objectives should not be merely the interests of *others,* but also the collective good, in which the fiduciary also has an interest.   To the extent that the law induces fiduciaries to work for the collective good, the law helps shape desirable social trends.

REFERENCES ON FIDUCIARY CONCEPTS

Adam Smith, The Wealth of Nations, Bk. V, Ch. I, Pt. III, Art. I (1776) Observations on the negligence of corporate directors.

Joseph Story, Commentaries on the Law of Agency § 210 (1839).   Exposition of agent's duty of zeal for the exclusive benefit of the principal.

Kaplan, Fiduciary Responsibility in the Management of the Corporation, 31 Bus.Law. 883 (1976).   An exposition of the variety of ways in which the fiduciary idea is invoked in corporation law.

Ballantine, Morbid Morality: A Standard for Galahad or "Reasonable Men"?   38 Am.Bar Assn.J. 298 (1952).   A caustic attack on elevating fiduciary standards above those of the market-place.

NOTE: SOME OTHER APPLICATIONS OF THE FIDUCIARY CONCEPT

The fiduciary concept has been greatly expanded by legal developments in the second half of the twentieth century.   In a book written to be read by the general public, the author attributes the growth of litigation to a shift from "contractual" to "fiduciary" responsibilities.   J.K. Lieberman, The Litigious Society (1981).

In the seminal case that inaugurated the implication of a private remedy from Rule 10b–5 under the Securities and Exchange Act of 1934, the court alluded to fiduciary principles as the source of the standards applied in implementing Rule 10b–5.   See Kardon v. National Gypsum Co., 73 F.Supp. 798, 803 (E.D.Pa.1947).   Later decisions have cast doubt on the applicability of fiduciary principles under this rule.   See Santa Fe Industries v. Green, 430 U.S. 462, 97 S.Ct. 1292, 51 L.Ed.2d 480 (1977).

A broad definition of "fiduciary" was introduced in the Employee Retirement Income Security Act (ERISA), which made it include anyone who exercised discretion or gave advice in connection with a retirement income plan. Fiduciaries were enjoined to exercise "care, skill, prudence and diligence."   29 U.S.C. §§ 1002(21) and 1104(a)(1).

REFERENCES

Proceedings, ABA National Institute, Fiduciary Responsibilities Under the Pension Reform Act (1975) 31 Business Lawyer 1–281 (special issue) (a comprehensive treatment).

Knickenbocher, Fiduciary Responsibility Under the Pension Reform Act (1975) 10 Real Prop. 495 (analysis from the preventive approach).

Wyatt, The Increasing Liabilities of Fiduciaries (1975) 114 Trusts & Estates 704, 755 (focus on estate and pension planning).

NOTE ON FIDUCIARY DUTY IN EUROPEAN LAW

European law systems do not appear to rely so heavily as US law on a general conception of "fiduciary duty," but they appear to reach similar results by invoking rules formulated in other terms. In France, Civil Code art. 1993 [1] provides:

> Any agent is required to render an accounting of his management, and to give satisfaction to the principal for all that he has received by virtue of his procuration, even when what he received was not due the principal.

The German Civil Code does not appear to include a parallel provision, but contains various "general clauses" from which responsibilities of a fiduciary type are derived. One of these is an innocuous-looking rule announcing that the scope of authority is defined by the terms of the communication creating it.[2] Case law has applied this rule to hold agents broadly accountable for abuse (*Missbrauch*) of their authority.[3] Another source of fiduciary-type duties is a provision that invalidates contracts in which an agent acts simultaneously for his principal and for himself.[4] This has been applied broadly to embrace cases in which corporate managers seize a corporate opportunity.[5] A third source is a provision which requires that all contracts be performed as required by good faith under the circumstances.[6] This provision has been applied in conjunction with other agency rules to require a high degree of accountability on the part of agents.[7]

SECTION 2. WHO IS A FIDUCIARY, AND FOR WHOM

SNEPP v. UNITED STATES

United States Supreme Court, 1980.
444 U.S. 507, 100 S.Ct. 763, 62 L.Ed.2d 704.

PER CURIAM.

Based on his experiences as a CIA agent, Snepp published a book about certain CIA activities in South Vietnam. Snepp published the account without submitting it to the Agency for prepublication review. As an express condition of his employment with the CIA in 1968, however, Snepp had executed an agreement promising that he would "not . . . publish . . . any information or material relating to the Agency, its activities or intelligence activities generally, either during or after the term of [his] employment . . . without specific prior approval of the Agency." Pet. 59a. The promise was an integral part of Snepp's concurrent undertaking "not to disclose any classified information relating to the Agency without proper authorization." Id., at 58a.[1] Thus, Snepp had pledged not to divulge *classified* information

---

1. As translated in J.H. Crabb, The French Civil Code (1977).

2. BGB § 167.

3. See J. von Staudinger, Kommentar zum BGB, § 167, Anm. 91–105 (12th ed. 1978).

4. BGB § 191.

5. H. Wiedemann, Gesellschaftsrecht I, 346 (1980).

6. "[W]ie Treu und Glauben mit Rucksicht auf die Verkehrssitte es erfordern." BGB § 242.

7. J. von Staudinger, op. cit., § 242, Anm. 164–181.

1. Upon the eve of his departure from the Agency in 1976, Snepp also executed a "termination secrecy agreement." That document reaffirmed his obligation "never" to reveal "any classified information, or any information concerning intelligence or CIA that has not been made public by CIA . . . without the express written consent of the Director of Central Intelligence or his representative." Pet. 61a.

and not to publish *any* information without prepublication clearance. The Government brought this suit to enforce Snepp's agreement. It sought a declaration that Snepp had breached the contract, an injunction requiring Snepp to submit future writings for prepublication review, and an order imposing a constructive trust for the Government's benefit on all profits that Snepp might earn from publishing the book in violation of his fiduciary obligations to the Agency. . . . The District Court . . . enjoined future breaches of Snepp's agreement and imposed a constructive trust on Snepp's profits.

The Court of Appeals accepted the findings of the District Court and agreed that Snepp had breached a valid contract. . . . Thus, the court upheld the injunction against future violations of Snepp's prepublication obligation. The court, however, concluded that the record did not support imposition of a constructive trust. The conclusion rested on the court's perception that Snepp had a First Amendment right to publish unclassified information and the Government's concession—for the purposes of this litigation—that Snepp's book divulged no classified intelligence.

. . .

Snepp's employment with the CIA involved an extremely high degree of trust. In the opening sentence of the agreement that he signed, Snepp explicitly recognized that he was entering a trust relationship. The trust agreement specifically imposed the obligation not to publish *any* information relating to the Agency without submitting the information for clearance. Snepp stipulated at trial that—after undertaking this obligation—he had been "assigned to various positions of trust" and that he had been granted "frequent access to classified information, including information regarding intelligence sources and methods." 456 F.Supp., at 178. Snepp published his book about CIA activities on the basis of this background and exposure. He deliberately and surreptitiously violated his obligation to submit all material for prepublication review. Thus, he exposed the classified information with which he had been entrusted to the risk of disclosure.

Whether Snepp violated his trust does not depend upon whether his book actually contained classified information. The Government does not deny—as a general principle—Snepp's right to publish unclassified information. Nor does it contend—at this stage of the litigation—that Snepp's book contains classified material. The Government simply claims that, in light of the special trust reposed in him and the agreement that he signed, Snepp should have given the CIA an opportunity to determine whether the material he proposed to publish would compromise classified information or sources. Neither of the Government's concessions undercuts its claim that Snepp's failure to submit to prepublication review was a breach of his trust.

. . .

The Government could not pursue the only remedy that the Court of Appeals left it without losing the benefit of the bargain it seeks to enforce. Proof of the tortious conduct necessary to sustain an award of punitive damages might force the Government to disclose some of the very confidences that Snepp promised to protect. . . .

A constructive trust, on the other hand, protects both the Government and the former agent from unwarranted risks. This remedy is the natural and customary consequence of a breach of trust. It deals fairly with both parties by conforming relief to the dimensions of the wrong. If the agent secures prepublication clearance, he can publish with no fear of liability. If the agent publishes unreviewed material in violation of his fiduciary and contractual obligation, the trust remedy simply requires him to disgorge the benefits of his faithlessness. Since the remedy is swift and sure, it is tailored to deter those who would place sensitive information at risk. And since the remedy reaches only funds attributable to the breach, it cannot saddle the former agent with exemplary damages out of all proportion to his gain. . . . We therefore reverse the judgment of the Court of Appeals in so far as it refused to impose a constructive trust on Snepp's profits, and we remand the case to the Court of Appeals for reinstatement of the full judgment of the District Court.

So ordered.

MR. JUSTICE STEVENS, with whom MR. JUSTICE BRENNAN and MR. JUSTICE MARSHALL join, dissenting.

. . .

The rule of law the Court announces today is not supported by statute, by the contract, or by the common law.

. . .

The Court has not persuaded me that a rule of reason analysis should not be applied to Snepp's covenant to submit to prepublication review. Like an ordinary employer, the CIA has a vital interest in protecting certain types of information; at the same time, the CIA employee has a countervailing interest in preserving a wide range of work opportunities (including work as an author) and in protecting his First Amendment rights. . . .

But even assuming that Snepp's covenant to submit to prepublication review should be enforced, the constructive trust imposed by the Court is not an appropriate remedy. If an employee has used his employer's confidential information for his own personal profit, a constructive trust over those profits is obviously an appropriate remedy because the profits are the direct result of the breach. But Snepp admittedly did not use confidential information in his book; nor were the profits from his book in any sense a product of his failure to submit the book for prepublication review. . . .

The Court's decision to dispose of this case summarily on the Government's conditional cross-petition for certiorari is just as unprecedented as its disposition of the merits.

. . .

The uninhibited character of today's exercise in lawmaking is highlighted by the Court's disregard of two venerable principles that favor a more conservative approach to this case.

First, for centuries the English-speaking judiciary refused to grant equitable relief unless the plaintiff could show that his remedy at law was inadequate. Without waiting for an opportunity to appraise the adequacy of the punitive damage remedy in this case, the Court has jumped to the conclusion that equitable relief is necessary.

Second, and of greater importance, the Court seems unaware of the fact that its drastic new remedy has been fashioned to enforce a species of prior restraint on a citizen's right to criticize his government.

POST–EMPLOYMENT CONFLICT OF INTEREST
18 United States Code § 207 (1984).

§ 207. Disqualification of Former Officers and Employees; Disqualification of Partners of Current Officers and Employees

(a) Whoever, having been an officer or employee of the executive branch of the United States Government, of any independent agency of the United States, or of the District of Columbia, including a special Government employee, after his employment has ceased, knowingly acts as agent or attorney for, or otherwise represents, any other person (except the United States), in any formal or informal appearance before, or, with the intent to influence, makes any oral or written communication on behalf of any other person (except the United States) to—

(1) any department, agency, court, court-martial, or any civil, military, or naval commission of the United States or the District of Columbia, or any officer or employee thereof, and

(2) in connection with any judicial or other proceeding, application, request for a ruling or other determination, contract, claim, controversy, investigation, charge, accusation, arrest, or other particular matter involving a specific party or parties in which the United States or the District of Columbia is a party or has a direct and substantial interest, and

(3) in which he participated personally and substantially as an officer or employee through decision, approval, disapproval, recommendation, the rendering of advice, investigation or otherwise, while so employed

shall be fined not more than $10,000 or imprisoned for not more than two years, or both.

[Omitted paragraphs penalize representation within two years after retirement in matters that were under the supervision of the former employee, and representation within one year in the department in which the representative was employed.]

REFERENCES

Rogers and Young, Public Office as a Public Trust: A Suggestion That Impeachment for High Crimes and Misdemeanors Implies a Fiduciary Standard (1975) 63 Geo.L.J. 1025 (a historical approach to support the view that impeachment should be based on a fiduciary standard—breach of trust—and not the need to prove actual criminal acts).

County of Cook v. Barrett, 36 Ill.App.3d 623, 344 N.E.2d 540 (1975) (county clerk held to be a fiduciary, and the county entitled to a constructive trust to recover $180,000 in bribes received by the clerk; the absence of any showing of damage to the county is immaterial).

United States v. Drisko, 303 F.Supp. 858 (E.D.Va.1969) (U.S. recovers from government employee the value of gifts received by employee from entrepreneur for furnishing information on government activities and investigations affecting the entrepreneur's business).

Reading v. Attorney-General, [1949] 2 All Eng.Rep. 68, [1951] 1 All Eng.Rep. 617 (British soldier who helped smugglers evade Egyptian taxes held accountable to British treasury); comment, 65 Harv.L.Rev. 502.

CHALUPIAK v. STAHLMAN

Pennsylvania Supreme Court, 1951.
368 Pa. 83, 81 A.2d 577.
Comments: 56 Dick.L.Rev. 357, 100 U.Penn.L.Rev. 448, 13 U.Pitts.L.Rev. 162.

Bill in equity by Paul Chalupiak and another against H.C. Stahlman and another to compel conveyance to plaintiffs of land purchased by named defendant at tax sale. The Court of Common Pleas of Beaver County . . . entered a final decree dismissing the bill and plaintiffs appealed.

ALLEN M. STEARNE, JUSTICE. Was the business relationship between the defendant, H.C. Stahlman and plaintiff, Paul Chalupiak of such a nature and character which required of defendant the duty of loyalty, fidelity and fair dealing and which precluded defendant from acquiring and enforcing an adverse title to real estate against plaintiff? The court below ruled that defendant owed no such duty and dismissed the bill. This appeal followed.

The commissioners of Beaver County purchased at the county treasurer's tax sale a tract of land assessed as "land of James Moore Heirs". There was no description by metes and bounds but eventually it was established that the area consisted of 54.088 acres. Adjoining this land was another tract which was also owned by the county commissioners. Plaintiff was desirous of acquiring the land formerly owned by the "James Moore Heirs" and purchased the same from the commissioners. At the suggestion of the commissioners plaintiff employed a registered engineer to prepare a survey and plan of the tract and he also had the title examined and approved by a lawyer. The survey and plan was inaccurate because it included approximately 30 acres of land not a part of the "Moore tract". Plaintiff, under the mistaken information thus furnished, was of the opinion that he owned 80 acres of land which he proceeded to subdivide into building lots and sold some of them to purchasers by deeds with general warranty of title. Such conveyances included part of the 30 acres of land to which plaintiff had no title.

It is obvious from his testimony that plaintiff is an unlettered man. Defendant, H.C. Stahlman, on the contrary, in addition to his employment in an adjacent factory or mill, was a justice of the peace and also the tax collector. He maintained a business office with a paid assistant. For fees he drew wills, contracts and other papers, took affidavits and acknowledgments and prepared income tax returns. Defendant was obviously a type of country squire, of some education, whom people of the area consulted for many purposes and in whom doubtless his client reposed a great confidence.

Some time in 1945, plaintiff called at defendant's office and requested him to prepare a deed for a subdivision of the land which plaintiff had sold to Adam Adamaitas. Plaintiff brought with him a sketch or plan prepared by his engineer. Defendant examined the plan and concluded that the land proposed to be conveyed did not appear to be a part of the "Moore Heirs" tract. Defendant asked plaintiff: "Are you sure that you own this ground?" Plaintiff replied that his engineer had drawn the plan and that his attorney informed plaintiff that he had good title. Defendant did not prepare the deed to Adamaitas and plaintiff employed an attorney for that purpose. However, from July 7 to September 15, 1945, defendant prepared four other deeds for such subdivisions, at plaintiff's request, from the engineer's survey. Defendant received $5.00 for each deed except one for which he received $3.00. Title to some of the land purported to be conveyed in these four deeds, as above stated, was then in the commissioners.

In July, 1946 plaintiff brought to defendant a petition to the commissioners to validate title to plaintiff's land for the purpose of acknowledgment. Defendant read to plaintiff the description of the land described in the petition and showed plaintiff on the borough map that the description indicated that plaintiff did not own the land for which he petitioned to have his title validated. As other errors appeared in the petition, it was not *then* acknowledged. Defendant informed plaintiff that the land to which title was in question was advertised for sale by the Beaver County Commissioners. Subsequently, on November 27, 1946, the acknowledgment to the petition was taken by defendant and filed March 5, 1947. *When plaintiff brought his petition to defendant on November 27, 1946 for acknowledgment, defendant did not inform plaintiff that defendant had already purchased the land in question.*

On August 28, 1946, *defendant* had purchased part of the property adjoining the "Moore Heirs" property *as agent for his sister* who resides in Asheville, North Carolina. On February 26, 1947, defendant purchased another portion of adjoining property in the joint names of himself and his sister. It was this land, or a portion of it, which defendant purchased but which plaintiff had mistakenly considered to be his own and had conveyed to the four individuals as stated above.

The court below found that any information obtained by defendant: ". . . as to ownership of land in Baden, was not secured by him from plaintiff. [Defendant] had such information before [plaintiff] came to him to prepare deeds. [Defendant] brought this information to the attention of [plaintiff] on several occasions. [Plaintiff], relying on advice of his engineer and counsel, refused to heed the information given by Stahlman [defendant]."

The fact that defendant, through borough plans, had knowledge of the ownership of lands in the borough is not controlling. Such maps or plans were available to all. It is, however, of paramount importance that—accepting such judicial finding of fact—it was plaintiff's request to defendant to draw a deed which caused the defendant, in examining the maps and plans of the borough, to recognize the fact that plaintiff's proposed transfers included land to which he had no title.

In the testimony it appears that defendant also prepared plaintiff's income tax returns. Defendant stated in this connection that "[defendant] wasn't even sure that that land didn't belong to [plaintiff], when [defendant] bought it."

The issue upon which this case revolves is the *capacity* in which defendant acted when he performed services for plaintiff. This in turn depends upon the *nature* and extent of the services rendered by defendant.

At the outset, it must be conceded that if all that defendant did for plaintiff was to act as a stenographer or clerk to fill in blanks in a deed form, defendant would not assume the duties and liabilities of a conveyancer. It is obvious, however, that defendant was employed as more than a stenographer or typist. While perhaps defendant was not acting as a conveyancer, with all the duties and liabilities of a lawyer in such a field: Ladner's Real Estate Conveyancing, Vol. 2, p. 497; La-Brum v. Commonwealth Title Company, 358 Pa. 239, 56 A.2d 246, yet the testimony is clear that he was more than a mere clerk and stenographer. He was plaintiff's agent and confidential adviser. . . .

Here defendant acted, at plaintiff's request and on plaintiff's behalf, in drawing the deeds in question, subject to plaintiff's control. Because of his knowledge as tax collector and as an agent or conveyancer, he was aware either that plaintiff had no title whatever to the 30 acres or at least plaintiff's title was doubtful. Defendant secured, *during the course of his service to plaintiff,* the knowledge that plaintiff was attempting to convey land which plaintiff did not own. *It was this knowledge that defendant utilized against the interests of plaintiff.* Defendant, on the basis of this knowledge, went to a commissioners' sale and purchased the land which he knew or suspected that plaintiff mistakenly thought he had already validly conveyed to others. It is manifest that had plaintiff never dealt with defendant the latter would never have been led to purchase the land in question. Defendant was no chance purchaser. . . . Defendant violated the duty of loyalty and fidelity he owed to plaintiff. . . .

It is not of controlling importance that defendant utilized information which related to defect in *title*. True, defendant was not employed to search *title* but to prepare or draw a deed. However, this Court, speaking through Justice Sharswood, stated in Smith v. Brotherline, 62 Pa. 461, 469, that "The relation between him and his client is confidential, and whether he acts upon information derived from him or from any other source, he is affected with a trust." See Restatement, Agency, sec. 395, supra, where it is stated that an agent cannot use information acquired by him during the course of his agency to the injury of the principal ". . . although such information does not relate to the transaction in which he is then employed." It is important that a full disclosure of information to the conveyancer or agent be required.

Defendant, seeking to avoid the consequences of his acts, maintains that since he fully warned plaintiff that his title was doubtful and fully informed plaintiff of the tax sale where defendant purchased the land in question, he is therefore relieved of his fiduciary obligations to plaintiff. We do not agree. It would defeat the very purpose of the rule to permit defendant, having learned during his service to plaintiff of a defect in plaintiff's title, to give plaintiff full warning that *he* was going to take advantage of the defect. It could easily be that even though plaintiff or his grantee were present at the commissioners' sale, that defendant could bid up the price to a point where plaintiff would be required to settle upon defendant's terms. . . .

Even if we did not attribute to defendant any conscious effort to defraud or take undue advantage of plaintiff, such a transaction cannot stand. It is said in Cleavinger v. Reimar, 3 Watts & S. 486, it is not on the ground of fraud, but upon the principles of public policy that transactions similar to the present are prohibited.

. . .

Decree reversed with direction to the court below to enter a decree in accordance with the prayer of the bill.

BELL, JUSTICE (dissenting). I very strongly dissent from the majority opinion's summation of the facts and its conclusions of law. I cannot find nor could the Chancellor who saw and heard the witnesses, nor the court en banc, any fraud, actual or legal, and certainly no confidential relationship.

. . . *Whatever information defendant acquired as to the ownership of the land was never secured by him from plaintiffs and plaintiffs never relied upon defendant* or on defendant's gratuitous information, but on the advice of plaintiffs' counsel and engineer (see particularly finding No. 33). How then could a confidential relationship arise? We can easily imagine the ridicule and scorn with which a lawyer would have showered plaintiffs if they had taken the opinion (or doubt) of a conveyancer, who received the colossal fee of $5.00 ahead of and in preference to the opinion and advice of plaintiffs' lawyer and engineer. *Defendant never made any false or fraudulent statement* (see particularly finding No. 24); on the contrary, defendant's warning plaintiffs of his doubt about their title and advising them of the pending Commissioners sale were, we believe, the actions of an honest man instead of that of a cheat or a defrauder. The Chancellor specifically found, as we have hereinabove set forth, and the evidence was overwhelming and uncontradicted that *plaintiff told defendant he was relying upon the advice of his lawyer and engineer instead of the defendant.* To hold under these facts, that defendant Stahlman occupied a confidential relationship to the plaintiffs with regard to the land which defendant Stahlman subsequently purchased at public sale seems so far fetched as to be incomprehensible.

MOSS v. VADMAN

Supreme Court of Washington, En Banc, 1969.
77 Wn.2d 396, 463 P.2d 159.

FINLEY, JUDGE. This action was brought by the plaintiffs, Darrell Moss and Robert Robbins (partners who bought and sold real estate) against Warren Vadman, (their accountant who also advised them from time to time on their real estate transactions). Their complaint was that he had failed to assign to them an option to purchase 1,163.30 acres of land referred to herein as the Mottman tract. The option was obtained by Vadman under circumstances and conditions hereinafter described.

This particular property had a special value in 1966, it being large enough to be an acceptable site for the campus of a new 4-year college which it was believed the 1967 legislature would establish in Thurston County.[2] Title to the property was in Mottman Mercantile Company, a corporation owned by the members of the Mottman family.

. . .

The trial court dismissed the action on the basis of its conclusions that Vadman was not the agent of the plaintiffs in procuring the option; that he breached no fiduciary relationship in assigning the option to the Swanson-Whisler group; and that consequently no constructive trust was established. From that dismissal, the plaintiffs have appealed.

. . .

Vadman was also the accountant for the Mottman Mercantile Company, as well as for some individual members of the Mottman family. We will refer to the corporation and the members of the family collectively as the Mottmans, except where differentiation may be important. Based upon the knowledge Vadman had acquired of the Mottmans, he suggested to the plaintiffs in November or December 1965, that the Mottmans might be willing to accept $1,000,000 for the tract of land here in question. The plaintiffs in March 1966, authorized Vadman to offer $5,000 for a 1-year option to purchase the tract for

2. The 1967 legislature did as anticipated, and the tract continued to have this potential until December 1967 when another site was selected.

$1,000,000.[3] It was agreed that Vadman was to receive a 2 per cent finder's fee if he was successful in acquiring the option and if the option was sold or exercised by them within the year. It was understood that the option would be taken in Vadman's name, and that the identity of Moss and Robbins was not to be disclosed to the Mottmans.[4]

This offer was not acceptable to the Mottmans, either as to purchase price or as to the amount to be paid for the option, but because of the interest shown they commissioned Mr. Hubert Hoffman to make a study of the property to determine its value.

The trial court's findings of fact cover quite concisely what followed thereafter.

On July 16, 1966, Mr. George Mottman, Mr. Hoffman and the defendant Vadman met at the store operated by Mottman Mercantile Company and tentatively agreed upon a price of $1,160,000.00 [5] for the tract and $60,000.00 for a one year option, and planned for a stockholders meeting later to obtain stockholder approval thereto. (Finding of fact 12.)

On July 18, 1966, the defendant Vadman reported to Plaintiffs the price and that Mottman would probably give an option for a year for $60,000.00. (Finding of fact 13.)

The defendant Vadman was sick from July 21 to August 7, 1966, and the Mottmans delayed the stockholders' meeting until August 8th so that he could be present. At the meeting on August 8, 1966, the Mottmans orally agreed to give the defendant Vadman an "Option" to the end of August. The defendant Vadman informed Mottmans that he was dealing with some undisclosed interested parties (plaintiffs) and that they were to have until the end of August to raise the $60,000.00. The defendant Vadman told Mottmans that he was also interested, and if the undisclosed parties then interested did not raise the money, he would find others, and it was agreed that he, Vadman, would have an additional day for himself or until September 1, 1966, at 5:00 P.M. (Finding of fact 14.)

That on or about August 8, 1966, plaintiffs were informed that they would have to the end of the month (August 31, 1966) to obtain from Vadman an assignment of his option right upon the payment of $60,000.00 for the option and a Finder's Fee of 2%. Later, on the evening of August 31, 1966, on a phone call from the plaintiffs, the

3. This authorization was in the form of a letter dated March 29, 1966, addressed to Vadman, and signed by the plaintiff Darrell F. Moss, which read as follows: "Please accept this letter as the authority to offer to the Mottman family for their Westside Olympia holdings, as set forth on the accompanying map,

ONE MILLION DOLLARS CASH ($1,000,000.00)

to be paid one year from the giving of an option for which we will place on deposit Five Thousand Dollars ($5000.00)."

4. Both the plaintiffs and Vadman were aware that the Mottmans would not be inclined to tie up their property for so long a time with parties of such limited financial means as the plaintiffs.

5. This was approximately $1,000 an acre.

defendant Vadman extended the time to 10:00 A.M., September 1, 1966. (Finding of fact 15.)

At this point, we interrupt our quotation of the trial court's findings to point out that the finding (No. 14) that Vadman had the day of September 1 for himself is a crucial finding in the case. The plaintiffs at all times have contended that their understanding was that they had until 5 p.m. on September 1, 1966 to raise the $60,000.

. . .

In their quest for the $60,000, the plaintiffs contacted the Swanson-Whisler group in the latter part of August.

We turn again to the findings as made by the trial court.

On August 24, 1966, the defendant Richard Swanson began dealing with the plaintiffs regarding the option and in what proportions they would contribute and who would have control. After several meetings they failed to agree. On August 29, 1966, the defendant Richard Swanson contacted the defendant Vadman and learned that plaintiffs had until the end of August to perform. On August 30, 1966, Richard Swanson informed the defendant Vadman that his group would put up option money and pay a finders' fee if plaintiffs did not. On the evening of August 31, 1966, the defendant Vadman told the defendant Richard Swanson that he had given plaintiffs until 9:00 or 10:00 A.M. on September 1, 1966 within which to produce the $60,000.00. On the morning of September 1, 1966, at 10:00 o'clock A.M., plaintiffs had not complied and the defendant Vadman accepted the Swanson-Whisler offer. (Finding of fact 17.)

. . .

That at a meeting which started at 2:00 P.M. on September 1, 1966, the option was signed by the Mottman Mercantile Company to the defendant Warren Vadman and delivered to him, and later, (July 27, 1967) transferred by him to the defendants Swanson and Whisler when an obligation was given to him evidencing a finder's fee of $25,000.00 less $1100.00 paid for attorney's fee, leaving a balance payable to him of $23,900.00. (Finding of fact 19.)

. . .

The trial court concluded that, on the basis of the facts as found, Vadman was not an agent of the plaintiffs and that there was no fiduciary relationship, and that when the plaintiffs failed to produce $60,000 by the end of August, or within the extension accorded to them, Vadman was at liberty to deal with the Swanson-Whisler group.

With these conclusions we are in accord. If there was an agency between the plaintiffs and Vadman, and we do not believe there was, it was for the limited purpose of presenting the original offer made by the plaintiffs to the Mottmans. When that offer was rejected, the agency, if any, terminated.

. . .

We have repeatedly held that a prerequisite of an agency is control of the agent by the principal. McCarty v. King County Medical Service Corp., 26 Wash.2d 660, 175 P.2d 653 (1946) and cases cited.

We have frequently cited the Restatement of Agency[7] for the proposition that an agency relationship results from the manifestation of consent by one person that another shall act on his behalf and subject to his control, with a correlative manifestation of consent by the other party to act on his behalf and subject to his control. Matsumura v. Eilert, 74 Wash.Dec.2d 369, 444 P.2d 806 (1968); Turnbull v. Shelton, 47 Wash.2d 70, 286 P.2d 676 (1955); Coombs v. R.D. Bodle Co., 33 Wash. 2d 280, 205 P.2d 888 (1949); McCarty v. King County Medical Service Corp., supra. Seavey on Agency states that an agency is a consensual relation between two persons created by law by which a principal has a right to control the conduct of the agent and the agent has a power to affect the legal relations of the principal. W. Seavey on Agency § 3 (1964).

. . .

Plaintiffs apparently intended to create an agency relationship. To that end they sent Vadman a letter of authority to make an offer for the option on the Mottman tract. This might be interpreted as a manifestation of consent by plaintiffs that Vadman act for them and subject to their control. Vadman, however had no intent to create an agency. He did not consent to the agency, and more importantly, he did not submit himself to the control of the plaintiffs as to any of his subsequent actions.

. . .

Having found no agency, we need not consider the question of a breach of fiduciary relationship by Vadman, or any participation in that breach by the Swanson-Whisler group or Evergreen Park, Inc.

The judgment appealed from is affirmed.

. . .

HILL, JUDGE (dissenting).

. . .

I would hold that there was an agency, and a fiduciary relationship between the plaintiffs and Vadman. While it is my view that the evidence preponderates that the plaintiffs were told by Vadman that they had until 5 p.m. on September 1, 1966 to produce the $60,000 and that they had the right to proceed on that assumption, I concede that there is evidence to support the trial court's finding that the plaintiffs had only until the end of August, and that Vadman had reserved for himself the extra day of September 1, 1966.

My dissent is therefore predicated on the proposition that the evidence establishes that there was a limited agency terminating at the end of August 1966, and that until that time Moss and Robbins had the

---

7. Both the original and Restatement of Agency, 2d § 1 (1958).

exclusive right as between Vadman and themselves to acquire for $60,000 a year's option to buy the Mottman tract for $1,160,000.

It seems clear to me that the defendant Vadman, who had acted as the agent of the plaintiffs in procuring that right, violated his fiduciary relationship with them when on August 29 he disclosed to the defendant Richard Swanson, representing the Swanson-Whisler group, that if that group could not make a deal with the plaintiff's during August, they could deal with him on September 1. This in effect ended any chance the plaintiffs had of acquiring financing through the Swanson-Whisler group and made Vadman liable for whatever he received in consequence of his subsequent dealing with the Swanson-Whisler group.

. . .

To Vadman's credit, as his testimony indicates, he made an effort to induce the Swanson-Whisler group to work with the plaintiffs; but he also told them the one thing they needed to know to take off any pressure to deal with the plaintiffs, i.e., that if they (the Swanson-Whisler group) did not deal with the plaintiffs, they could deal with Vadman on September 1. Vadman's insistence throughout that he could not dispose of the option until September 1 speaks eloquently of his own recognition of a fiduciary relationship with the plaintiffs until the end of August.

. . .

Consequently, I would direct the entry of a money judgment in favor of the plaintiffs against the defendant Vadman in the sum of $25,000, the amount received by him from the Swanson-Whisler group as a result of his transfer of the option to that group.[8]

NOTE ON ILLEGAL PURPOSE

It is commonly stated that no accounting of profits will be enforced among participants in an illegal enterprise. The theory is that the remedy being in equity, the plaintiff is barred from recovery by his "unclean hands." The doctrine is ascribed to the "Highwayman's Case" in which one highway robber brought a bill against another for an accounting; the case may be mythical (see Ashhurst v. Mason, 1875, L.R. 20 Eq. 225, 230), and has no citation.

A recent application of the doctrine is found in Johnston v. Senecal, 329 Mass. 556, 109 N.E.2d 467 (1952). Plaintiff was seeking an accounting of the assets of a partnership which had been in the business of selling parking meters to municipalities. The court found that part of the partnership business was to furnish entertainment and food and drink to those in power to purchase for the municipalities. This activity was held to be against public policy and the contract of partnership illegal. Plaintiff was denied any right of accounting under the illegal contract.

8. Although the prayer of the plaintiffs' complaint was for $23,000 the actual find-er's fee paid was $25,000, and recovery of that amount is authorized by CR 54(c).

REFERENCES

Waychoff v. Waychoff, 309 Pa. 300, 163 A. 670, 86 A.L.R. 190 (1932) (accounting denied to laymen who had agreement with attorney for splitting of fees on veterans' insurance claims).

Irwin v. Curie, 171 N.Y. 409, 64 N.E. 161, 58 A.L.R. 830 (1902) (accounting granted to layman who had fee-splitting agreement with attorney, since opposite result would merely reward the attorney, on whom lies primary duty of compliance).

Illegal purpose—agencies:

Harry Parker Limited v. Mason (England, Court of Appeal) [1940] 4 A.E.R. 199 (plaintiff cannot recover from defendant amounts which latter received to use in placing bets, where scheme was to place these bets and others in such a way as to falsify the odds).

Stone v. Freeman, 298 N.Y. 268, 82 N.E.2d 571 (1948) (client who gave broker money to bribe French Purchasing Mission cannot recover unused balance).

Willig v. Gold, 75 Cal.App.2d 809, 171 P.2d 754 (1946) (agent not accountable to principal for bonus received from third party for revealing principal's frauds); comment, 31 Minn.L.Rev. 293.

OPDYKE v. KENT LIQUOR MART, INC.

Delaware Supreme Court, 1962.
40 Del.Ch. 316, 181 A.2d 579.

SOUTHERLAND, CHIEF JUSTICE. The principal issue in this case concerns the ownership of certain shares of stock of the defendant, Kent Liquor Mart, Inc.

In the summer of 1959 Milton R. Opdyke, the plaintiff, and George M. Smith, one of the defendants, discussed a possible venture into the liquor business. They learned of a vacant store in a shopping center near Dover. They interviewed Glenn A. Richter, one of the defendants. Richter was one of two members of Richter and Meyer, which owned the shopping center. He told them that the store would be available if he were made a co-owner of the business. They agreed.

Opdyke and Smith retained Herman C. Brown, Esq., an attorney practicing in Dover, to incorporate the business. The corporation was formed in September, 1959. . . .

The store was opened in August, 1960. It did not prosper as its owners had hoped. At a meeting on October 9 Richter said he would be willing to get out of the business. . . .

After many efforts to agree on a settlement, Opdyke in March, 1961 offered to buy Smith's and Richter's shares. . . .

On the following Tuesday (March 28), Richter and Smith called to see Brown. Richter said that on that morning Opdyke had told him that the deal was off. Richter and Smith had a problem—a proposed sale of the corporation to a Mr. Behan for $30,000. To this Opdyke would not agree. . . . As they were leaving Brown said that he was sorry to see this happen, and that he would have some interest, on behalf of a client or of himself, in purchasing all or part of the corporation. . . .

Later that day, Brown called Richter . . .. Brown then offered $21,000 for the two-thirds of the stock under the same conditions. Richter said he would consult Smith and advise Brown. Later Richter confirmed the sale. . . .

Before leaving Brown requested Richter and Smith not to tell Opdyke of the sale because he (Brown) wanted to tell Opdyke himself. . . .

Opdyke's third point raises a very serious question. He asserts that Brown, as a lawyer, owed him a fiduciary duty; and that when Brown acquired Richter's stock he violated that duty. He contends that Brown by the purchase acquired an interest adverse to his client, and also that Brown, even if his fiduciary relation had theretofore terminated, made use of information acquired in a confidential relationship in a way adverse to the interest of his former client.

Brown replies that his fiduciary duty was to the corporation only, and not to any of its stockholders. When the dispute between them arose he advised them that he was not representing any of them but only the corporation. Consequently, he argues, he was free to buy stock in the corporation from any stockholder.

The Vice Chancellor sustained this defense. . . .

We observe at once that all of this reasoning is based upon the concept that the corporation has a separate existence from the individuals who are its stockholders. For purposes of corporation law this distinction is ordinarily sound, although even in that field the corporate fiction is on occasion disregarded.

But in determining the existence or nonexistence of the important relationship of attorney and client a broader approach is required. The question is, What in fact was the relationship between Brown and the three men? This is not a simple case, as defendants' counsel suggests, of an attorney for a corporation investing in its stock.

It is clear to us that Brown was at the beginning of the venture, and also at its end, the attorney for the three men. The corporation was simply a form for the carrying on of a joint venture. For our present purpose Brown must be regarded as the attorney for three joint adventurers. When they fell out he undertook to resolve their differences. He very properly told them that he could not represent any one of them against another. This was so, not because of the corporate form of the enterprise, but because of the well-settled rule that if a lawyer is retained by two clients and they get into a dispute he cannot ordinarily represent either. Indeed, Brown's justifiable insistence on this neutrality was a recognition, conscious or not, of his fiduciary duty to all three men. That he was acting in his capacity as a lawyer admits of no doubt. Why were they discussing the matter in his office if not to obtain his help and counsel in their difficulty? In fact it was Brown who succeeded in evolving a possible settlement of the whole matter—a commendable effort. . . .

When Brown bought the Richter stock, he acquired an interest in the subject matter of the dispute between his clients. It was an interest necessarily adverse to that of one of them—Opdyke. Moreover, even if it be assumed, as the Vice Chancellor found, that the relationship of attorney and client had ceased with the failure of the settlement, yet he is still liable in this case because his knowledge that the stock was for sale was acquired directly from his role as counselor. . . .

It is said that after learning of Brown's purchase Opdyke voiced no objection and had no criticism of Brown. His failure to assert his legal rights is of no moment. He was not represented by separate counsel, and he naturally did not realize his legal position. It was Brown's duty to enlighten him, but this duty was not performed. . . .

We regret that a member of our bar has succumbed to the temptation to put his own interest above that of his client. But that he did so we entertain no doubt. . . .

A judgment should be entered embodying appropriate relief, inter alia, declaring Brown a constructive trustee for Opdyke in respect of the interest acquired by him under sales contract with Richter and the others. . . .

MODEL RULES OF PROFESSIONAL CONDUCT
American Bar Association, 1984.

Rule 1.8   Conflict of Interest: Prohibited Transactions

(a) A lawyer shall not enter into a business transaction with a client or knowingly acquire an ownership, possessory, security or other pecuniary interest adverse to a client unless:

    (1) the transaction and terms on which the lawyer acquires the interest are fair and reasonable to the client and are fully disclosed and transmitted in writing to the client in a manner which can be reasonably understood by the client;

    (2) the client is given a reasonable opportunity to seek the advice of independent counsel in the transaction; and

    (3) the client consents in writing thereto.

(b) A lawyer shall not use information relating to representation of a client to the disadvantage of the client unless the client consents after consultation. . . .

SECTION 3. THE EXTENT OF FIDUCIARY DUTIES

MEINHARD v. SALMON

New York Court of Appeals, 1928.
249 N.Y. 458, 164 N.E. 545, 62 A.L.R. 1.
Comments: 29 Cal.L.Rev. 367, 42 Harv.L.Rev. 953, 13 Minn.L.Rev. 711, 3 St.
Johns L.Rev. 287, 38 Yale L.J. 782.

CARDOZO, C.J.   On April 10, 1902, Louisa M. Gerry leased to the defendant Walter J. Salmon the premises known as the Hotel Bristol at the northwest corner of Forty-second street and Fifth avenue in the city of New York.   The lease was for a term of twenty years, commencing May 1, 1902, and ending April 30, 1922.   The lessee undertook to change the hotel building for use as shops and offices at a cost of $200,000.   Alterations and additions were to be accretions to the land.

Salmon, while in course of treaty with the lessor as to the execution of the lease, was in course of treaty with Meinhard, the plaintiff, for the necessary funds.   The result was a joint venture with terms embodied in a writing.   Meinhard was to pay to Salmon half of the moneys requisite to reconstruct, alter, manage and operate the property.   Salmon was to pay to Meinhard 40 per cent of the net profits for the first five years of the lease and 50 per cent for the years thereafter.   If there were losses, each party was to bear them equally.   Salmon, however, was to have sole power to "manage, lease, underlet and operate" the building.   There were to be certain preemptive rights for each in the contingency of death.

The two were coadventurers, subject to fiduciary duties akin to those of partners, King v. Barnes, 109 N.Y. 267, 16 N.E. 332.   As to this we are all agreed.   The heavier weight of duty rested, however, upon Salmon.   He was a coadventurer with Meinhard, but he was manager as well.   During the early years of the enterprise, the building, reconstructed, was operated at a loss.   If the relation had then ended, Meinhard as well as Salmon would have carried a heavy burden.   Later the profits became large with the result that for each of the investors there came a rich return.   For each, the venture had its phases of fair weather and of foul.   The two were in it jointly, for better or for worse.

When the lease was near its end, Elbridge T. Gerry [1] had become the owner of the reversion.   He owned much other property in the neighborhood, one lot adjoining the Bristol Building on Fifth avenue and four lots on Forty-second street.   He had a plan to lease the entire tract for a long term to some one who would destroy the buildings then existing, and put up another in their place.   In the latter part of 1921, he submitted such a project to several capitalists and dealers.   He was

---

1. The familiar ring of this name may result from the fact that an Elbridge Gerry was a signer of the Declaration of Independence, governor of Massachusetts and fifth vice-president of the United States.   It was under his administration as Governor of Massachusetts in 1812 that the state was divided into new voting districts.   The outline of the new districts was thought to resemble a salamander—critics referred to them as a "gerrymander."

unable to carry it through with any of them. Then, in January, 1922, with less than four months of the lease to run, he approached the defendant Salmon. The result was a new lease to the Midpoint Realty Company, which is owned and controlled by Salmon, a lease covering the whole tract, and involving a huge outlay. The term is to be twenty years, but successive covenants for renewal will extend it to a maximum of eighty years at the will of either party. The existing buildings may remain unchanged for seven years. They are then to be torn down, and a new building to cost $3,000,000 is to be placed upon the site. The rental, which under the Bristol lease was only $55,000, is to be from $350,000 to $475,000 for the properties so combined. Salmon personally guaranteed the performance by the lessee of the covenants of the new lease until such time as the new building had been completed and fully paid for.

The lease between Gerry and the Midpoint Realty Company was signed and delivered on January 25, 1922. Salmon had not told Meinhard anything about it. Whatever his motive may have been, he had kept the negotiations to himself. Meinhard was not informed even of the bare existence of a project. The first that he knew of it was in February when the lease was an accomplished fact. He then made demand on the defendants that the lease be held in trust as an asset of the venture, making offer upon the trial to share the personal obligations incidental to the guaranty. The demand was followed by refusal, and later by this suit. A referee gave judgment for the plaintiff, limiting the plaintiff's interest in the lease, however, to 25 per cent. The limitation was on the theory that the plaintiff's equity was to be restricted to one-half of so much of the value of the lease as was contributed or represented by the occupation of the Bristol site. Upon cross-appeals to the Appellate Division, the judgment was modified so as to enlarge the equitable interest to one-half of the whole lease. With this enlargement of plaintiff's interest, there went, of course, a corresponding enlargement of his attendant obligations. The case is now here on an appeal by the defendants. . . .

[The paragraph omitted here is the one quoted by Professor Scott in Section 1 of this chapter.]

The owner of the reversion, Mr. Gerry, had vainly striven to find a tenant who would favor his ambitious scheme of demolition and construction. Baffled in the search, he turned to the defendant Salmon in possession of the Bristol, the keystone of the project. He figured to himself beyond a doubt that the man in possession would prove a likely customer. To the eye of an observer, Salmon held the lease as owner in his own right, for himself and no one else. In fact he held it as a fiduciary, for himself and another, sharers in a common venture. If this fact had been proclaimed, if the lease by its terms had run in favor of a partnership, Mr. Gerry, we may fairly assume, would have laid before the partners, and not merely before one of them, his plan of reconstruction. The pre-emptive privilege, or, better, the pre-emptive opportunity, that was thus an incident of the enterprise, Salmon appropriated to himself in secrecy and silence. He might have warned Meinhard that the plan had been submitted, and that either would be free to compete for the award. If he had done this, we do not need to say whether he would have been under a duty, if successful in the competition, to hold the lease so acquired for the benefit of a venture then about to end, and thus prolong by indirection its responsibilities and duties. The trouble about his conduct is that he excluded his coadventurer from any chance to compete, from any chance to enjoy the opportunity for benefit that had come to him alone by virtue of his agency. This chance, if nothing more, he was under a duty to concede. The price of its denial is an extension of the trust at the option and for the benefit of the one whom he excluded.

No answer is it to say that the chance would have been of little value even if seasonably offered. Such a calculus of probabilities is beyond the science of the chancery. Salmon, the real estate operator, might have been preferred to Meinhard, the woolen merchant. On the other hand, Meinhard might have offered better terms, or reinforced his offer by alliance with the wealth of others. Perhaps he might even have persuaded the lessor to renew the Bristol lease alone, postponing for a time, in return for higher rentals, the improvement of adjoining lots. We know that even under the lease as made the time for the enlargement of the building was delayed for seven years. All these opportunities were cut away from him through another's intervention. . . .

Little profit will come from a dissection of the precedents. None precisely similar is cited in the briefs of counsel. What is similar in many, or so it seems to us, is the animating principle. Authority is, of course, abundant that one partner may not appropriate to his own use a renewal of a lease, though its term is to begin at the expiration of the partnership, Mitchell v. Reed, 61 N.Y. 123, 19 Am.Rep. 252; 84 N.Y. 556. The lease at hand with its many changes is not strictly a renewal. Even so, the standard of loyalty for those in trust relations is without the fixed divisions of a graduated scale. There is indeed a dictum in one of our decisions that a partner, though he may not renew a lease, may purchase the reversion if he acts openly and fairly. Anderson v. Lemon, 8 N.Y. 236; cf. White & Tudor, Leading Cases in Equity [9th ed.], vol. 2, p. 642; Bevan v. Webb, 1905, 1 Ch. 620; Griffith v. Owen, 1907, 1 Ch. 195, 204, 205. It is a dictum, and no more, for on the ground that he had acted slyly he was charged as a trustee. The holding is thus in favor of the conclusion that a purchase as well as a lease will succumb to the infection of secrecy and silence. Against the dictum in that case, moreover, may be set the opinion of Dwight, C., in Mitchell v. Reed, where there is a dictum to the contrary (61 N.Y. at p. 143). . . .

We have no thought to hold that Salmon was guilty of a conscious purpose to defraud. Very likely he assumed in all good faith that with the approaching end of the venture he might ignore his coadventurer and take the extension for himself. He had given to the enterprise time and labor as well as money. He had made it a success. Meinhard, who had given money, but neither time nor labor, had already been richly paid. There might seem to be something grasping in his insistence upon more. Such recriminations are not unusual when coadventurers fall out. They are not without their force if conduct is to be judged by the common standards of competitors. That is not to say that they have pertinency here. Salmon had put himself in a position in which thought of self was to be renounced, however hard the abnegation. He was much more than a coadventurer. He was managing coadventurer, Clegg v. Edmondson, 8 D.M. & G. 787, 807. For him and for those like him, the rule of undivided loyalty is relentless and supreme. Wendt v. Fischer, supra; Munson v. Syracuse, etc., R.R. Co., 103 N.Y. 58, 74, 8 N.E. 355. . . .

A question remains as to the form and extent of the equitable interest to be allotted to the plaintiff. The trust as declared has been held to attach to the lease which was in the name of the defendant corporation. We think it ought to attach at the option of the defendant Salmon to the shares of stock which were owned by him or were under his control. The difference may be important if the lessee shall wish to execute an assignment of the lease as it ought to be free to do with the consent of the lessor. On the other hand, an equal division of the shares might lead to other hardships. It might take away from Salmon the power of control and management which under the plan of the joint venture he was to have from first to last. The number of shares to be allotted to the plaintiff should, therefore, be reduced to such an extent as may be necessary to preserve to the defendant Salmon the expected measure of dominion. To that end an extra share should be added to his half. . . .

ANDREWS, J. (dissenting). . . . It may be stated generally that a partner may not for his own benefit secretly take a renewal of a firm lease to himself. Mitchell v. Reed, 61 N.Y. 123, 19 Am.Rep. 252. Yet under very exceptional circumstances this may not be wholly true. (W. & T. Leading Cas. In Equity [9th ed.] p. 657; Clegg v. Edmondson, 8 D.M. & G. 787, 807.) In the case of tenants in common there is still greater liberty. There is said to be a distinction between those holding under a will or through descent and those holding under independent conveyance. But even in the former situation the bare relationship is not conclusive. Matter of Biss, 1903, 2 Ch. 20. . . .

Where the trustee or the partner or the tenant in common, takes no new lease but buys the reversion in good faith a somewhat different question arises. Here is no direct appropriation of the expectancy of renewal. Here is no off-shoot of the original lease. We so held in Anderson v. Lemon (8 N.Y. 236), and although Judge Dwight casts some doubt on the rule in Mitchell v. Reed, it seems to have the support of authority. (W. & T. Leading Cas. in Equity, p. 650; Lindley on

Partnership [9th ed.], p. 396; Bevan v. Webb, 1905, 1 Ch. 620.) The issue then is whether actual fraud, dishonesty, unfairness is present in the transaction. If so, the purchaser may well be held as a trustee. (Anderson v. Lemon, cited above.)

With this view of the law I am of the opinion that the issue here is simple. Was the transaction in view of all the circumstances surrounding it unfair and inequitable? I reach this conclusion for two reasons. There was no general partnership, merely a joint venture for a limited object, to end at a fixed time. The new lease, covering additional property, containing many new and unusual terms and conditions, with a possible duration of eighty years, was more nearly the purchase of the reversion than the ordinary renewal with which the authorities were concerned. . . .

REFERENCES ON FIDUCIARY DUTIES OF PARTNERS

Weller v. Simenstad, 24 Wis.2d 1, 127 N.W.2d 794 (1964) (one member of medical partnership received additional income as executive of private hospital linked with the partnership, and as county coroner; he was obliged to account to partnership for former, but not for latter because copartner had acquiesced with knowledge of the latter source).

NOTE ON FIDUCIARY OBLIGATIONS AND CONFLICTS OF INTEREST IN PARTNERSHIPS

In the absence of a provision in the partnership agreement, fiduciary obligations among partners will be governed by UPA §§ 21, 22 and 43, which you should now review. The ULPA, in both its original form and the 1976 revision, is strangely silent on the subject of fiduciary obligations. The revised act provides for application of the UPA in "any case not provided for in this Act" (RULPA § 1105), and the original act provides for application of "the rules of law and equity, including the law merchant" (ULPA § 29). Under either of these formulations, it would appear that the general partner(s) has a fiduciary obligation to the firm, but does a limited partner have similar obligations? The answer is unclear, but it would appear that the limited scope of permissible activities of the limited partners would make it unlikely that they would occupy the role of fiduciary.

Within the last fifteen years, use of limited partnerships to acquire and develop real estate, and to pursue certain other ventures (such as oil and gas exploration, motion picture distribution, etc.) expanded dramatically, largely for tax-motivated reasons. Public sale of limited partnership interests has been extensive, and in most instances the general partner of such partnerships manages other partnerships. A major section of the offering documents for such limited partnership interests is the disclosure of conflicts of interest, which limited partners necessarily consent to as a condition of their investment.

Consider the following excerpts of a recent prospectus for a real estate limited partnership. What remains of the fiduciary obligation of the general partners?

CONFLICTS OF INTEREST

The interests of the General Partners and their Affiliates may conflict with the interests of the Limited Partners in various ways. These conflicts include:

1. *Receipt of Commissions, Fees and Other Compensation by the General Partners and their Affiliates.* Partnership transactions involving the purchase, sale and management of the Partnership's properties will result in the realization by the General Partners and their Affiliates of substantial commissions, fees, compensation and other income. The General Partners have absolute discretion with respect to such transactions. The agreements and arrangements, including those relating to compensation, between the Partnership and the General Partners and their Affiliates are not the result of arm's length negotiations. . . .

2. *Competition with the Partnership from Affiliates of the General Partners for the Time and Services of Common Officers and Directors.* The officers and directors of the Managing General Partner and of W_____ Management are also officers and/or directors of F_____ and of certain of its subsidiaries and are general partners of 22 partnerships which are Affiliates of F_____. They will also be officers, directors and/or partners of corporations and partnerships to be formed in the future by F_____ and its Affiliates. Conflicts may arise in the allocation of the time of such persons between the Partnership and these other corporations and partnerships. Each General Partner is only required to devote such time to the affairs of the Partnership as is necessary for the proper performance of its duties under the Partnership Agreement, and neither the officers and directors of the Managing General Partner nor the partners of L_____ are expected to devote their full time to the performance of such duties. . . .

3. *Competition by the Partnership with Affiliates for Properties.* A substantial number of other partnerships organized to invest in a specific real property or properties are managed or advised by F_____ and its Affiliates. . . . F_____ is planning to form and to manage or advise, directly or through Affiliates, additional real estate investment partnerships or other entities, both private and public, some of which may have the same investment objectives as the Partnership. F_____ and its Affiliates, including the General Partners, may also purchase properties for their own accounts and will not give the Partnership a right of first refusal to purchase such properties unless they determine that such properties meet the investment objectives of the Partnership and all of the Net Proceeds have not already been invested. . . .

If an entity which is managed or advised by the General Partners or their Affiliates is doing well and another is doing poorly, the General Partners and such Affiliates may have an incentive to assign desirable properties to the entity performing poorly in order to equalize performance.

The interests of the Partnership and the interests of Affiliates of the General Partners may also conflict when the Partnership attempts to sell or lease its properties.

Affiliates of the General Partners may acquire properties adjacent to the Partnership's properties. It is possible that the value of such properties may be enhanced by their proximity to the Partnership's properties or that such properties may be in competition with the Partnership's properties for prospective tenants.

4. *Property Management Fee.* W_____ Management, an Affiliate of the General Partners, will serve as manager of the Partnership's properties and receive a fee with respect to each property managed by it . . . payable whether or not a property is generating Cash Available for Distribution or is otherwise held on a basis advantageous to the Partnership. Accordingly, a conflict of interest could arise if the retention of a property were advantageous to W_____ Management but detrimental to the Partnership. . . . in the future W_____ Management will serve as manager of properties owned or managed by other Affiliates of F_____.

5. *Participation by an Affiliate as Selling Agent of the Offering.* W_____ Securities Co., Inc., a broker-dealer which is a wholly owned subsidiary of F_____, will act as Selling Agent in connection with the offering. Any review of the structure, formation or operation of the Partnership performed by W_____ Securities Co., Inc. cannot be considered to represent an independent review, and such review may not be as meaningful as a review conducted by a nonaffiliated Selling Agent. . . .

6. *Lack of Separate Representation.* The Partnership and its Limited Partners and the General Partners and their Affiliates, except for the Selling Agent, are not represented by separate counsel. . . .

PATIENT CARE SERVICES, S.C. v. SEGAL
Appellate Court of Illinois, 1975.
32 Ill.App.3d 1021, 337 N.E.2d 471.

McNAMARA, JUSTICE:

Plaintiffs, Patient Care Services, S.C. (hereinafter referred to as Patient Care), an Illinois professional service corporation, and David A. Martinez, M.D., one of its two officers and directors, filed a three count complaint in the circuit court of Cook County against Medical Services, S.C. (hereinafter referred to as Medical Services), another Illinois professional service corporation, Marshall B. Segal, an officer and director of both of the above-named corporations, and Little Company of Mary Hospital, an Illinois corporation (hereinafter referred to as the hospital). The first count, sounding in equity, alleged that Segal violated his fiduciary duties owed to Patient Care by setting up a competing corporation while an officer and director of Patient Care and by seizing its business asset, requiring the court to impose a constructive trust upon the corporate funds of Segal and Medical Services and to order an accounting.

.   .   .

At the conclusion of all the evidence, the trial court, as trier of fact, entered judgment for defendants.

.   .   .

We find the pertinent facts to be as follows. Both Martinez and Segal are licensed doctors in Illinois. Segal additionally is a licensed attorney in Wisconsin and California. During the latter part of 1970 and the early months of 1971, Martinez worked part time in the emergency room of Little Company of Mary Hospital in Evergreen Park, Illinois. During this time the acting administrator of the hospital approached him and inquired whether he would be interested in reorganizing the hospital's out-patient clinic and in assuming some staff responsibilities at the hospital. In April, 1971, Martinez met Segal while both were working at another hospital. Martinez subsequently discussed the proposition offered to him, and the two doctors outlined a program of comprehensive medical planning services which they would offer the hospital. A professional service corporation would be set up to handle the program. . . .

The parties orally agreed on the basic elements of the proposal and the program commenced on July 1. Patient Care was incorporated by Segal and Martinez in the latter part of June or beginning of July, 1971. Each doctor owned 50% of the corporate shares and became a director of the corporation. Segal was named president and Martinez secretary-treasurer.

.   .   .

The hospital agreed to pay Patient Care $22.50 an hour for each hour a doctor employed by Patient Care worked in the emergency room. Additionally the hospital paid Patient Care $3800 a month for the health care planning preparation. Patient Care, in turn, paid the doctors employed by it $15 per hour for each hour of work in the emergency room, except for the two principals, who would each receive $21 per hour for this work. Segal and Martinez also drew monthly salaries of $4,000 each, and, subsequent to the commencement of their operation, the two principals agreed that the corporation would pay $185 per day to whichever one of them was in Chicago while the other was outside the city. During the year of its services at the hospital Segal received approximately $92,000 and Martinez $48,000.

Martinez testified that he made it clear in June, 1971, that he had been accepted at Harvard University some months earlier as a candidate for an advanced degree in public policy and that he would be in residence at Harvard for the first year of Patient Care's operation at the hospital. However, he stated at that time that he would commute to Chicago every second or third weekend as studies permitted.

. . .

In November Segal, bearing most of the administrative burden with Martinez away at Harvard, told Martinez he was unhappy with their financial arrangement. At the time the principals were drawing a monthly salary and getting paid for work either one performed in the emergency room. Martinez said that he eventually agreed on January 4, 1972, to the aforementioned $185 per day plan. The agreement was made retroactive to July 1, 1971.

. . .

Martinez asserted that Segal's unhappiness continued even after execution of their agreement. In Martinez' opinion Segal's dissatisfaction stemmed from Segal's desire for additional compensation, from Martinez' absence from the city, and from the length of time it was taking Martinez to develop the planning services. On February 21, 1972, Segal wrote Martinez that he had concluded that their association had reached an impasse requiring its termination. Segal further stated that the corporation's arrangement with the hospital would end on June 30, 1972, and that unless Martinez agreed to sell his interest in the company Segal would take steps to dissolve it.

. . .

The duties that an officer or director owe to his corporation are so well established as to need no citation of authority to support them. They include the requirement of undivided, unselfish, and unqualified loyalty, of unceasing effort never to profit personally at corporate expense, of unbending disavowal of any opportunity which would permit the fiduciary's private interests to clash with those of his corporation. These duties are rooted not only in elementary rules of equity but also in business morality and public policy.

. . .

It therefore follows that an officer or director who strays from faithful adherence to these precepts and actively engages in a rival or competing business to the detriment of his corporation must answer to the corporation for the injury sustained.

. . .

It must first be recognized that at least initially the finalization of a written contract to cover the first year of its operation of services at the hospital as well as the preparation and execution of a new one to embrace succeeding years constituted a corporate opportunity for Patient Care. Patient Care was organized for the purpose of providing comprehensive health services to a hospital. For the first year of its incorporation it was engaged in furnishing those services to the hospital, and the hospital was satisfied with those services. Obviously the very nature of its business necessitated a continuation and development of this relationship.

. . .

When such a corporate opportunity exists it is inherent in an officer's or director's fiduciary obligations to refrain from purchasing property for himself in which the corporation has an interest, actual or expectant, or which may hinder or defeat the plans and purposes of the corporation in the carrying on or development of the legitimate business for which it was created.

. . .

Viewed in this light, this court finds it indisputable that Segal blatantly violated those duties of loyalty and trust which he owed to Patient Care. While an officer and director of that corporation, he helped set up and subsequently took over control of a different corporation organized to perform the very similar, if not identical, services Patient Care was organized to perform. Based upon various disagreements that he had with Martinez, his co-officer and co-director of Patient Care, Segal wrote Martinez in February, 1972, and announced his intention to terminate his association with Martinez. Segal testified that he was familiar with the contents of a letter written soon thereafter by his personally retained attorney to Patient Care's attorney that Segal was intent on negotiating on his behalf to provide comprehensive medical services to the same hospital which was then under contract to Patient Care. Segal further admitted that it was around this time that he ceased any efforts to persuade the hospital to finalize a contract for the current and subsequent years with Patient Care. At the time Segal knew that Patient Care's contract with the hospital was the corporation's sole asset. When the first year of Patient Care's contract with the hospital concluded, Segal's new corporation, Medical Services, took over on a month-to-month basis. At the time of trial, almost a year after Medical Services had begun work at the hospital, Segal remained an officer and director of Patient Care.

The recital of these facts, all admitted by Segal, reveal a violation of his duties and loyalty to Patient Care. They not only signify a course of conduct bent on seizing his corporation's business but also evidence a willingness to destroy his corporation in the process.

Segal's response is to point out alleged breaches of contract by Martinez and to argue that any continuation of his relationship with Martinez would have resulted in his peonage to Patient Care. The disagreements with Martinez would still not condone the actions taken by Segal vis-a-vis Patient Care. If Segal felt undercompensated or taken advantage of, he could have resigned from Patient Care.

. . .

If he felt Martinez breached any contract with him and/or Patient Care, the proper recourse was, and is, for Segal to sue in the courts for breach of contract.

. . .

Defendants' case authority holding that a corporate officer or director violates his fiduciary duty to his corporation by failing to inform the corporation of a business opportunity he seized as his own has no applicability to the present case. The cases cannot be inverted to hold that once he gives notice he is ipso facto free to contest with the corporation the business opportunity.

. . .

In any event, it is clear that the determination of good faith rests upon the existence of many factors of which disclosure is only one.

. . .

Disclosure would appear to have more significant weight in initially discovering whether a corporation would be interested in expanding its activities into an area which would appear to be profitable and naturally extensive.

. . .

However, where an officer or director, as here, desires to seize the only asset his financially solvent corporation presently possesses, when the corporation has manifested its desire to retain it, and when the corporation obviously needs to retain it, the mere fact that such officer and director has announced his intention in advance to throw down the gauntlet and do battle with his corporation over the opportunity will not constitute good faith.

. . .

We note in passing that it makes no difference whether or not the corporate opportunity seizure took place at Segal's personal behest or through the vehicle of Segal's corporation.

. . .

The proper remedy is for the court to impress a constructive trust on defendants and to order an accounting.

. . .

Judgment reversed and remanded with directions.

DEMPSEY and MEJDA, JJ., concur.

FLIEGLER v. LAWRENCE

Supreme Court of Delaware, 1976.
361 A.2d 218.

McNEILLY, JUSTICE:

In this shareholder derivative action brought on behalf of Agau Mines, Inc., a Delaware corporation, (Agau) against its officers and directors and United States Antimony Corporation, a Montana corporation (USAC), we are asked to decide whether the individual defendants, in their capacity as directors and officers of both corporations, wrongfully usurped a corporate opportunity belonging to Agau, and whether all defendants wrongfully profited by causing Agau to exercise an option to purchase that opportunity. The Court of Chancery found in favor of the defendants on both issues. (1974). Reference is made to that opinion for a full statement of the facts; what follows here is but a brief resume of the events giving rise to this litigation.

I

In November, 1969, defendant, John C. Lawrence (then president of Agau, a publicly held corporation engaged in a dual-phased gold and silver exploratory venture) in his individual capacity, acquired certain antimony properties under a lease-option for $60,000. Lawrence offered to transfer the properties, which were then "a raw prospect", to Agau, but after consulting with other members of Agau's board of directors, he and they agreed that the corporation's legal and financial position would not permit acquisition and development of the properties at that time. Thus, it was decided to transfer the properties to USAC, (a closely held corporation formed just for this purpose and a majority of whose stock was owned by the individual defendants) where capital necessary for development of the properties could be raised without risk to Agau through the sale of USAC stock; it was also decided to grant Agau a long-term option to acquire USAC if the properties proved to be of commercial value.

In January, 1970, the option agreement was executed by Agau and USAC. Upon its exercise and approval by Agau shareholders, Agau was to deliver 800,000 shares of its restricted investment stock for all authorized and issued shares of USAC. The exchange was calculated on the basis of reimbursement to USAC and its shareholders for their costs in developing the properties to a point where it could be ascertained if they had commercial value. . . .

[USAC was unable to raise development funds by selling its own shares, and so Agau gave USAC warrants for Agau shares, which USAC pledged to secure a development loan. Agau also loaned some of its personnel to USAC for development purposes. By October 1970, the property had proved to be valuable, and Agau exercised its option by issuing 800,000 of its shares to the defendant officers and directors in exchange for shares of USAC. The plaintiff filed this suit on behalf of Agau to recover the 800,000 shares and for an accounting.]

II

The Vice-Chancellor determined that the chance to acquire the antimony claims was a corporate opportunity which should have been (and was) offered to Agau, but because the corporation was not in a position, either financially or legally, to accept the opportunity at that time, the individual defendants were entitled to acquire it for themselves after Agau rejected it.

We agree with these conclusions for the reasons stated by the Vice-Chancellor, which are based on settled Delaware law. *Guth v. Loft, Inc.*, Del.Supr., 23 Del.Ch. 255, 5 A.2d 503 (1939). Accordingly, Agau was not entitled to the properties without consideration.

III

Plaintiff contends that because the individual defendants personally profited through the use of Agau's resources, *viz.,* personnel (primarily Lawrence) to develop the USAC properties and stock purchase warrants to secure a $300,000, indebtedness (incurred by USAC because it could not raise sufficient capital through sale of stock), they must be compelled to account to Agau for that profit. This argument presupposes that defendants did in fact so misuse corporate assets; however, the record reveals substantial evidence to support the Vice-Chancellor's conclusion that there was no misuse of either Agau personnel or warrants. Issuance of the warrants in fact enhanced the value of Agau's option at a time when there was reason to believe that USAC's antimony properties had a "considerable potential", and plaintiff did not prove that alleged use of Agau's personnel and equipment was detrimental to the corporation.

Nevertheless, our inquiry cannot stop here, for it is clear that the individual defendants stood on both sides of the transaction in implementing and fixing the terms of the option agreement. Accordingly, the burden is upon them to demonstrate its intrinsic fairness. *Johnston v. Greene,* Del.Supr., 35 Del.Ch. 479, 121 A.2d 919 (1956) . . . We agree with the Vice-Chancellor that the record reveals no bad faith on the part of the individual defendants. But that is not determinative. The issue is where [sic] the 800,000 restricted investment shares of Agau stock, objectively, was a fair price for Agau to pay for USAC as a wholly-owned subsidiary.

A.

Preliminarily, defendants argue that they have been relieved of the burden of proving fairness by reason of shareholder ratification of the Board's decision to exercise the option. . . .

. . .

The purported ratification by the Agau shareholders would not affect the burden of proof in this case because the majority of shares voted in favor of exercising the option were cast by defendants in their capacity as Agau shareholders. . . .

Nor do we believe the Legislature intended a contrary policy and rule to prevail by enacting 8 Del.C. § 144, which provides, in part:

(a) No contract or transaction between a corporation and 1 or more of its directors or officers, or between a corporation and any other corporation, partnership, association, or other organization in which 1 or more of its directors or officers, are directors or officers, or have a financial interest, shall be void or voidable solely for this reason, or solely because the director or officer is present at or participates in the meeting of the board or committee which authorizes the contract or transaction, or solely because his or their votes are counted for such purpose, if:

(1) The material facts as to his relationship or interest and as to the contract or transaction are disclosed or are known to the board of directors or the committee, and the board or committee in good faith authorizes the contract or transaction by the affirmative votes of a majority of the disinterested directors, even though the disinterested directors be less than a quorum; or

(2) The material facts as [to] his relationship or interest and as to the contract or transaction are disclosed or are known to the shareholders entitled to vote thereon, and the contract or transaction is specifically approved in good faith by vote of the shareholders; or

(3) The contract or transaction is fair as to the corporation as of the time it is authorized, approved or ratified, by the board of directors, a committee, or the shareholders.

Defendants argue that the transaction here in question is protected by § 144(a)(2), which, they contend, does not require that ratifying shareholders be "disinterested" or "independent"; nor, they argue, is there warrant for reading such a requirement into the statute. See Folk, *The Delaware General Corporation Law—A Commentary and Analysis* (1972), pp. 85–86. We do not read the statute as providing the broad immunity for which defendants contend. It merely removes an "interested director" cloud when its terms are met and provides against invalidation of an agreement "solely" because such a director or officer is involved. Nothing in the statute sanctions unfairness to Agau or removes the transaction from judicial scrutiny.

B.

Turning to the transaction itself, we note at the outset that from the time the option arrangement was conceived until the time it was implemented, there occurred marked changes in several of the factors which formed the basis for the terms of the exchange. . . .

On the basis of these changed conditions and in light of the fact that the exchange price was originally calculated simply to reimburse the USAC shareholders for their costs, plaintiff argues that the issuance of 800,000 shares of Agau stock, having a market value of at least 1.2 million dollars, to acquire a corporation in which only $83,000 in cash had been invested, and whose property was subject to loans of $300,000, is patently unfair.

. . .

Viewing the two corporations as going concerns from the standpoint of their current and potential operational status presents a clearer and more realistic picture not only of what Agau gave up, but of what it received.

Agau was organized solely for the purpose of developing and exploring certain properties for potentially mineable gold and silver ore. The bulk of its cash, raised through a public offering, had been expended in "Phase I" exploration of the properties, which failed to establish a commercial ore body, although it did reveal "interesting" zones of mineralization which indicated to Lawrence that "Phase II" development and exploration might eventually be desirable. However, plans for further development had been temporarily abandoned as being economically unfeasible due to Agau's lack of sufficient funds to adequately explore the properties, as well as to the falling market price of silver. It further appears that other than a few outstanding unexercised stock purchase warrants, Agau did not have any ready sources of capital. Thus, as the Vice-Chancellor found, had the option not been exercised, Agau might well have gone out of business.

By comparison, the record shows that USAC, while still considered to be in the exploratory and development stage, could reasonably be expected to produce substantial profits. At the time in question, the corporation had established a sizeable commercial ore body, had proven markets for its product, and was in the midst of constructing a major ore separation facility expected to produce a high grade ore concentrate for market.

. . .

Considering all of the above factors, we conclude that defendants have proven the intrinsic fairness of the transaction. Agau received properties which by themselves were clearly of substantial value. But more importantly, it received a promising, potentially self-financing and profit generating enterprise with proven markets and commercial capability which could well be expected to provide Agau at the very least with the cash it sorely needed to undertake further exploration and development of its own properties if not to stay in existence. For those reasons, we believe that the interest given to the USAC shareholders was a fair price to pay. Accordingly, we have no doubt but that this transaction was one which at that time would have commended itself to an independent corporation in Agau's position.

Affirmed.

NOTE ON THE CORPORATE OPPORTUNITY DOCTRINE

The classical situation involving corporate opportunity is exemplified in Guth v. Loft, 23 Del.Ch. 255, 5 A.2d 503 (1939). Guth was president of Loft, Inc. which operated a chain of retail candy and soft drink stores; he became interested in reducing the tribute paid to the Coca-Cola Company for its syrups. Through his position in Loft, he became acquainted with the possibility of buying the formulas and processes of Pepsi-Cola, which he proceeded to do, using in part funds of Loft. He then formed a new Pepsi-Cola Company, with no funds of its own, to which he supplied the facilities, materials, credit, executives and employees of Loft, mostly without any payment. When Pepsi-Cola became a financial success, Guth denied that Loft had any interest in it.

The court ordered him to transfer his shares in Pepsi-Cola (now worth millions of dollars) to Loft.

An interesting contrast with Fliegler v. Lawrence, supra, is presented by Irving Trust Co. v. Deutsch, 73 F.2d 121 (2d Cir.1934), cert. denied 294 U.S. 708, 55 S.Ct. 405, 79 L.Ed. 1243 (1935). Acoustic Products Company contracted to buy shares in another company, but was unable to raise the money to complete the purchase, whereupon directors of Acoustic raised the necessary money and bought the shares for themselves. The court concluded that the directors were accountable because their decision not to complete the purchase on behalf of Acoustic was infected with a conflict of interest.

REFERENCES ON CORPORATE OPPORTUNITY

Walker, Legal Handles Used to Open or Close the Corporate Opportunity Door (1961) 56 Nw.Univ.L.Rev. 608. (A good basic introduction to the general area).

Orchard v. Covelli, 590 F.Supp. 1548 (W.D.Pa.1984), appeal dismissed 791 F.2d 916, 920 (3d Cir.1986) (majority shareholder of franchised restaurant did not violate duty to minority holder by taking renewal franchise for a corporation from which minority was excluded, when franchisor objected to renewing franchise to corporation that included minority).

Lash v. Lash Furniture Co., 130 Vt. 517, 296 A.2d 207 (1972) (director who had voted against corporation's acquisition of shares in it, and who later bought the shares for himself, was bound to hold them in trust for the corporation).

Am. Empire Life Insurance Co. v. McAdory, 319 So.2d 237 (Miss.1975) (three directors of life insurance company bought a judgment which was a lien against land of their company; although life insurance company had paid amount of judgment to a third party affiliated with directors, judgment remained unsatisfied and directors proceeded to execute; directors enjoined and ordered to hold judgment in trust for company).

Hartung v. Architects Hartung/Odle/Burke Inc., 157 Ind.App. 546, 301 N.E.2d 240 (1973) (former proprietor of architectural business incorporated self and employees; then resigned, and took over offices and contracts for himself; held liable for breach of fiduciary duty to corporation and to the other principals in it).

Johnston v. Greene, 35 Del.Ch. 479, 121 A.2d 919 (1956) (dominant shareholder of parent company did not violate fiduciary duty to subsidiary by withholding from it ownership of patents on products manufactured by subsidiary, when shareholder's ownership was not derived from relationship with subsidiary).

NOTE ON VALIDITY OF TRANSACTIONS IN WHICH DIRECTORS HAVE CONFLICTING INTERESTS

In addition to the question of what is a corporate opportunity, the *Fliegler* case, supra, raises the question whether contracts approved by corporate directors are valid when one or more of the directors have conflicting interests in regard to them. The Delaware statute quoted in that decision is fairly representative of state corporation statutes on the subject. The following section from the 1984 revision of the MBCA is a slightly more elaborate statement of the same principles.

The California revision of 1975 departed from the pattern in formally requiring that when validation is based on a vote of shareholders, the votes cast by interested director-shareholders be excluded, and that when validation is based on a vote of disinterested directors, the transaction be "just and reasonable." Cal.Gen.Corp.L. § 310.

The *Fliegler* case suggests, but does not answer, the further question, whether a corporation's decision to relinquish a potential opportunity is to be judged on the same basis as a transaction with a director or a person affiliated with the director.

MODEL BUSINESS CORPORATION ACT

Committee on Corporate Laws of the Section on Corporation, Banking and Business Law of the American Bar Association, 1984.

§ 8.31 Director Conflict of Interest

(a) A conflict of interest transaction is a transaction with the corporation in which a director of the corporation has a direct or indirect interest. A conflict of interest transaction is not voidable by the corporation solely because of the director's interest in the transaction if any one of the following is true:

(1) the material facts of the transaction and the director's interest were disclosed or known to the board of directors or a committee of the board of directors and the board of directors or committee authorized, approved, or ratified the transaction;

(2) the material facts of the transaction and the director's interest were disclosed or known to the shareholders entitled to vote and they authorized, approved, or ratified the transaction; or

(3) the transaction was fair to the corporation.

(b) For purposes of this section, a director of the corporation has an indirect interest in a transaction if (1) another entity in which he has a material financial interest or in which he is a general partner is a party to the transaction or (2) another entity of which he is a director, officer, or trustee is a party to the transaction and the transaction is or should be considered by the board of directors of the corporation.

(c) For purposes of subsection (a)(1), a conflict of interest transaction is authorized, approved, or ratified if it receives the affirmative vote of a majority of the directors on the board of directors (or on the committee) who have no direct or indirect interest in the transaction, but a transaction may not be authorized, approved, or ratified under this section by a single director. If a majority of the directors who have no direct or indirect interest in the transaction vote to authorize, approve, or ratify the transaction, a quorum is present for the purpose of taking action under this section. The presence of, or a vote cast by, a director with a direct or indirect interest in the transaction does not affect the validity of any action taken under subsection (a)(1) if the transaction is otherwise authorized, approved, or ratified as provided in that subsection.

(d) For purposes of subsection (a)(2), a conflict of interest transaction is authorized, approved, or ratified if it receives the vote of a majority of the shares entitled to be counted under this subsection. Shares owned by or voted under the control of a director who has a direct or indirect interest in the transaction, and shares owned by or voted under the control of an entity described in subsection (b)(1), may not be counted in a vote of shareholders to determine whether to authorize, approve, or ratify a conflict of interest transaction under subsection (a)(2). The vote of those shares, however, is counted in determining whether the transaction is approved under other sections of this Act. A majority of the shares, whether or not present, that are entitled to be counted in a vote on the transaction under this subsection constitutes a quorum for the purpose of taking action under this section.

REFERENCES

Marsh, Are Directors Trustees? Conflict of interest and corporate morality (1966) 22 Bus.Law. 35 (a part of a symposium on Duties and Liabilities of Directors—a good overview with extensive citations).

Note, The Fairness Test of Corporate Contracts with Interested Directors, (1948) 61 Harv.L.Rev. 335 (a standard analysis that has value—good review of early cases).

Non-profit corporations:

Stern v. Lucy Webb Hayes National School for Deaconesses and Missionaries, 381 F.Supp. 1003 (D.C.D.C.1974), noted (1975) 24 Catholic L.Rev. 657 (directors of charitable non-profit corporation held to same fiduciary duties as directors of business corporation).

NOTE: CORPORATE CONFLICTS OF INTEREST IN EUROPEAN LAW

French and German laws reveal a concern that is at least as acute as in the US about conflicts between the interests of corporate executives and of corporate investors, but the relevant legal provisions differentiate sharply between "public companies," whose shares are typically traded on stock exchanges, and "private companies," whose shares cannot be so traded, and are usually held by smaller numbers of investors.[1]

With regard to public companies, French and German regimes expressly nullify contracts between executives and their corporations which are not approved in some manner designed to eliminate conflicts of interest. This treatment contrasts with that of the MBCA which expressly validates contracts approved in a proper manner, but leaves open the validity of contracts that are not so approved.

The European procedures for validating dealings between executives and public corporations vary with the type of governing structure. In Germany, public companies are required to have a supervisory council (*Aufsichtsrat*) from which executives are excluded, and which hires and fires executives. In France, public companies may voluntarily have a similar council (called *conseil de surveillance*). In public companies that have a supervisory council, dealings between executives and the corporation must be conducted by the supervisory council.[2]

---

1. In the literature of comparative law, the "public companies" are commonly designated more precisely as "negotiable share companies," or "merchantable share companies." In French and German, their names are respectively *société anonyme* and *Aktiengesellschaft*. The companies that we here call "private" are more specifically designated "limited liability compa-nies," which is a literal translation of the French *société a responsabilité limitée* and the German (Gesellschaft mit beschränkter Haftung).

2. French Law on Commercial Companies, art. 143 (CCH, 1971); German Stock Corporation Law § 112 (Mueller/Galbraith, 1976).

French public companies that have not chosen to install a supervisory council must have a board of directors which, as in the US, may include executives. In these companies, contracts between executives and the company are subjected to a four-step routine. They must be approved by disinterested members of the board, reported to the independent auditors, reported by the auditors to the shareholders, and approved by the shareholders without counting the votes of the interested executives.[3]

In private companies, no special procedures are prescribed for the validation of contracts between the company and the managers. If managers abuse their powers, they are subject to the general principles mentioned earlier (pp. 334–335) regarding unfaithful agents. French law reinforces these principles of civil liability with criminal prohibitions directed expressly at corporate executives. Public company executives are liable to fines and imprisonment if they, "acting in bad faith, use the company's property or credit in a manner which they know to be contrary to the interests of the corporation, for personal ends . . . ."[4] A parallel provision applies to managers of private companies.[5]

The German Criminal Code contains a provision that prescribes fine and imprisonment for anyone who abuses a position of trust to injure the property interests of someone else,[6] but we have not found evidence of its being applied to contracts involving conflicts of interest.

REFERENCES

Warren, Comparative View of the New French Approach to Corporate Conflict of Interest (1969) 24 Bus.Law. 809.

Cowan, Company Directors: Their Powers, Duties and Responsibilities (1967) 2 Tasm. U.L.Rev. 361.

Prentice, Director's Fiduciary Duties—The Corporate Opportunity Doctrine (1972) 50 Canadian Bar Rev. 623.

NOTE ON DUAL REPRESENTATION

An unusual case of dual representation is Glenn v. Rice, 174 Cal. 269, 162 P. 1020 (1917), where the agent was not allowed to collect his commission even from the principal who knew of the double agency. Obviously this resulted in a windfall for the principal. The court explained:

"The authorities, with practical unanimity, declare that if an agent is engaged by both parties to effect a sale of property from one to the other, or an exchange between them, not as a mere middleman to bring them together, but actively in inducing each to make the trade, he cannot recover compensation from either party, unless both parties knew of the double agency at the time of the transaction. The reason for the rule is that he thereby puts himself in a position where his duty to one conflicts with his duty to the other, where his own interests tempt him to be unfaithful to both principals, a position which is against sound public policy and good morals. His contract for compensation being thus tainted, the law will not permit him to enforce it against either party. It is no answer to this objection to say that he did, in the particular case, act fairly and honorably to both. The infirmity of his contract does not arise from

---

3. French Law on Commercial Companies, supra, arts. 101–103.

4. French Law on Commercial Companies, supra, art. 437(3).

5. Id., art. 425(4).

6. Strafgesetzbuch § 266.

his actual conduct in the given case, but from the policy of the law, which will not allow a man to gain anything from a relation so conducive to bad faith and double dealing. And the fact that the party whom he sues was aware of the double agency and of the payment, or agreement to pay, compensation by the other party, and consented thereto, does not entitle him to recover. He must show knowledge by both parties. One party might willingly consent, believing that the advantage would accrue to him, to the detriment of the other. The law will not tolerate such an arrangement, except with the knowledge and consent of both, and will enter into no inquiry to determine whether or not the particular negotiation was fairly conducted by the agent. It leaves him as it finds him, affording him no relief. [Citing cases.]"

The rule against dual representation does not, however, condemn all undisclosed assistance to the opposite party. In Sessions v. Pacific Improvement Co., 57 Cal.App. 1, 206 P. 653 (1922), the vendor had succeeded, with the plaintiff's aid, in selling 156 acres of waterfront to the United States Shipping Board Emergency Fleet Corporation for $1,000,000. (This was in World War I.) Pending the transaction, the plaintiff took a job with the fleet corporation as engineering adviser. The court held that his employment was not irreconcilable with his position as agent for the seller. Among the reasons given were the following:

"It would thus appear that plaintiff's assistance furthered rather than dissuaded action, and there is nothing in the evidence to indicate the slightest breach of plaintiff's duty. On the contrary, he seems at all times to have been zealous in advancing the true interests of defendants. And in justice to defendants it should be said that there is nothing on their part suggestive of even a remote desire to conceal anything affecting the suitability of the property for the intended use.

"If there were known disadvantages of which the government had not been apprised, then fairness and good faith counseled full disclosure. At no time can a broker with a due sense of the ethics of his calling justify himself in deliberately withholding from a purchaser material facts known to the broker and not known or visible to the purchaser; nor would he rightly serve his principal in so doing. There is no breach of trust toward his employer in revealing the truth, and the law will not penalize commendable candor by forfeiting the broker's commission. The broker is employed to deal honestly. Evidence of 'honesty, truthfulness, and a good reputation' is a prerequisite to the issuance of a real estate license, and dishonest dealing furnishes a ground for revocation of a license. Willful concealment or suppression of material facts is sheer dishonesty; and every broker owes it to the seller as well as to the buyer, and none the less to himself, to oppose and shun everything smacking of fraud, sharp practice, or bad faith."

REFERENCES

Permissible dual representation:

Seigel v. Cambridge-Wendell Realty Co., 323 Mass. 598, 83 N.E.2d 262 (1949) (broker recovers commission despite dual representation, where buyer and seller knew and acquiesced).

Faultersack v. Clintonville Sales Corp., 253 Wis. 432, 34 N.W.2d 682 (1948) (auctioneer has duty to disclose to seller arrangements he has made to finance a bidder); comment, 33 Marq.L.Rev. 58.

Bell v. Strauch, 40 Tenn.App. 384, 292 S.W.2d 59 (1955) (broker who arranged exchange of real estate entitled to commissions from each party as he had fully disclosed his relationship to each).

Improper dual representation:

Sprathen, Harrington, Thomas, Inc. v. Hawn, 116 Ga.App. 175, 156 S.E.2d 402 (1967) (fee denied a mortgage banking concern acting as agent of borrowers from an insurance company; court held it violated its fiduciary duty in not informing borrowers that they were also to receive a fee from the insurance company).

Concurrent representation of competitors:

Hoffman v. M. Schwartz, Inc., 137 N.Y.S.2d 232 (1954) (manufacturer's representative was entitled to commissions despite concurrent representation of competing manufacturers).

Foley v. Mathias, 211 Iowa 160, 233 N.W. 106, 71 A.L.R. 696 (1930) (broker did not violate duty to one landlord by simultaneously representing another landlord in competition to rent to same prospective tenant).

SECTION 4. REMEDIES FOR BREACHES OF FIDUCIARY DUTY

Preceding cases have illustrated the most frequent remedies for breach of fiduciary duty—the loss of a right to compensation, and the imposition of a constructive trust. In this section we present a case on the cumulation of remedies, and a pair of cases that are peculiarly applicable to lawyers—the exclusion from some aspect of practice.

TARNOWSKI v. RESOP

Minnesota Supreme Court, 1952.
236 Minn. 33, 51 N.W.2d 801.
Comment: 37 Minn.L.Rev. 402.

KNUTSON, JUSTICE. Plaintiff desired to make a business investment. He engaged defendant as his agent to investigate and negotiate for the purchase of a route of coin-operated music machines. On June 2, 1947, relying upon the advice of defendant and the investigation he had made, plaintiff purchased such a business from Phillip Loechler and Lyle Mayer of Rochester, Minnesota, who will be referred to hereinafter as the sellers. The business was located at LaCrosse, Wisconsin, and throughout the surrounding territory. Plaintiff alleges that defendant represented to him that he had made a thorough investigation of the route; that it had 75 locations in operation; that one or more machines were at each location; that the equipment at each location was not more than six months old; and that the gross income from all locations amounted to more than $3,000 per month. As a matter of fact, defendant had made only a superficial investigation and had investigated only five of the locations. Other than that, he had adopted false representations of the sellers as to the other locations and had passed them on to plaintiff as his own. Plaintiff was to pay $30,620 for the business. He paid $11,000 down. About six weeks after the purchase, plaintiff discovered that the representations made to him by defendant were false, in that there were not more than 47 locations; that at some of the locations there were no machines and at others there were machines more than six months old, some of them being seven years old; and that the gross income was far less than $3,000 per month. Upon discovering the falsity of defendant's representations and those of the sellers, plaintiff rescinded the sale. He offered to return what he had received, and he demanded the return of his money. The sellers refused to comply, and he brought suit against them in the district court of Olmsted county. The action was tried, resulting in a verdict of $10,000 for plaintiff. Thereafter, the sellers paid plaintiff $9,500, after which the action was dismissed with prejudice pursuant to a stipulation of the parties.

In this action, brought in Hennepin County, plaintiff alleges that defendant, while acting as agent for him, collected a secret commission from the sellers for consummating the sale, which plaintiff seeks to recover under his first cause of action. In his second cause of action, he seeks to recover damages for (1) losses suffered in operating the route prior to rescission; (2) loss of time devoted to operation; (3) expenses in connection with rescission of the sale and his investigation in connection therewith; (4) nontaxable expenses in connection with prosecution of the suit against the sellers; and (5) attorneys' fees in connection with the suit. The case was tried to a jury, and plaintiff recovered a verdict of $5,200. This appeal is from the judgment entered pursuant thereto.

Defendant contends that after recovery of a verdict by plaintiff in his action for rescission against the sellers he cannot maintain this action against defendant. Principally, defendant argues that recovery in the action against the sellers is a bar to this action for the following reasons: (1) That plaintiff has elected one of alternative remedies and cannot thereafter pursue another; (2) that successful pursuit of one remedy constitutes a bar to another remedy for the same wrong, even though the outcome of the first action did not make plaintiff whole in point of actual loss; (3) that the satisfied verdict in the rescission case is a bar; and (4) that defendant and the sellers were joint tort-feasors, and the discharge of one discharged them all.

With respect to plaintiff's first cause of action, the principle that all profits made by an agent in the course of an agency belong to the principal, whether they are the fruits of performance or the violation of an agent's duty, is firmly established and universally recognized. Smitz v. Leopold, 51 Minn. 455, 53 N.W. 719. . . .

It matters not that the principal has suffered no damage or even that the transaction has been profitable to him. Raymond Farmers Elevator Co. v. American Surety Co., 207 Minn. 117, 290 N.W. 231, 126 A.L.R. 1351.

The rule and the basis therefor are well stated in Lum v. McEwen, 56 Minn. 278, 282, 57 N.W. 662, where, speaking through Mr. Justice Mitchell, we said: "Actual injury is not the principle the law proceeds on, in holding such transactions void. Fidelity in the agent is what is aimed at, and, as a means of securing it, the law will not permit him to place himself in a position in which he may be tempted by his own private interests to disregard those of his principal. . . ."

The right to recover profits made by the agent in the course of the agency is not affected by the fact that the principal, upon discovering a fraud, has rescinded the contract and recovered that with which he parted. Restatement, Agency, § 407(2). Comment e on Subsection (2) reads: "If an agent has violated a duty of loyalty to the principal so that the principal is entitled to profits which the agent has thereby made, the fact that the principal has brought an action against a third person and has been made whole by such action does not prevent the principal from recovering from the agent the profits which the agent has made. Thus, if the other contracting party has given a bribe to the agent to make a contract with him on behalf of the principal, the principal can rescind the transaction, recovering from the other party anything received by him, or he can maintain an action for damages against him; in either event the principal may recover from the agent the amount of the bribe."

It follows that, insofar as the secret commission of $2,000 received by the agent is concerned, plaintiff had an absolute right thereto, irrespective of any recovery resulting from the action against the sellers for rescission.

[The court also sustained the plaintiff's second cause of action.]

Affirmed.

REFERENCES

Liability of third party inducing agent's fraud:

Canadian Ingersoll Rand v. Loveman & Sons, 227 F.Supp. 829 (N.D.Ohio 1964) (defendant had conspired with chief buyer of plaintiff to charge plaintiff exorbitant prices).

American Life Insurance Co. v. Florida Anglers Association, 185 F.2d 460 (5th Cir. 1950) (defendant borrower had paid secret commission to agent of plaintiff lender to arrange favorable loan).

Measure of damages:

Dubern v. Girard Trust Bank, 454 F.2d 565 (3d Cir.1972) (bank serving as investment agent failed to remit funds promptly; principal died too soon to invest in a bond exempt from inheritance tax; bank liable for loss of avoidable tax).

Proof of damage:

Watson v. Limited Partners of WCKT, Limited, 570 S.W.2d 179 (Tex.Civ.App.1978), (general manager who wasted assets was liable to restore contributions to limited partners without proof of causation between his negligence and loss of assets).

COLUMBUS BAR ASSOCIATION v. GRELLE
Supreme Court of Ohio, 1968.
14 Ohio St.2d 208, 237 N.E.2d 298.

The respondent, Walter W. Grelle, Jr., was admitted to the practice of law in August 1938, and, with the exception of the four years that he served in the United States Navy during World War II, he has been engaged in practice in Columbus, Ohio, ever since. During his years of practice the respondent has been active in the bar associations and various fraternal, civic, and veterans' organizations. The complaint forming the basis of this disciplinary action is the only complaint that has ever been filed against the respondent.

The facts that led to the filing of this complaint by the Columbus Bar Association are as follows:

On April 23, 1963, the respondent filed a personal injury action on behalf of Lloyd I. Perine in the Franklin County Court of Common Pleas. On July 19, 1963, the respondent and his secretary witnessed the signing of a separation agreement between Lloyd I. Perine and his wife, Dorothy J. Perine. This agreement had been prepared by the respondent, but the terms had been previously agreed upon by the Perines, with little or no advice from the respondent. The part of this separation agreement that is relevant to this action provided that Mrs. Perine was to receive one-third of the net proceeds of Mr. Perine's personal injury case.

Mrs. Perine subsequently requested the respondent to obtain a divorce for her. It is clear that Mr. Perine knew of this request and acquiesced in it, and that Mrs. Perine knew that the respondent was representing her husband in the personal injury action. The testimony of Mrs. Perine and the respondent conflicted as to whether the respondent accepted the divorce case or declined it on the basis of conflict of interest. In any case, a divorce petition was filed in the Domestic Relations Division of the Franklin County Court of Common Pleas on behalf of Mrs. Perine in September of 1963. This petition was prepared by the respondent. It was signed, and the acknowledgment for it was taken by Richard J. Giovanetti, an attorney who rented office space in the same suite as respondent. The petition itself was in simple form, and it did not plead the facts constituting the alleged grounds of divorce.

At the hearing on the divorce petition on November 27, 1963, which was uncontested, the respondent appeared for Mrs. Perine, the reason given for his appearance being that attorney Giovanetti was out of town. A decree was granted which incorporated the terms of the separation agreement.

After the divorce, the former Mrs. Perine remarried and became Mrs. Pinto. She later obtained another attorney to enforce the child support order of $10 per week against Mr. Perine.

In February 1965, the personal injury action of Mr. Perine was settled by the respondent for $19,000, and respondent paid the net proceeds directly to Mr. Perine. On May 11, 1965, Mrs. Pinto called the respondent and asked about the personal injury case. Respondent then told her that the case had been settled, but refused to disclose the amount of the settlement without permission of Mr. Perine. On May 18, 1964, Mrs. Pinto filed a motion to reduce to a money judgment that part of the separation agreement which had formalized the agreement that she was to share in the net proceeds of the settlement. Respondent, representing Mr. Perine, successfuly resisted this motion. The propriety of the order dismissing this action is not before us.

Subsequently, Mrs. Pinto brought these facts to the attention of the Columbus Bar Association which filed the complaint in this case. On these facts, the Board of Commissioners on Grievances and Discipline concluded that the respondent had violated his oath of office and Canons 6 and 37 of the Canons of Professional Ethics. The recommendation of the commissioners was that the respondent be suspended for an indefinite period from the practice of law.

The matter is before us on the findings of the board and the respondent's objections thereto, and for disciplinary action if we conclude that the facts properly found require such action.

Per Curiam.

One of the major objections of respondent pertains to the conclusion of the board that his conduct violated Canon 6 of the Canons of Professional Ethics. Canon 6 reads as follows:

"Adverse Influences and Conflicting Interests.

"It is the duty of a lawyer at the time of retainer to disclose to the client all the circumstances of his relations to the parties, and any interest in or connection with the controversy, which might influence the client in the selection of counsel.

"It is unprofessional to represent conflicting interests, except by express consent of all concerned given after a full disclosure of the facts. Within the meaning of this canon, a lawyer represents conflicting interests when, in behalf of one client, it is his duty to contend for that which duty to another client requires him to oppose.

"The obligation to represent the client with undivided fidelity and not to divulge his secrets or confidences forbids also the subsequent acceptance of retainers or employment from others in matters adversely affecting any interest of the client with respect to which confidence has been reposed."

Respondent notes that there was no finding that he did not disclose to each of the Perines his representation of the other, and he argues that the evidence shows that there was, in fact, full disclosure of this mutual representation. We agree with respondent on this point. Dorothy Pinto testified at the hearing that when she went to the respondent's office it was with full knowledge and approval of her husband, Lloyd Perine. She also testified that she had previously agreed with Lloyd Perine that he would pay for any divorce received.

There was no misrepresentation by the respondent as to his position with respect to either of the parties. It appears that with respect to the separation agreement and the divorce appearance he was not primarily protecting anyone or advising anyone, but was rather carrying out the mutual wishes of the parties. Conflicting interests arose out of the separation agreement, but not until over a year after the divorce was final. Any representation of the wife by the respondent had long since ceased.

The agreement between the parties which had reference to a division of the net proceeds of the contemplated settlement of Mr. Perine's claim for damages contained no promise by the respondent to protect the rights assigned to Mrs. Perine at the time of distribution. There is no claim that there was any representation that attorney Grelle would represent her or protect her interest in that fund upon distribution. It is understandable, however, that Mrs. Perine might have concluded that this was to be one of Mr. Grelle's functions. The fact that such misunderstandings are likely to occur under such circumstances must lead to the conclusion that only in the clearest cases should counsel hazard to represent interests which are or may become adverse, even after disclosing his dual representation.

In retrospect, this was not such a case. Too many experienced lawyers have accepted such employment in separation or divorce matters under such circumstances, only to ultimately abandon the interest of one or the other of their clients. In such instances of dual representation, a party disappointed in the financial results, as was Mrs. Pinto, may validly argue after the fact that the dual representation brought about the omission from the agreement of specific language protecting her upon distribution of the anticipated settlement fund.

At all events, when Mrs. Pinto filed her motion to reduce to judgment that part of the agreement drawn by respondent which gave her a one-third interest in the proceeds of the personal injury settlement, Mr. Grelle should have withdrawn from the matter. His failure promptly to disclose to Mrs. Perine the fact that a settlement had occurred and that distribution to Perine had been made, and his ardent advocacy of the husband's adverse interest to the agreement violated the second paragraph of Canon No. 6, and was unprofessional conduct which justifies a reprimand.

We find, however, in view of all the facts of this case, including his full disclosure to the parties of his position and their consent to that position, that Mr. Grelle did not violate his oath of office. In view of the previously unblemished record of the respondent the reprimand which we here impose is judged to be suitable disciplinary action.

Judgment accordingly.

CANNON v. UNITED STATES ACOUSTICS CORP.

United States District Court, Northern District of Illinois, 1975.
398 F.Supp. 209 (N.D.Ill.1975), affirmed in part and reversed in part
532 F.2d 1118 (7th Cir.1976).

MARSHALL, DISTRICT JUDGE.

Charles B. Cannon, Richard L. Davis, John G. Marsh, and Jeffrey Ross brought this derivative shareholder's action, as well as personal claims, against the defendants, U.S. Acoustics Corporation (hereinafter

"Acoustics"), a Florida Corporation, and National Perlite Products, S.A., (hereinafter "Perlite"), a Panamanian Corporation. . . .

There are pending for decision cross-motions to disqualify counsel and a motion to disqualify Cannon as a party plaintiff. Shortly after Robert J. Gareis, Peter J. Mone and the firm of Baker & McKenzie filed their appearances on behalf of the corporate and individual defendants, plaintiffs moved to disqualify them from representing the corporate defendants and requested that the court appoint independent counsel. Plaintiffs base their motion on the theory that dual representation in a shareholder derivative suit creates a conflict of interest that the court can order terminated.

Concomitant with filing their answer to the plaintiffs' motion, defendants moved to strike Cannon as a party plaintiff and to strike the appearances of N.A. Giambalvo and Boodell, Sears, Sugrue, Giambalvo & Crowley as counsel for the plaintiff.

Defendants argue that by virtue of Canon 4 of the American Bar Association's Code of Professional Responsibility (hereinafter "CPR"), Cannon (who is a lawyer), and the lawyers and law firm which represent him, cannot maintain the pending suit because each previously represented the corporate defendants in legal matters that are substantially related to the present litigation.

I. *Plaintiffs' motion to strike the appearance of the attorneys on behalf of the corporate defendants*

. . .

In substance, the plaintiffs' complaint is a shareholder's derivative suit. . . . A derivative suit is, in legal effect, a suit brought by the corporation, but conducted by the shareholders. The corporation, although formally aligned as a defendant for historical reasons, is in actuality a plaintiff. . . . The stockholder is only a nominal plaintiff.

. . .

The preceding paragraph delineates the anomalous position of the corporation; it is both a defendant and a plaintiff. An examination of plaintiffs' complaint amply reveals this position. Count 1 alleges that beginning in 1968 and continuing to the present, the individual defendants committed numerous violations of Rule 10b–5: illegal stock options were allegedly granted, stock was issued and purchased upon false representations that the stock was for services, rent, and other expenses, stock was issued for little or no consideration, corporate opportunities were usurped, illegal profits were retained by certain officers and directors, and illegal and excessive compensation was paid to Stedman.

. . .

Even a cursory examination of the foregoing allegations demonstrates that should they be established at trial, Acoustics and Perlite will benefit substantially. For this reason plaintiffs argue that Mone, Gareis, and the firm of Baker & McKenzie cannot represent the alleged

wrongdoers and the ultimate beneficiaries of any judgment that might
be obtained.

Defendants' position is that although there is a theoretical conflict
of interest, no real conflict exists. They argue that the corporations are
really inactive participants in the lawsuit, and that should any conflict
arise they will withdraw their representation of the individual defendants and continue their representation of the corporations. Defendants further argue that their present position is that all the transactions complained of are legal and should be upheld.

.   .   .

When a single lawyer or law firm undertakes to represent both the
individual and corporate defendants in a derivative action, at least two
potential ethical problems arise. First, there exists, as previously
discussed, a potential conflict of interest between the individual and
corporate defendants, and second, there is the threat that confidences
and secrets obtained from each client may be jeopardized because of the
dual nature of the representation.   .   .   .

[The Court quoted and discussed Canon 5 and Ethical Consideration EC 5–18.]

Although EC5–18 is persuasive authority for plaintiffs' position,
EC5–15 is even more so:

> If a lawyer is requested to undertake or to continue representation
> of multiple clients having potentially differing interests, he must
> weigh carefully the possibility that his judgment may be impaired
> or his loyalty divided if he accepts or continues the employment.
> He should resolve all doubts against the propriety of the represen-
> tation. A lawyer should never represent in litigation multiple
> clients with differing interests; and there are few situations in
> which he would be justified in representing in litigation multiple
> clients with potentially differing interests. If a lawyer accepted
> such employment and the interests did become actually differing,
> he would have to withdraw from employment with likelihood of
> resulting hardship to the client; and for this reason it is preferable
> that he refuse the employment initially.

Taken together, these two ethical considerations convincingly establish
that in a derivative suit the better course is for the corporation to be
represented by independent counsel from the outset, even though
counsel believes in good faith that no conflict of interest exists.

.   .   .

As previously discussed the court is bound to apply the CPR to
lawyers practicing before it. The code is clear that multiple representation is improper when the client's interests are adverse. . . . This
solution, concededly, is not without its disabilities. The corporations'
rights to counsel of their choice are infringed and in a closely held
corporation, as here, the financial burden is increased. Nevertheless,
on balance, the corporations must obtain independent counsel. . . .

[The Court also held that the plaintiff Cannon was disqualified from maintaining the suit on the corporation's behalf because of his former service as attorney for the corporation. On appeal, the judgment was reversed in part to permit Cannon to continue in the case for the sole purpose of petitioning for allowance of attorney's fees; in other respects the judgment was affirmed.]

MODEL RULES OF PROFESSIONAL CONDUCT
American Bar Association, 1984.

Rule 1.7 Conflict of Interest: General Rule

(a) A lawyer shall not represent a client if the representation of that client will be directly adverse to another client, unless:

(1) the lawyer reasonably believes the representation will not adversely affect the relationship with the other client; and

(2) each client consents after consultation.

(b) A lawyer shall not represent a client if the representation of that client may be materially limited by the lawyer's responsibilities to another client or to a third person, or by the lawyer's own interests, unless:

(1) the lawyer reasonably believes the representation will not be adversely affected; and

(2) the client consents after consultation. When representation of multiple clients in a single matter is undertaken, the consultation shall include explanation of the implications of the common representation and the advantages and risks involved.

Rule 1.9 Conflict of Interest: Former Client

A lawyer who has formerly represented a client in a matter shall not thereafter:

(a) represent another person in the same or a substantially related matter in which that person's interests are materially adverse to the interests of the former client unless the former client consents after consultation; or

(b) use information relating to the representation to the disadvantage of the former client except as Rule 1.6 would permit with respect to a client or when the information has become generally known.

. . .

REFERENCES

Adverse interests:

Westinghouse Electric Corp. v. Kerr McGee Corp., 580 F.2d 1311 (7th Cir.1978), cert. denied 439 U.S. 955, 99 S.Ct. 353, 58 L.Ed.2d 346 (1978) (Chicago office of Kirkland, Ellis represented Westinghouse in antitrust suit against uranium producers, including Kerr McGee, Gulf and Getty Oil. Washington office of same firm represented the American Petroleum Institute, of which defendants were members, in statement to Congress and the public about oil company diversification, and gathered confidential information on extent of uranium interests. Court orders Kirkland, Ellis to cease representation of Westinghouse unless Westinghouse dismisses API members from the antitrust suit).

Firestone Tire & Rubber Co. v. Risjord, 449 U.S. 368, 101 S.Ct. 669, 66 L.Ed.2d 571 (1981) (order denying motion to disqualify attorney held nonappealable).

Note, A Brake on the Washington "Revolving Door"? (1980) 14 Ga.L.Rev. 378 (Disciplinary Rule 5–105(D) of the Code of Professional Responsibility flatly precludes participation by firm of which partner has conflict, but ABA Opinion 342 has approved participation although partner was formerly involved on behalf of the government, where "screening procedures" are used.)

Breitel, The Lawyer as Fiduciary, 31 Business Lawyer 3 (1975) (basic premise is that lawyers, as such, occupy quasi-public office).

Chapter 6

PARTNERSHIP

SECTION 1. THE VARIETIES AND USES OF PARTNERSHIP

INTRODUCTORY NOTE

To this point, we have studied problems and issues relevant to all forms of enterprise, and the cases and comments have involved individuals, proprietorships, partnerships, corporations and other entities interchangeably. Our examination now shifts to one of the major forms of business enterprise, the partnership. The word "business" has not crept in accidentally, for the partnership form in its very definition is limited to associations carrying on "a business for profit." [1]

Partnership organization takes a variety of forms. One of these, known as limited partnership, has been made the subject of special acts—most recently the Uniform Limited Partnership Act (ULPA) of 1916 and the Revised Uniform Limited Partnership Act (RULPA) of 1976. All other forms are generally conceded to be governed by the Uniform Partnership Act (UPA) of 1914. There is a difference of opinion as to whether transitory associations characterized as "joint ventures" are categorical partnerships, or whether they are similar organizations to which partnership law is applied by analogy, but both views lead to the same conclusion. The UPA is in effect in 45 states, and the Uniform Limited Partnership Act, either in its original form or as revised in 1976, is in effect in all the states. A majority of the states have now adopted the RULPA or variants thereof.

We have already seen that a partnership may be established without specific agreement, even inadvertently. A limited partnership requires filing of an agreement, but the agreement may be a very simple one. Our task in this chapter revolves about the partnership agreement or the lack thereof. In the absence of an agreement, the statutes provide certain assumptions applicable to the relations of the partners: division of profits, payment of salaries, control over partnership affairs, death, retirement and the like. Controversies that arise over these matters that have not been included in a partnership agreement provide most of the cases in this section.

More fundamental to our study is the avoidance of these controversies, and in particular the development of partnership agreements that embody the intentions of the partners and provide for effective treat-

---

1. UPA § 6(1).

ment of future eventualities. The value of studying the cases is that they provide a catalog of errors and omissions to be avoided by means of advance agreement.

There are controversies of two types that most frequently arise between partners. The first type involves questions of partnership compensation, management rights, and determination of what is a partnership asset—what is partnership property and what is individual property. The second set of controversies arises specifically in the context of termination of a partnership. What are the rights of the withdrawing partner? What rights, if any, do partners have to continue the business, and how does one evaluate partnership assets, including going concern value or good will? There are also apt to be special concerns when there are claims of creditors, both individual and partnership.

Most of the cases in this chapter, in fact, arise in a context of partnership termination. Termination inevitably brings to a head many problems which were not solved, and perhaps not even faced, as long as the partnership ran on. A partner can draw for his current needs, without knowing or even thinking very hard about the exact extent of his partnership interests; when the players get ready to pick up their money and go home, they have to decide who owns what. For this reason, termination brings up for decision many questions about fiduciary duty, compensation, and partnership property which arose long before, but were kicked under the rug until the day of final reckoning. This tendency for termination to bring the skeletons out of the closet is accentuated by a prevalent judicial attitude toward litigation among partners. Judges commonly feel the partners should settle their disputes among themselves, until cooperation has proved to be no longer possible. This supposition is expressed in an often repeated doctrine that one partner cannot sue another about partnership matters except in the course of a suit for final accounting on dissolution.[2] Although this rule is riddled with exceptions,[3] it expresses a genuine

---

2. L.H. Heiselt, Inc. v. Brown, 108 Colo. 562, 120 P.2d 644, 168 A.L.R. 1081 (1941); annot., 168 A.L.R. 1088; Mitchell Resort Enterprises v. C. & S. Builders, 570 S.W.2d 463 (Tex.Civ.App.1978). As a corollary of this doctrine, it has been held that the period of limitations or laches does not run against an intra-partnership claim until dissolution. Korziuk v. Korziuk, 13 Ill.2d 238, 148 N.E.2d 727 (1958); Einsweiler v. Einsweiler, 390 Ill. 286, 61 N.E.2d 377 (1945).

The same principle was held applicable to bar suit for breach of a joint venture agreement without an accounting, where the affairs of the joint venture were complex. Lau v. Valu-Bilt Homes, Limited, 59 Haw. 283, 582 P.2d 195 (1978).

The procedural treatment of limited partnerships is different. Under the ULPA, courts may even permit derivative suits by analogy to the law of corporations. See Note, Standing of Limited Partners to Sue Derivatively (1965) 65 Colum.L.Rev. 1463. The revised ULPA specifically provides for derivative actions by limited partners. RULPA §§ 1001–1004.

3. See Catron v. Watson, 12 Ariz.App. 132, 468 P.2d 399 (1970); Roberts v. Astoria Medical Group, 43 A.D.2d 138, 350 N.Y.S.2d 159 (1973) (member of medical partnership could sue firm for failure to obtain proper liability insurance for him).

judicial reluctance to settle one of a bag of controversies without settling all.

NOTE: "ACCOUNTING"

In most cases in this chapter disputes between partners or disputes between surviving partners and representatives of deceased partners are presented in an action for an "accounting." The UPA provides for a right to a formal account in § 22 and § 43. Except in rare instances an accounting is incident to a decree of dissolution of the partnership, or occurs after dissolution during the winding up process prior to extinguishment. In Weidlich v. Weidlich, 147 Conn. 160, 157 A.2d 910 (1960), the court described the mechanics of the final account as follows:

"Upon the termination of a partnership either by act of the parties or operation of law, an accounting usually becomes necessary. Mechem, Partnership (2d Ed.) 464. Unless there is an adjustment by agreement, an accounting must be made in court, and equity is the proper forum. Roberts v. Weiner (1951) 137 Conn. 668, 81 A.2d 115. Equity has plenary jurisdiction in the matter of partnership accounts which extends to all matters necessary to wind up partnership affairs. Maruca v. Phillips (1952) 139 Conn. 79, 83, 90 A.2d 159, 161; Gillett v. Hall (1840) 13 Conn. 426, 433. Equity has full jurisdiction of a suit for an accounting and settlement of partnership affairs. The petition may be brought either by the representatives of a deceased partner against the survivors or by the survivors against such representatives. 4 Pomeroy, Equity Jurisprudence (5th Ed.) p. 459.

"Where a partner presents a petition in equity against the other partners, stating that the accounts are unsettled and praying for an account, the usual course for the court is to appoint a committee or auditors before whom the parties can produce their accounts and be heard on oath and who will conduct a minute and patient examination of their claims. Beach v. Hotchkiss (1818) 2 Conn. 425, 429: see Rev.1958, c. 907. After the balance due and to whom it is due is ascertained, a report is made to the court, which has power to accept it or to reject it. If the report is accepted, a decree may be entered in favor of the partners who are entitled to it and executions will be issued accordingly, whether the debtors are plaintiffs or defendants in the case. 2 Swift, Digest, p. 145.

"Each partner owes to his associates the duty of rendering true accounts and full information about everything which affects the partnership. If he fails to perform this duty, his associates are entitled to maintain a suit for an accounting against him. Burdick, Partnership (3rd Ed.) p. 350. The account when rendered should be in writing and should be substantiated by the partner's oath. Sigourney v. Munn (1829) 7 Conn. 324, 332. Any partner may bring a petition in equity for the settlement of partnership affairs.

"A final account is the one great occasion for a comprehensive and effective settlement of all partnership affairs. All the claims and demands arising between the partners should be settled upon such an accounting. Mechem, Partnership (2d Ed.) 465, p. 404."

In this case judicial approval of the accounting was denied because of insufficient information about the original partnership assets and about transactions which had taken place during the winding up.

In reading about accounting in legal literature, one is often puzzled by subtle differences in the various ways in which the words "account" and "accounting" are used. Probably the primordial meaning of the term is simply to *report* the facts and figures to someone else; one *counts* to himself, and *accounts* to another.

Various extensions of this idea have developed. The most widely known is the development in the area of business administration, where accounting has grown into a complex science involving matters of record keeping, presentation and analysis. Very little of this accounting science appears in the cases and statutes on partnership accounting.

In legal literature "accounting" is frequently used to indicate the *paying over* of money shown to be due on the report of facts and figures. This usage is frequently encountered in the phrase "accounting for profits," which may denote the paying over of money due, with or without the necessity of a prior report. This meaning was encountered in Chapter 5.

In reading the partnership act and the cases, you will need to determine in each context whether "accounting" is used to designate the reporting of figures, or the paying of balances, or both.

NOTE: THE VARIETIES OF PARTNERSHIP

The term partnership ordinarily brings to mind a small organization of professionals or businesspeople. Typical among such partnerships would be law firms, medical practices, and small mercantile establishments. Until tax factors became predominant—and state corporation laws were changed to take account of that fact—partnership was the only form of organization available to collections of professionals. Even today, when it is common to find both small and large professional associations established as P.C.'s (professional corporations) or P.A.'s (professional associations), the partnership form remains predominant. So, for example, most of the major national CPA firms are partnerships, each with hundreds of partners resident in many states and countries. Many of the large law firms, even those with offices in several states, retain the partnership form. And, in a development best left for explanation by tax lawyers, recent years have seen the proliferation of "partnerships including professional corporations", professional organizations in which some or all of what once would be individual partners are individually incorporated. Note that § 6 of the UPA speaks of "persons" as partners, not individuals. This complex professional firm structure is an illustration of a partnership of corporations.

Interestingly, while the tax virtues of corporate status have attracted professionals who once used partnership form, other tax virtues have commended the partnership form for businesses that might otherwise have been incorporated. Although we have not collected the statistics, we can confidently say that the principal form of real estate development—whether shopping center, office building, rental complex or mobile home park—in the United States has been the limited partnership. These partnerships are very sizeable indeed, rivaling and often exceeding their corporate counterparts. Commonly, such partnerships raise $20 to $50 million from public investors. One exceptional case in recent years was the limited partnership that undertook the building of Detroit's $600 million Renaissance Center.

As you might expect, the structure of these partnerships will be tailored to their purposes. Complex partnership operations almost inevitably produce complex partnership structures, like their corporate counterparts. Consider the following organization chart, which is based on similar organizations appearing in public prospectuses.

ORGANIZATION CHART
DRY GULCH INVESTORS, LTD.

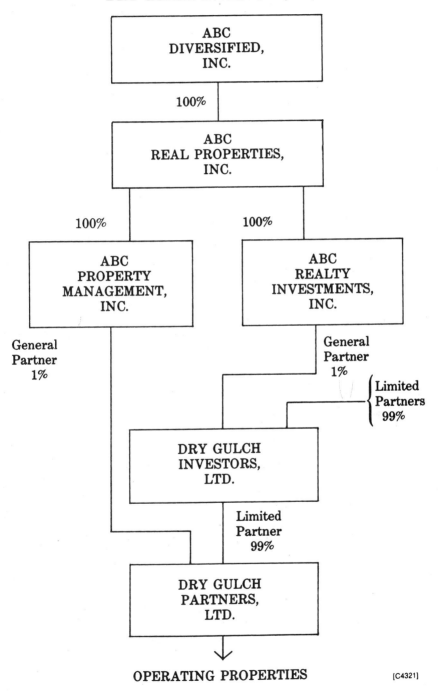

OPERATING PROPERTIES

[C4321]

You may wonder why it is necessary to create such a complex structure simply for the purpose of acquiring and developing a piece of real property, such as a shopping center. Each of the elements in the chart has a separate function.

We begin with Dry Gulch Partners, Ltd., the "operating partnership," which will acquire and develop the properties, operate them, and later sell them. It is organized as a limited partnership, with a corporate general partner. The limited partnership form assures that its investors (other than the general partner) will not be liable beyond their initial investment for the debts or obligations of the partnership.[1]

Dry Gulch Investors, Ltd., the "investment partnership," is also a limited partnership. It is the entity that raises money from outside investors for ultimate investment in the properties. Note that it also has a single general partner, which is a corporation. Why the need for two tiers of partnership?

Note that the general partner of the "operating partnership" is ABC Property Management, Inc. this corporation is a professional property manager, and manages for a fee the properties of a substantial number of limited partnerships. The ULPA and the RULPA forbid participation in management by limited partners,[2] so a corporation is formed to act as the general partner in several operating partnerships.

The general partner of the "investment partnership" is ABC Realty Investments, Inc., a different corporation. Its functions as a general partner are quite different from those of ABC Property Management, Inc., as it is involved with raising money and financial structuring. In many structures, however, there is but a single limited partnership that combines the functions of "operating" and "investment" partnerships. Incidentally, ABC Realty Investments, Inc. will serve as the general partner of several investment partnerships.

You may also wonder about the propriety of having a limited partnership in which the general partner is a corporation. Isn't this tantamount to having a corporation without corporate form? The Internal Revenue Service had the same doubts, and it promulgated a series of pronouncements that have the effect of categorizing this structure as a corporation for tax purposes unless the corporate general partner has sufficient assets to be effectively liable as a general partner on the debts of the partnership.[3]

We have added a few more tiers to the structure in the interests of realism. In many instances, the establishment and sale (or "syndication") of limited partnership interests will be done by large corporations whose subsidiaries are involved in investment and management in the appropriate fields (e.g., real estate, oil and gas exploration).

Another point might be added concerning the complex structure. The parent corporation receives, via its several subsidiaries, management and other fees at a number of the levels of this complex organization. In the case of Dry Gulch, fees are levied at both tiers of partnership. Moreover, the parent corporation may also own an investment adviser, brokerage house or investment banking firm that receives a commission on sale to the public of the limited partnership interests.

---

1. ULPA § 7, RULPA § 303.

2. ULPA § 7, RULPA § 303.

3. Rev.Proc. 72–13, 1972–1 Cum.Bull. 735; Rev.Proc. 74–17, 1974–1 Cum.Bull. 438.

In short, contemporary partnership structures are often no less complex—or profitable—than contemporary corporate organizations. The complex structures occasionally produce interesting litigation, as the following case demonstrates.

LAND INVESTMENT, INC. v. BATTLEGROUND ASSOCIATES

Vermont Supreme Court, 1980.
138 Vt. 316, 415 A.2d 753.

BARNEY, CHIEF JUSTICE.

This litigation is best understood as a suit by the plaintiff to collect money claimed to be due under transactions in part expressed in a certain $50,000 note. The matter is not as simple as that, but the note obligation is a handy reference point to keep track of the cause.

The action is further confused by the shifting identities involved in the various arrangements and commitments out of which it arose. The plaintiff's side gives little trouble. The named corporate plaintiff, Land Investment, Inc., was a business entity through which Nathan Smith handled real estate transactions and various financing agreements.

The defendant, Battleground Associates, presents a more complex picture. It was a limited partnership, with its general partner being a Delaware corporation, the Sugar River Company. Sugar River, in turn, was the wholly owned subsidiary of another Delaware corporation called Whitecaps. One man, William Murphy, the single largest shareholder in Whitecaps, was a director and chief executive officer of both Sugar River and Whitecaps, and was Battleground's chief operating officer. In part, the litigation involves the exact capacity in which Sugar River acted when it made certain commitments. As can be seen, there are certainly three possibilities: (1) it acted as general partner of Battleground Associates; (2) it acted on its own behalf; or (3) it acted in some capacity for the benefit of Whitecaps, its owner.

. . .

In 1970 through 1972, Whitecaps, acting through Sugar River, assembled about a hundred and fifty-five acres in Fayston, Vermont, for the development of a condominium project. Permits were obtained for 63 units to be built on part of the Sugar River holdings in Fayston, a 76.2 acre parcel. A consortium was put together to invest $250,000 in the project. That was to be done as soon as a limited partnership was formed to serve as the investment vehicle, and title to the 76.2 acre parcel was conveyed to that partnership. The defendant, Battleground Associates, is that partnership.

Prior to the formation of Battleground, in order to provide some short term financing for the condominium project, Murphy, in his capacity as president of Sugar River, approached Smith for a $25,000 loan from Land Investment. . . .

The second, and critical, deal between Smith and Murphy arose out of the sequence of events that followed the creation of Battleground

Associates. Sugar River participated as Battleground's general partner, with Whitecaps acting as guarantor of all of Sugar River's obligations as general partner. Murphy signed the partnership agreement on behalf of Sugar River, and the guarantee on behalf of Whitecaps. At this point, Sugar River conveyed to Battleground Associates the land on which the condominium project was to be built, with Murphy executing the deed on behalf of Sugar River.

. . .

[Certain financing was arranged, but additional financing was necessary.]

At this point, Murphy again turned to Smith. The latter eventually agreed that Land Investment would provide the necessary letter of credit. To implement their agreement, substantial documentation was required. It was prepared by Land Investment's attorney. Among these documents was a written memorandum of the agreement which was signed by Smith as president of Land Investment and by Murphy in the following form:

THE SUGAR RIVER COMPANY

by   s/William A. Murphy
     Its President

Therefore, the face of the document reflected an agreement solely between Sugar River and Land Investment. It recited that at the request of Sugar River and for the benefit of Whitecaps, Land Investment would use its line of credit to obtain issuance of a $38,000 letter of credit. It stated that plaintiff was charging $12,000, plus all costs and expenses it might incur, for the use of its credit. It further provided that if the letter of credit was called, Sugar River was to repay the amount called, plus interest, in addition to the $12,000.

To secure these obligations, the agreement required that Sugar River execute a $50,000 interest bearing note supported by two mortgages on Sugar River owned real estate in Fayston. The real estate was not further described. Sugar River subsequently executed a first mortgage on a 5.9 acre parcel adjacent to the condominium site and a second mortgage, subject to a prior interest held by the Vermont Federal Savings and Loan Association, on a 50 acre parcel across the road from it.

Whitecaps defaulted under the purchase agreement in March 1974, and the letter of credit was called just prior to its expiration. The plaintiff then sought to enforce its remedies under the note and contract.

One procedure was a suit on the note foreclosing the mortgages on the 5.9 acre and 50 acre parcels owned by Sugar River.

. . .

Almost simultaneously with the action against Sugar River, this action against Battleground Associates was begun. Its fundamental premise was simple enough. The plaintiff argued that all the activities involving the letter of credit arrangement were for the benefit of Battleground Associates and that Battleground received and still retains the benefits of that arrangement. Therefore, says the plaintiff, recovery of the note, fees, interest and damages directly from Battleground Associates is both legal and supported by the facts. In fact, it argues, there are several legal theories applicable, any one of which supports recovery. The trial court rejected each of these theories and rendered judgment for the defendant.

The first contention advanced to support reversal is that the acts of Sugar River in procuring the letter of credit were done as the general partner of Battleground Associates as part of carrying on the usual way the partnership proposes. In such a case, it is argued, the commitment of Sugar River to repayment of the letter of credit, together with its fees and interest, is effectively the commitment of the partnership.

As the general partner of Battleground, Sugar River is the partnership's agent. . . .

There being no dispute as to Sugar River's status as a partner of Battleground or as to Sugar River's authority to bind Battleground to such a contract, the next question is whether the act was for apparently carrying on Battleground's business.

. . .

. . . [T]he trial court had adequate factual foundation for determining that the letter of credit was, as it stated, a Whitecaps operation and properly so allocable. There was no place for the operation of any presumption in support of it being a partnership business, the specific facts being to the contrary. The participation of Sugar River quite clearly was in order to make available additional real estate security which Sugar River owned.

The plaintiff suggests, alternatively, that if it cannot prevail on the notion that the whole transaction was part of partnership business, it should then succeed on the theory of an undisclosed principal. . . . The evidence which has been previously discussed, relating to the first financing arrangement of this development entered into by the plaintiff, supports the conclusion that the existence of Battleground had been disclosed. The remedy is not available if the existence of the principal is known at the time of contracting, since it would then be presumed, for example, that a sale to the agent would rest on an acceptance of that person's credit without resort to others. . . .

Moreover, Battleground Associates was not a principal, disclosed or undisclosed, in this transaction. As we have already seen, the application to the plaintiff for credit assistance was on behalf of Whitecaps. Any incidental benefit to the condominium developer, Battleground Associates, does not change the express contractual situation between

Whitecaps, the plaintiff and the Worcester Bank. This doctrine is not a road to reach the assets of Battleground.

. . .

Affirmed.

NOTE: TAX MOTIVATIONS IN PARTNERSHIP STRUCTURE

With federal individual income tax rates running up to 50% before 1987 and corporate tax rates nearly that high, it stands to reason that tax effects have heavily motivated business structure. The fundamental difference between federal taxation of partnerships and corporations is that corporations are taxed as entities, whereas partnerships are not. In other words, a corporation pays tax on the income it earns, while a partnership as such pays no tax. Instead, the partners are treated as earning directly their distributive shares of the partnership income, and they are personally taxed on that income whether or not it is distributed to them.

The most obvious result of this difference is that partnership income is taxed only once, at the level of the partners personally. Corporate income, on the other hand, is taxed at the corporate level, and taxed once again upon distribution to shareholders as dividends. This fact, together with the fact that *losses* of a partnership are also treated as though they are incurred directly by partners, accounts for much of the use of the partnership form.

Until the 1986 Tax Reform Act, partnership losses served as a substantial motivating factor for wealthy investors. Individuals of substantial wealth and income would become limited partners in large limited partnerships, which would generally acquire and develop real estate, engage in mineral exploration, engage in research and development activities, or produce motion pictures. The combined effects of deductions for interest on borrowed money, depreciation, and other expenses—together with various tax credits—generally produced a tax loss in early years of operations. Investors welcomed these losses, which they offset against their taxable income from other sources.

The investors expected, of course, that the properties, motion pictures, oil wells, etc. would ultimately be sold by the partnership at a substantial profit. Often, but not always, they were. And, while the investors recognized substantial taxable income on such sales, they also recognized substantial real cash flows on the liquidation of their interests. In effect, these "tax shelters" resulted in the deferral of substantial income tax, with later payment of the tax generally timed to coincide with substantial profit on disposition of the partnership property.

The investments were risky, and the heavy tax motivation often resulted in partnership structures that were not only at the borders of legality from a tax viewpoint, but were also economically dubious. The days of "tax shelters" may well be at an end, by virtue of a myriad of tax changes effected by the Tax Reform Act of 1986. Although the basic partnership tax structure—in which partners are taxed as though they had directly earned or incurred income or losses—remains, many of the provisions that allowed recognition of substantial early losses have been changed.

However, it would be premature to report on the demise of limited partnerships as a form for investment in real estate and other ventures. Ultimately, even the early "tax shelter" partnerships depended upon the expectation of a true economic return (i.e., sale of a building at a profit) to justify investment. Today, with the primary tax motivation blunted if not removed, the economic justifications still remain.

REFERENCES ON PARTNERSHIP TAXATION:

General texts:

The two leading texts on partnership taxation are

Willis, Pennell & Postlewaite, Partnership Taxation (3d Ed.1981), 2 vols.

McKee, Nelson & Whitmire, Federal Taxation of Partnerships and Partners (1977, with 1986 Supp.), 2 vols.

SECTION 2. COMPENSATION, ALLOCATION OF PROFITS AND LOSSES, AND REIMBURSEMENT FOR CONTRIBUTIONS

NOTE ON PROFITS, SALARIES AND EXPENSES OF PARTNERS

Ordinarily, if partners take the time to prepare a written partnership agreement they will provide in it for the sharing of profits and losses, and for the payment of any salaries or compensation to which they agree. We explore in this note the nature of such agreements.

Suppose, however, that the partners make no agreement, or that the agreement is silent on profits, losses and compensation. The Uniform Partnership Act provides solutions where the partners have not spoken: profits and losses shall be divided equally,[1] salaries shall not be paid to partners,[2] and expenses incurred individually by partners in the partnership business shall be reimbursed.[3] These rules are rather rigid, and they produce unfortunate results in certain cases, as where one partner has worked long and hard on the firm's business, while another has enjoyed his leisure. The decisions that follow indicate how the courts have treated the inevitable litigation arising from such situations.

You might consider whether a better rule could be written than the UPA presumption. Would it be more appropriate to have a presumption that profits and losses will—in the absence of an agreement—be divided on the basis of relative effort and relative capital contributions? How would such a rule be administered?

Partnership agreements may call for profits to be divided equally, or in varying percentages, among the partners. Losses are generally divided in the same percentages, and the UPA so presumes unless otherwise provided,[4] but there may be reasons for using a different allocation of losses. Indeed, the profit percentage may also change with different levels of profit, and may change from year to year. Some complexities may develop in recalculation of the profit percentages when the members of the partnership change. For example, in large law firms the addition of a new partner, or the retirement or death of an existing partner, may require recalculation of all the profit percentages. As an alternative, many firms have adopted the "unit" method of calculation, in which each partner is assigned a certain number of units, and in which the total of the units becomes the denominator of the fraction for determining profit percentage.

1. UPA § 18(a).
2. UPA § 18(f).
3. UPA § 18(b).
4. UPA § 18(a).

Example: The ABC law firm uses a unit calculation for profits and losses. A is assigned 4 units, B 3 units, and C 1 unit. A's share of profits and losses is therefore ⁴⁄₈, B's is ³⁄₈, and C's is ¹⁄₈. If D is admitted as a new partner with a unit assignment of 2, the new shares become ⁴⁄₁₀ for A, ³⁄₁₀ for B, ¹⁄₁₀ for C, and ²⁄₁₀ for D.

Ordinarily, the members of a professional partnership will require that distributions be made to them periodically prior to the end of the year, and therefore before a final calculation may be made of the firm's profits. Distributions of this kind are usually called "drawings," and represent in most cases an advance against the partners' shares of the profits. Alternatively, the partners may agree to the payment of "salaries," though in a real sense these, too, represent the equivalent of a distribution of profits to them.

Setting the formula and structure for profit-allocation within a partnership can be a formidable task. Articles and books have been written on how profits should be allocated in law firms and other professional partnerships. In the case of real estate limited partnerships and other tax shelters, the provisions on profit allocations and fees to general partners frequently run several pages of small type.

If there is no agreement on profits, salaries and expenses, there is likely to be dispute not only as to the division thereof among the partners, but as to the character of individual expenditures. Are they reimbursable expenses, or are they disguised salaries? Consider the cases that follow.

REFERENCES ON LAW FIRM PARTNERSHIPS

Gilson & Mnookin, Sharing Among the Human Capitalists: An Economic Inquiry into the Corporate Law Firm and How Partners Split Profits (1985) 37 Stanford L.Rev. 313.

Cantor, How to Cut A Plump Melon (1972) 13 Law Office Econ. & Mgmt. 13.

Moldenhauer, Formula and Nonformula Systems for Distributing Partnership Net Income (1972) 13 Law Office Econ. & Mgmt. 21.

Giuliani, Financial Planning and Control for Lawyers, 63 ABAJ 61 (1977).

WAAGEN v. GERDE
Washington Supreme Court, 1950.
36 Wn.2d 563, 219 P.2d 595.
Comment, 49 Mich.L.Rev. 905.

DONWORTH, JUSTICE. This is a suit in which the plaintiff alleged that during a period of six years an equal partnership existed between him and the defendant Karl Gerde in the ownership and operation of a certain fishing vessel. Plaintiff prayed for an accounting of partnership earnings alleged to have been fraudulently withheld by the defendants in the amount of $20,000. . . . At the conclusion of the trial, the court took the case under advisement and wrote a memorandum decision holding in favor of the plaintiff. After having denied the defendants' motion for a new trial, the court granted plaintiff judgment for the sum of $11,916.44, from which the defendants have appealed. . . .

Appellant located the Princess in March, 1940, and arranged to purchase her for $8750 and to install a new engine for $700. He also obtained a loan of $5000 from the R.F.C. which was secured by a mortgage on the boat. Respondent sent $2500 to appellant for the purpose of their acquiring the boat and the purchase was consummated, appellant mortgaging his home to pay for his share.

In May, 1940, appellant wrote respondent asking for $50 to help pay interest on the mortgage and an insurance premium. Respondent sent him $100 and thereafter no further request for money was ever made by appellant, although respondent was able and willing to contribute his share. . . .

Whenever appellant was in charge of the boat he received the customary portion of the two-thirds of the "catch" to which the crew was entitled. This amounted to $19,755.09. In addition, appellant received $2,812.09 for services rendered as captain or co-captain. He and respondent each received half of the one-third of the "catch," to which the boat was entitled, amounting to $19,634.92 for each. As to these items there is no dispute.

In November, 1941, appellant conceived the idea of fishing for soupfin shark with gill nets. [After some experimentation, he constructed special nets for this purpose, and used them successfully.]

The total cost of these nets and of keeping them in repair during the period from January, 1942, to March, 1946, was $20,872.54. During this period appellant, without the knowledge of respondent, took one-half of the boat's one-third share of the "catch" as rental for the use of these nets. The gross amount received by him was $37,705.42. His theory appears to be that since respondent did not expressly authorize the purchase of the nets, they belonged exclusively to appellant and he was entitled to half of the boat's share as rental for their use. When the Princess was sold, appellant disposed of the nets for $7000 which he retained, in addition to the rental ($37,705.42). The profit resulting from the use and sale of these nets was $23,832.88, which was retained by appellant. Half of this sum is claimed by respondent in this suit.
. . .

When the Princess was sold in March, 1946, respondent received from appellant $9000 (being one-half of the sale price) and learned for the first time that appellant claimed to own the nets. Appellant's letter advising him of this claim was as follows:

Seattle, Wash. March 21, 1946

"Hallo Alfred:

"Thanks for the letter, which we received some time ago. Well I can now tell you that Princess is sold. I must say that I did not feel very much like selling, but as you know, it is impossible to get anybody you can trust to take care of the boat. I have had lots of trouble this year. This winter we have not earned anything, only expenses have we had. Weather bad all the time. We have some money coming yet from the Liver Po*l*l, will probably get them in a few months I am sending you a check for 9.000.—for half of the boat and all that was with the boat when we bought. The nets for shark fishing I have bought from the time we first started, have paid all expenses myself, there was lots of work with it, *so that if you should own part of it and pay for everything, I believe you would have been in debt.* I have been in the hole the two last winters. Last year I lost everything for 4000.—and this winter I have a loss of 1500.—. *So the profit is not big.* We have kept accounts and everything is squared now except a bit of money we still can expect from the po*ll.* All accounts are according to the regulations of the Union. If you some time come up here you can go through the books. Well, this will be all for now.

Best greetings from us all

Karl and family." (Italics ours).

When appellant wrote this letter he had received a profit from the use and sale of the shark nets (after deducting all costs of acquisition and expenses of repairs—exclusive of appellant's labor) amounting to $23,832.88. Consequently, his statement that, if respondent had owned an interest in the nets and had paid his share of the costs and expenses, "I believe you would have been in debt" was entirely false. The truth was that, instead of being "in debt" with respect to the nets, respondent would have had one-half of $23,832.88 or $11,916.44 as his profit. . . .

[The appellant's primary contention was that the parties were not partners, but only co-owners of the boat. This contention was rejected because of the parties' use of the terms "partnership" and "partner" in various communications, including their income tax returns. The appellant also contended that the nets were individual rather than partnership property, but lost on this issue because the expenses in connection with the nets were charged to partnership accounts.]

Appellant's final assignment of error is that the trial court erred in refusing to allow appellant any credit for work done by him in constructing the shark nets.

The evidence shows that appellant with some help from his two sons designed and built the shark nets. Respondent did not in any way assist him in his job. According to appellant, the value of this work was $2500 and he claims that, even though a partnership should be found to exist, he should be compensated for this work.

The general rule is clear that one partner is not entitled to extra compensation from the partnership, in the absence of an express or an implied agreement therefor. Each case must depend largely upon its own facts, and thus other cases are generally of little or no assistance in deciding the case at hand.

The exception to the general rule is well stated in 1 Rowley, Modern Law of Partnership 412, § 354, as follows: " 'Where it can be fairly and justly implied from the course of dealing between the partners, nor [or] from circumstances of equivalent force, that one partner is to be compensated for his services, his claim will be sustained.' [Emerson v. Durand, 64 Wis. 111, 24 N.W. 129, 54 Am.Rep. 593.] 'The partnership may be of such a peculiar kind, and the arrangements and the course of dealing of the partners in regard to it may be such as pretty plainly to show an expectation and understanding, without an express agreement upon the subject, that certain services of a copartner should be paid for. Such cases, presenting unusual conditions, are exceptions to the general rule [Hoag v. Alderman, 184 Mass. 217, 68 N.E. 199],' however."

While appellant's ingenuity and industry were largely responsible for the success of the Princess in shark fishing, we cannot find anything in the record from which an agreement to pay him special compensation could be implied. Appellant did inform respondent that he was busy getting the nets ready and that it would "be lots of work to fix" them, but never at any time did he inform respondent what the work actually entailed or that he expected any compensation for it. Since respondent had so little knowledge of the conduct of the net operations, there could not be any implied agreement for compensation. The trial court found no factual basis for such an allowance, and we can find none in the record. In re Levy's Estate, 125 Wash. 240, 215 P. 811, cited by appellant, this court did not set forth the factual situation under which extra compensation was allowed, and therefore that case cannot be held to be controlling in the present case. . . .

The facts as found by the trial court are adopted by this court. That court correctly applied the legal principles involved and we find no error in its disposition of the case. Upon our consideration of the entire record, it is ordered that the judgment and decree appealed from be and hereby is affirmed.

[The court does not appear to have considered the possibility that expenditures on the nets were additional capital contributions for which appellant might have been entitled to interest under UPA § 18(c).]

SIMPSON, C.J., and BEALS, SCHWELLENBACH and GRADY, JJ., concur.

ALTMAN v. ALTMAN
United States Court of Appeals, Third Circuit, 1981.
653 F.2d 755.

OPINION OF THE COURT

SEITZ, CHIEF JUDGE.

Ashley Altman appeals from a judgment of the district court ordering the dissolution of five partnerships and directing that the assets of the partnerships be liquidated and distributed to the partners. Pennsylvania law governs the disposition of this diversity action.

I.

From 1952 to 1973, Sydney Altman and Ashley Altman operated a number of partnerships engaged in real estate construction and management in southeastern Pennsylvania. During this period the two brothers shared equally in the management and control of the partnerships, and through their joint efforts they built the businesses into very profitable and substantial enterprises. Sydney and Ashley received identical salaries, and each brother was permitted to charge certain personal expenses to the partnerships. The brothers agreed that the amount of such expenses would be equal. Therefore, if one brother charged more personal expenses to the partnerships, he would pay to the other brother one-half the amount by which his personal expenses exceeded those of his brother.

. . .

[In January, 1973, Sydney moved to Florida to obtain a divorce, and for the first six months thereafter commuted weekly to Pennsylvania to work for two to three days. Beginning July, 1973, Sydney did not return to Pennsylvania, and in November he advised Ashley that he was considering retiring from the business. A dispute arose between the brothers as to whether this constituted dissolution, and Sydney ultimately brought judicial action for dissolution. The district court ordered dissolution.]

. . . The court found that Ashley's conduct had "progressed to a point which makes it impracticable for the partnerships to continue," and dissolution was ordered as of June 6, 1977, the date of the court's decision. In addition, Ashley was directed to pay Sydney $153,750.67 to equalize partnership distributions, salaries, and reimbursed personal expenses. . . .

. . .

III.

Ashley also challenges the district court's holding that he is not entitled to compensation beyond his share of the partnership profits for managing the partnerships between August 1973 and June 1977. The court found that Ashley breached the partnership agreements by unilaterally paying himself salaries from the partnerships in excess of what the brothers had agreed upon. The court concluded that under Pennsylvania law the services rendered by Ashley did not justify additional compensation.

The Pennsylvania Supreme Court has emphasized that "in the absence of an agreement to the contrary, a partner is not entitled to compensation beyond his share of the profits, for services rendered by him in performing partnership matters. . . . [A] right to compensation arises only where the services rendered extend beyond normal partnership functions." Rosenfeld v. Rosenfeld, 390 Pa. 39, 45, 133 A.2d 829, 832 (1957); see Kirby v. Kalbacher, 373 Pa. 103, 105, 95 A.2d 535, 540 (1953) (services required only for successful operation of existing partnership not beyond normal partnership functions). Ashley, however, does not expressly contend that the services he performed went beyond normal partnership functions. Instead, he relies on Greenan v. Ernst, 408 Pa. 495, 508–10, 184 A.2d 570, 577–78 (1962), in which the Pennsylvania Supreme Court concluded that it would be "highly inequitable" to deny compensation to an active partner who had assumed sole responsibility for the management of a partnership when the inactive partners either "could not or would not" assume any responsibility. The court noted that the "skill and efforts" of the active partner produced large profits for the partnership and therefore benefitted the other partners.

In contending that it would be highly inequitable in this case to deny compensation, Ashley emphasizes that after August 1973 the entire management and supervision of the partnerships were left to him. He asserts that he not only preserved the partnerships' properties but also maximized profits during this period. In addition, Ashley points to expert testimony at the trial emphasizing the high caliber of his management of the partnerships.

Ashley apparently is contending that compensation is awarded under Pennsylvania law whenever it would be highly inequitable not to do so. However, *Greenan* does not support this contention. The *Greenan* court reaffirmed the *Rosenfeld* rule, and it found that the services in question extended beyond normal partnership functions. Thus, Ashley must show more than the fact that a failure to award compensation would be highly inequitable; he must also show that his services extended beyond normal partnership functions.

In this case, the district court concluded that Ashley's services did not warrant compensation in excess of his share of the partnership profits. In reaching this decision, the court necessarily found that the services performed by Ashley did not extend beyond normal partnership functions. We recognize that in *Greenan* the Pennsylvania Supreme Court appeared to relax the definition of "beyond normal partnership functions" by allowing compensation to a partner who had assumed responsibility for the continued operation of an existing partnership. However, the critical factor in *Greenan* was that the active partner had taken an existing partnership and expanded it substantially beyond its previous size and scope. In contrast, the services rendered by Ashley maintained the operation of existing businesses in the same manner as they had been operated before Sydney's departure. In addition, unlike the situation in *Greenan,* the lack of participation in the partnerships by Sydney was with the consent of Ashley. Thus, the district court's factual finding that Ashley's services did not warrant compensation beyond his share of the partnership profits was not clearly erroneous. Although this result may appear harsh to some, we believe that the narrow scope of our review of the district court's factual findings and the relevant principles of Pennsylvania law require this conclusion.

IV.

The district court also directed Ashley to pay Sydney an amount equal to one-half of the personal expenses charged to the partnerships by Ashley between January 1974 and June 1977. The court found that this payment was necessary to equalize the distribution of partnership earnings. Ashley contends that this award was erroneous. He asserts that the practice of the brothers before 1974 was to charge such personal expenses to the partnerships, and that he merely continued this practice after Sydney moved to Florida. Ashley also notes that the partnership agreements provided that "the partners shall be reimbursed by the partnership for their out-of-pocket personal expenses." In addition, he apparently argues that the brothers' past practice of equalizing the amount of reimbursed personal expenses was altered by Sydney's agreement in January 1974 that his personal expenses would be charged against his capital account and not as expenses of the partnerships.

The district court found that prior to Sydney's move to Florida the brothers had an agreement that they would charge their personal expenses to the partnerships. The court also found that Sydney and Ashley had agreed that if one brother's personal expenses were greater than those of the other brother, a payment would be made to equalize the situation. When it ordered Ashley to pay Sydney an amount representing the personal expenses charged by Ashley after 1973, the district court referred to the equalization agreement and apparently held that it had not been altered by the brothers. We do not perceive any basis for holding otherwise. The January 1974 agreement between Sydney and Ashley clearly altered one aspect of their past practice—Sydney's personal expenses were to be charged against his capital account rather than as expenses of the partnership. However, the evidence does not reveal that the brothers even referred to the equalization practice in reaching this agreement. In addition, the decision to change the method of charging Sydney's personal expenses does not by itself indicate that the equalization agreement must have been modified. Thus, we conclude that the district court did not commit error when it awarded Sydney an amount equal to one-half of the personal expenses charged to the partnerships by Ashley.

.   .   .

VI.

The judgment of the district court will be affirmed.

NOTE ON ALTMAN v. ALTMAN

Though it is not once mentioned in the opinion of the Third Circuit, the Uniform Partnership Act is in effect in Pennsylvania. The applicable provision, UPA § 18(f), appears in Penn.Stat.Ann. tit. 59, § 51(f) (1964).

REFERENCES—COMPENSATION

Luff v. Luff, 158 F.Supp. 311 (D.C.D.C.1958) (compensation allocated among partners based on monetary value of each day's work; case decided prior to adoption of UPA).

Vangel v. Vangel, 51 Cal.2d 510, 334 P.2d 863 (1959) (compensation allowed to one whose fault caused the dissolution for managerial services rendered in continuing business after dissolution).

Chazan v. Most, 209 Cal.App.2d 519, 25 Cal.Rptr. 864 (1962) (§ 18 of the UPA allowing compensation to a "surviving partner" for services in winding up refers only to a partner who survives after the death of the other).

Wikstrom v. Davis, 211 Or. 254, 315 P.2d 597 (1957) (compensation denied to partner who wound up business after expulsion of co-partner).

Greenan v. Ernst, 408 Pa. 495, 184 A.2d 570 (1962) (partner entitled to reasonable compensation for managing partnership assets although he had fraudulently concealed profits from co-partner).

Timmermann v. Timmermann, 272 Or. 613, 538 P.2d 1254 (1975) (partnership continued eighteen months after one partner withdrew; continuing partners allowed compensation for labor and management).

Koenig v. Huber, 87 S.D. 507, 210 N.W.2d 825 (1973) (partner not entitled to added compensation for extra services contributed while co-partner served as deputy sheriff).

Interest and other charges:

Capitol Beef Co. v. Somerville Meat Co., 1 Mass.App. 505, 301 N.E.2d 825 (1973) (in joint venture accounting, charges for interest and for penalties should be charged against share of venturer responsible for that expense, rather than against revenue of the joint venture).

NOTE ON SHARING LOSSES; FOREIGN LAW

The Partnership Act (§ 18(a)) provides that partners share losses in proportion to their shares of profits. In a partnership where assets are important, profits are likely to be shared (by agreement) in proportion to capital contributions. So if P contributed 60, Q 30 and R 10, and the assets had doubled at dissolution, each would receive twice what he had put in; if the assets had lost half their value, each would receive half.

If however P contributes 100 while Q contributes nothing but his efforts, the agreement will probably divide profits in some other way—perhaps equally per capita. Under such an agreement, if the assets have doubled, they will be distributed 150 to P (for his capital plus one half of the profits), and 50 to Q. If the assets have been totally lost, Q would be obliged by UPA § 18(a) to contribute 50 to P to equalize their losses. If one can imagine one's self going assetless into a partnership from which he emerges not only without profit, but with a huge debt, one may feel that this result is unfair. Although some fairer rule may be written into the partnership agreement, assetless partners are the kind least likely to retain lawyers to protect their interests by contract clauses.

A neat solution to this problem is provided by the Civil Code of the Philippines (art. 1797), which provides that an "industrial partner" (meaning one who contributes only services) has no duty to contribute to losses; the commission's comment explains that he has already made a contribution by rendering services which yielded no profit.

In the Code Napoleon, the solution is quite capricious. A partner who contributes only services is treated, for purposes of sharing profits and losses, as if he had contributed the same amount as that co-partner who has contributed the smallest amount (but more than zero), and is bound to contribute to losses in this proportion (art. 1853). In a partnership of three who have contributed 80%, 20% and 0%, the non-contributor will be bound to make up one sixth of the loss; in a partnership of two who have contributed 100 and 0, the non-contributor will be bound to make up half the loss! This allocation can be modified by terms of the partnership agreement, but never to the extent of completely exonerating a partner from contribution (art. 1955). Thus the French Code forbids the solution which the Philippine Code prescribes.

REFERENCE

Ripert and Roblot, Traite de Droit Commercial (6th ed. 1968) I, 419–421.

SECTION 3. PARTNERSHIP PROPERTY AND PARTNERSHIP CONTROL

A. PROPERTY

NOTE: PARTNERSHIP PROPERTY

Identification of partnership property is important in establishing rights among partners, and also among individual and partnership creditors. An initial question asks whether the ownership of the property used was contributed to the partnership, or only its use. This kind of question presents itself to the courts most frequently with regard to real property, but it can arise also with regard to investments, or to a stock exchange seat, or to the goodwill accompanying a going concern.

If the ownership of the property in question has not been contributed to the partnership, it forms no part of the partnership estate. The only partnership question which can then arise is whether the owner is entitled to some sort of rental or other compensation for its use, in addition to his proportionate share of the profits.

If ownership of the property was contributed to the partnership, more complicated questions arise. At the outset, there is the question whether title can be held by a partnership. One hundred years ago, courts were prone to say that, since a partnership is not a legal entity, a conveyance to a partnership is a nullity; or that it operates (if at all) as a conveyance to the partners, or some of them, in their individual capacities. This hobgoblin is apparently laid to rest by the UPA.

Assuming that real estate can be held by a partnership, or by the partners in their capacity as such, one is ready for the question, on whom does the property devolve when the partnership is "dissolved"? On reading the Uniform Act, one might conclude that the question is rather simply answered there. But on turning to the post-UPA cases, one is met by an outpouring of curious lore which obviously flows from a more ancient source.

Before proceeding to the cases, please read carefully sections 8 and 24–28 of the Uniform Partnership Act.

IN RE ESTATE OF SCHAEFER

Supreme Court of Wisconsin, 1976.
72 Wis.2d 600, 241 N.W.2d 607.

DAY, JUSTICE.

The orders appealed from arise out of a single petition filed in probate court by Marilynn H. Schaefer, widow of the decedent, Ben G. Schaefer, concerning a large number of matters in the administration of the estate. . . . The principal issue concerns real estate inventoried as property of a business partnership between Ben Schaefer and his brother, Arthur Schaefer, and claimed by Marilynn Schaefer to have belonged to the brothers as tenants in common. . . .

Ben G. and Arthur E. Schaefer went into business together in 1933, each providing an equal capital share to start an automobile dealership in Racine, which came to be known as Schaefer Pontiac Sales. No written partnership agreement was ever executed. The brothers began acquiring real estate in 1944, making purchases through 1967 which included items 26 through 38 of the inventory, which are at issue here. The deeds to all 13 parcels are included in the record; nine of the deeds name the grantees simply as "Ben G. Schaefer and Arthur E. Schaefer;" three of the deeds name the grantees as "Ben G. Schaefer and Arthur E. Schaefer, as tenants in common," and one deed refers to "Ben G. Schaefer and Arthur E. Schaefer, a real estate partnership."

In 1947, the automobile sales activity was incorporated, and separated from the real estate business which became known as "Ben G. Schaefer and Arthur E. Schaefer, Real Estate Department." A separate checking account was maintained for the real estate business, titled "Ben G. Schaefer and Arthur E. Schaefer, Real Estate Trust Account, Partnership." The respondents introduced testimony by an accountant, retained to examine the business records, to the effect that all payments for real estate purchased, and all proceeds from real estate sold, and income from leases, came from or went into this checking account. When mortgage loans were obtained, the proceeds went into the "partnership" bank account, and the amortization payments came from that account. When improvements were made to property held by the business, they were paid for out of the "partnership" account. This testimony was uncontradicted, and was accepted as true by the trial court.

Various documents in the record provide additional evidence concerning the understanding of the Schaefer brothers as to ownership of the real estate. A mortgage on one of the parcels in question was given by "Ben G. Schaefer and Arthur E. Schaefer, as co-partners." Leases were introduced by the respondents as follows:

(1) Lease from "Ben G. Schaefer and Arthur E. Schaefer, d/b/a Schaefer Realty Company," signed by Arthur E. Schaefer alone;

(2) Lease from "Ben G. Schaefer and Arthur E. Schaefer," signed by Arthur E. Schaefer as "Partner," alone;

(3) Lease from "Arthur E. Schaefer and Ben G. Schaefer, co-partners," signed by Arthur E. Schaefer alone; and

(4) Lease from "Ben G. Schaefer and Arthur E. Schaefer, a partnership" signed by Arthur E. Schaefer as "partner," alone.

In an attempt to show that the real estate was not regarded as partnership property, Marilynn Schaefer introduced additional leases as follows:

(1) Lease with option to buy from "Arthur E. Schaefer and Colette Schaefer, his wife, and Ben G. Schaefer and Marilynn Schaefer, his wife," signed by all four lessors;

(2) Lease from "Ben G. Schaefer and Arthur E. Schaefer," signed by both of them;

(3) Lease from "Ben G. Schaefer and Arthur E. Schaefer," signed by Arthur E. Schaefer, alone.

Marilynn Schaefer also introduced documents relating to a condemnation proceeding which referred to "lands of Ben G. Schaefer and Marilynn Schaefer, his wife; Arthur E. Schaefer and Colette Schaefer, his wife," and a deed conveying some of the business property from the Schaefers and their wives, individually named. The proceeds of that condemnation, however (as well as prior rental income from that property), went into the "partnership" books, and were distributed to Ben and Arthur accordingly. Arthur testified that the wives' names were included "because the attorneys wanted them, not because they (the wives) had any interest," although he was referring to a deed not admitted into evidence.

Respondents also introduced testimony based on tax returns filed between 1948 and 1969 by the business on tax forms designed for partnerships, and by Ben G. Schaefer individually, showing that the income of the real estate operation was divided equally between Ben and Arthur, and that Ben's reported income coincided with the amount distributed by the business. This testimony was undisputed, except insofar as Marilynn extracted the concession that the partnership tax return forms might be used for non-partnership business arrangements.

On this evidence, the trial court found that a partnership existed, and that the real estate was partnership property. Marilynn Schaefer challenges the sufficiency of the evidence to support that finding, and makes legal arguments based on the statute of frauds and the form of the deeds of conveyance.

The evidence overwhelmingly supports the trial court's finding that a partnership did exist. . . .

Once the existence of a partnership is established, there is a statutory presumption that property purchased with partnership funds belongs to the partnership unless a "contrary intent" is shown. Sec. 178.05(2), Wis.Stats. [UPA § 8] The evidence in this case is plainly insufficient to establish a "contrary intent." The only evidence of intent not to operate as a partnership are the references to "tenants in common" on three of the thirteen deeds conveying the lands in question to Ben and Arthur, and the inclusion of the Schaefers' spouses as grantors on the two conveyances introduced. Even if this would be sufficient to overcome the statutory presumption, it must be weighed against the overwhelming mass of evidence showing that the lands were purchased with partnership funds, managed as a partnership activity, and sold for partnership benefits.

Marilynn Schaefer attacks the probative value of the respondents' evidence, in particular the testimony concerning the "partnership" tax returns. . . . This court has held that receipt of a share of business profits, as shown in tax returns, is prima facie evidence of partnership . . . In any case, there is ample evidence independent of the tax returns to support the trial court's finding that a partnership existed and owned the real estate in question. . . .

Marilynn Schaefer also argues that a partnership dealing in real estate is subject to the statute of frauds, and must be evidenced by a writing. It is true that this court has adopted the minority view that a partnership created to deal in real estate is void unless conforming to the statute of frauds . . .

There was admittedly no written partnership agreement in the present case. However, an exception to the statute of frauds is made where all parties have performed the contract, indicating their acquiescence in its terms. . . .

. . . This is a case where the Schaefer brothers purchased land out of a common fund, held record title in both of their names, took possession of, leased, and improved the land on a joint basis, and divided the profits between themselves. After such conduct of this business for over 20 years, it is now sought to wind up its affairs in a manner completely consistent with the long-standing "performance" of the firm. There is no evidence whatsoever that Ben Schaefer would have disputed the existence of a partnership; certainly his wife, in pursuit of a dower interest, should not now be permitted to claim that "performance" was insufficient to demonstrate that the Schaefer brothers fully intended that the remaining properties in inventory should be handled as had all the others.

. . .

Marilynn Schaefer also argues that because the deeds to the properties in question conveyed them as estates of inheritance (to Ben and Arthur Schaefer and "their heirs and assigns forever"), Ben and Arthur received estates of inheritance, as tenants in common, and did not take the lands as a business partnership. Words of inheritance, however, refer to the extent of the estate granted—a fee simple—and do not define the grantee. . . . The words "heirs and assigns forever" manifest no particular intent to create an estate of inheritance. Moreover, here the words of inheritance were part of the standard printed form of deed. They cannot be said, in light of the evidence of intent to create a partnership, to demonstrate any intent whatsoever to take the property as tenants in common.

Apart from the words of inheritance, Marilynn Schaefer argues that the muniment of title should govern; since the bulk of the deeds name as grantees simply Ben G. and Arthur E. Schaefer, the deeds acted to create a tenancy in common between them. Whatever presumption the muniment of title may ordinarily carry, this court has long held to the principle, now codified in sec. 178.05, Stats., supra, that property purchased with partnership funds and appropriated for partnership purposes is presumptively partnership property, regardless of the manner in which title is formally held.

. . . In the present case, the evidence established both that the real estate was purchased with partnership funds, and that it was purchased and used for partnership purposes. The fact that legal title was in the individual partners is immaterial under these circumstances.

In summary, the partnership of the Schaefer brothers was not subject to the statute of frauds because it was sufficiently performed to establish its existence. The words of inheritance used in the deeds, and the form in which legal title was held, are immaterial to the determination of whether the real estate in question was partnership property, since the evidence conclusively shows the purchase of the real estate with partnership funds, and its use for partnership purposes.

BALAFAS v. BALAFAS
Minnesota Supreme Court, 1962.
263 Minn. 267, 117 N.W.2d 20.

KNUTSON, CHIEF JUSTICE. This is an appeal from an order of the district court denying plaintiff's motion for a new trial and from the judgment entered pursuant to the court's order.

The action is brought for an accounting seeking to establish that certain property acquired jointly by two brothers, Chris and Michael M. Balafas, over a lifetime of working and dealing together constituted partnership property and that one-half thereof, upon the death of Michael M. Balafas, belonged to his estate. The court found that the property acquired by the brothers was considered partnership property during their lifetime but that there was an agreement, implied in fact, between them that upon the death of one the survivor would be the owner of all such joint property.

The appeal falls mainly into two separate aspects, namely: Does the evidence sustain the court's finding that there was an agreement, implied in fact, that upon the death of one of the brothers the property acquired by them jointly during their lifetime should belong to the survivor, and, if so, are there any legal impediments to the consummation and enforcement of such agreement? We will consider these in order.

Michael M. Balafas, referred to hereinafter as Mike, came to this country from Greece in 1907. He had about a second-grade education. In 1911, his brother Chris came from Greece and joined him in Stillwater, Minnesota, where they operated a shoeshine and shoe-repair business. They continued in business in Stillwater for about 25 years, after which they discontinued that business. They left Stillwater, Mike obtaining work in St. Paul and Chris in Minneapolis. Eventually they again went into the shoe-repair business in Minneapolis in 1941. At that time they purchased a house with an attached shop from which they operated their business.

Apparently to begin with they split the proceeds of the business evenly. Early in their business activities they began to purchase stock out of the joint fund of the brothers, putting most of the stock in the name of Chris. After leaving Stillwater they again began purchasing stock when business picked up, apparently each putting up half of the money, although it appears that more consistently they purchased the stock out of the joint fund. Practically all of the stock was purchased in the name of Chris. They made their income tax returns on a partnership form. Over all the years that they were in business together there was never any division of profits in the usual sense. Their living expenses, most of the money they spent for stock, and all other disbursements were made out of the joint fund.

Mike married plaintiff, Mary Balafas, in 1942. . . . Existence in the household may be characterized by its frugality. Mary was given a small sum of money to run the house, and, in addition to doing the housework, she helped in the shop. She also kept what books they had under the direction of Mike. Chris never did learn to read or write, so the business affairs were conducted largely by Mike. . . .

On September 26, 1959, Mike died after being ill with cancer for about 3 years. The property which the two brothers had amassed, largely corporate securities, amounted roughly to the sum of $700,000 at the time of Mike's death. The securities they held were either in the name of Chris or in the names of Mike and Chris as joint tenants. Shortly after Mike's death, Mary Balafas signed and filed a petition for the probate of Mike's estate, and his will was admitted to probate, but the estate, excluding the property owned jointly by the two brothers or in the name of Chris, amounted to only a nominal sum. In 1960, Mary was appointed special administratrix of Mike's estate to bring this action. She claimed that all the assets amassed during Mike's lifetime were purchased with partnership funds and that upon Mike's death one-half thereof belonged to his estate.

At the outset of the trial it was stipulated that Mike and Chris were engaged in a partnership during the time involved and that up to the death of Mike the assets acquired by the brothers were acquired with partnership funds. In addition to the facts stated above, there was other evidence that tended to establish the agreement found by the court. Oliver Eielson, a stockbroker who had handled the brothers' business for about 16 years prior to Mike's death, testified that he had asked Mike why most of the stock was in Chris' name. Mike replied that he did not want his wife, plaintiff herein, to get those stocks. . . .

In 1956, the two brothers executed new wills in which Mike made a specific bequest of $10,000 to Mary and left the remainder of his estate to Chris. Chris' will left everything to Mike. Eielson, the stockbroker, testified that when Mike told him of the provisions of the new will he had some discussion with Mike about it. He testified:

"In '56. He came into the office, and he told me he had this new will prepared, and he said, 'I am going to leave everything to Chris,' and I says, 'Well, Mike, that isn't right.' I says, 'You certainly want to leave some to your wife,' and he says, 'No, I am not going to leave her anything. I don't want to leave her anything.' "

In addition to the above testimony there is evidence of financial transactions in Mike's later years which add support to a finding that Mike planned that Chris should take all the property in Chris' name or in their joint names.

In 1957, a $50,000 savings certificate was procured from joint funds in the name of Mike in trust for his niece, Stamata Balafas; another was procured in the name of Mike or Mary Balafas for $10,000; and a savings account was opened for Mike in trust for Matheos Balafas. A few days before his death, Mike instructed Chris to take $50,000 from joint funds and place it in Mary's account. He had also set up a checking account of more than $4,000 in her name, and she received $3,400 cash from Chris for Mike's last expenses and funeral. In other words, during the last 2 years of his life, Mike gave Mary some $64,000, in addition to which she received $3,400 after his death. If he had not intended to leave the balance of his property which was already in the name of Chris or in the names of the two brothers as joint tenants to Chris upon his death, it is obvious that it would have been unnecessary to make these provisions for his wife, Mary. The only rational implication from all the facts taken together is that he intended to leave the securities that were carried in Chris' name or in the names of himself and Chris jointly to Chris upon his death, and the will of Chris leaving everything to Mike implements this conclusion that the brothers intended the survivor to have the securities which they owned jointly upon the death of one.

There is also evidence which shows that the relationship between Mike and Mary was at times quite strained. . . .

In spite of her denials at the time of this trial, the evidence shows quite clearly that she knew, during all the time that she was living with Mike, how the property was carried and that none of it was in her name. Even the house they lived in was in the names of Mike and Chris as joint tenants. Mary had attended school through the tenth grade and had a much better education than either of the brothers. She kept the books under the direction of Mike and could hardly have helped knowing how the securities were bought and carried.

After Mike's death, Mary talked to Oliver Eielson and stated to him that she had received everything to which she was entitled and more than she had expected and that she was satisfied. Apparently thereafter she saw an opportunity to acquire more, and, while many might feel that Mike could have been more liberal with Mary, the evidence clearly sustains the court's finding that the brothers intended that when one died the other would be the owner of all of the joint property carried in the name of Chris alone or in the names of Mike and Chris jointly. In fact, it is difficult to see how any other conclusion could be arrived at.

The question then arises: Are there any legal impediments to the enforcement of such agreement?

2. The nature and manner of proof of a contract implied in fact have been adequately discussed in prior decisions of this court. . . .

The difference between a contract implied in fact and an express contract lies mainly in the manner of proof. In Lombard v. Rahilly, 127 Minn. 449, 450, 149 N.W. 950, we said:

> "A contract implied in fact requires a meeting of the minds, an agreement, just as much as an express contract. The difference between the two is largely in the character of the evidence by which they are established. It is sometimes said that a contract implied in fact is established by circumstantial evidence. . . . The question whether there is such a contract is usually to be determined by the jury as an inference of fact."

Once a contract implied in fact is sufficiently established, it is as valid as any other contract.

3. Plaintiff contends that, inasmuch as the parties have stipulated and the court has found that the property jointly acquired and owned by the brothers during Mike's lifetime was acquired with partnership funds and held as partnership property, upon Mike's death his share of the partnership property belonged to his estate under the Uniform Partnership Act, which is the law of this state. Minn.St. 323.37, subd. 1, reads in part:

> "When dissolution is caused in any way, except in contravention of the partnership agreement, each partner, as against his copartners and all persons claiming through them in respect of their interests in the partnership, *unless otherwise agreed,* may have the partnership property applied. . . ." (Italics supplied.)

Minn.St. 323.39 reads in part:

> "In settling accounts between the partners after dissolution, the following rules shall be observed, *subject to any agreement to the contrary:* . . . ." (Italics supplied.)

Minn.St. 323.42 provides:

> "The right to an account of his interest shall accrue to any partner, or his legal representative, as against the winding up of partners or the surviving partners or the person or partnership continuing the business, at the date of dissolution, *in the absence of any agreement to the contrary.*" (Italics supplied.)

It is obvious that the rules governing accountings between partners upon dissolution and the rights of surviving partners are subject to agreements entered into between them which may be contrary to the usual statutory rules established in the absence of such agreements. In Block v. Schmidt, 296 Mich. 610, 296 N.W. 698, the facts are quite similar to those now before us. With respect to the contention now under discussion, the Michigan court said (296 Mich. 620, 296 N.W. 702):

> ". . . appellants' contention is not tenable that since all the property in suit was acquired by investments of partnership earnings, the property so acquired must be held under the Uniform Partnership Act to belong to the partners, notwithstanding there were no creditors of the partnership, and notwithstanding the two brothers took title to the respective portions of their properties as above noted. The Uniform Partnership Act does not provide in that particular an inflexible rule of law. Instead the act expressly provides for cases wherein a 'contrary intention appears.'"

That is true here. The Uniform Partnership Act does not preclude an agreement between partners that upon the death of one the survivor or survivors shall be the owners of the partnership property.

4. It is clear that during his lifetime Mike could have disposed of his personal property as he saw fit, even if the effect of it was to diminish his spouse's marital interests upon his death. . . .

While some courts have found difficulty with the disposition of partnership property on the death of one of the partners for the reason that it is frequently claimed that such dispositions are testamentary in character, the general rule followed by a great weight of authority is that an agreement between partners that the survivor shall be the owner of all partnership property is valid if untainted by fraud. The general rule is stated in 40 Am.Jur., Partnership, § 312, as follows:

> "A provision in a partnership agreement that on the death of one of the partners his interest in the partnership shall become the property of the other partners is not testamentary in nature, and the fact that the agreement is not executed according to the requirements of the statute of wills does not invalidate it."

While most of the cases dealing with this subject involve written agreements, the rule is as applicable to a contract implied in fact as to an express agreement once such contract is sufficiently established.

. . .

. . . It is doubtful that either of these uneducated men ever had a clear legal concept of ownership of this property as partners. It is more likely that they always considered their joint property as if it were mutually owned by the two of them. It is hardly to be expected that they would observe all the legal niceties that might be found in an agreement between lawyers or even laymen having better educations. In determining what their intentions were, we must look to all the dealings between them and judge them as they are, not as they might have been. When we do that, it is clear that they intended that when one died the other should have the property acquired jointly and held in the name of Chris or in the joint names of Chris and Mike. No effort was ever made to divide the earnings annually or otherwise. All expenditures were paid out of the common fund, no matter for whose benefit it was paid. . . . The method they chose for accomplishing the purpose of having the survivor become the owner of all may not have been the best from a legal standpoint, but the evidence amply sustains a finding that they did have such intention.

Affirmed.

REFERENCES

Matter of Estate of Allen, 239 N.W.2d 163 (Iowa 1976) (property purchased with partnership funds held not partnership property because of clear intent by parties that it be held individually).

Kozlowski v. Kozlowski, 164 N.J.Super. 162, 395 A.2d 913 (1978) (partnership not implied by cohabitation of unmarried man and woman, sharing his income).

Miller v. City Bank & Trust Co., 82 Mich.App. 120, 266 N.W.2d 687 (1978) (partnership not proved by wife who worked with husband in nursery business; assumed business name declared husband and wife to be partners, husband made weekly checks from partnership account to each in equal amounts, but all tax returns made by husband as sole owner).

MADISON NATIONAL BANK v. NEWRATH
Court of Appeals of Maryland, 1971.
261 Md. 321, 275 A.2d 495.

FINAN, JUDGE. In this appeal we are called upon to determine the nature of the interest which Robert B. Weiss, one of the defendants below, had in Pike Associates, styled as a joint venture (Pike Associates) and which owned a leasehold estate improved by the Pike Shopping Center, Montgomery County, Maryland. At various times Weiss pledged his interest in the leasehold estate and in Pike Associates as security for loans. . . .

The land on which Pike Shopping Center is located is leased on a long term basis to Messrs. Hafta, Weiss and Wine, trading as "Pike Associates, a Joint Venture." The joint venture was formed by agreement on July 9, 1965, whereby Haft, Weiss and Wine agreed "to invest, as their respective shares of the capital of the Joint Venture herein created, all of their respective rights, titles and interests in and to the aforesaid leasehold interest in the Property." The agreement also provided for the management and operation of the shopping center for a period of 25 years during which period the parties would share equally in the profits and losses of the business. . . .

In July, 1967, Fidelity Associates, Inc. (Fidelity) made Weiss a loan in the amount of $150,000; however, apparently to avoid the usury law, the maker of the note was the W. & W. Corporation, a corporation controlled by Weis. . . . Also, to secure this debt, Weiss and his wife executed a deed of trust to Walter D. Newrath and Henry S. Snyder, as trustees for the benefit of Fidelity, conveying "all of their rights, title, and interest" in the leasehold estate. . . .

Fidelity had previously sought to insure the validity of this deed of trust with the Capitol Title and Escrow Corporation. Capitol Title refused to insure this trust instrument (apparently because the leasehold was owned by the joint venture and not individually by the parties to the joint venture agreement). Fidelity sought to fortify its position by obtaining a security interest in Weiss' interest in Pike Associates. It did this by obtaining an assignment in trust dated July 19, 1967, of that interest. It should be noted that the parties to this appeal agree as to the validity of this last mentioned security interest; however, it was not perfected by the filing of a financing agreement as required by the Uniform Commercial Code (U.C.C.).

. . . In 1965, Madison lent $150,000 to W. & W. Corporation. The debt was extended by several renewal notes. On March 20, 1968, the debt was again extended to March 20, 1969. In consideration of this extension, Weiss (and his associate Wine) executed security agreements giving Madison a lien on their interests in Pike Associates. Each of these liens was perfected under the Uniform Commercial Code by the filing of the financing statement. . . .

Madison initiated action in the lower court by a suit to enjoin the foreclosure of the deed of trust held by Fidelity and further sought to have the court declare its own lien superior to that of Fidelity. The chancellor summed up his findings below by stating:

". . . The principal contention of the plaintiff is that the deed of trust [Fidelity's security interest] is invalid because a sale of a partnership asset on behalf of the one partner without the approval of the other partners is contrary to [Art. 73A], Section 25(2)(b) of the Uniform Partnership Act which says that 'a partner's right in a specific partnership property is not assignable except in connection with the assignment of the rights of all partners in the same property.' The defendants contend that the defendants, Weiss and wife, are not partners in the property described in the deed of trust but are joint venturers. A careful reading of the agreement between Haft, Wine and Weiss satisfies the Court that they are not partners but are joint venturers. See Vol. VIII, Maryland Law Review, page 22 to 40. Since the security agreements referred to in the Bill of Complaint were used for the sole purpose of additional security and no action has been taken under the same, it will not be necessary for the Court to pass upon its validity as such. The Court is, therefore, of the opinion that the deed of trust and note secured thereby are valid and subsisting liens on the property described in the deed of trust. . . ."

We disagree with the lower court's finding that Fidelity's deed of trust was a valid and subsisting lien on the leasehold property. The lower court erred not only in failing to find Pike Associates to be a partnership, but it begged the question in finding it a joint venture.

There is ample authority, including past decisions of this Court, holding that a joint venture and a partnership are indistinguishable; however, we would prefer to say that they *may* be indistinguishable and are in this case. Hobdey v. Wilkinson, 201 Md. 517, 525–527, 94 A.2d 625 (1953). . . .

The Uniform Partnership Act, which has been in effect in Maryland since 1916, defines a partnership as "an association of two or more persons to carry on as co-owners a business for a profit." . . . We think Pike Associates, serving the purpose of several individuals, who had contributed personal assets to bring it into being, for the building, financing, leasing, managing and operating for mutual profit a major shopping center over a period of 25 years or more, comes within the ambit of the Uniform Partnership Act. This being the case, the lower court's theory that Weiss' interest in the leasehold was that of a tenant in common and that he could convey it by way of a deed of trust as individually owned property does not hold water. Weiss' interest in the leasehold was contributed by him as his share of the capital contribution to Pike Associates, and, as such, it became partnership property.

. . .

[The court then quoted U.P.A. §§ 8(1), 25(1)(d, e).]

In view of what we have expressed, the deed of trust given by Weiss to Fidelity in July of 1967 to secure the $165,000 note is invalid, as he sought to convey, as individually owned property, that which was partnership property. . . .

[In omitted portions of the opinion, the court held that the trust assignment of Weiss' interest in the partnership was subordinated to the security interest of Madison, for lack of filing.]

Decree reversed and case remanded for the entry of a decree consistent with this opinion; appellees to pay costs.

BLOCK v. MYLISH

Pennsylvania Supreme Court, 1945.
351 Pa. 611, 41 A.2d 731.

JUSTICE JONES. This appeal arises out of a declaratory judgment proceeding instituted to settle a controversy between surviving partners and the personal representative of a deceased partner concerning the proceeds of insurance carried by the partnership on the life of the deceased partner.

In 1923, the firm of Mylish, Mann and Drucker, composed of Isaac D. Mylish, Alfred Mann and Jerome J. Drucker, took out a separate policy of insurance on the life of each of the partners in principal sums of $10,000 and, in 1930, took out three additional like policies for $50,000 each, making in all two policies for an aggregate amount of $60,000 of insurance on the life of each partner. The partnership was named beneficiary in all of the policies and, at all times, paid the premiums thereon with partnership funds, as business expenses.

. . .

Mann died on June 4, 1943, leaving a last will of which Gordon A. Block is executor. . . .

Mylish and Drucker duly exercised their option to purchase Mann's interest in the business pursuant to the provisions of the partnership agreement, but a dispute arose among the interested parties with respect to the extent to which the value of the business should be affected on account of the policies of insurance on Mann's life. His executor maintained that the life insurance proceeds became an asset of the partnership contemporaneously with Mann's death and should, therefore, be reflected *in toto* in a valuation of the business, while Mylish and Drucker contended that only the cash surrender value of the policies on Mann's life was a partnership asset at the date of his death and that the proceeds of the insurance were available to them under the partnership agreement for their personal use in purchasing Mann's interest in the business. The learned judge of the court below decided the controversy in favor of the deceased partner's estate and entered judgment accordingly from which the surviving partners have appealed.

. . .

The presently material portions of the partnership agreement are contained in paragraph 7 thereof and the three ensuing unnumbered paragraphs from which the following excerpts or summaries are taken:

In paragraph 7 it is provided that "In the event of the termination of the partnership by the death of any one of the partners, a complete inventory of the assets of the business shall be ascertained as soon after the death of said partner as possible, . . ." by appraisers to be selected as provided in the agreement.

The next succeeding paragraph provides that "From the gross assets of the business so ascertained, the liabilities shall be deducted which shall show the net worth of the business. The surviving partners shall have the right and are hereby granted the option of purchasing the deceased partner's interest in the partnership for the sum so arrived at as to his share (good-will not to be included), . . .". The same paragraph specifies the terms of payment for the deceased partner's interest, viz., $5,000 in cash at the time the surviving partners exercise their option to purchase, fifty per cent of the balance within six months of the date of death of the deceased partner, twenty-five per cent within nine months of the same date and the remaining twenty-five per cent within one year.

The next paragraph provides that "In the event that the proceeds of life insurance on the deceased partner's life shall be paid to the copartnership and is free and clear, or is partially so, then in that event the entire proceeds, or such portion thereof as is free and clear of the said life insurance, shall be turned over and paid by said partnership on account of the purchase price and applied against the above payments insofar as it can be."

. . .

The appellants base their claim to the proceeds of the insurance on Mann's life upon the clause above quoted to the effect, in material part, that "the entire proceeds [of the insurance on the deceased partner's life], or such portion thereof as is free and clear . . ., shall be turned over and paid by said partnership on account of the purchase price" for the deceased partner's share in the business. Because of this provision, which relates to the type of payments to be made in discharge of the liability for the purchase of the deceased partner's interest rather than to the valuation of the assets of the business, the surviving partners would have the agreement interpreted so as to mean that the proceeds of the insurance on the life of a deceased partner were to be the property of the surviving partners in their individual and personal right and not the property of the partnership. Such a construction is not admissible under any fair interpretation of the written agreement.

That the insurance policies on the lives of the partners were assets of the business, and as such partnership property, is not open to reasonable dispute. . . .

The purpose and intent of the provision respecting the use to be made of the proceeds of the insurance is readily apparent. Under the immediately preceding paragraph of the agreement, the surviving partners were required to make but a relatively small cash payment upon exercising their option to purchase a deceased partner's interest. Payment of the balance of the purchase price was deferred and was to be made in installments over the year succeeding the partner's death. The reason for that provision is obvious. It was designed to save the surviving partners from the necessity of converting partnership assets, to the possible impairment or disruption of the business, in order to pay the purchase price in cash forthwith. . . . In short, to the extent of the insurance money received by the partnership upon the death of a partner, his representatives were to receive (on account of the purchase price for his interest in the business) cash instead of notes of the surviving partners. That is the clearly expressed meaning of the provision. It was not intended to advantage the surviving partners pecuniarily at the expense of their deceased associate.

The element of wager, based upon the fortuity of survivorship, which the appellants' construction of the agreement would introduce, could serve to deny the right of the partners to a reciprocal insurable interest in the life of each other. This is, by no means, intended to suggest that partners do not have an insurable interest in the life of one another. . . . Under the present appellants' contention, a partner's expectation of benefit or advantage could lie not in the continuance of the lives of his partners but rather in the possibility of their deaths prior to his own. The impeachment of the basis for the insurance which the appellants' construction would thus inject would require that the contention be discountenanced. In interpreting a contract, a construction which would effect an unreasonable or unlawful end is to be avoided. . . .

The unreasonableness of the appellants' contention is further apparent. The construction of the partnership agreement, which they advocate, would not furnish a rule uniformly applicable. For example, had the surviving partners declined to exercise their option to purchase Mann's interest, then, under further terms of the partnership agreement, liquidation would have ensued. In that event, the value of the deceased partner's interest would have been fixed as of the date of the dissolution of the partnership. Wood v. Wood, 312 Pa. 374, 378, 167 A. 600; Froess v. Froess, 284 Pa. 369, 374, 131 A. 276. Mann's death worked a dissolution of the partnership. Act of March 26, 1915, P.L. 18, Part VI, § 31, 59 P.S. § 93. And, at the instant of dissolution, the cash proceeds of the matured policies on Mann's life forthwith became part of the partnership assets. The fact that the policies were not paid by the insurance companies for several weeks thereafter, pending the filing of required proofs, did not constitute the insurance a subsequently accruing asset. . . .

The judgment is affirmed.

REFERENCE ON INSURANCE POLICIES

Jones v. Simmons, 47 Mich.App. 654, 209 N.W.2d 840 (1973) (life insurance policies were taken on the life of each partner, payable to the other, and premiums paid from partnership "profits"; held, proceeds belonged to surviving partner, not to firm).

Emerson v. Arnold, 92 Mich.App. 345, 285 N.W.2d 45 (1979) (partners' practice of increasing life insurance on each other as value of partnership interests increased did not prove agreement to accept amount of insurance proceeds in payment for partnership interest).

NOTE: DEVOLUTION OF PARTNERSHIP REALTY

The devolution of partnership realty is today a rather simple subject, but it has a very complicated past. Even today, the judges seldom content themselves with the easy analysis of the Uniform Partnership Act, but employ a great deal of terminology which can be understood only after some review of earlier law.

We start with the fact that judges of two hundred years ago did not personify a partnership; it would have been as strange to them to speak of property owned by a partnership as to speak of property owned by a friendship.[1] Later, as merchants came to personify partnerships, they occasionally conveyed real estate to partnership names. Judges were startled; sometimes they found that the conveyance conveyed nothing at all; sometimes that it conveyed title to those partners whose names appeared in the firm name; a few thought it might convey to all the actual partners, but hardly any thought it could convey to the "partnership."[2]

---

1. See for example the opinion of Lord Chancellor Hardwicke in West v. Skip, 1 Vesey 239, 27 Eng.Repr. 1006 (1749).

2. American cases are collected in annotation, 1 A.L.R. 564.

Professor Burdick has traced the judicial concept of the partnership as a property-holding "entity" well back into the 19th century, debunking the myth that it was promulgated by Dean Ames, or by the National Bankruptcy Act. F.M. Burdick,

Under the uniform act it is clear that real property can be conveyed into and out of a partnership name (§ 8). But this does not necessarily solve the problem of devolution on death, since death dissolves the partnership in whose name the property is held (§ 31(4)). In any event, it is as true today as in the time of Lord Hardwicke that a partnership can act only through living persons, and the question must be answered, which persons may act when one of the original group is dead? [3]

Descent and distribution. You have probably read elsewhere about the two radically different systems which English case law evolved to govern the devolution of an individual's assets on his death. One was the system of *descent,* which applied to real estate, and which carried obvious markings of its feudal ancestry. The eldest son, without let or hindrance of court, possessed for himself the entire patrimony. He had no obligations either to the kin or the creditors of the deceased, although the law slowly developed some lame methods for the assertion of creditor's claims.[4]

On the other hand, personalty was ruled by the system called *distribution.* A representative known as an executor or administrator took charge of the assets he could find, with an affirmative obligation to pay off the decedent's debts, and distribute the remainder among the "next of kin" upon a plan which treated all the children equally.

Neither of these systems fit the partnership situation neatly. The objections to descent and primogeniture do not require elaboration.

Distribution by the executor or administrator was also objectionable, in that it would bring into the business of the surviving partners a stranger with whom they had never agreed to associate.[5]

The English courts solved the problem quite painlessly with respect to partnership personal estate. They promptly recognized that sole control and administration of the partnership goods should remain with the surviving partner. He was not, however, like a joint tenant, who as winner took all. The surviving partner had to account to the dece-

Some Judicial Myths (1909) 22 Harv.L.Rev. 393. But it seems clear that most of the judges before 1900 regarded a partnership as incapable of holding property. Burdick's earliest reference for an entity theory of partnership is 1832.

Cf. American Bank & Trust Co. v. Michael, 244 So.2d 882 (La.App.1971) (under Louisiana Civil Code, real estate cannot vest in partnership unless partnership articles are in writing; if partners' names appear in deed, title vests in partners individually).

3. It was early decided that property acquired by partners would not be deemed in joint tenancy, since one merchant would not be likely to intend a gift to be conferred on his partner at his death. Jeffereys v. Small, 1 Vernon 217, 23 Eng.Repr. 424 (1683). Although originally a rule of equity, this became a rule for interpreting conveyances at law. American Law of Real Property (1952) § 6.8.

4. See American Law of Real Property (1952) § 14.6.

5. American decisions and even critical writings frequently attribute the doctrine of "equitable conversion" of realty to a desire to escape primogeniture. In a scholarly and convincing article, Professor F.M. Burdick has characterized this explanation as "judicial myth." He contends that the desire to keep the real estate in the hands of the surviving partners was the dominant reason for "conversion." F.M. Burdick, Some Judicial Myths (1909) 22 Harv.L.Rev. 393.

dent's executor or administrator, who would in turn pay over the proceeds, like the proceeds of other personalty, to the decedent's next of kin.[6] The same system was followed by American courts.[7] Although it made the surviving partner play something of an executor's role, very little theory was ever spun about it.

Equitable conversion in England. The pattern of devolution adopted for partnership real estate was ultimately the same as had been followed for partnership chattels. The rights of use and disposition passed from the decedent to his surviving partners; the proceeds of liquidation were distributed by the administrator to the next of kin.[8]

This solution was obviously a revolutionary bit of judicial legislation. It not only shifted the power of disposition from the common-law pattern, but also snatched the fruits from the common-law beneficiary. Even where primogeniture had been abandoned, the partnership solution had the effect of depriving the deceased partner's widow of dower, since there is no dower in personalty.

Probably for these reasons, the adoption of a special pattern for devolution of partnership realty came later than for personalty, and seems always to have been regarded as a creature of equity. It was rationalized by saying that in the eyes of equity the realty of a partnership was converted into personalty, very much as a contract to sell real estate is said to convert it into personal estate.

Equitable conversion in the United States. By the time American decisions on partnership realty were called for, there was much less need for equitable conversion than there had been in England. Primogeniture had been abolished, and the heirs of real estate were in large measure the same as the inheritors of personal estate. On the other hand, it was still important that the partnership creditors should be paid off from the firm assets.

Many American courts accordingly decided that partnership real estate should be treated like partnership personalty only to the extent necessary for partnership purposes. If the real estate was needed to pay the firm debts, the surviving partners might sell it. But if the real estate was not needed, the deceased partner's share would descend as if the land were held by him, in common with the other partners, without any partnership. The practical incidents of this view were that in many instances the surviving partners could not sell the unneeded land, the executor did not account for it nor receive a commission on it (as he would on personal estate passing through his hands), and the widow's dower attached. Courts taking this view were prone to say that the real estate was equitably converted only if required for

---

6. Newell v. Townsend, 6 Sim. 419, 58 Eng.Repr. 651 (1834); Buckley v. Barber, 6 Exch.Rep. 164, 155 Eng.Repr. 498 (1851).

7. Holbrook v. Lackey, 54 Mass. (13 Metc.) 132 (1847).

8. Darby v. Darby, 3 Drewry 495, 61 Eng.Repr. 992 (1856).

partnership purposes, or that it was *re*converted when the partnership needs terminated.[9]

This American view introduced a whole host of problems as to the point at which conversion begins and ends; or when, as it was sometimes stated, "partnership purposes" require conversion. Where debts could not be paid without selling all the real estate, the question was easily answered. It was harder to answer if debts required some but not all of the real estate, or if there was a hard choice between selling real and personal estate. If the real estate was bought for the purpose of being sold (like building lots in a subdivision), it was often held that the partnership purposes required conversion, regardless of the amount of debts.[10]

All that can be said with certainty about equitable conversion in the United States before the Uniform Act is that there was the widest variation not only among states but also within states as to the circumstances in which equitable conversion occurred.[11]

With this background, you may profitably reread UPA § 25 and consider what happens to partnership property on death of a partner under the Uniform Act, in practice and in theory. Then turn to the cases which illustrate application of the Act.

REFERENCE

Matter of Havemeyer, 17 N.Y.2d 216, 270 N.Y.S.2d 197, 217 N.E.2d 26 (1966) (value of interest in partnership taxable as personalty in state of decedent owner, although assets consisted partly of real estate, taxable as such in Connecticut); comment, 35 Fordham L.Rev. 346.

CULTRA v. CULTRA

Tennessee Supreme Court, 1949.
188 Tenn. 506, 221 S.W.2d 533.
Noted: 21 Tenn.L.Rev. 202, 98 U.Penn.L.Rev. 269.

Suit by George Cultra and others against Sayre Elizabeth Cultra and others, to determine whether realty owned by partnership descended to heirs of deceased partner, or continued to be personalty and subject to the laws of distribution. From a decree that realty was to be disposed of as personalty, an appeal was taken.

BURNETT, JUSTICE. This case presents the question of whether or not the real estate owned by a partnership, purchased by said partnership with partnership funds for partnership purposes, and not needed to pay partnership debts, descends to the heirs of a deceased partner or continues to be personalty and subject to the laws of distribution.

9. For an exhaustive collection and discussion of American authorities, see Rowley, Modern Law of Partnership (1916) §§ 624, 625.

10. Buckley v. Doig, 188 N.Y. 238, 80 N.E. 913, 11 Ann.Cas. 263 (1907).

11. Authorities are collected in annotation: Partnership Land as Real or Personal Property for Purposes of Descent and Distribution, 25 A.L.R. 389.

The cause was heard below on bill, answer and on a stipulation of facts. It is shown, and was found by the chancellor, that four people (Cultras) were partners doing business under the trade name "Morning Star Nursery," the interest being $\frac{1}{3}$ in one of the four and $\frac{2}{9}$ in [each of] the other three. These partners for the purpose of the partnership acquired three tracts of land. Two of these tracts of land were acquired in the name of the four partners, "Trading and doing business as Morning Star Nursery," while the third tract was merely acquired in the names of the individuals, the trade name not being inserted in the deed. It is shown though, without question, that this third tract was acquired by partnership out of partnership funds and for partnership purposes.

Two of the partners have died. The question here is raised by the after-born child of one of these partners. This child through her guardian ad litem takes the position that the property descends as realty to her to the exclusion of the widow, that is, the interest of her deceased father. The chancellor held that this property, all having been acquired with partnership funds and for the use of the partnership, upon the death of the partners, their interest therein was to be disposed of as personalty and that the surviving partners had a right to sell this land and then distribute the proceeds thereof as other partnership property.[1]

Prior to the enactment of the Uniform Partnership Law in 1917, . . . the courts of this State have uniformly held that it is a rule of property that real estate of a partnership is held as personalty for the purposes of the partnership but where not needed for such purposes it descends, as other real estate, to the heirs. Williamson v. Fontain, Ex'r, 66 Tenn. 212.

In thus holding the courts of this State were in line with the majority of the cases in the United States. These cases hold that the real estate, in equity, is regarded as personal property so long as it was necessary to use the real estate in settling and paying debts of the partnership and in adjusting the equities between the partners, but after this was done, any real estate remaining descends as real estate and was subject to laws of descent and distribution. See the full and copious Annotation, 25 A.L.R. 389, 414, where cases from practically every state in the Union are cited and many are digested, setting forth the respective rules as adopted by various states.

Since the adoption of the Uniform Partnership Act, above referred to, the courts of this State have not passed upon the question. . . .

Courts of other states, in construing the Uniform Partnership Act, adopt the rule of "out and out" conversion, that is, that when the property is acquired by the partnership, from the partnership fund, for

---

1. (Ed. note). Under the laws of descent of Tennessee then in effect, land of a decedent descended to the children, with no interest in the widow (except dower, where applicable); personalty descended to the widow and children, the widow receiving a "child's share." Tenn.Code of 1934 §§ 8380, 8389; Tenn.Code of 1955 §§ 31–101, 31–201.

partnership purposes, it becomes personalty for all purposes. The most notable of these cases is Wharf v. Wharf, 306 Ill. 79, 137 N.E. 446, 449.

These cases, and the holdings last above referred to, in effect adopt the English rule. This rule is that partnership realty must be regarded as personalty for all purposes, including descent and distribution. Real estate purchased and used for partnership purposes is an "out and out" conversion to personalty so that it will be distributed as such. See 25 A.L.R. at page 405. . . .

Those courts that have considered the Uniform Partnership Act in reference to realty, used and purchased for partnership purposes, have considered the same with reference "to the sections of the Act to the effect that: (1) The title to the firm realty vests in the surviving partner and, if there is none, in the personal representative of the deceased partner, (Code Section 7864(2)(d)); (2) A partner's interest is only a share in the profits and surpluses, the same being personal property; (Code Section 7865); (3) A partner's interest in specific partnership property is not subject to dower, curtesy, or allowance to the next of kin; (Code Section 7864(2)(e)); and (4) The debts of the partnership are to be paid and the surplus paid in cash to the partners. (Code Section 7877(1))." 16 Tenn.Law Review, 886.

The Supreme Court of Illinois in Wharf v. Wharf, supra, in commenting on these various sections of the Uniform Partnership Act (the Act of Illinois being identical with that of Tennessee) said: "It seems that the legislative intention was to adopt the English rule that real estate which becomes personal property for the purposes of a partnership remains personal property for the purpose of distribution."

It is true that in the Wharf case the partnership was solely for the purpose of dealing in real estate and that the general rule is that real estate partnerships are considered as personalty, and must be distributed as such. See list of cases in 25 A.L.R. at the bottom of page 403. We considered the reasoning in the Wharf case, that is, that the rule is changed as to all partnerships, whether real estate or otherwise, by reason of the passage of the Uniform Partnership Act, is the most reasonable rule and is one that we should adopt and do adopt as the applicable rule in this State.

In this construction and application of the Uniform Partnership Act we are meeting and reaching the intent of the Legislature in passing this Act. By so doing the conversion of real estate into personalty for certain purposes and then when those purposes have been met, reconverting the real estate back into realty is done away with by this Act. By this construction when a partnership once acquires real estate, with partnership funds and for partnership purposes, it then becomes personalty for all purposes and can be conveyed according to the terms of the Act as other partnership property. This seems a sound rule to apply and we are applying it here.

From what has been said above, it results that the decree of the Chancellor must be affirmed. The cause will be remanded so that the Chancellor may fix solicitors' fees in the case.

All concur.

REFERENCES ON DEVOLUTION

Bear v. Bear, 151 Colo. 188, 377 P.2d 538 (1962) (surviving partner entitled to mining property because he held as joint tenant).

Todd v. Todd, 250 Iowa 1084, 96 N.W.2d 436 (1959) (property conveyed to one partner by his co-partners held to be partnership property).

Harmon v. Martin, 395 Ill. 595, 71 N.E.2d 74 (1947) (conveyance by surviving joint venturer valid).

La Russo v. Paladino, 109 N.Y.S.2d 627 (1951), affirmed by memorandum 280 App. Div. 988, 116 N.Y.S.2d 617 (suit for share of assets of partnership not maintainable by heirs of deceased partner).

Jones v. Shatina, 2 Wn.App. 873, 471 P.2d 110 (1970) (mining property deed to three mining partners devolved on survivors on death of one; his heirs had only a claim for money value of decedent's interest in firm equity).

Maltzman, Characterization of Partnership Property upon the Death of one of the Partners (1961) 16 U. of Miami L.Rev. 92 (discusses and contrasts the UPA and Florida law).

Note:

Farm Partnership: Ownership and Use of Real Property (1962), 47 Iowa L.Rev. 689 (discusses and contrasts the UPA and Iowa law).

REFERENCES ON EXECUTION AGAINST PARTNERSHIP PROPERTY

Cases:

Sherwood v. Jackson, 121 Cal.App. 354, 8 P.2d 943 (1932) (execution issued on judgment against a partner, and levied on partnership property; levy vacated).

Townsend v. L.J. Appel Sons, 164 Md. 255, 164 A. 679 (1933) (execution issued on judgment against partner, and levied on partnership property; vacated, although firm did not use firm name, or otherwise disclose partnership relation).

Schultz v. Ziegenfuss, 105 N.J.Super. 468, 253 A.2d 180 (1969) (judgment entered against A and B without mentioning partnership did not create lien on property held in name of partnership consisting of A and B).

Articles:

Gose, Charging Order under the UPA (1953) 28 Wash.L.Rev. 1.

Richardson, Creditors' Rights and the Partnership (1952) 40 Ky.L.J. 243.

REFERENCES ON TAXATION OF PARTNERSHIP PROPERTY

Under prevailing rules on jurisdiction to tax, a state may tax tangible property within its territory, and may tax intangible property which belongs to its residents regardless of the location of intangible property's contacts. If a partner living in state A is a member of a partnership with tangible assets in state B, have both states jurisdiction to impose death duties? Does it make any difference whether either or both has adopted the UPA, with its separation of "rights in specific partnership property" from a partner's "interest in the partnership"?

Blodgett v. Silberman, 277 U.S. 1, 48 S.Ct. 410, 72 L.Ed. 749 (1927) (where member of partnership with land and other assets in New York was resident of Connecticut, Connecticut could impose inheritance tax on his entire interest in the partnership although New York also taxed some or all of assets of partnership).

Estate of Havemeyer, 17 N.Y.2d 216, 270 N.Y.S.2d 197, 217 N.E.2d 26 (1966), reversing 24 A.D.2d 477, 261 N.Y.S.2d 277 (1964), which affirmed 42 Misc.2d 585, 248 N.Y.S.2d 412 (1963) (where N.Y. resident was member of New York partnership owning real estate in Connecticut, New York could impose estate tax on resident's entire interest in partnership, although Connecticut had imposed inheritance tax on real estate).

B. CONTROL

SUMMERS v. DOOLEY

Idaho Supreme Court, 1971.
94 Idaho 87, 481 P.2d 318.

DONALDSON, JUSTICE.

This lawsuit, tried in the district court, involves a claim by one partner against the other for $6,000. The complaining partner asserts that he has been required to pay out more than $11,000 in expenses without any reimbursement from either the partnership funds or his partner. The expenditure in question was incurred by the complaining partner (John Summers, plaintiff-appellant) for the purpose of hiring an additional employee. The trial court denied him any relief except for ordering that he be entitled to one half $966.72 which it found to be a legitimate partnership expense.

The pertinent facts leading to this lawsuit are as follows. Summers entered a partnership agreement with Dooley (defendant-respondent) in 1958 for the purpose of operating a trash collection business. The business was operated by the two men and when either was unable to work, the non-working partner provided a replacement at his own expense. In 1962, Dooley became unable to work and, at his own expense, hired an employee to take his place. In July, 1966, Summers approached his partner Dooley regarding the hiring of an additional employee but Dooley refused.

Nevertheless, on his own initiative, Summers hired the man and paid him out of his own pocket. Dooley, upon discovering that Summers had hired an additional man, objected, stating that he did not feel additional labor was necessary and refused to pay for the new employee out of the partnership funds. Summers continued to operate the business using the third man and in October of 1967 instituted suit in the district court for $6,000 against his partner, the gravamen of the complaint being that Summers has been required to pay out more than $11,000 in expenses, incurred in the hiring of the additional man, without any reimbursement from either the partnership funds or his partner. After trial before the court, sitting without a jury, Summers was granted only partial relief [1] and he has appealed. He urges in essence that the trial court erred by failing to conclude that he should be reimbursed for expenses and costs connected in the employment of extra help in the partnership business.

1. The trial court did award Summers one half of $966.72 which it found to be a legitimate partnership expense.

The principal thrust of appellant's contention is that in spite of the fact that one of the two partners refused to consent to the hiring of additional help, nonetheless, the non-consenting partner retained profits earned by the labors of the third man and therefore the non-consenting partner should be estopped from denying the need and value of the employee, and has by his behavior ratified the act of the other partner who hired the additional man.

The issue presented for decision by this appeal is whether an equal partner in a two man partnership has the authority to hire a new employee in disregard of the objection of the other partner and then attempt to charge the dissenting partner with the costs incurred as a result of his unilateral decision.

. . .

In the instant case the record indicates that although Summers requested his partner Dooley to agree to the hiring of a third man, such requests were not honored. In fact Dooley made it clear that he was "voting no" with regard to the hiring of an additional employee.

An application of the relevant statutory provisions and pertinent case law to the factual situation presented by the instant case indicates that the trial court was correct in its disposal of the issue since a majority of the partners did not consent to the hiring of the third man. I.C. § 53–318(8) provides:

> "Any difference arising as to ordinary matters connected with the partnership business may be decided by a *majority of the partners*. . . ." (emphasis supplied)

. . . A careful reading of the statutory provision indicates that subsection 5 bestows *equal rights in the management and conduct of the partnership business* upon all of the partners.[4] The concept of equality between partners with respect to management of business affairs is a central theme and records throughout the Uniform Partnership Law, I.C. § 53–301 et seq., which has been enacted in this jurisdiction. Thus the only reasonable interpretation of I.C. § 53–318(8) is that business differences must be decided by a majority of the partners provided no other agreement between the partners speaks to the issues.

A noted scholar has dealt precisely with the issue to be decided.

". . . if the partners are equally divided, those who forbid a change must have their way." Walter B. Lindley, A Treatise on the Law of Partnership, Ch. II, § III, ¶ 24–8, p. 403 (1924). See also, W. Shumaker, A Treatise on the Law of Partnership, § 97, p. 266.

See also, Clarke et al. v. Slate Valley R. Co., 136 Pa. 408, 20 A. 562 (1890) for a discussion of this rule.

In the case at bar one of the partners continually voiced objection to the hiring of the third man. He did not sit idly by and acquiesce in

---

4. In the absence of an agreement to the contrary. . . . In the case at bar, there is no such agreement and thus I.C. § 53–318(5) and each of the other subsections are applicable.

the actions of his partner. Under these circumstances it is manifestly unjust to permit recovery of an expense which was incurred individually and not for the benefit of the partnership but rather for the benefit of one partner.

Judgment affirmed. Costs to respondent.

NOTE: CONTROL DISPUTES IN THE TWO–PERSON PARTNERSHIP

As the principal case points out, the Uniform Partnership Act creates a presumption of equal control in the absence of an agreement otherwise by the partners. UPA § 18(e), 18(h). A number of courts have faced the question whether, in a two-person partnership, one of the partners may act contrary to the wishes of the other and still bind the partnership. The principal case is particularly interesting because it suggests that an ordinary partnership transaction—the hiring of an additional person—may be vetoed by one of the partners. Is this consistent with UPA § 9?

Compare the decision in National Biscuit v. Stroud, 249 N.C. 467, 106 S.E.2d 692 (1959). In that case, one partner gave notice to a third party (and to his partner) that he would not be responsible for any further purchases by his partner. Purchases were nevertheless made, and the court held that since purchases were within the scope of partnership business (citing UPA §§ 9, 15) the partner's authority could not be restricted and the defendant was liable. UPA § 18(e) and 18(h) were relied upon for the court's view that one equal partner cannot restrict another. The case is noted in 1960 Duke L.J. 150.

A third view of the two-partner dispute appears in the pre-UPA decision of Bank of Bellbuckle v. Mason, 139 Tenn. 659, 202 S.W. 931 (1918). One partner notified his bank that payments of partnership checks should not be honored unless there were sufficient funds in the partnership account. The bank nevertheless honored an overdraft by the other partner, and was denied recovery against the partner who had given notice. The court relied on language similar to UPA § 9, holding that the notice to the bank terminated the agency authority of the second partner.

Suppose that a partnership has three members, and one of them, being outvoted on a point of partnership policy, notifies third parties that he will not be bound. If the other two, on behalf of the partnership, negotiate the disputed contract, is the minority member liable? Compare Johnston & Co. v. Dutton's Administrator, 27 Ala. 245 (1855) (minority member liable), with O.L. Standard Dry Goods Co. v. Hale, 148 Va. 640, 139 S.E. 300 (1927) (not liable).

Apart from agreement in advance, the solution to the dilemma of who controls lies in dissolution of the partnership. Dissolution is always available under UPA § 31, although in some instances damages may be assessed against the dissolving partner; see UPA § 38(2). If the appropriate notice is then given under UPA § 35, the objecting former partner will no longer be bound to future partnership obligations.

REFERENCES

Dissent in contravention of articles of partnership:

Wipperman v. Stacy, 80 Wis. 345, 50 N.W. 336 (1891) (where dissenting partner attempted to terminate purchasing authority conferred by articles of partnership, held liable).

Eduardo Fernandez Y Compania v. Longino & Collins, 199 La. 343, 6 So.2d 137 (1942) (under Louisiana statute, attempt of one partner to terminate another's power to sell firm merchandise, conferred by written agreement, held ineffective).

Powers of partners in dissolved partnership:

Bell v. Porter, 261 Mich. 97, 246 N.W. 93 (1932) (partner's admission of debt of firm admissible in evidence, although made after dissolution).

Cotton v. Keen, 120 N.J.L. 491, 1 A.2d 8 (1938) (partners bound by liquidating partner's promise to pay attorney to collect receivables).

Breach after dissolution of agreement made before:

Goerig v. Continental Casualty Co., 167 F.2d 930 (9th Cir.1948) (while defendant was a dormant partner, partnership agreed to indemnify plaintiff surety company in case of default; after dormant partner retired, partnership defaulted, surety paid; defendant held liable, although surety never knew of or relied upon his membership in firm).

PLASTEEL PRODUCTS CORP. v. HELMAN

Reread this case and the note following it, reproduced ante at p. 29.

FRIGIDAIRE SALES CORP. v. UNION PROPERTIES, INC.
Court of Appeals of Washington, 1976.
14 Wn.App. 634, 544 P.2d 781.

CALLOW, JUDGE.

The plaintiff, Frigidaire Sales Corporation, appeals from a superior court judgment dismissing its claim against defendants Leonard Mannon and Raleigh Baxter. The sole issue presented on appeal is whether individuals who are limited partners become liable as general partners when they also serve as active officers or directors, or are shareholders of a corporation which is the managing general partner of the limited partnership.

The parties agreed on the facts. On January 15, 1969, Frigidaire Sales Corporation entered into a contract with Commercial Investors, a limited partnership, for the sale of appliances to Commercial. The contract was signed on behalf of Commercial Investors by defendants Mannon and Baxter in their respective capacities as president and secretary-treasurer of Union Properties, Inc., the corporate general partner of Commercial Investors. Mannon and Baxter were also directors of Union Properties, Inc., and each owned 50 percent of the outstanding shares of Union Properties, Inc. In their capacities as directors and officers of Union Properties, Inc., the defendants exercised the day-to-day management and control of Union Properties, Inc. Both defendants also held one limited partnership unit out of a total of 52 outstanding partnership investment units in Commercial Investors.

Frigidaire Sales Corporation, as the creditor, instituted this action against the general partner Union Properties, Inc. and the defendants Mannon and Baxter individually when Commercial Investors, as the debtor and as the purchaser of the appliances, failed to pay the November 1970 installment and all subsequent installments due on the contract. The trial court entered judgment for the plaintiff against

Union Properties, Inc., but dismissed the plaintiff's claim against Mannon and Baxter. The plaintiff appeals the dismissal of the individual defendants.

LIMITED PARTNERSHIPS

. . .

RCW 25.08.070(2)(a) assumes that a corporation can be a general partner of a limited partnership when it states that a limited partner shall not be deemed to take part in control by possessing or exercising the power to vote on the transfer of a majority of the voting stock of a "corporate general partner." Cf. *Bassan v. Investment Exch. Corp.*, 83 Wash.2d 922, 524 P.2d 233 (1974). With this premise in mind, we note that RCW 25.08.120 provides:

> (1) A person may be a general partner and a limited partner in the same partnership at the same time.

> (2) A person who is a general, and also at the same time a limited partner, shall have all the rights and powers and be subject to all the restrictions of a general partner; except that, in respect to his contribution, he shall have the rights against the other members which he would have had if he were not also a general partner.

IS THE DOMINANT CONSIDERATION CREDITOR RELIANCE OR PROHIBITED CONTROL?

The plaintiff contends that the defendants, as limited partners, controlled the business because they were (1) sole shareholders of Union Properties, Inc., the general partner; (2) on the board of directors of Union Properties, Inc.; (3) president and secretary of Union Properties, Inc.; and (4) exercised the day-to-day management of Union Properties, Inc. The defendants contend, on the other hand, that the limited partnership was controlled by its general partner Union Properties, Inc., a distinct and separate legal entity, and not by the defendants in their individual capacities.

. . .

The issue recently received attention in Texas. In *Delaney v. Fidelity Lease Ltd.*, 526 S.W.2d 543 (Tex.1975), the limited partners controlled the business of the limited partnership as officers, directors and stockholders of the corporate general partner. The Texas Supreme Court held at 545:

> [T]hat the personal liability, which attaches to a limited partner when "he takes part in the control and management of the business," cannot be evaded merely by acting through a corporation.

The opinion overrules the decision of the Texas Court of Civil Appeals, in which it had been stated:

> The logical reason to hold a limited partner to general liability under the control prohibition of the Statute is to prevent third

parties from mistakenly assuming that the limited partner is a general partner and to rely on his general liability. However, it is hard to believe that a creditor would be deceived where he knowingly deals with a general partner which is a corporation. That in itself is a creature specifically devised to limit liability. The fact that certain limited partners are stockholders, directors or officers of the corporation is beside the point where the creditor is not deceived.

Delaney v. Fidelity Lease Ltd., 517 S.W.2d 420, 425 (Tex.Civ.App.1974).

The Supreme Court opinion in *Delaney* was concerned that the statutory requirements of at least one general partner with general liability in a limited partnership could be circumvented by limited partners operating the partnership through the corporation with minimum capitalization and, therefore, with limited liability. The fear is, however, not peculiar to a limited partnership with a corporate general partner. An individual may form a corporation with limited capitalization and thereby attempt to avoid personal liability. When one acts in such fashion, however, the inadequate capitalization is a factor in determining whether to disregard the corporate entity. . . . If a corporate general partner in a limited partnership is organized without sufficient capitalization so that it was foreseeable that it would not have sufficient assets to meet its obligations, the corporate entity could be disregarded to avoid injustice. We find no substantive difference between the creditor who does business with a corporation that is the general partner in a limited partnership and a creditor who simply does business with a corporation. In the absence of fraud or other inequitable conduct, the corporate entity should be respected. . . .

We note that the decision of the Supreme Court of Texas in *Delaney* relies upon the reasoning of the dissent filed in the Texas Court of Civil Appeals. We believe that the dissent, however, is based in part upon the incorrect premise that a corporation may not be a general partner under the Uniform Limited Partnership Act. We have shown that this is not so under the Washington act. Moreover, the dissent based its reasoning upon the assumption that, because the limited partners acted as officers of the corporate general partner, they "were obligated to their other partners to so operate the corporation as to benefit the partnership." 517 S.W.2d at 426. We find no inherent wrong in this. Persons in the position of the individual defendants in this case would be bound to act in the best interests of both the corporate general partner and the limited partners under the guidelines of RCW 25.08.120. The dual capacities are not inimical as asserted.

. . .

Moreover, a literal reading of RCW 25.08.070 that disregards the existence of the corporate entity as a general partner is not justified. The consideration of the issue must inquire not only whether a limited partner has participated in a forbidden control, but also whether the corporate entity should be regarded or disregarded. . . .

Here, there was an overt intention to regard the corporate entity and no showing of the violation of any duty owing to the creditor. The creditor dealt with the corporate general partner in full awareness of the corporate status of the general partner. There is no showing of any fraud, wrong or injustice perpetrated upon the creditor, merely that RCW 25.08.070 provides that a limited partner becomes liable as a general partner if he takes part in the control of the business. . . . When these are the circumstances, we hold that the corporate entity should be upheld rather than the statute applied blindly with no inquiry as to the purpose it seeks to achieve. . . .

A limited partner is made liable as a general partner when he participates in the 'control' of the business in order to protect third parties from dealing with the partnership under the mistaken assumption that the limited partner is a general partner with general liability. See Feld, *The 'Control' Test for Limited Partnerships*, 82 Harv.L.Rev. 1471, 1479 (1969). If a limited partnership certificate pursuant to RCW 25.08.020(2) is properly prepared and filed and the limited partner does not participate in the control of the business, it is unlikely that third parties will be misled as to the limited liability of the limited partners. The underlying purpose of the control prohibition of RCW 25.08.070 is not furthered, however, by prohibiting limited partners from forming a corporation to act as the sole general partner in a limited partnership. A third party dealing with a corporation must reasonably rely on the solvency of the corporate entity. It makes little difference if the corporation is or is not the general partner in a limited partnership. In either instance, the third party cannot justifiably rely on the solvency of the individuals who own the corporation.

We hold that limited partners are not liable as general partners simply because they are active officers or directors, or are stockholders of a corporate general partner in a limited partnership.

Affirmed.

FRIGIDAIRE SALES CORP. v. UNION PROPERTIES, INC.
Supreme Court of Washington, 1977.
88 Wn.2d 400, 562 P.2d 244.

HAMILTON, ASSOCIATE JUSTICE.

Petitioner, Frigidaire Sales Corporation, sought review of a Court of Appeals decision which held that limited partners do not incur general liability for the limited partnership's obligations simply because they are officers, directors, or shareholders of the corporate general partner. . . .

Petitioner cites *Delaney v. Fidelity Lease Ltd.*, 526 S.W.2d 543 (Tex. 1975), as support for its contention that respondents should incur general liability under RCW 25.08.070 for the limited partnership's obligations. That case also involved the issue of liability for limited partners who controlled the limited partnership as officers, directors, and shareholders of the corporate general partner. The Texas Supreme Court reversed the decision of the Texas Court of Civil Appeals and found the limited partners had incurred general liability because of their control of the limited partnership. . . .

We find the Texas Supreme Court's decision distinguishable from the present case. In *Delaney,* the corporation and the limited partnership were set up contemporaneously, and the sole purpose of the corporation was to operate the limited partnership. The Texas Supreme Court found that the limited partners who controlled the corporation were obligated to their other limited partners to operate the corporation for the benefit of the partnership. . . . This is not the case here. The pattern of operation of Union Properties was to investigate and conceive of real estate investment opportunities and, when it found such opportunities, to cause the creation of limited partnerships with Union Properties acting as the general partner. Commercial was only one of several limited partnerships so conceived and created. Respondents did not form Union Properties for the sole purpose of operating Commercial. Hence, their acts on behalf of Union Properties were not performed merely for the benefit of Commercial.

. . .

[W]e agree with our Court of Appeals analysis that this concern with minimum capitalization is not peculiar to limited partnerships with corporate general partners, but may arise any time a creditor deals with a corporation. . . . Because our limited partnership statutes permit parties to form a limited partnership with a corporation as the sole general partner, this concern about minimal capitalization, standing by itself, does not justify a finding that the limited partners incur general liability for their control of the corporate general partner. . . . If a corporate general partner is inadequately capitalized, the rights of a creditor are adequately protected under the 'piercing-the-corporate-veil' doctrine of corporation law. . . .

Furthermore, petitioner was never led to believe that respondents were acting in any capacity other than in their corporate capacities. The parties stipulated at the trial that respondents never acted in any direct, personal capacity. When the shareholders of a corporation, who are also the corporation's officers and directors, conscientiously keep the affairs of the corporation separate from their personal affairs, and no fraud or manifest injustice is perpetrated upon third persons who deal with the corporation, the corporation's separate entity should be respected. . . .

There can be no doubt that respondents, in fact, controlled the corporation. However, they did so only in their capacities as agents for their principal, the corporate general partner. Although the corporation was a separate entity, it could act only through its board of directors, officers, and agents. . . . In the eyes of the law it was

Union Properties, as a separate corporate entity, which entered into the contract with petitioner and controlled the limited partnership.

Further, because respondents scrupulously separated their actions on behalf of the corporation from their personal actions, petitioner never mistakenly assumed that respondents were general partners with general liability. . . . Because petitioner entered into the contract knowing that Union Properties was the only party with general liability, and because in the eyes of the law it was Union Properties, a separate entity, which controlled the limited partnership, there is no reason for us to find that respondents incurred general liability for their acts done as officers of the corporate general partner.

The decision of the Court of Appeals is affirmed.

NOTE ON DELANEY v. FIDELITY LEASE, LTD.

After *Delaney* was decided, in 1979, the Texas limited partnership act was amended. Among the changes was the addition of a clause providing that a limited partner does not take part in control by acting as an officer, director or shareholder of a corporate general partner. Furthermore, the act was amended to require that the creditor seeking personal liability establish that he reasonably believed the limited partner was a general partner.

Compare Revised ULPA § 303, which is somewhat less clear on the corporate general partner issue (see, e.g., § 303(b)(1), which refers to being "an agent or employee" of the general partner), but also includes a reliance requirement.

BOXER v. HUSKY OIL CO.
Delaware Chancery Court, 1981.
429 A.2d 995.

HARTNETT, VICE CHANCELLOR.

. . .

I

Husky Exploration Limited was a Colorado limited partnership formed for the purpose of investment in oil and mineral resources. The plaintiffs in this action are the limited partners of Husky Exploration Limited who seek to assert claims against defendant Husky Petroleum Corporation, the general partner, and defendant Husky Oil Company, the owner of the general partner. The complaint alleges, in part, that defendant Husky Petroleum Corporation, the general partner, breached its fiduciary duty to the limited partners, as well as violated the terms of the Partnership Agreement, by causing the sale of the limited partners' interests at a price it knew or should have known to be totally inadequate.

The Partnership Agreement, under which Husky Exploration Limited was formed as a limited partnership, granted defendant Husky Petroleum Corporation, the general partner, an option to purchase the interests of all the limited partners. The Partnership Agreement also provided that the general partner could assign this option to another. On January 1, 1980, the date of the partnership's termination, the assets of the limited partnership included an interest in Husky Canadian Exploration Company and an interest in Husky Minerals Ltd. Defendant Husky Petroleum Corporation, the general partner, pursuant to the option, assigned to Husky Oil Operations, Ltd. the partnership's interest in Husky Canadian Exploration Company. The general partner valued this asset at approximately 10 million dollars. The partnership's interest in Husky Minerals Ltd. which was valued by the general partner at $78,480. was assigned by the general partner to defendant Husky Oil Company. Defendant Husky Oil Company owns the general partner and controls Husky Canadian Exploration Company. It therefore stood on both sides of the transactions. The plaintiffs assert that these valuations by the general partner were far below the actual value of the assets transferred.

. . .

II

[The defendant moved to dismiss on grounds of lack of equity jurisdiction.]

III

The complaint alleges a breach of a fiduciary duty on the part of the general partner as a basis for equity jurisdiction. The Uniform Limited Partnership Act, which has been adopted in both Delaware and Colorado, provides that a general partner has all the rights and powers and is subject to all the restrictions and liabilities of a partner in a partnership without limited partners. [The court here quotes § 9 of the ULPA.]

The Uniform Partnership Act, which has also been adopted in both Delaware and Colorado makes a partner accountable as a fiduciary. [The court here quotes § 21 of the UPA.]

When the provisions of the Uniform Partnership Act and the Uniform Limited Partnership Act are read together, it is clear that the general partner in a limited partnership owes a fiduciary duty to the limited partners. See Homestake Mining Co. v. Mid-Continent Exploration Co., 10th Cir., 282 F.2d 787 (1960); Gundelach v. Gollehon, Colo. App., 598 P.2d 521 (1979); Bassan v. Investment Exchange Corp., 83 Wash.2d 922, 524 P.2d 233 (1974). It is also clear that a partner owes a fiduciary duty to the other partners at common law. Newburger, Loeb & Co., Inc. v. Gross, 2nd Cir., 563 F.2d 1057 (1977); Meinhard v. Salmon, N.Y.Ct.App., 249 N.Y. 458, 164 N.E. 545 (1928). See generally Crane and Bromberg, Law of Partnership § 68 (1968); Note, Fiduciary Duties of Partners, 48 Iowa L.Rev. 902 (1963).

The duty of the general partner in a limited partnership to exercise the utmost good faith, fairness, and loyalty is, therefore, required both

by statute and common law. This fiduciary duty of partners is often
compared to that of corporate directors:

> "Furthermore, the fiduciary duty of fair dealing by a general
> partner to a limited partner is no less than that owed by a
> corporate director to a shareholder. The form of the enterprise
> does not diminish the duty of fair dealing by those in control of the
> investments." Miller v. Schweickart, S.D.N.Y., 405 F.Supp. 366
> (1975).

IV

An alleged breach of fiduciary duty has historically served as a
basis for equitable jurisdiction. . . . Where the relationship between
the parties imposes an equitable obligation to account, equity has
always taken jurisdiction over the controversy, even where there may
be an adequate remedy at law. . . .

[The Court did not reach the merits of the alleged breach.]

SANDERSON v. COOKE
New York Court of Appeals, 1931.
256 N.Y. 73, 175 N.E. 518.

CRANE, J.

Charles D. Barney & Co. is an old established brokerage house with
which the plaintiff became connected in 1911. By articles of partnership, dated February 1, 1911, he, with six others, became general
partners of the firm with one special partner. The partnership was
continued by another agreement dated November 29, 1912. Again, on
the 1st day of February, 1915, articles of general partnership were
signed, under which the firm continued until December 31, 1918, at
which time, either by agreement dated that day, or January 1, 1919,
the firm was dissolved and a new firm formed, in which the plaintiff
and J. Horace Harding became special partners. This special partnership was continued by agreements dated December 23, 1919, and June
29, 1920, and terminated by agreement in writing dated the 14th day of
January, 1921.

As a special partner, Mr. Sanderson's rights were limited to a
return of his capital contribution, and a fixed percentage thereon.
These he received upon retirement. His interests as general partner,
prior to 1918, were disposed of by the agreements referred to, and by
settlement. He at no time has claimed, and does not now claim, that
any of the partnerships owe him $1, or that the settlements were unfair
or fraudulent. He never has made, and does not now make, any claim
of any kind or nature upon any of his former associates or the
partnership of Barney & Co. . . .

This litigation arises out of a supposed property right which the
plaintiff claims to have in the old books of account. . . . The books,
which included cash books, blotters, purchase and sales books, ledgers,

stock records, journals, and bond ledgers, were passed on from firm to firm and used in continuity; that is, the new or succeeding firm did not open new or fresh books actually, but continued to write and make entries in the old books until all the pages were used up. One book, therefore, might contain the business of more than one of these firms. The fact is beyond dispute—because Mr. Sanderson himself says so— that the business could not be carried on without the information contained in all these records. The books of the previous firm were necessary to carry on the business as a going concern. . . .

In 1926, Mr. Sanderson asked to see and examine the books of the old firms, which were then in the possession of Charles D. Barney & Co., and was afforded the opportunity, not only of inspecting the books personally, but of having them examined by public accountants, Barrow, Wade, Guthrie & Co. . . . The defendants were willing to have the plaintiff inspect these personally, but refused to permit him to make and take copies of them.

The plaintiff thereupon, on the 15th day of November, 1928, or eight years after his final termination of all relationships with Charles D. Barney & Co., commenced this action, basing it solely upon the claim that the books belonged to him, were his property the same as a desk or a chair could be property; that he was entitled as a matter of right to see, inspect, and copy all or any part of the books in question. . . .

The general rule regarding business partnerships is that books should be kept open to the inspection of any partner at all reasonable times, even after dissolution, subject, however, to special agreement. Lindley on Partnership (Amer. Ed., Ewell), §§ 404, 420; Rowley on Partnership, § 913; Partnership Law, Consol. Laws, c. 39, §§ 41, 99. Even under these broad statements of the law, a partner's rights are not absolute. He may be restrained from using the information gathered from inspection for other than partnership purposes. Trego v. Hunt, L.R. [1896] A.C. 7. The employment of an agent to make the inspection does not authorize the selection of anybody he may choose for the purpose. The agent employed must be a person to whom no reasonable objection can be taken, and the purpose for which he seeks to use the right of inspection must be one consistent with the main purposes and the well-being of the whole partnership. Bevan v. Webb, L.R. [1901] 2 Ch. 59. The right of inspection by an agent is not so absolute as the right to a personal inspection, and may be refused if the court is satisfied that the assistance of an agent is not reasonably required, or that the inspection is wanted for an improper purpose. An agent may be required to give an undertaking that the information acquired will not be improperly used. Lindley on Partnership (9th Ed.) p. 492. Howlett v. Hall, 55 App.Div. 614, 67 N.Y.S. 267, recognizes that the right is not a strict property right the same as part ownership in other personal property, but is confined within limitations. Motive plays a part, which, of course attaches to the ownership of no other kind of property, for in this case it was stated that the application to examine the books may be refused, if it be made in bad faith. . . .

We are not treating here, however, with a partnership in existence, a going concern, nor with an action for a partnership accounting and the inspection incident thereto, nor with joint partnership property left on dissolution, for safe-keeping, in the custody of the other partner or partners. We have much more than this. Whatever may be the property right of a partner in the partnership books, he may transfer and dispose of it like his right to any other bit of property by express, or necessarily implied, agreement. This is succinctly and forcibly stated in a short opinion by Mr. Justice Albert Cardozo, in Platt v. Platt, 61 Barb. 52, page 53. Writing of a former partner, whose executors claimed a right to inspect partnership books, the justice said: "Nathan C. Platt had parted with his interest in the partnership, and conveyed it to the defendant. While that sale stands, the plaintiffs have no rights in the property. While that sale stands, the books belong to no one but the defendant; and while they belong exclusively to him, no one else has the right to a general inspection of them."

. . .

The trial judge has found that there was nothing in any of the partnership agreements with the plaintiff which refers to the books, records, and correspondence. Neither was there any reference to office furniture and fixtures in all of the agreements. The plaintiff has never made any claim to be a part owner or have a property interest in these. He says at one point that the furniture, and the making over of the offices were very expensive. What became of his property interest in these assets? They passed, as he intended that they should pass, to the firms continuing the business, and which, of necessity, were obliged to have the office equipment to carry on the business. The books and the records and the files were much more necessary for the continuance of that business. We find expressions running through all these various partnership agreements clearly indicating that it was the intention that every succeeding firm continuing the business of Charles D. Barney & Co. should take as its property the books, records, files, and office chattels used by the preceding firm.

. . .

We therefore conclude that the plaintiff, in the formation of the limited partnership January 1, 1919, transferred his property interest in the books to the new firm, in which he became a limited partner, and that he is not entitled absolutely, as matter of right, to an examination of them. His property interest in them has ceased. This, however, does not mean that he may not at any time have an examination of the books for any sufficient reason recognized by law. Equity is very liberal in permitting a partner to examine the partnership books, even when the property in them has passed into other hands. Any plausible or sufficient reason for the protection and enforcement of rights or for the preservation of evidence will move the court. Equity will not, however, in the absence of such property right, direct the extensive examination here demanded in the absence of any reason or necessity therefor, or without any excuse other than the mere desire of the plaintiff to exercise a naked right.

For the reasons here stated, the judgment of the Appellate Division and that of the Special Term should be reversed, and a new trial granted, with costs to abide the event.

CARDOZO, C.J., and LEHMAN, KELLOGG, and O'BRIEN, JJ., concur.

NOTE: INSPECTION RIGHTS OF PARTNERS

The inspection rights of partners and the duties of partners to render full information on partnership matters are set forth in UPA §§ 19 and 20, which you should read. Sanderson v. Cooke is one of few decisions elaborating on these rights, and while it does not refer to the UPA, that act was adopted by New York in 1919. The inspection rights of a limited partner appear to be essentially the same as those of a general partner. See ULPA § 10(a), (b). Much more specific provisions on the inspection rights of limited partners appear in RULPA § 105. Do these convey greater or lesser rights than the UPA and ULPA formulations?

Attempts may be made to define or limit the inspection rights of partners by means of the partnership agreement. The syntax of UPA § 19 leaves unclear whether the agreement may restrict such rights, or whether the agreement may simply specify where the books shall be kept. Section 20 does not refer at all to modification by the partnership agreement. One decision suggests, in a limited setting, that the agreement may limit unqualified access to the books. See People v. Phillips, 207 Misc. 205, 137 N.Y.S.2d 697 (1955).

On the question of inspection rights of former partners, apart from the principal case, see Price v. Briggs, 160 Cal.App.2d 524, 325 P.2d 573 (1958).

SECTION 4. PARTNERSHIP CHANGES AND TERMINATION

INTRODUCTORY NOTE

One of the most salient characteristics of a partnership is its impermanence—its terminability. Inevitably, termination creates new problems; there is a problem of how much the retiring partners or their survivors are entitled to, and of priorities when there is not enough for all. At the same time, termination provides a means of solving problems; if the parties cannot agree about how to run the business, they can put an end to their disagreements by terminating and splitting up.

Termination as used here includes the whole process of bringing an association to an end. First, there is the happening of the event—a mutual agreement, a unilateral act, or an unwilled event like death—which starts the process of termination. Then there are the mechanics of terminating affairs—selling the assets, paying the debts, and settling the accounts among members. Eventually, the moment comes when the bundle of rights and duties called "partnership" no longer exist, because the last right has been transferred and the last duty discharged.

Various names may be applied to the various stages. The Uniform Partnership Act, however, is quite specific in applying the term "dissolution" only to the first step—the act or event precipitating termination (Sections 29–30). The process of turning assets into money to pay off creditors and partners, or of partitioning the remaining assets, and of paying off the obligations of partners to each other is called "winding up"—an English term which in other American contexts is often replaced by "liquidation". The conclusion of the process is not named in the Act; we will call it "extinguishment".

Moreover, according to the UPA, dissolution occurs regardless of the parties' contrary agreement, when death or withdrawal intervenes (Section 31). Granted the definition of "dissolution", this conclusion seems inevitable; no agreement can prevent the severing of the partnership relationship with a man who is dead. However, California and some other states have modified the Act to say that dissolution is caused in the situations enumerated in Section 31 only if the agreement does not otherwise provide.[1] This raises an interesting question. If the severance of partnership by death is not called "dissolution" in California, what is it called?

What happens after a partnership is "dissolved"? The Uniform Partnership Act deals expressly with two possibilities. (1) The partnership may be "wound up"; provisions relating to this process appear in sections 33–40 and 43, which should be studied carefully. (2) The business of the partnership may be continued with the consent of the retiring partner, or of a deceased partner's personal representative, and without the consent of a partner who has wrongfully withdrawn or been justifiably expelled. These contingencies are referred to in sections 38(2), 41, 42 and 43, which should likewise be studied. There is a third possibility which the draftsmen of the Act seem to have overlooked. (3) The business may be continued without consent under conditions other than those stated in section 38(2). Whether or not the remaining partners are *entitled* to continue it under such conditions may be debated (re-read sections 37 and 38(1)), but this is what has actually happened in a good many of the cases.

With respect to the first two alternatives, the law provides clearly differentiated formulas for determining what the parties get.

The difference between the formulas makes it quite important to ascertain in a given case which alternative has been followed. This is not as easy as it seems, since business enterprises do not wind themselves up automatically like a steel tape. It takes time to sell assets on advantageous terms, and to get all the debts ascertained and paid, so that even in the clearest cases of "winding up" there has usually been a

---

1. West's Ann.California Corp.Code
§ 15031; 54 Okl.St.Ann. § 231; Vernon's
Tex.Ann.Civ.St. art. 6132b.

considerable continuance of operations. Furthermore, parties commonly defer going to court until an eventual liquidation has occurred, so that even in the clearest cases of "continuation" there has been, by the time of the court's decision, a winding up. What the court usually has to decide is whether the business was wound up as promptly as practicable, or was continued longer than necessary.

A. TERMINATION OF THE PARTNERSHIP— "WINDING UP"

McGEE v. RUSSELL'S EXECUTORS

Virginia Supreme Court of Appeals, 1928.
150 Va. 155, 142 S.E. 524.

PRENTIS, P. Without undertaking to state in detail every fact shown by this record, the fundamental facts appear to be these:

About 1890, Charles H. Russell and his son W.H. Russell, both of whom are now dead, formed a partnership for the purpose of manufacturing wagons. The name of the partnership was C.H. Russell & Son, the plant was located at Clarksville, Virginia, and the father, C.H. Russell, owned a two-thirds interest, while the other one-third was owned by his son, W.H. Russell. Charles H. Russell died December 14, 1919, testate. The executors named in his will were his son, W.H. Russell, and William Leigh, of Danville, but William Leigh died before the testator, so that upon his death W.H. Russell took charge of his separate estate as his executor, and of the partnership property as surviving partner.

The will made several specific bequests—among them one to his son, W.H. Russell, of $15,000 "in value of my two-thirds interest, in moneys and accounts due to the firm of C.H. Russell & Son, and in stock and material and machinery in hand belonging to said firm, said fifteen thousand dollars in value to be set apart and delivered to him out of my said interest in the money and accounts due to said firm, and in the stock and material on hand, and machinery belonging to said firm, the property given him under this clause of my will to be his absolute property." The testator had in his lifetime given to his daughters, Annie A. McGee and Alice L. Russell, each $15,000, and so it is apparent that this bequest to his son was for the purpose of producing equality among his children. He directed that the residuum of his estate be equally divided among his three children, his son and his two daughters.

There are many letters in the record showing intense enmity of the brother towards his two sisters. This enmity is expressed in the most unrestrained language, and perhaps accounts for this unfortunate controversy. This rancor, so plainly manifested, however, supplies no facts which are helpful in determining the rights of the parties, and we shall make no further allusion to it.

The legal question involved, and the point emphasized by the appellants, is based upon section 42 of the Uniform Partnership Act (Acts 1918, p. 541; Code, § 4359 [42]), quoted in the margin.

Relying thereon, the appellants claim that the surviving partner, without the consent of his sisters and against their wishes, continued the business, and that, in consequence of this action on his part, the value of the share of the deceased partner must be ascertained as of the date of the dissolution of the partnership by Charles H. Russell's death; whereas, for the appellee it is contended that section 42, so relied upon, is not applicable, because the business was not so continued under any of the conditions set forth in section 41(1, 2, 3, 5, 6), or section 38(2b), and they further maintain that the business of the copartnership was only continued as authorized by sections 30 and 33 of the Uniform Partnership Act, and merely for the purpose of closing up its business and distributing its assets. These sections are also quoted in the margin.

There is little difference between the contending parties as to the law, but the controversy arises out of their conflicting views as to the facts.

Adverting now to these facts, it appears that, at the time of the death of the elder Russell, the concern owed some debts, had goods ordered which had not been delivered, and had a very large stock of materials on hand, consisting of various unassembled parts of wagons which could be marketed to the best advantage only after they had been assembled and manufactured into wagons. All of the parties recognized the fact that it would be disastrous to offer these unfinished parts of wagons for sale at public auction, or otherwise, in bulk. They promptly employed counsel, and voluminous correspondence ensued, the purpose of which was to induce an agreement by which the surviving partner would pay to his sisters the value of their interests in the partnership property. . . . Efforts to reconcile the views of the parties continued until the latter part of November, 1920, and shortly thereafter this suit was brought by the executor and surviving partner for the settlement of his accounts and for general directions.

In the interval there had occurred a general business depression, and the prospects of financial success had diminished. Additional parts of wagons which had been missing had been in the meantime bought, and many wagons had been manufactured.

The case was referred to a commissioner for a settlement of the partnership accounts, and the position which is taken here for the appellants was there taken; but the commissioner was evidently of opinion that all of the acts of the surviving partner were in good faith and done only for the purpose of closing up the affairs of the partnership. His position was not an easy one. A sale of the materials on hand in bulk would have been disastrous. His own interest as a partner and the one-third interest therein bequeathed him by his father gave him a five-ninths interest in the concern. He had every motive for conserving the assets and for prudent action.

Exceptions to the commissioner's report were taken, and the trial court agreed with the commissioner.

Taking a general view of the facts as we have indicated them, we discover no good reason for any contrary view. Every proposition of law urged by the appellants may be acceded to, but they are all based upon the averment that the surviving partner, without any agreement on the part of the others interested, continued the partnership business; whereas, under our view of the facts, the surviving partner only continued the partnership business in order to avoid a destruction of the value of the assets, because driven thereto by the necessities of the situation and because, in his own judgment, formed under the advice of counsel, it was necessary to do so in order to close up its affairs properly so as to make proper distribution of its assets. There is no reason to doubt that that was in fact the best course to pursue, and that it was taken for the purpose of winding up its affairs. Though assumed in argument, there is nothing to show that any different course would have yielded any better results.

Before the final decree, the surviving partner filed a written statement with the commissioner, which, if true, is quite convincing. He was afterwards sworn as a witness, subjected himself to cross-examination, and offered to submit his books for inspection. There is no allegation or suggestion of any fraudulent conversion, or proof of any sacrifice of the assets. Full and complete inventories were promptly taken, copies thereof sent to all the parties interested, and there is no indication of any concealment at any time.

The appellants, by their counsel, greatly emphasize the fact that the inventory of the stock of unfinished wagon parts, materials on hand, and other personal property of the copartnership shows that these were listed at $35,719.56, but the appraisers who made that report stated this therein at the time:

"Should same be subjected to sale, there would be a great reduction, due to the fact that wagon parts made at one factory cannot be judiciously used at any other factory. We further think that it would take at least three years to make up and dispose of the stock, and this would involve the purchase of a large quantity of other materials and parts."

And one of the appraisers testified that, if this property had been then sold, it would hardly have brought more than 25 per cent. of this appraisement.

The proper conclusions seem to us to be quite obvious. It would be a great wrong to hold the surviving partner responsible as the purchaser of the property at such an appraisement and under the circumstances shown. It was afterwards sold, after proper advertisement, under the order of court in this cause, the sale was confirmed without objection, and the price then paid for it by the surviving partner as the highest bidder therefor is the best evidence of its true value.

Affirmed.

REFERENCES

Lebanon Trotting Association v. Battista, 37 Ohio App.2d 61, 306 N.E.2d 769 (1972) (limited partnership formed for 20 years to operate race track; in last year of partnership term, renewed lease for term of unstated duration extending beyond term of partnership; after dissolution by expiration, partnership was entitled to continue operation for duration of lease if this was most economical way of winding up).

Paciaroni v. Crane, 408 A.2d 946 (Del.Ch.1979) (after dissolution of partnership, majority had right to manage race horse, which was the principal property of the partnership, pending sale).

PLUTH v. SMITH
California District Court of Appeal, 2d District, 1962.
205 Cal.App.2d 818, 23 Cal.Rptr. 550.

Action for an accounting. The Superior Court, Los Angeles County, George A. Dockweiler, J., entered judgment unsatisfactory to defendants and they appealed. . . .

FIELS, JUSTICE. This is an appeal from a judgment in favor of the estate of a deceased partner against the surviving partners after an accounting. The undisputed facts which form the background for this action are as follows:

John L. Thies and defendant Joseph Smith had been in business together since about 1931. On January 6, 1939, Thies and Smith and Smith's wife, the defendant Hazel Smith, entered into a written partnership agreement. . . . The 1939 agreement provided that "each partner will confine his entire time, efforts and talent to the business," salaries and drawings were to be equal, and profits were to be shared equally. The agreement stated: "This partnership shall continue for a period of twenty (20) years". . . .

On October 30, 1959, Hattie Pluth, a niece, was appointed guardian of the person and estate of Thies. On November 24, 1959, Thies, through his guardian, commenced this action against the two Smiths for dissolution of the partnership and for an accounting. This complaint did not mention the written agreement, the guardian apparently being uninformed of it at that time. . . .

After a trial the court made findings of fact and an interlocutory judgment declaring that the partnership was "terminated" on November 27, 1959, and appointing a receiver and referee to liquidate the assets and take the accounting. . . .

After the referee reported the court made new findings which included all of the interlocutory findings with some elaboration; and added new matter taken from the referee's report. It found that as of November 27, 1959, there was due to Thies as his share of profits withheld each year back to 1942, a total of $23,590.82; that the net worth of the partnership as of November 27, 1959, was $122,579.55, of which plaintiff was entitled to one-third, or $40,859.85. The court then made a final judgment ordering the receiver to sell the property and distribute the proceeds to the parties. Defendants are appealing from that judgment. . . .

On November 27, 1959, Thies' guardian, through her attorney, sent a letter to defendants declaring the partnership terminated. The trial judge found that "said partnership was terminated and dissolved on November 27, 1959." Defendants criticize this use of the word "terminated," pointing out that on dissolution the partnership is not terminated, but continues until the winding up of partnership affairs is completed, (Corp.Code, § 15030). No harm is done by this misuse of a word. It is abundantly clear that the trial court treated November 27, 1959, as the date of dissolution, this being the date on which it became the duty of defendants to cease carrying on, as distinguished from winding up the business. (Corp.Code, §§ 15029, 15033.)

The final judgment ordered that the receiver sell the partnership business and distribute the proceeds, after payment of partnership obligations and receivership expenses, as follows:

(a) To plaintiff, the sum of $71,069.20 with interest at 7 per cent per annum from November 27, 1959, to the date of payment. This sum was made up from the following items:

(1) One-third of the net worth as determined by the court's appraiser as of November 27, 1959 . . . . $40,859.85

(2) The amount by which one-half of the defendants' total drawings exceeded the drawings of Thies during the term of the partnership 23,590.82

(3) Interest on the deficiency in Thies' drawing to November 27, 1959 . . . . 6,618.53

Total $71,069.20

(b) To defendants, any remaining money up to a total of $51,510.35.

(c) If any amount remains, one-third to plaintiff and two-thirds to defendants . . .

The provision of the judgment that plaintiff receive the appraised value of the partnership cannot be supported under the circumstances of this case. When dissolution is caused in any way except in contravention of the partnership agreement, each partner may have the partnership property applied to discharge its liabilities and the surplus applied to pay in cash the net amount owing to the respective partners. (Corp.Code, § 15038, subd. (1).) This is the relief demanded by plaintiff in the complaint, the amended complaint and in the notice of dissolution. When a partnership is liquidated the assets are sold and the proceeds divided, or the assets may be distributed in kind, but it is ordinarily improper to require one partner to pay the other the appraised value of an asset. (Harper v. Lamping (1867), 33 Cal. 641, 649; Rice v. Watkins (1948), 85 Cal.App.2d 44, 51, 191 P.2d 810).

Corporation Code, section 15042, provides that if the business is continued under specified conditions the retiring partner may have the value of his interest as of the date of dissolution ascertained, and shall receive as an ordinary creditor an amount equal to this value with interest or a proportion of the profits after dissolution. The conditions under which that section may be applied include the assignment of a partnership interest, the continuation of the business by consent of both the retiring and continuing partners, continuation by innocent partners after wrongful dissolution by another, and expulsion of a partner. None of those conditions exist in this case.

Casida v. Roberts (1959), 51 Cal.2d 853, 337 P.2d 829, cited by plaintiff, falls within the literal reading of section 15042 because the partnership was dissolved through the expulsion of the plaintiff. Defendant had the benefit of continuing the business so long as he saw fit, and the Supreme Court held that plaintiff was entitled to the value of his interest as of the date of expulsion under section 15042.

Two circumstances make it improper to give to plaintiff here the appraised value of the assets—as distinguished from the proceeds of liquidation. The first is that Thies himself, in the exercise of his rights, demanded the dissolution and liquidation. The second is that defendants have not received the benefit of keeping the business after dissolution. We may assume that even in cases not falling literally within section 15042 it may be equitable to require a partner who retains the business as a going concern to pay off the retiring partner on an appraised valuation. (See Nuland v. Pruyn (1950), 99 Cal.App.2d 603, 222 P.2d 261; Wikstrom v. Davis (1957) 211 Or. 254, 315 P.2d 597.) In such case the going-concern value is preserved and the appraisal method would give the retiring partner his fair share. Where the business is to be liquidated, the award of an appraised value, plus interest, is a harsh and drastic remedy, for it casts upon one party the full risk that the property may not bring at forced sale the amount of the appraisal.

In the present case the trial court on September 23, 1960, made an interlocutory order taking the business away from defendants and placing it in the hands of a receiver who is ordered to liquidate it as soon as the judgment becomes final. In determining the value of the partnership assets as of the date of dissolution the trial court included $30,000 for good will. There is no evidence that any of this good will value could be converted into cash at the receiver's sale. The court-appointed appraiser included nothing for good will in his appraisal of the market value of the business. The harshness of the judgment is augmented by the provision that plaintiff share in the excess if the property brings in more than the amount of the appraisal plus expenses.

Plaintiff argues that defendants should be treated as trustees who converted the trust property as of the date of dissolution. The trial court made no finding, and the evidence does not indicate any basis for finding that defendants did anything wrongful after the notice of dissolution on November 27, 1959, except to defer winding up the business. This delay occurred because of the dispute between the parties as to whether plaintiff was entitled to a winding-up. The civil action to resolve this dispute was commenced by plaintiff three days before the dissolution, and was resolved as quickly as the trial court was able to dispose of it. By continuing to operate the service station, defendants were preserving it as a going business, pending a decision in court. The assets, as they stood on the date of dissolution, are intact, along with subsequently earned profits. Plaintiff's interest was subjected to the claims of creditors during that ten months' period, but the exposure was harmless as the business earned a profit, and the liabilities, as the receiver's report shows, were less than two per cent of the amount which the court found to be the market value of the assets. The legal controversy which has delayed the liquidation is a difficult one. There is no reason to penalize defendants in the liquidation. Defendants' failure to pay Thies his share of the drawings was reprehensible, and for this plaintiff is entitled to a recovery of money, plus interest. The dissolution itself is on a different basis. It arises not from wrong-doing, but as a result of the contract which the partners made. In liquidation plaintiff is entitled only to the one-third which the contract contemplates. . . .

As so modified, the judgment is affirmed.

SHINN, P.J., and FORD, J., concur.

REFERENCES

Block, Death of a Partner: Liquidating the Interest in a Personal Service Firm (1965) 104 Trusts and Estates 104.

Bateh v. Brown, 289 Ala. 699, 271 So.2d 833 (1973) (lower court attempted to liquidate by ordering distribution of property between partners in kind, after paying creditors; reversed, because partners did not agree on valuation of items; UPA not in force).

Wolf v. Murrane, 199 N.W.2d 90 (Iowa 1972) (where two of four partners retired, and others desired to continue business, it was proper for receiver to "wind up" by selling business as going concern to partners who wished to continue, without liquidating and paying debts; goodwill should be included).

Wikstrom v. Davis, 211 Or. 254, 315 P.2d 597 (1957) (expelled partner is creditor, entitled to payment of his share in priority to partners who continued business).

Smith v. Kennebeck, 502 S.W.2d 290 (Mo.1974) (two of three partners dissolved and sold business to corporation consisting of themselves; court treats as "continuation" without considering why it was not a liquidation).

NOTE: THE RIGHT TO DEMAND A WINDING UP

Read sections 37, 38 and 43 of the Uniform Partnership Act. The act deals fairly clearly with the rights of a living former partner who has rightfully retired, and one who has wrongfully quit or earned expulsion. To which group does the act assimilate the representative of a deceased partner, the guardian of an incompetent partner, or the trustee of a bankrupt partner? In section 38(1), line 3, is "all persons" a coordinate subject (with "each partner") or a coordinate object of the preposition "against"? What is "cause" under section 37, line 5? What is comprised in the right to an account given by section 43?

Consider also the legislative provisions on a partner's death in California and Washington. Do they evidence consistent or inconsistent tendencies? Should their provisions (or the best of them) be incorporated in the UPA?

Consider also the variation of section 31 in California, Oklahoma and Texas, which states that the various causes of dissolution apply only if the partnership agreement does not provide otherwise. Has this a bearing on the right or duty to wind up?

CALIFORNIA PROBATE CODE

§ 421. Surviving Partner

The surviving partner of a decedent must not be appointed administrator of the estate if any person interested in the estate objects to his appointment.

§ 571. Acquisition of Estate and Collection of Debts; Partnership Property

. . . When, at the time of his death, a partnership existed between the decedent and any other person, the surviving partner has the right to continue in the possession of the partnership, and to settle its business, but the interest of the decedent in the partnership must be included in the inventory, and be appraised as other property. The surviving partner must settle the affairs of the partnership without delay, and account to the executor or administrator, and pay over such balances as may from time to time be payable to him, in right of the decedent. . . .

WASHINGTON REVISED CODE

11.64.030 Survivor May Purchase Deceased's Interest—Protection Against Partnership Liabilities

The surviving partner or the surviving partners jointly, shall have the right at any time to petition the court to purchase the interests of a deceased partner in the partnership. Upon such petition being presented to the court shall, in such manner as it sees fit, learn and by order fix the value of the interest of the deceased over and above all partnership debts and obligations, and the terms and conditions upon which the surviving partner or partners may purchase, and thereafter the surviving partner or partners shall have the preference right for such length of time as the court may fix, to purchase the interest of the deceased partner at the price and upon the terms and conditions fixed by the court. If any such surviving partner be also the executor or administrator of the estate of the deceased partner, such fact shall not affect his right to purchase, or to join with the other surviving partners to purchase such interest in the manner hereinafter provided.

The court shall make such orders in connection with such sale as it deems proper or necessary to protect the estate of the deceased against any liability for partnership debts or obligations.

11.64.04 Surviving Partner May Operate Under Agreement With Estate—Termination

The court may, in instances where it is deemed advisable, authorize and direct the personal representative of the estate of a deceased partner to enter into an agreement with the surviving partner or partners under which the surviving partner or partners may continue to operate any going business of the former partnership until the further order of the court. The court may, in its discretion, revoke such authority and direction and thereby terminate such agreement at any time by further order, entered upon the application of the personal representative or the surviving partner or partners or any interested person or on its own motion.

HUNTER v. STRAUBE

Supreme Court of Oregon, 1975.
273 Or. 720, 543 P.2d 278.

McAllister, Justice.

This suit was filed by the plaintiffs, Dr. Arthur F. Hunter and Dr. O.D. Haugen, to dissolve a three-man medical partnership in which the defendant, Dr. Kurt R. Straube, was the third member. The three doctors were radiologists practicing in Portland under the firm name of Lloyd Center X–Ray. The partnership was created by a partnership agreement dated July 26, 1969 and a written addendum dated November 24, 1971 which added the plaintiff Haugen to the partnership.

On September 11, 1974 the plaintiffs filed this suit in Multnomah County to dissolve the partnership and prayed for the appointment of a receiver and the winding up of the partnership. The defendant counterclaimed, alleging that he was entitled to continue the partnership business, to recover damages from plaintiffs for the breach of the partnership agreement, and to settle with the plaintiffs as withdrawing partners as provided by the partnership agreement.

. . .

The trial court found that by the filing of this suit the plaintiffs "did not cause by express will a dissolution of their partnership with defendant." The court further found that since "the partnership continues as an entity," the court had no jurisdiction to wind up the affairs of the partnership. The court also dismissed the counterclaims of defendant because "no dissolution had occurred."

The pertinent portions of the partnership agreement read as follows:

3. TERM: The partnership shall continue until the partnership is dissolved as herein provided.

16. TERMINATION: In the event of the death of retirement of any Partner or the voluntary liquidation of the partnership, the following procedure shall be observed:

A. *Death:*

(1) The death of any Partner *shall not dissolve the partnership as to the other Partners, * * *.* (Emphasis added.)

B. *Retirement:*

The retirement of any Partner *shall not dissolve the partnership as to the other Partners,* and each Partner hereby does bind his estate, heirs or personal representatives to receive the sums as in this paragraph computed as full acquittance and payment of his interest in this partnership and all undistributed or uncollected earnings therein and does hereby agree to execute such receipts and bills of sale, deeds, or other instruments of conveyance or satisfaction as may be required to carry out the terms, conditions and stipulations herein set forth. (Emphasis added.)

(1) Upon the voluntary or involuntary retirement of a Partner from the partnership, *or upon the withdrawal of a Partner from the partnership,* the books of the partnership shall be closed as of the first day of the month in which the retirement or withdrawal becomes effective, and such Partner shall be entitled to receive the following sums and no more, all subject to Paragraph 16B(2) hereof:

(a) An amount equal to the capital account of the withdrawing or retiring Partner as of the close of the last fiscal year of the partnership, adjusted for additional capital investment subsequent thereto and reduced by any distributions during the current fiscal year of net profits in excess of said net profits. The capital amount, as so determined, shall be paid in forty-eight (48) equal monthly installments, with the first installment payable on the fifth (5th) day of the fourth (4th) month following the closing date and remaining installments on the fifth (5th) day of the ensuing months, all without interest.

(b) An amount equal to the retiring or withdrawing Partner's share in the undistributed net profits, if any, of the partnership as of the closing date determined as provided in said Partnership Agreement reduced by any accounts payable relating to the collection of accounts receivable. The amount of such undistributed profits shall be paid as soon as reasonably practical.

(c) A share in future income of the partnership, as evidenced by the accounts receivable for services of the partnership as of the closing date, computed as provided in this subparagraph. Accounts receivable shall be valued at 75%, except that accounts which were first billed more than one year prior to the closing date shall be valued at zero. The amount to which the retiring or withdrawing partner shall be entitled shall be computed on the basis of the following formula:

Percentage of participation in net profits of partner	X	Value of Accounts as computed	X	Number of full years as Partner of partnership, or predecessor partnerships, as of the first day of the current partnership year
				20

For example, if the total value of such accounts receivable is $40,000, and the retiring or withdrawing Partner is entitled to 25% of the net profits on the closing date, such Partner would receive $500 for each of such full years as a Partner. The amount thus determined shall be paid as a distribution of income in forty-eight (48) equal installments, without interest, at the same times as provided for under subparagraph (a) above. (Emphasis added.)

(2) *Non-Competition:*

If a Partner shall voluntarily withdraw or retire and shall engage in the practice of medicine or participate in any association, group or clinic so engaged within a forty-mile radius of the City of Portland, Oregon, during a period of three years from the effective date of withdrawal or retirement, such Partner shall have no right to receive any distributions under Paragraph B(1) above, from the date he so engages in the practice of medicine. (Emphasis added.)

(3) *Procedure re Retirement:*

(a) Any Partner voluntarily resigning from the Partnership shall give six months' written notice to each of the other Partners of his desire to retire, and such retirement shall take effect six months from the date of delivery of such notice to the other Partners.

Plaintiffs contend that they expressed their will to dissolve the partnership by the filing of this suit, citing *Carrey v. Haun et al.,* 111 Or. 586, 592, 227 P. 315 (1924). We agree with this contention. See *Clark v. Allen et al.,* 215 Or. 403, 410, 333 P.2d 1100 (1959). However, we disagree with the contention of the plaintiffs that by the filing of this suit they are entitled to a dissolution in accordance with the Uniform Partnership Law. The plaintiffs ignore the provision of the partnership agreement that limits the dissolution to the withdrawing partners and expressly provides that "the retirement of any Partner shall not dissolve the partnership as to the other Partners".

The power to dissolve a partnership is governed by ORS 68.530 and provides for dissolution both without violation of the partnership agreement and in contravention of the partnership agreement. In either case, it is clear that *if* the partnership agreement provides for the distribution of the partnership property the rights of the partners are governed by the partnership agreement rather than by the Uniform Partnership Law. See provisions in ORS 68.310, 68.420, 68.440, 68.590, 68.600 and 68.620.[1]

In the case at bar the plaintiffs had the power to dissolve the partnership by electing to withdraw as partners, a choice which they made by filing this suit. Plaintiffs, however, did not have the right to dissolve the partnership without complying with the terms of the partnership agreement. As was succinctly stated in *Straus v. Straus,* 254 Minn. 234, 94 N.W.2d 679, 686 (1959):

> A distinction must be recognized between the power to dissolve a partnership and the right to dissolve a partnership. Any partner may have the power to dissolve a partnership at any time * * * and this is true even though such dissolution is in contravention of the partnership agreement * * * If a partner exercises his power to dissolve a partnership, but does not have the right to do so, he must suffer the penalties * * *.
>
> . . .

We think the plaintiffs cannot, by merely calling their withdrawal a dissolution, escape from the liabilities which they assumed when they executed the partnership agreement. The plaintiffs have not cited a single authority in support of their contention.

. . .

In *Devlin v. Rockey,* 295 F.2d 266 (7th Cir.1961), the partnership agreement provided for termination upon a two-thirds majority vote of all the partners or upon the unanimous consent of all the partners. Two of the ten partners sought a decree declaring they had effected a dissolution of the partnership, alleging that the partnership was one at will and therefore subject to dissolution by any partner at any time. The court held that, despite use of the word dissolution by the plaintiffs, it was clear that they were to be treated as withdrawing partners under the agreement, the partnership was not dissolved, and distribution to the plaintiffs was to be controlled by the partnership agreement provisions pertaining to withdrawal of a partner. 295 F.2d at 269.

Similarly, in *Adams v. Jarvis,* 23 Wis.2d 453, 127 N.W.2d 400 (1964), the partnership agreement specifically provided that the partnership would not terminate upon the withdrawal of a partner. The plaintiff withdrew but contended this effected a dissolution under a Wisconsin statute identical to ORS 68.510. The court refused to construe the statute so as to invalidate an otherwise enforceable contract. In one sense plaintiff's withdrawal constituted a dissolution, the court said, but the partnership was not wholly dissolved so as to require

---

1. All the provisions cited, relating to the rights and duties of the partners, make clear that they are subject to any agreement between the parties to the contrary. For example, ORS 68.620 provides 'Rules for distribution. In settling accounts between the partners after dissolution, the following rules shall be observed, subject to any agreement to the contrary: * * *.'

complete winding up. The partnership continued to exist under the terms of the agreement. 127 N.W.2d at 403–404.

Gibson v. Angros, 30 Colo.App. 95, 491 P.2d 87 (1971), involved a covenant not to compete upon withdrawal of a partner from the partnership. Plaintiff argued that his notice to resign from the partnership operated as a dissolution and he was therefore no longer bound by the restrictive covenant. The court held that plaintiff's actions constituted a voluntary retirement under the terms of the partnership agreement, and the terms of the agreement which became operative upon such retirement were not rendered nugatory by the dissolution of the partnership. 491 P.2d at 91.

We hold that the filing of this suit by the plaintiffs was an election by each of them to withdraw from the partnership in contravention of the partnership agreement. Under those circumstances the withdrawal entitles the defendant to continue the partnership business and to settle the affairs of the partnership in accordance with the terms of the partnership agreement. The defendant also has the right to any damages he may have suffered on account of the plaintiffs' breach of the provision for six months' notice of withdrawal.

This suit is reversed and remanded to the court below for further proceedings consistent with this opinion.

Reversed and remanded.

POLIKOFF v. LEVY
Illinois Appellate Court, 1971.
132 Ill.App.2d 492, 270 N.E.2d 540.

CRAVEN, JUSTICE. This is an appeal from a decree entered on plaintiff's motion for a summary decree ordering a judicial sale of all of the assets of a joint venture, its windup, and distribution of the net sale proceeds to joint venture members. The decree also approved accountings filed by the defendants of the operations of the joint venture.

.   .   .

The subject-matter of this case has been the focal point of much litigation.[1] . . .

A joint venture of some forty-nine persons, known as the "State House Inn," located in Springfield, Illinois, was formed in 1959, acquired land and constructed a motor motel thereon known as the "State House Inn." Plaintiff, Ben Polikoff, was one of the original members of this joint venture.

.   .   .

1. Ed. note: The suit was filed in 1962, and included charges of securities acts violations. Dismissal of these was affirmed in the appellate court ((1965) 55 Ill.App. 229, 204 N.E.2d 807) and petitions for appeal or certiorari denied by Illinois and U.S. Supreme Courts ((1965) 382 U.S. 903, 86 S.Ct. 237). A related suit by the defendants' corporation to confirm its title to the motel was dismissed and the dismissal affirmed (State House Inn v. Polikoff (1967) 86 Ill. App.2d 97, 230 N.E.2d 283).

Count II, in Chancery, charged a wrongful dissolution of the joint venture by the principal defendants in conveying and transferring all of the joint venture assets to the new corporation. The State House Inn Corporation, without the consent of and over the objection of Ben Polikoff, plaintiff. It prayed that the court wind up the affairs of the joint venture and for such other and further relief as might be just and equitable.

Upon separate motion of both plaintiff and defendants for a summary decree in their respective favors, the court ordered the joint venture to be wound up by a public judicial sale of all of its assets and the distribution of the net proceeds of such sale to the joint venture members. It also approved the accountings filed by the defendants.

The motion for summary decree by plaintiff was supported by the affidavit of plaintiff. This motion set forth that all of the property of the joint venture was purportedly transferred to the defendant-corporation, The State House Inn Corporation; that this transfer was without the consent and over the objection of the plaintiff—joint venturer; . . . and that, as a matter of law, the plaintiff was entitled to a decree declaring the joint venture dissolved and winding up the joint venture. . . .

. . .

On the issue of law, it is clear that defendants have no right to buy plaintiff, Ben Polikoff's interest in the joint venture. A co-venture is governed substantially by the same rules which govern a partnership. The settled law is that where, as here, a partner or joint venturer retired without himself causing a wrongful dissolution, the copartners or co-venturers have no right to buy the retired partner's or co-venturer's interest. Lindley, Partnership (11th ed. 1950), p. 660; Story, Partnership (2d ed. 1846), sec. 351, pp. 528–530; Reinhardt v. Reinhardt, 271 Ill.App. 287 (4th Dist.1933). Plaintiff here did not wrongfully withdraw from the joint venture nor cause a wrongful dissolution. Section 42 of the Illinois Uniform Partnership Act is not applicable here since plaintiff did not cause a wrongful dissolution.

. . .

The established procedure in winding up a dissolved joint venture where the dissolution was not caused in contravention of the agreement, unless the agreement creating the joint venture provides otherwise or all joint venturers agree otherwise, is to convert its assets into cash by sale, discharge its liabilities, and distribute the surplus, if any, to its members. Section 38(1) of the Illinois Uniform Partnership Act so provides. Such was the rule of partnership law prior to the statute. (Lindley, Partnership (11th ed. 1950), p. 657; Story, Partnership 2d ed. 1846), sec. 347, pp. 520, 527–528; Rowley, Partnership (2d ed. 1960), Vol. 1, pp. 670, 696, 709, 736; 68 C.J.S. Partnership, sec. 388, p. 902). Neither section 38(2) nor section 43 of the Illinois Uniform Partnership Act is applicable to this case.

Where the co-venturers cannot agree on the method of sale at dissolution, a public judicial sale is the only available method of conversion of the assets. Equitable principles and possible unfavorable results of a forced judicial public sale cannot compel disregard for the application of the ordinary and traditional methods of final settlement of a business relationship. The parties have failed to provide by their agreement a possibly more favorable method of liquidation. The trial court properly decreed a public judicial sale in the instant case.

. . .

. . . The judgment of the Circuit Court of Cook County is affirmed in part and reversed in part. . . .[2]

REFERENCES ON "FREEZE–OUTS" OF PARTNERS

Page v. Page, 55 Cal.2d 192, 10 Cal.Rptr. 643, 359 P.2d 41 (1961) (reversing a judgment holding a partnership to be for a term, rather than at will). Discussing the matter of leaving a partnership, the Court stated:

> A partner at will is not bound to remain in a partnership, regardless of whether the business is profitable or unprofitable. A partner may not, however, by use of adverse pressure "freeze out" a copartner and appropriate the business to his own use. A partner may not dissolve a partnership to gain the benefits of the business for himself, unless he fully compensates his copartner for his share of the prospective business opportunity. In this regard his fiduciary duties are at least as great as those of a shareholder of a corporation.

Zeibak v. Nasser, 12 Cal.2d 1, 82 P.2d 375 (1938) (discussing the operation of UPA § 38 in the context of wrongful dissolution).

Prentiss v. Sheffel, 20 Ariz.App. 411, 513 P.2d 949 (1973) (in partnership at will, 2 of 3 partners dissolved, and sold partnership business as going concern at public auction to themselves; held, they had a right to squeeze out third partner and to bid at their own sale).

MAHAN v. MAHAN
Supreme Court of Arizona, 1971.
107 Ariz. 517, 489 P.2d 1197.

Plaintiff is the widow of Terrell B. Mahan, who died 15 July 1966, in Prescott, Arizona. She is suing Gordon Mahan in her own right and as executrix of Terrell Mahan's estate, which is being probated in Yavapai County, Arizona.

When plaintiff married Terrell Mahan in 1948, a construction and agriculture partnership existed between Terrell and his brothers, Gordon and Merwin. (Merwin withdrew from the partnership in 1962 and is not involved in the lawsuit.) The partnership was an equal one in the sense that the profits were divided on an equal basis, first three ways, and then two.

At about this time (1964–1965), the partnership became inactive, and it remained inactive through Terrell's death in 1966 and the bringing of the present lawsuit in 1969. Gordon, the surviving partner,

2. Ed. note: The reversal related to the sufficiency of the defendants' accounting.

did nothing toward settling the affairs of the partnership and accounting to the executrix until Terrell's widow brought this suit.

The principal partnership asset at Terrell's death and the time of the lawsuit was the remainder of a block of Coconino County land bought in 1950 and known as the Red Lake Ranch. In 1960, the partnership sold a portion of the ranch for $80,000, leaving 1,752.34 acres of patented land, plus 1,843 acres of State leased land. In December, 1961, the partnership made an aborted sale of practically the same block owned at Terrell's death. The sale, for $284,200 fell through in 1963, and the Mahan brothers regained the land. In 1963, an appraiser valued the land at $43,868.44, and in 1965 an accountant, for federal tax purposes lowered the value on the partnership books to $15,622.61.

. . .

The defendant advanced, and the trial court accepted, the contention that since Terrell's capital account was reduced by $23,000 to $4,005.45 and was one-eighth of the value of the total capital account ($31,308.06), Terrell's widow should receive, in distribution, one-eighth of $33,274.31 or $4,159.29.

. . .

The answer to the question of whether the court erred in accepting the book value of the assets can be answered by looking at the figures we have reconstructed. Every single component of the $33,274.61 book value has been strongly contested. The Red Lake Ranch, for example, was sold in 1961 for over $280,000, but has an arbitrary book value of $15,622.61. An "investment" valued at $9,150 is made up of two investments, one worthless and the other worth only $900. In short, the book values are completely arbitrary and should not have been used.

. . . The normal rule is that book value is only used in ascertaining the respective shares when there is an explicit contractual provision to that effect, and even then is not used where the facts of the case make it inequitable to do so. . . . Here there was no contractual provision mandating the use of book value, and even if there were, the facts show book value in this case to be so disproportionate to possible real values that it would be inequitable for it to be used anyway.

Having decided that book value should not be used in valuing the partnership assets, we are forced to conclude that the trial court should have granted plaintiff's wish to have the assets liquidated.

. . .

We hold that the partnership assets must be liquidated, and that the general creditors be paid first. If the assets are insufficient for this purpose, the estate and Gordon should be charged equally for the losses. If the assets are more than sufficient then the surviving partner should be paid first up to the amount of $23,297.16 to set off the withdrawal from the capital account by Terrell. Any amount left over should be equally divided between Terrell's estate and the surviving partner, Gordon Mahan.

. . .

REFERENCES ON RIGHT TO WIND UP

Detroit Bank & Trust Co. v. Dickson, 78 Mich.App. 12, 259 N.W.2d 228 (1977) (court confirms order of winding up entered against surviving partner on suit of executor of deceased partner, because UPA does not give survivor a right to buy out estate, and there was no buy-out provision in the partnership agreement).

Maras v. Stilinovich, 268 N.W.2d 541 (Minn.1978) (court orders liquidation of partnership by selling the business to one of the partners with payment in installments over a ten-year period with 6% interest).

Nicholes v. Hunt, 273 Or. 255, 541 P.2d 820 (1975) (in absence of an express contrary agreement the partnership may be dissolved at the will of any of the parties; court entitled to distribute assets based on equities without resort to sale).

Haynes v. Allen, 482 S.W.2d 85 (Mo.App.1972) (medical partnership agreement provided that on dissolution "by agreement" laboratory equipment and accounts receivable would vest free of debts in majority wanting to carry on clinic; member who was expelled without cause was entitled to value of his share of all assets [about $27,000] rather than share of remaining assets under "agreement" clause [about $7,000]).

Adams v. Jarvis, 23 Wis.2d 453, 127 N.W.2d 400 (1964) (withdrawing partner had no right to compel liquidation where agreement provided for continuation). Comment, 48 Marq.L.Rev. 253.

Note, Right of a Surviving Partner to Purchase a Deceased Partner's Interest Under the Uniform Partnership Act (1963), 62 Mich.L.Rev. 106 (the author argues that the U.P.A. does not demand liquidation and that a court approved sale of partnership assets to the surviving partner should be permitted).

B. CONTINUATION OF THE PARTNERSHIP—RIGHTS OF FORMER PARTNERS

As will be seen, the rights of former partners after a continuation of the business usually arise when the business has been finally liquidated, after the disputed continuation. Is it necessary to wait so long, or can a partner proceed to some remedy without obtaining, or awaiting, final liquidation?

Even if payment is made as promptly as possible, some difficult questions arise as to the amount. How does one determine the value of an unliquidated share? Is going concern value, including the expectation of future profits, included? What about the changes in value which take place between the dissolution and the payment?

If payment is long delayed while the business runs merrily on, further complications arise. There may be extensive losses; from whose shares should they be deducted? There may be profits; to whose shares should they be added? Does it make any difference whether the withdrawn partner's successors have consented, or acquiesced, or have fought bitterly for liquidation, and finally obtained it?

MATTER OF BROWN
New York Court of Appeals, 1926.
242 N.Y. 1, 150 N.E. 581, 44 A.L.R. 510.

CARDOZO, J.   Vernon C. Brown & Company were stockbrokers for many years in the city of New York. Stephen H. Brown, one of the partners, died. The survivors, denying that there was any good will to be accounted for, continued the business at the old stand and in the old name. The executors acquiesced. For so acquiescing they have been held to be at fault, and their accounts have been surcharged accordingly. The question is whether the decree may be sustained.

The Browns, Vernon and Stephen, were brothers. They began business in 1895 with one Watson, under the name of Watson & Brown. In 1901 Watson withdrew, and the brothers went on. "Vernon C. Brown & Company" became the name of the continued partnership. New members were admitted from time to time, but the firm name remained unchanged. Good will was not mentioned in the partnership articles or in any books of account. Incoming members did not pay anything for it. One member, Mr. Schoonmaker, retired while Stephen Brown was alive. If good will was an asset, he was entitled to share in it. The evidence is uncontradicted that nothing was paid him. We may infer that in the thought of the partners nothing was due.

. . . The business was lucrative, though it was run, one would gather, in a more or less old-fashioned and conservative way, without advertising in newspapers or solicitation of accounts. It had four branches or departments: (1) The general commission business; (2) the so-called "odd lot" business, which proved to be the most lucrative of all; (3) the so-called "two-dollar" business; and (4) speculative business transacted for the firm itself. There is a finding that all the branches of the business except the last had in them an element of good will for which the survivors were accountable. The net profits of the three branches were averaged for a period of three years, allowance being made for interest on capital and for the personal services rendered by the partners. The value of the good will was fixed at two years' purchase price of the profits so computed. On this basis, the value was $103,891.60, of which 15%, $15,583.74, was the share due to the estate. The surrogate, confirming the report of a referee, held that the accounts of the executors were to be surcharged for failing to collect this amount from the survivors. The Appellate Division unanimously affirmed.

The books abound in definitions of good will (People ex rel. Johnson Co. v. Roberts, 159 N.Y. 70, 80, 53 N.E. 685; Von Bremen v. MacMonnies, 200 N.Y. 41, 47, 93 N.E. 186). There is no occasion to repeat them. Men will pay for any privilege that gives a reasonable expectancy of preference in the race of competition (cf. Walton Water Co. v. Village of Walton, 238 N.Y. 46, 50, 143 N.E. 786). Such expectancy may come from succession in place or name or otherwise to a business that has won the favor of its customers. It is then known as good will. Many are the degrees of value. At one extreme there are expectancies so strong that the advantage derived from economic opportunity may be said to be a certainty. At the other are expectancies so weak that for any rational mind they may be said to be illusory. We must know the facts in any case.

Good will, when it exists as incidental to the business of a partnership, is presumptively an asset to be accounted for like any other by those who liquidate the business (Slater v. Slater, 175 N.Y. 143, 67 N.E. 224; Matter of David & Matthews, 1899, 1 Ch. 378; Witkowsky v. Affeld, 283 Ill. 557, 119 N.E. 630). The course of dealing, however, can stamp it with a different quality. Partners may contract that good will, though it exist, shall not "be considered as property or as an asset of the co-partnership" (Douthart v. Logan, 190 Ill. 243, 252, 60 N.E. 507, 510; Witkowsky v. Affeld, supra). The contract may "be expressly made," or it may "arise by implication, from other contracts and the acts and conduct of the parties" (Douthart v. Logan, supra). The implication will be drawn the more readily when the good will, if any, is tenuous or doubtful. Upon this appeal, the form of the findings precludes us from adjudging that the distribution of what would otherwise be an asset has been varied by agreement. We state, however, for the guidance of the trial court, that evidence exists from which such an agreement may be gathered. The trier of the facts might not unreasonably infer from the course of dealing between the partners when new members came in and old ones went out that by tacit understanding there was to be no accounting for good will. No doubt there must be caution before property interests of value are thus excluded by implication. The life of the business must be scrutinized for every relevant circumstance affecting the intention of the partners. The inference is one of fact, to be drawn, if at all, when intention is thus appraised and probabilities are measured.

Assuming for present purposes that the disposition of good will has not been varied by agreement, we reach the question whether there was any good will to be disposed of upon the facts recited in the findings. To answer that question, we must consider at the outset what rights would have passed to a buyer of the good will if the surviving partners had sold it in the course of liquidation. The chief elements of value upon any sale of a good will are, *first,* continuity of place, and, *second,* continuity of name (People ex rel. Johnson Co. v. Roberts, 159 N.Y. 70, at p. 83, 53 N.E. 685). There may indeed at times be others, e.g., continuity of organization. That element is of value in business of a complex order. Where the business is simple, the benefits of organization are slight and not so easily transmitted. Confining ourselves now to the two chief elements of value, we may assume that the buyer of this good will would have been reasonably assured of continuity of place. The firm offices were the same from the beginning of the business till the death of Stephen Brown and later. There is nothing to show that the survivors, genuinely endeavoring to dispose of the good will, would have been unable to deliver possession to a buyer of the lease. A more difficult question is presented when we ask to what extent there would have been continuity of name. "Vernon C. Brown & Co." was not an arbitrary symbol, like The Snyder Mfg. Co., e.g., in Snyder Mfg. Co. v. Snyder (54 Ohio St. 86, 43 N.E. 325). It had not gained a secondary meaning supplanting a primary meaning which had been descriptive of a man or men, and instead identifying impersonally an organization or a product. Writ large in this style or title was the name of a living man who had done nothing by word or act to give the name a reality or a significance external to himself. A buyer of the good will would gain no right to the use of any style or title whereby this man would be represented as still a partner in the business. We assume that in conducting the new business he would be privileged to describe himself, subject, however, to the rules of the Exchange, as the "successor" to the old one (Moore v. Rawson, 199 Mass. 493, 497, 499, 85 N.E. 586). He would not be suffered to go farther. One who writes his name at large in the style or title of a partnership does not dedicate to the partnership, by force of that act alone without other tokens of intention, the right to sell the name at auction upon every change of membership.

We do not overlook the provisions of the statute (Partnership Law, § 80, subd. 1; formerly Partnership Law, § 20 [Cons.Laws, ch. 39]) whereby partnership names are made capable of transfer to the successors to a business.[1] The sole effect of that provision is to give the approval of the law to a use that would otherwise be criminal though a transfer were attempted (Slater v. Slater, supra, at p. 149; Caswell v. Hazard, 121 N.Y. 484, 496, 24 N.E. 707). The statute tells us what the partners are at liberty to assign. It does not tell us what they are under a duty to assign. . . .

We have said that the members of the old firm might compete without restraint, after a sale of the good will, with the members of the new one. There are distinctions in that regard between voluntary and involuntary sales (Von Bremen v. MacMonnies, 200 N.Y. 41, 93 N.E. 186). After a voluntary sale, the seller, though he may compete, may not drum up or circularize the customers of the business. After a sale *in invitum,* he is not subject to a disability so heavy. For the purpose of this distinction, a sale by surviving partners upon a liquidation of the business, is a sale coerced by law (Hutchinson v. Nay, 187 Mass. 262, 72 N.E. 974; Moore v. Rawson, supra). The survivors may indeed be bound as upon a voluntary sale if they have given the transaction such

---

1. This statute, which is not part of the Uniform Partnership Act, and does not appear to be in frequent use in other states, provides that the use of a partnership or business name may be continued (1) when the former owner of the name did interstate or international business, and the business is being carried on by some of the former partners or assignees, or (2) where a majority of the former owners consent to use of the name by a new organization, or (3) where the name was that of a sole trader doing interstate or international business, and has been sold as a part of his estate. The statute is traced to a New York statute of 1854, and has been repeatedly amended, before and after the decision of the principal case.

an aspect in the eyes of the buyer (Caswell v. Hazard, 121 N.Y. 484, 495, 24 N.E. 707; Lindley on Partnership, p. 543). The representative of the deceased partner, however, has no cause for complaint if by appropriate recitals or reservations they disclose its involuntary quality and thus limit its effect. Their duty as liquidators is done when they convey what would be conveyed upon a sale by a receiver (Hutchinson v. Nay, supra).

We conclude, then, that a buyer of this good will, if it had been put up for sale by the liquidating partners, would have had the benefit at most of continuity of place and of such continuity of name as would belong to a "successor." We have next to consider the relation of these benefits to the several branches or departments in which the business was conducted.

There is a finding, unanimously affirmed, that appurtenant to the general commission branch was an element of good will not incapable of conveyance. We cannot say that this finding is qualified by others to such an extent that as a matter of law it must be disregarded as erroneous. The buyer of the good will would take over the firm records, which would give the names of the old customers. He would be in a position to notify them that he had succeeded to the business. True the old partners might send out notices that they were still in business for themselves. None the less, some customers might wander into the old place from forgetfulness or habit. Once there, inertia might lead them to give an order to brokers whom they found established in possession (Hill v. Fearis, 1905, 1 Ch. 466, stockbrokers; Rutan v. Coolidge, 241 Mass. 584, 136 N.E. 257, architects; Witkowsky v. Affeld, 283 Ill. 557, 119 N.E. 630, insurance brokers). The relation is not so distinctly personal or professional that good will is excluded either for reasons of public policy or as an inference of law (Bailly v. Betti, 241 N.Y. 22, 148 N.E. 776; Blakely v. Sousa, 197 Penn.St. 305, 47 N.E. 286; Messer v. Fadettes, 168 Mass. 140, 46 N.E. 407). We may doubt whether a privilege so uncertain would be worth a great deal. The surrogate would have been justified in placing the value at a much lower figure than he did, or even at a nominal amount (Rutan v. Coolidge, supra). The question is not whether the buyer would be willing to pay much or would be making a wise bargain. The question is whether a reasonable man would be willing to pay anything.

The odd lot business stands on a different basis. Its essential characteristics are established by the findings. There is a rule of the New York Stock Exchange by which the unit of trading on the floor of the Exchange is declared to be one hundred shares. Dealings in smaller numbers of shares are known as odd lot transactions. Most stockbrokers do not transact an odd lot business, but there are some that do, and Vernon C. Brown & Company was one of them. Orders for odd lots do not come through the office. They are given on the floor of the Exchange to the individual member or members of the firm who are its floor representatives. They come invariably from other brokers communicating with fellow-members of the Exchange whom they know as individuals.

A buyer of the good will would gain nothing in respect of this branch of the business from continuity of place. There was no relation between such orders and the place where the firm business was transacted. He would gain nothing from the privilege of announcing himself the successor to the business without continuity of name. The individual brokers who had been accustomed to receive these orders from fellow-members of the Exchange would still be on hand to receive them as before. The findings suggest no reason why business so individual and personal should be diverted or diminished. Very likely the new firm, when announcing its succession to the business, would advertise the fact that its board members, if there were any, would buy and sell odd lots. It might advertise a like readiness though the business it was starting had no relation of succession to any that had gone before. The appeal to favor would be hardly stronger in one case than in the other. The situation would be different if the old partners had been about to withdraw from the field of competition. While they remained in the arena, the tie of succession was too attenuated to give to the buyer in transactions so individual and personal a fair promise of advantage. One cannot gain a foothold upon a ledge of opportunity so narrow. Expectancy in such conditions may be said to have reached the vanishing point at which it merges in illusion.

The "two-dollar" or "specialist" business is personal and individual like the department just considered. The specialist is a broker who remains at one post of the Exchange where particular stocks are dealt in and there executes orders received from other brokers. He receives a commission of $2.50 for every 100 shares. Good will does not attach to business of this order for the same reason that none attaches to dealings in odd lots.

. . .

The order of the Appellate Division and the decree of the Surrogate's Court, so far as such decree is appealed from, should be reversed, and a rehearing ordered, with costs to abide the event.

Order reversed, etc.

REFERENCES: PARTNERSHIP GOODWILL

Bailey v. McCoy, 187 Neb. 618, 193 N.W.2d 270 (1971) (holds that a partnership engaged in performing services may have goodwill).

Wolf v. Murrane, 199 N.W.2d 90 (Iowa 1972) (where receiver sold business as a going concern, goodwill was properly included in sale).

Collins v. Merrick, 202 Kan. 276, 448 P.2d 1 (1968) (partnership at will to conduct annual Grand National Jalopy Races was dissolved by expulsion of one partner while others continued races; held, there was insufficient evidence that partnership possessed any goodwill for which they should account to expelled partner).

Clements v. Clements, 2 Mich.App. 370, 139 N.W.2d 918 (1966) (brothers operated parking lot rented from parents; although business was profitable, court holds there was no salable goodwill since continuation of lease depended on whim of decedent's parents).

Wikstrom v. Davis, 211 Or. 254, 315 P.2d 597 (1957) (nothing allowed for goodwill because no proof of its value was offered).

Hartsock v. Strong, 21 Md.App. 100, 318 A.2d 237 (1974) (partnership agreement provided for survivor on dissolution to pay $7500 for share of good will unless amended; later parties increased insurance pursuant to brokers recommendation based on valuation of good will at $40,000 apiece; this effectuated amendment of agreement, so that $40,000 must be paid to decedent's partner's estate).

Block, Death of a Partner: Liquidating the Interest in a Personal Service Firm (1965) 104 Trusts and Estates 104 (valuation of intangibles, including good will and work in progress).

NOTE: FURTHER REFLECTIONS ON GOING CONCERN VALUE

Matter of Brown illustrates an early and greatly oversimplified view of the nature of going concern value. Perhaps most importantly it indicates the need for a provision in the partnership agreement setting forth a formula for determination of the value of the firm.

In contemporary financial thinking, it is not sound to approach the valuation of a business by adding up the value of its physical assets and then assigning a separate value to "goodwill", or going concern value. Instead, a more realistic value for the firm is determined by capitalizing the expected stream of future earnings, or discounting the future cash flow. Description and evaluation of these techniques, and others, can be found in the references below.

Perhaps the fundamental flaw in Matter of Brown is its identification of "goodwill" with continuity of name, place and organization. The phenomenon of going concern value is far more complex. For example, "human assets," in the form of an existing base of personnel familiar with the firm's procedures and operations, form a part of going concern value.[1] Executive talent, management procedures, pricing policies, customer loyalty and other factors also enter into the value of the business. One need only reflect on the fact that some companies are highly profitable, while others in the same business are not, to realize that earning power—going concern value—cannot be captured in a few words.

In analyzing the question of going concern value, three questions may be asked. (1) Is there going concern value, in the sense that the value of the business as a whole is greater than the value of its individual assets? (2) Does the partnership agreement provide for, or preclude, the payment of going concern value to a retired partner or the estate of a deceased partner? (3) Does a portion of the going concern value leave the partnership as the result of the death, or retirement, of the withdrawn partner?

REFERENCES ON VALUATION OF BUSINESSES

Brudney & Chirelstein, Corporate Finance (2d Ed. 1979), Part I.

Weston & Copeland, Managerial Finance (8th ed. 1986), Ch. 23.

Herwitz, Business Planning (Temporary 2nd ed. 1984), Ch. 1.

1. See Pyle, Monitoring Human Resources—"On Line", 22 Mich.Bus.Rev. 19 (1970).

M. & C. CREDITORS CORP. v. PRATT

New York Supreme Court, N.Y. County, 1938.
172 Misc. 695, 17 N.Y.S.2d 240.
Affirmed without opinion 255 App.Div. 838, 7 N.Y.S.2d 662 (1938), affirmed 281
N.Y. 804, 24 N.E.2d 482 (1939).

GEORGE SYLVESTER, REFEREE. In this action for an accounting, plaintiff seeks, in effect, to recover back an alleged overpayment made in 1929 to the executors of Dallas B. Pratt, who, prior to his death on October 9, 1929, was a partner in the private banking firm of Maitland, Coppell & Company (hereinafter referred to as the old firm). Upon Pratt's death, the surviving partners organized a new firm under the same name to continue the business. The payment in question, amounting to $424,394.11, was made by the new firm and was intended to represent Pratt's interest in the firm as of the date of his death.

Plaintiff contends that ascertainment of Pratt's interest was improperly made as of the date of his death; that liquidation was essential in order to determine the amount due; and that, in any event, his estate should have been charged with the depreciation in the value of the firm's securities which occurred between the date of his death and the date of payment.

[The stock market crash of 1929 had occurred between Pratt's death and the principal payment to his executors, on December 13. In 1932 the succeeding firm became bankrupt, and its assets were sold to the plaintiff.]

Upon dissolution of a partnership, the surviving partners are required to close up the partnership affairs, dispose of the assets, pay all creditors, and remit the decedent's share to his representatives. Williams v. Whedon, 1888, 109 N.Y. 333, 16 N.E. 365, 4 Am.St.Rep. 460; Preston v. Fitch, 1893, 137 N.Y. 41, 33 N.E. 77; N.Y. Partnership Law, Sec. 74 [UPA § 43].

The plaintiff contends that the continuance of the business does not affect the obligation of the firm to liquidate; that, without such liquidation, no payment could properly be made to Pratt's estate, since the surplus available for partners could not be determined until the assets had been sold and all liabilities paid. No direct authority is cited in support of this view. Plaintiff is satisfied to refer to cases holding that the representatives of a deceased partner have the right to require liquidation; that, until such liquidation is completed, they have no interest in the assets of the partnership; that legal title is vested in surviving partners and that the right of the executors remains a contingency, a mere chose in action, until liquidation.

Plaintiff's interpretation would require the representatives of the deceased partner to force a liquidation, thus jeopardizing the continued business; or, in the alternative, to wait indefinitely for payment of the decedent's interest. Ordinary considerations of fairness and justice require that plaintiff's views should not prevail unless rendered unavoidable by decisive authority. No such authority has been cited to the referee nor has he been able to discover any.

On the contrary, Section 73 of the Partnership Law explicitly provides: [the court quoted UPA § 42].

Section 72 [UPA § 41], referred to in Sec. 73, is designed to protect the creditors of a partnership which, dissolved by a change in membership, nevertheless proceeds with its business. Subdivision 3 is applicable here [quoting it].

The reference here to continuance of the business "as set forth in subdivisions one and two" is to the continuance of business "without liquidation of the partnership affairs."

Section [42] is decisive of the plaintiff's contention, unless it be said that the absence of consent of Pratt's executors to the continuance in business renders this provision inoperative.

The purpose of Section [41], subdivision 3 is to render available to creditors the share of the deceased partner in the assets of the firm where his representatives have consented to the continuance of the business. In this case, the rights of creditors are not involved. Section [42] provides that where the rights of creditors are not involved, the representatives of the deceased partner may have his share of the assets ascertained as of the date of death. The requirement of consent by the decedent's representatives to a continuance of the business is a prerequisite to subjecting the decedent's interest to creditors of the continuing business. It could not have been intended to limit the rights of the representatives to require payment of the decedent's interest as of the date of death.

This construction of Sec. [42] has been indicated in Cahill v. Haff, 1928, 248 N.Y. 377, at page 380, 162 N.E. 288, where Judge Andrews said: "It is clear that the surviving partner may be required to account for the firm transactions and for transactions requisite to wind up the firm business. That at least he must do. . . . If the son, for example, continues the partnership business, with no accounting, retaining and using therein capital belonging to the estate of the father, with the consent, express or implied, of his representatives, the latter are entitled at their option to receive the profits attributable to the use of his rights in the property of the dissolved partnership. [Uniform] Partnership Law [§ 42], merely a statement of the pre-existing law; Pollock on Partnership, p. 133. *Probably the same thing is true if there be no consent.*" (Referee's italics.)

As indicated by Judge Andrews, Section [42] is expressive of the common law rule that where the surviving partners of a business continue to use the interest of a deceased partner in the conduct of the firm's affairs, they must account to the representatives of the decedent, not only for the value of his share at the date of his death, but also for profits earned which may be attributed to that value. On the other hand, all losses are required to be borne entirely by the surviving partners.

It is said that the language of the Court in Cahill v. Haff, supra, simply means that the decedent's representatives are entitled to a liquidation to ascertain the value at the date of death and not to an appraisal or other computation, not based on actual liquidation. The Court's opinion is to the contrary, 248 N.Y. at pages 385, 386, 162 N.E. at page 290:

"The executrix, therefore, at her election, is entitled to receive the profits attributable to the use of this capital, and for it also the son must account at least to the date of any new trial. At the time of his death, therefore, did the deceased have capital therein? . . .

"As appears by the referee's report, on February 22, 1919 [date of death], the assets of the firm amounted to $265,160.90. Its liabilities were $241,076.25. The balance is $24,084.65. If this were all it would seem that the father at his death still had invested therein $12,042.33."

Thus, it appears that the Court took the valuation at the date of death without requiring liquidation. . . .

The rule is stated as follows in 2 Rowley's Modern Law of Partnership, Sec. 638: "A surviving partner has no authority to continue the business, but must wind it up, and if he does continue it, he is answerable for all debts which he incurs and for loss and depreciation thus occasioned."

In Froess v. Froess, 1925, 284 Pa. 369, 131 A. 276, the surviving partner had continued the business for some time following the death of one of the partners. The Court, in applying a provision identical with that here involved, said, per Sadler, J., 284 Pa. at page 374, 131 A. at page 278: "The determination of the right of the deceased partner, where there has been no agreement to continue the business or dispose of the estate's interest for a fixed sum . . . may be controlled by an election of the personal representative of the decedent to take a share of the assets and profits which have been gained by the use of the property prior to actual settlement [citing cases]. Or, in lieu of the latter, interest may be demanded on the value of the property, estimated as of the date of dissolution."

Quoting from Brown's Appeal, 89 Pa. 139, at page 147, the Court continued: "If the survivors of a partnership carry on the concern, and enter into new transactions with the partnership funds, they do so at their peril . . . .. If no profits are made, or even if a loss is incurred, they must be charged with interest on the funds they use, and the whole loss will be theirs."

In Mattson v. Wagstad, 1926, 188 Wis. 566, 206 N.W. 865, 869, the Court construed a provision identical with Partnership Law, Sec. 73, as conferring an option upon the deceased partner's representatives to "the value of the interest at the date of the dissolution."

This doctrine is also established by statute in England (English Partnership Act, 1890; 53–54 Victoria, ch. 39). . . .

The defendants are entitled to judgment dismissing the complaint upon the merits, with costs. Submit findings and judgment in accordance herewith.

REFERENCES ON AGREED VALUATION

Mundy v. Holden, 42 Del.Ch.84, 204 A.2d 83 (1964) (agreed value of $40,000 for partner's share held binding on estate, despite evidence that book value of the interest was substantially greater).

Emerson v. Arnold, 92 Mich.App. 345, 285 N.W.2d 45 (1979) (partners agreed to pay for shares on dissolution a stated value to be adjusted annually, provided it had been adjusted within two years of dissolution; they failed to make adjustment; payment was ordered at value determined independently of agreed amount).

BLUT v. KATZ

New Jersey Supreme Court, 1953.
13 N.J. 374, 99 A.2d 785.
Comments: 23 Ford.L.Rev. 211, 67 Harv.L.Rev. 1271, 38 Minn.L.Rev. 553, 29 N.Y.U.L.Rev. 1151, 63 Yale L.J. 709.

The opinion of the court was delivered by WACHENFELD, J. . . . .

In 1925 five partners executed a partnership agreement under which they conducted the United Shop Cap Company. The term was for a period of one year. Amongst other things, it provided for even distribution of the profits, weekly allowances to the partners, and the paying off of any partner who should voluntarily withdraw.

Before 1940 two partners withdrew, but no further agreement was executed by the remaining partners, and from that date until the death of the decedent they operated the business as equal one-third partners.

In 1946 the plaintiff's husband became ill and thereafter, until his death in 1949, rendered no services to the partnership business. During this time, however, he continued to receive his customary weekly salary and his share of other withdrawals, amounting in all to some $60,000. He also had free access to the books of the business and complete information as to its operation, and apparently approved the various financial reports.

After his death the widow instituted this action as executrix against the two surviving partners, seeking a dissolution of the partnership, an accounting, and the appointment of a receiver. A counterclaim was filed seeking to charge the account of the deceased partner with the cost of providing substitute help during his illness from 1946 to 1949. To avoid the appointment of a receiver, the defendants deposited $25,000 with the court to secure payment of whatever sum might be determined to be due to the plaintiff.

At the trial level, judgment was entered in the amount of $19,153 and interest for the plaintiff to the date of the defendants' deposit into court, and the counterclaim was dismissed. Blut v. Katz, 14 N.J.Super. 121, 81 A.2d 406 (Ch.Div.1951). The sum so arrived at represented the deceased partner's interest in the capital account at the time of his death. Good will was excluded as an asset of the partnership in calculating the deceased partner's interest.

On cross-appeals to the Appellate Division, it was there determined good will should have been included, and the cause was remanded to the Chancery Division to determine the value thereof, 24 N.J.Super. 165, 93 A.2d 775, 777. Both sides are dissatisfied with the results and each appeals.

The first issue to be decided is the denial by both lower tribunals of the plaintiff's demand for an option to recover the profits earned after the dissolution which might be attributable to the use of her husband's capital by the defendants in continuing the partnership business. The demand was made pursuant to R.S. 42:1–42, N.J.S.A. [UPA § 42], and the briefs are replete with discussion of the meaning of the statute.

The statute referred to deals with the liability of persons continuing partnership business without liquidation. It is obviously designed to protect the estate of a deceased partner from the demands of creditors in the event the executors see fit to liquidate. If the executor gives consent to the continuation of the partnership business without liquidation, then the estate's interest in the partnership is subjected to the claims of any new creditors.

It is contended the statutory plan requiring consent as therein outlined consistently provides that the *quid pro quo* is the right to a proportionate share of the profits of the new partnership if the personal representative so chooses, for the assumption of the additional risk of claims of the new creditors. Without the personal representative's consent, it is said, no additional risk is assumed and the Legislature by its enactment, therefore, gave no right to a share of the profits.

R.S. 42:1–42, N.J.S.A., entitled "Ascertaining value of interest of retired or deceased partner," giving the right to profits, refers to "conditions set forth in paragraph . . . 3 . . . of section 42:1–41 of this title . . .." Paragraph 3 of R.S. 42:1–41, N.J.S.A., provides:

"When any partner retires or dies and the business of the dissolved partnership is continued as set forth in paragraphs '1' and '2' of this section, with the consent of the retired partners or the representative of the deceased partner . . .."

R.S. 42:1–42, N.J.S.A., pointedly refers to paragraph 3 of R.S. 42:1–41, N.J.S.A., which, in turn, specifically provides for the consent of the retired partner or the representative of the deceased partner.

This is the manner in which the statute was construed by both lower tribunals, and in that construction we concur, even though research fails to disclose judicial adjudications in other jurisdictions buttressing this interpretation.

The only contrary thoughts we have encountered are expressed in an opinion construing the New York Partnership Act, identical with our own, M. & C. Creditors Corp. v. Pratt, 172 Misc. 695, 17 N.Y.S.2d

240 (Sup.Ct.1938), affirmed 255 App.Div. 838, 7 N.Y.S.2d 662 (1938), appeal denied 255 App.Div. 962, 8 N.Y.S.2d 990 (1938), affirmed, no opinion, 281 N.Y. 804, 24 N.E.2d 482 (Ct.App.1939), where the writer, referring to the sections already discussed, says they could not have been intended to limit the rights of the representatives to require payment of the decedent's interest as of the date of death. Also, in Cahill v. Haff, 248 N.Y. 377, 162 N.E. 288, 289 (Ct.App.1928), the court, although finding consent express or implied by the representative and holding he was therefore entitled to receive the profits attributable to the use of his rights in the property of the dissolved partnership, by way of dictum opined: "Probably the same thing is true if there be no consent."

However, we have concluded in the case *sub judice* that the statutory plan involves the giving of consent to the continuation of the partnership business before a deceased partner's representative can exercise the option to profits. Furthermore, consideration of merely the broad equitable doctrines applicable, without recourse to the statute, brings us to the same end result.

There is much authority sustaining the principle that, where one or more partners of a firm continue the business after the death of one of the partners, the legal representative of the deceased partner is entitled to his share of the profits made, Phillips v. Reeder and Prior, 18 N.J.Eq. 95 (Ch. 1866); Drapkin v. Klebanoff, 137 A. 432, 5 N.J.Misc. 531 (Ch.1927), but this principle is not universally applied; it has many limitations and qualifications and is always subject to equitable considerations.

So, where the main success of the firm is due to the skill, time and diligence of the remaining partners, the application of the rule has been withheld upon the ground that it would be inequitable to do otherwise. Profits having been denied, interest on the amount involved is substituted in its place. Phillips v. Reeder and Prior, supra; Laterra v. Laterra, 134 N.J.Eq. 162, 34 A.2d 289 (E. & A.1943).

Here the success of the business, from the record, appears to be due to the personal element and efforts, the plaintiff's husband having made no contribution to its continuance for a long period of time while he was ill. Under the circumstances and the proof, it would be inequitable to permit the plaintiff to participate in the profits made after the dissolution, to which she contributed nothing, as determined by the trial court.

Assuming consent to be a prerequisite to her right to elect to receive profits in lieu of interest, the plaintiff insists the findings of the trial court and the Appellate Division that she did not give consent to the continued operation of the partnership business were erroneous, as "all the evidence in the case is to the contrary."

This lavish assertion, however, finds little support in the record. There is an abundance of evidence sustaining the conclusions arrived at below. Being purely a fact issue, decided adversely to the plaintiff by both lower courts, we will not ordinarily make an independent finding unless a miscarriage of justice is imminent. Midler v. Heinowitz, 10 N.J. 123, 89 A.2d 458 (1952). We do not conceive that to be the situation here.

[In omitted portions of the opinion, the court held that the surviving partners were entitled to no credit for payments made to a substitute for the decedent during his illness, since no claim for such payment had been made before death; and that good will should be included in the valuation, in view of firm earnings of $28,000 to $73,000.]

For the reasons herein cited, the judgment of the Appellate Division is affirmed and the cause remanded to the Chancery Division for disposition not inconsistent with these views.

For affirmance: JUSTICES OLIPHANT, WACHENFELD, BURLING, JACOBS and BRENNAN—5.

For modification: CHIEF JUSTICE VANDERBILT and JUSTICE HEHER—2.

HEHER, J. (dissenting in part). I agree that the proofs do not sustain the contention that the plaintiff representative of the deceased partner consented to the continuance of the partnership business after his death. But this does not defeat her right, if she so elects to recover the profits earned after the dissolution of the partnership fairly attributable to the use of the deceased partner's capital in the continuance of the partnership business. If this be the representative's right where such consent is given, and R.S. 42:1–41 N.J.S.A. and R.S. 42:1–42, N.J. S.A., expressly so provide, then *a fortiori* this is so where the business is continued without consent; for it would seem that on the plainest principles of equity and justice the surviving partners should account for the profits ensuing from their unauthorized use of the deceased partner's capital. The principle of unjust enrichment has peculiar application in such circumstances. It is not the capital risk that determines the right, but rather the reaping of a profit from the use of the capital.

The statutory provisions cited supra have reference to the rights of creditors where consent is given to continue the partnership business.

I would modify the judgment in this regard also.

REFERENCES

Time of election:

Hurst v. Hurst, 86 Ariz. 242, 344 P.2d 1001 (1959) (former partner allowed to elect interest in lieu of profits during the course of trial).

Essay v. Essay, 175 Neb. 689, 123 N.W.2d 20 (1963) (allowed former partner to elect profits when there was demand for winding up, but would have limited her to interest if she had asked for the value at the time of dissolution).

Moseley v. Moseley, 196 F.2d 663 (9th Cir.1952) (partner's election between profits and interest may be made after the accounting is taken).

Election of profits where consent withheld:

Moseley v. Moseley, 196 F.2d 663 (9th Cir.1952) (excluded partner entitled to elect profits regardless of consent).

Nuland v. Pruyn, 99 Cal.App.2d 603, 222 P.2d 261 (1950) (excluded partner entitled to elect profits notwithstanding dissent to exclusion in view of terms of partnership agreement).

Ruppe v. Utter, 76 Cal.App. 19, 243 P. 715 (1925) (excluded partner entitled to elect profits).

Determination of profits attributable to use of capital:

Hilgendorf v. Denson, 341 So.2d 549 (Fla.App.1977) (when one partner withdrew from two-member real estate brokerage partnership, profits pending final settlement held wholly attributable to efforts of remaining partner, and none to use of capital).

Timmermann v. Timmermann, 272 Or. 613, 538 P.2d 1254 (1975) (on dissolution of farming partnership, value of services of remaining partners must be deducted before determining profits attributable to use of capital of retired partner).

Vangel v. Vangel, 51 Cal.2d 510, 334 P.2d 863 (1959) (services of partners rendered after dissolution must be deducted before determining profit attributable to capital. After remaining partners deposited retiring partner's share in court, no profits were attributable to use of retiring partner's right in the partnership property).

C. RIGHTS OF CREDITORS, OLD AND NEW

HORN'S CRANE SERVICE v. PRIOR

Nebraska Supreme Court, 1967.
182 Neb. 94, 152 N.W.2d 421.

WHITE, C.J. The district court sustained a general demurrer and a motion to dismiss an amended petition, dismissed the action, and plaintiff appeals. We affirm the judgment.

Plaintiff, a seller of equipment and supplies, in two causes of action in his amended petition seeks a personal judgment against the defendants, and each of them, for liability arising out of specific sums due under a written contract with (first cause of action) and for supplies and services furnished (second cause of action) a partnership or joint adventure comprised of the two defendants, Wendell H. Prior and Orie Cook, and one C.E. Piper, the manager who, being a resident of Colorado, was not joined in the action. The partnership or joint adventure was formed for the purpose of operating a quarry and rock-crushing business for profit and the written contract was entered into and the supplies and services furnished pursuant thereto. Defendants' ultimate liability for personal judgment flowed out of the partnership's or joint adventure's original liability as a separate entity in the transactions.

. . . In neither the original nor amended petition is it alleged, either directly or by inference that the partnership or joint adventure property was insufficient to satisfy its debts, or that there was no partnership property, and there is no allegation of dissolution or insolvency of said joint adventure or partnership. This was fatal.

In an action seeking a personal judgment against the individual members of a partnership or a joint adventure the petition does not state a cause of action if it fails to state that there is no partnership property or that it is insufficient to satisfy the debts of the partnership or joint adventure. . . .

There are several reasons for the rule. One of the most obvious is that credit having been extended to the partnership or firm, the members ought to have a right to insist that the partnership property be exhausted first. And to permit a firm creditor to by-pass the partnership property and exhaust the assets of an individual member leaving the partnership property extant, would be an obvious injustice, permit the other partners to profit at his expense, and place him in an adverse position with relation to his copartners.

No problem arises out of the plaintiff's allegation that this is a joint adventure. Both parties consider it as a partnership in their briefs. Plaintiff alleges that the defendants and Piper jointly entered into an enterprise for the purpose of acquiring and operating a business; that they contributed money and property thereto; that they all exercised control but that Piper was the manager; and that the plaintiff entered into said contracts on the representation of the defendants that they were an existing partnership. The substance of plaintiff's theory, which he affirms in his brief, is that defendants were members of a partnership and individually and jointly liable on that basis. We further note that section 67–306, R.R.S.1943, defines a partnership as "an association of persons organized as a separate entity to carry on a business for profit." Under the facts alleged and the theory presented by the plaintiff, the law of partnership applies. With reference to joint adventures, this court, in Soulek v. City of Omaha, 140 Neb. 151, 299 N.W. 368, said as follows: "The principal distinction between a partnership and a joint adventure is that the latter may relate to a single transaction. . . . The law of partnership applies to the questions arising between the parties and among the parties in relation to third parties." The district court was correct in sustaining the demurrer and dismissing the action on the ground that the petition did not state a cause of action.

. . .

Affirmed.

SMITH, J., dissenting.

The asserted obligations of the partnership are the kind for which members of a firm are liable jointly under the Uniform Partnership Act, § 67–315(b), R.R.S.1943. . . .

Plaintiff is denied an adjudication on the merits because the firm is presumably solvent. That formula strangely enough derives color of support from equitable rules written into statutes a century ago. Writ of execution on a judgment against the firm itself is issued against partnership property. If the judgment is not satisfied, the creditor may file a bill in equity against the partners. The prescribed allegations of the bill are the judgment and the insufficiency of partnership property. §§ 25–313, 25–314, and 25–316, R.R.S.1943. An alternative remedy for the creditor's benefit—not an obstacle to a direct action against partners—was probably intended. . . .

Does the businessman intend primarily to extend credit to the firm? Two writers gave negative answers in 1915. See, Williston, "The Uniform Partnership Act . . .," 63 U.Pa.L.Rev., 196, 209; Lewis, "The Uniform Partnership Act . . .," 29 Harv.L.Rev., 158, 166; Lewis, "The Uniform Partnership Act," 24 Yale L.J., 617, 639. An affirmative answer is not obvious even in 1967.

The need of a partner for protection against inroads on firm assets should be evaluated with other considerations. By hypothesis the firm is solvent in some sense. A general partner runs the risk that he will be compelled ultimately to pay all partnership debts. The partnership creditor in pursuit of a remedy will at times view this need with a healthy skepticism, which I share.

McCown, J., joins in this dissent.

REFERENCES

Stone v. Stone, 293 So.2d 523 (La.App.1974) (suit against partners on partnership obligation was not maintainable without joining partnership as defendant under Louisiana statute providing "The partners of an existing partnership may not be sued on a partnership obligation unless the partnership is joined as a defendant.").

Richard Matthews, Jr., Inc. v. Vaughan, 91 Nev. 583, 540 P.2d 1062 (1975) (suit against general partner in limited partnership did not justify judgment and execution against limited partnership assets, unless limited partnership was named as a defendant).

NOTE: ORDER OF SUIT AND EXECUTION

Horn's Crane Service suggests two separable problems—(1) in what order partners and the partnership should be sued on partnership obligations, and (2) in what order execution should be levied pursuant to judgment on partnership obligations.

The first question could not arise at common law, since there was no way of suing the "partnership"; one must sue the partners.[1] As recently as 1919, a New York court struck off as surplusage the name of the partnership which had been joined with the partners as defendants in a suit on a firm obligation.[2]

However, the common law recognized a distinction between firm property and individual property. If property of both kinds was before the same court, the court would apply firm property first to firm debts and individual property first to individual debts.[3] With respect to separate executions, a few common law courts held—as the UPA has since decreed—that individual creditors could not proceed at all against firm property; they could only attach the proceeds of

---

1. Crane and Bromberg, Partnership (1968) § 58; see X–L Liquors v. Taylor (1955) 17 N.J. 444, 111 A.2d 753.

2. Calumet & Hecla Mining Co. v. Equitable Trust Co., 186 App.Div. 328, 174 N.Y.S. 317 (1919). The law was changed in the following year to permit suits against

partnership and other unincorporated associations (N.Y.Gen.Assns. L., § 12); this was reenforced in 1945 by N.Y.Civ. CPLR § 1025.

3. Crane and Bromberg, Partnership § 91A (1968); acc., UPA § 40(h).

distribution.[4] Firm creditors could levy on individual property,[5] but some courts held that they must exhaust firm property first.[6]

Because of these distinctions, it was important to indicate whether the creditor sought a judgment against the partners as individuals or as members of a firm. Before suit in the firm name was authorized, attorneys for firm creditors commonly prayed judgment against the named defendants as individuals and as partners; e.g., "Elizabeth Taylor and Robert Taylor, individually and as copartners doing business as Taylor Wine Co."[7] Innumerable cases of suit in this form appear in the reports, without a hint that the individual judgment must await unsatisfied execution on the firm judgment.

However, plaintiff's counsel in *Horn's Crane* seem to have omitted any prayer for judgment against the defendants *as partners,* or against the firm. If a purely individual judgment were entered against the defendants, the plaintiffs would not be able to issue execution on firm property;[8] consequently if Nebraska followed the rule of "firm property first,"[9] the creditors would not be able to execute on individual property, either. Therefore, the decision to deny judgment against the defendants as individuals was probably justified.[10]

However, the court seems to say that even if the plaintiff had sued the defendants as partners, he could not simultaneously have sued them as individuals. This goes beyond any known authority,[11] and calls for a regrettable circuity of procedure. Possibly the court will disown the breadth of its declaration when presented with a properly drawn complaint against the partnership and the partners as individuals.

REFERENCES

Cases involving joint venture as a basis of liability:

Bond v. O'Donnell, 205 Iowa 902, 218 N.W. 898, 63 A.L.R. 901 (1928) (three friends contributed to buy land on speculation with one taking title and signing mortgage note for part of price; all jointly liable to creditor).

Chisholm v. Gilmer, 81 F.2d 120 (4th Cir.1936), certiorari granted 298 U.S. 648, 56 S.Ct. 682, 80 L.Ed. 1377 (1936), affirmed 299 U.S. 99, 57 S.Ct. 65, 81 L.Ed. 63 (1936), rehearing denied 299 U.S. 623, 57 S.Ct. 229, 81 L.Ed. 458 (1936) (bank directors bought

4. Id. § 43; UPA § 25(2)(c).

5. Richardson, Creditors' Rights and the Partnership (1951) 40 Ky.L.J. 243, 254–60.

6. Seligman v. Friedlander, 199 N.Y. 373, 92 N.E. 1047 (1910); May v. McGowan, 194 F.2d 396 (2d Cir.1952).

7. Cf. X–L Liquors v. Taylor, 17 N.J. 444, 111 A.2d 753 (1955). This form of caption was proper, but the sheriff erred in returning service on "the partnership," which was not a servable party.

See also Schloss v. Silverman, 172 Md. 632, 192 A. 343 (1937), where with superabundance of caution plaintiff's counsel sued "Toney Schloss and Dan Schloss, copartners trading as the Baltimore Lumber Company, as members of the partnership and as individuals, and the partnership."

8. UPA § 25(2)(c).

9. As in cases cited supra, note 6.

10. As authority for its decision, the court cited early Nebraska cases in which suit against individual partners was brought on the basis of another state's judgment against the partnership, sued in its firm name. Judgment was given for defendants, on the ground that there should first be an execution issued and returned against the firm. Ruth v. Lowrey, 10 Neb. 260, 4 N.W. 977 (1880); Leach v. Milburn Wagon Co., 14 Neb. 106, 15 N.W. 232 (1883). To the present authors, the decisions seem correct on the broader ground that if the out-of-state judgment was not against the defendants as individuals, it could not form the basis of a suit for an in-state individual judgment.

11. But see note 10 supra.

stock together to increase capital of bank in which they were interested, anticipating no direct profit from resale of stock; held jointly liable for assessments against stock).

Rae v. Cameron, 112 Mont. 159, 114 P.2d 1060 (1941) (defendants liable as joint venturers despite lack of express agreement to share losses).

Geisenhoff v. Mabrey, 58 Cal.App.2d 481, 137 P.2d 36 (1943) (individuals who invested in ice rink were joint venturers, even though they filed incorporation papers, where they never transferred assets or liabilities to corporation).

Wood v. Western Beef Factory, Inc., 378 F.2d 96 (10th Cir.1967) (where W financed feeding of cattle which G selected and purchased, and both expected to split profits, they were joint venturers).

Dubuque Stone Products Co. v. Fred L. Gray Co., 356 F.2d 718 (8th Cir.1966) (where parties signed agreement committing themselves to "joint venture" but limiting one party's contribution, latter party was fully liable to third party for joint venture debts).

Are joint ventures partnerships?

Frank L. Mechem, Law of Joint Adventures (1931) 15 Minn.L.Rev. 644 (yes).

Nichols, Joint Ventures (1950) 36 Va.L.Rev. 425 (yes).

Note, Joint Venture—Problem Child of Partnership (1950) 38 Calif.L.Rev. 860 (yes).

Note, Joint Venture or Partnership (1949) 18 Ford.L.Rev. 114 (no).

Note, A Partnership and a Joint Venture Distinguished (1920) 33 Harv.L.Rev. 852 (no).

Note, Joint Ventures—Extent to Which Partnership Law Applies (1936) 35 Mich.L. Rev. 297 (yes).

Note, The Business Joint Venture in Louisiana (1951) 25 Tulane L.Rev. 382 (yes, in Louisiana).

Note, Apparent Authority and the Joint Venture—Reducing the Scope of Agency Between Business Associates, 13 U.C.Davis L.Rev. 824 (1980).

TUPPER v. KROC

Supreme Court of Nevada, 1972.
88 Nev. 146, 494 P.2d 1275.

BATJER, JUSTICE:

.   .   .

Lloyd G. Tupper, appellant, and Ray A. Kroc, respondent, entered into three limited partnerships for the purpose of holding title to and leasing parcels of real estate. Tupper was the general partner, Kroc was the limited partner and each held a fifty percent interest.

Kroc filed an action alleging that Tupper had mismanaged and misappropriated funds from these partnerships and requested that they be dissolved and that a receiver be appointed. Pending the final outcome of that action the trial court appointed a receiver to manage the three business organizations. Prior to the date on which the complaint for dissolution had been filed, Tupper had on several occasions been unable to pay his share of the partnerships' obligations. Kroc on those occasions personally contributed the total amounts owed by the partnerships, and in return accepted interest bearing notes from Tupper in amounts equal to one-half of the partnerships' debts paid by him. Kroc thereafter filed an action against Tupper to recover on those notes and was awarded a summary judgment in the amount of $54,609.02.

In an effort to collect on that judgment, Kroc filed a motion pursuant to NRS 87.280 [UPA § 28] requesting the district court to charge Tupper's interest in the partnerships with payment of the judgment and for the sale of Tupper's interest to satisfy the judgment. On June 12, 1969, a charging order was entered directing the sheriff to sell all of Tupper's "right, title and interest" in the three partnerships and to apply the proceeds against the unsatisfied amount of the judgment. Tupper was served with notice of the sale, but he took no action to redeem his interest. The sale was held on June 27, 1969, and Kroc purchased Tupper's interest for $2,500.

Kroc filed a motion to terminate the receivership on March 12, 1970, contending that he was the sole owner of the partnerships and that the need for a receiver had ceased. On May 18, 1970, the appellants filed an objection to the respondents' motion to terminate the receivership, and a motion to set aside the sale conducted pursuant to the charging order. The trial court denied the appellants' motion to set aside the sale, and granted the respondents' motion to terminate the receivership and discharge the receiver. It is from these two orders that this appeal is taken.

The appellants contend that the trial court erred when it confirmed the sale of Tupper's interest in the three partnerships because (1) Kroc failed to affirmatively show that a sale of Tupper's interest in the partnerships was necessary; (2) a partner's interest in a partnership is not subject to a sale in satisfaction of a judgment; (3) it was improper to nominate the sheriff to conduct the sale which was irregularly and improperly held; (4) the sheriff's sale was inequitable in that the price paid for Tupper's partnership interest was grossly inadequate; (5) it was impermissible to conduct the sale of Tupper's interest in the partnerships while they were in receivership; and (6) the sale was in violation of the partnerships' agreements. Furthermore, the appellants contend that it was improper to discharge the receiver because Tupper retained such an equity in the partnership business and assets as to compel continuation of the receivership.

. . .

The charging order was properly entered by the district court against Tupper's interest in the three partnerships. . . . Pursuant to the provisions of [UPA § 28] the district court was authorized to appoint a receiver to act as a repository for Tupper's share of the profits and surplus for the benefit of Kroc, or as the court did here, order the sale of Tupper's interest. . . . In Kroc's application for the order charging Tupper's interest in the partnerships he requested an order directing a sale of that interest. Likewise in the notice to Tupper and his attorneys they were advised that Kroc was seeking a sale of Tupper's interest. The application and notice afforded Tupper an opportunity to take whatever steps he deemed necessary to either limit the charging order or prevent the sale.[2] Tupper was allowed 30 days to file an appeal from the order charging his interest in the partnerships and ordering the sale. NRCP 73. He did not appeal from that order, but instead waited nearly a year after the sale was made before filing a motion to set it aside. The appellants are now estopped to question the propriety of the charging order.

Although the appellants concede that the charging order is not under attack they continue a collateral attack by insisting that the sale of Tupper's interest in the partnerships authorized by the charging order was void. One of those contentions of irregularity is based upon the fact that an accounting "to determine the nature and extent of the interest to be sold" was not required by the district court before it entered its order authorizing the sale. In support of this contention the appellants rely upon *Balaban v. Bank of Nevada,* [86 Nev. 862, 477 P.2d 860 (1970)]. Although we declared the sale in that case to be void and ordered an accounting, it is inapposite to support a claim that the sale in this case is void. In Balaban the notice of sale advised that "said sale will include all physical assets." This was impermissible and for that reason we set the sale aside. Furthermore, *Balaban* concerned a dissolution of a partnership by death, its winding up and the interplay of the Uniform Partnership Act (NRS Ch. 87) and the probate code (NRS Chs. 143 and 148). Within those chapters are found special provisions and requirements for an accounting (NRS 143.040; NRS 87.430; NRS 148.210) which are not found in the statute authorizing the charging order (NRS 87.280). An accounting prior to the sale of Tupper's interest was not compelled in this case.

The appellants also contend that Tupper's interest in the partnership was inadequately described. Anyone reading or relying on the notice of sale was, as a matter of law, deemed to understand that by statute the sale of Tupper's interest in the partnerships consisted of a sale of his share of the profits and surplus and no more. NRS 87.240; NRS 87.260; NRS 87.280. Any further or more extensive description would have been confusing or redundant. An accounting might have revealed the amount of current profits, if any, or the estimated value of the surplus, if any, but it would not have added anything to the description of Tupper's interest beyond that found in NRS 87.260.

Pursuant to NRS 87.280(1) the district court was authorized to make any order which the circumstances of the case required. That statute authorized the appointment of the sheriff of Clark County to sell Tupper's interest in the partnerships, and authorized Tupper's

---

2. If only a charging order had been entered or had the court in the charging order appointed a receiver under NRS 87.280, to receive Tupper's share of the partnerships' profits or upon dissolution his share of the surplus instead of ordering a sale, then upon receipt by Kroc of an amount sufficient to satisfy the judgment against Tupper entered on April 30, 1969, Tupper would have been restored to his right to receive his share of the profits or upon dissolution his share of the surplus; however, when his interest in the partnerships was sold he was forever foreclosed from receiving any profits or surplus from the three partnerships.

interest to be sold in accordance with the provisions of NRS 21.130(2) at a time certain on June 27, 1969. . . .

The appellants' contention that the price paid by Kroc for Tupper's interest in the three partnerships is inadequate, is without merit. The mode for determining the value of Tupper's interest in the partnerships was by a public sale. See *McMillan v. United Mortgage Co.*, 82 Nev. 117, 412 P.2d 604 (1966). The fair market value of $2,500 was established by Kroc's bid at the sheriff's sale. The respondents were under no duty or obligation to support or justify that price and the entire burden was upon the appellants to prove its inadequacy. . . .

The appellants . . . claim that it was impermissible to conduct the sale of Tupper's interest in the partnerships' assets and business but not the interest of a partner in the partnerships. Tupper's interest in the partnerships, i.e. his right and title in the profits and surplus, were his personal property and not partnership property in the custody of the receiver. NRS 87.260. [UPA § 26]

The appellants contend that the sale amounted to an involuntary assignment of Tupper's interest in the partnerships and is in violation of the partnership agreements which preclude a partner from assigning his interest. We do not agree. A sale made pursuant to a charging order (NRS 87.180) of a partner's interest in a partnership is not an assignment of an interest in a partnership. See NRS 87.270. Furthermore, the partnership agreements could not divest the district court of its powers provided by statute to charge and sell an interest of a partner in a partnership.

Finally the appellants contend that because Tupper retained an equity in the partnerships' business and assets, the district court erred when it discharged the receiver. Unfortunately for the appellants this is not true. After Kroc bought all of Tupper's interest in the partnerships, i.e. all of his right and title to the profits and surplus, Kroc was entitled to all of the profits and all of the surplus. . . . After the sale Tupper had no immediate or future rights to any profits or surplus or any equity whatever in the partnership property, and therefore he had no valid reason to insist on a continuation of the receivership.

Although as a matter of law the respondents were entitled to have the receivership terminated and the receiver discharged, the wisdom of that request, short of the dissolution of the partnerships, is questionable, for as soon as the receiver was discharged Tupper had the authority under NRS Ch. 87, as well as the partnerships' agreements, to assert his right to participate in the management. By purchasing Tupper's interest in the partnerships Kroc did not divest Tupper of his other property rights. (NRS 87.240).

The receiver was appointed at the request of Kroc, now Tupper wants the receiver to be reappointed to protect Tupper as a general partner from liability that might be incurred through excessive partnership debts. At a glance it might seem that Tupper's fears have some merit. However, as a matter of law, at the moment the receiver was discharged Tupper's right to participate in the management of the partnerships (NRS 87.240) was restored, and as the general partner he would, at least theoretically, be able to prevent the partnerships from incurring liabilities in excess of assets.

The orders of the district court from which these appeals have been taken are affirmed.

REFERENCES ON CHARGING ORDERS

Gose, The Charging Order Under the Uniform Partnership Act (1953), 28 Wash.L. Rev. 1.

Axelrod, The Charging Order—Rights of a Partner's Creditors (1983), 36 Ark.L.Rev. 81.

IN RE JERCYN DRESS SHOP

United States Court of Appeals, Second Circuit, 1975.
516 F.2d 864.

ROBERT P. ANDERSON, CIRCUIT JUDGE:

Leslie Fay Sales, a division of Leslie Fay, Inc., Falchick Dress Co., Inc., and Campus Juniors, Inc., three creditors of Jercyn Dress Shop (Jercyn), a partnership, appeal from the district court's decision and order affirming the bankruptcy court's dismissal of appellants' involuntary petition in bankruptcy to the extent that it was addressed against Jercyn's partners, Jack A. Scherer and Eva Scherer, husband and wife, as opposed to the partnership entity itself, on the ground that these partners had not committed an act of bankruptcy within the contemplation of § 3(a) of the Bankruptcy Act (the Act), 11 U.S.C. § 21(a).[1]

The facts are not in dispute and may be briefly summarized. On October 19, 1972 the Scherers signed and executed an indenture whereby "Jercyn Dress Shop, a co-partnership comprised of Jack A. Scherer and Eva Scherer," made a general assignment of its assets to Bernard Sands for the benefit of its creditors. The assignment was recorded on October 20, 1972 in the office of the Clerk of Kings County, New York.

On November 15, 1972, the appellants filed an involuntary petition in bankruptcy in the United States District Court for the Eastern District of New York against "Jercyn Dress Shop, A Partnership, and

1. 11 U.S.C. § 21(a) provides:

"(a) Acts of bankruptcy by a person shall consist of his having (1) concealed, removed, or permitted to be concealed or removed any part of his property, with intent to hinder, delay, or defraud his creditors or any of them, or made or suffered a transfer of any of his property, fraudulent under the provisions of section 107 or 110 of this title; or (2) made or suffered a preferential transfer, as defined in subdivision a of section 96 of this title; or (3) suffered or permitted, while insolvent, any creditor to obtain a lien upon any of his property through legal proceedings or distraint and not having vacated or discharged such lien within thirty days from the date thereof or at least five days before the date set for any sale or other disposition of such property; or (4) made a general assignment for the benefit of his creditors; or (5) while insolvent or unable to pay his debts as they mature, procured, permitted, or suffered voluntarily or involuntarily the appointment of a receiver or trustee to take charge of his property; or (6) admitted in writing his inability to pay his debts and his willingness to be adjudged a bankrupt."

Jack A. Scherer, and Eva Scherer, as General Partners, Jointly." The petition alleged only the following act of bankruptcy:

"4. Within four months next preceding the filing of this petition, the alleged bankrupts committed an act of bankruptcy in that the alleged bankrupts did heretofore to wit, on or about October 20, 1972, make an assignment for the benefit of creditors to Bernard Sands, which assignment was recorded in the office of the Clerk of the County of Kings, State of New York, on October 20, 1972."

On December 6, 1972, Jercyn consented in writing to its adjudication in bankruptcy but the Scherers filed a joint answer denying the material allegations of the involuntary petition and moving for dismissal of the petition against them as individual partners. They asserted, as an affirmative defense, that paragraph 4 of appellants' petition alleged an act of bankruptcy solely by the partnership, and that they personally had committed no act of bankruptcy as defined in § 3(a) of the Act which would subject them to adjudication.

In an opinion dated April 3, 1973, the Referee in Bankruptcy held that the assignment for the benefit of creditors relied on by appellants as an act of bankruptcy was executed by the partnership as an entity and not by the Scherers as individuals, and that as a matter of law "this partnership act could not be imputed *ipso facto* to them and thus be used as an act of bankruptcy against them." He, therefore, dismissed the petition against the Scherers individually by order dated April 5, 1973, which was affirmed after review by the district court in a decision and order dated August 14, 1974. This appeal followed.

Appellants do not allege that the Scherers are individually insolvent, have executed general assignments of their individual properties, or have committed any acts of bankruptcy apart from their role as partners in the making of the general assignment by the partnership. The sole issue on appeal, therefore, is whether a general assignment by a partnership of its assets for the benefit of its creditors is *ipso facto* an act of bankruptcy by the individual partners as well. This court holds that it is not.

As reflected *inter alia* by §§ 1(23), 5a and 5j of the Bankruptcy Act, 11 U.S.C. §§ 1(23), 23(a), 23(j),[2] Congress has adopted the "entity theory" of partnership bankruptcies by which "a partnership may be adjudged a bankrupt as a separate entity without reference to the

---

2. 11 U.S.C. § 1(23) provides, in relevant part, that " 'Persons' shall include . . . partnerships . . .."

11 U.S.C. § 23(a) provides:

"(a) A partnership, including a limited partnership containing one or more general partners during the continuation of the partnership business or after its dissolution and before the final settlement thereof, may be adjudged a bankrupt either separately or jointly with one or more or all of its general partners."

11 U.S.C. § 23(j) provides:

"(j) The discharge of a partnership shall not discharge the individual general partners thereof from the partnership debts. A general partner adjudged a bankrupt either in a joint or separate proceeding may, pursuant to the provisions of this title, obtain a discharge from both his partnership and individual debts."

bankruptcy of the partners as individuals." Liberty National Bank v. Bear, 276 U.S. 215, 220–221, 48 S.Ct. 252, 72 L.Ed. 536 (1928). See also 1A Collier, Bankruptcy ¶ 5.03, at 694–698 (14th ed. 1975). Under § 5b of the Act (11 U.S.C. §123(b)),[3] a partnership may be adjudged a bankrupt either upon its filing of a voluntary petition or upon the filing of an involuntary petition against it. In keeping with the entity theory, therefore, the partnership must be able to commit at least some acts of bankruptcy (see 11 U.S.C. § 21(a)) separate and distinct from personal acts of bankruptcy committed by its partners.

. . .

Appellants object that under this interpretation preferential transfers by the individual partners, should they later become bankrupt, and by the partnership will bear different dates to the possible detriment of partnership creditors. It is apparent, however, that any differences in such filing dates can also work to the advantage of partnership creditors.

. . .

Furthermore, partnership creditors are adequately protected by other provisions of the Act. Any conversion of partnership property into property of an individual partner, for example, must have been *bona fide* and without intent to hinder, delay, or defraud creditors. Where an insolvent partnership has made a fraudulent transfer in order to conceal assets from its creditors, those assets belong to the insolvent partnership and its creditors. See 1A Collier, Bankruptcy ¶ 5.28, at 738 (14th ed. 1975). Also the partnership trustee cannot prevent the partnership creditors from obtaining in an appropriate forum *in personam* judgments against the individual partners on unpaid partnership debts.

. . .

Most importantly, Rule 108(c) requires each unadjudicated general partner to file a statement of his personal assets and liabilities within 10 days of the qualification of the trustee in the partnership bankruptcy proceedings (see 1A Collier, Bankruptcy ¶ 5.25, at 734 (14th ed. 1975)), and the bankruptcy court in appropriate circumstances may administer the personal estates (Francis v. McNeal, 228 U.S. 695, 33 S.Ct. 701, 57 L.Ed. 1029 (1913); 1A Collier, Bankruptcy ¶ 5.25, at 734 (14th ed. 1975)) in order to insure that property in excess of each individual's debts is available for payment of the partnership debts (see In re Ira Haupt & Co., 240 F.Supp. 369 (S.D.N.Y.1965); 1A Collier, Bankruptcy ¶ 5.25, at 734.1–734.2 (14th ed. 1975)) even though the nonadjudged general partners have not personally committed an act of

---

3. 11 U.S.C. § 23(b) provides:

"(b) A petition may be filed by one or more or all of the general partners in the separate behalf of a partnership or jointly in behalf of a partnership and of the general partner or partners filing the same: *Provided, however,* That where a petition is filed in behalf of a partnership by less than all of the general partners, the petition shall allege that the partnership is insolvent. A petition may be filed separately against a partnership or jointly against a partnership and one or more or all of its general partners."

bankruptcy and cannot obtain a discharge. . . . Thus even though the individual partners are not automatically placed in bankruptcy along with the partnership entity, the partnership creditors still have ample protection.

The judgment of the district court is affirmed.

REFERENCES

Hanley, Partnership Bankruptcy Under the New Act (1978) 31 Hastings L.J. 149.

Levy, Partnerships in Bankruptcy (1971) 76 Com.L.J. 289.

Kennedy, New Deal for Bankruptcy (1960) 60 Colum.L.Rev. 610.

BANKRUPTCY REFORM ACT OF 1978
11 U.S. Code §§ 101–151302.

§ 101. Definitions

. . .

(29) "insolvent" means—

. . .

(B) with reference to a partnership, financial condition such that the sum of such partnership's debts is greater than the aggregate of, at a fair valuation—

(i) all of such partnership's property, exclusive of property of the kind specified in subparagraph (A)(i) of this paragraph; and

(ii) the sum of the excess of the value of each general partner's nonpartnership property, exclusive of property of the kind specified in subparagraph (A)(ii) of this paragraph, over such partner's nonpartnership debts;

. . .

(33) "person" includes individual, partnership, and corporation, but does not include governmental unit;

. . .

§ 548. Fraudulent Transfers and Obligations

. . .

(b) The trustee of a partnership debtor may avoid any transfer of an interest of the debtor in property, or any obligation incurred by the debtor, that was made or incurred on or within one year before the date of the filing of the petition, to a general partner in the debtor, if the debtor was insolvent on the date such transfer was made or such obligation was incurred, or became insolvent as a result of such transfer or obligation.

. . .

§ 723. Rights of Partnership Trustee Against General Partners

(a) If there is a deficiency of property of the estate to pay in full all claims which are allowed in a case under this chapter concerning a partnership and with respect to which a general partner of the partnership is personally liable, the trustee shall have a claim against such general partner for the full amount of the deficiency.

(b) To the extent practicable, the trustee shall first seek recovery of such deficiency from any general partner in such partnership that is not a debtor in a case under this title. Pending determination of such deficiency, the court may order any such partner to provide the estate with indemnity for, or assurance of payment of, any deficiency recoverable from such partner, or not to dispose of property.

(c) Notwithstanding section 728(c) of this title, the trustee has a claim against the estate of each general partner in such partnership that is a debtor in a case under this title for the full amount of all claims of creditors allowed in the case concerning such partnership. Notwithstanding section 502 of this title, there shall not be allowed in such partner's case a claim against such partner on which both such partner and such partnership are liable, except to any extent that such claim is secured only by property of such partner and not by property of such partnership. The claim of the trustee under this subsection is entitled to distribution in such partner's case under section 726(a) of this title the same as any other claim of a kind specified in such section.

(d) If the aggregate that the trustee recovers from the estates of general partners under subsection (c) of this section is greater than any deficiency not recovered under subsection (b) of this section, the court, after notice and a hearing, shall determine an equitable distribution of the surplus so recovered, and the trustee shall distribute such surplus to the estates of the general partners in such partnership according to such determination.

SENATE REPORT No. 95–989

July 14, 1978 [on Bankruptcy Reform Act of 1978].
U.S. Code Cong. & Adm. News (1978) No. 11C, Leg.Hist. pp. 97–98.

Section 723. Rights of Partnership Trustee Against General Partners

This section is a significant departure from present law. It repeals the jingle rule, which, for ease of administration, denied partnership creditors their rights against general partners by permitting general partners' individual creditors to share in their estates first to the exclusion of partnership creditors. The result under this section more closely tracks generally applicable partnership law, without a significant administrative burden.

Subsection (a) specifies that each general partner in a partnership debtor is liable to the partnership's trustee for any deficiency of partnership property to pay in full all administrative expenses and all claims against the partnership.

Subsection (b) requires the trustee to seek recovery of the deficiency from any general partner that is not a debtor in a bankruptcy case. The court is empowered to order that partner to indemnify the estate or not to dispose of property pending a determination of the deficiency.

The language of the subsection is directed to cases under the bankruptcy code. However, if, during the early stages of the transition period, a partner in a partnership is proceeding under the Bankruptcy Act while the partnership is proceeding under the bankruptcy code, the trustee should not first seek recovery against the Bankruptcy Act partner. Rather, the Bankruptcy Act partner should be deemed for the purposes of this section and the rights of the trustee to be proceeding under title 11.

Subsection (c) requires the partnership trustee to seek recovery of the full amount of the deficiency from the estate of each general partner that is a debtor in a bankruptcy case. The trustee will share equally with the partners' individual creditors in the assets of the partners' estates. Claims of partnership creditors who may have filed against the partner will be disallowed to avoid double counting.

Subsection (d) provides for the case where the total recovery from all of the bankrupt general partners is greater than the deficiency of which the trustee sought recovery. This case would most likely occur for a partnership with a large number of general partners. If the situation arises, the court is required to determine an equitable redistribution of the surplus to the estate of the general partners. The determination will be based on factors such as the relative liability of each of the general partners under the partnership agreement and the relative rights of each of the general partners in the profits of the enterprise under the partnership agreement.

NOTE ON PRIORITIES

Please read carefully section 41 of the UPA.

To a modern student, this section may seem to expend a lot of words in stating the obvious. But its purpose becomes clear when one remembers that jurists in the formative era of partnership law generally regarded a partnership not as an entity, but as a group of individuals who chose to acquire certain joint rights and obligations. Whenever a member dropped out or a new one was added, a different joint group was involved.

To illustrate, a partnership of P, Q and R might incur a joint debt to creditor C. Then P might drop out and be replaced by S; the new partnership of Q, R and S borrows money from D. What are the respective rights of creditors C and D?

Under the rules of sections 25 and 40, partnership creditors have priority over individual creditors in enforcing claims against partnership property. If these rules were applied without modification, C would have a prior claim to that part of the present partnership property which was received from the P-Q-R firm, while D would have a prior claim to property of Q-R-S which never belonged to P-Q-R. One can easily imagine the difficulty of sorting out the items of firm property, and the fanciful arguments which would be used to prove that the money now in the bank account is really the money received from P-Q-R, or is new money generated by Q-R-S. These are the problems which the Uniform Commissioners, in their note to section 41, called "inexecrable confusion" (betraying some etymological confusion between *inextricable* and *execrable!*).

The Commissioners solved the most glaring part of this problem by providing that the creditors of the preceding partnership become creditors of the succeeding partnership. They seem to have been a little nervous about the solution, since they avoided enunciating it as a general principle, and instead stipulated four circumscribed situations to which it would apply. They left some uncertainty about situations in which the business is continued without express consent, but with some sort of acquiescence or mere failure to interfere. As one might guess, situations of the latter sort are quite frequent, and supply grist for the mills of justice.

BLUMER BREWING CORP. v. MAYER

Wisconsin Supreme Court, 1936.
223 Wis. 540, 269 N.W. 693, 111 A.L.R. 1087.

This action was begun on May 21, 1935, by the plaintiff, Blumer Brewing Corporation, against M.F. Mayer, administrator of the estate of Charles R. Einbeck and C.A. Roderick, administrator de bonis non of the estate of Hugo Einbeck, to wind up the affairs of a partnership known as Einbeck Bros., Monroe, Wis., and to procure an accounting between the various parties interested in the estates and for the appointment of a receiver. There was a trial, the court found against the plaintiff, and from the judgment entered on March 12, 1936, dismissing the action, the plaintiff appeals.

From some time prior to 1921, Hugo Einbeck and Charles R. Einbeck were doing business as partners under the firm name of Einbeck Bros., sometimes described, however, as the Monroe Bottling Works. On November 28, 1928, Hugo Einbeck died. The surviving partner, Charles R. Einbeck, was duly appointed administrator of the Hugo Einbeck Estate. . . . Charles R. Einbeck made income tax returns for himself personally, for Einbeck Bros. and as administrator of the Estate of Hugo Einbeck, all of which disclose that the partnership business was being continued as before the death of Hugo and that the Estate of Hugo Einbeck was being credited with profits and charged with losses of the business. . . .

The trial court directed judgment dismissing the action on the ground that Charles R. Einbeck was without authority to continue the business and that the assets of the estate of Hugo Einbeck were not chargeable with the liabilities of Einbeck Bros., incurred after the death of Hugo Einbeck.

ROSENBERRY, CHIEF JUSTICE. The principal question for decision is, Did Charles R. Einbeck as surviving partner under the circumstances of this case have authority to continue the partnership business after the dissolution of the partnership brought about by the death of Hugo Einbeck? The defendants contend that a partnership business may be continued after the death of a partner under the following circumstances and no other: (1) If it is provided by the partnership agreement and such agreement is binding on the estate of the deceased partner; (2) if it is so directed in the will of the deceased partner; (3) pursuant to order of the court first obtained; (4) by agreement by the surviving partner and legal representatives of the deceased partner, provided the legal representative has been given by the will of decedent the necessary power or the agreement is approved by the court.

The plaintiff does not seriously contest these propositions as matters of general law but contends that the propositions of general law have been modified by the provisions of the Uniform Partnership Act, chapter 123, Wisconsin Stats. It is to be noted in this case that the administrator did not assume, or attempt to assume, the duties of an active partner. All that was done in this case was to permit the interest of Hugo Einbeck, the deceased partner, to remain in the partnership business and to be thereafter administered by Charles R. Einbeck as surviving partner. The estate in no sense became a partner in the business and its liability under any theory of the law was limited to the interest of Hugo Einbeck in the partnership assets.

A determination of the issue raised in this case depends upon the interpretation given to section 123.36(1), (2) and (3) [section 41(1), (2), and (3) of the Uniform Partnership Act] relating to rights and liabilities on continuing the business of a partnership after dissolution without liquidation.

The obvious purpose of this section is to continue the partnership business without the disruption and confusion which resulted at common law when a partner retired or died. . . . Under subsection (3) when a partner dies and his personal representatives consent to a continuation of the business, the law takes hold of the situation and the consent of the personal representative has the same effect as if an effective assignment had been made and subjects the interest of the deceased partner in the partnership property to the claims of existing and future creditors.

Did Charles R. Einbeck, as administrator of the estate of Hugo Einbeck, have power to give such consent? The interest of Hugo Einbeck in the partnership property was personal property. Section 123.05, Wis.Stats. Mattson v. Wagstad (1926) 188 Wis. 566, 206 N.W. 865. Charles R. Einbeck, as administrator of the estate of Hugo Einbeck, had power to sell and dispose of the personal estate without order of court, and to pass good title thereto. Munteith v. Rahn (1861) 14 Wis. 210; Williams v. Cobb (1916) 242 U.S. 307, 37 S.Ct. 115, 61 L.Ed. 325.

We are not called upon to consider here and do not consider to what extent if at all an administrator may make himself personally liable in dealing with the assets where he proceeds without an order of the court. It would seem to require no argument to show that an administrator who had power to sell and dispose of an estate—in this case, the interest of Hugo Einbeck in the partnership business—had power to consent to the retention of the assets by the surviving partner in the continuation of the business. While the Uniform Partnership Act deals with partnership law and we are unable to discover any intention on the part of the Legislature in adopting that act to enlarge or affect in any way the power of administrators and executors, the statute must be construed with regard to the purpose its framers sought to attain. In the past, there have been numerous instances in which the interest of the deceased partner in the partnership business has been allowed to continue. Where the partnership venture proved successful, of course no questions arose, every one concerned was benefited. When, however, the partnership venture proved unsuccessful, many difficult questions were presented for solution growing out of the fact that at common law as under the statute the death of a partner dissolved the partnership. Claims of existing creditors were against the partnership as it then stood. Claims of future creditors were against the business as subsequently continued and the determination of the rights of the various classes of creditors presented problems very difficult of solution and upsetting to business transactions. The framers of the act said: "The neglect of the retiring partners or of the representatives of the deceased partner should not as at present create inexecrable confusion between the creditors of the first and second partnership in regard to their respective rights in the property employed in the business. Both classes of creditors should be ahead of the claim of such retired partner or the representative of the deceased partner, and both classes of creditors should also have equal rights in the property. This paragraph probably effects a change in the present law, though the same result is often now brought about by implying a promise to pay the debts of the dissolved partnership on the part of the person or partnership continuing the business." [Commissioners' Note, 7 U.L.A. 231.]

It is considered that under this section it is not necessary for the administrator to be authorized by the court to give his consent. The situation which is dealt with by the statute is one where with the knowledge and acquiescence of the administrator, the surviving partner is permitted to retain the interest of the deceased partner in the business and to continue it. When that happens, it operates as an assignment of the interest of the deceased partner to the surviving partner or partners. If the statute be not so construed, the principal purpose of its framers will be defeated. What is sought is not an enlargement of the power of an administrator but protection of the partnership creditors and a definition of their rights. That an administrator had such power even at common law is established by Hoyt v. Sprague (R.I.1881) 103 U.S. 613, 26 L.Ed. 585, and Big Four Implement Co. v. Keyser, 99 Kan. 8, 161 P. 592, L.R.A.1917C, 166. . . .

It is considered that the court was in error in holding that the interest of Hugo Einbeck in the partnership property was not liable for subsequent debts of the partnership business continued by Charles R. Einbeck in the name of Einbeck Bros. . . .

The judgment appealed from is reversed, and cause remanded for further proceedings as indicated in the opinion.

IN RE HESS

United States District Court, W.D. Pennsylvania, 1923.
1 F.2d 342.

[Weir, S.G. Ligo, Hess and Hanna were partners; Weir sold his interest to the other partners, they undertaking a partnership obligation to pay Weir. Ligo then sold to Hess and Hanna, in consideration of their notes payable to J.E. Ligo; soon after the sale, they changed the firm name to "Hess and Hanna". The firm of Hess & Hanna was later adjudicated bankrupt. Weir and Ligo sought to prove their claims for payment pro rata with those of other creditors. The referee disallowed their claims.]

GIBSON, DISTRICT JUDGE. . . . The learned referee has placed considerable stress upon the fact that the claim [of Weir] is filed against the estate in bankruptcy of Hess & Hanna, while the obligation was that of Hess, Hanna, and Ligo, doing business as Weir, Ligo & Co. But Hess and Hanna, then doing business under the name of Weir, Ligo & Co., beyond all contradiction, assumed the debts of the partnership composed of Hess, Hanna, and Ligo, and continued the business without any liquidation of its affairs. Considering the matter only from the standpoint of Hess and Hanna, the firm is bound by section 41, par. 1, of the Pennsylvania Partnership Act (Purd.Dig. vol. 6, p. 7060 [Pa.St. 1920, § 16636]), which reads as follows: [quoting UPA § 41(1)].

In view of the assumption of the debt of the preceding partnership by Hess and Hanna as Weir, Ligo & Co., we are of opinion that Mr. Weir's claim was, subject to certain qualifications to be later discussed, a proper claim against the bankrupt partnership.

The claim of J.E. Ligo, who stands in the place of S. Garvin Ligo, is based upon a direct obligation assumed by the bankrupt partnership. True, the judgment notes to J.E. Ligo were signed by the firm name of "Weir, Ligo & Co.," as well as by the individual partners, but the firm was then composed of Hess and Hanna, and the business was conducted by them without liquidation of the affairs of Weir, Ligo & Co.; the name only being changed. This claim, in our opinion, is also properly provable against the bankrupt partnership.

But the claims of both Thomas D. Weir and J.E. Ligo, while provable against the bankrupt estate, may not be entitled to participate in the distribution of the fund in the hands of the trustee [in bankruptcy]. The claimants cannot enter into competition for the fund with their own creditors. Mr. Ligo, representing S. Garvin Ligo, cannot participate in the distribution until Mr. Weir has been fully paid, as the latter is his creditor. Nor may he compete with other creditors of the bankrupt firm whose claims date back to a time prior to his retirement from Weir, Ligo & Co. Mr. Weir, also, is not entitled to participate with any persons, if any there be, whose claims arose prior to his retirement, until such claims have been paid. It may be that certain creditors of the partnership, whose claims arose after the retirement of either Mr. Weir or Mr. Ligo, may be able to establish as a fact that one (or both) of the claimants, by his conduct, has estopped himself from entering into the distribution until their claims have been fully paid. Unfortunately, the record is silent as to the financial condition of Weir, Ligo & Co., when either Mr. Weir or Mr. Ligo retired; also as to the dates of claims of other creditors, and of the notices given at the respective times the claimants retired from the partnership. In view of this fact, we feel unable to make final order allowing the claims in the manner sought by claimants. The matter is remanded to the referee, to take such further proceedings as may be required in the premises, having in mind the opinions herein expressed.

NOTE: QUESTIONS REGARDING IN RE HESS

The case of In re Hess is the principal authority on the distribution of assets in an insolvent partnership estate among creditors and *former* partners. It enunciates certain principles, but the opinion does not make clear just how the principles were applied.

In order to show what is at issue, consider the following simplified summary of the facts. Weir, Ligo, Hess and Hanna were members of a partnership of which A was a creditor. Weir assigned his interest to Ligo, Hess and Hanna, who agreed to pay him for it. Ligo, Hess and Hanna continued the business, incurring a debt to B. Ligo later assigned his interest to Hess and Hanna, who agreed to pay Ligo. Hess and Hanna continued the business, incurring debts to C and others, and became bankrupt.

In the bankruptcy it appears that the following are creditors of Hess & Hanna:

A, because creditors of a partnership are creditors of successor partnership which carries on the business;

B, for the same reason;

C, because he extended credit directly to Hess & Hanna;

Weir, because the agreement of Ligo, Hess and Hanna made him their creditor, and because Hess and Hanna are a successor partnership to Ligo, Hess and Hanna;

Ligo, because Hess and Hanna undertook a partnership obligation to him.

However, A has a priority over Weir; A and B and Weir have priorities over Ligo; Ligo and C are both "ordinary creditors" of Hess and Hanna; but C's rights as a creditor of Hess and Hanna are equal to those of A and B and Weir.

How did the court resolve this problem of "circuitous priorities"? Although the published opinion reveals that the court recognized these priorities, it is not quite clear how they were carried out in distribution. At least two possible methods find some support in the language of the opinion.

First method: Put A and B and C in class 1, since they are not deferred to anyone; pay them in full or pro rata with assets available.

Put Weir in class 2, because he is deferred to A.

Put Ligo in class 3, because he is deferred to A and B and Weir.

Second method: Calculate a tentative distribution to A, B, C, Weir, and Ligo, since all are creditors.

Reassign Ligo's share among A, B, and Weir to the extent necessary to pay them in full.

Reassign Weir's share (with its augmentation from Ligo) to A to the extent necessary to repay him in full.

The differences between the methods could be fairly substantial. Assume that each has a claim for 10 thousand dollars, that there are no other creditors, and that the estate amounts to 40 thousand dollars.

First method: A, B, and C each gets 10.

Weir gets the next 10.

Ligo gets nothing.

Second method: Assign to each a tentative distribution of 8.

Reassign 6 of Ligo's 8 to A, B, and Weir, giving each a total of 10, and leaving Ligo with a net of 2.

C's 8 remain unaffected.

No reassignment of Weir's share is necessary, since A is fully paid.

If the estate assets are assumed to be 30 instead of 40, the first method results in giving 10 each to A, B, and C, and nothing to Weir or Ligo. The second method gives 10 to A (after reassignment of shares of Ligo and Weir), 8 to B (after reassignment from Ligo), and 6 each to Weir and C (Weir recovering from Ligo what he loses to A). Ligo again gets nothing.

The following language is from the rehearing by the referee in the case of In re Hess. Does it answer the above questions?

"Pursuant to the order of the Court further hearings were held before the Referee; but very little material evidence was introduced. There was only one other creditor who attempted to show that his claim predated the retirement of either Mr. Weir or Mr. Ligo. This was the claim of J.J. Dean who supplied gasoline to all the different partnerships. This gasoline was sold under a running account with continual payments and continual delivery of gasoline to all the different partnerships. . . .

Under the facts in this case, the Referee is of the opinion that the indebtedness of the partnership of which Weir was a member to J.J. Dean has been fully paid. . . .

The Referee, therefore, holds that Thomas D. Weir was a creditor of the partnership of which . . . Ligo was a member and as stated by the District court, Mr. Ligo cannot participate in the distribution until Mr. Weir has been fully paid.

For the reason stated above, the Referee orders the dividend that would otherwise be payable to Mr. Ligo on the distribution be paid to apply on the claim of Thomas D. Weir. As this dividend will not be sufficient to pay Mr. Weir's claim in full, there can be no payment to Mr. Ligo from the assets of the partnership."

REFERENCES ON PRIORITIES

Raeburn, The So-Called Lien of a Partner (1949) 12 Mod.L.Rev. 432 (priority of firm debts over former partner's claim).

Note, Order of Distribution to Partners under the UPA (1951) 23 Rocky Mtn.L.Rev. 331 (tabular presentation of distribution).

Note, Right of a Partner's Separate Creditors to Share in Distribution of Assets (1952) 17 Mo.L.Rev. 185.

William v. Stevens, 11 A.2d 433 (1939) (current partnership held not liable for debt of prior partnership as there was no agreement to pay by the current partnership and no evidence that any of the assets of the old partnership remained).

Stuart v. Willis, 244 F.2d 925 (9th Cir.1957) (government not allowed to claim set off for taxes due from one joint venturer against contract claim of the joint venture).

Limited partner:

Securities & Exchange Commission v. duPont Homsey Co., 204 F.Supp. 944 (D.Mass. 1962) (defrauded limited partner is subordinated to creditors in seeking restitution from bankrupt firm; applying UPA § 39).

ULPA 23(1) as it existed before the 1976 revision contained some surprises. Limited partners who held debt claims ranked equally with other creditors, in respect to their debt claims. Their claims for capital and profits preceded not only the general partners' claims for capital and surplus, but also the general partners' debt claims. Most surprising of all, although without real significance, was the provision that limited partners' profit claims preceded their own capital claims.

In re Haupt & Co., 343 F.2d 726 (1965), certiorari denied 382 U.S. 890, 86 S.Ct. 182, 15 L.Ed.2d 148 (1965) (limited partner not entitled to vote as a "creditor" for trustee in bankruptcy).

Klebanow v. N.Y. Produce Exchange, 232 F.Supp. 965 (S.D.N.Y.1964), reversed 344 F.2d 294 (2d Cir.1965) (limited partners not entitled to sue derivatively on behalf of partnership to recover treble damages for Sherman Act violation).

Liability of retired partners:

DeNunzio v. Gaian, 43 A.D.2d 673, 349 N.Y.S.2d 974 (1973) (partners who had retired, with agreement that successors would pay debts, remained liable to holders of claims which existed before partners' retirement).

Fox Valley Builders Corp. v. Day, 71 Wis.2d 785, 238 N.W.2d 748 (1976) (partner personally liable for partnership obligation arising prior to an agreement to dissolve, because creditor had not participated in agreement).

UNIFORM PARTNERSHIP ACT (1914)

[As of 1987, the Uniform Partnership Act had been adopted in all U.S. states except Georgia and Louisiana.]

PART I. PRELIMINARY PROVISIONS

PART II. NATURE OF A PARTNERSHIP

PART III. RELATIONS OF PARTNERS TO PERSONS DEALING WITH THE PARTNERSHIP

PART IV. RELATIONS OF PARTNERS TO ONE ANOTHER

PART V. PROPERTY RIGHTS OF A PARTNER

PART VI. DISSOLUTION AND WINDING UP

PART I

PRELIMINARY PROVISIONS

§ 1. Name of Act

This act may be cited as Uniform Partnership Act.

§ 2. Definition of Terms

In this act, "Court" includes every court and judge having jurisdiction in the case.

"Business" includes every trade, occupation, or profession.

"Person" includes individuals, partnerships, corporations, and other associations.

"Bankrupt" includes bankrupt under the Federal Bankruptcy Act or insolvent under any state insolvent act.

"Conveyance" includes every assignment, lease, mortgage, or encumbrance.

"Real property" includes land and any interest or estate in land.

§ 3. Interpretation of Knowledge and Notice

(1) A person has "knowledge" of a fact within the meaning of this act not only when he has actual knowledge thereof, but also

when he has knowledge of such other facts as in the circumstances shows bad faith.

(2) A person has "notice" of a fact within the meaning of this act when the person who claims the benefit of the notice:

(a) States the fact to such person, or

(b) Delivers through the mail, or by other means of communication, a written statement of the fact to such person or to a proper person at his place of business or residence.

§ 4. Rules of Construction

(1) The rule that statutes in derogation of the common law are to be strictly construed shall have no application to this act.

(2) The law of estoppel shall apply under this act.

(3) The law of agency shall apply under this act.

(4) This act shall be so interpreted and construed as to effect its general purpose to make uniform the law of those states which enact it.

(5) This act shall not be construed so as to impair the obligations of any contract existing when the act goes into effect, nor to affect any action or proceedings begun or right accrued before this act takes effect.

§ 5. Rules for Cases Not Provided for in This Act

In any case not provided for in this act the rules of law and equity, including the law merchant, shall govern.

PART II

NATURE OF A PARTNERSHIP

§ 6. Partnership Defined

(1) A partnership is an association of two or more persons to carry on as co-owners a business for profit.

(2) But any association formed under any other statute of this state, or any statute adopted by authority, other than the authority of this state, is not a partnership under this act, unless such association would have been a partnership in this state prior to the adoption of this act; but this act shall apply to limited partnerships except in so far as the statutes relating to such partnerships are inconsistent herewith.

§ 7. Rules for Determining the Existence of a Partnership

In determining whether a partnership exists, these rules shall apply:

(1) Except as provided by section 16 persons who are not partners as to each other are not partners as to third persons.

(2) Joint tenancy, tenancy in common, tenancy by the entireties, joint property, common property, or part ownership does not of itself establish a partnership, whether such co-owners do or do not share any profits made by the use of the property.

(3) The sharing of gross returns does not of itself establish a partnership, whether or not the persons sharing them have a joint or common right or interest in any property from which the returns are derived.

(4) The receipt by a person of a share of the profits of a business is prima facie evidence that he is a partner in the business, but no such inference shall be drawn if such profits were received in payment:

(a) As a debt by installments or otherwise,

(b) As wages of an employee or rent to a landlord,

(c) As an annuity to a widow or representative of a deceased partner,

(d) As interest on a loan, though the amount of payment vary with the profits of the business,

(e) As the consideration for the sale of a good-will of a business or other property by installments or otherwise.

§ 8. Partnership Property

(1) All property originally brought into the partnership stock or subsequently acquired by purchase or otherwise, on account of the partnership, is partnership property.

(2) Unless the contrary intention appears, property acquired with partnership funds is partnership property.

(3) Any estate in real property may be acquired in the partnership name. Title so acquired can be conveyed only in the partnership name.

(4) A conveyance to a partnership in the partnership name, though without words of inheritance, passes the entire estate of the grantor unless a contrary intent appears.

PART III

RELATIONS OF PARTNERS TO PERSONS DEALING WITH THE PARTNERSHIP

§ 9. Partner Agent of Partnership as to Partnership Business

(1) Every partner is an agent of the partnership for the purpose of its business, and the act of every partner, including the execution in the partnership name of any instrument, for apparently carrying on in the usual way the business of the partnership of which he is a member binds the partnership, unless the partner so acting has in fact no authority to act for the partnership in the particular matter, and the person with whom he is dealing has knowledge of the fact that he has no such authority.

(2) An act of a partner which is not apparently for the carrying on of the business of the partnership in the usual way does not bind the partnership unless authorized by the other partners.

(3) Unless authorized by the other partners or unless they have abandoned the business, one or more but less than all the partners have no authority to:

(a) Assign the partnership property in trust for creditors or on the assignee's promise to pay the debts of the partnership,

(b) Dispose of the good-will of the business,

(c) Do any other act which would make it impossible to carry on the ordinary business of a partnership,

(d) Confess a judgment,

(e) Submit a partnership claim or liability to arbitration or reference.

(4) No act of a partner in contravention of a restriction on authority shall bind the partnership to persons having knowledge of the restriction.

§ 10. Conveyance of Real Property of the Partnership

(1) Where title to real property is in the partnership name, any partner may convey title to such property by a conveyance executed in the partnership name; but the partnership may recover such property unless the partner's act binds the partnership under the provisions of paragraph (1) of section 9, or unless such property has been conveyed by the grantee or a person claiming through such grantee to a holder for value without knowledge that the partner, in making the conveyance, has exceeded his authority.

(2) Where title to real property is in the name of the partnership, a conveyance executed by a partner, in his own name, passes the equitable interest of the partnership, provided the act is one within the authority of the partner under the provisions of paragraph (1) of section 9.

(3) Where title to real property is in the name of one or more but not all the partners, and the record does not disclose the right of the partnership, the partners in whose name the title stands may convey title to such property, but the partnership may recover such property if the partners' act does not bind the partnership under the provisions of paragraph (1) of section 9, unless the purchaser or his assignee, is a holder for value, without knowledge.

(4) Where the title to real property is in the name of one or more or all the partners, or in a third person in trust for the partnership, a conveyance executed by a partner in the partnership name, or in his own name, passes the equitable interest of the partnership, provided the act is one within the authority of the partner under the provisions of paragraph (1) of section 9.

(5) Where the title to real property is in the names of all the partners a conveyance executed by all the partners passes all their rights in such property.

§ 11. Partnership Bound by Admission of Partner

An admission or representation made by any partner concerning partnership affairs within the scope of his authority as conferred by this act is evidence against the partnership.

§ 12. Partnership Charged With Knowledge of or Notice to Partner

Notice to any partner of any matter relating to partnership affairs, and the knowledge of the partner acting in the particular matter, acquired while a partner or then present to his mind, and the knowledge of any other partner who reasonably could and should have communicated it to the acting partner, operate as notice to or knowledge of the partnership, except in the case of a fraud on the partnership committed by or with the consent of that partner.

§ 13. Partnership Bound by Partner's Wrongful Act

Where, by any wrongful act or omission of any partner acting in the ordinary course of the business of the partnership or with the authority of his co-partners, loss or injury is caused to any person, not being a partner in the partnership, or any penalty is incurred, the partnership is liable therefor to the same extent as the partner so acting or omitting to act.

§ 14. Partnership Bound by Partner's Breach of Trust

The partnership is bound to make good the loss:

(a) Where one partner acting within the scope of his apparent authority receives money or property of a third person and misapplies it; and

(b) Where the partnership in the course of its business receives money or property of a third person and the money or property so received is misapplied by any partner while it is in the custody of the partnership.

§ 15. Nature of Partner's Liability

All partners are liable

(a) Jointly and severally for everything chargeable to the partnership under sections 13 and 14.

(b) Jointly for all other debts and obligations of the partnership; but any partner may enter into a separate obligation to perform a partnership contract.

§ 16. Partner by Estoppel

(1) When a person, by words spoken or written or by conduct, represents himself, or consents to another representing him to any one, as a partner in an existing partnership or with one or more persons not actual partners, he is liable to any such person to whom such representation has been made, who has, on the faith of such representation, given credit to the actual or apparent partnership, and if he has made such representation or consented to its being made in a public manner he is liable to such person, whether the representation has or has not been made or communicated to such person so giving credit by or with the knowledge of the apparent partner making the representation or consenting to its being made.

(a) When a partnership liability results, he is liable as though he were an actual member of the partnership.

(b) When no partnership liability results, he is liable jointly with the other persons, if any, so consenting to the contract or representation as to incur liability, otherwise separately.

(2) When a person has been thus represented to be a partner in an existing partnership, or with one or more persons not actual partners, he is an agent of the persons consenting to such representation to bind them to the same extent and in the same manner as though he were a partner in fact, with respect to persons who rely upon the representation. Where all the members of the existing partnership consent to the representation, a partnership act or obligation results; but in all other cases it is

the joint act or obligation of the person acting and the persons consenting to the representation.

§ 17. Liability of Incoming Partner

A person admitted as a partner into an existing partnership is liable for all the obligations of the partnership arising before his admission as though he had been a partner when such obligations were incurred, except that this liability shall be satisfied only out of partnership property.

PART IV

RELATIONS OF PARTNERS TO ONE ANOTHER

§ 18. Rules Determining Rights and Duties of Partners

The rights and duties of the partners in relation to the partnership shall be determined, subject to any agreement between them, by the following rules:

(a) Each partner shall be repaid his contributions, whether by way of capital or advances to the partnership property and share equally in the profits and surplus remaining after all liabilities, including those to partners, are satisfied; and must contribute towards the losses, whether of capital or otherwise, sustained by the partnership according to his share in the profits.

(b) The partnership must indemnify every partner in respect of payments made and personal liabilities reasonably incurred by him in the ordinary and proper conduct of its business, or for the preservation of its business or property.

(c) A partner, who in aid of the partnership makes any payment or advance beyond the amount of capital which he agreed to contribute, shall be paid interest from the date of the payment or advance.

(d) A partner shall receive interest on the capital contributed by him only from the date when repayment should be made.

(e) All partners have equal rights in the management and conduct of the partnership business.

(f) No partner is entitled to remuneration for acting in the partnership business, except that a surviving partner is entitled to reasonable compensation for his services in winding up the partnership affairs.

(g) No person can become a member of a partnership without the consent of all the partners.

(h) Any difference arising as to ordinary matters connected with the partnership business may be decided by a majority of the partners; but no act in contravention of any agreement between the partners may be done rightfully without the consent of all the partners.

§ 19. Partnership Books

The partnership books shall be kept, subject to any agreement between the partners, at the principal place of business of the partnership, and every partner shall at all times have access to and may inspect and copy any of them.

§ 20. Duty of Partners to Render Information

Partners shall render on demand true and full information of all things affecting the partnership to any partner or the legal representative of any deceased partner or partner under legal disability.

§ 21. Partner Accountable as a Fiduciary

(1) Every partner must account to the partnership for any benefit, and hold as trustee for it any profits derived by him without the consent of the other partners from any transaction connected with the formation, conduct, or liquidation of the partnership or from any use by him of its property.

(2) This section applies also to the representatives of a deceased partner engaged in the liquidation of the affairs of the partnership as the personal representatives of the last surviving partner.

§ 22. Right to an Account

Any partner shall have the right to a formal account as to partnership affairs:

(a) If he is wrongfully excluded from the partnership business or possession of its property by his co-partners,

(b) If the right exists under the terms of any agreement,

(c) As provided by section 21,

(d) Whenever other circumstances render it just and reasonable.

§ 23. Continuation of Partnership Beyond Fixed Term

(1) When a partnership for a fixed term or particular undertaking is continued after the termination of such term or particular undertaking without any express agreement, the rights and duties of the partners remain the same as they were at such termination, so far as is consistent with a partnership at will.

(2) A continuation of the business by the partners or such of them as habitually acted therein during the term, without any

settlement or liquidation of the partnership affairs, is prima facie evidence of a continuation of the partnership.

PART V

PROPERTY RIGHTS OF A PARTNER

§ 24. Extent of Property Rights of a Partner

The property rights of a partner are (1) his rights in specific partnership property, (2) his interest in the partnership, and (3) his right to participate in the management.

§ 25. Nature of a Partner's Right in Specific Partnership Property

(1) A partner is co-owner with his partners of specific partnership property holding as a tenant in partnership.

(2) The incidents of this tenancy are such that:

(a) A partner, subject to the provisions of this act and to any agreement between the partners, has an equal right with his partners to possess specific partnership property for partnership purposes; but he has no right to possess such property for any other purpose without the consent of his partners.

(b) A partner's right in specific partnership property is not assignable except in connection with the assignment of rights of all the partners in the same property.

(c) A partner's right in specific partnership property is not subject to attachment or execution, except on a claim against the partnership. When partnership property is attached for a partnership debt the partners, or any of them, or the representatives of a deceased partner, cannot claim any right under the homestead or exemption laws.

(d) On the death of a partner his right in specific partnership property vests in the surviving partner or partners, except where the deceased was the last surviving partner, when his right in such property vests in his legal representative. Such surviving partner or partners, or the legal representative of the last surviving partner, has no right to possess the partnership property for any but a partnership purpose.

(e) A partner's right in specific partnership property is not subject to dower, curtesy, or allowances to widows, heirs, or next of kin.

§ 26. Nature of Partner's Interest in the Partnership

A partner's interest in the partnership is his share of the profits and surplus, and the same is personal property.

§ 27. Assignment of Partner's Interest

(1) A conveyance by a partner of his interest in the partnership does not of itself dissolve the partnership, nor, as against the other partners in the absence of agreement, entitle the assignee, during the continuance of the partnership, to interfere in the management or administration of the partnership business or affairs, or to require any information or account of partnership transactions, or to inspect the partnership books; but it merely entitles the assignee to receive in accordance with his contract the profits to which the assigning partner would otherwise be entitled.

(2) In case of a dissolution of the partnership, the assignee is entitled to receive his assignor's interest and may require an account from the date only of the last account agreed to by all the partners.

§ 28. Partner's Interest Subject to Charging Order

(1) On due application to a competent court by any judgment creditor of a partner, the court which entered the judgment, order, or decree, or any other court, may charge the interest of the debtor partner with payment of the unsatisfied amount of such judgment debt with interest thereon; and may then or later appoint a receiver of his share of the profits, and of any other money due or to fall due to him in respect of the partnership, and make all other orders, directions, accounts and inquiries which the debtor partner might have made, or which the circumstances of the case may require.

(2) The interest charged may be redeemed at any time before foreclosure, or in case of a sale being directed by the court may be purchased without thereby causing a dissolution:

(a) With separate property, by any one or more of the partners, or

(b) With partnership property, by any one or more of the partners with the consent of all the partners whose interests are not so charged or sold.

(3) Nothing in this act shall be held to deprive a partner of his right, if any, under the exemption laws, as regards his interest in the partnership.

PART VI

DISSOLUTION AND WINDING UP

§ 29. Dissolution Defined

The dissolution of a partnership is the change in the relation of the partners caused by any partner ceasing to be associated in

497

the carrying on as distinguished from the winding up of the business.

§ 30. Partnership Not Terminated by Dissolution

On dissolution the partnership is not terminated, but continues until the winding up of partnership affairs is completed.

§ 31. Causes of Dissolution

Dissolution is caused:

(1) Without violation of the agreement between the partners,

(a) By the termination of the definite term or particular undertaking specified in the agreement,

(b) By the express will of any partner when no definite term or particular undertaking is specified,

(c) By the express will of all the partners who have not assigned their interests or suffered them to be charged for their separate debts, either before or after the termination of any specified term or particular undertaking,

(d) By the expulsion of any partner from the business bona fide in accordance with such a power conferred by the agreement between the partners;

(2) In contravention of the agreement between the partners, where the circumstances do not permit a dissolution under any other provision of this section, by the express will of any partner at any time;

(3) By any event which makes it unlawful for the business of the partnership to be carried on or for the members to carry it on in partnership;

(4) By the death of any partner;

(5) By the bankruptcy of any partner or the partnership;

(6) By decree of court under section 32.

§ 32. Dissolution by Decree of Court

(1) On application by or for a partner the court shall decree a dissolution whenever:

(a) A partner has been declared a lunatic in any judicial proceeding or is shown to be of unsound mind,

(b) A partner becomes in any other way incapable of performing his part of the partnership contract,

(c) A partner has been guilty of such conduct as tends to affect prejudicially the carrying on of the business,

(d) A partner wilfully or persistently commits a breach of the partnership agreement, or otherwise so conducts himself in matters relating to the partnership business that it is not reasonably practicable to carry on the business in partnership with him,

(e) The business of the partnership can only be carried on at a loss,

(f) Other circumstances render a dissolution equitable.

(2) On the application of the purchaser of a partner's interest under sections 28 or 29 [should read 27 or 28];

(a) After the termination of the specified term or particular undertaking,

(b) At any time if the partnership was a partnership at will when the interest was assigned or when the charging order was issued.

§ 33. General Effect of Dissolution on Authority of Partner

Except so far as may be necessary to wind up partnership affairs or to complete transactions begun but not then finished, dissolution terminates all authority of any partner to act for the partnership,

(1) With respect to the partners,

(a) When the dissolution is not by the act, bankruptcy or death of a partner; or

(b) When the dissolution is by such act, bankruptcy or death of a partner, in cases where section 34 so requires.

(2) With respect to persons not partners, as declared in section 35.

§ 34. Rights of Partner to Contribution From Co-partners After Dissolution

Where the dissolution is caused by the act, death or bankruptcy of a partner, each partner is liable to his co-partners for his share of any liability created by any partner acting for the partnership as if the partnership had not been dissolved unless

(a) The dissolution being by act of any partner, the partner acting for the partnership had knowledge of the dissolution, or

(b) The dissolution being by the death or bankruptcy of a partner, the partner acting for the partnership had knowledge or notice of the death or bankruptcy.

§ 35. Power of Partner to Bind Partnership to Third Persons After Dissolution

(1) After dissolution a partner can bind the partnership except as provided in Paragraph (3).

(a) By any act appropriate for winding up partnership affairs or completing transactions unfinished at dissolution;

(b) By any transaction which would bind the partnership if dissolution had not taken place, provided the other party to the transaction

(I) Had extended credit to the partnership prior to dissolution and had no knowledge or notice of the dissolution; or

(II) Though he had not so extended credit, had nevertheless known of the partnership prior to dissolution, and, having no knowledge or notice of dissolution, the fact of dissolution had not been advertised in a newspaper of general circulation in the place (or in each place if more than one) at which the partnership business was regularly carried on.

(2) The liability of a partner under Paragraph (1b) shall be satisfied out of partnership assets alone when such partner had been prior to dissolution

(a) Unknown as a partner to the person with whom the contract is made; and

(b) So far unknown and inactive in partnership affairs that the business reputation of the partnership could not be said to have been in any degree due to his connection with it.

(3) The partnership is in no case bound by any act of a partner after dissolution

(a) Where the partnership is dissolved because it is unlawful to carry on the business, unless the act is appropriate for winding up partnership affairs; or

(b) Where the partner has become bankrupt; or

(c) Where the partner has no authority to wind up partnership affairs; except by a transaction with one who

(I) Had extended credit to the partnership prior to dissolution and had no knowledge or notice of his want of authority; or

(II) Had not extended credit to the partnership prior to dissolution, and, having no knowledge or notice of his want of authority, the fact of his want of authority has not been advertised in the manner provided for advertising the fact of dissolution in Paragraph (1b II).

(4) Nothing in this section shall affect the liability under Section 16 of any person who after dissolution represents himself or consents to another representing him as a partner in a partnership engaged in carrying on business.

§ 36. Effect of Dissolution on Partner's Existing Liability

(1) The dissolution of the partnership does not of itself discharge the existing liability of any partner.

(2) A partner is discharged from any existing liability upon dissolution of the partnership by an agreement to that effect between himself, the partnership creditor and the person or partnership continuing the business; and such agreement may be inferred from the course of dealing between the creditor having knowledge of the dissolution and the person or partnership continuing the business.

(3) Where a person agrees to assume the existing obligations of a dissolved partnership, the partners whose obligations have been assumed shall be discharged from any liability to any creditor of the partnership who, knowing of the agreement, consents to a material alteration in the nature or time of payment of such obligations.

(4) The individual property of a deceased partner shall be liable for all obligations of the partnership incurred while he was a partner but subject to the prior payment of his separate debts.

§ 37. Right to Wind Up

Unless otherwise agreed the partners who have not wrongfully dissolved the partnership or the legal representative of the last surviving partner, not bankrupt, has the right to wind up the partnership affairs; provided, however, that any partner, his legal representative or his assignee, upon cause shown, may obtain winding up by the court.

§ 38. Rights of Partners to Application of Partnership Property

(1) When dissolution is caused in any way, except in contravention of the partnership agreement, each partner, as against his co-partners and all persons claiming through them in respect of their interests in the partnership, unless otherwise agreed, may have the partnership property applied to discharge its liabilities, and the surplus applied to pay in cash the net amount owing to the respective partners. But if dissolution is caused by expulsion of a partner, bona fide under the partnership agreement and if the expelled partner is discharged from all partnership liabilities, either by payment or agreement under section 36(2), he shall receive in cash only the net amount due him from the partnership.

(2) When dissolution is caused in contravention of the partnership agreement the rights of the partners shall be as follows:

(a) Each partner who has not caused dissolution wrongfully shall have,

I. All the rights specified in paragraph (1) of this section, and

II. The right, as against each partner who has caused the dissolution wrongfully, to damages for breach of the agreement.

(b) The partners who have not caused the dissolution wrongfully, if they all desire to continue the business in the same name, either by themselves or jointly with others, may do so, during the agreed term for the partnership and for that purpose may possess the partnership property, provided they secure the payment by bond approved by the court, or pay to any partner who has caused the dissolution wrongfully, the value of his interest in the partnership at the dissolution, less any damages recoverable under clause (2a II) of this section, and in like manner indemnify him against all present or future partnership liabilities.

(c) A partner who has caused the dissolution wrongfully shall have:

I. If the business is not continued under the provisions of paragraph (2b) all the rights of a partner under paragraph (1), subject to clause (2a II), of this section,

II. If the business is continued under paragraph (2b) of this section the right as against his co-partners and all claiming through them in respect of their interests in the partnership, to have the value of his interest in the partnership, less any damages caused to his co-partners by the dissolution, ascertained and paid to him in cash, or the payment secured by bond approved by the court, and to be released from all existing liabilities of the partnership; but in ascertaining the value of the partner's interest the value of the good-will of the business shall not be considered.

§ 39. Rights Where Partnership Is Dissolved for Fraud or Misrepresentation

Where a partnership contract is rescinded on the ground of the fraud or misrepresentation of one of the parties thereto, the party entitled to rescind is, without prejudice to any other right, entitled,

(a) To a lien on, or a right of retention of, the surplus of the partnership property after satisfying the partnership liabilities to third persons for any sum of money paid by him for the purchase of an interest in the partnership and for any capital or advances contributed by him; and

(b) To stand, after all liabilities to third persons have been satisfied, in the place of the creditors of the partnership for any payments made by him in respect of the partnership liabilities; and

(c) To be indemnified by the person guilty of the fraud or making the representation against all debts and liabilities of the partnership.

§ 40. Rules for Distribution

In settling accounts between the partners after dissolution, the following rules shall be observed, subject to any agreement to the contrary:

(a) The assets of the partnership are:

I. The partnership property,

II. The contributions of the partners necessary for the payment of all the liabilities specified in clause (b) of this paragraph.

(b) The liabilities of the partnership shall rank in order of payment, as follows:

I. Those owing to creditors other than partners,

II. Those owing to partners other than for capital and profits,

III. Those owing to partners in respect of capital,

IV. Those owing to partners in respect of profits.

(c) The assets shall be applied in the order of their declaration in clause (a) of this paragraph to the satisfaction of the liabilities.

(d) The partners shall contribute, as provided by section 18(a) the amount necessary to satisfy the liabilities; but if any, but not all, of the partners are insolvent, or, not being subject to process, refuse to contribute, the other partners shall contribute their share of the liabilities, and, in the relative proportions in which they share the profits, the additional amount necessary to pay the liabilities.

(e) An assignee for the benefit of creditors or any person appointed by the court shall have the right to enforce the contributions specified in clause (d) of this paragraph.

(f) Any partner or his legal representative shall have the right to enforce the contributions specified in clause (d) of this paragraph, to the extent of the amount which he has paid in excess of his share of the liability.

(g) The individual property of a deceased partner shall be liable for the contributions specified in clause (d) of this paragraph.

(h) When partnership property and the individual properties of the partners are in possession of a court for distribution, partnership creditors shall have priority on partnership property and separate creditors on individual property, saving the rights of lien or secured creditors as heretofore.

(i) Where a partner has become bankrupt or his estate is insolvent the claims against his separate property shall rank in the following order:

I.   Those owing to separate creditors,

II.   Those owing to partnership creditors,

III.   Those owing to partners by way of contribution.

§ 41. Liability of Persons Continuing the Business in Certain Cases

(1) When any new partner is admitted into an existing partnership, or when any partner retires and assigns (or the representative of the deceased partner assigns) his rights in partnership property to two or more of the partners, or to one or more of the partners and one or more third persons, if the business is continued without liquidation of the partnership affairs, creditors of the first or dissolved partnership are also creditors of the partnership so continuing the business.

(2) When all but one partner retire and assign (or the representative of a deceased partner assigns) their rights in partnership property to the remaining partner, who continues the business without liquidation of partnership affairs, either alone or with others, creditors of the dissolved partnership are also creditors of the person or partnership so continuing the business.

(3) When any partner retires or dies and the business of the dissolved partnership is continued as set forth in paragraphs (1) and (2) of this section, with the consent of the retired partners or the representative of the deceased partner, but without any assignment of his right in partnership property, rights of creditors of the dissolved partnership and of the creditors of the person or partnership continuing the business shall be as if such assignment had been made.

(4) When all the partners or their representatives assign their rights in partnership property to one or more third persons who promise to pay the debts and who continue the business of the dissolved partnership, creditors of the dissolved partnership are also creditors of the person or partnership continuing the business.

(5) When any partner wrongfully causes a dissolution and the remaining partners continue the business under the provisions of section 38(2b), either alone or with others, and without liquidation of the partnership affairs, creditors of the dissolved partnership are also creditors of the person or partnership continuing the business.

(6) When a partner is expelled and the remaining partners continue the business either alone or with others, without liquidation of the partnership affairs, creditors of the dissolved partner-

ship are also creditors of the person or partnership continuing the business.

(7) The liability of a third person becoming a partner in the partnership continuing the business, under this section, to the creditors of the dissolved partnership shall be satisfied out of partnership property only.

(8) When the business of a partnership after dissolution is continued under any conditions set forth in this section the creditors of the dissolved partnership, as against the separate creditors of the retiring or deceased partner or the representative of the deceased partner, have a prior right to any claim of the retired partner or the representative of the deceased partner against the person or partnership continuing the business, on account of the retired or deceased partner's interest in the dissolved partnership or on account of any consideration promised for such interest or for his right in partnership property.

(9) Nothing in this section shall be held to modify any right of creditors to set aside any assignment on the ground of fraud.

(10) The use by the person or partnership continuing the business of the partnership name, or the name of a deceased partner as part thereof, shall not of itself make the individual property of the deceased partner liable for any debts contracted by such person or partnership.

§ 42. Rights of Retiring or Estate of Deceased Partner When the Business Is Continued

When any partner retires or dies, and the business is continued under any of the conditions set forth in section 41(1, 2, 3, 5, 6), or section 38(2b) without any settlement of accounts as between him or his estate and the person or partnership continuing the business, unless otherwise agreed, he or his legal representative as against such persons or partnership may have the value of his interest at the date of dissolution ascertained, and shall receive as an ordinary creditor an amount equal to the value of his interest in the dissolved partnership with interest, or, at his option or at the option of his legal representative, in lieu of interest, the profits attributable to the use of his right in the property of the dissolved partnership; provided that the creditors of the dissolved partnership as against the separate creditors, or the representative of the retired or deceased partner, shall have priority on any claim arising under this section, as provided by section 41(8) of this act.

§ 43. Accrual of Actions

The right to an account of his interest shall accrue to any partner, or his legal representative, as against the winding up partners or the surviving partners or the person or partnership continuing the business, at the date of dissolution, in the absence of any agreement to the contrary.

PART VII

MISCELLANEOUS PROVISIONS

§ 44. When Act Takes Effect

This act shall take effect on the _____ day of _____ one thousand nine hundred and _____.

§ 45. Legislation Repealed

All acts or parts of acts inconsistent with this act are hereby repealed.

UNIFORM LIMITED PARTNERSHIP ACT (1916)

[As of 1987, the Uniform Limited Partnership Act of 1916 was in effect in the following states: Alaska, District of Columbia, Florida, Georgia, Hawaii, Illinois, Indiana, Kentucky, Maine, Mississippi, Missouri, Nevada, New Hampshire, New Jersey, New Mexico, New York, North Carolina, North Dakota, Ohio, Oregon, Pennsylvania, Rhode Island, South Carolina, South Dakota, Tennessee, Texas, Utah, Vermont, Virginia.]

§ 1. Limited Partnership Defined

A limited partnership is a partnership formed by two or more persons under the provisions of Section 2, having as members one or more general partners and one or more limited partners. The limited partners as such shall not be bound by the obligations of the partnership.

§ 2. Formation

(1) Two or more persons desiring to form a limited partnership shall

(a) Sign and swear to a certificate, which shall state

I. The name of the partnership,

II. The character of the business,

III. The location of the principal place of business,

IV. The name and place of residence of each member; general and limited partners being respectively designated,

V. The term for which the partnership is to exist,

VI. The amount of cash and a description of and the agreed value of the other property contributed by each limited partner,

VII. The additional contributions, if any, agreed to be made by each limited partner and the times at which or events on the happening of which they shall be made,

VIII. The time, if agreed upon, when the contribution of each limited partner is to be returned,

IX. The share of the profits or the other compensation by way of income which each limited partner shall receive by reason of his contribution,

X. The right, if given, of a limited partner to substitute an assignee as contributor in his place, and the terms and conditions of the substitution,

XI. The right, if given, of the partners to admit additional limited partners.

XII. The right, if given, of one or more of the limited partners to priority over other limited partners, as to contributions or as to compensation by way of income, and the nature of such priority,

XIII. The right, if given, of the remaining general partner or partners to continue the business on the death, retirement or insanity of a general partner, and

XIV. The right, if given, of a limited partner to demand and receive property other than cash in return for his contribution.

(b) File for record the certificate in the office of [here designate the proper office].

(2) A limited partnership is formed if there has been substantial compliance in good faith with the requirements of paragraph (1).

§ 3. Business Which May Be Carried On

A limited partnership may carry on any business which a partnership without limited partners may carry on, except [here designate the business to be prohibited].

§ 4. Character of Limited Partner's Contribution

The contributions of a limited partner may be cash or other property, but not services.

§ 5. A Name Not to Contain Surname of Limited Partner; Exceptions

(1) The surname of a limited partner shall not appear in the partnership name, unless

(a) It is also the surname of a general partner, or

(b) Prior to the time when the limited partner became such the business had been carried on under a name in which his surname appeared.

(2) A limited partner whose name appears in a partnership name contrary to the provisions of paragraph (1) is liable as a general partner to partnership creditors who extend credit to the partnership without actual knowledge that he is not a general partner.

§ 6. Liability for False Statements in Certificate

If the certificate contains a false statement, one who suffers loss by reliance on such statement may hold liable any party to the certificate who knew the statement to be false.

(a) At the time he signed the certificate, or

(b) Subsequently, but within a sufficient time before the statement was relied upon to enable him to cancel or amend the certificate, or to file a petition for its cancellation or amendment as provided in Section 25(3).

§ 7. Limited Partner Not Liable to Creditors

A limited partner shall not become liable as a general partner unless, in addition to the exercise of his rights and powers as a limited partner, he takes part in the control of the business.

§ 8. Admission of Additional Limited Partners

After the formation of a limited partnership, additional limited partners may be admitted upon filing an amendment to the original certificate in accordance with the requirements of Section 25.

§ 9. Rights, Powers and Liabilities of a General Partner

(1) A general partner shall have all the rights and powers and be subject to all the restrictions and liabilities of a partner in a partnership without limited partners, except that without the written consent or ratification of the specific act by all the limited partners, a general partner or all of the general partners have no authority to

(a) Do any act in contravention of the certificate,

(b) Do any act which would make it impossible to carry on the ordinary business of the partnership.

(c) Confess a judgment against the partnership,

(d) Possess partnership property, or assign their rights in specific partnership property, for other than a partnership purpose,

(e) Admit a person as a general partner,

(f) Admit a person as a limited partner, unless the right so to do is given in the certificate,

(g) Continue the business with partnership property on the death, retirement or insanity of a general partner, unless the right so to do is given in the certificate.

§ 10. Rights of a Limited Partner

(1) A limited partner shall have the same rights as a general partner to

(a) Have the partnership books kept at the principal place of business of the partnership, and at all times to inspect and copy any of them.

(b) Have on demand true and full information of all things affecting the partnership, and a formal account of partnership affairs whenever circumstances render it just and reasonable, and

(c) Have dissolution and winding up by decree of court.

(2) A limited partner shall have the right to receive a share of the profits or other compensation by way of income, and to the return of his contribution as provided in Sections 15 and 16.

§ 11. Status of Person Erroneously Believing Himself a Limited Partner

A person who has contributed to the capital of a business conducted by a person or partnership erroneously believing that he has become a limited partner in a limited partnership, is not, by reason of his exercise of the rights of a limited partner, a general partner with the person or in the partnership carrying on the business, or bound by the obligations of such person or partnership; provided that on ascertaining the mistake he promptly renounces his interest in the profits of the business, or other compensation by way of income.

§ 12. One Person Both General and Limited Partner

(1) A person may be a general partner and a limited partner in the same partnership at the same time.

(2) A person who is a general, and also at the same time a limited partner, shall have all the rights and powers and be subject to all the restrictions of a general partner; except that, in respect to his contribution, he shall have the rights against the other members which he would have had if he were not also a general partner.

§ 13. Loans and Other Business Transactions With Limited Partner

(1) A limited partner also may loan money to and transact other business with the partnership, and, unless he is also a general partner, receive on account of resulting claims against the partnership, with general creditors, a pro rata share of the assets. No limited partner shall in respect to any such claim

(a) Receive or hold as collateral security any partnership property, or

(b) Receive from a general partner or the partnership any payment, conveyance, or release from liability, if at the time the assets of the partnership are not sufficient to discharge partnership liabilities to persons not claiming as general or limited partners.

(2) The receiving of collateral security, or a payment, conveyance, or release in violation of the provisions of paragraph (1) is a fraud on the creditors of the partnership.

§ 14. Relation of Limited Partners Inter Se

Where there are several limited partners the members may agree that one or more of the limited partners shall have a priority over other limited partners as to the return of their contributions, as to their compensation by way of income, or as to any other matter. If such an agreement is made it shall be stated in the certificate, and in the absence of such a statement all the limited partners shall stand upon equal footing.

§ 15. Compensation of Limited Partner

A limited partner may receive from the partnership the share of the profits or the compensation by way of income stipulated for in the certificate; provided, that after such payment is made, whether from the property of the partnership or that of a general partner, the partnership assets are in excess of all liabilities of the partnership except liabilities to limited partners on account of their contributions and to general partners.

§ 16.   Withdrawal or Reduction of Limited Partner's Contribution

(1) A limited partner shall not receive from a general partner or out of partnership property any part of his contribution until

(a) All liabilities of the partnership, except liabilities to general partners and to limited partners on account of their contributions, have been paid or there remains property of the partnership sufficient to pay them,

(b) The consent of all members is had, unless the return of the contribution may be rightfully demanded under the provisions of paragraph (2), and

(c) The certificate is cancelled or so amended as to set forth the withdrawal or reduction.

(2) Subject to the provisions of paragraph (1) a limited partner may rightfully demand the return of his contribution

(a) On the dissolution of a partnership, or

(b) When the date specified in the certificate for its return has arrived, or

(c) After he has given six months' notice in writing to all other members, if no time is specified in the certificate either for the return of the contribution or for the dissolution of the partnership.

(3) In the absence of any statement in the certificate to the contrary or the consent of all members, a limited partner, irrespective of the nature of his contribution, has only the right to demand and receive cash in return for his contribution.

(4) A limited partner may have the partnership dissolved and its affairs wound up when

(a) He rightfully but unsuccessfully demands the return of his contribution, or

(b) The other liabilities of the partnership have not been paid, or the partnership property is insufficient for their payment as required by paragraph (1a) and the limited partner would otherwise be entitled to the return of his contribution.

§ 17. Liability of Limited Partner to Partnership

(1) A limited partner is liable to the partnership

(a) For the difference between his contribution as actually made and that stated in the certificate as having been made, and

(b) For any unpaid contribution which he agreed in the certificate to make in the future at the time and on the conditions stated in the certificate.

(2) A limited partner holds as trustee for the partnership

(a) Specific property stated in the certificate as contributed by him, but which was not contributed or which has been wrongfully returned, and

(b) Money or other property wrongfully paid or conveyed to him on account of his contribution.

(3) The liabilities of a limited partner as set forth in this section can be waived or compromised only by the consent of all members; but a waiver or compromise shall not affect the right of a creditor of a partnership who extended credit or whose claim arose after the filing and before a cancellation or amendment of the certificate, to enforce such liabilities.

(4) When a contributor has rightfully received the return in whole or in part of the capital of his contribution, he is nevertheless liable to the partnership for any sum, not in excess of such return with interest, necessary to discharge its liabilities to all creditors who extended credit or whose claims arose before such return.

§ 18. Nature of Limited Partner's Interest in Partnership

A limited partner's interest in the partnership is personal property.

§ 19. Assignment of Limited Partner's Interest

(1) A limited partner's interest is assignable.

(2) A substituted limited partner is a person admitted to all the rights of a limited partner who has died or has assigned his interest in a partnership.

(3) An assignee, who does not become a substituted limited partner, has no right to require any information or account of the partnership transactions or to inspect the partnership books; he is only entitled to receive the share of the profits or other compensation by way of income, or the return of his contribution, to which his assignor would otherwise be entitled.

(4) An assignee shall have the right to become a substituted limited partner if all the members (except the assignor) consent

thereto or if the assignor, being thereunto empowered by the certificate, gives the assignee that right.

(5) An assignee becomes a substituted limited partner when the certificate is appropriately amended in accordance with Section 25.

(6) The substituted limited partner has all the rights and powers, and is subject to all the restrictions and liabilities of his assignor, except those liabilities of which he was ignorant at the time he became a limited partner and which could not be ascertained from the certificate.

(7) The substitution of the assignee as a limited partner does not release the assignor from liability to the partnership under Sections 6 and 17.

§ 20.   Effect of Retirement, Death or Insanity of a General Partner

The retirement, death or insanity of a general partner dissolves the partnership, unless the business is continued by the remaining general partners

(a) Under a right so to do stated in the certificate, or

(b) With the consent of all members.

§ 21.   Death of Limited Partner

(1) On the death of a limited partner his executor or administrator shall have all the rights of a limited partner for the purpose of settling his estate, and such power as the deceased had to constitute his assignee a substituted limited partner.

(2) The estate of a deceased limited partner shall be liable for all his liabilities as a limited partner.

§ 22.   Rights of Creditors of Limited Partner

(1) On due application to a court of competent jurisdiction by any judgment creditor of a limited partner, the court may charge the interest of the indebted limited partner with payment of the unsatisfied amount of the judgment debt; and may appoint a receiver, and make all other orders, directions, and inquiries which the circumstances of the case may require.

In those states where a creditor on beginning an action can attach debts due the defendant before he has obtained a judgment against the defendant it is recommended that paragraph (1) of this section read as follows:

On due application to a court of competent jurisdiction by any creditor of a limited partner, the court may charge the interest of the indebted limited partner with payment of the unsatisfied amount of such claim; and may appoint a receiver, and make all other orders, directions, and inquiries which the circumstances of the case may require.

(2) The interest may be redeemed with the separate property of any general partner, but may not be redeemed with partnership property.

(3) The remedies conferred by paragraph (1) shall not be deemed exclusive of others which may exist.

(4) Nothing in this act shall be held to deprive a limited partner of his statutory exemption.

§ 23. Distribution of Assets

(1) In settling accounts after dissolution the liabilities of the partnership shall be entitled to payment in the following order:

(a) Those to creditors, in the order of priority as provided by law, except those to limited partners on account of their contributions, and to general partners,

(b) Those to limited partners in respect to their share of the profits and other compensation by way of income on their contributions,

(c) Those to limited partners in respect to the capital of their contributions,

(d) Those to general partners other than for capital and profits,

(e) Those to general partners in respect to profits,

(f) Those to general partners in respect to capital.

(2) Subject to any statement in the certificate or to subsequent agreement, limited partners share in the partnership assets in respect to their claims for capital, and in respect to their claims for profits or for compensation by way of income on their contributions respectively, in proportion to the respective amounts of such claims.

§ 24. When Certificate Shall Be Cancelled or Amended

(1) The certificate shall be cancelled when the partnership is dissolved or all limited partners cease to be such.

(2) A certificate shall be amended when

(a) There is a change in the name of the partnership or in the amount or character of the contribution of any limited partner,

(b) A person is substituted as a limited partner,

(c) An additional limited partner is admitted,

(d) A person is admitted as a general partner,

(e) A general partner retires, dies or becomes insane, and the business is continued under Section 20,

(f) There is a change in the character of the business of the partnership,

(g) There is a false or erroneous statement in the certificate,

(h) There is a change in the time as stated in the certificate for the dissolution of the partnership or for the return of a contribution,

(i) A time is fixed for the dissolution of the partnership, or the return of a contribution, no time having been specified in the certificate, or

(j) The members desire to make a change in any other statement in the certificate in order that it shall accurately represent the agreement between them.

§ 25. Requirements for Amendment and for Cancellation of Certificate

(1) The writing to amend a certificate shall

(a) Conform to the requirements of Section 2(1a) as far as necessary to set forth clearly the change in the certificate which it is desired to make, and

(b) Be signed and sworn to by all members, and an amendment substituting a limited partner or adding a limited or general partner shall be signed also by the member to be substituted or added, and when a limited partner is to be substituted, the amendment shall also be signed by the assigning limited partner.

(2) The writing to cancel a certificate shall be signed by all members.

(3) A person desiring the cancellation or amendment of a certificate, if any person designated in paragraphs (1) and (2) as a person who must execute the writing refuses to do so, may petition the [here designate the proper court] to direct a cancellation or amendment thereof.

(4) If the court finds that the petitioner has a right to have the writing executed by a person who refuses to do so, it shall order the [here designate the responsible official in the office designated in Section 2] in the office where the certificate is recorded to record the cancellation or amendment of the certificate; and where the certificate is to be amended, the court shall also cause to be filed for record in said office a certified copy of its decree setting forth the amendment.

(5) A certificate is amended or cancelled when there is filed for record in the office [here designate the office designated in Section 2] where the certificate is recorded

(a) A writing in accordance with the provisions of paragraph (1), or (2) or

(b) A certified copy of the order of court in accordance with the provisions of paragraph (4).

(6) After the certificate is duly amended in accordance with this section, the amended certificate shall thereafter be for all purposes the certificate provided for by this act.

§ 26. Parties to Actions

A contributor, unless he is a general partner, is not a proper party to proceedings by or against a partnership, except where the object is to enforce a limited partner's right against or liability to the partnership.

§ 27. Name of Act

This act may be cited as The Uniform Limited Partnership Act.

§ 28. Rules of Construction

(1) The rule that statutes in derogation of the common law are to be strictly construed shall have no application to this act.

(2) This act shall be so interpreted and construed as to effect its general purpose to make uniform the law of those states which enact it.

(3) This act shall not be so construed as to impair the obligations of any contract existing when the act goes into effect, nor to affect any action or proceedings begun or right accrued before this act takes effect.

§ 29. Rules for Cases Not Provided for in This Act

In any case not provided for in this act the rules of law and equity, including the law merchant, shall govern.

§ 30. Provisions for Existing Limited Partnerships

(1) A limited partnership formed under any statute of this state prior to the adoption of this act, may become a limited partnership under this act by complying with the provisions of Section 2; provided the certificate sets forth

(a) The amount of the original contribution of each limited partner, and the time when the contribution was made, and

(b) That the property of the partnership exceeds the amount sufficient to discharge its liabilities to persons not claiming as general or limited partners by an amount greater than the sum of the contributions of its limited partners.

(2) A limited partnership formed under any statute of this state prior to the adoption of this act, until or unless it becomes a limited partnership under this act, shall continue to be governed

by the provisions of [here insert proper reference to the existing limited partnership act or acts], except that such partnership shall not be renewed unless so provided in the original agreement.

§ 31. Act (Acts) Repealed

Except as affecting existing limited partnerships to the extent set forth in Section 30, the act (acts) of [here designate the existing limited partnership act or acts] is (are) hereby repealed.

REVISED UNIFORM LIMITED PARTNERSHIP ACT (1976)

[As of 1987, the Revised Uniform Limited Partnership Act had been adopted, occasionally with variations in substance and language, in the following states: Alabama, Arizona, Arkansas, California, Colorado, Connecticut, Delaware, Idaho, Iowa, Kansas, Maryland, Massachusetts, Michigan, Minnesota, Montana, Nebraska, New Jersey, Oklahoma, Washington, West Virginia, Wisconsin, Wyoming.]

ARTICLE 1. GENERAL PROVISIONS

ARTICLE 2. FORMATION; CERTIFICATE OF LIMITED PARTNERSHIP

ARTICLE 3. LIMITED PARTNERS

ARTICLE 4. GENERAL PARTNERS

519

ARTICLE 5. FINANCE

ARTICLE 6. DISTRIBUTIONS AND WITHDRAWAL

ARTICLE 7. ASSIGNMENT OF PARTNERSHIP INTERESTS

ARTICLE 8. DISSOLUTION

ARTICLE 9. FOREIGN LIMITED PARTNERSHIPS

ARTICLE 10. DERIVATIVE ACTIONS

ARTICLE 11. MISCELLANEOUS

ARTICLE 1

GENERAL PROVISIONS

§ 101. Definitions

As used in this Act, unless the context otherwise requires:

(1) "Certificate of limited partnership" means the certificate referred to in Section 201, and the certificate as amended.

(2) "Contribution" means any cash, property, services rendered, or a promissory note or other binding obligation to contribute cash or property or to perform services, which a partner contributes to a limited partnership in his capacity as a partner.

(3) "Event of withdrawal of a general partner" means an event that causes a person to cease to be a general partner as provided in Section 402.

(4) "Foreign limited partnership" means a partnership formed under the laws of any State other than this State and having as partners one or more general partners and one or more limited partners.

(5) "General partner" means a person who has been admitted to a limited partnership as a general partner in accordance with the partnership agreement and named in the certificate of limited partnership as a general partner.

(6) "Limited partner" means a person who has been admitted to a limited partnership as a limited partner in accordance with the partnership agreement and named in the certificate of limited partnership as a limited partner.

(7) "Limited partnership" and "domestic limited partnership" means a partnership formed by 2 or more persons under the laws of this State and having one or more general partners and one or more limited partners.

(8) "Partner" means a limited or general partner.

(9) "Partnership agreement" means any valid agreement, written or oral, of the partners as to the affairs of a limited partnership and the conduct of its business.

(10) "Partnership interest" means a partner's share of the profits and losses of a limited partnership and the right to receive distributions of partnership assets.

(11) "Person" means a natural person, partnership, limited partnership (domestic or foreign), trust, estate, association, or corporation.

(12) "State" means a state, territory, or possession of the United States, the District of Columbia, or the Commonwealth of Puerto Rico.

§ 102. Name

The name of each limited partnership as set forth in its certificate of limited partnership:

(1) shall contain without abbreviation the words "limited partnership";

(2) may not contain the name of a limited partner unless (i) it is also the name of a general partner or the corporate name of a corporate general partner, or (ii) the business of the limited partnership had been carried on under that name before the admission of that limited partner;

(3) may not contain any word or phrase indicating or implying that it is organized other than for a purpose stated in its certificate of limited partnership;

(4) may not be the same as, or deceptively similar to, the name of any corporation or limited partnership organized under the laws of this State or licensed or registered as a foreign corporation or limited partnership in this State; and

(5) may not contain the following words [here insert prohibited words].

§ 103. Reservation of Name

(a) The exclusive right to the use of a name may be reserved by:

(1) any person intending to organize a limited partnership under this Act and to adopt that name;

(2) any domestic limited partnership or any foreign limited partnership registered in this State which, in either case, intends to adopt that name;

(3) any foreign limited partnership intending to register in this State and adopt that name; and

(4) any person intending to organize a foreign limited partnership and intending to have it register in this State and adopt that name.

(b) The reservation shall be made by filing with the Secretary of State an application, executed by the applicant, to reserve a specified name. If the Secretary of State finds that the name is available for use by a domestic or foreign limited partnership, he shall reserve the name for the exclusive use of the applicant for a period of 120 days. Once having so reserved a name, the same applicant may not again reserve the same name until more than 60 days after the expiration of the last 120-day period for which that applicant reserved that name. The right to the exclusive use of a reserved name may be transferred to any other person by filing in the office of the Secretary of State a notice of the transfer, executed by the applicant for whom the name was reserved and specifying the name and address of the transferee.

§ 104. Specified Office and Agent

Each limited partnership shall continuously maintain in this State:

(1) an office, which may but need not be a place of its business in this State, at which shall be kept the records required by Section 105 to be maintained; and

(2) an agent for service of process on the limited partnership, which agent must be an individual resident of this State, a domestic corporation, or a foreign corporation authorized to do business in this State.

§ 105. Records to Be Kept

Each limited partnership shall keep at the office referred to in Section 104(1) the following: (1) a current list of the full name and last known business address of each partner set forth in alphabetical order, (2) a copy of the certificate of limited partnership and all certificates of amendment thereto, together with executed copies of any powers of attorney pursuant to which any certificate has been executed, (3) copies of the limited partnership's federal, state, and local income tax returns and reports, if any, for the 3 most recent years, and (4) copies of any then effective written partnership agreements and of any financial statements of the limited partnership for the 3 most recent years. Those records are subject to inspection and copying at the reasonable request, and at the expense, of any partner during ordinary business hours.

§ 106. Nature of Business

A limited partnership may carry on any business that a partnership without limited partners may carry on except [here designate prohibited activities].

§ 107. Business Transactions of Partner With the Partnership

Except as provided in the partnership agreement, a partner may lend money to and transact other business with the limited partnership and, subject to other applicable law, has the same rights and obligations with respect thereto as a person who is not a partner.

ARTICLE 2

FORMATION; CERTIFICATE OF LIMITED PARTNERSHIP

§ 201. Certificate of Limited Partnership

(a) In order to form a limited partnership two or more persons must execute a certificate of limited partnership. The certificate shall be filed in the office of the Secretary of State and set forth:

(1) the name of the limited partnership;

(2) the general character of its business;

(3) the address of the office and the name and address of the agent for service of process required to be maintained by Section 104;

(4) the name and the business address of each partner (specifying separately the general partners and limited partners);

(5) the amount of cash and a description and statement of the agreed value of the other property or services contributed by each partner and which each partner has agreed to contribute in the future;

(6) the times at which or events on the happening of which any additional contributions agreed to be made by each partner are to be made;

(7) any power of a limited partner to grant the right to become a limited partner to an assignee of any part of his partnership interest, and the terms and conditions of the power;

(8) if agreed upon, the time at which or the events on the happening of which a partner may terminate his membership in the limited partnership and the amount of, or the method of determining, the distribution to which he may be entitled respecting his partnership interest, and the terms and conditions of the termination and distribution;

(9) any right of a partner to receive distributions of property, including cash from the limited partnership;

(10) any right of a partner to receive, or of a general partner to make, distributions to a partner which include a return of all or any part of the partner's contribution;

(11) any time at which or events upon the happening of which the limited partnership is to be dissolved and its affairs wound up;

(12) any right of the remaining general partners to continue the business on the happening of an event of withdrawal of a general partner; and

(13) any other matters the partners determine to include therein.

(b) A limited partnership is formed at the time of the filing of the certificate of limited partnership in the office of the Secretary of State or at any later time specified in the certificate of limited partnership if, in either case, there has been substantial compliance with the requirements of this section.

§ 202. Amendment to Certificate

(a) A certificate of limited partnership is amended by filing a certificate of amendment thereto in the office of the Secretary of State. The certificate shall set forth:

(1) the name of the limited partnership;

(2) the date of filing of the certificate; and

(3) the amendment to the certificate.

(b) Within 30 days after the happening of any of the following events an amendment to a certificate of limited partnership reflecting the occurrence of the event or events shall be filed:

(1) a change in the amount or character of the contribution of any partner, or in any partner's obligation to make a contribution;

(2) the admission of a new partner;

(3) the withdrawal of a partner; or

(4) the continuation of the business under Section 801 after an event of withdrawal of a general partner.

(c) A general partner who becomes aware that any statement in a certificate of limited partnership was false when made or that any arrangements or other facts described have changed, making the certificate inaccurate in any respect, shall promptly amend the certificate, but an amendment to show a change of address of a limited partner need be filed only once every 12 months.

(d) A certificate of limited partnership may be amended at any time for any other proper purpose the general partners may determine.

(e) No person has any liability because an amendment to a certificate of limited partnership has not been filed to reflect the occurrence of any event referred to in subsection (b) of this Section if the amendment is filed within the 30-day period specified in subsection (b).

§ 203. Cancellation of Certificate

A certificate of limited partnership shall be cancelled upon the dissolution and the commencement of winding up of the partnership or at any other time there are no limited partners. A certificate of cancellation shall be filed in the office of the Secretary of State and set forth:

(1) the name of the limited partnership;

(2) the date of filing of its certificate of limited partnership;

(3) the reason for filing the certificate of cancellation;

(4) the effective date (which shall be a date certain) of cancellation if it is not to be effective upon the filing of the certificate; and

(5) any other information the general partners filing the certificate determine.

§ 204. Execution of Certificates

(a) Each certificate required by this Article to be filed in the office of the Secretary of State shall be executed in the following manner:

(1) an original certificate of limited partnership must be signed by all partners named therein;

(2) a certificate of amendment must be signed by at least one general partner and by each other partner designated in the certificate as a new partner or whose contribution is described as having been increased; and

(3) a certificate of cancellation must be signed by all general partners;

(b) Any person may sign a certificate by an attorney-in-fact, but a power of attorney to sign a certificate relating to the admission, or increased contribution, of a partner must specifically describe the admission or increase.

(c) The execution of a certificate by a general partner constitutes an affirmation under the penalties of perjury that the facts stated therein are true.

§ 205. Amendment or Cancellation by Judicial Act

If a person required by Section 204 to execute a certificate of amendment or cancellation fails or refuses to do so, any other partner, and any assignee of a partnership interest, who is adversely affected by the failure or refusal, may petition the [here designate the proper court] to direct the amendment or cancellation. If the court finds that the amendment or cancellation is proper and that any person so designated has failed or refused to execute the certificate, it shall order the Secretary of State to record an appropriate certificate of amendment or cancellation.

§ 206. Filing in Office of Secretary of State

(a) Two signed copies of the certificate of limited partnership and of any certificates of amendment or cancellation (or of any judicial decree of amendment or cancellation) shall be delivered to the Secretary of State. A person who executes a certificate as an agent or fiduciary need not exhibit evidence of his authority as a prerequisite to filing. Unless the Secretary of State finds that any certificate does not conform to law, upon receipt of all filing fees required by law he shall:

(1) endorse on each duplicate original the word "Filed" and the day, month, and year of the filing thereof;

(2) file one duplicate original in his office; and

(3) return the other duplicate original to the person who filed it or his representative.

(b) Upon the filing of a certificate of amendment (or judicial decree of amendment) in the office of the Secretary of State, the certificate of limited partnership shall be amended as set forth therein, and upon the effective date of a certificate of cancellation (or a judicial decree thereof), the certificate of limited partnership is cancelled.

§ 207. Liability for False Statement in Certificate

If any certificate of limited partnership or certificate of amendment or cancellation contains a false statement, one who suffers loss by reliance on the statement may recover damages for the loss from:

(1) any person who executes the certificate, or causes another to execute it on his behalf, and knew, and any general partner who knew or should have known, the statement to be false at the time the certificate was executed; and

(2) any general partner who thereafter knows or should have known that any arrangement or other fact described in the certificate has changed, making the statement inaccurate in any respect within a sufficient time before the statement was relied upon reasonably to have enabled that general partner to cancel or amend the certificate, or to file a petition for its cancellation or amendment under Section 205.

§ 208. Notice

The fact that a certificate of limited partnership is on file in the office of the Secretary of State is notice that the partnership is a limited partnership and the persons designated therein as limited partners are limited partners, but it is not notice of any other fact.

§ 209. Delivery of Certificates to Limited Partners

Upon the return by the Secretary of State pursuant to Section 206 of a certificate marked "Filed," the general partners shall promptly deliver or mail a copy of the certificate of limited partnership and each certificate to each limited partner unless the partnership agreement provides otherwise.

ARTICLE 3

LIMITED PARTNERS

§ 301. Admission of Additional Limited Partners

(a) After the filing of a limited partnership's original certificate of limited partnership, a person may be admitted as an additional limited partner:

(1) in the case of a person acquiring a partnership interest directly from the limited partnership, upon the compliance with the partnership agreement or, if the partnership agreement does not so provide, upon the written consent of all partners; and

(2) in the case of an assignee of a partnership interest of a partner who has the power, as provided in Section 704 to grant the assignee the right to become a limited partner, upon the exercise of that power and compliance with any conditions limiting the grant or exercise of the power.

(b) In each case under subsection (a), the person acquiring the partnership interest becomes a limited partner only upon amendment of the certificate of limited partnership reflecting that fact.

§ 302. Voting

Subject to Section 303, the partnership agreement may grant to all or a specified group of the limited partners the right to vote (on a per capita or other basis) upon any matter.

§ 303. Liability to Third Parties

(a) Except as provided in subsection (d), a limited partner is not liable for the obligations of a limited partnership unless he is also a general partner or, in addition to the exercise of his rights and powers as a limited partner, he takes part in the control of the business. However, if the limited partner's participation in the control of the business is not substantially the same as the exercise of the powers of a general partner, he is liable only to persons who transact business with the limited partnership with actual knowledge of his participation in control.

(b) A limited partner does not participate in the control of the business within the meaning of subsection (a) solely by doing one or more of the following:

(1) being a contractor for or an agent or employee of the limited partnership or of a general partner;

(2) consulting with and advising a general partner with respect to the business of the limited partnership;

(3) acting as surety for the limited partnership;

(4) approving or disapproving an amendment to the partnership agreement; or

(5) voting on one or more of the following matters:

(i) the dissolution and winding up of the limited partnership;

(ii) the sale, exchange, lease, mortgage, pledge, or other transfer of all or substantially all of the assets of the limited partnership other than in the ordinary course of its business;

(iii) the incurrence of indebtedness by the limited partnership other than in the ordinary course of its business;

(iv) a change in the nature of the business; or

(v) the removal of a general partner.

(c) The enumeration in subsection (b) does not mean that the possession or exercise of any other powers by a limited partner constitutes participation by him in the business of the limited partnership.

(d) A limited partner who knowingly permits his name to be used in the name of the limited partnership, except under circumstances permitted by Section 102(2)(i), is liable to creditors who extend credit to the limited partnership without actual knowledge that the limited partner is not a general partner.

§ 304. Person Erroneously Believing Himself Limited Partner

(a) Except as provided in subsection (b), a person who makes a contribution to a business enterprise and erroneously but in good faith believes that he has become a limited partner in the enterprise is not a general partner in the enterprise and is not bound by its obligations by reason of making the contribution, receiving distributions from the enterprise, or exercising any rights of a limited partner, if, on ascertaining the mistake, he:

(1) causes an appropriate certificate of limited partnership or a certificate of amendment to be executed and filed; or

(2) withdraws from future equity participation in the enterprise.

(b) A person who makes a contribution of the kind described in subsection (a) is liable as a general partner to any third party who transacts business with the enterprise (i) before the person withdraws and an appropriate certificate is filed to show withdrawal, or (ii) before an appropriate certificate is filed to show his status as a limited partner and, in the case of an amendment, after expiration of the 30-day period for filing an amendment relating to the person as a limited partner under Section 202, but in either case only if the third party actually believed in good faith that the person was a general partner at the time of the transaction.

§ 305. Information

Each limited partner has the right to:

(1) inspect and copy any of the partnership records required to be maintained by Section 105; and

(2) obtain from the general partners from time to time upon reasonable demand (i) true and full information regarding the state of the business and financial condition of the limited partnership, (ii) promptly after becoming available, a copy of the limited partnership's federal, state, and local income tax returns for each year, and (iii) other information regarding the affairs of the limited partnership as is just and reasonable.

ARTICLE 4

GENERAL PARTNERS

§ 401. Admission of Additional General Partners

After the filing of a limited partnership's original certificate of limited partnership, additional general partners may be admitted only with the specific written consent of each partner.

§ 402. Events of Withdrawal

Except as approved by the specific written consent of all partners at the time, a person ceases to be a general partner of a limited partnership upon the happening of any of the following events:

(1) the general partner withdraws from the limited partnership as provided in Section 602;

(2) the general partner ceases to be a member of the limited partnership as provided in Section 702;

(3) the general partner is removed as a general partner in accordance with the partnership agreement;

(4) unless otherwise provided in the certificate of limited partnership, the general partner: (i) makes an assignment for the

benefit of creditors; (ii) files a voluntary petition in bankruptcy; (iii) is adjudicated a bankrupt or insolvent; (iv) files a petition or answer seeking for himself any reorganization, arrangement, composition, readjustment, liquidation, dissolution, or similar relief under any statute, law, or regulation; (v) files an answer or other pleading admitting or failing to contest the material allegations of a petition filed against him in any proceeding of this nature; or (vi) seeks, consents to, or acquiesces in the appointment of a trustee, receiver, or liquidator of the general partner or of all or any substantial part of his properties;

(5) unless otherwise provided in the certificate of limited partnership, [120] days after the commencement of any proceeding against the general partner seeking reorganization, arrangement, composition, readjustment, liquidation, dissolution, or similar relief under any statute, law, or regulation, the proceeding has not been dismissed, or if within [90] days after the appointment without his consent or acquiescence of a trustee, receiver, or liquidator of the general partner or of all or any substantial part of his properties, the appointment is not vacated or stayed, or within [90] days after the expiration of any such stay, the appointment is not vacated;

(6) in the case of a general partner who is a natural person,

(i) his death; or

(ii) the entry by a court of competent jurisdiction adjudicating him incompetent to manage his person or his estate;

(7) in the case of a general partner who is acting as a general partner by virtue of being a trustee of a trust, the termination of the trust (but not merely the substitution of a new trustee);

(8) in the case of a general partner that is a separate partnership, the dissolution and commencement of winding up of the separate partnership;

(9) in the case of a general partner that is a corporation, the filing of a certificate of dissolution, or its equivalent, for the corporation or the revocation of its charter; or

(10) in the case of an estate, the distribution by the fiduciary of the estate's entire interest in the partnership.

§ 403. General Powers and Liabilities

(a) Except as provided in this Act or in the partnership agreement, a general partner of a limited partnership has the rights and powers and is subject to the restrictions of a partner in a partnership without limited partners.

(b) Except as provided in this Act, a general partner of a limited partnership has the liabilities of a partner in a partnership without limited partners to persons other than the partnership and the other partners. Except as provided in this Act or in the partnership agreement, a general partner of a limited partnership has the liabilities of a partner in a partnership without limited partners to the partnership and to the other partners.

§ 404. Contributions by a General Partner

A general partner of a limited partnership may make contributions to the partnership and share in the profits and losses of, and in distributions from, the limited partnership as a general partner. A general partner also may make contributions to and share in profits, losses, and distributions as a limited partner. A person who is both a general partner and a limited partner has the rights and powers, and is subject to the restrictions and liabilities, of a general partner and, except as provided in the partnership agreement, also has the powers, and is subject to the restrictions, of a limited partner to the extent of his participation in the partnership as a limited partner.

§ 405. Voting

The partnership agreement may grant to all or certain identified general partners the right to vote (on a per capita or any other basis), separately or with all or any class of the limited partners, on any matter.

ARTICLE 5

FINANCE

§ 501. Form of Contribution

The contribution of a partner may be in cash, property, or services rendered, or a promissory note or other obligation to contribute cash or property or to perform services.

§ 502. Liability for Contributions

(a) Except as provided in the certificate of limited partnership, a partner is obligated to the limited partnership to perform any promise to contribute cash or property or to perform services, even if he is unable to perform because of death, disability or any other reason. If a partner does not make the required contribution of property or services, he is obligated at the option of the limited partnership to contribute cash equal to that portion of the value (as stated in the certificate of limited partnership) of the stated contribution that has not been made.

(b) Unless otherwise provided in the partnership agreement, the obligation of a partner to make a contribution or return money or other property paid or distributed in violation of this Act may be compromised only by consent of all the partners. Notwithstanding the compromise, a creditor of a limited partnership who extends credit, or whose claim arises, after the filing of the certificate of limited partnership or an amendment thereto which, in either case, reflects the obligation, and before the amendment or cancellation thereof to reflect the compromise, may enforce the original obligation.

§ 503. Sharing of Profits and Losses

The profits and losses of a limited partnership shall be allocated among the partners, and among classes of partners, in the manner provided in the partnership agreement. If the partnership agreement does not so provide, profits and losses shall be allocated on the basis of the value (as stated in the certificate of limited partnership) of the contributions made by each partner to the extent they have been received by the partnership and have not been returned.

§ 504. Sharing of Distributions

Distributions of cash or other assets of a limited partnership shall be allocated among the partners, and among classes of partners, in the manner provided in the partnership agreement. If the partnership agreement does not so provide, distributions shall be made on the basis of the value (as stated in the certificate of limited partnership) of the contributions made by each partner to the extent they have been received by the partnership and have not been returned.

ARTICLE 6

DISTRIBUTIONS AND WITHDRAWAL

§ 601. Interim Distributions

Except as provided in this Article, a partner is entitled to receive distributions from a limited partnership before his withdrawal from the limited partnership and before the dissolution and winding up thereof:

(1) to the extent and at the times or upon the happening of the events specified in the partnership agreement; and

(2) if any distribution constitutes a return of any part of his contribution under Section 608(b), to the extent and at the times or upon the happening of the events specified in the certificate of limited partnership.

§ 602. Withdrawal of General Partner

A general partner may withdraw from a limited partnership at any time by giving written notice to the other partners, but if the withdrawal violates the partnership agreement, the limited partnership may recover from the withdrawing general partner damages for breach of the partnership agreement and offset the damages against the amount otherwise distributable to him.

§ 603. Withdrawal of Limited Partner

A limited partner may withdraw from a limited partnership at the time or upon the happening of events specified in the certificate of limited partnership and in accordance with the partnership agreement. If the certificate does not specify the time or the events upon the happening of which a limited partner may withdraw or a definite time for the dissolution and winding up of the limited partnership, a limited partner may withdraw upon not less than 6 months' prior written notice to each general partner at his address on the books of the limited partnership at its office in this State.

§ 604. Distribution Upon Withdrawal

Except as provided in this Article, upon withdrawal any withdrawing partner is entitled to receive any distribution to which he is entitled under the partnership agreement and, if not otherwise provided in the agreement, he is entitled to receive, within a reasonable time after withdrawal, the fair value of his interest in the limited partnership as of the date of withdrawal based upon his right to share in distributions from the limited partnership.

§ 605. Distribution in Kind

Except as provided in the certificate of limited partnership, a partner, regardless of the nature of his contribution, has no right to demand and receive any distribution from a limited partnership in any form other than cash. Except as provided in the partnership agreement, a partner may not be compelled to accept a distribution of any asset in kind from a limited partnership to the extent that the percentage of the asset distributed to him exceeds a percentage of that asset which is equal to the percentage in which he shares in distributions from the limited partnership.

§ 606. Right to Distribution

At the time a partner becomes entitled to receive a distribution, he has the status of, and is entitled to all remedies available to, a creditor of the limited partnership with respect to the distribution.

§ 607. Limitations on Distribution

A partner may not receive a distribution from a limited partnership to the extent that, after giving effect to the distribution, all liabilities of the limited partnership, other than liabilities to partners on account of their partnership interests, exceed the fair value of the partnership assets.

§ 608. Liability Upon Return of Contribution

(a) If a partner has received the return of any part of his contribution without violation of the partnership agreement or this Act, he is liable to the limited partnership for a period of one year thereafter for the amount of the returned contribution, but only to the extent necessary to discharge the limited partnership's liabilities to creditors who extended credit to the limited partnership during the period the contribution was held by the partnership.

(b) If a partner has received the return of any part of his contribution in violation of the partnership agreement or this Act, he is liable to the limited partnership for a period of 6 years thereafter for the amount of the contribution wrongfully returned.

(c) A partner receives a return of his contribution to the extent that a distribution to him reduces his share of the fair value of the net assets of the limited partnership below the value (as set forth in the certificate of limited partnership) of his contribution which has not been distributed to him.

ARTICLE 7

ASSIGNMENT OF PARTNERSHIP INTERESTS

§ 701. Nature of Partnership Interest

A partnership interest is personal property.

§ 702. Assignment of Partnership Interest

Except as provided in the partnership agreement, a partnership interest is assignable in whole or in part. An assignment of a partnership interest does not dissolve a limited partnership or entitle the assignee to become or to exercise any rights of a partner. An assignment entitles the assignee to receive, to the extent assigned, only the distribution to which the assignor would be entitled. Except as provided in the partnership agreement, a partner ceases to be a partner upon assignment of all his partnership interest.

§ 703. Rights of Creditor

On application to a court of competent jurisdiction by any judgment creditor of a partner, the court may charge the partnership interest of the partner with payment of the unsatisfied amount of the judgment with interest. To the extent so charged, the judgment creditor has only the rights of an assignee of the partnership interest. This Act does not deprive any partner of the benefit of any exemption laws applicable to his partnership interest.

§ 704. Right of Assignee to Become Limited Partner

(a) An assignee of a partnership interest, including an assignee of a general partner, may become a limited partner if and to the extent that (1) the assignor gives the assignee that right in accordance with authority described in the certificate of limited partnership, or (2) all other partners consent.

(b) An assignee who has become a limited partner has, to the extent assigned, the rights and powers, and is subject to the restrictions and liabilities, of a limited partner under the partnership agreement and this Act. An assignee who becomes a limited partner also is liable for the obligations of his assignor to make and return contributions as provided in Article 6. However, the assignee is not obligated for liabilities unknown to the assignee at the time he became a limited partner and which could not be ascertained from the certificate of limited partnership.

(c) If an assignee of a partnership interest becomes a limited partner, the assignor is not released from his liability to the limited partnership under Sections 207 and 502.

§ 705. Power of Estate of Deceased or Incompetent Partner

If a partner who is an individual dies or a court of competent jurisdiction adjudges him to be incompetent to manage his person or his property, the partner's executor, administrator, guardian, conservator, or other legal representative may exercise all of the partner's rights for the purpose of settling his estate or administering his property, including any power the partner had to give an assignee the right to become a limited partner. If a partner is a corporation, trust, or other entity and is dissolved or terminated, the powers of that partner may be exercised by its legal representative or successor.

ARTICLE 8

DISSOLUTION

§ 801. Nonjudicial Dissolution

A limited partnership is dissolved and its affairs shall be wound up upon the happening of the first to occur of the following:

(1) at the time or upon the happening of events specified in the certificate of limited partnership;

(2) written consent of all partners;

(3) an event of withdrawal of a general partner unless at the time there is at least one other general partner and the certificate

of limited partnership permits the business of the limited partnership to be carried on by the remaining general partner and that partner does so, but the limited partnership is not dissolved and is not required to be wound up by reason of any event of withdrawal if, within 90 days after the withdrawal, all partners agree in writing to continue the business of the limited partnership and to the appointment of one or more additional general partners if necessary or desired; or

(4) entry of a decree of judicial dissolution under Section 802.

§ 802. Judicial Dissolution

On application by or for a partner the [here designate the proper court] court may decree dissolution of a limited partnership whenever it is not reasonably practicable to carry on the business in conformity with the partnership agreement.

§ 803. Winding Up

Except as provided in the partnership agreement, the general partners who have not wrongfully dissolved a limited partnership or, if none, the limited partners, may wind up the limited partnership's affairs; but the [here designate the proper court] court may wind up the limited partnership's affairs upon application of any partner, his legal representative, or assignee.

§ 804. Distribution of Assets

Upon the winding up of a limited partnership, the assets shall be distributed as follows:

(1) to creditors, including partners who are creditors, to the extent otherwise permitted by law, in satisfaction of liabilities of the limited partnership other than liabilities for distributions to partners under Section 601 or 604;

(2) except as provided in the partnership agreement, to partners and former partners in satisfaction of liabilities for distributions under Section 601 or 604; and

(3) except as provided in the partnership agreement, to partners *first* for the return of their contributions and *secondly* respecting their partnership interests, in the proportions in which the partners share in distributions.

ARTICLE 9

FOREIGN LIMITED PARTNERSHIPS

§ 901. Law Governing

Subject to the Constitution of this State, (1) the laws of the state under which a foreign limited partnership is organized govern its organization and internal affairs and the liability of its limited partners, and (2) a foreign limited partnership may not be denied registration by reason of any difference between those laws and the laws of this State.

§ 902. Registration

Before transacting business in this State, a foreign limited partnership shall register with the Secretary of State. In order to register, a foreign limited partnership shall submit to the Secretary of State, in duplicate, an application for registration as a foreign limited partnership, signed and sworn to by a general partner and setting forth:

(1) the name of the foreign limited partnership and, if different, the name under which it proposes to register and transact business in this State;

(2) the state and date of its formation;

(3) the general character of the business it proposes to transact in this State;

(4) the name and address of any agent for service of process on the foreign limited partnership whom the foreign limited partnership elects to appoint; the agent must be an individual resident of this State, a domestic corporation, or a foreign corporation having a place of business in, and authorized to do business in this State;

(5) a statement that the Secretary of State is appointed the agent of the foreign limited partnership for service of process if no agent has been appointed under paragraph (4) or, if appointed, the agent's authority has been revoked or if the agent cannot be found or served with the exercise of reasonable diligence;

(6) the address of the office required to be maintained in the State of its organization by the laws of that State or, if not so required, of the principal office of the foreign limited partnership; and

(7) if the certificate of limited partnership filed in the foreign limited partnership's state of organization is not required to include the names and business addresses of the partners, a list of the names and addresses.

§ 903. Issuance of Registration

(a) If the Secretary of State finds that an application for registration conforms to law and all requisite fees have been paid, he shall:

(1) endorse on the application the word "Filed", and the month, day, and year of the filing thereof;

(2) file in his office a duplicate original of the application; and

(3) issue a certificate of registration to transact business in this State.

(b) The certificate of registration, together with a duplicate original of the application, shall be returned to the person who filed the application or his representative.

§ 904. Name

A foreign limited partnership may register with the Secretary of State under any name (whether or not it is the name under which it is registered in its state of organization) that includes without abbreviation the words "limited partnership" and that could be registered by a domestic limited partnership.

§ 905. Changes and Amendments

If any statement in the application for registration of a foreign limited partnership was false when made or any arrangements or other facts described have changed, making the application inaccurate in any respect, the foreign limited partnership shall promptly file in the office of the Secretary of State a certificate, signed and sworn to by a general partner, correcting such statement.

§ 906. Cancellation of Registration

A foreign limited partnership may cancel its registration by filing with the Secretary of State a certificate of cancellation signed and sworn to by a general partner. A cancellation does not terminate the authority of the Secretary of State to accept service of process on the foreign limited partnership with respect to [claims for relief] [causes of action] arising out of the transactions of business in this State.

§ 907. Transaction of Business Without Registration

(a) A foreign limited partnership transacting business in this State may not maintain any action, suit, or proceeding in any court of this State until it has registered in this State.

(b) The failure of a foreign limited partnership to register in this State does not impair the validity of any contract or act of the foreign limited partnership or prevent the foreign limited partnership from defending any action, suit, or proceeding in any court of this State.

(c) A limited partner of a foreign limited partnership is not liable as a general partner of the foreign limited partnership solely by reason of having transacted business in this State without registration.

(d) A foreign limited partnership, by transacting business in this State without registration, appoints the Secretary of State as its agent for service of process with respect to [claims for relief] [causes of action] arising out of the transaction of business in this State.

§ 908. Action by [Appropriate Official]

The [appropriate official] may bring an action to restrain a foreign limited partnership from transacting business in this State in violation of this Article.

ARTICLE 10

DERIVATIVE ACTIONS

§ 1001. Right of Action

A limited partner may bring an action in the right of a limited partnership to recover a judgment in its favor if general partners with authority to do so have refused to bring the action or if an effort to cause those general partners to bring the action is not likely to succeed.

§ 1002. Proper Plaintiff

In a derivative action, the plaintiff must be a partner at the time of bringing the action and (1) at the time of the transaction of which he complains or (2) his status as a partner had devolved upon him by operation of law or pursuant to the terms of the partnership agreement from a person who was a partner at the time of the transaction.

§ 1003. Pleading

In a derivative action, the complaint shall set forth with particularity the effort of the plaintiff to secure initiation of the action by a general partner or the reasons for not making the effort.

§ 1004. Expenses

If a derivative action is successful, in whole or in part, or if anything is received by the plaintiff as a result of a judgment, compromise, or settlement of an action or claim, the court may award the plaintiff reasonable expenses, including reasonable attorney's fees, and shall direct him to remit to the limited partnership the remainder of those proceeds received by him.

ARTICLE 11

MISCELLANEOUS

§ 1101. Construction and Application

This Act shall be so applied and construed to effectuate its general purpose to make uniform the law with respect to the subject of this Act among states enacting it.

§ 1102. Short Title

This Act may be cited as the Uniform Limited Partnership Act.

§ 1103. Severability

If any provision of this Act or its application to any person or circumstance is held invalid, the invalidity does not affect other provisions or applications of the Act which can be given effect without the invalid provision or application, and to this end the provisions of this Act are severable.

§ 1104. Effective Date, Extended Effective Date and Repeal

Except as set forth below, the effective date of this Act is _____ and the following Acts [list prior limited partnership acts] are hereby repealed:

(1) The existing provisions for execution and filing of certificates of limited partnerships and amendments thereunder and cancellations thereof continue in effect until [specify time required to create central filing system], the extended effective date, and Sections 102, 103, 104, 105, 201, 202, 203, 204 and 206 are not effective until the extended effective date.

(2) Section 402, specifying the conditions under which a general partner ceases to be a member of a limited partnership, is not effective until the extended effective date, and the applicable provisions of existing law continue to govern until the extended effective date.

(3) Sections 501, 502 and 608 apply only to contributions and distributions made after the effective date of this Act.

(4) Section 704 applies only to assignments made after the effective date of this Act.

(5) Article 9, dealing with registration of foreign limited partnerships, is not effective until the extended effective date.

§ 1105. Rules for Cases Not Provided for in This Act

In any case not provided for in this act the provisions of the Uniform Partnership Act govern.

*

GENERAL PARTNERSHIP AGREEMENT *

AGREEMENT made _____ 1975, among _____ of _____, Ohio; _____ of _____, Ohio; _____ of _____, Ohio; _____ of _____, Ohio; _____ of _____, Ohio; and _____ of _____, Ohio (all of such parties are hereinafter sometimes referred to as "Partners"):

1. **Name of Business:** The parties do hereby form a partnership under the name of _____.

2. **Office:** The office of the partnership shall be located at _____ or at such other location or locations as the Managing Partners may from time to time designate.

3. **Term:** The term of the partnership shall begin on _____ 1975, and shall continue until _____, 1975, unless sooner terminated as herein provided.

4. **Capital:** The capital of the partnership shall be Sixty Thousand Dollars ($60,000.00).

5. **Capital Contribution of Partners:** The following persons shall be partners and shall contribute to the capital of the partnership the cash amounts set opposite their names:

Partner	Contribution	Percentage
	$12,000.00	20%
	12,000.00	20%
	12,000.00	20%
	12,000.00	20%
	6,000.00	10%
	6,000.00	10%
	$60,000.00	100%

The initial capital accounts of the Partners shall be equivalent to their respective contributions of such capital of the partnership as set forth hereinabove. If at any time or times hereafter the Managing Partners should unanimously determine that further capital is required in the interests of the partnership, and that the capital of the partnership should be increased, the additional capital shall be contributed by the Partners in the respective percentages hereinabove set forth. No interest shall be paid on the initial or on any subsequent contributions to the capital of the partnership. (See Paragraph 17.)

* © Copyright 1976, American Law Institute. Reprinted by permission from M. Volz and A. Berger, The Drafting of Partnership Agreements (1976), pp. 147–159.

6. **Profit and Loss:** The net profit of the partnership shall be divided among the Partners and the net losses of the partnership shall be borne by the Partners pro rata, in the respective percentages of their capital contributions.

For the purposes of this agreement in determining the share of partnership net profits to which each Partner shall be entitled, the partnership profits shall be determined without taking into account any deduction for depreciation.

For income tax purposes all depreciation deductions shall be allocated among the partners in proportion to their dollar cash capital contributions.

7. **Mortgage Refinancing:** In the event that as a result of refinancing any mortgage constituting a lien against the real property held by the partnership, net proceeds, in excess of the then remaining principal balance of the mortgage prior to such refinancing, are received by the partnership, then such net proceeds shall be distributable among the Partners in the same ratio as set forth in Paragraph 5 hereof.

8. **Management Duties and Restrictions:** _____ shall be the Managing Partners. The Managing Partners shall have full charge of the management, conduct and operation of the partnership in all respects and in all matters, including but not limited to, full power to purchase, sell and convey personal and real property on such terms as they may determine, to lease such property or any part thereof on such terms and for such period as they may determine, to borrow money on behalf of the partnership, and to mortgage personal and real property, whether such mortgage be a first or second mortgage lien, as well as to make any agreement modifying any contract, lease, note or mortgage.

A majority of the Managing Partners shall be authorized and empowered to determine all questions relating to the conduct and management of the partnership business, and the determination of a majority of the Managing Partners on any such question (excepting, and not including, the determination of the interest or share of any Partner in the capital, net profits, or net losses of the partnership, or the claims of any Partner against the partnership, or its claims against such Partner) shall be binding on all Partners. None of the Managing Partners shall be authorized or empowered without the consent of a majority of the Managing Partners (but with such consent, shall be authorized and empowered), on behalf of the partnership, to borrow (from any partner or third party) or make, deliver, or accept any commercial paper, or execute any mortgage, bond, lease, deed, release, or agreement, or purchase or contract to purchase, or sell or contract to sell any property, or compromise or release any of its claims or debts. No Partner shall, except with the consent of all other Partners, withdraw his capital contribution, in whole or in part, or assign, mortgage, or sell his share in the partnership or in its capital, assets, or property, or enter into any agreement as a result of which any other person, firm, or corporation shall become interested with him in the partnership, or do any act detrimental to the best interests of the partnership, or which would make it impossible to carry on the purpose of the partnership.

Each Managing Partner may have other interests and may engage in any business or trade, profession, or employment whatsoever, whether such business, trade, profession, or employment is similar or competing with the purpose of the partnership, on his own account, or in partnership with or as an employee of or as an officer, director or stockholder of any other person, firm or corporation, and he shall not be required to devote his entire time to the partnership. No Managing Partner shall be obligated to devote more time and attention to the conduct of the partnership than shall be deemed, by all of the Managing Partners including such Partner, to be required for the partnership. The Managing Partners shall receive reasonable compensation for services to be rendered by them in the management of the partnership affairs. In the event of death of a Managing Partner or Partners, the remaining Managing Partners shall conduct the affairs of the partnership under the provisions of this paragraph, except as hereinafter provided.

The Managing Partners, on behalf of the partnership, may purchase and sell real and personal property from and to any Partner, whether he be a Managing Partner, or otherwise, provided, however, such purchase or sale shall be for fair market value.

9. **Books:** The partnership shall maintain full and accurate books of account which shall be kept at the principal partnership office. Each Managing Partner shall cause to be entered in such books all transactions of or relating to the partnership. Each Partner shall have access to and the right to inspect and copy such books and all other partnership records.

10. **Annual Accounting:** As of the last day of December of each year during the continuance of the partnership, commencing December 31, 1975, a full, true and accurate account shall be made in writing of all of the assets and liabilities of the partnership, and of all of its receipts and disbursements, and the assets, liabilities and income, both gross and net, shall be ascertained, and the net profits or net losses shall be fixed and determined; and the account of each Partner shall thereupon be credited or debited, as the case may be, with his share (as specified in Paragraphs 5 and 6) of such net profits or losses. In preparing such account, there shall be charged all expenses of the partner-

ship, and also, all losses and other charges incident or necessary to the carrying on of the purpose of the partnership.

Any Partner may withdraw his share of the net profits (less his share of principal payments on any notes or mortgages) at the end of each or any fiscal year. For the purposes of determining net profits, depreciation shall not be considered as an operating expense. The period commencing _____, 1975, and ending December 31, 1975, and each succeeding twelve (12) month period ending on December 31 of each year thereafter, shall be deemed a fiscal year of the partnership for this purpose and for all other purposes of this agreement. If any Partner shall not withdraw the whole, or any part of his share of the net profits, such Partner shall not be entitled to receive any interest upon any such undrawn profits, nor shall any such profits so undrawn be deemed an increase of his capital, or entitle such party to an increase in the share of the profits of the partnership, without the express written consent of all other Partners.

11. **Death of a Partner:** The death of any Partner shall not operate to dissolve said partnership, but the partnership shall be conducted by the survivors until the expiration of the term of said partnership, as herein provided. An inventory and appraisement of the partnership assets and a sale of the deceased Partner's interest therein is hereby dispensed with. The capital of said partnership shall remain unimpaired and shall not be withdrawn by the administrators or executors of a deceased Partner until the expiration of said term.

The executors, administrators, heirs, legatees, devisees, and distributees of a deceased Partner shall be Partners and shall have all the rights of such deceased Partner hereunder, including the right to examine the books, papers, and documents of the firm; the right to be present and participate in taking and signing the annual accounts, and the right to receive all net profits accruing to the interest of such deceased Partner.

Notwithstanding anything to the contrary contained herein, in the event two or more of the Managing Partners are deceased, the partnership shall be terminated and liquidated and the remaining Partners shall thereupon proceed with reasonable promptness to liquidate the partnership, the procedure as to liquidation and distribution of the partnership assets to be as provided in Paragraph 13.

12. **Retirement of a Partner:** Any Partner shall have the right to retire and withdraw from the partnership before the end of the term fixed for its duration. If any Partner shall thus elect to retire from the partnership, he shall serve written notice of such election upon all of the remaining Partners as provided in Paragraph 15. Upon the mailing of such notices of election to

546

retire, the remaining Partners shall have the right either to purchase the entire interest or share of the retiring Partner in the partnership (hereinafter called his "entire partnership interest"), or to terminate and liquidate the partnership.

If the remaining Partners (or one or more of them) elect to purchase such retiring Partner's entire partnership interest, they shall give written notice of their election to the retiring Partner before the expiration of the period (hereinafter called "acceptance period") of six (6) months from the date of their receipt of his notice of intention to retire, or if such notices are received by the remaining Partners on different dates, then from the latest date of receipt by the remaining Partners of the retiring Partner's notice of intention to retire. In such event the amount of the purchase price and the method of computing the same, the percentages and manner of business of such retiring Partner's entire partnership interest, the method of payment and the other rights and obligations of the retiring Partner and the remaining Partners and incidental consequences shall be as follows.

If the remaining Partners thus elect to purchase the retiring Partner's entire partnership interest, the purchase price shall be the book value thereof as it appears upon the books and records of the partnership as of the close of business on the date of mailing by such retiring Partner to the remaining Partners of written notice of his election to retire (or if such notices be mailed on different dates, then the latest of such dates) as adjusted by substituting the fair market value as of such date in place of the book value of any real estate owned by the partnership. Such book value adjusted as provided shall be computed by the certified public accountant regularly employed by the partnership in accordance with accounting practices regularly followed by the partnership, and in cases not covered by such practices, in accordance with good accounting practice. No allowance shall be made for goodwill or other intangible assets, except as those assets have been reflected on the partnership books immediately prior thereto. Such book value shall include and reflect the retiring Partner's capital account as at the end of the last accounting year as shown on the partnership books, increased by the retiring Partner's share of partnership profits or decreased by his share of partnership losses for the period from the beginning of the accounting year in which notice is received until said notice is received, and increased by contributions and decreased by withdrawals during such period. In making the adjustment for the fair market value of the real estate, the accountant shall rely on and use the written appraisal of a licensed real estate appraiser selected by the accountant for that purpose at the expense of the partnership. A statement showing such book value as thus adjusted and the

547

supporting items and computations (including without limitation a copy of the real estate appraisal relied on) shall be completed by the accountant and copies delivered to the retiring Partner and to the remaining Partners. Such book value as adjusted as set out in the accountant's statement shall constitute and be deemed to be the purchase price for the retiring Partner's entire partnership interest, binding upon all parties hereto unless and until changed by written agreement of the parties or by arbitration award as hereinafter provided.

In the absence of any other agreement between them, each remaining Partner shall have the primary right to purchase that portion of the retiring Partner's entire partnership interest computed by the proportion which such remaining Partners' percentage interest in the profits of the partnership bears to the percentage interests of the other remaining Partners in such profits, and also a secondary right to purchase any remaining portion of the retiring Partner's partnership interest not desired for purchase by any other remaining Partner in the exercise of his primary rights; if there is more than one remaining Partner desiring to exercise secondary rights to purchase any such remaining portion, they shall be entitled to purchase the same in equal parts. Notwithstanding the foregoing, the election of the remaining Partners to purchase portions not aggregating the retiring Partner's entire partnership interest shall be of no effect.

If the retiring Partner's entire partnership interest is accepted for purchase by two (2) or more remaining Partners, the portion of the purchase price payable by each remaining Partner shall be the sum determined by multiplying the purchase price for the entire partnership interest by the fraction representing the portion thereof purchased by such remaining Partner.

The purchase price due from each purchasing remaining Partner (hereinafter sometimes called "Purchaser") shall be paid by such Purchaser to the retiring Partner's personal representatives, as follows: thirty per cent (30%) thereof, in cash, on the Closing Date as hereinafter defined; the balance, by such Purchaser's execution and delivery of twelve (12) promissory notes, each dated as of the Closing Date, each in the principal amount of one-twelfth of the balance of such purchase price, each payable with interest at the rate of six per cent (6%) per annum to the order of the retiring Partner, the first of such notes to be payable on the thirtieth day of January following the calendar year in which the Closing Date falls, and the remaining eleven notes to be payable successively, one every three months thereafter. Such notes shall provide for the privilege of prepayment at any time without premium or penalty, and shall recite that all such notes shall become due at the option of the holder if all or any part of the principal or interest due on any such note remains unpaid for thirty (30) days after the date on which the same becomes due by the terms of such note. The Closing Date shall be the thirtieth day after the expiration of the "acceptance period," provided however, that the Purchaser shall have the right to advance the date of closing on five (5) days' written notice to the retiring Partner. The closing shall be held at the then principal office of the partnership or at any other place agreed to by the parties.

Simultaneously with the delivery to the retiring Partner by the respective Purchasers of the purchase price notes and the initial cash payments above provided for, the retiring Partner shall deliver to the respective Purchasers appropriate duly executed instruments of transfer and assignment, assigning and transferring good and marketable title to the portion or portions of the retiring Partner's entire partnership interest thus purchased, free from any liens or encumbrances or rights of others therein. The retiring Partner's entire partnership interest thus transferred shall comprise all of his right, title, and interest in and to the partnership, its firm name and all assets thereto, including but not limited to, the retiring Partner's capital account as of the date of notice, his share of any undrawn profits for any fiscal year up to, and his share of net profits from the beginning of, the fiscal year in which his retirement occurs and for all periods after his retirement. The retiring Partner's entire partnership interest shall not be deemed to include any debts and liabilities of the partnership to the retiring Partner for loans and advances (other than by way of capital contributions) made by him, which shall be repaid by the partnership as required by the terms of such loans and advances and by law. The percentage of each Purchaser in the profits and losses of the partnership shall be increased by that portion of the retiring Partner's percentage therein equal to the fraction of the retiring Partner's entire partnership interest purchased by such Purchaser.

If the remaining Partners do not elect before the expiration of the "acceptance period" and in the manner herein provided, to purchase the retiring Partner's entire partnership interest, the remaining Partners shall thereupon proceed with reasonable promptness to liquidate the business of the partnership, the procedure as to liquidation and distribution of the partnership assets to be as provided in Paragraph 13.

13. **Procedure on Liquidation:** At the termination of this partnership by the expiration of its term, and whenever liquidation of the partnership is otherwise provided for hereunder, the Managing Partners (or the surviving Managing Partners) shall proceed with reasonable promptness to liquidate the partnership.

The profits and losses during the period of liquidation shall be divided among or be borne by the Partners (or the then remaining or surviving Partners, as the case may be), including the estate of any deceased Partner, in the respective percentages in which they shared in the profits and losses prior to the event which resulted in such liquidation. After the payment of partnership debts, expenses of liquidation, and any loans by Partners to the partnership, the proceeds of liquidation, as realized, shall be distributed, first, in discharge of the undrawn profits of the Partners and of the estate of any deceased Partner, and then proportionately in discharge of the respective capital accounts. Any excess shall be distributed among the surviving Partners and the estate of any deceased Partner in the respective percentages in which they shared partnership profits immediately prior to the event which resulted in such liquidation. In connection with such liquidation, the Managing Partners shall have the sole discretion as to whether to sell any partnership asset, including but not limited to real estate, and if so, whether at public or private sale and for what amount and on what terms, or whether (if sale thereof is not required to enable payment of debts, expenses of liquidation, loans by Partners, and undrawn profits of the Partners) to distribute and transfer the same to and among the Partners and the estate of any deceased Partner, in kind, by transferring interest therein in the respective percentages in which profits and losses were shared immediately prior to the event which resulted in such liquidation. In the event that the Managing Partners determine to sell any real property, they shall not be required to sell the same promptly, but they shall have full right and discretion to determine the time, place, and manner in which such sale or sales shall be had, having due regard to the activity and condition of the real estate market and general financial and economic conditions.

14. **Arbitration:** Any controversy or claim arising out of or relating to this Agreement, or to the interpretation, breach, or enforcement thereof, shall be submitted to three (3) arbitrators and settled by arbitration, in accordance with the rules, then obtaining, of the American Arbitration Association; provided, however, and notwithstanding any other provision of such rules, if the matter submitted to arbitration shall involve a dispute as to the adjusted book value of a deceased, incompetent, or retiring Partner's entire partnership interest, such arbitration shall be held before three (3) arbitrators, one (1) of whom shall be a certified public accountant and the other two (2) of whom shall be licensed real estate appraisers. Any award made by a majority of such arbitrators shall be final, binding, and conclusive on all parties hereto for all purposes, and judgment may be entered thereon in any court having jurisdiction thereof.

15. **Notices:** Wherever provision is made in this Agreement for the giving, service, or delivery of any notice, statement, or other instrument, such notice shall be deemed to have been duly given, served, and delivered if mailed by United States registered or certified mail, addressed to the party entitled to receive the same at his address written at the head of this Agreement; provided, however, that each party hereto may change his mailing address by giving to each other party hereto, by United States registered or certified mail, written notice of election to change such address and of such new address. Except where otherwise specified in this Agreement, any notice, statement, or other instrument shall be deemed to have been given, served, and delivered on the date on which such notice was mailed as herein provided.

16. **Corporate Partners:** Wherever and whenever required by this Agreement or by the Managing Partners, all notices to a corporate partner shall be deemed to have been received if sent to the President thereof; and all notices sent by such corporate partners shall be accompanied by a certified copy of a resolution authorizing and approving the contents of such notice, whether same be for information, decision or otherwise.

17. **Additional Contributions to Partnership:** In the event that any call for additional capital contributions is made upon the Partners, such call shall be made in good faith, shall be reasonably necessary for the carrying out of the purpose of the partnership, and shall be applied to the Partners in proportion to their respective capital contributions. No Partner shall be obligated to satisfy any such call, however. In the event that any Partner does not agree to contribute the additional contribution called for, the partnership interest of such Partner shall be diminished to the ratio which his total partnership contribution bears to the total contribution made by all Partners.

18. **Merger of Prior Agreements:** This Agreement contains the sole and entire agreement and understanding of the parties with respect to the entire subject matter hereof. Any and all prior discussions, negotiations, commitments, and understandings relating thereto are hereby merged herein. This Agreement cannot be changed or terminated orally.

19. **Benefit:** The covenants and agreements herein contained shall inure to the benefit of and be binding upon the parties hereto and their respective executors, administrators, successors, and assigns.

IN WITNESS WHEREOF, the parties hereto have hereunto set their names and seals, all as of the day and year first above written.

GENERAL PARTNERSHIP AGREEMENT

Signed in the presence of:

_____   _____ [*Seal*]
Witness

_____   _____ [*Seal*]
Witness

_____   _____ [*Seal*]
Witness

INDEX

References are to Pages

†